AF778047

To our wives,
Nancy Gaertner
and
Maryvonne Cooper

and our children,
Scott, Denise and Amanda Gaertner
and
Chris and Danielle Cooper

Also, in memory of Lloyd Morrison.

CONTENTS

PREFACE xiii

1 THE NATURE OF CONTEMPORARY ACCOUNTING 1

ORIENTATION
THE USES OF ACCOUNTING INFORMATION
Managerial decisions. Investment decisions. Public policy decisions.
THE ACCOUNTING PROFESSION
Certified public accountant (CPA). Certificate in management accounting (CMA).
ACCOUNTING PRACTICE
Public accounting. Private accounting. Governmental accounting.
THE DEVELOPMENT OF ACCOUNTING STANDARDS AND PRINCIPLES
FORMS OF BUSINESS ORGANIZATION
Sole proprietorship. Partnership. Corporation.
BASIC ACCOUNTING EQUATION AND TERMINOLOGY

2 ACCOUNTING METHODOLOGY 15

ORIENTATION
BASIC ILLUSTRATION: SMITH TRUCKING COMPANY
The entity principle.
THE BALANCE SHEET

REVENUES AND EXPENSES
Net income (or profit). Various revenues and expenses.
ACCRUAL CONCEPT
EFFECT OF REVENUE AND EXPENSES ON THE ACCOUNTING EQUATION
SMITH TRUCKING COMPANY EXAMPLE, CONTINUED
THE INCOME STATEMENT
DEBITS AND CREDITS
DIVIDENDS
COMMON ACCOUNT CLASSIFICATIONS

3 BASIC ELEMENTS OF AN ACCOUNTING SYSTEM 41

ORIENTATION
DOCUMENTS AND CONTROLS
Accounting controls. Source documents.
THE ACCOUNTING CYCLE
THE JOURNAL
The general journal.
THE LEDGER
TRIAL BALANCE
ADJUSTING ENTRIES
The periodicity principle and the matching principle. Principal types of transactions requiring adjustment.
ADJUSTING ENTRIES ILLUSTRATED
Recorded costs. Unrecorded costs. Recorded revenue. Unrecorded revenue. The need for adjusting entries.
FINANCIAL STATEMENTS
CLOSING ENTRIES
Real and nominal accounts.

4 THE ACCOUNTING CYCLE COMPLETED 74

ORIENTATION
COMPREHENSIVE ILLUSTRATION
Journal entries. Posting. Trial balance. Adjusting journal entries. Financial statements prepared. Closing entries. Post-closing trial balance.
METHODS OF EXPEDITING ACCOUNTING RECORD KEEPING
Subsidiary ledgers. Special journals. Sales journals. Cash receipts journals. Other journals. Worksheet.
DATA PROCESSING IN ACCOUNTING
Microcomputers in accounting. Other methods of processing data.
LOCATING ERRORS
Transpositions and slides.

5 CASH AND SHORT-TERM MARKETABLE SECURITIES 122

ORIENTATION
CASH
Administration of cash. Cash control. Petty cash. Bank reconciliations. Cash-basis accounting. Cash statement. Comparison of cash-basis and accrual-basis accounting. Cash budgeting. Analysis of the cash position. Electronic funds transfer. Point-of-sale (POS) terminals.
MARKETABLE SECURITIES
FASB Statement No. 12. Lower-of-cost-or-market rule illustrated. Sale of securities.

6 REVENUES AND RECEIVABLES 154

ORIENTATION
THE NATURE OF REVENUE
REVENUE RECOGNITION AND MEASUREMENT
RECORDING REVENUES AND RECEIVABLES
Sales discounts. Sales taxes.
UNCOLLECTIBLE ACCOUNTS: A SPECIAL PROBLEM OF RECEIVABLES VALUATION
Direct write-off method. Allowance method.
CREDIT CARD SALES
PLEDGING, ASSIGNING, AND FACTORING ACCOUNTS RECEIVABLE
LONG-TERM CONSTRUCTION CONTRACTS
Percentage-of-completion method. Complete-contract method.
NOTES RECEIVABLE
Defaulting on notes. Discounting notes receivable. Contingent liability.

7 INVENTORY AND COST OF SALES 186

ORIENTATION
MERCHANDISE COSTS
Cost of goods sold. Gross profit
The importance of accurate inventory valuation.
ITEMS OF INVENTORY COST
Goods in transit. Freight-in. Purchase discounts. Purchase returns and allowances.

PERPETUAL INVENTORY SYSTEM
PERIODIC INVENTORY SYSTEM
TRADE DISCOUNTS
COST FLOW ASSUMPTIONS
Effects of alternative cost-assignment methods: specific identification, weighted average, first-in, first-out (FIFO), last-in, first-out (LIFO). FIFO and LIFO contrasted. LIFO and taxes.
LOWER OF COST OR MARKET (LCM)
Illustration of lower of cost or market.
THE EFFECT OF INFLATION ON INVENTORIES
ESTIMATING ENDING INVENTORIES—THE GROSS PROFIT METHOD
CONSIGNED MERCHANDISE

8 PLANT ASSETS: Acquisition and Depreciation 224

ORIENTATION
ACQUISITION OF PLANT ASSETS
Noncash acquisitions. Lump-sum (basket) purchases.
DEPRECIATION
Book value.
DEPRECIATION METHODS
Straight-line method. Double declining-balance method. Sum-of-the-years' digits method. Production-unit method. Service-hours method. Comparison of depreciation methods. Depreciation for less than one year. Two common misconceptions concerning depreciation.
CAPITAL AND REVENUE EXPENDITURES
REPAIRS, RENEWALS, AND IMPROVEMENTS OF PLANT ASSETS
Scrap value and maintenance cost in optimum life determination: illustration.
DEPRECIATION AND INCOME TAXES
Acclerated Cost Recovery System (ACRS).
LEASING PLANT ASSETS

9 PLANT ASSETS: Trade-ins, Natural Resources, Intangibles, and Other Assets 255

ORIENTATION
DISPOSAL OF PLANT ASSETS
Asset trade-ins.
NATURAL RESOURCES
Capitalization of a natural resource. Depletion. Percentage depletion.
INTANGIBLE ASSETS

Patents. Trademarks. Copyrights. Franchises. Organization costs. Goodwill. Inconsistencies between financial and tax accounting for intangible assets.
OTHER ASSETS AND DEFERRED CHARGES
Cash surrender value of life insurance.

10 PRESENT VALUES AND LIABILITIES 282

ORIENTATION
PRESENT VALUES
Future value of $1. Present value of $1. Future value of an annuity of $1. Present value of an annuity of $1.
LIABILITIES
Current liabilities. Long-term debt. Deferred income taxes. Long-term leases. Pensions. Contingent liabilities.

11 BOND CONTRACTS 323

ORIENTATION
TERMINOLOGY
ILLUSTRATION: BASIC BOND CONTRACTS
BOND VALUATION AND INTEREST DETERMINATION
BOND ISSUANCE AND DISCOUNT (OR PREMIUM) AMORTIZATION
Discount. Discount amortization. Premium
Premium amortization.
SEMIANNUAL INTEREST PAYMENTS
COMPARISON OF EFFECTIVE INTEREST AND STRAIGHT-LINE AMORTIZATION
BONDS REDEEMED BEFORE MATURITY
SERIAL BONDS
BONDS ISSUED BETWEEN INTEREST PAYMENT DATES
BOND SINKING FUND

12 OWNERS' EQUITY 195

ORIENTATION
FORMS OF BUSINESS ORGANIZATION
UNINCORPORATED BUSINESS FIRMS
Accounting for sole proprietorships. Accounting for partnerships. Characteristics common to sole proprietorships and partnerships.
CORPORATION ACCOUNTING
Issuance of corporate securities. Par and no-par stock. Preferred stock and cummulative preferred stock. Dividends in general.

Property and script dividends. Stock dividends. Stock splits
Treasury stock. Authorized stock. Convertible securities
Retained earnings. Unrealized gains and losses taken directly to owners' equity. Special stock equity accounts or conditions
Balance sheet disclosure of corporate equities.

13 STATEMENT OF CHANGES IN FINANCIAL POSITION 379

ORIENTATION
INTRODUCTION TO THE STATEMENT
WORKING CAPITAL APPROACH TO STATEMENT OF CHANGES
Determining the activities affecting working capital. Working capital provided by operations.
CASH BASIS APPROACH TO STATEMENT OF CHANGES
Cash provided by operations.
EVALUATION OF THE STATEMENT OF CHANGES IN FINANCIAL POSITION
Cash basis versus working capital basis for the financial changes statement.

14 FINANCIAL STATEMENT ANALYSIS 410

ORIENTATION
BASIC ANALYTICAL PROCEDURES
Horizontal analysis. Vertical analysis. Common-size statements. Standards of comparison. Quality of earnings.
RATIO ANALYSIS
Tests of profitability. Tests of liquidity and solvency. Market and other tests. Summary evaluation of Karparts Corporation.

15 THE EMERGING ISSUES: Inflation Accounting, Accounting for International Activity and Accounting Theory 439

ORIENTATION
FINANCIAL REPORTING AND CHANGING PRICES
Historical cost profits—a "true" profit? Two approaches to the problem: constant-dollar accounting and current-value accounting.

FASB Statement No. 33 requirements. Purchasing power gains and losses. Accounting for inflation—a final comment.
INTERNATIONAL ACCOUNTING
Basic international monetary system. The International Monetary Fund. Foreign exchange trading. Premiums, discounts, and spread. Instruments of foreign exchange. Accounting for foreign exchange transactions. Foreign shipment terms. Accounting for foreign trade. Exchange gains and losses. Foreign subsidiaries. International accounting standards.
BASIC ACCOUNTING THEORY
The development of accounting standards. The objectives of financial reporting. Basic principles. Final comments.

APPENDIX: Financial Statements of a Company Listed on the New York Stock Exchange 477

INDEX 537

PREFACE

This financial accounting textbook is intended to serve as an introduction to the academic study of accounting. Its primary purpose is to communicate the basic objectives, methodologies, and underlying concepts of financial accounting. The book explains how accounting data are accumulated and presented, describes many of the fundamental principles and concepts that underlie accounting information, and initiates the reader into the effective use of such data.

The text material is presented with the use of frequent examples, and with a careful focus on terminology. It will provide the reader with a good basic business vocabulary. Following each chapter are numerous questions, exercises, and problems which are designed to reinforce concepts and procedures presented in the body of the chapter. In general, the approach and material treatment of the book reflect the authors' goal of writing a highly readable, interesting, and instructive financial accounting textbook.

The text is thorough and comprehensive, yet selective in what is presented. The coverage is very comprehensive in the areas of asset trade-in and accounting for bond contracts. In most previously published introductory texts these areas have needlessly received meager treatment. This text gives more coverage to the subject and in so doing gives more of a real-world treatment to the subject. (Conversely, certain other areas are not covered in detail in this text, because of the inappropriateness of the topic for a first course in accounting.)

We have purposely made this text very contemporary and up to date; it exposes the reader to several areas which are new or emerging in financial accounting. For example, there is a discussion of the new Treasury Department rules pertaining to the disclosure of supplementary information computed using the LIFO inventory method. The Accelerated Cost Recovery System (ACRS), which is a part of the Economic Recovery Act of 1981, is discussed as it relates to the depreciation issue. Certain provisions of the Tax Equity and Fiscal Responsibility Act (TEFRA) passed in September of 1982 are briefly discussed as well.

FASB Statement No. 52, "Foreign Currency Translation" (which is effective for fiscal years beginning after December 15, 1982), is covered in the section on international accounting. Again, in an effort to be more than a "how to do it" text, a brief discussion of the conceptual complexities involved in this issue are presented.

The concept of the "present value of money" is discussed from a procedural viewpoint. Typically the student will have been exposed to courses in which the derivation of similar formulas is explained. There is no discussion in this area on how the present value formulas were derived; rather the focus is on how the present value tables can be used, and what they can do for the student. The reader is introduced to this concept in Chapter 10, and the tables are used later in that chapter and several additional times throughout the remainder of the book.

The final chapter of the text provides an exposure to two emerging issues in financial accounting: accounting for inflation and international accounting. The issue of accounting for inflation is certainly still in the evolutionary stages, with current rules requiring that only very large, publicly held companies present supplemental data in this regard. It is likely that these requirements will change in the future, and that this will be a provocative topic in financial accounting for years to come.

The area of international accounting is an emerging area to which tomorrow's accountants should be exposed. In the first half of the twentieth century, the United States went from a group of regional economies to a national economy. In the second half of this century, we are rapidly moving from a national to an international economy. Organizations such as the American Assembly of Collegiate Schools of Business (AACBS) and the American Accounting Association (AAA) have emphasized the need to internationalize the business and accounting curriculum at all levels. The international accounting section of Chapter 15 is an effort to follow these recommendations, and in so doing, to sensitize the student to the type of business world that he or she will actually encounter.

This book is organized into four sections. The first four chapters deal with the basic nature of accounting, accounting methodology, and details of the accounting cycle.

The second section of the book (Chapters 5 to 9) focuses on assets and income statement items which are related to those assets. For example, sales and accounts receivable are covered in the same chapter; as are inventories and cost of goods sold. Accounting for the acquisition and depreciation of depreciable assets is covered in Chapter 8; and asset trade-ins as well as natural resources and intangibles are presented in Chapter 9.

The third section of the book (Chapters 10 to 12) deals with present values and the "credit side" of the balance sheet, that is, liabilities and owners' equity. Chapter 11, Bond Contracts, is very comprehensive, and emphasizes that accounting for bonds from the purchaser/investor viewpoint is essentially the "mirror image" of the entries of the issue/seller.

The owners' equity chapter focuses on the corporation; although sufficient attention is devoted to partnership equity to provide the student with a working knowledge of the area. The emerging concept of taking unrealized gains and losses directly to the owners' equity section is mentioned. This is currently required for noncurrent marketable securities and in foreign currency translation. Earnings per share is covered at a basic level, giving the student enough information to be prepared for more detailed coverage in later courses.

Section four of the text (Chapters 13 to 15) deals with the uses of accounting information and the emerging issues in financial accounting. Chapter 13 is a thorough coverage of the statement of changes in financial position (both working capital and cash concepts). Chapter 14, Financial Statement Analysis, includes a thorough coverage of ratio and percentage analysis.

The final chapter focuses on emerging issues in the field (accounting for inflation and international accounting), and includes a short elaboration on the principles which underlie financial accounting. This accounting theory section is presented so that the reader is completely aware that, although there are certain very well-defined procedures to be followed in the preparation of financial statements, the discipline of accounting is a provocative and dynamic area of study.

The question might be asked: Why another introductory text? The answer to that question revolves around the fact that there are so many recent changes in financial accounting that the basic structure of the discipline is changing. Evidence of this abounds in inflation accounting, the extensive use of present values, the international character of the contemporary business world, and the acceptability of carrying certain income and loss items directly to the balance sheet. These basic changes result in a need for new, contemporary texts which present these revolutionary changes in a clear, concise way. At the same time the reader should be provided with an appreciation of some of the ambiguity which surrounds many of these important issues. This then prepares the student to be better able to accommodate the changes he or she will encounter in accounting in the coming years. This text does present the most contemporary issues in a very pragmatic and readable manner. At the same time it exposes the reader to some of the basic concepts which underlie the entire process, thereby allowing the student to better accommodate to changes that are yet to come.

To summarize, the text is very readable, uses frequent examples, has a traditional conventional approach, is comprehensive yet selective, does contain an element of the conceptual, and is completely contemporary.

ACKNOWLEDGMENTS

This text has benefited greatly from the comments of our reviewers. Special thanks are due to Shirley M. Arbesfeld, Rutgers University; Frank Bird, University of Richmond; Janice Carr, California Polytechnic State University; Michael J. Cerullo, University of Wyoming; Janet Daniels, University of Hartford; Dan R. Hines, East Carolina University; W. Elbert Jones, University of South Carolina; Jack Miller, St. Louis Community College at Florissant Valley; Marvin W. Tucker, Southern Illinois University at Carbondale; Thomas S. Wetzel, Northern Illinois University; and Norlin Rueschhoff, The University of Notre Dame.

Our thanks also go to the graduate students and typists who assisted the authors. A special thanks to Charles Dougherty and Nancy Smith in the preparation of the book.

Suggestions and comments from the users of this book are invited.

James F. Gaertner
S. Kerry Cooper

THE NATURE OF CONTEMPORARY ACCOUNTING

1

ORIENTATION

The primary objective of this chapter is to introduce the general aspects and the nature of contemporary accounting to the beginning accounting student. A synopsis of professional opportunities, professional organizations and regulatory bodies, and a historical tracing of accounting thought and practice adds to the basic framework. The chapter includes an introduction to the primary forms of business organization, and concludes with an introduction to the basic accounting equation.

In business the word *accounting* refers to a method of communicating financial information about enterprises to interested parties. Just as there is an insatiable demand for information of all kinds in the modern world, there is an insatiable demand on the part of business managers, investors, and others for financial information bearing on the past successes and failures and future prospects of business organizations. It is the function of accounting to identify, measure, record, and report information (mostly financial in nature) about the activities of a business enterprise or other societal entity. An organization, whether profit making or nonprofit, has financial activities and a responsibility to report its financial activities to interested parties.

Since accounting is concerned with communicating, it is natural that accounting terms reflect the idea of reporting. The word *account* means the recitation of things that have taken place, often implying someone's responsibility for the results. Accounting terms such as *journal* and *journalize* refer to the record of events. The word *statement* as used in the term *financial statement* means the results and conclusions drawn from a record of events.

Good reporting, however, should recount the activities and results of the past primarily as a basis for future action. It is particularly important that reporting be unbiased, inclusive of all significant happenings, and thorough in its analysis of the meaning of the reported data. Thus, accounting involves a system of putting data together in a meaningful way, assuring its propriety and completeness, and reporting the resulting information to interested parties. Unfortunately, like most devices fashioned by human beings, accounting systems are not perfect, and elements of bias and errors of omission and commission do exist. In order to evaluate the adequacy of accounting information, one must take into consideration the needs of the users of accounting data and the general economic climate, as well as the accounting procedures relating to the recording, verification, and reporting of the financial information.

Accounting serves a crucial role in modern industrialized society, especially in a free enterprise economy. The availability of economic resources in business enterprises is determined, to a large extent, by the decisions of many individuals to invest in those enterprises. If the economy is to be prosperous and productive, resources must be placed in the custody of firms which are efficient producers of goods that consumers want. In a competitive system, a firm's operating results and financial strength will indicate if it is using its resources to meet society's needs. A firm that is producing goods that no one wants to buy cannot make a profit. Since investors want to share in the profits of business enterprise, they will place their funds with firms they consider likely to be profitable, and they will withhold their funds from unprofitable firms. Thus, if investors make the right decisions, productive resources will be channeled into business firms which are efficient producers of the goods and services that society wants. Efficient decisions by investors, and efficient management of resources committed to a firm's use, may result from good accounting information; neither is likely to result without it.

Accounting, then, is a process of measurement and communication. It has often been called the "language of business."

THE USES OF ACCOUNTING INFORMATION

In the last several years accountants have become much more aware of the fact that they are creating a product (financial statements) for which there is a user or consumer. The accounting process extends beyond the creation of accounting reports; it extends to the analysis and interpretation of the information generated by the system. It is important that the accountant be aware of the various types of potential uses of the financial statements that he or she generates.

Some users of financial reports (such as owners, creditors, management, and the like) have a direct interest in the activities of the enterprise; while others (such as financial analysts, stock exchanges, regulatory agencies) have an indirect interest. In general terms, accounting information has three major uses: (1) managerial decisions, (2) investment decisions, (3) public policy matters.

Managerial Decisions

Many decisions made by management are made largely on the basis of accounting data. Decisions such as whether to open or close a plant, whether to introduce a new product, and what pay increases to give in the next year are all determined largely on the basis of data provided by accounting reports.

Investment Decisions

Should an individual, a mutual fund, or a life insurance company invest a large amount of money in a particular company? Should they divest themselves of an investment made previously? These decisions and other similar ones are typically made largely on the basis of information provided by accounting reports. Many investment decisions are made daily largely on the basis of accounting data.

Public Policy Decisions

Does the United States actually have an adequate inventory of gasoline and heating oil for the upcoming year? Are we entering a recession, or a period of prosperity? Is a segment of our business community being monopolized by one company? Is another segment in need of federal assistance? Information concerning these public policy decisions is provided by accounting systems throughout the United States. To a large extent, the taxes used to provide government services are collected on the basis of accounting systems in use throughout the country.

THE ACCOUNTING PROFESSION

The term *profession* is probably one of the more abused terms in the English language. It is used to describe many occupations ranging from physician and clergy to actor and virtually any other classifiable occupation.

If accounting is currently a profession in the true sense of the word (as opposed to an occupation), it is a relatively new profession. For many years, the world existed without an accounting profession just as it existed without a legal profession. Many years ago, as the human race began to congregate into social organizations, the need for a set of rules to govern human behavior began to emerge; hence the beginning of laws and the legal profession. Similarly, contemporary economic society has become extremely complex in a very short period of time. All societies engage in the basic economic activities of production, income distribution, saving, and consumption. In highly developed economies like the United States, these activities have become very complex, intertwined, and specialized. Our economic, and therefore our social well-being depends on an orderly conduct of these sophisticated activities. A major factor in this conduct is the availability of adequate, accurate, and reliable financial information. The profession of accountancy has emerged to fill this need for society.

Certified Public Accountants (CPAs)

There are certain professional designations for those accountants who, in addition to meeting specified academic requirements, have passed a rigorous examination and are licensed by the state. The first of these designations is that of the certified public accountant (CPA). This designation was first established in New York in 1896 and spread quickly throughout the country. Currently there are more than 200,000 CPAs in the United States.

Although the CPA requirements vary somewhat among states, generally they include high moral character; a college degree with sufficient accounting courses; over one year of actual accounting experience; and the successful completion of a two-and-a-half-day examination. This examination, which is prepared and administered by the American Institute of Certified Public Accountants (AICPA), is scheduled in each state simultaneously, and is given semiannually each May and November.

In recent years, several states have enacted laws requiring CPAs to participate in a program of continuing professional education. Obviously states will differ as to the details of the requirements, such as the number of hours of formal education required. The rules adopted by several State Boards of Accountancy require forty hours per year.

Certificate in Management Accounting (CMA)

The Institute of Management Accounting, which is an affiliate of the National Association of Accountants, now grants the certificate in management accounting (CMA) as evidence of professional competence in that field. Requirements for the CMA designation include a college degree or equivalent, two years' experience in management accounting, and successful completion of a two-and-a-half-day examination. A program of continuing education is required for renewal of the certificate.

ACCOUNTING PRACTICE

Generally accountants tend to specialize into subareas of the discipline. In terms of the practice of accounting, the field may be divided into three broad areas: (1) public accounting, (2) private (or managerial) accounting, and (3) governmental accounting.

Public Accounting

Public accounting is the domain of the CPA. The principal function of the CPA in public accounting is *auditing.* In conducting an audit, public accountants examine the records supporting the financial reports of an enterprise and express an opinion regarding the statement's fairness and reliability. This function is often referred to as the *attest function.* Its purpose is to lend credibility to the financial reports; that is, to provide assurance that they are dependable.

Tax accounting encompasses the preparation of tax returns for clients as well as the consideration of tax consequences of alternative courses of action. The increasing multinational nature of contemporary business has created a new field of international taxation in which the accountant is called upon to render tax advice to the multinational corporation. To render tax services, the CPA must have extensive knowledge of tax laws, regulations and interpretations, and court decisions, as well as a thorough knowledge of accounting.

Some CPA firms offer *management advisory services* to their clients. In the past, when CPA firms discovered problems in a client's business during the course of an audit, they often made suggestions for corrective action. As a result, public accounting firms found themselves becoming increasingly involved in management consulting work. The services are generally accounting-based and include such activities as cost-effectiveness studies, financial advice, computer installation and applications, and operational analysis.

When an individual enters public accounting, he or she often joins a large firm in a staff accountant position. After a period of time, generally one or two years, the position of senior accountant is normally attained. A senior accountant supervises a group of staff accountants on one particular project or job. The next step in the career path is manager or supervisor (the exact names vary among firms). A manager generally has the responsibility of several projects or jobs which are being run by the seniors that report to him or her. The final step in the career path of an accountant choosing public accounting with a large firm is partner. A partner, as the name implies, is an owner of the firm. Some of the very large firms may have several hundred partners scattered throughout the world. Instead of receiving a straight salary, the partners are generally compensated by receiving some part of the profits of the firm. Of course not all of the individuals entering public accounting will achieve the partnership position. In a large firm it often takes ten or more years to achieve partnership status.

Private Accounting

Many accountants, including CPAs, are employed outside of public accounting by profit-making and nonprofit organizations. Generally these accountants are referred to as management accountants. The progression "up the ladder" in private accounting is not as well defined as in the public sector. However, the chief accounting officer in industry is normally called the *controller.* He or she manages the work of the accounting department and is also an integral part of the management team of the business. The accountants in the private sector must record transactions and prepare the financial statements for the enterprise. This general realm of accounting includes not only the preparation of financial statements but other areas such as system design, determination of product cost, forecasting, and budgeting.

Governmental Accounting

The complex operations of the many governmental units result in a need for competent accountants to organize, control, and report on operations. Accountants employed in the public sector often perform functions very similar to their private sector counterparts. The Internal Revenue Service (IRS), the Securities and Exchange Commission (SEC), and the General Accounting Office (GAO), utilize accountants in the various services that they perform for the government.

THE DEVELOPMENT OF ACCOUNTING STANDARDS AND PRINCIPLES

Record keeping is thought to have begun about 4000 B.C., though the oldest known commercial documents are clay tables from Babylonia dating back to about 3000 B.C. In early accounting there was no systematic accounting for all transactions of a particular entity, only for specific selected activities.

It appears likely that "contemporary" double-entry bookkeeping originated in Italy around the fourteenth century. The first society of accountants was formed in Venice in the late sixteenth century and, gaining a virtual monopoly over practice, prescribed a six-year apprenticeship for candidates.

The first known description of existing bookkeeping systems was published in Italy in 1494. The book, *Summa,* contained several chapters on bookkeeping as it existed at that time; it was written by Luca Pacioli, a Franciscan friar who had taught at several universities in Italy.

For centuries accountants essentially "did their own thing" with the records of the firms for which they worked. It is obvious, however, that if creditors, investors, and society in general are to rely on these records at some point in time, a need develops for a logical and consistent set of standards to govern accounting. The establishment of these rules has been an evolutionary process, from the days of Pacioli to the present.

Certainly the Industrial Revolution, the rise of the corporate form of business organization, the enactment of the income tax law in the United States in 1913, and the depression of the 1930s, all resulted in tremendous stimulus to accounting activity. Research to develop accounting principles and practices which will keep pace with changes in economic activity is a major activity of professional accountants and accouting educators.

The professional organization of CPAs, the American Institute of Certified Public Accountants (AICPA), for many years was the source of authoritative pronouncements on the nature of accounting methods and techniques to be employed. Before 1959, the Committee on Accounting Procedure of the AICPA performed this function by the occasional issuance of Accounting Research Bulletins. From 1959 to 1973, the Accounting Principles Board (APB) carried on this task. The term *APB Opinions* refers to the recommendations of this body. In 1973, the Financial Accounting Standards Board (FASB) which is independent of the AICPA, replaced the Accounting Principles Board. As accounting thought continues to evolve and develop, and as new accounting problems emerge, the FASB will issue Statements of Financial Accounting Standards which will alter and enlarge the body of accepted accounting procedures. Throughout this book, you will see occasional references to "generally accepted accounting principles" (or GAAP). This term refers to the structure of conceptual and applied principles built up out of such recommendations which, in effect, prescribes accounting methods to be employed in given situations. Accouting principles for business enterprises are greatly influenced by the organizational form of firms.

FORMS OF BUSINESS ORGANIZATION

A business enterprise can be organized as either (1) a sole proprietorship, (2) a partnership, or (3) a corporation.

Sole Proprietorship

A business owned by one person is a sole (or single) proprietorship. Often the owner acts as the manager of the business. Legally, the business and the owner are not separate entities; however from an accounting standpoint, the business is an entity entirely separate from the owner. It owns its own property and has its own debts.

Partnership

An unincorporated business owned by two or more persons is a partnership. The organization of a partnership requires only an agreement (preferably written) which is sometimes referred to as *articles of copartnership.* This contract specifies such matters as the division of profits, duties, and responsibilities of the various partners; admission and retirement of partners; and terms of dissolution. Each partner is legally responsible for the debts of the business; however, as in the case of the sole proprietorship, accounting views the partner's personal activities as separate from those of the partnership.

Corporation

A business which is incorporated under the laws of one of the fifty states, with the owners known as stockholders, is referred to as a corporation. Ownership is represented by shares of stock which can be freely bought and sold. The owners of the stock are the *stockholders* (or *shareholders*), and they exercise control over the management of corporate affairs indirectly by electing a *board of directors.* This board meets periodically to determine corporate policies and to select corporate officers who, in turn, manage the corporation. The chart below here depicts this relationship.

Accounting focuses on the conduct of corporate business, not on the directors and managers as individuals. The stockholders enjoy what is called *limited liability;* they are liable for the debts of the corporation only to the extent of their investment.

The corporation is the most important form of business organization in the United States. Nearly all large businesses, and many small ones, are organized as corporations. This dominant role of the corporation in our economy is due to such advantages as the relative ease of accumulating large amounts of money from investors, the limited liability of owners, the transferability of

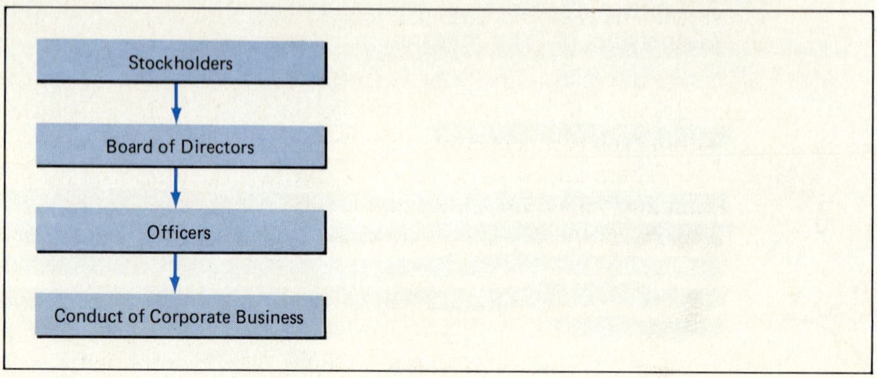

shares of ownership, and the continuity of existence. Disadvantages of incorporating include the difficulties of incorporating, the cost of incorporating, and the fact that a corporation is usually taxed directly on its own corporate income. Because of its dominant role, *we shall emphasize the corporate form of business in this book.* The accounting concepts, principles, and standards generally apply to the sole proprietorship and partnership forms of business as well.

BASIC ACCOUNTING EQUATION AND TERMINOLOGY

The first book on accounting, published by Luca Pacioli in 1494, had as its basis an accounting equation which continues to be the foundation of all contemporary accounting. This basic equation is:

$$A = E$$

or

Assets equal Equities

Assets are items of value, or, in other words, economic resources which are owned by a business and expected to benefit future operations.

Some commonly encountered assets are:

- — Cash
- — Land
- — Buildings
- — Accounts receivable (money owed us)
- — Supplies
- — Merchandise (inventories)

It is important to note that if a company buys an asset (for example, land) for \$50,000 and its value subsequently increases to say, \$75,000, the company does not increase its value in the accounting records to represent the current market value. The company maintains its basic accounting records based on historic costs. This is referred to as the *cost principle* in accounting. This principle helps insure the objectivity of the information being presented. *Equities* are defined as claims to those items of value. So the basic accounting equation states that within each business entity the items of value equal the claims to those items.

There are two general types of equities: equities of the creditors of the company, called *liabilities;* and equities of the owneis of the business, called *owners' equity.* Therefore our basic accounting equation can be expanded to:

$$A = L + OE$$

or

Assets equal Liabilities plus Owners' Equity

Liabilities are debts, what a company owes; the economic obligations of a business entity or individual. Some commonly encountered liabilities are:

- Accounts payable Amounts owed to creditors as a result of purchases of goods and services.
- Notes payable Amounts owed as a result of borrowing money.
- Wages payable Amounts owed to workers for their labor services.
- Taxes payable Amounts owed to some governmental body.

Many, but not all, liabilities include the word *payable.* Owners' equity is a residual amount. As the name implies, it is the equity of the owners of the business in that entity. The fact that it is a residual amount can be demonstrated by moving the L in the equation to the left-hand side of the equal sign, and we get:

$$A - L = OE$$

or

Assets minus Liabilities equals the equity of the owners of the business

Owners' equity increases when the owners invest more in the business, and when the business firm earns profits. Conversely, owners' equity is decreased by withdrawals by owners and by losses incurred by the business. An entire chapter will be devoted to owners' equity later in this book. It is useful now, however, to achieve a basic understanding of some of the commonly used terminology relating to owners' equity.

When owners invest in a corporation they generally do so by the purchase of *capital stock.* The owners of that stock are referred to as *stockholders.* When a corporation earns a profit, it can choose either to keep it in the business, or to distribute it to the stockholders. Earnings (profits) of a business that are kept in the business are referred to as *retained earnings;* whereas earnings that are distributed to owners are referred to as *dividends.* Therefore, owners' equity has basically two component parts: 1) the amount paid in by investors (often called *paid-in capital*), and 2) the amount of earnings retained in the business (often called *retained earnings*).

SUMMARY

There is an insatiable demand on the part of managers, investors, and others for financial information bearing on the past successes and future prospects of business organizations. It is the function of accounting to identify, measure, record, and report information about the activities of a business enterprise or other societal entity. Accounting involves a system of putting data together in a meaningful way, assuring its propriety and completeness, and reporting the resulting information to interested parties. In order to evaluate the adequacy of accounting information, the needs of users of the accounting data, as well as the accounting procedures used in the recording, verifying, and reporting of financial information, must be taken ito consideration. The basic accounting equation, Assets = Equities, which was first presented in the late fifteenth century, continues to be the foundation of all contemporary accounting.

KEY POINTS

1. Accounting information has three major uses:

a. Managerial decisions
b. Investment decisions
c. Public policy matters

2. Certified public accountant (CPA) is a professional designation for those accountants who have 1) met specified academic requirements, 2) passed a rigorous examination prepared by the American Institute of Certified Public Accountants (AICPA), and 3) are licensed by the state.

3. A certificate in management accounting (CMA) is awarded by the Institute of Management Accounting as evidence of professional competence in the field of managerial accounting.

4. In terms of the practice of accounting, the field may be classified into three broad areas:

a. Public accounting
b. Private or managerial accounting
c. Governmental accounting

5. The principal functions of public accounting are auditing, accounting, and management advisory services.

6. Accountants employed outside of public accounting, by profit-making and nonprofit organizations, are generally referred to as management accountants.

7. A business enterprise can be organized as either:

a. Sole proprietorship
b. Partnership
c. Corporation

8. The basic accounting equation is: Assets = Equities, meaning that within a business all things of value (Assets) are equal to the claims (equities) on those same things of value.

9. There are two types of Equities:

a. Liabilities: Equities of creditors
b. Owners' equity: Equities of the owners (a residual amount)

10. The basic accounting equation is now expanded to: Assets = Liabilities + Owners' Equity

QUESTIONS

1. Why is accounting considered to be a socially useful discipline?

2. Distinguish between accounting and bookkeeping.

3. What are some examples of accounting information that would be useful to a firm's management in making decisions about operations? To investors? To other interested parties?

4. Describe in general terms the requirements that an individual must meet to become a CPA.

5. Distinguish between certified public accountant (CPA) and certified management accountant (CMA).

6. Describe the primary functions of public accounting.

7. Why must financial statements be reviewed by auditors?

8. How can a CPA help management in its decision-making process?

9. Identify the following organizations:

   a. Financial Accounting Standards Board
   b. Accounting Principles Board
   c. American Institute of Certified Public Accountants
   d. Institute of Management Accounting

10. In general, what are the responsibilities of the controller in a business?

11. What are the three principal services provided by pubic accountants?

12. Distinguish the primary forms of business organizations.

13. What is meant by "generally accepted accounting principles"?

14. Would you describe the development of accounting principles and standards as an evolutionary or revolutionary process? Discuss.

15. List and briefly discuss several historical events which you believe have had an impact on the development of accounting over the years.

16. What is meant by the "accounting equation"? List and define its component parts.

E1-1 Each year, publicly owned companies publish reports on their operating performance. Explain why each of the following individuals may be interested in examining the published financial statements.

a. Management
b. Stockholders
c. Creditors
d. Potential stockholders
e. Internal Revenue Service
f. Securities and Exchange Commission
g. Employer's union
h. Consumer groups
i. Economic adviser to the President of the United States

E1-2 Since Frank Jones began a small bakery business in a local mall 2 years ago, his sales volume has increased each year. The business is operated as a sole proprietorship. Located next door is a coffee shop operated by Pam Gilbert. Pam has suggested that the two enterprises combine by means of a partnership. Frank likes the idea of the larger enterprise but thinks incorporation would be the wiser choice.

a. Distinguish among the forms of business: sole proprietorship, partnership, and corporation.
b. What are the advantages and disadvantages of partnership?
c. What are the advantages and disadvantages of incorporation?

E1-3 Daniel and Carol are both accounting majors at a major university. Daniel has researched employment opportunities in accounting with large industrial firms. Carol has examined possibilities in public accounting.

a. Suggest possible career paths in Daniel's chosen field.
b. Trace Carol's career path and responsibilities in public accounting.

E1-4 Harwood Helm, a senior anthropology major, was willed a small plant shop by his wealthy aunt. Because he had not made any plans for a career, he decides to try running the business, but he is unsure of where to start. A friend who attends business school suggests contacting a certified public accountant.

a. What may have prompted his friend's suggestion.
b. How would a certified public accountant be of assistance?

E1-5 Classify each of the following items as either an *Asset, Liability,* or *Owners' Equity* item:

a. Cash
b. Mortgage payable
c. Office supplies
d. Capital stock
e. Salaries payable
f. Equipment (used in manufacturing a product)
g. Microcomputers
h. Retained earnings
i. Amount due IRS for back taxes plus a penalty

j. Interest due on loan from Friendly National Bank
k. Money owed to our company from a supplier who was inadvertently overpaid

E1-6 Marge Drew began her consulting business 3 years ago. At that time she and several of her friends invested a total of $5,000 in the business. Each of the founding stockholders were issued an amount of stock proportionate to their investment. Marge has never found the time to establish a formal accounting system for her business until now, when she asks for your help in setting up a basic system. Your examination of her business has determined that she presently has the following (listed alphabetically):

Accounts payable	$900 L
Capital stock	$5,000 O
Cash in bank	$10,200 A
Microcomputer	$2,800 A
Note payable: First Bank	$4,500 L
Office supplies	$2,500 A

REQUIRED:

1. What is the total amount of the assets in Marge Drew's business?
2. What is the total amount of liabilities?
3. What is the total amount of owners' equity?
4. What should the retained earnings of the business be at present?

ACCOUNTING METHODOLOGY 2

ORIENTATION

The purpose of this chapter is to expand, elaborate, and refine the basic accounting equation presented in Chapter 1. The underlying foundation and basic methodology of accounting practice is established through the introduction of basic accounting terminology. Fundamental financial statements are introduced along with the concepts of accrued accounting and double-entry bookkeeping. The concept of debits and credits and a listing of common account classifications complete this foundation chapter.

BASIC ILLUSTRATION: SMITH TRUCKING COMPANY

The Entity Principle

The basic accounting equation, Assets = Liabilities + Owners' Equity, was introduced in Chapter 1. To illustrate how this equation can be applied to a business situation, let us assume that Bob Smith and some of his friends decide to start a trucking business, and we are to perform the accounting for the business. It is important to remember that we will only be accounting for the

DATE	TRANSACTION	ASSETS	=	LIABILITIES	+	OWNERS' EQUITY
Jan. 2	Smith Trucking received $50,000 invested by the owners and issued stock to these owners	Cash + $50,000				Capital stock + $50,000
Jan. 3	Bought truck for $12,500	Cash − 12,500 Truck + 12,500				
Jan. 5	Bought land for $10,000 and building for $25,000	Cash − 35,000 Land + 10,000 Building + 25,000				
Jan. 18	Bought supplies on account for $2,400	Supplies + 2,400		Accounts payable + $2,400		
Jan. 22	Borrowed $5,000 from Friendly National Bank	Cash + 5,000		Note payable + 5,000		
Jan. 30	Paid creditor the amount owed for supplies purchased ($2,400)	Cash − 2,400		Accounts payable − 2,400		
	Totals	$55,000	=	$5,000	+	$50,000

trucking company *entity,* not for the person Bob Smith, or his friends, or other entities in which they might be involved.

The preceding example illustrates the effect of certain transactions on the accounting equation.

The total assets of $55,000 represents the following individual assets amounts:

Cash	$5,100	($50,000 − 12,500 − 35,000 + 5,000 − 2,400)
Truck	12,500	
Land	10,000	
Building	25,000	
Supplies	2,400	
	$55,000	

There is only one liability at the end of the month: Notes Payable, $5,000; and only one owners' equity item: Capital Stock, $50,000.

With this information we can now prepare a balance sheet.

THE BALANCE SHEET

The purpose of a *balance sheet* is to show the financial position of a business at a particular moment in time. It is a listing of the assets, liabilities, and owners' equity of a business *as of a given date.* Most businesses prepare balance sheets periodically, either monthly, quarterly, or annually. Obviously, the more often businesses prepare balance sheets, the more frequently there will be current information available to use in making decisions.

The balance sheet as of the end of January 19X1 for Smith Trucking Company would be as shown in Figure 2-1.

FIGURE 2-1

Smith Trucking Company, Inc.
Balance Sheet
as of January 31, 19X1

ASSETS		LIABILITIES AND OWNERS'S EQUITY	
Cash	$ 5,100	Liabilities: Notes payable	$ 5,000
Supplies	2,400	Owners' equity: Capital stock	50,000
Truck	12,500		
Land	10,000		
Buildings	25,000		
	$55,000		$55,000

Note that the heading of the balance sheet contains three items:

1. the name of the entity (Smith Trucking Company, Inc.);
2. the name of the statement (Balance Sheet); and
3. the date of the balance sheet.

Below this heading is the body of the balance sheet, which contains the listing of the assets, liabilities, and owners' equity of the business. It is essentially a formal representation of the basic equation Assets = Equities.

REVENUES AND EXPENSES

Most companies are in existence to make a profit. Heretofore we have only looked at transactions that involved trading among assets, liabilities, and capital stock. Now we will examine transactions which result in a profit or a loss to the corporation.

Net Income (or Profit)

A profit (or *net income*) is an increase in owners' equity resulting from the operations of the business. It can also be considered the excess of the revenues of an enterprise over expenses. If expenses exceed revenue, a loss occurs and owners' equity decreases.

Various Revenues and Expenses

In general, the amount charged to customers for the goods or services sold to them is called *revenue.* Examples of revenues are: fees earned by doctors, lawyers, CPAs, and other professional people; commissions earned by stockbrokers; interest earned by banks on loans to customers; and sales of companies selling merchandise rather than performing services for their customers. Revenues increase owners' equity. *Expenses* are the cost of the goods and services used up in the process of generating revenue. Common examples of expenses would be the cost of utilities to heat and cool the building, salaries paid to employees, depreciation on assets employed in the business, and the cost of merchandise that a company sells. Costs and expenses are not synonymous. For example, office supplies might cost a company $500, but that is not an expense until the company uses up those supplies. Because expenses are the cost of goods and services used up, they are referred to as *expired costs.* Expenses decrease owners' equity.

ACCRUAL CONCEPT

It is important to note that in the measurement of company profit, accounting does *not* merely measure money taken in versus money spent.[1] In accrual accounting, a commitment on the part of a customer to pay money in the future is considered revenue. Similarly, a commitment on the part of a company to pay out money in the future can be considered an expense. In addition, not all cash receipts are considered revenue, and not all cash payments are considered expenses. For example, a company might sell merchandise for $1,800 on December 20, 19X1, and not receive payment until February 2, 19X2. The sale of the merchandise would result in an increase in the assets of the firm (accounts receivable) of $1,800, and an increase in owners' equity of the same amount, *although no cash has been received.* However, when the cash payment is received on February 2, 19X2, this would *not* result in revenue. It would result in an increase in one asset (cash) and a decrease in another asset (accounts receivable).

Similarly, expenses and cash payments are not identical. Examples of cash payments which are not expenses include the purchase of land for cash (an increase in one asset—land, and a decrease in another asset—cash); the payment of an account payable (a decrease in a liability); and the payment of cash dividends.

EFFECT OF REVENUE AND EXPENSES ON THE ACCOUNTING EQUATION

It was mentioned earlier that revenues increase owners' equity and expenses have the opposite effect. Because that is the case, the accounting equation can now be expanded to:

$$A = L + [OE + (R - E)]$$

It is important to note that an increase in revenue increases the right side of the equation; but an increase in expenses decreases the right side of the equation because expenses have a negative (−) sign. So if a company pays utility expenses with cash, cash is decreased on the left side of the equation, and utility expense is increased on the right side. However, the equation remains in balance because expenses are subtracted on the right-hand side of the equation.

---

[1] There is an unsophisticated system of accounting known as *cash basis accounting* which essentially does measure revenue and expenses in terms of cash received and paid. The cash basis of accounting does not give a good picture of profitability. For example, it generally considers all money spent as an expense even if the money was spent to purchase an asset, and all money received as revenue even if it is for services to be rendered in the future.

SMITH TRUCKING COMPANY EXAMPLE, CONTINUED

We will now continue with the Smith Trucking Company example in its second month of operation. This time, however, we will list each asset, liability, and owners' equity item individually.

Note in Figure 2-2 that the accounting equation has been written across the top, with each individual asset, liability, and so on, to be used listed below. The beginning balances for the Smith Trucking Company example used previously are then inserted to begin the month.

Assume that, during the month of February 19X1, the following transactions occur:

Feb. 4	Hauled dirt for customer; customer paid $650
Feb. 6	Filled truck with gas; paid $45
Feb. 10	Hauled gravel for ABX, Inc.; sent them a bill for $875
Feb. 15	Had minor repair work done on truck; received bill for $190
Feb. 18	Hauled boxes for PDQ, Inc.; sent them a bill for $295
Feb. 22	Paid monthly note at bank Principal $45 Interest 50 Total $95
Feb. 23	ABX paid amount due: $875
Feb. 28	Supplies on hand: $1,950 Paid utility bill: $115 Depreciation on truck: $300 Depreciation on building: $200

Most of the examples in Figure 2-2 are self-explanatory; several items, however, deserve elaboration.

Date of Transaction	*Elaboration/Explanation*
Feb. 4	Received money for work performed; increase cash and fees revenue.
Feb. 6	Paid cash for gasoline; decrease cash and add gas expense which is a negative item on right side of equation.
Feb. 10	Performed the work, but did not receive cash. Because this is an accrual accounting system, an asset (accounts receivable) is increased, and revenues are also increased.
Feb. 15	Another example of accrual accounting. Money did not change hands, but Smith Trucking Company has incurred a commitment to transfer funds in the future. Thus an expense is increased and a liability is increased as well. (Again, increasing the expense has the effect of decreasing the right side of the equation.)
Feb. 18	Same as the Feb. 10 transaction.
Feb. 22	Paid cash to bank for two things: interest on $5,000 loan and

FIGURE 2-2

Smith Trucking Company, Inc.

DATE	ASSETS									LIABILITIES	
	Cash	***Accts. rec.***	***Supplies***	***Truck***	***Acc. dep. truck***	***Land***	***Building***	***Acc. dep. bldg.***		***Accts. pay.***	***Notes pay.***
Beg. Bal.	$5,100		$2,400	$12,500		$10,000	$25,000				$5,000
Feb. 1, 19X1											
Feb. 4	+650										
Feb. 6	− 45										
Feb. 10		+875									
Feb. 15										+190	
Feb. 18		+295									
Feb. 22	− 95										−45
Feb. 23	+875	−875									
Feb. 28			−450								
	−115										
					−300						
								−200			
	$6,370	$295	$1,950	$12,500	−$300	$10,000	$25,000	−$200	=	$190	4,955
					$55,615						

FIGURE 2-2

Smith Trucking Company, Inc.

DATE	OWNERS' EQUITY +	REVENUE −			EXPENSES				
								Depreciation	
	Cap. stock	*Fees*	*Gas*	*Repairs*	*Supplies*	*Interest*	*Utilities*	*Trucks*	*Bldg.*
Beg. Bal. 19X1	$50,000								
Feb. 4		+650							
Feb. 6			+ 45						
Feb. 10		+875							
Feb. 15				+ 190					
Feb. 18		+295							
Feb. 22						+ 50			
Feb. 23									
Feb. 28					+ 450				
							+ 115		
								+ 300	
									+ 200
	$50,000	$1,820	−$45	−$190	−$450	−$50	−$115	−$300	−$200
				$55,615					

repayment of principal. So, a reduction of cash is required along with a deduction of the note payable and increase in interest expense.

Feb. 23 Smith Trucking Company received cash in payment of an account receivable. Notice that revenue is not increased as the cash is received. To do so would be to record it twice, because under accrual accounting the revenue was increased when the commitment to convey cash was incurred on Feb. 10.

Feb. 28 (1) The company determined that the supplies on hand totaled \$1,950. This means that supplies used totaled \$450 (\$2,400 − \$1,950). It is thus necessary to reduce the asset, Supplies, to \$1,950 and to increase the Supplies Expense item by \$450.

Feb. 28 (2) The company paid cash of \$115 for utilities expense for the month.

Feb. 28 (3) It was determined that the truck depreciated by \$300 and the building by \$200. (The method of determining depreciation will be discussed in a later chapter). The expense item, Depreciation Expense, is increased and a *contra-asset* account, Accumulated Depreciation, is increased. The contra asset Accumulated Depreciation will be shown as a deduction from the related asset account when the balance sheet is presented. It should be noted that essentially the same results would have occurred had we reduced the assets accounts (truck and building) directly, instead of recording the depreciation in an accompanying contra asset. However, by recording the depreciation as we have done, we have additional information in that we will know at all times the original cost of the assets and the accumulated depreciation on those assets.

The total of each side of the equation is \$55,615. On the asset side this number is determined by adding the assets and subtracting the contra assets (accumulated depreciation). On the equity side of the equation, the liabilities, owners' equity, and revenues are added, and the expenses are subtracted.

THE INCOME STATEMENT

The *income statement* is a listing of the revenues minus the expenses of an entity for a specific period of time such as a month, quarter, or year. As mentioned earlier in the chapter, *profit* or *net income* is the difference between the revenues and expenses for the specified period. Figure 2-3 presents the income statement for February 19X1 for Smith Trucking Company.

As with the balance sheet, the heading for the income statement contains three items: (1) the name of the business, (2) the name of the statement (Income Statement), and (3) the time period covered by the statement. Unlike the balance sheet, which is as of a particular day, an income statement is prepared for a period or block of time such as a month, a quarter, or a year.

FIGURE 2-3

Smith Trucking Company, Inc.
Income Statement
for the month ended February 28, 19X1

Revenues:			
	Hauling fees		$1,820
Expenses:			
	Gas	$ 45	
	Repairs	190	
	Supplies	450	
	Interest	50	
	Utilities	115	
	Depreciation: Truck	300	
	Depreciation: Building	200	
	Total expenses		1,350
Net income			$ 470

DEBITS AND CREDITS

The system that we have used up to now for recording transactions has been useful, but obviously could become cumbersome for a larger company. Consequently a system utilizing *accounts, debits,* and *credits* is actually used in accounting. In most accounting systems you will find separate *accounts* for each asset, liability, and so forth. An account can be a space in the storage capacity of a computer, but for the sake of learning, it is best thought of as a sheet of paper having two sides: a left or *debit* side, and a right or *credit* side. Increases in the account are always recorded on one side, and decreases are always recorded on the other. Figure 2-4 represents the way the Cash account may appear for a company.

It is important to note that in manual accounting systems, accounts look very much like the illustration in Figure 2-4.

Exactly the same principle exists in computer-based accounting systems, but the information in such systems is kept in the storage capacity of the computer rather than on a sheet of paper. For learning purposes, it is useful to think of the account in the manual method just described: as a sheet of paper with a left and a right side.

As mentioned previously, debit simply means left side of the account, and credit means right side. However, debits signify increases for assets and expenses, and decreases for liabilities, owners' equity, and revenue. Credits signify

FIGURE 2-4

Account for: CASH

Left or *Debit* side (Increases)	Right or *credit* side (Decreases)

FIGURE 2-5

Accounting Equation:

	Assets	= *Liabilities*	+ *Owners' equity*	+ *Revenues*	− *Expense*
To Increase:	Debit	Credit	Credit	Credit	Debit
To Decrease:	Credit	Debit	Debit	Debit	Credit

decreases for assets and expenses, and increases for liabilities, owners' equity and revenue. This relationship of debits and credits to the accounting equation is summarized in Figure 2-5.

Therefore to increase an asset, such as cash, we would debit it; or, in other words, place the amount of the transaction on the left side of the account. To increase a revenue account, such as hauling fees, we would credit it, or place the amount on the right side of the account. So to record the transaction on February 4, 19X1, in which Jones Trucking Company received $650 for hauling dirt we would:

Debit (dr.): Cash (Asset) for $650
Credit (cr.): Fees (Revenue) for $650

Often debits are abbreviated by "dr." and credits by "cr."

The accounts for Cash and Fees would appear as follows after the previous transaction was recorded:

Cash

Debit		Credit
(Beginning balance)	$5,100	
(Feb. 4)	650	

Fees

Debit	Credit	
	$650	(Feb. 4)

For each transaction, (1) debits will always equal credits; and (2) the accounting equation will always remain in balance. This dual balancing feature helps assure the mathematical accuracy of the accounting function.

DIVIDENDS

Dividends are distributions of the corporation's earnings to stockholders. When it is determined that the dividends are to be paid, the accountant debits (thereby increasing) the Dividends account, and credits (thereby increasing), the Dividends Payable account. When the dividends are actually paid, the accountant debits (thereby reducing) Dividends Payable, and credits (thereby reducing) Cash. Dividends are not an expense, but have the effect of reducing owners' equity.

COMMON ACCOUNT CLASSIFICATIONS

Figure 2-6 lists several frequently encountered account classifications relating to the accounting equation. You will notice that assets and liabilities are divided into two categories, current and noncurrent.

Current assets are defined as cash or items which will be converted into cash (i.e., Accounts Receivable) or consumed (i.e., Prepaid Expenses) within one year. Occasionally, current assets include items which will be converted into cash or consumed over a period longer than one year. This procedure is normally followed in cases where the company's *operating cycle* exceeds one year. An operating cycle is the average period of time between the acquisition of merchandise for resale and the conversion of this merchandise back into cash.

FIGURE 2-6

Common Account Classifications

I. ASSETS
- A. Current assets:
  - Cash
  - Short-term investments
  - Accounts receivable (from customers)
  - Merchandise inventory
  - Prepaid expenses
- B. Long-term investments
- C. Plant assets:
  - Land
  - Buildings
  - Machinery, equipment
- D. Intangible assets:
  - Patents
  - Franchises
  - Goodwill

II. LIABILITIES
- A. Current liabilities:
  - Accounts payable (to supplies)
  - Notes payable (short-term)
  - Wages payable
  - Taxes payable
  - Interest payable
  - Dividends payable
- B. Long-term liabilities:
  - Mortgage payable
  - Bonds payable
  - Notes payable (long-term)

III. OWNERS' EQUITY
- Capital stock
- Retained earnings

IV. REVENUES
- Sales of services (Fees)
- Sales of merchandise
- Other income (such as interest income)

V. EXPENSES
- A. Cost of merchandise sold
- B. Selling expenses:
  - Sales salaries
  - Advertising expense
  - Delivery expense
  - Miscellaneous selling expense
- C. Administrative and general expenses:
  - Administrative salaries
  - Office salaries
  - Utilities expense
  - Depreciation expense
  - Insurance expense
  - Interest expense
  - Rent expense
  - Miscellaneous administrative and general expense
- D. Federal Income tax expense

The series of transactions normally included in the operating cycle are: (1) purchase of merchandise, (2) sale of merchandise for credit, (3) collection of the account receivable from the customer. By showing these assets in a separate category on the balance sheet, we are able to inform the reader of the short-term debt paying ability of an entity. Some of the other asset categories include such items as long-term investments, plant assets, and intangibles.

Current liabilities are those obligations whose retirement is anticipated to require the use of current assets or the creation of new current liabilities. So, realistically, most current liabilities are those which will be paid off within one year. Long-term liabilities are all other debts of the entity.

Figure 2-6 is not intended to be a completely comprehensive listing. More detailed explanations of some of the subclassifications and accounts and additional account titles will follow later in the book.

SUMMARY

As with any field of knowledge, the understanding of accounting theory and methodology is based on the grasp of the underlying tenets and principles. The central identity and relationships of accounting are reflected in the basic equation: Assets equal Liabilities plus Equities. The introduction of basic terminology allows for consistency and conformity in practice. The basic financial statements—balance sheet and income statement—are the end product of the accounting function. The foundations of contemporary accounting methodology are based on the accrual concept and double-entry bookkeeping utilizing debits and credits to indicate increases and decreases in the various accounts.

KEY POINTS

1. The purpose of the **balance sheet** is to show the financial position of a business at a particular moment in time. It is a formal representation of the basic accounting equation.

2. A **profit** (or net income) is an increase in the owners' equity resulting from the operations of the business. It can be considered the excess of revenues over expenses.

3. A **loss** occurs when expenses exceed revenues and therefore owners' equity is decreased.

4. An extension of the basic accounting equation to reflect revenues and expenses is: Assets equal Liabilities plus Owners' Equity plus Revenues minus Expenses.

5. The **income statement** is a listing of the revenues minus the expenses of an entity for a specified period of time.

6. **Revenue** is the amount charged to customers for goods or services sold them.

7. **Expenses** are the cost of goods and services used up in the process of generating revenue. Expenses are often referred to as *expired costs,* and they result in a decrease in owners' equity.

8. An **account** is best considered to be a sheet of paper having two sides: a *debit* (left) side, and a *credit* (right) side. A separate account is kept for each asset, liability, owners' equity, revenue, and expense item.

9. **Current assets** are cash or items which will be converted into cash within the length of one year or the normal operating cycle of the business.

10. **Current liabilities** are obligations whose retirement is anticipated to require the use of current assets or the creation of new current liabilities.

QUESTIONS

1. Define the following terms:

   a. Revenue
   b. Expense
   c. Profit
   d. Current asset
   e. Current liability
   f. Account
   g. Debit
   h. Credit

2. Why is the change in a firm's cash balance not necessarily the same as earnings for the period?

3. An expense may be shown on the income statement even if payment of the amount did not occur during the accounting period covered by that income statement. Explain.

4. In reporting assets on a company's balance sheet, why is no distinction made between those provided by creditors and those provided by owners?

5. Why is the balance sheet sometimes called the statement of financial position?

6. Why are earnings added to (and losses subtracted from) the owners' contributions to the firm to arrive at the total amount of owners' claims to firm assets?

7. What are the two primary sources of owners' equity in a business?

8. How does the income statement relate to the balance sheet?

9. Explain the relationship of debits and credits to the elements of the accounting equation.

10. Why is a systematic framework of accounting essential to business firms? Why is knowledge of this framework vital for an understanding of the financial statements of business firms?

EXERCISES

E2-1 Dynamo Janitorial Services Corporation does various cleaning jobs for business firms. Most of these sales of services are on account (on a credit basis). At the beginning of 19X1, the firm's customers owe it a total of $6,000. During 19X1, the firm's credit sales amount to $49,000. Collections from customers totaled $59,000 of which $9,000 represented cash sales. Operating costs amounted to $60,000. What is the profit or loss for 19X1? What amount is owed the firm by its customers at the end of 19X1?

E2-2 The Ventura Company reported assets amounting to $100,000 and liabilities amounting to $45,000 on its December 31, 19X2 balance sheet. Assets of $85,000 and liabilities of $50,000 had been reported on the December 31, 19X1 balance sheet. Dividends of $5,000 were paid to stockholders in 19X2. There were no additional contributions of capital stockholders in 19X2. What was the amount of net earnings (or net loss) for the Ventura Company in 19X2?

E2-3 The Ringgold Corporation began operations in January 19X0, when $250,000 of capital stock was issued to stockholders. During its first 3 years of operations, net earnings amounted to $60,000 and there was no dividend distribution to stockholders. In 19X1, an additional $50,000 of capital stock was issued. On December 31, 19X2, reported assets held amounted to $550,000. How much is owed to creditors by the firm on that date?

E2-4 Based on the following information, indicate whether the items appear as assets (A), liabilities (L), or owners' equity (OE) on the balance sheet:

a. Delivery equipment	$24,000	______
b. Land	50,000	______
c. Cash	25,000	______
d. Liabilities, long-term	40,000	______
e. Marketable securities	10,000	______
f. Buildings	52,000	______
g. Liabilities, current	25,000	______
h. Capital stock	62,000	______
i. Retained earnings	32,000	______
j. Receivables	36,000	______

E2-5 **REQUIRED:**

For each transaction described next, indicate in each column whether the total is increased, decreased, or not changed by the transaction.

	Total Assets	Total Liabilities	OWNERS' EQUITY Capital Stock	OWNERS' EQUITY Retained Earnings
a. Payment in cash of interest expense				
b. Purchase of supplies on credit				
c. Depreciation recorded on assets				
d. Collection of accounts receivable				
e. Borrowing money from bank				
f. Recording of income tax for year—part paid in cash; remainder payable next year				
g. Sale of plant asset at a gain; that is, for more than its undepreciated value				

E2-6 Using the same format as in E2-5, classify the following transactions:

a. Purchased office equipment on credit
b. Paid a liability of the business
c. Owner invested cash in the business
d. Obtained a loan from the bank for business use
e. Purchased a delivery truck for cash
f. Returned for credit some defective office equipment purchased on credit but not paid for

E2-7 Using the format from E2-5, classify the effects of the following transactions:

a. Owner invests cash in business
b. Collection of an account receivable
c. Purchased typewriter on credit
d. Purchased office supplies for cash
e. Paid a liability
f. Sold land for a price in excess of cost

E2-8 The Falcone Corporation is in the process of preparing a balance sheet at the end of 19X1. The following amounts have been determined:

Retained earnings at the start of 19X1	$74,000
Cash dividends paid to stockholders during 19X1	40,000
Net income (after income taxes) for 19X1	48,000

Determine the amount of retained earnings at the end of 19X1.

E2-9 From the following information, prepare a balance sheet in good form:

Accounts payable	$40,000	Capital stock	$100,000
Building	80,000	Accounts receivable	50,000
Supplies	10,000	Equipment	40,000
Cash	20,000	Retained earnings	60,000

E2-10 Dabney Real Estate, Inc., which has been operating for the past 7 years, is owned by four investors. Coleman Dabney owns 55 percent of the stock (5,500 shares) and is the manager in charge. On December 31, 19X2, the following financial information was determined:

Commissions earned and collected in cash	$200,000
Commissions earned and uncollected	20,000
Rental service fees collected and earned	36,000
Salaries expense paid	100,000
Commissions expenses paid	80,000
Payroll taxes paid	6,000
Rent paid—11 months (not including December, yet to be paid) at $200 per month	2,200
Utilities expenses paid	1,000
Promotion and advertising paid	11,600
Miscellaneous expenses paid	400
Office furniture cost $6,000 when acquired and has an estimated useful life of 10 years.	
Depreciation calculated	600
The corporate income tax rate is 22 percent, resulting in a tax of	11,880
During the year, the company paid the owners cash dividends "out of profit," totaling	$20,000

Prepare an income statement for 19X2.

E2-11 The How-To Bookstore was organized by Chuck Cuttie and Dave Wrigley as a corporation with each contributing $30,000 to provide the initial capital. The store ended its first year of operations on December 31, 19X2. On that date, the following financial information was available:

Cash on hand in the bank	$44,000
Due from customers from sale of books	2,000
Store and office equipment, purchased January 1, 19X2 for $60,000 (estimated useful life 10 years), depreciation for the year was calculated to be	6,000
Amounts owed to publishers for books purchased	8,000
A note payable to the local bank	4,000
The first year's profit totaled.	28,000

None of it was paid out in dividends during the year.

REQUIRED:

Prepare a balance sheet for How-To Bookstore as of December 31, 19X2.

PROBLEMS

P2-1 The following selected transactions for Amanda Company are summarized in equation form in the following table, with each of its eight transactions identified by letter.

Assets = Liabilities + Owners' Equity

	CASH	+ ACCOUNTS RECEIVABLE	+ BUILDING	+ EQUIPMENT	= ACCOUNTS PAYABLE	+ AMANDA CAPITAL
	$ -0-	$ -0-	$ -0-	$ -0-	$ -0-	$ -0-
a.	+30,000					+30,000
	$30,000					+30,000
b.	−26,000		+26,000			
	$ 4,000	-0-	$26,000	-0-	-0-	$30,000
c.				+8,000	$8,000	
	$ 4,000	-0-	$26,000	$8,000	$8,000	$30,000
d.	+ 6,000					+ 6,000
	10,000	-0-	26,000	8,000	8,000	36,000
e.		+5,000				+5,000
	10,000	5,000	26,000	8,000	8,000	41,000
f.	− 2,000				− 2,000	
	8,000	5,000	26,000	8,000	6,000	41,000
g.	+1,000	−1,000				
	9,000	4,000	26,000	8,000	6,000	41,000
h.	− 600					− 600
	$8,400	$4,000	$26,000	$8,000	$6,000	$40,400

Write an explanation of the nature of each transaction. Assume that item a. is the only contribution or withdrawal of capital by the owner, and that the company does not use revenue and expense accounts but rather records such items directly into the capital account.

P2-2 From the following information about Jay's Lakeside Paradise, prepare a balance sheet at August 31. Also prepare a new balance sheet after the transactions of September 21 and a third after the transaction of October 1.

Accounts payable	$ 24,000	Office equipment	$15,840
Accounts receivable	33,880	Buildings	57,200
Cash	?	Notes payable	6,820
Capital stock	116,380	Land	26,400

Sept. 21 Fifty percent of the land was sold at a price of $13,200, which was equal to its cost. A down payment of $4,400 in cash was received and the buyer agreed to pay the balance within 10 days.

Oct. 1 Cash totaling $8,800 was received from collection of an account receivable as final settlement from the buyer of the land. In addition, a cash payment of $2,400 was made on an account payable.

P2-3 Scholastic Paper, Inc., is a service enterprise to students. Its owner, Mike Quinn, has only a limited knowledge of accounting. He prepared the following balance sheet which, although arranged satisfactorily, has errors relating to the concepts of business entity and asset valuation. The amount of capital was determined by subtracting total liabilities from total assets.

Scholastic Papers, Inc.
Balance Sheet
November 30, 19X2

ASSETS		LIABILITIES AND OWNERS' EQUITY	
Cash	$ 2,520	Notes payable	$150,000
Notes receivable	2,000	Accounts payable	36,000
Accounts receivable	9,130	Total liabilities	$186,000
Land	90,000		
Building	122,050		
Office furniture	13,686	Owners' equity	71,916
Other assets	18,530		
	$257,916		$257,916

In discussions with Quinn, and by inspection of the accounting records, the following facts are discovered:

a. One of the accounts receivable, amounting to $6,000, is an IOU which Quinn received in a backgammon tournament 5 years ago. The IOU bears only initials and Quinn does not know either the name or the address of the maker.

b. Office furniture includes an antique desk purchased November 29 of the current year at a cost of $3,600. Quinn explains that he is not required to pay for the desk until January, and accordingly he did not include this debt among the liabilities.

c. Also included in the amount for office furniture is a word processor costing $950, which Quinn gave his son as a birthday present.

d. The item Other Assets, of $18,530, represents the total amount of income taxes paid to the federal government over a period of years. Quinn believes the tax to be unconstitutional and believes he will be able to recapture it once his son completes law school.

e. The land was acquired at a cost of $50,000 but the balance sheet entry was increased to $90,000 when a friend offered to pay that much if the building could be moved from the lot.

Prepare a corrected balance sheet for November 30, 19X2.

For each of the five sets of additional information, explain the appropriate generally accepted accounting principle which governs the proper treatment.

P2-4 Jonas Jewelers is developing the annual financial statements for 19X2. The following amounts have been verified at December 31, 19X1:

Cash	$39,000
Accounts receivable	11,200
Merchandise inventory	320,000
Investment in stock of the Randex Corp. (long-term)	20,000
Store equipment	64,000
Used store equipment held for disposal	27,000
Accumulated depreciation on store equipment	19,200
Accounts payable	52,800
Long-term notes payable	80,000
Income taxes payable	10,200
Retained earnings	109,000
Common stock, 10,000 shares outstanding, sold at $21 per share	

Prepare a classified balance sheet at December 31, 19X1.

P2-5 A list of balance sheet items appear here for Harry Calvin Lodge at November 30, 19X3. Prepare a classified balance sheet for November 30, 19X3 including a figure for total liabilities. Owners' equity must be calculated.

Accounts payable	$37,500	Buildings	$156,000
Accounts receivable	33,750	Cash	29,250
Vehicles	30,600	Note payable	60,000
Land	75,000	Equipment	75,000
Accumulated depreciation: Vehicles	6,000	Owners' Equity	?

P2-6 Transactions of the Webb Company are summarized here in equation form. For each transaction, a. through g., write a separate sentence explaining the nature of the transaction. Webb does not use revenue or expense accounts but rather includes such items directly in capital. There were no owner contributions to, or withdrawals from, the business during the period.

	ASSETS					= LIABILITIES + EQUITY	
	Cash	+ Accounts Receivable	+ Land	+ Building	+ Equipment	= Accounts Payable	+ T. Webb Capital
Balance	$6,200	$12,800	$42,000	$114,200	$ -0-	$18,200	$157,000
a.	+1,000	− 1,000					
Balance	7,200	11,800	42,000	114,200	-0-	18,200	157,000
b.	−2,400				+ 2,400		
Balance	4,800	11,800	42,000	114,200	2,400	18,200	157,000
c.	+4,000						+ 4,000
Balance	8,800	11,800	42,000	114,200	2,400	18,200	161,000
d.					+ 3,200	+ 3,200	
Balance	8,800	11,800	42,000	114,200	5,600	21,400	161,000
e.	− 800				+ 4,800	+ 4,000	
Balance	8,000 +	11,800 +	42,000 +	114,200 +	10,400 =	25,400	161,000
f.	−1,000						− 1,000
Balance	7,000 +	11,800 +	42,000 +	114,200 +	10,400 =	25,400 +	160,000
g.	−1,200					− 1,200	
	$5,800 +	$11,800 +	$42,000 +	$114,200 +	$10,400 =	$24,200 +	$160,000

P2-7 Balance sheet items for Blueberry Valley Coffee Shop on October 1 were as follows:

Accounts payable	$ 16,800	Accounts receivable	$ 1,260
Building	184,000	Cash	19,320
Furniture	109,200	Land	105,000
Note payable	151,200	Supplies	11,760
Capital stock	100,000	Retained earnings	?

During the next 2 days, the following transactions occurred:

Oct. 2 (1) The owner invested an additional $63,000 cash in the business. (2) The accounts payable were paid in full. (No payment was made on the note payable).

Oct. 3 (1) Dining-room furniture was purchased at a cost of $37,800 to be paid within 10 days. (2) Supplies were purchased for $2,100 at a fire sale for a supply outlet. If purchased through regular channels, these supplies would have cost $3,780.

Prepare balance sheet for October 1 and October 3.

P2-8 Steve Paisley resigned from his position with a national firm of certified public accounts to establish his own public accounting practice. The following events occurred during September, the first month of operation. Some of the events relate to the business entity, Steve Paisley, CPA, while others are personal in nature and have no effect on the business entity.

- **Sept. 1** Sold personal investments consisting of an apartment building and some IBM stock for a total of $196,000 cash. Deposited $150,000 of this cash in a bank account in the name of the practice, Steve Paisley, CPA.
- **Sept. 2** Bought some gold bars for $12,000, which he placed in a safe deposit box rented under his name.
- **Sept. 2** Purchased land with a small office building suitable for his accounting practice. Total cost was $180,000 of which $100,000 was paid from the business bank account as a cash down payment. Paisley signed a note payable for the balance calling for payment in 5 years or less. The county property tax assessor had indicated that the land had a current fair value 50 percent greater than the value of the office building. (Divide the total cost between land and office building).
- **Sept. 3** Purchased office equipment for cash, $10,400.
- **Sept. 3** Moved his personal accounting library from his home to the office with the purpose of investing this library as an asset of the business. Fair market value of the library was $1,700.
- **Sept. 5** Agreed to employ a recent college graduate as staff assistant at a monthly salary of $1,500. The staff assistant was to report for work on October 1.
- **Sept. 6** Purchased a dirt track motorcycle which he planned to use on weekend trips. He turned in an old motorcycle and paid a balance of $1,600 in cash.
- **Sept. 7** Returned a defective chair included in the September 3 purchase of office equipment for full credit of $470. Received in exchange another model chair priced at $420 and a cash refund of $50.
- **Sept. 8** On Sunday, while visiting a friend who was going out of business and entering military service, Paisley had an opportunity to buy for $1,200 cash some office supplies which had originally cost $2,000. Paisley used a personal check to pay for the supplies.
- **Sept. 9** Brought to his office the office supplies purchased the previous day.

a. List those transactions which are personal in nature, and which should not be included in the balance sheet of the business entity.
b. Prepare a balance sheet for the business entity at September 9, 19X2.

P2-9 The B Corporation shows the following total amounts in its accounts on December 31, 19X1. It operates on a calendar-year basis.

Assets, December 31, 19X1	$598,300
Expenses for year 19X1	467,500
Dividends in 19X1	15,000
Liabilities, December 31, 19X1	183,900
Owners' equity: Capital stock, December 31, 19X1	250,000
Stockholders' equity: Retained earnings, January 1, 19X1	141,400
Revenue for year 19X1	505,500

REQUIRED:

1. Express the above figures in accordance with equation

$$A = L + OE + (R - E)$$

2. Determine the December 31, 19X1, amount of total owners' equity.
3. What is the amount of the earnings for 19X1?
4. If the owners decided to liquidate the firm and they could dispose of the assets for $540,000 on December 31, 19X1, what would the creditors receive in the dissolution and what would the stockholders receive?

P2-10 After the first 5 months of operations in calendar year 19X2, the G Corporation's accounting records show the following amounts on June 1, 19X2:

Assets	$87,000
Expenses	43,000
Dividends	6,000
Liabilities	23,000
Owners' equity: Capital stock	40,000
Owners' equity: Retained earnings	18,000
Revenues	55,000

The retained earnings amount is taken as of December 31, 19X1—the last date on which the accounting records have been adjusted and closed. All the other amounts reflect the operations of 19X2 up to June 1. The following events took place during the month of June:

a. The G corporation purchased from its suppliers, on account, merchandise costing $15,000.
b. Capital stock was issued in exchange for a new building valued at $25,000.
c. The G Corporation sold merchandise that had cost $20,000 to customers, on account, for $35,000.
d. Wages and other costs of operations amounting to $8,000 were paid.

REQUIRED:

1. Show the effects of each of these events on the assets, expenses, dividends, liabilities, stockholders' equity, and revenue of the G Corporation.
2. Calculate the amount of earnings for the first 6 months of 19X2.
3. Calculate the amount of stockholders' equity as of June 30, 19X2.

P2-11 Harry Sethna established a corporation engaged in environmental consulting, on July 16 of the current year. During the remainder of the month, the following business transactions were completed:

July 16 Sethna transferred from a personal bank account to the corporation, in exchange for stock, $10,000

16	Purchased equipment on account, $1,500
16	Purchased supplies for cash, $350
17	Paid rent for period of July 16 to end of month, $700
18	Purchased a truck for $18,000, paying $3,000 cash and giving a note payable for the remainder
19	Received cash for job completed, $800
22	Purchased supplies on account, $250
23	Paid wages of employees, $1,200
23	Paid 1-year premium on property and casualty insurance, $850
25	Paid creditor for equipment purchased on July 16, $1,500
26	Recorded sales on account and sent invoices to customers, $7500
29	Received cash for job completed, $820, the sale had not been recorded previously
29	Received an invoice for truck expense, to be paid in August, $184
30	Paid utilities expense, $210
30	Paid miscellaneous expenses, $90
31	Received cash from customers on account, $4,500
31	Paid wages of employees, $1,300

REQUIRED:

Record each of the transactions in a manner similar to the illustration in Figure 2-2 in the text.

P2-12 You will find here several accounts with numbered transactions for the month of October that have already been recorded. You will also find a list of transaction descriptions with a letter identification. You are required to make a list of the transaction numbers, and place a letter opposite each to identify the type of transaction that took place.

Cash

Debit	Credit
(1) 50,000	(6) 200,000
(2) 400,000	(7) 8,000
(4) 60,000	(12) 3,000
	(13) 15,000

Accounts Receivable

Debit	Credit
(3) 80,000	(4) 60,000
	(9) 5,000

Notes Receivable

Debit	Credit
(9) 5,000	

Interest Receivable

Debit	Credit
(10) 150	

Merchandise

Debit	Credit
(5) 40,000	

Equipment

Debit	Credit
(6) 200,000	(8) 5,000

Accounts Payable

Debit	Credit
(13) 15,000	(5) 40,000

Rent Payable

Debit	Credit
	(11) 500

Taxes Withheld

Debit	Credit
	(7) 1,000

Capital Stock	
	(2) 400,000

Sales	
	(1) 50,000
	(3) 80,000

Advertising Expense	
(12) 3,000	

Salaries Expense	
(7) 8,000	

Rent Expense	
(11) 500	

Depreciation Expense	
(8) 5,000	

Interest Income	
	(10) 150

Transaction descriptions:

- **a.** Payroll paid
- **b.** Equipment purchased
- **c.** Purchases on account
- **d.** Collection on account
- **e.** Sale on account
- **f.** Capital stock issued for cash
- **g.** Cash sale
- **h.** Depreciation recognized
- **i.** Note taken on account
- **j.** Accrual of rent
- **k.** Paid on advertising expense
- **l.** Accrual of interest income
- **m.** Paid on account

P2-13 Assume that you are a practicing certified public accountant and that you receive the following letter from an acquaintance, on January 7, 19X2.

> Dear Joe:
> Our company is trying to get a bank loan so that we can broaden our product line. The bank wants a balance sheet for the business before they will consider extending us any additional credit. I have gathered the information as of December 31, 19X1, that I think is needed.
>
> Our building and equipment cost $80,000 total. We have taken $12,000 in depreciation expense on our income tax returns since we started the business. We still owe $15,000 on our mortgage note to the bank for the building (our installment payments are $100 a month), but the equipment is fully paid for. The cash balance for the company was $8,000 on December 31. Our customers owe us $11,000 and we expect to collect every dollar of it. The merchandise inventory on hand on December 31 cost $25,000. The lot our building is on cost $6,000. We bought the lot next to it a couple of years ago for $5,000 and we expect to build a small warehouse on it someday, but we haven't made use of this land yet. We owe $14,000 on account to our suppliers and a $1,500 note to the bank due on March 31, 19X2.

As you know, my father-in-law, my brother, and I own all the capital stock in our firm. Altogether, we put up $50,000 for the 5,000 shares of $10 par value stock issued when we organized the company. We haven't issued any stock since, but we've retained most of our earnings in the business since then.

I would like you to prepare a balance sheet for our company in the best form you can from this information. Of course, I don't expect you to accept any responsibility for the amounts reported.

Signed Max M. Bucks
President

From the information provided, prepare a balance sheet in good form for December 31, 19X1.

BASIC ELEMENTS OF AN ACCOUNTING SYSTEM

3

ORIENTATION

This chapter examines the methodology employed to address the primary task of an accounting system — to bring order to the mass of data generated in daily business activities in an accurate and economical fashion. The procedures employed are essential to assure that all the information is recorded in proper sequence, that the impact of the data is measured and appropriately allocated, and that data accumulation is without errors or omissions. Proper accounting controls are crucial to a good accounting system. The *accounting cycle* reflects this control methodology.

DOCUMENTS AND CONTROLS

The preceding chapters have served to introduce the nature and functions of accounting and have indicated that accounting plays an integral and essential role in business enterprise. Indeed, it is virtually impossible to operate even the simplest business without some form of accounting system. Anyone who has observed the operations of a business firm knows how much data are generated in day-to-day business activities.

It is the task of an accounting system to bring order to this mass of data, and to do so in an accurate and economical fashion. An accounting system is first a record-keeping system, and it must provide for orderly handling of data in a series of necessary elaborate procedures. These procedures must be such that there is assurance that all of the data are recorded in proper sequence, that the impact of the data is measured and appropriately allocated, and that the data are accumulated without omissions or errors in classification.

Accounting Controls

Control of data is essential throughout the entire record-keeping process to prevent errors and to help prevent and detect fraud. *Accounting controls* were defined as follows in *Statement on Auditing Standards No. 1* of the American Institute of Certified Public Accountants:

> Accounting controls comprise the plan of organization and all methods and procedures that are concerned mainly with, and relate directly to, the safeguarding of assets and the reliability of the financial records. They generally include such controls as the systems of authorization and approval, separation of duties concerned with record-keeping and accounting reports from those concerned with operations or asset custody, physical controls over assets, and internal auditing.

Source Documents

A good accounting system, then, must be characterized by proper accounting controls. Data which indicate the effects of business events must be brought under immediate control by being recorded in the system as the events occur. Such events invariably generate documents such as sales and purchase invoices, remittance advices, checks, and shipping orders. These documents provide the initial information concerning the financial impact of an event that is formally recorded in the accounting records. These *source documents* should be serially numbered to ensure their proper use and to avoid errors.

THE ACCOUNTING CYCLE

Ultimately, the objective of accounting activity is to produce financial statements for the business entity. The preparation of financial statements requires the careful accumulation of the data of business transactions, and the systematic rearrangement of data into patterns that will highlight important information about past events, and provide management, owners, and other interested parties with a basis for predicting future events. Through the centuries, the accounting models used in implementing those procedures have become fairly well established in terms of the specific routines that must be followed and the controls that are needed in order to ensure that all data have been properly included and properly combined.

The procedures utilized to accumulate and summarize the data into financial statements are often referred to as the *accounting cycle.* Basically, they are as follows:

1. Transactions are analyzed.
2. Transactions are recorded in a journal.
3. Transactions are posted from the journal to the ledger.
4. A trial balance is prepared.
5. Adjusting entries are recorded and posted.
6. Financial statements are prepared.
7. Closing entries are recorded.
8. A post-closing trial balance is prepared.

A worksheet is often prepared to facilitate the preparation of the financial statements. The worksheet is not an essential step in the accounting cycle, but rather an effort to expedite the process. The worksheet is illustrated in Chapter 4. In addition, an adjusted trial balance is often prepared in conjunction with the preparation of financial statements. As the name indicates, it is a trial balance prepared immediately after adjusting entries are posted. An adjusted trial balance is illustrated in Chapter 4 in conjunction with the worksheet.

THE JOURNAL

The General Journal

A *journal* is a chronological listing of all business transactions that will go into the accounting system. There are several types of journals to record several specific types of transactions. We will briefly examine the various kinds of journals in the next chapter. However, an accounting system always includes a *general journal* which we will use for all activities in this chapter.

The general journal of an enterprise would appear as follows:

GENERAL JOURNAL				PAGE NO.
Date	**Account Titles and Explanation**	**Acct. No.**	**Dr.**	**Cr.**

For each transaction recorded, a date would be inserted in the left-hand column; then the account to be debited is written in the Account Title column. The account to be credited is written on the line below, with an indention to indicate that it is a credited item. The amounts are then inserted in the Dr. and Cr. columns. For example, if on October 1, 19X1, Z corporation is formed by the investing of $75,000 in cash for shares in the firm, the transaction would be recorded in the journal as follows:

JOURNAL				PAGE NO. 1
Date	**Account Titles and Explanation**	**Acct. No.**	**Dr.**	**Cr.**
19X1 Oct. 1	Cash Common stock To record initial investment in the business		75,000	 75,000

You will notice that the Acct. No. column is not filled in at this time. This is not done until the amounts in the journal are transferred to accounts in the ledger, at which time the ledger numbers for cash and common stock would be recorded in the Acct. No. column.

Recording transactions in the manner just illustrated is known as *journalizing,* and each transaction recorded in the journal is referred to as a *journal entry.* Because the journal is the place where each transaction is first recorded, it is known as the book of *original entry.* In contrast the ledger is known as the book of *final entry.*

THE LEDGER

The ledger is a series of accounts for the business entity. It is useful to think of each account as being a separate page in the ledger. The process of transferring the information contained in the journal to the ledger is called *posting.* The posting of the accounts is normally done monthly, although it can easily be done more, or less, frequently.

In posting debits and credits recorded in the journal, entries are transferred directly to the appropriate accounts in the ledger. Ledger accounts can be arranged in a number of different ways. However, they all contain the basic elements of an account (title, debit side, and credit side) as illustrated in Chapter 2. The posting of the journal entry to record the initial investment in the Z Corporation would appear as follows:

Cash (Acct. No. 101)	
19X1	
Oct. 1 75,000	

Common Stock (Acct. No. 301)	
	19X1
	Oct. 1 75,000

The account numbers (101 and 301) would then be recorded in the Acct. No. column in the journal to indicate that the amounts had been posted.

As you can see, each account in the ledger is like a "pigeon hole" into which the figures generated by the business events (and first recorded in the journal) are sorted. Because of the very large number of figures that must be handled, even in a small business firm, this orderly procedure is necessary to ensure that all of the financial data of the business events are recorded accurately, and that the data is arranged in meaningful patterns.

The simple ledger accounts that were just illustrated are often referred to as *T-accounts,* and are used primarily for illustrative purposes. The T-account form is used for illustration throughout this book. Actual accounts in a business ledger follow the exact principle of the T-account, but are usually in a somewhat more elaborate form. A common account form found in accounting practice is the three-column form, which would be constructed as follows:

CASH (ACCOUNT NO. 101)					
Date	**Explanation**	**Reference**	**Dr.**	**Cr.**	**Balance**

The date of the transaction would be posted in the Date column. The Explanation column is not frequently used, but is often provided to make notations when necessary. The Reference column will contain the page of the journal from which the entry is posted. (In turn, the account number from the ledger is entered in the Account Number column of the journal.) This provides a cross-reference between these two records.

Journalizing and posting by hand is used only to a limited extent in this book because of its limited use in business. With the increased availability of relatively inexpensive microcomputers, the manual approach of posting the accounts is used only in the smallest and most unsophisticated business firms.

In business firms having a large volume of transactions, where the chance for error is great, the posting process is usually performed by accounting machines or a computer. In these more sophisticated systems, transactions may actually be recorded simultaneously in the journal and ledger.

TRIAL BALANCE

The trial balance is a listing of the balances of the various accounts at the end of an accounting period (month, quarter, or year). It is prepared to determine that the debits equal the credits as of the end of an accounting period, after all normal transactions have been recorded. The trial balance will be illustrated in Chapter 4.

ADJUSTING ENTRIES

The financial statements that have been introduced previously are normally prepared at the end of each *fiscal year* (which may or may not correspond to the calendar year). Often financial statements are prepared more frequently, such as semiannually, quarterly, or monthly. Regardless of when constructed, the balance sheet must include all of the organization's financial resources as well as its liabilities on a particular date. Likewise, the income statement must present all revenue and expense information that is properly assignable to a particular period in the institution's life.

The Periodicity Principle and the Matching Principle

This breaking up of a continuous stream of business activity into artificial segments known as *accounting periods* (the *periodicity principle*) creates substantial measurement and allocation problems in the accounting process.

At the end of each accounting period, after the normal entries are completed, the accountant must determine whether any *adjusting entries* must be made to apportion certain items into the proper accounting period. Generally, adjusting entries must be made to update the accounting records because the passage of time has caused something recorded in one way to need to be modified. Adjusting entries are necessary, for example, because the recorded cost of assets, such as buildings or equipment, are gradually expiring with the passage of time. Before financial statements are prepared, the accounts must be brought up to date with respect to this depreciation of assets and several other items.

Another principle that is important to consider in the preparation of adjusting entries for any particular period of time is the *matching principle.* This principle holds that the revenue generated during an accounting period is matched with expenses incurred in generating that revenue. Stated differently, in matching revenue and expenses for a period, we first show all of the revenue earned during the period and then deduct from that revenue all expenses incurred in generating the revenue. This principle of matching revenues and expenses for a particular time period is the theoretical basis for most of the adjusting entries that are made.

Principal Types of Transactions Requiring Adjustment

There are four basic types of transactions that often cause adjusting entries to be made at the end of the accounting period:

COSTS

— *Recorded costs* which must be apportioned between two or more accounting periods. Example: Cost of an asset (such as equipment) which is used in business operations.

— *Unrecorded costs* that nevertheless must be identified within the current accounting period. Example: Interest cost on money borrowed, with the payment of interest to occur in a subsequent period.

REVENUE

— *Recorded revenue* which must be apportioned between two or more accounting periods. Example: Money received by a publisher from subscriptions to a magazine covering more than one accounting period.

— *Unrecorded revenue* that was earned in the current period but is to be collected in a subsequent period. Example: Rent revenue earned in the current period but uncollected at the end of the period.

Two terms, *accrued* and *deferred,* are frequently used in accounting in conjunction with adjusting entries. Accrued means built up or accumulated; deferred refers to postponement until a future time. Therefore, for example, an accrued expense is an expense incurred but not yet paid, such as salaries to be paid in the future. An example of an accrued revenue item is interest earned on loaned funds which has not yet been collected. An example of a deferred revenue is a revenue collected but not yet earned, such as advance receipt of payment for a service to be provided in the future; thus revenue recognition is postponed until the receipts are earned.

ADJUSTING ENTRIES ILLUSTRATED

Recorded Costs

Organizations often make payments in advance for items that will benefit future accounting periods. At the end of the current accounting period, a portion of the expenditure will have been consumed and the remainder of the expenditure will be unexpired (or still prepaid). That portion which has expired must be allocated into the current accounting period as an expense, and that portion which is unused represents an asset at the balance sheet date which will become an expense in due course.

Depreciation Illustration

On January 1, 19X1, Systems, Inc., purchased a computer from MBI, Inc., for $27,000. The asset has an estimated useful life of five years and an estimated *salvage value* (or trade-in value) of $3,000 at the end of that time. The series of entries would be:

Entry on purchase date:			
Jan. 1, 19X1	Computer equipment	$27,000	
	Cash		$27,000
	To record acquisition of computer equipment		
ADJUSTING ENTRY:			
Dec. 31, 19X1	Depreciation expense: Computer equipment	$ 4,800	
	Accumulated depreciation: Computer equipment		$ 4,800
	To record annual depreciation on computer equipment ($27,000 − $3,000 = $24,000 ÷ 5 = $4,800)		

The adjusting entry would be repeated at the end of each year over the life of the asset. The estimated amount of salvage value is deducted from the cost of the asset in arriving at annual depreciation expense. If financial statements are prepared more frequently than annually, the amount of the depreciation adjustment is reduced accordingly. For example, if statements are prepared monthly, the depreciation adjustment on January 31, 19X1, would be:

ADJUSTING ENTRY:		
Depreciation expense: Computer equipment	$400	
Accumulated depreciation: Computer equipment		$400
To record monthly depreciation on computer equipment ($4,800 ÷ 12 months = $400)		

This example assumes the straight-line depreciation method, in which the total cost minus salvage value is divided by the anticipated life of the asset. This and other methods of depreciation will be explained in more detail in Chapter 8.

Again, it is important to emphasize that the adjusting entry just illustrated serves two purposes: (1) It transfers the amount of expired cost to an expense account, and (2) it reduces the net amount in the asset account (by increasing a contra asset) to the amount which is unexpired.

Insurance Illustration

On August 31, 19X1, Systems, Inc., paid $3,600 for a two-year fire insurance policy covering their building. The series of entries would be:

Entry on purchase date:			
Aug. 31, 19X1	Prepaid insurance	$3,600	
	Cash		$3,600
	To record the acquisition of fire insurance policy		
ADJUSTING ENTRY:			
Dec. 31, 19X1	Insurance expense	$600	
	Prepaid insurance		$600
	To write off prepaid insurance		
	($3,600 ÷ 24 months = $150 per month × 4 months = $600)		

The adjusting entry would be repeated on December 31, 19X2 in the amount of $1,800 ($150 per month for 12 months); and on August 31, 19X3, the end of the policy life, the following entry would be made:

Aug. 31, 19X3	Insurance expense	$1,200	
	Prepaid insurance		$1,200
	To write off prepaid insurance ($150 × 8 months)		

Supplies Illustration

On June 15, 19X1, Systems, Inc., purchased supplies at a cost of $3,200. At the date of purchase they were placed in a special supplies closet to be used as needed. At the end of 19X1, an inventory of the supply closet indicated that $1,950 of supplies were still on hand. So, $1,250 ($3,200 − $1,950) worth of supplies were used up during the year. The series of entries would be:

Entry on purchase date:			
June 15, 19X1	Office supplies	$3,200	
	Cash (or Accounts payable)		$3,200
	To record acquisition of office supplies		
ADJUSTING ENTRY:			
Dec. 31, 19X1	Supplies expense	$1,250	
	Office supplies		$1,250
	To adjust office supplies account		

The adjusting entry results in the year-end accounting records reflecting the appropriate balance in the Office Supplies (asset) account, and in the Supplies Expense account.

Unrecorded Costs

Unrecorded costs are *accrued* liabilities that have been incurred during the year but not yet recorded. Accordingly, they represent liabilities at the end of the period; and the related debits for such items are included in the income statement as expenses. Depicted graphically they would appear as follows:

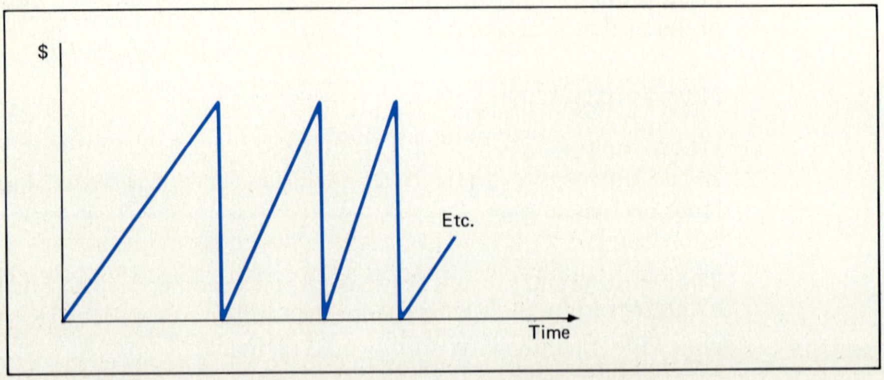

For such items (such as interest and salaries expense), the balance begins at zero, and as time goes on the liability and related expense increase until such time as payment is made and the liability amount drops immediately to zero. There is no problem in the proper accounting for these items except when the end of an accounting period occurs. It then becomes necessary to make adjusting entries in order to properly reflect expense and liability in the accounts.

Interest (Payable) Illustration

On October 30, 19X1, Systems, Inc., borrowed $100,000 cash from the Friendly National Bank on a six-month note with annual interest at 15 percent. The principal plus interest is due in six months. The sequence of entries is:

Borrowed the funds:			
Oct. 30, 19X1	Cash	$100,000	
	Note payable: Friendly National Bank		$100,000
	To record loan		
ADJUSTING ENTRY:			
Dec. 31, 19X1	Interest expense	$2,500	
	Interest payable		$2,500
	To record accrued interest payable ($100,000 × 15/100 × 2/12 = $2,500)		
Date of payment of principal and interest:			
Apr. 30, 19X2	Note payable: Friendly National Bank	$100,000	
	Interest payable	2,500	
	Interest expense	5,000	
	Cash		$107,500
	To record payment of loan (Total interest: $100,000 × 15/100 × 6/12 = $7,500)		

The adjusting entry made on December 31, 19X1, records the fact that the company owes $2,500 interest at that time, although it will not be paid until April 30, 19X2. It also apportions the proper amount of expense into 19X1, two months, leaving four months of interest to be charged to 19X2.

The payment on April 30, 19X2 reduces the note payable ($100,000) and interest payable ($2,500) to zero; debits the appropriate amount ($5,000 or 4 months interest) to the interest expense account, and reduces cash by the total of the principal and interest payments ($107,500).

Wages Illustration

When employees are paid on a monthly basis on the last day of the month, there are no unrecorded (or accrued) wages at the end of the accounting period. However, when wages are paid on a weekly or biweekly basis, the payment date rarely coincides with the end of the accounting period and it is therefore often necessary to make an adjusting entry for wages earned but not paid at the end of the period.

Assume that Systems, Inc., pays wages every Friday for a five-day week, and that total weekly payroll is $5,000. If December 31, 19X1 falls on Wednesday, the employees worked 60 percent (or three-fifths) of a week at that time. The adjusting entry on December 31, 19X1 would be:

ADJUSTING ENTRY:			
Dec. 31, 19X1	Wages expenses	$3,000	
	Wages payable		$3,000
	To record accrued wages as of December 31, 19X1 ($5,000 × 60%)		

This entry results in the balance sheet containing a liability for Wages Payable at year-end of $3,000; and the income statement containing Wage Expense for $3,000 which represents wages earned by employees the last three days of the year.

Recorded Revenue

When a payment for a service or product is received in advance of its being earned, the amount applicable to future periods is deferred to future periods. The amount which is unearned is considered a liability because it represents an obligation to perform a service or deliver a product in a future period.

Rent Illustration

Assume that Systems, Inc., owned a building which it rented out for $9,600 for four years, beginning September 1, 19X1, to a tenant who paid the full four-year amount in advance. The following entries would be made to record the transaction:

Entry to record the payment:			
Sept. 1, 19X1	Cash	$9,600	
	Unearned rent income		$9,600
	To record receipt of rent income in advance		
ADJUSTING ENTRY:			
Dec. 31, 19X1	Unearned rent income	$800	
	Rent income		$800
	To adjust for unearned rent expired for the period ($9,600 ÷ 48 months = $200 per month × 4 months = $800)		

The adjusting entry reduces the Unearned Rent Income account to the appropriate balance, $8,800 ($9,600 − $800). It also results in recording the four months' rent as income in the current period. Unearned Rent Income appears as a liability on the balance sheet as of December 31, 19X1.

The adjusting entry in December 31, 19X2, 19X3, and 19X4 would be in the amount of $2,400 ($200 × 12 months), leaving $1,600 to be adjusted in 19X5.

Unrecorded Revenue

Adjusting entries must be made for items of revenue that have been earned during the period but not collected. The adjustment records the amount which has been earned as an asset (a receivable) and a revenue item. Common examples of this type of situation are interest and rent receivable.

Interest Receivable Illustration

On December 1, 19X1, Systems, Inc., loaned $50,000 to a subsidiary company at 18 percent interest for one year. The principal and interest are to be repaid on December 1, 19X2. The entries associated with these are as follows:

Entry at the date of the loan:			
Dec. 1, 19X1	Notes receivable	$50,000	
	Cash		$50,000
	To record loan		
ADJUSTING ENTRY:			
Dec. 31, 19X1	Interest receivable	$750	
	Interest revenue		$750
	To adjust for interest receivable ($50,000 × 18/100 × 1/12 = $750)		

As a result of this entry, an asset of $750, Interest Receivable, appears on the balance sheet disclosing the amount due as interest from the loan as of December 31, 19X1. The income statement contains Interest Revenue of $750, the amount which has been earned in the current year.

The entry to record the receipt of the payment of the loan on December 1, 19X2 would be:

Dec. 1, 19X2	Cash	$59,000	
	Interest income		$ 8,250
	Interest receivable		750
	Note receivable		50,000
	To record receipt of loan payment		

This entry records the amount of cash received as principal ($50,000) and interest ($\$50{,}000 \times {}^{18}/_{100} \times {}^{12}/_{12} = \$9{,}000$); the interest income for 19X2 (11 months × $750 per month = $8,250); and the reduction to zero of the Interest Receivable ($750) and Note Receivable ($50,000) accounts.

The Need for Adjusting Entries

Because of the need for current accounting information to facilitate managerial decision making, and to generate financial statements for other uses, the continuous stream of business activity is broken down into artificial time segments. This results in substantial measurement, allocation, and matching problems. Proper valuation is required but difficult to ascertain. Adjusting entries must be made to recognize the appropriate period costs in accordance with accrual methodology and the matching of revenues and expenses.

FINANCIAL STATEMENTS

After all the adjusting entries have been journalized and posted to the accounts in the general ledger, the accounts reflect the amounts needed for the statements, and statements are prepared from those balances. The common statements which are prepared are: the income statement, the retained earnings statement, and the balance sheet. The income statement and balance sheet have been illustrated in Chapter 2. The retained earnings statement, which is merely a reconciliation between beginning and ending retained earnings balances, will be illustrated in Chapter 4. It is important to note that the preparation of the financial statements is the focal point of all of the recording, summarizing, and classification activity that occurs in an accounting period.

CLOSING ENTRIES

The final step in the accounting cycle is the preparation of the closing entries for the period. Closing entries have two purposes:

1. To bring to zero certain account balances
2. To transfer profit or loss into the Owners' Equity account

To fully understand this process, it is useful to be acquainted with real and nominal accounts.

Real and Nominal Accounts

A *real account* is a permanent account that appears on the balance sheet. These are accounts which will *not* be brought to zero (closed) at the end of each accounting period. Assets, liabilities,and owners' equity items fall into this category. *Nominal accounts* are temporary accounts and they generally appear on the income statement (The Dividends account is an exception.). These are items which measure for a given period of time, usually a fiscal year. At the end of that period, they are "closed" (reset to zero). Revenues, expenses, and dividends fall into this category. To understand why nominal accounts are closed and real accounts are not, one must realize that it is more useful for a company to know what its sales and expenses were for the most recent year, rather than from the inception of the business. So, periodically, as a part of the closing process, the balance in the sales and expense accounts are reduced to zero so that the company can begin again to measure them for the next period.

Nominal accounts are closed into Retained Earnings (Owners' Equity) through a temporary account called *Expense and Revenue Summary.* As the basic accounting equation indicates, revenues and expenses are only temporary extensions of owners' equity, and the closing entries are the process by which net income or loss is transferred into owners' equity.

To illustrate the closing process, assume that on June 30, 19X1, the end of the Gray Company's fiscal year, the ledger accounts appear as follows:

Summarized General Ledger

Account	Debit	Credit
All Assets	22,850	
All Liabilities		10,055
Common Stock		5,000
Retained Earnings		7,575
Dividends	1,000	
Sales		5,520
Salaries Expense	2,780	
Depreciation Expense	550	
Utilities Expense	725	
Miscellaneous Expense	245	

As stated previously, the asset, liability, and owners' equity accounts are not closed; only the revenue, expense, and dividend accounts are closed. Revenue accounts have credit balances, and dividend and expense accounts have debit balances. Therefore to close the revenue accounts, they must be debited; and to close the expense accounts, they must be credited. The only revenue account that the Gray Company has is Sales, which has a credit balance of $5,520 as of December 31, 19X1. The journal entry necessary to close this account is as follows:

Date	Account	Debit	Credit
June 30, 19X1	Sales	$5,520	
	Expense and revenue summary		$5,520
	To close the sales account		

The four expense accounts each have normal debit balances. Four separate journal entries could be made to close these four accounts; however, making one *compound entry* is easier and more efficient. The journal entry necessary to close Gray Company's expense accounts as of June 30, 19X1 is as follows:

Date	Account	Debit	Credit
June 30, 19X1	Expense and revenue summary	$4,300	
	Salaries expense		$2,780
	Depreciation expense		550
	Utilities expense		725
	Miscellaneous expense		245
	To close the expense accounts		

Posting the closing entries is illustrated next. (For convenience of notation, closing entries are denoted with an "X.")

All Assets	
22,850	

All Liabilities	
	10,055

Common Stock	
	5,000

Retained Earnings	
	7,575

Dividends	
1,000	

Sales	
(X) 5,520	5,520
-0-	-0-

Salaries Expense	
2,780	(X) 2,780
-0-	-0-

Depreciation Expense	
550	(X) 550
-0-	-0-

Utilities Expense	
725	(X) 725
-0-	-0-

Miscellaneous Expense	
245	(X) 245
-0-	-0-

Expense and Revenue Summary

Debit	Credit
(X) 4,300	(X) 5,520
	1,220 Balance

After these closing entries have been posted, the Sales and Expense accounts have zero balances. The Expense and Revenue account has two entries: a credit for $5,520 and a debit of $4,300. This results in a credit balance in that account of $1,220 ($5,520 − $4,300). Although no formal income statement was prepared for Gray Company, it is obvious that the $1,220 is equal to the company's net income for the period. This will always be true: The balance in the Expense and Revenue Summary, after closing the Revenue and Expenses, will always equal the net income or loss of the entity. If expenses had exceeded revenues, the balance in Expense and Revenue Summary, after closing those items into it, would have been a debit, and would have indicated a loss for the period.

The balance in Expense and Revenue Summary is now closed into Retained Earnings by debiting Expense and Revenue Summary for $1,220 and crediting Retained Earnings for the same amount. The final closing entry to be made is to close the Dividends account into Retained Earnings by debiting Retained Earnings and crediting Dividends for $1,000. These two entries are illustrated next:

June 30, 19X1	Expense and revenue summary	$1,220	
	Retained earnings		$1,220
	To close the expense and revenue summary account into retained earnings		
June 30, 19X1	Retained earnings	$1,000	
	Dividends		$1,000
	To close the dividends account		

Note that the Dividends account is not an expense or revenue account but is instead a nominal account reflecting the change in retained earnings for a period which is attributable to dividend declaration.

Posting the two entries just given is illustrated in the Gray Company ledger as follows:

All Assets

Debit	Credit
22,850	

All Liabilities

Debit	Credit
	10,055

Common Stock

Debit	Credit
	5,000

Retained Earnings

Debit	Credit
	7,575
	(X) 1,220
(X) 1,000	
	7,795 Balance

Dividends

Debit	Credit
1,000	(X) 1,000
-0-	-0-

Sales

Debit	Credit
(X) 5,520	5,520
-0-	-0-

Salaries Expense	
2,780	(X) 2,780
-0-	-0-

Depreciation Expense	
550	(X) 550
-0-	-0-

Utilities Expense	
725	(X) 725
-0-	-0-

Miscellaneous Expense	
245	(X) 245
-0-	-0-

Expense and Revenue Summary	
(X) 4,300	(X) 5,520
(X) 1,220	
-0-	-0-

Notice that the revenue, expense, and dividend accounts are reduced to zero balances and the retained earnings account is up to date to start the next year. Remember that revenue, expense, and dividend accounts show how Retained Earnings changed over the year. When the year is over, those accounts have served their purpose and their net effect (sales less expenses and dividends) must be transferred to retained earnings to make way for the new entries for the following year.

The closing (and adjusting) entries are dated as of the last day of the accounting period. It is obvious, however, that in most cases they could not actually be prepared on that day because there would not be enough time to accumulate all the data necessary for those entries by that date. In practice, closing and adjusting entries are normally prepared sometime during the month immediately following the end of the period, although they are dated as of the last day of the period for which statements are being prepared.

Gray Company
Post-closing Trial Balance
as of June 30, 19X1

	DR.	CR.
All assets	$22,850	
All liabilities		$10,055
Common stock		5,000
Retained earnings		7,795
Totals	$22,850	$22,850

SUMMARY

A business unit is an active economic entity. The financial statements presented for a business unit are descriptions of what the entity's financial position appears to be at a given point in time, and of the effectiveness of its activities. Business activities consist of transactions between a given firm and other firms and individuals. These transactions take place daily, and often in great numbers.

Accounting is based upon the same requirements for careful data accumulation that a research scientist faces when handling data regarding a laboratory experiment. In accumulating the data for the reports, the accountant must first determine the type of information needed by management and others to carry on the operations of the firm, and then follow a system for breaking down data of the transactions into the parts that are needed. The first step is the recording (journalizing) of the events of the firms as they occur, in order to get the information under immediate control. The data of the events must then be sorted according to the scheme of accounting classification used (posted to the accounts), to determine the dollar effects of the significant events. From these classified data, statements are prepared which are given to the decision makers.

KEY POINTS

1. **Accounting controls** comprise the plan of organization and all methods and procedures that are concerned with the safeguarding of assets and the reliability of the financial records.

2. The **accounting cycle** refers to the procedures utilized to accumulate and summarize the data into financial statements.

3. The components of the accounting cycle are:
   a. Recording business transactions in the journal
   b. Posting to the ledger
   c. Preparing a trial balance
   d. Making adjusting entries and posting to the ledger
   e. Preparing statements
   f. Making closing entries
   g. Preparing a post-closing trial balance

4. **Journal** A record which is arranged in a time sequence indicating the effects of the transactions of a firm on the accounts in the accounting classification.

5. **Account** A record of the changes in a business element in terms of monetary increases and decreases in that element.

6. **General ledger** A record made up of all the accounts used to provide the information for the principal financial statements.

7. **Trial balance** A schedule listing the names and the debit or credit balances of all accounts in the ledger.

8. **Posting** The transferring of amounts in the journal to accounts in the ledger.

9. **An entry** The record in a journal of a transaction. A monetary amount in an account (other than a balance or a total) is also referred to as an entry.

10. Adjusting entry An end-of-period entry, required in order to reflect assets, liabilities, revenues, and expenses not recorded in the transaction entries. Many adjusting entries reflect changes that have occurred through the passage of time but, at the time of the entry, have not yet appeared in the records. For example, adjusting entries are used to reflect allocations of past costs to expense, or the utilization of goods or services which have been recognized as prepaid or which will be paid for in succeeding accounting periods.

11. Closing entries End-of-period entries designed to

a. bring the temporary or nominal accounts (mainly revenue, expense, and dividends) to a zero balance, and
b. transfer the net amount of these accounts into retained earnings.

12. Post-closing trial balance A trial balance prepared after the temporary accounts have been closed.

QUESTIONS

1. What is the primary task of an accounting system?

2. What are accounting controls? Give three examples.

3. Why is the name "accounting cycle" appropriate?

4. Explain the purpose of each of the steps of the accounting cycle:
   a. Journalizing
   b. Posting
   c. Adjusting entries
   d. Closing entries
   e. Post-closing trial balance

5. What role is played in the accounting process by source documents such as sales slips, invoices, and remittance advices?

6. What is the purpose of indentation in journal entries?

7. What is the relationship between the journal and the ledger?

8. What is the difference between a real or a permanent account, and a nominal or temporary account?

9. Why can some assets be considered as expenses that have not expired?

10. All of the cases shown next are related to careless handling or manipulation of the basic business documents.
    a. A regular customer comes into the store and buys an item for $25 on account. The clerk is busy and tells the customer that he will write up the charge later. The clerk completely forgets the transaction and it is never

written up. What effect does this have on the records and statements? Will any evidence indicate that there has been an omission?

b. A clerk records a credit sale to a customer as a cash sale on the sales invoice. What effect will this error have on the records and on the statements? What evidence will bring this error to light?

c. A clerk records a cash sale as a credit sale on the sales invoice. What effect will this error have on the records and on the statements? What evidence will bring this error to light?

d. The general cashier of a firm takes $100 in cash from the register and "adjusts" the summary of cash register readings by $100. What is the effect of this manipulation on the records and on the statements? What evidence will bring this to light?

e. Merchandise is ordered from the C Corporation for $500 and an invoice is received from the C Corporation for the goods, but the goods are never shipped and are not received by the firm. The bookkeeper sets up an accounts payable for the amount and subsequently the accounts payable is paid. What is the effect of this error on the records and on the statements? What evidence will bring this to light?

f. A clerk mistook Mr. Jones for Mr. Smith and charged a credit sale to Mr. Smith that Mr. Jones had purchased. What would be the effect on the records and the statements? What evidence would bring this error to light?

g. In preparing the cash register receipts summary for February 8, a mistake of $99 was made in adding the total of the cash received. When the deposit in the bank was being prepared, the extra cash was noticed and an entry was made crediting Cash Over or Short for the amount. How will this affect the records and the statements? What evidence will bring this to light?

11. Explain the purpose of the two accounts: Depreciation Expense and Accumulated Depreciation. Is it customary for the two accounts to have identical balances? In which financial statements will each appear?

12. At the end of the fiscal year, the usual adjusting entry to accrue interest payable is inadvertently omitted. Which items will be erroneously stated because of the income statement for the year and the balance sheet as of the end of the year? Also, will net income be overstated or understated for the period?

13. What type of accounts are closed by transferring their balances to Expense and Revenue Summary as a debit? As a credit?

14. To what account in the ledger is the Dividends account periodically closed?

15. Identify the accounts from the following list that should be closed at the end of the fiscal year:

a. Accumulated depreciation
b. Cash
c. Miscellaneous expense
d. Sales

e. Equipment
f. Accounts payable
g. Supplies expense
h. Prepaid rent
i. Retained earnings
j. Dividends
k. Capital stock

16. Are adjusting and closing entries in the journal actually prepared the last day of the fiscal period? Explain.

17. Which of the following ledger accounts will appear in a post-closing trial balance:

a. Cash
b. Dividends
c. Retained earnings
d. Salaries expense
e. Interest revenue
f. Supplies
g. Capital stock
h. Accumulated depreciation
i. Accounts receivable
j. Prepaid insurance
k. Utilities expense

18. After Exot Company had closed all revenue and expense accounts into Expense and Revenue Summary, that account had a debit balance of $155,000. Did Exot have net income or a loss for the period? What will be the disposition of that $155,000 balance in Expense and Revenue Summary?

EXERCISES

E3-1 Give the journal entries to record the following transactions of the X Corporation:

a. Capital stock is issued for $100,000 on February 1, 19X2.
b. Equipment is purchased for $25,000 cash on July 1, 19X2.
c. Supplies costing $5,000 are purchased from vendors on open account on March 15, 19X2.
d. Wages of $40,000 for the month of January were paid to employees on January 31, 19X2.

E3-2 The Alpha Company maintains a "cashbook" in which it records cash receipts and payments and keeps track of the cash balance. Entries in the cashbook for the month of January 19X1 are as follows:

Cash balance, Jan. 1	$25,000
Sale, Jan. 5	4,000
Sale, Jan. 10	6,000
Salaries paid, Jan. 15	1,500
Sale, Jan. 22	2,000
Building rental payment, Jan. 30	2,500
Salaries paid, Jan. 30	1,500

REQUIRED:

1. Record the transactions indicated by the checkbook entries in journal entry form.
2. Construct a cash T-account, enter the January 1 beginning balance, post the journal entries to this account, and show the January 31 ending balance.

E3-3 Give the appropriate adjusting journal entry on the books of the Y Corporation on December 31, 19X2 for each of the following cases:

a. Wages earned by employees in December, but not yet paid as of December 31, 19X2 total $12,000.

b. Depreciation on plant equipment in 19X2 is calculated as $50,000.

E3-4 Three journal entries, for February, April, and August, found in the books of the H Corporation, are shown. You are to indicate the effects of the debits and credits and to explain the transaction that took place, as shown in the following example:

Cash	$1,000	
Notes payable to banks		$1,000

The debit to Cash shows that Cash is increasing because of the event, and the credit to Notes Payable to Banks indicates that there is an increase in liabilities, that is, Notes Payable, because of the event. The transaction is simply the borrowing of money from a bank.

The entries are:

a.	Feb. 4	Cash	$ 20,000	
		Bonds payable		$20,000
b.	Apr. 9	Accounts payable	$ 2,560	
		Cash		$ 2,560
c.	Aug. 21	Land	$ 30,000	
		Buildings	150,000	
		Mortgage bonds payable		$90,000
		Cash		90,000

E3-5 On January 1, 19X2, Jim Hart and Joan Hillbrecht organized the H & H Service Company as a corporation. The transactions of the company for the first 45 days are listed here. Analyze each transaction and record the appropriate journal entry.

Jan. 1	Cash invested by the owners: Hart $20,000; Hillbrecht, $10,000.
3	Paid monthly rent, $400.
15	Purchased equipment for use in business, costing $30,000; paid one-third down and signed a 6% note payable for the balance. Monthly payments comprised of part principal and part interest are to be paid on the note.
30	Paid cash for operating expenses amounting to $16,000; in addition, operating expenses of $4,000 were incurred on credit.
30	Service fees earned amounted to $34,000, of which $28,000 was collected, and the balance was on credit.
Feb. 10	Collected $2,000 on account for service fees previously performed on credit.
15	Paid $500 on the equipment note, including $100 interest expense.

E3-6 P. Sainz Company is in the process of preparing its trial balance on December 31, 19X1. Unfortunately, the Retained Earnings account in the ledger was damaged during an office fire, and is not legible.

REQUIRED:

Complete the trial balance, calculating the correct balance for the retained earnings account. The other ledger accounts are as follows:

ACCOUNT TITLE	AMOUNT
Cash	$28,000
Accounts receivable	52,000
Inventory	74,000
Prepaid expense	4,000
Land	48,000
Building	116,000
Accumulated depreciation: Building	38,000
Equipment	62,000
Accumulated depreciation: Equipment	40,000
Accounts payable	42,000
9% bonds payable	80,000
Common stock	120,000
Additional paid-in capital	30,000
Retained earnings	?

E3-7 The following accounts are selected from the general ledger of Jayscot Corporation. Relate the figures found in the accounts to determine the events that are recorded in the accounts.

Cash

Jan. 5	100,000	Jan. 8	3,000
19	250		

Capital Stock (Stockholders' equity)

		Jan. 5	100,000

Utilities Expense

Jan. 8	3,000		

Accounts Receivable

Jan. 12	500	Jan. 19	250

Sales

		Jan. 12	500

To give an example: On the basis of the entry for January 5, we can determine that on January 5 investors contributed $100,000 in cash to start the business. They thereby became stockholders of the firm. What happened on January 8, January 12, and January 19?

E3-8 Express the following transactions for Denleigh Retail Outlet, a corporation, in journal entry form.

a. The owners contribute $30,000 cash to provide start-up funds, and receive common stock from the corporation.
b. A 60-day, 18% note is signed in return for a $10,000 bank loan.
c. Annual building rental of $12,000 is paid in advance.
d. A check is issued for shelves and fixtures costing $16,000.

PROBLEMS

P3-1 Royce Kincaid opened a real estate agency called RK Real Estate Company.

a. He began his business by contributing the following assets to the business, for which he received stock.

Cash	$11,000
Land	2,000
Building	30,000
Automobile	4,800

b. Paid $300 for an advertisement announcing the opening of the agency.
c. Purchased office equipment on credit for $3,800 from PALL Furniture Company.

d. Earned and collected a commission of $2,400 from the sale of a house.
e. Purchased supplies for $1,200.
f. Paid one-half of the amount owed PALL Furniture Company.
g. Placed $150 advertisement in the newspaper.
h. Paid his secretary $280.
i. Billed Eric Smith $1,800 for the commission on selling his house.
j. Paid the utility bill, $140.
k. Received the bill for advertising, $150, to be paid.
l. Paid his secretary $280.
m. Received a partial payment from Eric Smith, $400.
n. Sold a house for a commission of $2,000, one-half of which was collected in cash and the other half of which is to be collected next month.
o. Purchased a 3-year insurance policy, $960.

REQUIRED:

1. Set up the following T-accounts: Cash, Accounts receivable, Supplies, Prepaid insurance, Land, Building, Automobile, Office equipment, Accounts payable, Capital stock, Commission revenue, Office salary expense, Advertising expense, Utility expense.
2. Record the transactions by entering debits and credits directly in the T-accounts, using the transaction letters to identify each debit and credit.
3. Prepare a trial balance using the current date.

P3-2 Horatia Doolittle, M.D., completed the following transactions during April 19X2:

Apr. 1 Began a practice by investing $5,000 to form a professional corporation.

2 Received a loan and signed a note to the bank for $20,000.

4 Purchased equipment on account, $5,600.

6 Received cash from patients, $1,600.

7 Billed patients for medical services, $1,400.

8 Paid salaries:
Nurse $360
Receptionist $300

10 Purchased medical supplies on account, $500.

11 Paid 2 months' rent in advance, $600.

12 Paid 2-year insurance policy, $560.

14 Returned for credit $80 of defective medical supplies purchased on April 10.

15 Paid cash to creditors from whom the equipment was purchased, $1,000.

16 Received cash from customers previously billed, $1,300.

20 Sold supplies to another doctor, at cost, as a courtesy, $100.

22 Paid salaries:
Nurse $360
Receptionist $300

23 Received bill for monthly laboratory expenses, $750.
26 Paid utilities, $200.
27 Billed patients for medical services, $1,600.
28 Received cash for services, $1,600.

REQUIRED:

1. Set up the following T-accounts: Cash, Accounts receivable, Medical supplies, Prepaid rent, Prepaid insurance, Equipment, Accounts payable, Notes payable, Capital stock, Medical fees earned, Nursing salaries, Office salaries, Laboratory expense, Utility expense.
2. a. Prepare journal entries to record the above transactions in the general journal.
   b. Post the entries to the T-accounts.
   c. Prepare a trial balance as of April 30, 19X2.

P3-3 The Kelly Delivery Service was organized as a corporation on June 1, 19X1. The management decided that the fiscal year for the company would be June 1 to May 31. The following transactions were selected from the first year for cash purposes. For convenience the letter identification has been used as the date:

a. Cash invested was $20,000 and capital stock was issued.
b. Three new delivery vehicles were purchased at a total cost of $20,000. One-half was paid in cash and an 8% note payable was signed for the balance.
c. Operating supplies costing $600 were purchased for cash. These supplies are to go into Operating Supplies Inventory and will be used gradually.
d. Delivery revenues earned amounted to $120,000, of which $20,000 was yet uncollected.
e. Operating expenses incurred amounted to $80,000, of which $14,000 was not yet paid in cash.
f. Paid cash for a 3-year insurance premium in advance to insure the delivery equipment, $1,200.
g. Collected $12,000 on the credit extended for delivery services (See item d.)
h. Paid $8,000 on the obligations for operating expenses (See item e.)
i. An inventory count showed that two-thirds of the operating supplies purchased (item c.) had been used by May 31, 19X2.
j. Paid $2,000 on the note given on the delivery vehicles (item b.), plus 12 months' interest (on $10,000).
k. Computed depreciation on the delivery vehicles for 1 year (up to May 31, 19X2, assuming a 5-year useful life).
l. On May 31, insurance for 1 year had expired.

REQUIRED:

1. Set up a journal and journalize each item.
2. Post the journal entries to ledger accounts; number the ledger accounts starting with 101 for Cash.
3. Prepare a trial balance at May 31, 19X2.

P3-4 Given the following general ledger for the S Corporation for the year ended December 31, 19X2, prepare an income statement and a balance sheet for the year. Also, prepare the closing entries as of December 31, 19X2.

Cash	
Bal. 20,000	

Accounts Receivable	
Bal. 25,000	

Equipment	
Bal. 38,000	

Accounts Payable	
	Bal. 22,000

Capital Stock	
	Bal. 40,000

Retained Earnings	
	Bal. 6,000

Sales	
	Bal. 98,000

Salaries Expense	
Bal. 51,000	

Miscellaneous Expense	
Bal. 32,000	

P3-5 On June 1, 19X2, Sal Scotti organized Superior Moving Company to provide long-distance moving of household furniture. The transactions shown below occured during June and were recorded in the following ledger accounts:

Cash	1	Accounts payable	30
Accounts receivable	3	Sal Scotti, capital	50
Land	5	Sal Scotti, drawing	51
Buildings	7	Income summary	60
Accumuated depreciation:		Moving service revenue	62
Building	8	Salaries expense	70
Trucks	10	Gasoline expense	72
Accumulated depreciation: Trucks	11	Repairs expense	74
Office equipment	13	Depreciation expense: Buildings	76
Accumulated depreciation:		Depreciation expense: Trucks	78
Office equipment	14	Depreciation expense: Office equipment	80

June 1 Scotti deposited $240,000 cash in a bank account in the name of the business, Superior Moving Company.

3 Purchased land and building for a total price of $146,400 of which $60,000 was applicable to the land, and $86,400 to the building. Paid cash for full amount.

5 Purchased three trucks from Dawson Motors at a cost of $34,560 each. A cash down payment of $48,000 was made, the balance to be paid by July 12.

6 Purchased office equipment for cash, $5,760.

6 Moved furniture for Mr. and Mrs. Alan Jonas from Sacramento to Hartford for $4,044. Collected $1,104 in cash with the balance to be paid within 30 days (credit Moving Service Revenue).

11 Moved furniture for various clients for $7,764. Collected $4,404 in cash, balance to be paid within 30 days.

15 Paid salaries to employees for first half of the month, $3,624.

24 Moved furniture for various clients for a total of $6,480. Cash collected in full.

30 Salaries expense for the second half of the month amounted to $3,180.

30 Received a gasoline bill for the month of June from Atlantic Oil Company in the amount of $9,200, to be paid before July 10.

30 Received bill of $300 for repair work on trucks during June by Century Motor Company.

30 The owner withdrew $1,440 cash for his personal use.

Scotti estimated a useful life of 20 years for the building, 4 years for the trucks, and 10 years for the office equipment.

INSTRUCTIONS:

a. Prepare journal entries. (Number pages and enter the proper journal page number in the Ref. column of the ledger accounts as each debit or credit is posted.)
b. Post to ledger accounts. (As each journal entry is posted to the ledger, enter the identification number of the ledger account debited or credited in the LP column of the journal. This will show that the amount has been posted and will provide a cross-reference between journal and ledger.)
c. Prepare a trial balance as of June 30, 19X2.
d. Prepare adjusting entries and post to ledger accounts.
e. Prepare an adjusted trial balance.
f. Prepare an income statement for June, and a balance sheet at June 30, 19X1.
g. Prepare closing entries and post to ledger accounts.
h. Prepare a post-closing trial balance.

P3-6 Robert Lowell, M.D., after completing his medical education, established his own practice on May 1. The following transactions occurred during the first month:

May 1	Opened a bank account in the name of his practice, Robert Lowell, M.D., by making a deposit of $7,800, and receiving stock.
1	Paid office rent for May, $455.
2	Purchased office equipment for cash, $2,496.
3	Purchased medical equipment from Niles Instruments, Inc., at a cost of $10,530. A cash down payment of $1,430 was made and a note payable was signed which required a payment of $4,550 on July 3 of the current year and a final payment of $4,550 on September 2.
3	Retained by Brandon Merchandising, Inc., to be on call for emergency service at a monthly fee of $195. The fee for May was collected in cash.
15	Excluding the retainer of May 3, fees earned during the first 15 days of the month amounted to $813, of which $137 was in cash and $676 was in accounts receivable.
15	Paid Mary Hester, R.N., her salary for the first half of May, $585.
19	Treated Michael Tracy for injuries received in an accident during his employment at Brandon Merchandising, Inc., Completed medical portions of insurance and industrial accident reports.
27	Treated Cynthia Knight, who paid $13 cash for an office visit and who agreed to pay $31 on June 1 for laboratory medical tests completed May 27.
31	Excluding the treatment of Cynthia Knight on May 27, fees earned during the last half of the month amounted to $1,378, of which $273 was in cash and $1,105 was in accounts receivable.
31	Paid Mary Hester, R.N., $585 salary for the second half of the month.
31	Received a bill from McGraw Medical Supplies in the amount of $312, representing the amount of medical supplies used during May (debit Medical Supplies Expense).
31	Paid utilities bill for the month, $43.

Other information: Dr. Lowell estimated the useful life of medical instruments at 9 years, and of office equipment at 8 years. The account titles to be used and the account numbers are as follows:

Cash	10	Capital stock	40
Accounts receivable	13	Retained earnings	41
Medical instruments	20	Expense and revenue summary	45
Accumulated depreciation: Medical instruments	21	Fees earned	49
Office equipment	22	Medical supplies expense	50
Accumulated depreciation: Office equipment	23	Rent expense	51
Notes payable	30	Salaries expense	52
Accounts payable	31	Utilities expense	53
		Depreciation expense: Medical instruments	54
		Depreciation expense: Office equipment	55

INSTRUCTIONS:

a. Journalize the previous transactions. (Number journal pages to permit cross-reference to ledger.)
b. Post to ledger accounts. (Use running balance form of ledger accounts to permit cross-reference to journal.)
c. Prepare a trial balance at May 31, 19X2.
d. Prepare adjusting entries and post to ledger accounts. (Round amounts to nearest dollar.)
e. Prepare an adjusted trial balance.
f. Prepare an income statement and a balance sheet in report form.
g. Prepare closing entries and post to ledger accounts.
h. Prepare post-closing trial balance.

P3-7 The accounting records of Placid Lake, Inc., are maintained on the basis of a fiscal year ending June 30. The following facts are to be used as a basis for making adjusting entries at June 30, 19X1:

a. Depreciation on the buildings for the year ended June 30 amounted to $28,250.
b. A 36-month fire insurance policy had been purchased on June 1. The premium of $2,880 for the entire life of the policy had been paid on June 1 and recorded as Unexpired Insurance.
c. A portion of the land owned had been leased on June 16 of the current year to a service station operator at a yearly rental rate of $9,600. One year's rent was collected in advance at the date of the lease and credited to Unearned Rental Revenue.
d. A small bus to carry guests to and from the airport had been rented on June 19 from Eazy Rentals, Inc., at a daily rate of $42. No rental payment had yet been made.
e. Among the assets owned by Placid Lake, Inc., were government bonds in the face amount of $50,000. Accrued interest receivable on the bonds at June 30 was computed to be $1,950.
f. A 3-month bank loan in the amount of $200,000 had been obtained on June 1 at an annual interest rate of 9%. No interest expense has been recorded.
g. The company signed an agreement on June 30 to lease a truck from Lowe Motors for a period of 1 year beginning July 1 at a rate of 36 cents a mile and with a clause providing for a minimum monthly charge of $600.
h. Salaries earned by employees but not paid amounted to $6,600.

Prepare the appropriate adjusting entries.

P3-8 Shown here is a four-column schedule consisting of the trial balance and the adjusted trial balance of Nancar Company at June 30, 19X1, the end of the fiscal year. The pair of adjustments columns which would normally appear between the Trial Balance columns and the Adjusted Trial Balance columns have purposely been omitted.

	TRIAL BALANCE		ADJUSTED TRIAL BALANCE	
	Debit	**Credit**	**Debit**	**Credit**
Cash	$84,000		$84,000	
Commission receivable	25,560		25,560	
Office supplies	5,400		1,320	
Office equipment	158,400		158,400	
Accumulated depreciation: Office equipment		$34,560		$35,880
Notes payable		120,000		120,000
Accounts payable		15,600		15,600
Salaries payable				13,200
Interest payable				1,800
Unearned commissions		10,200		7,800
Common stock		78,000		78,000
Commission earned		28,200		30,600
Salaries expense	13,200		26,400	
Interest expense			1,800	
Office supplies expense			4,080	
Depreciation expense: Office equipment			1,320	
	$286,560	$286,560	$302,880	$302,880

INSTRUCTIONS:

Prepare the adjusting entries which will explain the changes from the amounts in the Trial Balance columns to the amounts in the Adjusted Trial Balance columns. Include an explanation as part of each journal entry.

P3-9 Bad Work, Inc., was incorporated on March 31, 19X1. The company prepared the following trial balance at the end of its first quarter of operations:

Bad Work, Inc.
Trial Balance
June 30, 19X1

	Dr.	Cr.
Cash	$ 3,000	
Accounts receivable	36,000	
Supplies and parts	—	
Prepaid rent	—	
Unexpired insurance	—	
Land	18,000	
Construction equipment	180,000	
Accumulated depreciation: Equipment	—	
Accounts payable		$ 17,000
Accrued wages payable	—	
10% bonds payable		80,000
Interest payable		—
Common stock		145,000
Retained earnings, Mar. 31, 19X1		—
Paving contracts		125,000
Premixed concrete	41,000	
Wage expense	36,000	
Oil and gas purchases	17,000	
Construction supplies and parts expense	12,000	
Repair expense	9,000	
Rent expense	6,000	
Insurance expense	9,000	
Depreciation expense	—	
Financial expense	—	
	$367,000	$367,000

Additional information:

a. Construction supplies and parts which cost $1,600 are on hand at June 30, 19X1.
b. Rent on special equipment, covering the rental value for 6 months from June 1, 19X1, was paid on June 4.
c. Insurance covering operations for 3 years was acquired on April 1, 19X1.
d. Depreciation on construction equipment amounted to $5,000 per month. The equipment was acquired on March 31, 19X1.

e. Workers have been paid through June 28. An additional $1,500 is due on workers for the period since June 28.

f. Premixed concrete purchases, oil and gas purchases, and repair expenses of $2,500, $1,800, and $600, respectively, are unpaid at the end of June, 19X1.

g. The 10% Bonds Payable were issued on March 31—interest is payable September 30 and March 31 of each year—with the face amount of the bonds to be repaid March 31, (in 20 years.)

REQUIRED:

Based on the trial balance and additional information for Bad Work, Inc., prepare:

1. T-accounts using the figures on the original trial balance.
2. Journal entries to make the adjustments required on June 30, 19X1.
3. Post to the T-accounts the journal entries recorded in item b.

P3-10 After posting all adjusting entries, the account balances at year end for Bluehoe Company were as follows:

Cash	$10,000
Accounts receivable	12,300
Equipment	60,000
Accumulated depreciation	5,000 cr.
Notes payable	7,400 cr.
Accounts payable	5,650 cr.
Common stock	15,000 cr.
Retained earnings	37,500 cr.
Dividends	1,500
Sales (revenue)	50,000 cr.
Wages expense	25,500
Depreciation expense	2,500
Utilities expense	7,500
Miscellaneous expense	1,250

REQUIRED:

1. Prepare the closing entries for Bluehoe as of the year end.
2. Prepare a post-closing trial balance for Bluehoe as of the year-end.

THE ACCOUNTING CYCLE COMPLETED

4

ORIENTATION

This chapter reviews the procedures outlined in Chapter 3 by means of an illustration which includes all seven steps in the accounting cycle. In addition several methods of expediting and simplifying record keeping are discussed. These methods include the use of subsidiary ledgers, special journals, and worksheets. It is necessary to learn the basic techniques and theory of accounting before computer applications become applicable. This chapter introduces some of these basic computer applications. Finally, the location of errors and the preparation of financial statements without closing the books are discussed.

COMPREHENSIVE ILLUSTRATION

In this chapter we will attempt to "pull together" the accounting cycle by means of a single, yet fairly complete, illustration. This illustration will include all of the steps of the accounting cycle mentioned in Chapter 3. Those steps were:

Step 1: Journalize entries
Step 2: Post to ledger
Step 3: Prepare trial balance

Step 4: Prepare adjusting journal entries (and post)
Step 5: Prepare financial statements
Step 6: Prepare closing entries (and post)
Step 7: Prepare post-closing trial balance

As our illustration, let us assume that the Y Corporation, a computer consulting company, is formed on March 1, 19X1 and that the following events took place in the succeeding twelve-month period:

March 19X1	4	Stockholders paid in $80,000 in cash for shares in the firm.
	8	Rent for two years was paid for the use of buildings, $18,000.
	9	Data processing equipment was purchased for $50,000 cash and is expected to last for five years with a negligible salvage value.

Transactions for the remainder of the year are summarized next. (In an actual business situation, these transactions would be recorded individually.)

Consulting revenue billed on account for the year totaled $116,000; collections of accounts receivable totaled $92,000.

Salaries and wages paid for the year totaled $72,000. In addition there were accrued wages of $5,000 payable on February 28, 19X2 (the end of Y's fiscal year).

Utilities expense for the year totaled $6,500.

Dividends of $4,000 were declared and paid during the year.

On Februrary 28, 19X2, a $25,000 short-term loan was obtained from the Yoho State Bank, and the necessary adjusting entries were made.

Journal Entries

Y Corporation Journal *Page No. 1*

DATE		ACCT. NO.	DEBITS	CREDITS
19X1				
Mar. 4	Cash	[a]	80,000	
	Capital stock			80,000
	To record issuance of stock for cash			
8	Prepaid rent		18,000	
	Cash			18,000
	To record rent payment for 2 years' of use of a building			
9	Data processing equipment		50,000	
	Cash			50,000
	To record purchase of equipment and software expected to give annual service over 5 years			

[a] The Account No. would be inserted in this column when the amounts are posted to the ledger.

Y Corporation Journal (Continued)

DATE		ACCT. NO.	DEBITS	CREDITS
Various dates	Accounts receivable		116,000	
	Counseling revenues			116,000
	To record consulting revenue for the year			
Various dates	Cash		92,000	
	Accounts receivable			92,000
	To record the collection of accounts receivable for the year			
Various dates	Salaries and wages expense		72,000	
	Cash			72,000
	To record wages for the year			
Various dates	Utilities expense		6,500	
	Cash			6,500
	To record utilities expense for the year			
Various dates	Dividends		4,000	
	Dividends payable			4,000
	Dividends payable		4,000	
	Cash			4,000
	To record the declaration and payment of dividends during the year			
19X2				
Feb. 28	Cash		25,000	
	Note payable: Yoho State Bank			25,000
	To record loan obtained from Yoho State Bank			

Posting

The journal entries just recorded will now be posted to the ledger. In an actual business situation these postings would commonly take place monthly; however, in our simplified illustration we will post all journal entries at year end.

Cash 100

DATE	EXPLANATION	REFERENCE	DEBIT	CREDIT	BALANCE
19X1					
Mar. 4		J1	80,000		80,000 Dr.
8		J1		18,000	62,000 Dr.
9		J1		50,000	12,000 Dr.
Various		J1	92,000		104,000 Dr.
"		J1		72,000	32,000 Dr.

Cash 100 (Continued)

DATE	EXPLANATION	REFERENCE	DEBIT	CREDIT	BALANCE
"		J1		6,500	25,500 Dr.
"		J1		4,000	21,500 Dr.
19X2 Feb. 28		J1	25,000		46,500 Dr.

Accounts Receivable 110

DATE	EXPLANATION	REFERENCE	DEBIT	CREDIT	BALANCE
Various		J1	116,000		116,000 Dr.
"		J1		92,000	24,000 Dr.

Prepaid Rent 120

DATE	EXPLANATION	REFERENCE	DEBIT	CREDIT	BALANCE
19X1 Mar. 8		J1	18,000		18,000 Dr.

Equipment 130

DATE	EXPLANATION	REFERENCE	DEBIT	CREDIT	BALANCE
19X1 Mar. 9		J1	50,000		50,000 Dr.

Accumulated Depreciation: Equipment 131

DATE	EXPLANATION	REFERENCE	DEBIT	CREDIT	BALANCE

Notes Payable 200

DATE	EXPLANATION	REFERENCE	DEBIT	CREDIT	BALANCE
19X2					
Feb. 28		J1		25,000	25,000 Cr.

Dividends Payable 210

DATE	EXPLANATION	REFERENCE	DEBIT	CREDIT	BALANCE
Various		J1		4,000	
"		J1	4,000		-0-

Wages Payable 220

DATE	EXPLANATION	REFERENCE	DEBIT	CREDIT	BALANCE

Common Stock 300

DATE	EXPLANATION	REFERENCE	DEBIT	CREDIT	BALANCE
19X1 Mar. 4		J1		80,000	80,000 Cr.

Retained Earnings 310

DATE	EXPLANATION	REFERENCE	DEBIT	CREDIT	BALANCE

Dividends 320

DATE	EXPLANATION	REFERENCE	DEBIT	CREDIT	BALANCE
Various		J1	4,000		4,000 Dr.

Consulting Revenue 400

DATE	EXPLANATION	REFERENCE	DEBIT	CREDIT	BALANCE
Various		J1		116,000	116,000 Cr.

Salaries and Wages Expense 500

DATE	EXPLANATION	REFERENCE	DEBIT	CREDIT	BALANCE
Various		J1	72,000		72,000 Dr.

Utilities Expense 510

DATE	EXPLANATION	REFERENCE	DEBIT	CREDIT	BALANCE
Various		J1	6,500		6,500 Dr.

Rent Expense 520

DATE	EXPLANATION	REFERENCE	DEBIT	CREDIT	BALANCE

Depreciation Expense 530

DATE	EXPLANATION	REFERENCE	DEBIT	CREDIT	BALANCE

Expense and Revenue Summary 900

DATE	EXPLANATION	REFERENCE	DEBIT	CREDIT	BALANCE

In posting the accounts, the date of the original journal entry is entered in the Date column. The journal page number (J1) is entered in the Reference column, and at the same time the account number (e.g., 100 for Cash) would be entered in the Acct. No. column of the journal.

Trial Balance

As stated previously, a trial balance verifies the equality of debits and credits of the entries that have been journalized and posted during the accounting period. It is prepared by simply taking the account balances in the ledger and listing them in debit or credit columns. The trial balance for Y Corporation as of February 28, 19X2 would appear as follows:

Y Corporation
Trial Balance
as of February 28, 19X2

ACCOUNT NO.	ACCOUNT NAME	DEBIT	CREDIT
100	Cash	$46,500	
110	Accounts receivable	24,000	
120	Prepaid rent	18,000	
130	Equipment	50,000	
200	Notes payable		$25,000
300	Common stock		80,000
320	Dividends	4,000	
400	Consulting revenue		116,000
500	Wages and salaries expense	72,000	
510	Utilities expense	6,500	
		$221,000	$221,000

Adjusting Journal Entries

After the trial balance is prepared, adjusting journal entries are prepared and posted. An examination of the information from the Y Corporation reveals the need for three adjusting entries at year end:

1. To record annual depreciation
2. To write off expired prepaid rent
3. To accrue salary and wage expense at year end

These journal entries are illustrated next:

Y Corporation Journal (Continued) *Page No. 2*

DATE		ACCT. NO.	DEBITS	CREDITS
19X2	*Adjusting Entries*			
Feb. 28	Depreciation expense	[a]	10,000	
	Accumulated depreciation: Equipment			10,000
	To record annual depreciation ($50,000 ÷ 5 years = $10,000 per year)			
Feb. 28	Rent expense		9,000	
	Prepaid rent			9,000
	To write off expired prepaid rent for the period ($18,000 ÷ 2 years = $9,000 per year)			
Feb. 28	Salaries and wages expense		5,000	
	Salaries and wages payable			5,000
	To accrue wages at fiscal year end			

[a] Account Number would be filled in when posting is done.

The adjusting entries are now posted to the ledger accounts as follows:

Cash 100

DATE	EXPLANATION	REFERENCE	DEBIT	CREDIT	BALANCE
19X1					
Mar. 4		J1	80,000		80,000 Dr.
8		J1		18,000	62,000 Dr.
9		J1		50,000	12,000 Dr.
Various		J1	92,000		104,000 Dr.
"		J1		72,000	32,000 Dr.
"		J1		6,500	25,500 Dr.
"		J1		4,000	21,500 Dr.
19X2					
Feb. 28		J1	25,000		46,500 Dr.

Accounts Receivable 110

DATE	EXPLANATION	REFERENCE	DEBIT	CREDIT	BALANCE
Various		J1	116,000		116,000 Dr.
"		J1		92,000	24,000 Dr.

Prepaid Rent 120

DATE	EXPLANATION	REFERENCE	DEBIT	CREDIT	BALANCE
19X1					
Mar. 8		J1	18,000		18,000 Dr.
Feb. 28		J2		9,000	9,000 Dr.

Equipment 130

DATE	EXPLANATION	REFERENCE	DEBIT	CREDIT	BALANCE
19X1					
Mar. 9		J1	50,000		50,000 Dr.

Accumulated Depreciation: Equipment 131

DATE	EXPLANATION	REFERENCE	DEBIT	CREDIT	BALANCE
19X2					
Feb. 28		J2		10,000	10,000 Cr.

Notes Payable 200

DATE	EXPLANATION	REFERENCE	DEBIT	CREDIT	BALANCE
19X2 Feb. 28		J1		25,000	25,000 Cr.

Dividends Payable 210

DATE	EXPLANATION	REFERENCE	DEBIT	CREDIT	BALANCE
Various		J1		4,000	
"		J1	4,000		-0-

Wages Payable 220

DATE	EXPLANATION	REFERENCE	DEBIT	CREDIT	BALANCE
19X2 Feb. 28		J2		5,000	5,000 Cr.

Common Stock 300

DATE	EXPLANATION	REFERENCE	DEBIT	CREDIT	BALANCE
19X1 Mar. 4		J1		80,000	80,000 Cr.

Retained Earnings 310

DATE	EXPLANATION	REFERENCE	DEBIT	CREDIT	BALANCE

Dividends 320

DATE	EXPLANATION	REFERENCE	DEBIT	CREDIT	BALANCE
Various		J1	4,000		4,000 Dr.

Consulting Revenue 400

DATE	EXPLANATION	REFERENCE	DEBIT	CREDIT	BALANCE
Various		J1		116,000	116,000 Cr.

Salaries and Wages Expense 500

DATE	EXPLANATION	REFERENCE	DEBIT	CREDIT	BALANCE
Various		J1	72,000		72,000 Dr.
19X2					
Feb. 28		J2	5,000		77,000 Dr.

Utilities Expense 510

DATE	EXPLANATION	REFERENCE	DEBIT	CREDIT	BALANCE
Various		J1	6,500		6,500 Dr.

Rent Expense 520

DATE	EXPLANATION	REFERENCE	DEBIT	CREDIT	BALANCE
19X2 Feb. 28		J2	9,000		9,000 Dr.

Depreciation Expense 530

DATE	EXPLANATION	REFERENCE	DEBIT	CREDIT	BALANCE
19X2 Feb. 28		J2	10,000		10,000 Dr.

Expense and Revenue Summary 900

DATE	EXPLANATION	REFERENCE	DEBIT	CREDIT	BALANCE

Financial Statements Prepared

This step is the focal point of the entire process. All other steps in the accounting cycle are done so that financial statements can be prepared. The three financial statements to be prepared are the income statement, the retained earnings statement, and the balance sheet. These three statements for Y Corporation are illustrated next.

Y Corporation
Income Statement
for the year ended February 28, 19X2

Consulting revenue		$116,000
Salaries and wages expense	$77,000	
Utilities expense	6,500	
Rent expense	9,000	
Depreciation expense	10,000	
Total expenses		102,500
Net income		$13,500

A *Retained Earnings Statement* is a listing of the activity in retained earnings during the year. Although the net income and dividends have not yet been closed into retained earnings the Retained Earnings Statement is prepared in anticipation of this occurring. The Retained Earnings Statement for Y Corporation would appear as follows:

Y Corporation
Retained Earnings Statement
for the year ended February 28, 19X2

Retained earnings as of March 1, 19X1	$ -0-
Add: Net income for the period	13,500
Less: Dividends for the period	(4,000)
Retained earnings as of February 28, 19X2	$9,500

This ending retained earnings amount ($9,500) is now used in the balance sheet.

Y Corporation
Balance Sheet
as of February 28, 19X2

ASSETS		
Cash		$ 46,500
Accounts receivable		24,000
Prepaid rent		9,000
Equipment	$50,000	
Less accumulated depreciation: Equipment	10,000	40,000
Total assets		$119,500
LIABILITIES AND OWNERS' EQUITY		
Liabilities:		
Notes payable	$25,000	
Wages payable	5,000	
Total liabilities		$30,000
Owners' equity:		
Common stock	$80,000	
Retained earnings	9,500	
Total owners' equity		89,500
		$119,500

Closing Entries

The next step in the accounting cycle is the preparation of closing entries. The closing entries for Y Corporation are illustrated here:

Y Corporation Journal *Page No. 3*

DATE		ACCT. NO.	DEBITS	CREDITS
19X2	*Closing Entries*			
Feb. 28	Consulting revenue	a	116,000	
	Expense and revenue summary			116,000
	To close revenue account			
Feb. 28	Expense and revenue summary		102,500	
	Salaries and wages expense			77,000
	Utilities expense			6,500
	Rent expense			9,000
	Depreciation expense			10,000
	To close expense accounts			

Y Corporation Journal (Continued) *Page No. 3*

DATE		ACCT. NO.	DEBITS	CREDITS
Feb. 28	Expense and revenue summary		13,500	
	Retained earnings			13,500
	To close expense and revenue summary into retained earnings			
Feb. 28	Retained earnings		4,000	
	Dividends			4,000
	To close dividends account into retained earnings			

[a] To be filled in when posted to the ledger.

The closing entries would be posted to the ledger as follows:

Cash 100

DATE	EXPLANATION	REFERENCE	DEBIT	CREDIT	BALANCE
19X1					
Mar. 4		J1	80,000		80,000 Dr.
8		J1		18,000	62,000 Dr.
9		J1		50,000	12,000 Dr.
Various		J1	92,000		104,000 Dr.
"		J1		72,000	32,000 Dr.
"		J1		6,500	25,500 Dr.
"		J1		4,000	21,500 Dr.
19X2					
Feb. 28		J1	25,000		46,500 Dr.

Accounts Receivable 110

DATE	EXPLANATION	REFERENCE	DEBIT	CREDIT	BALANCE
Various		J1	116,000		116,000 Dr.
"		J1		92,000	24,000 Dr.

Prepaid Rent 120

DATE	EXPLANATION	REFERENCE	DEBIT	CREDIT	BALANCE
19X1					
Mar. 8		J1	18,000		18,000 Dr.
Feb. 28		J2		9,000	9,000 Dr.

Equipment 130

DATE	EXPLANATION	REFERENCE	DEBIT	CREDIT	BALANCE
19X1					
Mar. 9		J1	50,000		50,000 Dr.

Accumulated Depreciation: Equipment 131

DATE	EXPLANATION	REFERENCE	DEBIT	CREDIT	BALANCE
19X2					
Feb. 28		J2		10,000	10,000 Cr.

Notes Payable 200

DATE	EXPLANATION	REFERENCE	DEBIT	CREDIT	BALANCE
19X2					
Feb. 28		J1		25,000	25,000 Cr.

Dividends Payable 210

DATE	EXPLANATION	REFERENCE	DEBIT	CREDIT	BALANCE
Various		J1		4,000	
″		J1	4,000		-0-

Wages Payable 220

DATE	EXPLANATION	REFERENCE	DEBIT	CREDIT	BALANCE
19X2					
Feb. 28		J2		5,000	5,000 Cr.

Common Stock 300

DATE	EXPLANATION	REFERENCE	DEBIT	CREDIT	BALANCE
19X1					
Mar. 4		J1		80,000	80,000 Cr.

Retained Earnings 310

DATE	EXPLANATION	REFERENCE	DEBIT	CREDIT	BALANCE
19X2					
Feb. 28		J3		13,500	
Feb. 28		J3	4,000		9,500 Cr.

Dividends 320

DATE	EXPLANATION	REFERENCE	DEBIT	CREDIT	BALANCE
Various		J1	4,000		4,000 Dr.
19X2					
Feb. 28		J3		4,000	-0-

Consulting Revenue 400

DATE	EXPLANATION	REFERENCE	DEBIT	CREDIT	BALANCE
Various		J1		116,000	116,000 Cr.
19X2					
Feb. 28		J3	116,000		-0-

Salaries and Wages Expense 500

DATE	EXPLANATION	REFERENCE	DEBIT	CREDIT	BALANCE
Various		J1	72,000		72,000 Dr.
19X2					
Feb. 28		J2	5,000		77,000 Dr.
Feb. 28		J3		77,000	-0-

Utilities Expense 510

DATE	EXPLANATION	REFERENCE	DEBIT	CREDIT	BALANCE
Various		J1	6,500		6,500 Dr.
19X2					
Feb. 28		J3		6,500	-0-

Rent Expense 520

DATE	EXPLANATION	REFERENCE	DEBIT	CREDIT	BALANCE
19X2					
Feb. 28		J2	9,000		9,000 Dr.
Feb. 28		J3		9,000	-0-

Depreciation Expense 530

DATE	EXPLANATION	REFERENCE	DEBIT	CREDIT	BALANCE
19X2					
Feb. 28		J2	10,000		10,000 Dr.
Feb. 28		J3		10,000	-0-

Expense and Revenue Summary 900

DATE	EXPLANATION	REFERENCE	DEBIT	CREDIT	BALANCE
19X2					
Feb. 28		J3		116,000	
Feb. 28		J3	102,500		13,500 Cr.
Feb. 28		J3	13,500		-0-

Post-Closing Trial Balance

The final step in the accounting cycle is the preparation of the post-closing trial balance. The post-closing trial balance for Y Corporation as of February 28, 19X2 is illustrated next:

Y Corporation
Post-Closing Trial Balance
as of February 28, 19X2

	DR.	CR.
Cash	$46,500	
Accounts receivable	24,000	
Prepaid rent	9,000	
Equipment	50,000	
Accumulated depreciation		$10,000
Notes payable		25,000
Wages payable		5,000
Common stock		80,000
Retained earnings		9,500
Totals	$129,500	$129,500

The post-closing trial balance provides the starting point for the accounting activities of the next accounting period.

METHODS OF EXPEDITING ACCOUNTING RECORD KEEPING

There are several methods by which the record keeping in accounting can be simplified or expedited.

Three of the most common means of simplifying accounting record keeping and statement preparation are by the use of (1) subsidiary ledgers, (2) special journals, and (3) worksheets. These techniques are used both with manual and computer-based accounting systems.

Subsidiary Ledgers

The ledger that we have referred to thus far in this text is commonly called the *general ledger.* This is true because companies often have satellite or *subsidiary ledgers* for certain accounts. When this is the case, the primary account in the general ledger is known as the *control* account, and the detail of that account is kept in a subsidiary ledger. For example, it is not enough merely to know the total amount of accounts receivable and accounts payable. The firm must know how much is owed by each customer and to each creditor. Subsidiary (or detail) ledgers for accounts receivable and accounts payable serve to provide this information.

The accounts receivable subsidiary ledger consists of accounts for each customer, with the dates of sales and collection, and the balance due. The accounts payable subsidiary (or detail) ledger consists of accounts for each creditor (vendor), with the dates of purchases and payments and the balance owed. Small firms may substitute for these ledgers by maintaining files of sales invoices by customer, and purchase invoices by vendor.

Depending on the nature and needs of the particular firm, various other subsidiary ledgers may be utilized. For example, a merchandise subsidiary ledger will contain details, by merchandise types, of quantities and costs; while a plant asset subsidiary ledger will contain detailed information on machinery, equipment, buildings, and so forth.

The existence of subsidiary ledgers makes additional posting necessary. For example, a credit sale to a customer must be posted to that customer's account in the accounts receivable subsidiary ledger. This posting step is in addition to posting the amount in the general ledger accounts. The same holds for a purchase of merchandise on credit from a supplier: The amount must be posted to the supplier's account in the accounts payable detail ledger and to the merchandise subsidiary ledger, if one is employed.

Special Journals

The journalizing and posting of accounting data is greatly simplified by the use of special journals. Special journals are made possible by the fact that many business transactions frequently recur, and are journalized in the same fashion. For example, the journal entries for credit sales recorded in the basic two-column form as used previously may be simplified as shown in Figure 4-1.

Note that the inclusion of account titles in column headings makes it unnecessary to write account titles opposite the amounts; a transaction may be recorded on one line. This modification conserves space and speeds up the journalizing process. The posting process is simplified by the posting of totals rather than individual amounts to the accounts in the general ledger. This saves time and reduces the opportunity for error. No information is lost by use of this modified procedure, since the data are still in time sequence, and are still readily available. Both of these factors are significant in the design of record-keeping systems.

This same sales record may be further simplified as shown in Figure 4-2.

FIGURE 4-1

TWO-COLUMN (GENERAL) JOURNAL

Accounts receivable	50	
Sales		50
Accounts receivable	75	
Sales		75
Accounts receivable	40	
Sales		40

Can be reduced to:

Accounts Receivable Dr.	Sales Cr.
50	50
75	75
40	40
165	165

These totals may be posted instead of the individual figures.

Sales Journals

The journal illustrated in Figure 4-2 is called a *sales journal.* When sales are made on account, several copies of the sales invoice are prepared. The customer usually receives two copies, and at least one copy goes to the seller's accounting department. This sales invoice is the basis for entries made in the sales journal. The information listed on a sales invoice usually includes the date of the sale, the serial number of the invoice, credit terms, customer name, and amount of

FIGURE 4-2

TWO-COLUMN (GENERAL) JOURNAL

Jan. 3	Accounts receivable (Jones)	50	
	Sales		50
14	Accounts receivable (Smith)	75	
	Sales		75
29	Accounts receivable (Drake)	40	
	Sales		40

SALES JOURNAL

Date	Customer	Accounts Receivable Dr. Sales Cr.
Jan. 3	Jones	50
14	Smith	75
29	Drake	40
	Total	165

Post the total as a debit to the Accounts Receivable account and as a credit to the Sales account.

the sale. Only sales on credit are entered in a sales journal. When sales are made for cash, the transaction is usually recorded in a cash receipts journal which will be discussed later in this chapter.

The sales journal is easily used in conjunction with an accounts receivable subsidiary ledger. This is illustrated in Figure 4-3. This illustration uses the same three sales as were used in the previous illustration, but in a more elaborate, and realistic journal.

Note that each of the three sales transactions is recorded without indention to indicate a credit. Each entry consists of a debit to accounts receivable. The offsetting credit to Sales is understood without the indention, because sales on account are the only transactions recorded in this type of special journal.

Each entry in the sales journal represents a debit to a customer's account. The changes to a customer's account should be posted to the subsidiary ledger daily so that each customer's account will be completely current and useful in making decisions relating to further credit extensions and collectability of

FIGURE 4-3

SALES JOURNAL

Date	Account Debited		Invoice No.	Amount
19X1				
Jan. 3	Jones	✓	4011	50
14	Smith	✓	4012	75
29	Drake	✓	4013	40
				165
				(110) (400)

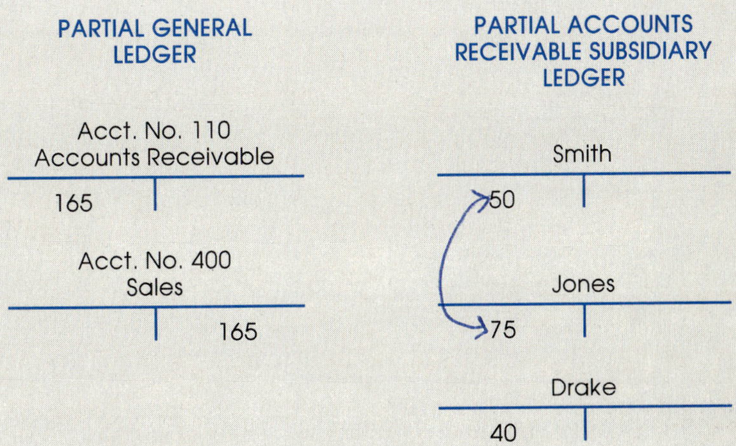

amounts. A check mark (✓) is placed in the sales journal opposite each amount posted to a customer's account, to indicate that the posting has been made. The invoice number (4011, 4012, 4013) is normally listed in the sales journal as a part of each entry. An entry in the sales journal indicates sale date, customer name, invoice number, and amount, but generally includes much less writing than would be required to record a sales transaction in the general journal. As the number of sales transactions mount, the time saved in recording and posting transactions in this expeditious manner becomes more important.

Direct Posting from Sales Invoices

If a company uses serially numbered sales invoices, a file or binder of duplicate invoices arranged in numerical order may take the place of a formal sales journal. At the end of the month, the invoices are totaled on an adding machine, and a general journal entry is made debiting Accounts Receivable and crediting Sales in the general ledger for the total of the period's sales. Obviously the amount of each sale from the individual sales invoices will be posted to the individual customer accounts in the subsidiary ledger as the sales are made.

Cash Receipts Journal

When a *cash receipts journal* is employed, it is used to record all cash receipts, regardless of source. In a typical business, the most frequent sources of cash are likely to be collections from customers on accounts and cash sales.

The cash receipts journal always has one column which represents a debit to Cash. The nature and frequency of the various types of transactions in which cash is received will determine the titles of other columns. However, it will almost always have a Sales credit column and an Accounts Receivable credit column. In addition, a Sundry (or Other) credit column may be utilized. A typical cash receipts journal is illustrated in Figure 4-4.

In this simulated cash receipts journal there were seven debits to cash for the month of November 19X1. Their total of $76,504 will be posted in one "lump sum" into the cash account in the ledger. The entries on November 8, 18, and 25 were the result of customers paying an account receivable. The total credit into accounts receivable of $9,779 will be posted into the general ledger, and each entry will be posted individually into the accounts receivable subsidiary ledger. When this is done, a check mark is placed in the reference column.

The company illustrated in Figure 4-4 probably accumulated the cash sale records and made an entry in the cash receipts journal bimonthly (on November 15 and 30). The total of these two amounts, $21,725, was posted to the Sales account in the ledger.

There were two Sundry items which were included in the cash receipts journal for the month. The first, on November 17 for $25,000, was obviously the result of the company borrowing money. The Sundry account credited was Notes Payable (Account No. 200). The second Sundry receipt of cash for the

FIGURE 4-4

Y Corporation
Cash Receipts Journal

				CREDITS		
DATE	ACCOUNTS CREDITED	REF.	CASH DR.	Accounts Receivable	Sales	Sundry
19X1						
Nov. 8	B. A. Raines		4,000	4,000		
15	Sales		10,500		10,500	
17	Note payable (12%, 90-day)		25,000			25,000
18	Jacobs & Dillon		2,512	2,512		
22	Common stock		20,000			20,000
25	Leigh, Inc.		3,267	3,267		
30	Sales		11,225		11,225	
			76,504	9,779	21,725	45,000

month resulted from the issuance of common stock on November 25. As with the previous Sundry item, when this amount is posted, the account title will be inserted in the reference column (Account No. 300). When all items from the Sundry column are posted, a check mark is placed below the total as an indication that the individual amounts which constitute that total have been posted.

The flow of data from the cash receipts journal to the ledgers of Y Corporation is illustrated in Figure 4-5.

Other Journals

Several other specialized journals are often used in businesses. The most common of these are the *cash payments journal* and the *purchases journal.*

Every transaction entered in the cash payments journal represents a credit to Cash and a debit to another account. The most common debit account is Accounts Payable, with others such as Purchases or various expense accounts used as well.

The purpose of the purchases journal is to record entries for all purchases of merchandise for resale on account. Every invoice received for the purchase of merchandise is the basis for an entry into the purchases journal. The purchases journal is normally very similar in arrangement and operation to the sales journal.

In addition to the two journals illustrated in this chapter (sales journal and cash receipts journal) and the two just mentioned (cash payments and purchases journals), other specialized journals may be required by various businesses. For example, a bank would probably have a notes receivable journal (as well as a notes receivable subsidiary ledger). A business that has a large volume

FIGURE 4-5

Y Corporation
Cash Receipts Journal

				CREDITS		
DATE	ACCOUNTS CREDITED	REF.	CASH DR.	Accounts Receivable	Sales	Sundry
19X1						
Nov. 8	B. A. Raines	✓	4,000	4,000		
15	Sales	✓	10,500		10,500	
17	Note payable (12%, 90-day)	200	25,000			25,000
18	Jacobs & Dillon	✓	2,512	2,512		
22	Common stock	300	20,000			20,000
25	Leigh, Inc.	✓	3,267	3,267		
30	Sales	✓	11,225		11,225	
			76,504	9,779	21,725	45,000
			(100)	(110)	(400)	(✓)

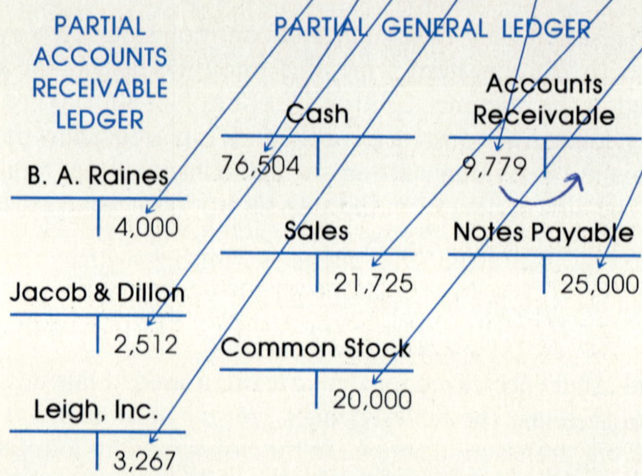

of sales returns might have a specially constructed journal for that purpose. On the other hand, many businesses have no need for certain journals. A fast-food restaurant would certainly have no need for a sales journal in which only sales on account are recorded.

Therefore, there is no established rule for businesses to follow in choosing the specific kind of special journals to be used in their accounting system. Each business will select the types of journals which will result in the greatest convenience and time saving in processing transactions. The design of the journals and ledgers is an integral part of the overall design of the accounting system.

In addition to the advantages of special journals which have previously been discussed, other advantages occur. For example, the duties can be divided among several employees, and the recording of entries in special journals can be handled by employees with little training. Another advantage is that errors can be quickly located, since they are usually discovered in the process of checking the equality of debits and credits in the journals.

Worksheet

A useful device often employed by a firm's accountants as well as independent auditors is the worksheet. The worksheet serves to summarize quickly, and modify (as appropriate), the output of an accounting system. There are many kinds of worksheets employed by practicing accountants, but the basic one, illustrated in Figure 4-6, serves especially well to provide a review of the process of preparing financial statements from the accounts.

Note the following points concerning the format of the worksheet:

1. The balances of all accounts in the general ledger before adjustments (the trial balance) are written out in the first set of columns. This serves as a trial balance; that is, it demonstrates equality of debits and credits in terms of dollar values.
2. Any adjusting entries required to bring accounts up to date are entered in the second set of columns.
3. The third set of columns shows the account balances after all necessary adjustments have been made. This is referred to as an *adjusted trial balance.*
4. The adjusted account balances are then separated into income statement accounts and balance sheet accounts.
5. In the set of columns for the income statement accounts, expenses will appear as debits, and revenues as credits. The difference between the totals of the debits and credits will be the profit or loss for the period. In the example given, revenues exceed expenses by $20,000 and this amount is the earnings for January (19X1). This represents an increase in retained earnings (an owners' equity account) and is thus carried to the credit side of the set of columns for the balance sheet.
6. In the set of balance sheet columns, assets appear as debits and equities as credits. After the addition of the income for the period to the equities side (as just detailed) the debits will equal credits.
7. Financial statements can then be prepared directly from the last two sets of columns on the worksheet, as shown.

By using the data produced in the previous worksheet, we may construct a set of statements for the X Corporation:

X Corporation
Income Statement
For the month of January 19X1
(last three zeros omitted)

Sales		$420
Expenses		
Utilities expense	$204	
Wages	68	
Other	128	
Total		400
Net income		$ 20

FIGURE 4-6

X Corporation Worksheet:
January 19X1
(last three zeros omitted)

	TRIAL BALANCE		ADJUSTMENTS		ADJUSTED TRIAL BALANCE		DATA FOR INCOME STATEMENT		DATA FOR BALANCE SHEET	
	Debit	**Credit**	**Debit**	**Credit**	**Debit**	**Credit**	**Debit**	**Credit**	**Debit**	**Credit**
Cash	55				55				55	
Accounts receivable	85				85				85	
Other current assets	110				110				110	
Equipment	150			(a) 12	138				138	
Accounts payable		75				75				75
Wages payable				(b) 8		8				8
Capital stock		200				200				200
Retained earnings		85				85				85
Sales		420				420		420		
Utilities expense	204				204		204			
Wages expense	60		(b) 8		68		68			
Other expenses	116		(a) 12		128		128			
Totals	780	780	20	20	788	788	400	420	388	368
Net income to be reported as an addition to retained earnings							20			20
Totals							420	420	388	388

Note: The X Corporation accounts were closed on December 31, 19X0. Depreciation on equipment was $12 during January. Wages owed to employees at the end of January amounted to $8.

X Corporation
Balance Sheet
As of January 31, 19X1
(last three zeros omitted)

ASSETS		LIABILITIES AND OWNERS' EQUITY		
Current assets		Curient liabilities		
Cash	$ 55	Accounts payable		$ 75
Accounts receivable	85	Wages payable		8
Other current assets	110	Total		$ 83
Total	$250	Owners' equity		
Equipment	138	Capital stock	$200	
		Retained earnings	105	
		Total owners' equity		305
Total assets	$388	Total equities		$388

In addition to being a handy summary device for the preparation and audit of annual statements, the worksheet is also useful for the preparation of *interim (monthly or quarterly) financial statements.* A firm will not ordinarily be content to wait for annual statements to know how operations are progressing, and statements will often be prepared quarterly or monthly. Worksheets are useful for these interim reports, since the formal accounting records need not be adjusted for the preparation of the statements. Adjusting entries need be recorded only on the worksheet, and closing entries need not be made. If interim statements were to be prepared directly from the accounts in the general ledger, it would be necessary to record adjusting and closing entries monthly in the journal and in the accounts, which would clutter the accounting records with such things as depreciation entries and wage accounts. By using the worksheet for interim statement preparation, these entries need be made only once a year in the formal accounting records.

DATA PROCESSING IN ACCOUNTING

The phrase *electronic data processing* (EDP) refers to the processing of information by electronic computers. It is important to note that a computer-based accounting system processes information relating to that system in much the same way as does a manual system. The difference is that in a computer-based system many of the steps (such as posting) are done internally, within the computer and peripheral equipment, and therefore the activity is not "visible" in the traditional sense. The starting point in either system is the source document, and transactions are recorded initially from these documents. However, the computer is capable of incredibly swift data manipulation, as well as having a vast data storage capacity. This combination of characteristics made it inevitable that the computer would be harnessed for the performance of recurring accounting tasks that involve processing voluminous quantities of data.

A computer has three basic capabilities: it can store data, transfer and otherwise manipulate data, and perform calculations with data. It must have an input unit to receive data, a storage unit to "memorize" data and instructions, and an output unit to transmit processed information to the user. Input devices convert coded data on punched cards, paper tape, magnetic tape, and disks into computer language for storage and processing. (A particularly impressive input device is the optical scanner, which can "read" printed data and convert it directly into computer language.) Coded data may also be input directly to the computer by means of keyboards.

The computer is instructed on how to store and manipulate the input data by means of a program. A program is simply a series of instructions previously prepared by a programmer which is given to the computer and stored in the computer's memory unit. The program also tells the computer what output to generate and in what form. The output may be in the form of printed material (such as financial statements), punched cards, tape, or disks which will be used in further processing.

In the design of EDP accounting systems, accountants may be inclined by their familiarity with manual accounting systems to force the EDP system into the same mold. This is a mistake if it is overdone. However, many of the features of a manual system do fit well into an EDP system, since the fundamental nature of the general ledger is the same in any accounting system. There must be "input" to the ledger, and the input must be properly controlled to insure accuracy and prevent fraud; it must be possible to demonstrate the validity of the input by some sort of audit procedure; and there must be "output"—from the ledger to the accounting reports—which is reliable and verifiable. In many cases the source documents may be accumulated according to much the same pattern under either system, although there is a trend toward eliminating the use of some of the source documents in computerized systems by having the original transaction information fed directly into the computer.

Computerized accounting systems achieve the same results as manual systems and achieve those results rapidly and economically, though such systems may bear little outward similarity to manual systems. The basic steps in the accounting process under a manual system and a computerized system may be compared:

MANUAL RECORD KEEPING	COMPUTERIZED RECORD KEEPING
1. A source document (or originating document), such as a check, a sales slip, or an invoice, is prepared for each transaction, and filed.	Source documents are usually prepared and filed as a basis for data input into the system, but direct input with no document involved is sometimes employed. Such direct input methods include optical scanning and terminals connected to the computer.

(Continued)

MANUAL RECORD KEEPING	COMPUTERIZED RECORD KEEPING
2. Transaction data is entered in various journals by means of journal entries.	Transaction data is recorded in machine-sensible form by means of punched cards, punched paper tape, magnetic tape, and disks.
3. Journal entry data is posted periodically to the general ledger from the various journals.	The transaction data on the input medium (cards or tape) is placed in the computer's memory unit or is stored on disks or tape by machine operation.
4. Account balances are maintained in the general ledger.	All the debits and credits for each account are stored in computer memory.
5. Adjusting journal entries are prepared and posted to the general ledger.	The computer program includes procedures for routine adjusting entries such as accrual of wages, interest payable, and depreciation. Data for special adjusting entries must be fed into the computer.
6. Statements are prepared from the account balances in the general ledger.	The arithmetic section of the computer calculates the account balances and the output prints out the statements in the form prescribed by the program.
7. The accounts are closed by posting the closing journal entries to the general ledger.	The computer transfers entries of the past period to a memory file for later audit purposes and carries balances forward.
8. For audit review purposes, the source documents and the accounting records are carefully preserved. This provides an audit trail which is easy to follow but requires many time-consuming audit procedures.	Maintaining an audit trail of originating documents and paper printouts is often necessary but results in additional costs. The computer can be programmed, however, to perform many of the audit procedures, thus saving time and expense.

While the same basic accounting steps are involved under the manual and the computerized system, it should be noted that computerized systems vary considerably according to the capabilities of the particular computers used, and the extent to which the firm utilizes the computer in the record-keeping process. It must be noted further that the computer can be programmed to produce additional internal and special purpose reports that may be of considerable value to management.

Microcomputers in Accounting

The microcomputer, or minicomputer, is currently making an impact on accounting, and many feel that it is just beginning to be used effectively. Many large public accounting firms are providing their professional staff with unlimited access to these machines. Examples of applications include budgetary, financial planning, depreciation schedules, mailing lists, trial balance preparations, fee estimates, and many tax applications.

To be more specific as to the applications of a microcomputer, suppose that a CPA is asked by a client to prepare a profitability projection for five years of a hotel he is planning to build. If the CPA prepares these projections at one assumed interest rate for borrowing and then the client wants to know what effect another interest rate might have on the projections, the CPA could feasibly "feed" the new interest rate into the microcomputer. The computer would make the necessary mathematical computations and the CPA would have the new projections immediately. This could even be done at the client's office if the computer is small enough to be portable.

Other Methods of Processing Data

Accounting or Bookkeeping Machines

Accounting or bookkeeping machines are basically posting machines operated by clerical personnel. These machines (which are simple by today's standards) make it possible to neatly post a transaction to several records. For example, a sales invoice can be recorded in the sales journal that is posted to the subsidiary accounts receivable ledger at the same time. Summary totals are then periodically posted manually to the sales account and accounts receivable control account in the general ledger. The primary benefits of these bookkeeping machines are that the posting process is faster and neater, and the equality of debits and credits is assured.

Punched-Card or Tape Equipment

A punched-card or tape system is one step up from bookkeeping machines. It generally involves data which is punched into cards (or tapes) by means of holes arranged in a definite pattern. The patterns of holes identify such things as the name of a customer or supplier, item sold or bought, the date, the amount, and other things such as credit terms and shipping information. These cards are then processed through different types of equipment to arrive at the proper grouping and necessary summarized totals. Different types of machinery that reproduce, verify, collate, and tabulate the punched cards facilitate the analysis. The advantages are similar to that of bookkeeping machines. However, they provide additional flexibility in that many different procedures can be employed on one card to develop different types of information.

LOCATING ERRORS

Regardless of the type of accounting system employed, clerical errors will occur. Their detection is possible in many ways, including chance discovery and through the medium of the trial balance. If the debit and credit totals of the trial balance are not equal, the reason for the difference should be determined before proceeding further into the accounting cycle.

The amount of the difference between the two totals of a trial balance often provides a clue as to the nature of the error or where it occurred. For example, a difference that is evenly divisible by 2, is often the result of posting a debit as a credit, or vice versa. This can be illustrated with the following brief example. Say that the debit and credit totals of a trial balance are $40,616 and $40,010 respectively. The difference of $606 may indicate that a credit posting of that amount was omitted or that a credit of $303 was erroneously posted as a debit.

Transpositions and Slides

Transpositions and *slides* are two other common types of errors. A transposition is the incorrect arrangement of digits in a number, such as writing $736 as $763 or $376. A slide is the misplacement of a decimal point, such as writing $252.00 as $25.20 or as $25,200.00. If either a transposition or slide has occurred and there are no other errors, the discrepancy between the two trial balance totals will be evenly divisible by 9.

An initial examination following the ideas outlined above will frequently reveal the error. If it does not, the common procedure is to retrace the various steps in the accounting process, beginning with the last step and working back to the original journal entries.

SUMMARY

The first part of this chapter was designed to pull together many of the concepts which were introduced in Chapter 3. The illustration included each step in the basic accounting cycle:

- Journalizing entries
- Posting to the ledger
- Preparation of a trial balance
- Adjusting journal entries
- Preparation of financial statements
- Preparation of closing entries
- Preparation of post-closing trial balance

Subsidiary ledgers and special journals are primarily methods of expediting the record-keeping process. The principal types of special journals are: sales journals, cash receipts journals, purchases journals, and cash payment journals. The principal subsidiary ledgers are accounts receivable and payable. Each subsidiary ledger has a control account in the general ledger. The control account contains the balance of the account in total, and the subsidiary ledgers contain the detail of that account. For example, the accounts receivable control account on a given date will provide the total balance owed by all customers. The subsidiary accounts receivable ledger will tell what each individual customer owes.

A worksheet is a handy device to aid in the preparation of financial statements. It is particularly useful in the preparation of interim (quarterly or monthly) financial statements. If a worksheet is used in this regard, adjusting and closing entries need not actively be made in the accounts, but rather they can be made on the worksheet only, thus avoiding a certain amount of clutter in the accounting records.

The computer is a device which also expedites the record-keeping function in accounting. A computer-based accounting system follows essentially the same steps as a manual system. The difference is that in a computer-based system many steps (such as posting) are done internally, within the computer memory, and therefore the activity is not visible in the traditional sense. Microcomputers are fairly recent additions to the scene in accounting, and they are being used more and more in the contemporary accounting environment. One obvious advantage of a microcomputer is its portability. It can often be taken to a client's office and operated in much the same way as a portable electric typewriter.

KEY POINTS

1. **Retained earnings statement** A reconciliation of beginning and ending retained earnings.

2. **Subsidiary ledgers** Satellite or detail ledgers which provide a summarized listing of items in one control account in the general ledger.

3. **Sales journal** A special journal used only to record sales to customers on account.

4. **Cash receipts journal** A special journal used to record all cash receipts.

5. **Purchases journal** A special journal used to record the purchase of merchandise for resale on account.

6. **Cash payments journal** A special journal used to record all cash payments.

7. **Worksheet** A columnar sheet designed to conveniently arrange all accounting data required for the preparation of financial statements.

8. **Electronic data processing** The processing of information by electronic computers.

9. **Microcomputers** Small, portable electronic computers used in processing data.

QUESTIONS

1. Distinguish between accrued and deferred.

2. What is the difference between an adjusting entry and a correcting entry?

3. Assuming the use of the sales journal and the cash receipts journal illustrated in this chapter, and a two-column general journal, indicate the journal in which each of the following should be recorded:

   a. Receipt of cash refund for an overcharge by a supplier.
   b. Investments of additional cash in the business by stockholders.
   c. Sale of merchandise on account.
   d. Sale of supplies on account, at cost, to an affiliated company.
   e. Adjustment to record depreciation expense for the year.
   f. Receipt of cash in payment of principal and interest on a note.
   g. Sale of merchandise for cash.
   h. Closing of the owners' drawing account at the end of the year.
   i. Adjusting entry for accrued wages payable at year end.

4. Describe briefly how the sales journal and the cash receipts journal used in question 3 will be posted.

5. Describe the principal similarities and differences between a manual and a computerized accounting system.

6. What are the basic elements of a worksheet? Explain.

7. In preforming the regular end-of-period accounting procedures, does the preparation of the worksheet precede or follow the posting of adjusting entries to ledger accounts?

8. Do the totals of the balance sheet ordinarily agree with the totals of the balance sheet columns of the worksheet? Why or why not?

9. How do special journals save time in entering and posting adjustments?

10. What term is applied to each of the following: A ledger comprising each individual customers' account? The single summarizing account for accounts receivable?

11. Which of the following would generally be considered as a source document which serves as the basis for an accounting entry?

   a. Sales invoice
   b. Tax return
   c. Purchase order
   d. Debit memo (from your bank)
   e. Repair estimate

12. In recording 5,000 individual sales on account during the month, how many times would it be necessary to write "Accounts Receivable" if the transactions are recorded in a general journal? Or if each sale is recorded in a sales journal?

13. Referring to question 12, how many individual postings to the Sales account are necessary if the general journal is used, or if the sales journal is used? How many individual postings to customer accounts in the accounts receivable subsidiary ledger are necessary if the general journal is used, or if the sales journal is used?

14. Assume Adams Company uses only a general journal, a ledger, and a subsidiary accounts receivable ledger. In posting from the general journal to the ledger, the bookkeeper inadvertently posted a debit of $800 to the customer's account as a credit. The posting to the accounts receivable subsidiary ledger was correct. No other errors occurred during the period. Will the debits and credits in the trial balance equal? If not how much will the difference be? What other records will be in disagreement?

EXERCISES

E4-1 Ludema Company rents its delivery equipment, paying rent at a rate of $2,400 per month for its six vans. On November 1, 19X2, the company pays the rent on its delivery equipment for 3 months in advance. Assuming the company does not charge expense until service is used, prepare appropriate entries as of November 1 (when payment was made), and December 31, 19X1 (the end of the company's accounting year).

E4-2 During September 19X2, the White Company experienced the following events:

a. Rent for September and October, in the total amount of $2,000, was paid Rental Realty Company during September.
b. A comprehensive insurance policy was purchased from the Torch Insurance Company for a 6-month period starting September 1. Cash payment of $600 is made for this coverage.
c. Supplies to be used in wrapping goods for customers were purchased from Cover-up Company for $800 during September, and the cost of supplies on hand on September 30, 19X2, equaled $160.

Assuming that the White Company records these expenditures as being prepaid, prepare the appropriate entry to record each of these events, and to record the adjustments required as of September 30, 19X2.

E4-3 Simcox Company is in the midst of preparing its financial statements for the year ending December 31, 19X2. The company's management has asked you, as their accountant, to determine what adjusting journal entries are necessary as of December 31, 19X2.

a. Simcox Co. moved into a new office on November 1, 19X2. Under the terms of their lease, a $12,000 payment was made on November 1 covering the first 6 months' rent. No entries have been made in the prepaid rent account since the payment was made.

b. On November 1, 19X2 the company took out a 3-year fire and theft insurance policy covering the office and its contents. The $7,200 cost of the insurance policy was debited to prepaid insurance on November 1. No other entry has been made in the prepaid insurance account since that date.

c. Simcox Co. had a supplies inventory of $10,000 on January 1, 19X2. During the year, additional supplies costing $60,000 were purchased, with the debit being made to Supplies Inventory. At the end of 19X2, the cost of supplies on hand was determined to be $16,000.

d. Salary payments of $350,000 were made to employees of Simcox Co. during 19X2. Unpaid salaries owed to employees at the end of 19X2 amounted to $16,000. There were no unpaid salaries at the end of 19X1.

E4-4 Phil's Outlet Store is in the process of completing the accounting process for the year just ended, December 31, 19X1. The worksheet has been started and the following data in respect to adjusting entries are available:

a. Office supplies purchased and debited to Office Supplies Inventory during the year amounted to $720. The year-end inventory showed $160 worth of supplies on hand.

b. Wages earned but unpaid and unrecorded at December 31, 19X1 amounted to $2,200.

c. Three-fourths of the basement of the store is rented to another merchant, Ron Lee, who sells compatible, but not competitive, merchandise. On November 1, 19X1, the store collected 6 months' rent in advance, amounting to $7,200, which was credited to Rent Income.

d. The rest of the basement is rented to Rick Jones; rent of $500 per month is payable monthly. On December 31, 19X1, the rent for November and December 19X1 had not yet been collected.

Prepare the appropriate adjusting entries.

E4-5 Philos Company, on August 1, 19X1 in order to meet a cash shortage, obtained a $12,000, 18% loan from a local bank. The principal, plus interest, was payable at the end of 12 months. The annual fiscal period for Philos ends on December 31, 19X1.

REQUIRED:

1. Give the journal entry on the date of the loan, August 1, 19X1.
2. Give the adjusting entry required on December 31, 19X1.
3. Give the journal entry on date of payment, July 31, 19X2.

E4-6 Assume that the worksheet at December 31, 19X2 for Delap Real Estate Corporation has been completed through the Adjusted Trial Balance and we are ready to extend each amount to several columns to the right. These columns are listed here with code letters:

CODE NO.	COLUMNS
a	Income statement, debit
b	Income statement, credit
c	Balance sheet, debit
d	Balance sheet, credit

Next are listed representative accounts to be extended on the worksheet of Delap Real Estate Corporation. You are to give a code letter for each account indicating the proper worksheet column to the right of Adjusted Trial Balance, to which the amount in each account is to be extended.

ACCOUNTS	CODE NO.
Cash	
Inventory of office supplies	
Interest payable	
Capital stock	
Commissions earned	
Rent collected in advance	
Salary expense	
Retained earnings, beginning credit balance	
Building	
Mortgage payable	
Income taxes payable	
Sales commissions receivable	
Accumulated depreciation on building	
Unearned sales commissions	
Income tax expense	
Net income:	
Code number for the debit	
Code number for the credit	
Net loss:	
Code number for the debit	
Code number for the credit	

E4-7 A company uses a one-column sales journal, a one-column purchases journal, a cash receipts journal, a cash payments journal, and a general journal in recording its transactions.

Indicate in which journal each of the following transactions would be recorded: (a) sold merchandise on credit; (b) sold merchandise for cash; (c) gave a customer credit for merchandise purchased on credit and returned; (d) paid a creditor; (e) paid office salaries; (f) customer paid for merchandise previously purchased on credit; (g) recorded adjusting and closing entries; (h) purchased merchandise on credit; (i) purchased sales department supplies on credit; (j) purchased office equipment for cash; (k) returned merchandise purchased on credit; (l) paid taxes.

E4-8 The items listed next are from the Adjustments columns of a worksheet as of December 31.

Prepare adjusting journal entries from the information.

	ADJUSTMENTS	
	Debit	**Credit**
Prepaid insurance		(a) $ 240
Office supplies		(b) 630
Accumulated depreciation: Office equipment		(c) 1,400
Accumulated depreciation: Store equipment		(d) 2,200
Office salaries expense	(e) $ 240	
Store salaries expense	(e) 480	
Insurance expense	(a) 240	
Office supplies expense	(b) 630	
Depreciation expense: Office equipment	(c) 1,400	
Depreciation expense: Store equipment	(d) 2,200	
Salaries payable		(e) 720
	$5,190	$5,190

E4-9 The following information is derived from the Income Statement columns of the worksheet of the Qwik-Fix Store on December 31.

	INCOME STATEMENT	
	Debit	**Credit**
Repair revenue		$48,480
Wages expense	$15,680	
Rent expense	2,400	
Supplies used	8,520	
Insurance expense	1,830	
Depreciation expense: Repair equipment	2,690	
	31,120	48,480
Net income	17,360	
	$48,480	$48,480
Dividends for the year totaled $20,000		

REQUIRED:

Journalize the closing entries for Qwik-Fix as of December 31.

E4-10 Garvey Company uses a cash receipts journal, a sales journal, a purchases journal, and a general journal. Indicate which journal should be used to record each of the following transactions:

(a) Adjusting entry to record depreciation
(b) Purchase of delivery truck for cash
(c) Purchase of merchandise on account
(d) Return of merchandise by a customer company for credit to its account.
(e) Payment of property taxes
(f) Purchase of typewriter on account
(g) Sale of merchandise on account
(h) Sale of merchandise for cash
(i) Refund to a customer who returned merchandise
(j) Return of merchandise to a supplier for credit

E4-11 The accounting system used by Omega Company includes a general journal and also four special journals for cash receipts, cash payments, sales, and purchases of merchandise. On January 31, the accounts receivable control account in the general ledger had a debit balance of $32,000, and the accounts payable control account had a credit balance of $96,000. During February, the sales journal included transactions which totaled $192,000. The purchases journal included transactions totaling $112,000. In the cash receipts journal, the accounts receivable column showed a credit total for February of $153,600. In the cash payments journal, the Accounts Payable column showed a debit total of $134,400.

a. What posting would be made of the total of the $153,600 Accounts Receivable column total in the cash receipts journal at February 28?
b. What posting would be made of the $192,000 total of the sales journal at February 28?
c. What posting would be made of the $112,000 total of the purchases journal at February 28?
d. Based on this information, state the balances of the accounts receivable control account and the accounts payable control account in the general ledger after completion of posting at February 28.

E4-12 Mode Company maintains its sales journal and accounts receivable subsidiary ledger by EDP. Each day the accounting department prepares a control total of total credit sales and sends the sales invoices to the EDP department. The sales data are keypunched by the EDP department, and the punched cards and a control figure representing the total number of sales transactions (per the invoices) are entered into the computer.

The computer prepares the sales journal, posts to the accounts receivable ledger (maintained on magnetic tape), and performs an item count. Any discrepancy in the item count is printed out on an error report. A copy of the sales journal for each day is sent back to the accounting department in comparison with the daily control totals.

What control procedure will first detect the following independent errors?

a. A sales invoice of $889 is accidentally keypunched as $8,890.
b. A sales invoice is lost on the way from the accounting department to the EDP department.
c. Several punched cards are lost before being processed by the computer.

PROBLEMS

P4-1 Cantcount Company determined its net income for the year ended December 31, 19X2, to be $80,000. None of the following items had been considered in computing the income figure:

a. Customers owed Cantcount Company $12,000 for purchases which were made late in 19X2. These accounts receivable had not been included when the revenue was determined. There are no accounts receivable at the beginning of 19X2.
b. The rent expense included $6,000, which represented payments covering the first 2 months of 19X3.
c. Store equipment, which was purchased for $28,000 4 years ago, is expected to last for only 7 years. No depreciation expense was used in computing the 19X2 income. The equipment is expected to be worthless at the end of 7 years.
d. On July 1, 19X2, Cantcount Company borrowed $120,000 to remodel its store. Although interest was stated to be at the rate of 10% per year, none was paid during 19X2, therefore, no interest expense was included among the expenses.

REQUIRED:

Based on information for the Cantcount Company:

1. Prepare the adjusting journal entries as of December 31, 19X2.
2. Determine the correct net income for 19X2.

P4-2 The Eazy Trucking Company (a corporation) is now in the process of completing the information-processing cycle for the year ended December 31, 19X2. The adjusting entries are now to be entered on the worksheet. The following data that must be considered have been developed from the records and related documents:

a. On September 1, 19X2, a 3-year insurance premium on certain equipment was paid, amounting to $1,440, which was debited to Prepaid Insurance.

b. During the year, office supplies amounting to $2,400 were purchased for cash and debited to Supplies Inventory; at the end of 19X2, an inventory of supplies showed $600. There was no inventory of supplies on hand at January 1, 19X2.

c. On December 31, 19X2, Phil's Garage completed repairs on a truck at a cost of $900; the amount was payable by January 30, 19X3.

d. In December 19X2, the tax bill on equipment for 19X2 amounting to $1,000 was received from the city; the taxes are due February 15, 19X3.

e. On December 31, 19X2, Eazy completed a hauling contract for an out-of-state company. The bill was for $5,400, payable within 30 days. No entry has been made.

f. On July 1, 19X2, Eazy purchased a new hauling van at a cash cost of $14,200. The estimated useful life of the van to Eazy was 5 years, with an estimated residual value at the time of $2,200. Compute depreciation for 6 months.

g. On October 1, 19X2, Eazy borrowed $12,000 from the local bank on a 1-year, 8% note payable. The principal and interest is payable at the end of 12 months.

REQUIRED:

Prepare the adjusting entries to be made at year end relating to the transactions just described.

P4-3 Babcock, Inc., which was organized on January 1, 19X1, use only a general journal and no subsidiary ledgers. The following transactions, some in summary form, occurred during Babcock's first year of operation:

Jan. 1	Investors purchased $50,000 of common stock.
Jan. 2	The company purchased equipment totaling $28,000. It has an estimated life of 10 years and an estimated salvage value of $3,000.
Jan. 3	A suitable building was rented for 3 years. The full rent was paid in advance, $7,200.
Various dates	Revenues (all on account) during the year totaled $68,000
Various dates	Expenses during the year (all cash) totaled $45,000. For illustrative purposes we will assume that all expenses are recorded in an account.
Various dates	Collections on account totaled $52,000
Dec. 31	Dividends were paid, $5,000
Dec. 31	Adjustment data: a. Equipment depreciation (data from previous entry) b. Prepaid rent (data from previous entry) c. Accrued wages as of December 31, 19X1, $2,000.

REQUIRED:

1. Journalize the transactions just listed.
2. Post to the ledger accounts.
3. Prepare a trial balance.
4. Prepare the necessary adjusting entries.
5. Prepare an income statement, retained earnings statement, and balance sheet for the period.
6. Prepare the necessary closing entries.
7. Prepare a post-closing trial balance.

P4-4 The trial balance of Jackson Laundromat at December 31, 19X1 (the end of the current fiscal year), and data needed to determine year-end adjustments are presented next.

Jackson Laundromat
Trial Balance
December 31, 19X1

Cash	$ 2,436	
Laundry supplies	3,950	
Prepaid insurance	1,198	
Laundry equipment	45,400	
Accumulated depreciation		$11,200
Accounts payable		730
Capital stock		10,000
Retained earnings		16,224
Dividends	12,440	
Laundry revenue		49,830
Wages expense	15,670	
Rent expense	3,640	
Utilities expense	2,230	
Miscellaneous expense	1,020	
	$87,984	$87,984

Adjustment data:

a. Inventory of laundry supplies at December 31	$ 810
b. Insurance premiums expired during the year	730
c. Depreciation on equipment during the year	3,620
d. Wages accrued but not paid at December 31	170

REQUIRED:

1. Record the trial balance on an eight-column worksheet.
2. Complete the worksheet.
3. Prepare financial statements for the company for the year.

P4-5 Listed next is the adjusted trial balance of Craig Corporation as of December 31, 19X1.

Craig Corporation
Adjusted Trial Balance
December 31, 19X1

	DEBITS	CREDITS
Cash	$ 41,280	
Notes receivable	59,600	
Accounts receivable	35,200	
Prepaid expenses	2,760	
Land	24,000	
Buildings	300,000	
Accumulated depreciation: Buildings		$ 100,000
Equipment	209,400	
Accumulated depreciation: Equipment		96,400
Notes payable		13,780
Accounts payable		43,800
Salaries payable		6,160
Unearned revenue		4,000
Mortgage payable		126,000
Common stock, 10,000 shares		160,000
Retained earnings, 12/31/X0		104,100
Service revenue		786,300
Wage and salary expenses	510,740	
Office expenses	107,200	
Transportation and travel expenses	80,000	
Depreciation expense	16,800	
Repairs and maintenance expenses	6,400	
Interest expense	5,440	
Income tax expense	21,720	
Dividends	20,000	
Totals	$1,440,540	$1,440,540

REQUIRED:

Use the adjusted trial balance to prepare an income statement, a retained earnings statement, and a balance sheet for Craig Corporation on December 31, 19X1.

P4-6 On September 1, 19X1, Jad Moving Co. was organized to provide transportation of household furniture. During September the following transactions occurred:

Sept. 1 Cash of $2,000,000 was received in exchange for common stock par value capital stock.

5 Purchased land for $500,000 and building for $720,000, paying $420,000 cash and signing a $800,000 mortgage payable bearing interest at 9%.

8 Purchased six trucks from G. W. Motors at a total cost of $864,000. A cash down payment of $400,000 was made, the balance to be paid by January 12.

9 Purchased office equipment for cash, $48,000.

9 Moved furniture for Mr. and Mrs. W. Bird from Chicago to San Antonio for $33,700. Collected $9,700 in cash, balance to be paid within 30 days (credit Moving Service Revenue).

10 Moved furniture for various clients for $64,700. Collected $36,700 in cash, balance to be paid within 30 days.

15 Paid salaries to employees for the first half of the month, $30,200.

25 Moved furniture for various clients for a total of $54,000. Cash collected in full.

30 Salaries expense for the second half of September amounted to $26,500.

30 Received a gasoline bill for the month of September from Good Company in the amount of $35,000, to be paid by October 15.

30 Received bill of $2,500 for repair work on trucks during September by Poor Repair Company.

30 Paid $10,000 to the holder of the mortgage payable. This $10,000 payment included $6,000 interest expense for September and $4,000 reduction in the liability.

30 Declared a $20,000 cash dividend, payable December 15.

Estimated useful life of the building was 20 years, trucks 4 years, and office equipment 10 years. The account titles to be used and the account numbers are as follows:

Cash	100	Retained earnings	310
Accounts receivable	105	Dividends	350
Land	110	Moving service revenue	400
Building	120	Salaries expense	500
Accumulated depreciation: Building	130	Gasoline expense	510
Trucks	150	Repairs and maintenance expense	520
Accumulated depreciation: Trucks	160	Interest expense	530
Office equipment	180	Depreciation expense: Building	540
Accumulated depreciation: Office equipment	190	Depreciation expense: Trucks	550
Accounts payable	200	Depreciation expense: Office equipment	560
Dividends payable	210	Expense and revenue summary	900
Mortgage payable, 9%	220		
Capital stock	300		

INSTRUCTIONS:

a. Prepare journal entries in general journal form. (Number journal pages to permit cross-reference to ledger.)
b. Post to ledger accounts. (Number ledger accounts to permit cross-reference to journal.)
c. Prepare a trial balance at September 30, 19X1.
d. Prepare adjusting entries and post to ledger accounts.
e. Prepare an adjusted trial balance.
f. Prepare an income statement for September, a retained earnings statement and a balance sheet at September 30, 19X1.
g. Prepare closing entries and post to ledger accounts.
h. Prepare a post-closing trial balance.

P4-7 Krack Repair Service Company, Inc., maintains a general journal, a sales journal, and a cash receipts journal. It also maintains an accounts receivable subsidiary ledger. Krack closes accounts and prepares financial statements monthly. The post-closing balance sheet for Krack as of December 31, 19X1 is prepared next.

Krack, Inc.
Post-Closing Trial Balance
As of December 31, 19X1

Cash	$ 200	
Accounts receivable (Note 1)	14,500	
Supplies	2,500	
Equipment	85,000	
Accumulated depreciation: Equipment		$ 15,000
Accounts payable		5,200
Capital stock		50,000
Retained earnings		32,000
	$102,200	$102,200

Note 1: Consists of three customers:

Ace, Co.	$ 7,500
Bat, Inc.	4,300
Crow, Inc.	2,700
	$14,500

Transactions for the month of January 19X2 and adjustment data are presented next.

REQUIRED:

1. Journalize the transactions utilizing the proper journal at all times.
2. Post to the general ledger accounts and the accounts receivable subsidiary ledger.
3. Prepare a trial balance.

4. Journalize and post the adjusting entries.
5. Prepare an income statement, a retained earnings statement, and a balance sheet for the period.
6. Journalize and post closing entries.
7. Prepare a post-closing trial balance as of January 31, 19X2.

TRANSACTIONS:

19X2	
Jan. 2	Borrowed $10,000 from Good State Bank for 1 year at 18%.
4	Did repair work for Bat, Inc., and sent them a bill, $3,850.
5	Paid accounts payable, $5,200.
6	Purchased additional equipment on account, $5,500.
6	Paid rent for month, $700.
7	Collected amount due from Ace, Co. on account, $7,500.
9	Discovered that equipment purchased on January 6 was unsuitable for our line of work; sold it to a competitor at cost, $5,500.
10	Paid gasoline expense for the month, $580.
15	Collected amount due from Bat, Inc., from previous month, $4,300.
20	Did repair work for Crow, Inc., and sent them a bill, $6,000.
30	Paid monthly wages, $3,000.
30	Paid monthly utility bill, $620.
30	Cash sales for the month totaled $1,400.

ADJUSTMENT DATA:

Depreciation for the month is calculated to be $250. An inventory of supplies reveals that supplies on hand at the end of the month total $1,650. Accrued interest payable on January 31, totals $150.

CASH AND SHORT-TERM MARKETABLE SECURITIES

5

ORIENTATION

The main features of the chapter are a survey of some of the problems and procedures involved in the analysis and administration of cash (including cash planning and cash control) and a discussion of short-term marketable securities.

Cash is treated in a separate chapter, not because it poses serious measurement and reporting problems for accounting, but because of its crucial significance in business activities. Possibly, the single most important aspect of financial statements is their usefulness in developing forecasts of future cash flows from business operations. This chapter shows why the mere reporting of past cash flows is insufficient for that purpose, and what the significance of cash planning and control is for a firm's management. Short-term marketable securities are often called "secondary cash resources" because if cash is needed for operating purposes, these securities may quickly be converted into cash. In the meantime these investments are often preferable to cash because of the dividend revenue which they produce and their potential for appreciation.

CASH

Economists tell us that cash is a medium of exchange. The conduct of business operations includes a wide variety of exchanges which are greatly facilitated by an adequate stock of cash or ready access to cash through an established credit position. Even transactions in which cash does not appear to be involved, have cash bases. A stockholder who contributes property other than cash for his stock very likely paid out cash for that property and hopes that the firm will be able to produce cash through the use of the property. When a firm takes property on the sale of its merchandise, the expectation is that the property will be sold for cash or used to produce cash. Yet cash itself is said to be a nonproductive asset. Though it is cash that is used to convey the wealth of a firm to the stockholders, it is the command over goods and services that causes the cash to be desired by the stockholders. Cash is a medium of exchange and is useful in other ways, but its movements tell little about changes in the real underlying wealth of a firm.

If cash is defined as a medium of exchange, then only those instruments that serve as a medium of exchange can be classified as cash. Included as cash are coins and currency, checks, money orders, bank drafts, and amounts on deposit in checking accounts. All of these items are readily taken by others in discharge of obligations and acquisitions of goods and services. Savings account balances are not literally cash because they are not ordinarily transferable to others in normal trade practice. Whether savings account balances are treated as cash or short-term investments has little effect on the analysis of financial statements, but it is important that assets which are merely readily salable or acceptable as collateral should not be treated as cash.

For accounting purposes, the value of one dollar is one dollar. Cash is valued in terms of the current value of money rather than in terms of its anticipated use in the operations of the firm. There are certain valuation problems concerning cash produced by a cash sale or collection from customers. For example, checks received from customers, although treated as cash, may prove to be uncollectible or subject to collection problems. If checks returned by the bank marked "Not Sufficient Funds" are deemed to be ultimately collectible, the amounts involved should be removed from the cash total and treated as a receivable.

Restricted cash may not have the same value to a firm as freely usable cash. Banks frequently require that firms which borrow money from them maintain a certain minimum balance (compensating balance) in a checking account in the lending bank. Other contractual restrictions on cash may exist arising from agreements with creditors, taxing authorities, employees, and others. Such "frozen" cash is still cash but, in the footnotes to the financial statements, comments on the restrictions should explain to the balance sheet readers that this portion of the cash is not freely available for business use.

Administration of Cash

Management has three basic responsibilities concerning cash: (1) to have enough cash at any point in time to conduct business operations, (2) not to have too much cash on hand at any point in time, and (3) to adequately safeguard and protect the cash that the company has. A normal balance of cash is an active asset; the net result of incoming and outflowing cash. Even a slight impediment in the inflowing cash stream may cause the cash balance to be wiped out quickly. As a firm's sales decline, the inflow of cash may not fall off as rapidly (because of receivable collections) as the outflow of cash, and the cash balance may actually tend to build up. As business activity grows, the outflow of cash tends to speed up more quickly than the inflow of cash. This often tends to shrink the cash balance below safe levels, so that temporary loans may be required until the firm can carry out long-term plans to increase its sources of capital.

Good cash management involves the investment of cash generated by operations. Cash temporarily available at low points in the seasonal pattern of activities should be invested in short-term investments (such as certificates of deposit) that can be converted back to cash readily and without much risk of loss. Balances that will be investible for longer periods should be committed to securities which yield a higher rate of return (such as corporate bonds or stocks). Such securities should often be treated as long-term investments since they are no longer serving as working capital.

Foreign currency possessed by an American firm is often available as a medium of exchange. When such currencies are held, the amounts must be translated into dollar equivalents in order to carry the cash as a single sum in the balance sheet. Exchange quotations are easily obtained and no difficulty is involved in translating Mexican pesos, Italian lira, or British pounds to dollar equivalents. When foreign currency amounts are held through a change in exchange rates, the firm will experience a gain or loss as a result.

It should be pointed out that the holding of any monetary amount while the value of money is declining (as a result of a rise in price levels) involves a loss of purchasing power. The reader of comparative balance sheets must bear this in mind when the balance of cash held at the end of the current period is compared with the balance held on earlier balance sheets. One hundred dollars held at the current year does not mean the same thing as one hundred dollars held at the end of a year ten or fifteen years ago unless the balance sheets have been translated into current dollar equivalents by using an index of purchasing power.

Cash Control

Many assets are susceptible to the risk of fraud or error, but cash is particularly susceptible since it is universally desired and easily transferred. A good system of cash control is therefore essential.

There are a number of general rules and procedures in any good control system. Immediate physical control should be obtained by depositing cash receipts intact in the bank daily. The duties of those responsible for cash or cash records should be separated in such a manner that two or more persons would have to collude in order to perpetrate a fraud. Those who maintain records should have no physical contact with the items reflected in the records, and there should be regular comparisons of the amounts shown in the records with the physical existence of the items reflected. There must be safeguards to see that all items are properly ordered, received, and handled, and that all items are disposed of only for legitimate business purposes.

Various indirect checks give implicit verification of cash. For example, audits of accounts receivable verify cash collections, and audits of various costs that are incurred verify some of the payments.

Disbursements are safeguarded by paying out all amounts by check or through the imprest system (petty cash) which is explained next. The balance of cash on hand is safeguarded by periodic checks. The bank balance is checked by preparing a reconciliation of the bank balance and the cash account.

Petty Cash

Disbursing by check is relatively safe but it is also expensive because of the safeguarding procedure involved. In some operations, the process of drawing a check may well cost several dollars, which is obviously uneconomical where small amounts are involved. Furthermore, the process may take some time, and the newsboy, the taxicab driver, or the post office cannot be expected to render a bill and wait a week to be paid. In practice, then, there is no way to avoid making some payments in cash rather than by check.

Long ago in England, a system was devised in which small amounts of cash were given to individuals to disburse for business purposes. This small amount of cash became known as petty cash. Measures devised to safeguard the petty cash became known as the imprest system. Currently, the system is referred to equally as the *petty cash system* or the *imprest system.* The usual procedure is a simple one. A person is selected to be responsible for the petty cash and the amount designated for petty cash (for example, between \$50 and \$500) is placed in his or her custody. The person selected is held strictly accountable to show at any time the amount entrusted to his or her care, or to show reasonable evidence that amounts expended were for business purposes.

From an accounting point of view, the petty cash fund is handled by first establishing the fund. The journal entry to establish a petty cash fund of \$200 would be:

Petty cash	\$200	
Cash		\$200

At that time a check for $200 would be cashed, and the funds would be handed over to the person responsible for the fund.

Later, as petty cash is disbursed, receipts (sometimes called vouchers) are collected and held, but no entries are made in the accounting records. For example, during a period of time, assume the following activities occurred relating to the petty cash fund:

1. Purchased stamps from the post office, paid from petty cash, $25.
2. Reimbursed the company president from the petty cash fund for expenses associated with taking a customer to lunch, $35.
3. Made a cash contribution to a charitable organization which solicited at our office, $10.
4. Paid a miscellaneous expense, $42.

At the end of the accounting period, or when the cash in the fund is reduced to a level which makes it inadequate to handle payments, the person in charge of the fund turns the receipts over to the company cashier or to the responsible individual. The cashier analyzes the disbursements and prepares a check to reimburse the petty cash fund. The entry to record the reimbursement given the facts in the previous example would be:

Postage expense	$25	
Lunches and entertainment expense	35	
Contributions expense	10	
Miscellaneous expense	42	
Cash		$112
To reimburse the petty cash fund		

The check in the amount of $112 will be cashed and the money put back into the petty cash fund. The balance of the fund will now be back up to $200. It is important to note that under a petty cash system, it is not necessary to make entries to reflect individual petty cash transactions. All payments are reflected in the accounts at the point of reimbursement. No entry is made to petty cash except to change its size. However, at any time during the period it is possible to verify the balance in petty cash by merely adding the total of the receipts, which reflect disbursements, to the cash balance of the fund.

If the fund has had significant activity for a period, it is possible that the receipts in the fund will not equal the amount by which the fund needs to be reimbursed. If this is the case, a temporary account, Cash Over and Short, should be debited or credited. For example, in our previous illustration if the cash balance of the fund before the reimbursement was $85, the check to be written for $112 would not bring the fund back up to the required $200 balance ($85 + $112 = $197). In this case the fund was $3 ($200 − $197) short. Under this circumstance a check would be written for $115, an amount sufficient to bring the fund up to the $200 balance, and the $3 should be debited to Cash Over and Short. This journal entry would appear as follows:

Postage expense	$25	
Lunches and entertainment expense	35	
Contributions expense	10	
Miscellaneous expense	42	
Cash over and short	3	
Cash		$115
To reimburse the petty cash fund		

If the petty cash fund is over (in other words, the cash balance exceeds what it should be), the Cash Over and Short account is credited by the amount of the overage. Generally, the balance in the Cash Over and Short account is debited or credited to Miscellaneous Expense at the end of the year.

In practice many variations of the petty cash or imprest system are used. The Cash Over and Short account is also used in the handling of over-the-counter cash receipts where errors in making change will inevitably occur. These errors will cause a cash shortage or overage at the end of the day when the cash is counted and compared with the cash register reading. Such a shortage or overage is debited or credited to Cash Over and Short. Other variations of the system are used for the travel funds given to salesmen and other agents of the firm. A common variation, used when the account involved is large, is to deposit the fund in a bank and allow the person in charge to draw checks on his or her own signature without the elaborate proof procedure required for the regular company disbursements by check. Some imprest systems involve very large sums of money and require quite elaborate safeguards and accounting procedures.

Bank Reconciliations

When a bank statement is received by a firm, the indicated ending cash balance on the statement will seldom agree with the amount shown in the general ledger for cash in the bank. There are three basic reasons for the difference: (1) a timing problem, (2) items of which the firm or the bank are not aware, and (3) errors.

Timing Problems

Outstanding checks are checks issued by the firm which have not been cleared by the bank. *Deposits in transit* are deposits which have been made by the firm but have not yet been recorded by the bank in its account for the firm. Neither outstanding checks nor deposits in transit are errors; they are the result of the fact that there is often a difference (time lag) between the time that the firm adds to or subtracts from the bank account and the time at which the bank is aware of the transaction.

Items of which the Firm is Unaware

Often the bank will increase or decrease the firm's account and wait to notify the firm with the bank statement. The most frequent adjustment of this kind is the *bank service charge,* which is a charge to the firm for the bank's services in handling the customer's account. *Debit* and *credit memoranda* often accompany the bank statement. (Since the firm's account is a liability to the bank, credits indicate increases and debits decreases in the account.) Typical debit and credit memoranda items include NSF checks returned (Not Sufficient Funds), loans collected by the bank, and automatic payments deducted from the firm's account.

Errors

Obviously, errors can be made by the firm or the bank when dealing with a large number of cash transactions. The bank reconciliation should reveal most of the possible errors on either side and this, in effect, results in the bank serving as an independent check on the cash accounting activities of the firm.

Form of the Reconciliation

The bank reconciliation should begin with (1) the cash balance per the bank statement and (2) the cash balance per the ledger. Additions and subtractions are then made to either balance when appropriate, resulting in (1) an adjusted balance per bank, and (2) an adjusted balance per ledger. The two adjusted balances should equal. The form should then be as follows:

X Corporation
Bank Reconciliation
Date

Balance per bank		xxx	Balance per ledger		xxx
Add:	Deposits in transit	xx	Add:	Bank credit memo	xx
	Other items	xx		Other items	xx
Subtract:	Outstanding checks	xx	Subtract:	Bank service charges and debit memos	xx
	Other items	xx		Other items	xx
Adjusted balance		xxx	Adjusted balance		xxx
		↑	(Should be equal)		↑

Bank Reconciliation Illustrated

To illustrate, the balance indicated in the cash account of the Dunlap Company on December 31, 19X1 was $28,750. The bank statement on that date showed that the company's cash balance on that date was $39,342. The following items were discovered as the bank reconciliation was being prepared:

1. Outstanding checks (total), $4,454.
2. Deposit in transit, $2,917.
3. Bank service charge, $5.
4. An NSF check in the amount of $2,700 was returned with the bank statement. Dunlap Company had included it in a deposit, but it was returned to the bank because of insufficient funds.
5. The bank collected a note plus interest for Dunlap totaling $10,150 and credited the company's account for that amount. They then debited the company's account for a $10 collection fee.
6. Included in the canceled checks was a check written by Dunlop, Inc., for $230. This amount was shown on the bank statement as charged to Dunlap Company's bank account.
7. A check for $222 had been erroneously recorded in the company's cash and accounts payable accounts as $2,222.
8. A check for $150 was returned in the bank statement and had not been recorded in the company's accounts.

The bank reconciliation for the Dunlap Company as of December 31, 19X1 would appear as follows:

Dunlap Company
Bank Reconciliation
December 31, 19X1

Balance per bank statement		$39,342	Balance per ledger		$28,750
Add: Deposit in transit	$2,917		Add: Loan collected by bank	$10,150	
Bank error: Dunlop check charged to Dunlap Company	230	3,147	Error check recorded as $2,222 instead of $222	2,000	12,150
Subtract: Outstanding checks		(4,454)	Subtract: Service charge	$5	
			Collection fee	$10	
			NSF check returned	2,700	
			Error, unrecorded check	150	(2,865)
Adjusted balance		$38,035	Adjusted balance		$38,035

In effect, the reconciliation has brought the balance for cash and the balance per the bank statement up to date as of the date of the statement. If the balances do not agree after the effects of outstanding checks, deposits in transit, and all debit and credit memoranda have been considered, it is obvious that an error exists and must be corrected. In the previous reconciliation, several errors were discovered when the bank reconciliation was being prepared.

After the bank reconciliation is successfully completed, it is usually necessary to prepare a journal entry to correct the cash account. This correcting journal entry will give effect to all of the adjustments to the cash account which appeared on the right-hand side of the previous reconciliation. The debit or credit to cash will be the difference between the beginning (unadjusted) book balance and the adjusted balance: in the case above a $9,285 ($38,035 − $28,750) debit. Assuming that the errors dealt with accounts receivable or accounts payable items, the journal entry to adjust the cash balance would appear as follows:

Cash	$9,285	
Bank service charge	5	
Miscellaneous expense (collection fee)	10	
Accounts receivable (2,700 + 150)	2,850	
Notes receivable		$10,000
Interest income		150
Accounts payable		2,000
To record adjustments to cash discovered by bank reconciliation		

The bank reconciliation statement is a tool of cash control; it has no particular value for financial analysis. It serves to explain why the cash balance shown as being on deposit by the bank differs from the balance shown as being on deposit by the depositor. It also shows the amount of cash actually on deposit that should be reflected as the balance of cash in the bank account. Not infrequently, the bank reconciliation brings to light errors on the part of the bank or the firm.

Similar reconciliation steps are often necessary for other business elements. The amount of individual accounts receivable as shown in the detail ledger must be reconciled with the amounts that customers show as payable to the firm. Likewise, accounts payable must be reconciled with the amounts shown as due on statements rendered by vendors. Such reconciliations are necessary due to confusion about the amount being allowed for returns of merchandise, discounts allowed on purchases, and so forth.

Cash-Basis Accounting

The case for accrual-basis accounting was made in Chapter 2. Accrual-basis accounting is concerned with the recognition and recording of the business events relating to the firm's activities independent of the time when cash is received or paid. The measurement of the net earnings of a firm under the accrual accounting model thus involves the consideration of revenues (such as sales on account) and expenses (such as wages payable to employees) which have not yet resulted in a cash inflow or outflow.

Cash-basis accounting is simpler, but generally less useful, than accrual-basis accounting. In the strictest sense, cash-basis accounting is cash-flow accounting—with all cash inflows and cash outflows (and *only* cash inflows and outflows) being considered in relation to their effect on the cash balance.

Such an approach is hardly suitable for measuring the profitability of a business firm's operations, since cash inflows may include borrowed funds and contributions by owners and cash outflows may include repayments of debt and dividends. However, a modified cash basis of accounting is widely used as a measure of "earnings" by individuals and some small business firms (particularly for federal income tax purposes).

According to this modified cash basis for measurement of "earnings," capital contributions and borrowed funds are not treated as revenues and, dividends and debt repayment are not treated as expenses. The cost of plant assets acquired is not treated as an expense when paid, but is allocated over the time periods benefited (depreciated) as in accrual accounting. Contrary to the accrual model, however, sales revenue is not recognized (considered to be revenue) until the cash has been received from the customer, and operating expenses for wages and other items are recognized (considered to be expenses) only as the payments are made to employees and others. The difference between these "revenues" and "expenses" is thus income under the cash basis.

Cash Statement

The principal statement for the cash-basis accountant is the Statement of Cash Receipts and Disbursements, which is the statement of the cash account. This statement starts with the cash balance carried over from the past period, adds the cash received, deducts the cash disbursed, and ends with the ending balance of cash.

X Corporation
Statement of Cash Receipts and Disbursements
March 19X1

Balance of cash on hand on March 1		$ 52,890
Receipts of cash in March		
Cash sales	$783,650	
Collections from customers	316,350	
Contributions by stockholders	200,000	
Proceeds of sale of property	45,670	
Proceeds of bond issue	74,330	
Total cash received		1,420,000
Total cash available during March		$1,472,890
Disbursements of cash in March		
Payments to vendors	$497,428	
Payments of operating expenses	502,572	
Payments of long-term debt	100,000	
Payments of dividends	50,000	
Investment of securities	90,000	
Acquisition of plant assets	160,000	
Total disbursements		1,400,000
Balance of cash on hand on March 31		$ 72,890

The cash basis of reporting is subject to the serious objection that cash does not always flow inward as the firm performs its services nor flow outward as efforts are made to produce sales or services. Net cash inflow is an important figure, but it does not measure the effectiveness of the activities of a firm in increasing its command of economic resources, nor does it measure the creativity of the firm. The treatment of inflows of cash as revenue, without consideration of related costs that have not yet resulted in outflows of cash, may produce a misleading profit determination. But the principal difference between the modified cash basis and the accrual basis is timing. In the very long run, both methods produce the same net results.

Comparison of Cash-Basis and Accrual-Basis Accounting

While the comparison of cash-basis with accrual-basis accounting demonstrates the superiority of the latter, in cases where a firm's financial statements indicate that it may be having liquidity problems (that is, having problems raising the cash needed to pay debts coming due), analysts may desire a cash statement as a supplement to the conventional accrual statements. The principal components of a cash statement may be constructed from statements prepared on the accrual basis by reversing the accrual process. This process involves treating increases and decreases on the balance sheet as adjustments of earnings statement data to arrive at the total of cash receipts and disbursements. An adjustment of the sales figure for changes in accounts receivable is necessary to determine the amount of cash collected from customers. An adjustment of the cost of goods sold to take into account the changes in merchandise inventory and the changes in accounts payable is necessary to determine the amount paid out to vendors during the period. In the following illustration, there are no prepayments of wages or wages payable; if there had been such balances, it would have been necessary to adjust wages expense for changes in prepayments or accruals in order to determine the cash paid out to employees.

Suppose the treasurer of B Corporation submitted the following statements:

B Corporation
Balance Sheets
on December 31, 19X1 and on December 31, 19X2

ASSETS	19X1	19X2	INCREASE (DECREASE)
Cash	$ 15,000	$ 20,000	$ 5,000
Accounts receivable	28,000	40,000	12,000
Merchandise inventory	45,000	60,000	15,000

B Corporation
Balance Sheets
on December 31, 19X1 and on December 31, 19X2 *(continued)*

ASSETS	19X1	19X2	INCREASE (DECREASE)
Equipment	50,000	90,000	40,000
Less: Accumulated depreciation	(19,000)	(23,000)	(4,000)[a]
Total assets	$119,000	$187,000	$68,000
EQUITIES			
Accounts payable	$ 40,000	$ 35,000	$(5,000)
Notes payable to banks	30,000	25,000	(5,000)
Bonds payable (long-term)	-0-	30,000	30,000
Capital stock	40,000	76,000	36,000
Retained earnings	9,000	21,000	12,000
Total equities	$119,000	$187,000	$68,000

[a] Any increase in accumulated depreciation represents a decrease in asset values.

B Corporation
Income Statement
For the year ended 19X2

Sales		$500,000
Operating expenses		
Cost of goods sold	$300,000	
Wages	130,000	
Depreciation of equipment	4,000	
Other expenses, interest, and taxes	42,000	
Total operating expenses		476,000
Net income		$ 24,000

Dividends declared and paid for the year were $12,000.

The balance sheet data and income statement data given by the treasurer may be used to construct a statement of cash receipts and disbursements:

B Corporation
Statement of Cash Receipts and Disbursements
for the year 19X2

Cash receipts:		
Collections from customers[a]	$488,000	
Issuance of bonds payable	30,000	
Issuance of capital stock	36,000	
Total receipts		$554,000

B Corporation
Statement of Cash Receipts and Disbursements
for the year 19X2 *(continued)*

Cash disbursements:		
Payments to vendors for merchandise[b]	$320,000	
Payment of wages (wage expense)	130,000	
Payment of other operating expenses	42,000	
Payment of portion of notes payable	5,000	
Purchase of equipment	40,000	
Payment of dividends	12,000	
Total disbursements		549,000
Increase in cash balance (see balance sheet)		$ 5,000

[a] Collections from customers were $12,000 less than total sales since accounts receivable increased by $12,000.
[b] It was necessary to purchase $15,000 more goods than the cost of goods sold in order to increase merchandise on hand by $15,000. Thus purchases amounted to $315,000. Since accounts payable was reduced by $5,000, it was necessary to pay $5,000 more than the purchases, or $320,000.

Using the data developed in the cash statement, the earnings statement for this firm can be reported on a cash basis:

B Corporation
Cash-Basis Earnings Statement
for the year 19X2

Revenue (collections from customers)		$488,000
Expenses (disbursements)		
Amounts paid to vendors for merchandise	$320,000	
Wages paid	130,000	
Payment of other operating expenses	42,000	
Total		492,000
Net loss		$ 4,000

Notice that on the cash basis, the earnings statement for B Corporation shows a loss of $4,000. This is in contrast to the earnings of $24,000 shown in the accrual-basis income statement.

Through a combination of changes, the B Corporation's cash statement shows an unfavorable earnings pattern, although the effect of these changes is in fact to improve B Corporation's financial position. A larger balance of accounts receivable indicates an increase in future cash inflows, and an increase in merchandise inventory and a decrease in the amount owed to vendors indicates an improved ability to provide goods for customers. Thus the B Corporation experienced a substantial growth in favorable economic factors that the cash-basis reports cannot show. On the other hand, the cash-basis report does contain some interesting information. In Chapter 13 we will return to this point to introduce statements which are intended to show similar financial changes in a more complete fashion than the traditional income statement.

Cash Budgeting

From an internal administration point of view, analysis of the adequacy of cash is primarily a matter of cash budgeting. The treasurer or other financial officer is responsible for maintaining adequate cash balances in order that the firm's actions will not be unduly restricted by lack of cash, and in order to maintain the firm's credit rating and avoid losing discounts offered for early payment of invoices. The best utilization of the sources of capital available to the firm in accordance with the cash needs of the firm will help to maximize earnings and minimize the costs of capital. Good cash planning is essential to good cash administration. Accountants play an important part in the process of formulating financial plans and in putting the plans together in a budget pattern in which the *cash budget* plays a central role. There are many obvious advantages in setting up a cash budget. If the management of a firm did not plan its needs for cash, it might issue excessive amounts of new stock or bonds and be saddled with idle funds, or it might issue too little, and not have enough funds to achieve its goals.

Analysis of the Cash Position

The ordinary outside investor is not much interested in the cash balance, nor in the cash budget. Good management implies good budgeting and the investor is interested in good management. The investor may have a speculative interest in such matters as changes in dividend patterns and scope of operations. Cash and marketable securities balances that are larger than normal may lead to some conjecture that the firm is about to increase dividends or is about to carry out some sort of expansion program. Occasionally an undue accumulation of cash and marketable securities may tend to indicate inefficient management since an excess of cash resources, like an excess of any other asset, does not generate satisfactory earnings. Clues as to the adequacy of cash balances are obtainable by examining the comparative balance sheets for a period of time. An increasing percentage of cash to total assets may mean, however, that a firm is simply strengthening its cash position, or is moving toward a new program.

Electronic Funds Transfer

There are currently several new systems for transferring funds electronically rather than by delivery of physical documents. Probably the field that is most affected by this innovation is banking. In this field, automated clearinghouses and other advances in electronic funds transfer may someday eliminate the need for physical delivery of voluminous bundles of documents each day.

Without *electronic funds transfer* (EFT), if a customer of Bank X draws a check on that bank to pay, for example, a credit card bill, the credit card company has traditionally deposited the check in its bank (Bank Z). Bank Z would then deliver the customer's check along with many others to Bank X in order to collect. Bank X will be doing the same thing, as will thousands of other banks all over the country. Most frequently, the activity will not occur between only the two banks involved, but rather through a complex system of clearinghouses and the check-clearing facilities of the Federal Reserve System. Electronic equipment now exists which enables banks to transfer funds from the account of one customer in Bank X to the account of another customer in Bank Z without this expensive and cumbersome exchange of physical documents. This is done frequently in both domestic and international financial transactions.

Point-of-Sale (POS) Terminals

To cut down on paperwork in supermarkets and other similar stores that cash many checks, banks can issue plastic identification cards to depositors who are also frequent customers of these stores. The depositor can then have the store use this card at a computer terminal to pay for purchases, or even to obtain cash from the store. The terminal is connected to the bank's computer system, which will approve the transaction and electronically transfer funds immediately from the customer's account to the store's account in the bank.

With the increasing use of plastic bank cards, electronic funds transfer, and other similar advancements there is some indication that we are moving in the direction of a "no cash, no check" society. In such a society everyone would have a bank card (or a series of cards) and use them for all purchases. The card would even be accepted at vending machines. Similarly, a company would pay its employees by delivering payroll information to its bank on magnetic tape or other similar input medium. The bank's computer would then automatically transfer funds from the employer's account into the various employees' accounts.

The further rapid movement toward a "no cash, no check" society is problematic. Although the technology for such a system already exists, impediments exist in the form of governmental and legislative restrictions, as well as public attitudes. It is safe to say that a considerable portion of the public is not currently comfortable with the thought of a rapid move toward such a national system.

MARKETABLE SECURITIES

A company may have cash on hand in an amount considerably in excess of its immediate requirements. Investments of such excess idle cash in *marketable securities* converts the unproductive cash into an earning asset while retaining the advantage of *liquidity*.

For example, a large corporation may wish to invest $10 million of excess cash over a normal two-day weekend in certain government securities yielding 12 percent annual interest. The income earning from such a two-day investment would be $6,667 as determined below:

$$\$10{,}000{,}000 \times \tfrac{12}{100} \times \tfrac{2}{360} = \$6{,}667$$

FASB Statement No. 12

Marketable securities are recorded at cost, including brokerage and related fees, when originally acquired. They are presented on subsequent balance sheets at their cost or current market price, whichever is lower, in accordance with FASB Statement No. 12. This presentation requirement is referred to as the *lower-of-cost-or-market* rule. Generally the rules of FASB Statement No. 12 can be summarized as follows:

1. Use an allowance (contra-asset) account to record write-downs from original cost to current market;
2. Use an "unrealized loss" account to record losses on write-downs from original cost to current market;
3. Use an "unrealized gain" account to record gains on write-ups from original cost to current market, *but only to the extent of previously recorded losses.*

The following is an illustration of the process just outlined.

Lower-of-Cost-or-Market Rule Illustrated

Assume that on December 1, 19X1, the Chan Corporation purchased 5,000 shares of Albert Corporation at $12, and 10,000 shares of Black, Inc., at $8 including brokerage fees. The total cost of the Chan Corporation investment in short-term marketable securities is:

Albert	5,000 shares @ $12 =	$ 60,000
Black	10,000 shares @ $ 8 =	80,000
		$140,000

The composite journal entry to record the acquisition is:

19X1			
Dec. 1	Investment in short term marketable securities	$140,000	
	Cash		$140,000
	To record acquisition of securities		

On December 31, 19X1, if the securities have increased in value above the $140,000 amount, no journal entry is made. By not recording the increased value of the securities and continuing to present them at $140,000, the rule of presenting the securities at the *lower* of the cost or market is being followed.

If, however, the value of the securities has dropped below the $140,000 amount, this fact must be acknowledged in the accounting records. For example, if, on December 31, 19X1, the market values Albert at $13 per share and Black at $6 per share, the current total market value would be:

Albert	5,000 shares @ $13 =	$ 65,000
Black	10,000 shares @ $ 6 =	60,000
		$125,000

or a decline in value of $15,000 ($140,000 − $125,000). This $15,000 downward revaluation of the short-term marketable securities portfolio is recorded by (1) recognizing an unrealized loss in the income statement; and (2) writing down the recorded cost of the portfolio by means of a contra-asset allowance account, as follows:

Dec. 31, 19X1	Unrealized loss on short-term marketable securities	$15,000	
	Valuation allowance for marketable securities		$15,000
	To record decline in fair market value of short-term securities		

The portfolio of marketable securities would be reflected in the current asset section of Chan Corporation's balance sheet at December 31, 19X1 as follows:

Marketable securities (cost)	$140,000
Less: Valuation allowance for marketable securities	15,000
	$125,000

The $125,000 is frequently referred to as the portfolio's *carrying value* as of December 31, 19X1.

The loss from the decline in the market value of the securities is termed an *unrealized* loss to distinguish it from a loss which results from the actual sale of securities. The $15,000 unrealized loss on short-term marketable securities is reflected in the income statement for the period ended December 31, 19X1.

Subsequent Year Activity

If in 19X2 the total value of the portfolio continues to decline and on December 31, 19X2 the market value is below the $125,000 carrying value on December 31, 19X1, an entry is made to record the decline. For example, if, on December 31, 19X2, Albert's market value per share is $12.50 and Black's is $6, the market value of the portfolio would be:

Albert	5,000 shares @ $12.50 =	$ 62,500
Black	10,000 shares @ $ 6.00 =	60,000
		$122,500

This market value drop of $2,500 ($125,000 − $122,500) during 19X2 would be recorded as follows:

Dec. 31, 19X2	Unrealized loss on short-term marketable securities	$2,500	
	Valuation allowance for marketable securities		$2,500
	To record decrease in fair market value of short-term securities		

The unrealized loss of $2,500 appears in the income statement for 19X2 and the valuation allowance (contra asset) is increased to $17,500 ($15,000 + $2,500) thereby reducing the 19X2 carrying value of the portfolio to $122,500 ($140,000 − $17,500).

If, however, during 19X2 the portfolio had increased in value, the fact must be recorded in the accounts. In this regard two possible situations could have occurred: (1) The market value of the portfolio increased less than the previously recorded write-down of $15,000 (to a total amount of less than the original cost of $140,000); or (2) the market value of the portfolio increased more than the previously recorded write-down of $15,000 (to a total amount of more than $140,000).

To illustrate the accounting for each situation, assume first that on December 31, 19X2 market quotations show Albert at $14 and Black at $6.50. In this case the market value of the portfolio would be:

Albert	5,000 shares @ $14.00 =	$ 70,000
Black	10,000 shares @ $ 6.50 =	65,000
		$135,000

The market value increase of $10,000 ($135,000 − $125,000) during 19X2 would be recorded as follows:

Dec. 31, 19X2	Valuation allowance for marketable securities	$10,000	
	Unrealized gain on marketable securities		$10,000
	To record increase in value of short-term securities		

The unrealized gain of $10,000 appears in the income statement for 19X2 and the valuation allowance (contra asset) is decreased to a net amount of $5,000 ($15,000 − $10,000) thereby increasing the 19X2 carrying value of the portfolio to $135,000 ($140,000 − $5,000).

To illustrate the second possibility mentioned previously, assume that the market value of the portfolio increased to an amount above the original cost of $140,000, and thereby to a greater extent than the $15,000 write-down in 19X1. Because of the lower cost or market value it is not permissible to write up the value of the securities above the original cost of $140,000. Therefore, the amount of the journal entry to record the increased portfolio value is limited to $15,000. To illustrate the accounting for this situation, assume now that on December 31, 19X2 the market values of the portfolio are Albert at $18 and Black at $7. In this case the total market value of the portfolio would be:

Albert	5,000 shares @ $18 =	$ 90,000
Black	10,000 shares @ $ 7 =	70,000
		$160,000

As mentioned previously, the unrealized gain can only be recorded to the extent of the balance in the allowance account, so the journal entry to record the increased value of the portfolio would be:

Dec. 31, 19X2	Valuation allowance for marketable securities	$15,000	
	Unrealized gain on marketable securities		$15,000
	To record increase in the fair market value of short-term securities		

In this case, the unrealized gain of $15,000 would appear on the income statement for 19X2, and the valuation allowance account would be reduced to zero resulting in a carrying value of the portfolio of the $140,000 cost of the securities. *Unrealized* increases and decreases in the value of securities are not gains and losses for income tax purposes. It should be noted that in most cases, if it is the intent of management to hold marketable securities for longer than one year, they will be classified as a long-term investment and not as a *current* asset. In the preceding illustration the securities were assumed to be held for longer than one year only for the purpose of illustrating the various possibilities relating to the increase and decrease in the market price of those securities.

Sale of Securities

When marketable securities are sold, a *realized gain or loss* is determined by comparing the proceeds from the sale with the original cost of the securities sold. Such a realized gain or loss is reported for tax purposes.

To illustrate the accounting for the sale of short-term marketable securities, we will go back to our previous illustration in which we assumed that on

December 1, 19X1, Chan Corporation had purchased 5,000 shares of Albert Corporation at $12, and 10,000 shares of Black, Inc., at $8 including all brokerage fees. The total cost of the investment was recorded as follows:

19X1			
Dec. 1	Investment in short-term marketable securities	$140,000	
	Cash		$140,000
	To record acquisition of securities		

Assume that on December 15 the price of Black, Inc., had dropped to $7 per share and it was decided to sell 5,000 shares of that stock. The brokerage fee on the sale was $750; therefore the proceeds of the sale will be:

5,000 × $7 =	$35,000
Less brokerage fee −	750
Total	$34,250

The sale would be recorded as follows:

Cash	$34,250	
Realized loss on sale of short-term marketable securities	5,750	
Investment in short-term marketable securities		$40,000
To record sale of short-term marketable securities		

The loss is the difference between the cost of the securities and the proceeds from their sale ($40,000 − $34,250 = $5,750).

After the sale, Chan holds securities with the following *cost:*

Albert	5,000 shares @ $12 =	$ 60,000
Black	5,000 shares @ $ 8 =	40,000
Total		$100,000

On December 31, 19X1, assume Albert Corporation had a market price of $13, and Black, Inc., had a market price of $6. The total carrying value of the securities at that time would be:

Albert	5,000 shares @ $13 =	$65,000
Black	5,000 shares @ $ 6 =	30,000
Total		$95,000

In this case the market value of the securities ($95,000) is less than their cost ($100,000), so the following journal entry must be made:

Dec. 31, 19X1	Unrealized loss on marketable securities	$5,000	
	Valuation allowance for marketable securities		$5,000
	To record decline in fair market value of short-term securities		

Any dividends received on short-term marketable securities held would be credited to Dividend Income. Such an entry would be:

Cash	XXX	
Dividend income		XXX

SUMMARY

Cash is the beginning and the end result of nearly all business endeavors. Yet idle cash holdings are a nonproductive asset. Cash itself does not produce new wealth, rather it is the utilization of cash for investment purposes that produces new values which flow into the business enterprise. Cash in amounts required to carry on business operations effectively is productive in this sense. *Excessive* cash, *excessive* inventories, *excessive* plant assets, and so forth are *nonproductive* assets in any sense.

The details of cash receipts and disbursements are generally not as useful to analysts and investors as the details of the earnings statement. Management, however, must have cash receipt and disbursement details on a daily basis in order to operate effectively and avoid difficulties. Moreover, the proper budgeting of cash is essential to good cash administration and to good financial position results.

Control of cash is of considerable significance since errors and fraud are particularly likely to occur in handling cash. Cash control involves the proper division of duties among employees, control of cash receipts, safeguarding cash on hand, and control of cash disbursements. Ideally, cash receipts should be deposited intact daily and cash should be disbursed by check. Documentary support for check disbursements is desirable through some sort of voucher system. A petty cash system should be used to safeguard the small disbursements of cash. The preparation of bank reconciliations monthly by a responsible officer serves to reveal fraud and errors of certain kinds and call attention to events that have not yet been recorded by the firm.

Excess cash is often converted into marketable securities. Such investments are initially recorded at cost and are presented on subsequent balance sheets at the lower of their cost or current market price. Fluctuations in the market price of marketable securities result in *unrealized* gains and losses to the investing company, as opposed to *realized* gains and losses which result from the actual sale of marketable securities.

KEY POINTS

1. Financial instruments and resources which serve as media of exchange or as immediately available purchasing power are properly termed cash.

2. Some financial instruments thought to be available for spending may actually be subject to various restrictions. In the case of a firm engaging in foreign activities, cash itself may be in a variety of currencies and such currencies must be translated to dollar equivalents. The purchasing power of the dollar may vary so that it is difficult to compare the current balance of cash with older balances.

3. The statement of cash receipts and disbursements is significant for internal management but not very significant for outside investors.

4. The cash basis of accounting, as modified, does not measure achievement as effectively as the accrual system for most firms of any size and complexity. The cash basis measures only a limited set of business events.

5. Poor cash planning may lead to inefficient management of inventories, receivables, and other items, or it may unduly restrict investment in these items. Poor cash planning may well affect the whole financial fabric of the firm.

6. To prevent errors and fraud from impacting on cash management, cash must be safeguarded as it is received, while it is held, and as it is disbursed. Cash receipts should be deposited daily, bank balances reconciled periodically, and cash disbursements controlled by proper use of checks, petty cash systems, and voucher systems.

7. Valuation of short-term securities is based on the lower-of-cost-or-market rule.

QUESTIONS

1. What is cash and how is it valued?

2. Does the expression "efficient management of cash" mean anything more than procedures to prevent losses from fraud or theft? Explain.

3. What are the primary characteristics of an effective internal control system for cash?

4. Why is a separation of duties necessary to insure sound internal control?

5. Explain how each of the following can contribute to internal control over cash:

   a. Bank reconciliation
   b. Petty cash fund

c. Cash register with printed receipts
d. Printed, prenumbered cash sales receipts
e. A regular vacation for the cashier
f. Two signatures on checks
g. Prenumbered checks

6. Describe how an imprest system of petty cash is operated.

7. Should a petty cash fund be replenished as of the last day of the accounting period? Explain.

8. Why is a bank reconciliation prepared?

9. In preparation of a bank reconciliation, how is each of the following items handled?

a. Outstanding checks
b. Deposits in transit
c. Customer's check deposited but returned by the bank as NSF
d. Note receivable collected by the bank
e. Bank service charge

10. What accounting entry or entries are necessary to properly record a NSF check returned by the bank?

11. At the close of business on a particular day, the combined count of cash for all cash registers reveal a cash shortage of $12.65. In what account would this cash shortage be recorded? Should the account be debited or credited?

12. Why does a company make temporary investments and how are they shown on the balance sheet?

13. Is a marketable security always a temporary investment? Explain.

14. What is the rationale for application of the lower-of-cost-or-market basis to temporary investments?

15. On which accounting statement would each of the following accounts appear?

a. Unrealized loss on short-term marketable securities
b. Investment in short-term marketable securities
c. Valuation allowances for marketable securities
d. Unrealized gain on short-term marketable securities

EXERCISES

E5-1 Which of the following items should be included as cash on a firm's balance sheet using generally accepted accounting principles?

a. Customers' checks returned by the bank marked NSF, which the issuers have agreed to make good.
b. Customers' checks that are to be deposited.
c. Cash received as advance payments on special contracts.
d. Notes receivable which have been turned over to a bank for collection.
e. A customer's check that has been postdated beyond the statement date.
f. Deposits in savings accounts under the firm's name.
g. Postage stamps received from customers to prepay mailing costs.
h. Cash advanced to salesmen for travel expenses.
i. Deposits in foreign banks where there are no currency restrictions.
j. An overdraft at the bank on the company's payroll account.

E5-2 Developing a convenient means of providing sales representatives with cash for their incidental expenses, such as entertaining a client at lunch, is a problem many companies face. One company has a plan whereby the sales representatives receive advances in cash from the petty cash fund. Each advance is supported by an authorization from the sales manager. The representative returns the receipt for the expenditure and any unused cash and replaces them in the petty cash fund. The cashier of the petty cash fund is responsible for seeing that the receipt and the cash returned equal the advance. At the time that the petty cash fund is reimbursed, the amount of the representative's expenditure is debited to Direct Sales Expense.

a. What is the weak point of the procedure, and what fundamental principle of internal control has been ignored?
b. What improvement in the procedure can you suggest?

E5-3 An accountant and his assistants are responsible for the following procedures: (1) receipts of all cash; (2) maintenance of the general ledger; (3) maintenance of the accounts receivable ledger; (4) maintenance of the journals for recording sales, cash receipts, and purchases; and (5) preparation of monthly statements to be sent to customers. As a service to customers and employees, the company allows the accountant to cash checks of up to $50 with money from the cash receipts. The accountant may approve the cashing of such a check for current employees and customers. When the deposits are made, the checks are included in the place of the cash receipts.

What weakness in internal control exists in this system?

E5-4 The Porter Company established a petty cash fund of $300 on June 1. On June 20, the fund was replenished for the payments made to date as shown by the following petty cash vouchers:

a. Freight-in, $19.00
b. Postage, $92.00
c. Telephone expense, $6.40
d. Repairs, $63.40
e. Miscellaneous expense, $44.00

Prepare journal entries in general journal form to record the establishment of the fund on June 1 and its replenishment on June 20.

E5-5 On January 1, 19X2, Cobb Corp. established a petty cash fund amounting to $200 by writing a check to "Petty Cash." The fund was assigned to Fred Doyle, an employee, to administer as custodian. At the end of January there was $10 cash remaining in the fund. Signed receipts for expenditures during January were summarized as follows:

a. Postage, $46
b. Office supplies, $36
c. Transportation, $12
d. Newspapers, $28
e. Miscellaneous, $8

REQUIRED:

1. Give entry to establish the fund.
2. Give entry to replenish the fund.
3. What balance would be reflected in the Petty Cash account in the ledger at January 31? Explain.

E5-6 The Waggoner Brothers Corporation received a bank statement for the month of March (dated March 31) showing a balance of $1,670.39. The Cash in Bank account shows a balance of $1,121.50 as of March 31. An analysis reveals the following reconciling items:

a. A deposit of $413.10 on March 31 was not recorded on the bank statement.
b. A credit memorandum attached to the bank statement indicates that the bank collected a note for Waggoner Brothers and credited the proceeds of $200 to their account. This has not been recorded on the books of the Waggoner Brothers.
c. Bank service charges (debit memorandum) were $1.50 for the month of March.
d. Checks outstanding as of March 31 totaled $772.49.
e. A check for $432 paid to a supplier had been incorrectly entered in the cash payments journal as $423.

REQUIRED:

a. Prepare a bank reconciliation statement to reconcile the balance per the bank statement with the balance of cash per the Cash in Bank account.
b. Make any necessary entries to adjust the accounts in general journal form.

E5-7 During the reconciliation of the Tortucial Company's checking account with the Easy Lend Bank, it is discovered that:

a. Checks outstanding amount to $4802.40
b. Bank service charges for the past month are $7.80
c. Deposits in transit are $690.02
d. Check no. 221 was recorded as a debit to accounts payable and a credit to cash for $480 when the check was correctly written for $840

Record the necessary entries on the books to adjust the accounts to their correct balance.

E5-8 The Dorsil Company, in view of some idle cash, decided to purchase some common stock in OX Corporation as a temporary investment. The following transactions reflect what happened following this decision:

Feb. 1, 19X2	Purchased for cash 5,000 shares of OX Corporation common stock at a cost of $39,200. Brokerage and related fees also were paid, amounting to $800.
Aug. 15, 19X2	Received a cash dividend on the OX stock of $.30 per share.
Dec. 30, 19X2	Sold 1,500 shares of the OX stock at $7.20 per share (including brokerage fees).
Dec. 31, 19X2	End of the fiscal year for accounting purposes.

REQUIRED:

1. Give appropriate journal entries for each date for the temporary investment in OX stock.
2. How would the temporary investment be reported on the balance sheet at December 31, 19X2? The market value did not change on December 31.

E5-9 The Futvest Company, in order to use some idle cash, in March 19X2 acquired 100 shares of common stock in each of three corporations:

a. Corporation A, cost $10,000
b. Corporation B, cost $8,000
c. Corporation C, cost $14,000

At the end of the fiscal period, December 31, 19X2, the quoted market prices per share were:
Corporation A, $104; Corporation B, $80; and Corporation C, $126.

REQUIRED:

1. Give entry to record the acquisition of the temporary investments.
2. Give entry to reflect the temporary investments at lower of cost or market. Show computations.
3. Show how the temporary investments would be reported on the balance sheet at December 31, 19X2.

PROBLEMS

P5-1 Portage Service Company maintains a petty cash fund to control small cash expenditures. The company does not use a voucher system. The operation of the fund during September, the last month of the company's fiscal year, is shown here.

Sept. 1 A check for $1,320 was issued and cashed to establish a petty cash fund.

Sept. 22 A count of the fund showed petty cash vouchers and cash on hand as follows:

Office supplies expense	$200.86
Postage expense	147.84
Telephone and telegraph expense	46.20
Miscellaneous expense	132.88
Currency and coin	792.22

In view of the fact that the fund was less than half depleted after the first three weeks, management decided to reduce the fund permanently to the amount of $880. A check was issued in the amount necessary to replenish the fund and establish it at the new authorized level.

Sept. 30 At September 30 the fund comprised the following items. However, through oversight, the fund was not replenished.

Office supplies expense	$158.40
Postage expense	211.20
Telephone and telegraph expense	55.00
Miscellaneous expense	150.48
Currency and coin	304.92

INSTRUCTIONS:

a. Prepare entries in general journal form to record the previous information. Include an entry at September 30 to record the expenditures to that date even though the fund was not replenished.

b. What is the amount of the asset account, Petty Cash, at the close of business on September 30? Explain the circumstances which led to this balance, and indicate the action management will probably take early in the next fiscal year.

P5-2 In order to handle small cash disbursements in an efficient manner, Braxton Company established a petty cash fund on July 1, 19X2. The following transactions occured relating to petty cash:

July 1 A check for $500 was issued and cashed to establish a petty cash fund.

July 15 The fund was replenished after a count which revealed the following cash and petty cash vouchers for disbursements:

Office supplies expense	$ 78.50
Postage expense	130.00
Travel expense	156.24
Miscellaneous expense	42.00
Telephone and telegraph expense	63.50
Currency and coin	29.76

July 31 A count of the fund at month-end disclosed the following:

Office supplies expense	$118.80
Postage expense	120.00
Travel expense	118.76
Miscellaneous expense	81.24
Currency and coin	61.20

A check was issued on July 31 to replenish the petty cash fund and to increase the amount of the fund to $750.

INSTRUCTIONS:

a. Prepare entries in general journal form to record the previous transactions.

b. Explain why the petty cash fund should be replenished at the end of the accounting period even though the fund contains considerable cash.

P5-3 The Riverside Pool Company established a petty cash fund in its snack bar so that payment can be made for small deliveries upon receipt. The following transactions occurred:

Oct. 1 The fund was established in the amount of $400 from the proceeds of a check drawn for that purpose.

31 The petty cash fund has cash of $21.42 and the following receipts on hand:

Merchandise received	$220.30
Office supplies	65.74
Laundry service	84.00
Miscellaneous expense	8.54

A check was drawn to replenish the fund.

Nov. 30 The petty cash fund has cash of $45 and the following receipts on hand:

Merchandise	$196.84
Delivery charges	76.30
Laundry service	84.00
Miscellaneous expense	7.86

The petty cash custodian cannot account for the fact that there is an excess of $10 in the fund. A check is drawn to replenish the fund.

Record each of the transactions in proper journal entry form.

P5-4 The following information comes from the records of Northrich Company:

FROM THE CASH RECEIPTS JOURNAL — PAGE NO. 17

Date	Debit Cash
Sept. 1	1,828
7	2,024
14	6,480
21	5,292
30	3,884
	19,508

FROM THE CASH PAYMENTS JOURNAL — PAGE NO. 20

Date	Check Number	Credit Cash
Aug. 28	813	28
Sept. 2	814	566
3	815	832
4	816	54
5	818	10
10	819	11,492
11	820	1,418
20	821	2,492
21	822	152
		17,044

The bank statement for Northrich Company appears as follows:

PATRIOT NATIONAL BANK — **STATEMENT OF NORTHRICH COMPANY MAIN AND 2ND STREETS**

Date	Checks and Other Debits		Deposits	Balance
Sept. 1	Balance brought forward			7,570.00
2	200.00	1,000.00	1,828.00	8,198.00
4	920.00	28.00		7,250.00
6	832.00			6,418.00
8	54.00		2,024.00	8,388.00
12	10.00	30.00 NSF		8,348.00
15			6,480.00	14,828.00
22			5,292.00	20,120.00
24	11,492.00			8,628.00
26	152.00		816.00 CM	9,292.00
30	8.00 SC			9,284.00

Code: CM—Credit Memo, DM—Debit Memo, NSF—Not Sufficient Fund, SC—Service Charge

The NSF check was received from F. Standish, a customer, for merchandise. The credit memorandum represents an $800 note collected by the bank plus interest. Check no. 820 for a purchase of merchandise was incorrectly recorded in the cash payments journal as $1,418 instead of as the correct amount of $1,814.

FROM THE GENERAL LEDGER

Cash — **Account No. 111**

Date	*Item*	*Post. Ref.*	*Debit*	*Credit*	*Balance Debit*	*Balance Credit*
Aug. 31	Balance				4,930	
Sept. 30		CR7	19,508		24,438	
30		CR10		17,044	7,394	

On September 1, there were only the following outstanding checks as reconciling items: check no. 792 at $200, check no. 799 at $1,000, check no. 811 at $520, and check no. 812 at $920.

REQUIRED:

1. Prepare a bank reconciliation as of September 30, 19X2.
2. Prepare adjusting entries in general journal form.
3. What amount should appear on the balance sheet for cash as of September 30, 19X2?

P5-5 Alsatial Company, a large merchandising concern that stocks over 170,000 different items in inventory, has just installed a sophisticated computer system for inventory control. The computer's data storage system has random access processing and carries all pertinent data relating to individual items of inventory. The system is equipped with fifteen remote computer terminals, distributed at various locations throughout the warehouse and sales areas. Using terminals, employees can obtain information from the computer system about the status of any inventory item. To make an inquiry, they use a keyboard, similar to that of a typewriter, that forms part of the remote terminal. The answer is relayed back instantaneously on a screen, which is also part of the terminal. As inventory is received, shipped, or transferred, employees update the inventory records in the computer system by means of the remote terminals.

REQUIRED:

1. What potential weakness in internal control exists in the system?
2. What suggestions do you have for improving the internal control?

P5-6 Montaigne Company reports the following information concerning cash balances and cash transactions for the month of September:

(a) Cash balance per bank statement as of September 30 was $17,586.50.

(b) Two debit memoranda accompanied the bank statement: one for $8 was for service charges for the month; the other for $129.20 was attached to an NSF check from P. Jordan.

(c) The paid checks returned with the September bank statement disclosed two errors in the cash records. Check no. 832 for $912.60 had been erroneously recorded as $930.60 in the cash payments journal, and check no. 851 for $154.88 had been recorded as $89.54. Check no. 832 was issued in payment for a store display counter: check no. 851 was for telephone expense.

(d) A collection charge for $252.00 (not applicable to Montaigne Company) was erroneously deducted from the account by the bank.

(e) Cash receipts of September 30 amounting to $1,170.50 were mailed to the bank too late to be included in the September bank statement.

(f) Checks outstanding as of September 30 were as follows: check no. 860 for $303.86; check no. 867 for $164.92; and check no. 869 for $247.22.

(g) The Cash account showed the following entries during September:

CASH						111
Sept. 1	Balance		12,683.64	Sept. 30	CD7	23,029.26
30		CR5	28,823.16			

INSTRUCTIONS:

a. Prepare a bank reconciliation at September 30.
b. Prepare the necessary adjusting entries in general journal form.

P5-7 The Drastic Company, in order to use idle cash, usually acquires common stock as a temporary investment. This case focuses on the purchase of three different common stocks during 19X2. The annual fiscal period for accounting purposes ends December 31. The sequence of transactions was:

Apr. 2, 19X2 Purchased for cash, as a temporary investment, the following common stocks:

CORPORATION	NUMBER OF SHARES	TOTAL PRICE PER SHARE
A	200	$ 80
B	400	$100
C	100	$140

Sept. 8, 19X2 Received a cash dividend of $6.60 per share on Corporation C stock.

Dec. 30, 19X2 Sold the stock in Corporation B for $112 per share.

Dec. 31, 19X2 Quoted market prices on this date were: Corporation A stock, $76; Corporation B stock, $112; and Corporation C stock, $750.

REQUIRED:

1. Give appropriate entry on each date.
2. Illustrate how the temporary investment should be reflected on the balance sheet at December 31, 19X2.

P5-8 The Philistine Pricing Company produces and sells one main product. There is seasonality in demand and the unit price is relatively high. The fiscal year for accounting purposes ends December 31. Typically, in the high months of the cycle the company generates cash which is idle during the low months. As a consequence, they consistently acquire temporary investments in order to earn a return on the otherwise idle cash. Recently, the company purchased 1,000 shares of common stock in each of two other corporations, designated for case purposes as Corporation X and Y. The prices per share, including fees and related costs, were: X $56, and Y $128. The sequence of transactions was:

Mar. 15, 19X2 Purchased the common stock of Corporation X and Y.

Oct. 3, 19X2 Received a cash dividend of $.80 per share on the stock of Corporation Y.

Dec. 30, 19X2 Sold 600 shares of the stock of Corporation X at $48 per share and 500 shares of the stock of Corporation Y at $132 per share.

Dec. 31, 19X2 End of fiscal period.

REQUIRED:

1. Give appropriate entries at each of the dates. Omit any closing entries.
2. Illustrate how the temporary investment would be reported on the balance sheet at December 31, 19X2.

REVENUES AND RECEIVABLES

6

ORIENTATION

This chapter is concerned with the concept of revenue, revenue-related receivables, and with the accounting problems related to the recognition and measurement of revenue.

We begin by discussing the revenue concept and the accounting problems associated with it, and then go on to describe the treatment of revenue and related asset items in the accounts. Particular emphasis is placed on proper valuation of accounts receivable through the appropriate handling of sales discounts, returns and allowances, sales taxes, and uncollectible accounts.

The dominant aspect of many business entities is the selling function. Generally sales are recognized and recorded when goods are delivered to customers and the customers have taken ownership title to the goods. Sales are made up of cash sales, sales on account, and sales to customers who have previously paid in advance. Where sales are recognized before the customers have paid for the goods, problems arise in determining revenue because it is unlikely that the firm will collect the full amount billed to all customers. Factors which must be considered as corrections of sales and accounts receivable are sales returns, bad debts, and various other items.

THE NATURE OF REVENUE

It is well accepted in business that the cash basis of accounting is not suitable for any but the simplest business organizations. Recognition of revenues and expenses on an accrual basis is complex and less objective than on a cash basis, but is required in order to give a better picture of the earnings and financial position of a firm. Where the accrual system is in use, the pattern employed for the recognition of revenue tends to set the pattern for the recognition of expenses (although there are a few cases where the opposite is true). The interrelated nature of revenue and expense recognition results from the matching of the revenues and expenses for a particular period to determine earnings for that period. This chapter is concerned with revenue recognition and measurement, and with the measurement and management of the corresponding inflow of assets. Subsequent chapters are concerned with similar problems relating to the various cost and expense factors.

It should be emphasized that the pattern to be adopted for the recognition of revenue cannot be determined without considering whether related expenses can be ascertained with reasonable accuracy. In the matching of revenues and expenses which culminates in the closing process, there is a matching of the values assigned to the inflowing assets with the values assigned to the outflowing assets to develop the amount of net earnings or growth in stockholders' equity. Cost must be anticipated (accrued), or held in abeyance as assets (deferred), until they can be matched as expenses against the revenues according to the system of revenue recognition followed by the firm. Thus, the establishment of an appropriate and meaningful basis for the recognition of revenue serves to establish the basis for the solving of many other timing problems found in accounting.

Revenue is the increase in assets (or decrease in liabilities) resulting from the sale of goods and services to customers. Revenue is generally measured by the values assigned to the assets flowing in from customers. The term *revenue* so defined includes interest on loans extended by the firm, rent charged to tenants, and other items resulting from rendering services to the firm's customers. Special gains, such as those from disposal of assets other than merchandise, are measured and reported as the excess of the proceeds of the sale over the book value (cost minus accumulated depreciation).

REVENUE RECOGNITION AND MEASUREMENT

The earning of revenues by a business enterprise often involves a great many steps over a considerable span of time. Indeed, all revenues can logically be traced back to the inception of the enterprise as a first cause.

However, the span of events encompassing the earning of revenue can be narrowed somewhat by viewing revenue as the amount of economic utility rendered to society by the firm. The price ultimately paid to the firm for the product or service it sells offers a measure of this increment in economic utility. While the revenue-earning process often includes many phases prior to sale, objective measurement of the revenue is quite difficult until the sale itself provides a measure. Even at the time of sale, measurement problems may exist if the sale is on credit and collection is uncertain.

The recognition (that is, the crediting of a revenue account in the accounting records) for accounting purposes implies its measurement, for values must be assigned to the appropriate accounts at the point of recognition. Revenue may be recognized and measured (perhaps estimated) at a number of different points in the revenue-earning process: at the time of cash collection from the customer, at the time of sale to the customer, when production is completed, while production takes place, or while an accretion or growth in the value of a product is occurring (timber growth, liquor aging, and so on). In choosing one of these events or changes as the basis on which to recognize, measure, and record revenue, the accountant must bear in mind that the amount of reported revenues is an important statistic for the assessment of the success of the enterprise. It is essential that the determination of revenues be a credible and reliable process. An objective basis must exist for the recognition of revenue.

A merchandising concern which sells merchandise in much the same condition as when it was purchased will normally recognize revenue at the point of sale. A sale is the most significant event in the sequence of steps comprising the revenue-earning process for such firms. At that point, the firm obtains either cash or a claim against the buyer for cash, and the amount of this cash or claim provides a measurement of the revenue earned. If the sale is on credit and a great deal of uncertainty exists about collection (as is true of some installment sales), it may be advisable to defer the recognition of revenue until collection is made. Normally, however, the amount of collectible credit sales can be determined by taking into account estimates of uncollectibles and sales returns and allowances.

A case can be made for revenue recognition prior to sale for firms engaging in mining, construction, and some other areas where sale is virtually assured. A mining firm, for example, which mines ores, such as gold, that have a ready market at established prices is justified in recognizing revenue as the ore is mined. The crucial event in the revenue-earning process for such firms is production, not sales. Construction contractors engaged in a construction project which requires a number of accounting periods for completion are permitted to recognize revenue as the work progresses. Such construction contracts usually involve an established fee which will be paid in full upon satisfactory completion. Revenue is recognized on the basis of *percentage of completion;* the ratio of costs-to-date and total estimated costs of the project provides a measure of percentage of completion. This method will be illustrated later in the chapter.

Most manufacturing concerns recognize revenue at the *point of sale* of the finished product. Periodic fluctuations in sales and changes in sales prices due to shifts in market conditions make revenue recognition prior to sale a dubious approach.

Ideally, revenue should be recognized as soon as possible after the completion of the various significant steps in the revenue-generating process. These steps, the relative significance of which varies among firms, may include securing the means to sell (and perhaps produce) goods and services, producing, selling, collecting and satisfying warranty requirements on items sold. Practical problems include the measurement of the revenue, the likelihood of collection, and the determination of the related expenses for matching purposes in earnings determination. Revenue recognition is thus desirable when revenue has been "earned" (that is, when the revenue-generating process is essentially complete) and the ultimate proceeds from the customer can be determined objectively and with reasonable accuracy.

RECORDING REVENUES AND RECEIVABLES

In accordance with the *revenue principle,* a sale is generally considered to be realized, and is therefore recorded, when title passes to the buyer from the seller, regardless of when cash is collected. Thus, sales would be recorded in the following manner:

Cash sales:		
Cash	xxx	
Sales (revenue)		xxx
Credit sales:		
Account receivable	xxx	
Sales (revenue)		xxx

Accounts Receivable include amounts due and collectible from customers in return for goods and services the customers have received from the firm. These are termed *open accounts* to indicate that the claims are supported by the sales transaction and are not evidenced by promissory notes. An amount of a claim against a customer is an account receivable, and is an asset only to the extent that it is collectible. A claim against a bankrupt individual which has no standing in law and which the individual cannot or will not pay is not an asset. An account must be potentially collectible in order to be recognized as an account receivable.

Receivables from officers and employees should not be merged with ordinary accounts receivable unless the firm is dealing with them on exactly the same basis as with ordinary customers. Generally, accounts with officers and employees are subject to special collection problems and often are not charged on the same pricing basis as accounts due from customers. A more important reason for separate statement treatment of accounts with officers is the possibility that such people may misuse their positions to make personal use of company funds. The amounts due from officers and employees should ordinarily be displayed separately in an appropriate section of the assets category depending upon the terms and likelihood of collection.

Sales Discounts

It is common for sellers to offer special terms to encourage early payment of cash on account. For example, the terms "2/10,n/30" appearing on a sales invoice mean that 2 percent may be deducted from the amount of the invoice if the account is settled within ten days of the date of the invoice and that the gross amount of the invoice must be remitted within thirty days of the date of the invoice. The "n" signifies net of trade discounts and the net figure price. (*Trade discounts* are deductions from the suggested retail price of items in order to arrive at the invoice price to the nonretail buyer.) The most common (and simplest) method of recording sales and related sales discount transactions is to enter the receivable and sale at the gross amount. Sales discounts are then recognized in the accounts only when payment is received within the discount period. Sales discounts would then be shown as a contra-revenue item. Specifically, it would be shown as a deduction from gross sales in the income statement to arrive at net sales.

Another approach to accounting for sales discounts holds that these discounts are, in reality, penalties added to the cost of merchandise sold to encourage prompt payment. Customers normally take sales discounts and, in accounting, the normal situation should govern accounting procedure. If this approach is adopted, sales and receivables are recorded net, of sales discounts, and any discounts not taken are credited to an "other income" account, such as "Sales Discounts Forfeited."

GROSS METHOD			NET METHOD		
Sales of $5,000, terms 2/10,n/30:					
Accounts receivable	5,000		Accounts receivable	4,900	
Sales		5,000	Sales		4,900
			[5,000 − .02 (5,000) = 4,900]		
Payment of $3,000 within discount period:					
Cash	2,940		Cash	2,940	
Sales discount	60		Accounts receivable		2,940
Accounts receivable		3,000			
[3,000 − .02 (3,000)] = 2,940					
Payment of $2,000 after discount period:					
Cash	2,000		Cash	2,000	
Accounts receivable		2,000	Sales discounts Forfeited		40
			Accounts receivable		1,960

To illustrate the two methods of accounting for sales discounts assume that (1) Boat Company makes a sale for $5,000, terms 2/10,n/30; (2) $3,000 is paid within the discount period and the discount is deducted; (3) $2,000 is paid after the expiration of the discount period.

Although the net method is generally considered preferable from a theoretical viewpoint, it is not used as often as the gross method because it requires additional analysis and bookkeeping.

Other similar sales discounts frequently offered such as 1/15,n/e.o.m.—meaning 1 percent discount if paid in 15 days, and net due at the *e*nd *o*f the *m*onth.

Sales Taxes

In most states, sales taxes are assessed as sales are made and collected from the customer by the merchant, who then remits them to the state. Such collections are neither revenue nor expense to the firm; it is merely acting as a collecting agent for the state government. To illustrate an appropriate accounting treatment of sales taxes, assume that a firm has sales of $70,000 (all on account), of which $50,000 has been collected. The 3 percent sales tax need not be remitted until the seller collects from the customer. Entries (in summary form) are as follows:

To record the sales and sales tax liability:		
Accounts receivable	$72,100	
Sales		$70,000
Sales tax payable (@ 3%)		2,100
To record collections on account: $50,000 + .03(50,000)		
Cash	$51,500	
Accounts receivable		$51,500
To record the remittance of sales tax: (.03/1.03) × 51,500		
Sales tax payable	$1,500	
Cash		$1,500

UNCOLLECTIBLE ACCOUNTS: A SPECIAL PROBLEM OF RECEIVABLES VALUATION

Uncollectible accounts receivable is an important problem in the valuation of receivables, and often a significant item in financial statements. There are several ways of treating uncollectible accounts receivable in the accounts.

One method for dealing with the effect of bad debts is the simple *direct write-off method* which merely calls for a debit to a Bad Debt Expense or some similar account and a credit to Accounts Receivable, in the period when the account is demonstrated to be uncollectible.

While the direct write-off method has the virtue of simplicity, its use results in two significant errors which would appear in the periodic financial statements of virtually any firm with a large volume of credit sales. The nature of these errors can be demonstrated by the following illustration.

Direct Write-off Method

On December 15, 19X1, the Carver Company sells merchandise, which cost $750, to the Dixon Company for $1,000 on account. The sale is recorded:

Accounts receivable	$1,000	
Sales		$1,000
To record sale on account		

The books are adjusted and closed on December 31, 19X1 and the financial statements are prepared. Clearly, revenues and receivables as reported are larger by $1,000 as a result of this sale.

On April 15, 19X2, it is determined that the account owed by the Dixon Company will never be collected. Under the direct write-off method, the following entry is made:

Bad debt expense	$1,000	
Accounts receivable—Dixon Co.		$1,000
To write off Dixon Co. receivable		

When financial statements are prepared for the year ending December 31, 19X2, reported net earnings will be lower by $1,000 as a result of this treatment. Notice that an account originating in 19X1 and treated as a sale of 19X1 is offset against 19X2 sales as an expense—an obvious mismatching of revenues and expenses.

Bad debts or uncollectible accounts are not unexpected events properly treated as losses. When sales are made on account, management is aware that a portion of the accounts will not be collected. It is not logical or meaningful to relate the amount of the accounts finally determined to be uncollectible this year, but originating in some previous year, as a deduction from this year's revenue in arriving at net earnings. The following accounting errors are introduced by the use of the direct write-off method in the previous example:

	19X1	19X2
Balance sheet	Assets (accounts receivable) are overstated by $1,000	
Income statement	Revenue and net earnings are overstated by $1,000	Expenses are overstated and earnings are understated by $1,000

The direct write-off method is generally not an acceptable way of accounting for bad debts. The errors involved in the direct write-off method justify the use of a more precise method to record the effects of bad debts.

Allowance Method

In practice, the allowance method of accounting for uncollectible accounts is used to minimize errors in matching bad debt expenses and revenues. This method involves using previous experience with uncollectible accounts to develop a basis for estimating the amount of bad debts, and using this estimate to adjust current assets and earnings. A proper journal entry to accomplish this is:

Bad debt expense	xxx	
Allowance for uncollectible accounts		xxx

The Bad Debt Expense account is obviously a selling expense which will appear on the income statement. The Allowance for Uncollectible Accounts is a contra asset which will appear on the balance sheet as a deduction from Accounts Receivable.

There are four phases to the allowance method of accounting for uncollectibles:

1. Estimating the amount of the accounts receivable that will not be collected due to inability or unwillingness of the customer.
2. Adjusting the accounts to reflect the uncollectibility estimate.
3. Determining the particular accounts that will not be collected and writing off these bad accounts.
4. Correcting the accounts when the adjustment or write-offs are found to be in error.

Two different estimating procedures are used to determine the amount of the bad debts. The first method involves determining the average percentage of credit sales of the past few years that have been uncollectible. From this analysis, an average or normal rate of loss is developed which is modified to take into account any changes in credit-granting policy and changes in business conditions. The rate thus determined should be applied to the total credit sales to produce the amount to be charged to Bad Debts Expense.

The second method of estimating uncollectibles starts with a detailed analysis of accounts receivable. The accounts are *aged,* which means that they are classified by the length of time they have been outstanding. Experience will give clues as to the collectibility of accounts in the various age groups. Records of efforts made to collect the accounts and the opinions of the collection personnel about the collectibility of the older accounts offer a basis for calculating the percentage of the accounts likely to be collected in each age group. The sum of the products of the collection percentage for each group and the total of each group will provide an estimate of the collectible amount that should be reflected in the accounts. The balance of the Allowance for Uncollectible Accounts must then be adjusted to reflect the probable amount uncollectible of the balance of Accounts Receivable. The debit accompanying the adjustment of the uncollectible balance is to Bad Debts Expense.

Allowance Method Illustration

Grant company starts the current year with the following account balances:

Accounts receivable (Dr.)	$90,000
Allowance for uncollectible accounts (Cr.)	$26,000

During the current year the following events occur:

1. The firm sells $400,000 on account.

Accounts receivable	$400,000	
Sales		$400,000

2. The firm collects $360,000 of the accounts receivable.

Cash	$360,000	
Accounts receivable		$360,000

3. The firm discovers individual accounts totaling $20,000 that are not collectible.

Allowance for uncollectible accounts	$ 20,000	
Accounts receivable		$ 20,000

(Note that individual accounts in the subsidiary ledger would also be credited.)

Prior to adjusting and closing entries, the relevant accounts appear as follows:

Accounts Receivable

Beginning bal.	90,000	Collections (2)	360,000
Sales (1)	400,000	Write-offs (3)	20,000

(Note that the balance of this account is $110,000)

Sales

	400,000 (1)

Allowance for Uncollectible Accounts

Write-off (3)	20,000	Beginning bal.	26,000

(Note that the balance of this account is $6,000)

Bad Debt Expense

Write-offs of uncollectible accounts (item 3) are accomplished by debiting the Allowance for Uncollectible Accounts account and crediting Accounts Receivable. The amount of *net* Accounts Receivable is unchanged so that, in effect, specific accounts have been written off in place of the general deduction from Accounts Receivable that is represented by the Allowance for Uncollectible Accounts account. These write-offs may relate to accounts originating in the previous year as well as in the current year.

Adjusting the Allowance Based on Sales

The Bad Debts Expense and the Allowance for Uncollectible Accounts account must now be adjusted. If the first of the two methods is used, and supposing that Grant Company's experience indicates that 2 percent of credit sales will be uncollectible, the adjusting entry will be:

Bad debts expenses (.02 × 400,000)	$8,000	
Allowance for uncollectible accounts		$8,000
To record bad debt expense for the year		

The balance of the Bad Debts Expense account, like the Sales account, will be closed to the Retained Earnings account. The ending balance of the Allowance for Uncollectible Accounts account, $14,000, will appear on the balance sheet as a deduction from Accounts Receivable. The accounts will now show:

Accounts Receivable

Bal.	90,000	(2)	360,000
(1)	400,000	(3)	20,000
Bal.	110,000		

Allowance for Uncollectible Accounts

(3)	20,000	Beginning	26,000
		(4)	8,000
		Bal.	14,000

Sales

(X)	400,000	(1)	400,000

Bad Debts Expense

(4)	8,000	(X)	8,000

Retained Earnings

(X)	8,000	(X)	400,000

Closing entries are indicated by (X).

Adjusting the Allowance Based on Aging Receivables

The use of the second of the two methods for the adjustment of estimated uncollectible accounts involves analyzing the $110,000 balance of Accounts Receivable by age groups. The aging analysis results in the following schedule:

Grant Company
Accounts Receivable—Aging Schedule

AGE (DAYS)	AMOUNT	ESTIMATED PERCENT UNCOLLECTIBLE	ESTIMATED UNCOLLECTIBLE AMOUNT
0–30	$ 40,000	2%	$ 800
31–60	30,000	6	1,800
61–90	20,000	15	3,000
91–120	8,000	25	2,000
121+	12,000	50	6,000
	$110,000		$13,600

The adjusting entry would then be an amount to bring the balance in the Allowance for Uncollectible Accounts up to the revised current estimate of $13,600, or $7,600 ($13,600 – $6,000):

Bad debts expense	$7,600	
Allowance for uncollectible accounts		$7,600
To record bad debt expense for the year		

This entry serves to establish the ending balance of the account at $13,600.

Irrespective of which of the two methods is used to estimate bad debt losses, complete accuracy is impossible. Two types of errors arise in the process of accounting for bad debts on an estimated basis. One type of error results quite simply from underestimating or overestimating the amount to be added to the Allowance for Uncollectible Accounts account (the estimate of the overall losses.) The other type of error occurs when a particular account is written off, but is collected later. When a firm collects an account that has been written off, the account should be reestablished by a debit to Accounts Receivable and a credit to Allowance for Uncollectible Accounts. This entry is followed by the regular collection entry. In this manner, the customer's account will show the complete record of what happened and will be more meaningful for credit purposes.

Recovery of an Account Written Off: Illustration

		Debit	Credit
1.	An account for $83 appears to be uncollectible and is written off.		
	Allowance for uncollectible accounts	$83	
	Accounts receivable: A. B. Johnson		$83
	To write off uncollectible account		
2.	The customer tenders payment and the account is reestablished.		
	Accounts receivable: A. B. Johnson	$83	
	Allowance for uncollectible accounts		$83
	To reestablish account receivable		
3.	The collection is treated as a regular collection on account.		
	Cash	$83	
	Accounts receivable: A. B. Johnson		$83
	To record receipt of cash on account		

In account form, this appears as follows:

Cash			
(3)	83		

Accounts Receivable			
Bal.	XXX	(1)	83
(2)	83	(3)	83

Allowance for Uncollectible Accounts			
(1)	83	Bal.	XXX
		(2)	83

In the customer's ledger, Johnson's account will show:

A. B. Johnson's			
Balance due	83	Bad debt write-off	83
Write-off restored	83	Collection on account	83

Note that Johnson's account in the detailed customer's records shows a complete record of the transactions. Such information may be useful in determining the firm's future credit-granting policy toward Johnson. In all cases, care must be taken to assure that write-off entries posted to customer accounts do not appear to be collections.

CREDIT CARD SALES

Most retail stores now allow customers to use a credit card of some type to pay for purchases. The businesses benefit primarily by avoiding the risk of uncollectible accounts when customers make their purchases with known cards such as Mastercard and Visa; in these cases, it is the issuer of the credit card (a financial institution) which extends credit—not the seller. Normally when a person makes a purchase using one of these cards they must sign a multiple-copy form which includes a *credit card draft.* This draft is very similar to a check which is drawn upon the assets of the credit card company (rather than the personal bank account of the customer). The retailer periodically sends these drafts to the credit card company and they pay the merchant in cash, less any discount. The credit card company then bills the card holder monthly for all drafts it has received during the month. If the card holder fails to pay the amount owed, it is the credit card company which sustains the loss.

In addition to avoiding the potential loss from uncollectible accounts, merchants who accept credit cards often receive cash more promptly than otherwise. They also avoid the expenses of investigating customers' credit standing as well as collection and bookkeeping expenses.

PLEDGING, ASSIGNING, AND FACTORING ACCOUNTS RECEIVABLES

When receivables are *pledged,* one party (the pledgor) uses accounts receivable as security for a loan. The party granting the loan (the pledgee) is empowered to sell the accounts receivable if the debt is not paid. No formal entry is made in the accounting records to record the pledge of accounts receivable.

When accounts receivable are *assigned,* one party (the assignor) actually transfers the receivable rights under contract to another party (the assignee). This is normally done when the assignor is attempting to obtain a loan from a finance company or bank. To insure that there is sufficient collateral, receivables in excess of the amount borrowed are generally assigned; and the borrowing company retains control of the assigned receivables. When collections are made on the assigned receivables, those monies are used to pay the amount borrowed. The journal entry which would be made to record the assigning of accounts receivable would be:

Accounts receivable assigned	XXX	
Accounts receivable		XXX

To record the assignment of accounts receivable as collateral for a loan from XYZ Finance Company

If accounts receivable are *factored,* it essentially means that they are sold. Companies purchasing accounts receivable are known as factors. Factors are financial institutions that buy receivables for a fee and then collect the remittances directly from the customer. The normal journal entry to be made by the company selling its receivables to a factor would be:

Cash	XXX	
Financing expense	XX	
Accounts receivable		XXX
To record the factoring of accounts receivable		

LONG-TERM CONSTRUCTION CONTRACTS

As mentioned previously in this chapter, there are certain situations in which revenue is recognized at a time other than the point of sale. One of these situations is in long-term construction contracts, such as the construction of a large building, power plant, dam, or similar asset. Such construction projects often take several years to complete, and it is generally thought to be misleading to postpone the recognition of profit on such projects until the end of construction. In such cases a technique for recognizing revenue called the *percentage-of-completion* method is often used. Under this method an estimate of the proportion of work done on the project is estimated each accounting period, and profit on the project is then recognized in that proportion.

Percentage-of-Completion Method

To illustrate the percentage-of-completion method, assume that L. T.Builders Company enters into a construction project in year 19X1 which lasts into 19X3. The contract price is $3,400,000 and the company, at the project's inception, expects to earn a profit on the project of $400,000; therefore original estimated total costs are $3,000,000 ($3,400,000 − $400,000). It is obvious, however, that the original expense estimate will not hold true throughout the project. The following schedule shows the actual costs incurred and the amount of profit to be recognized in each of the three years of the project using the percentage-of-completion method:

	YEAR		
	19X1	**19X2**	**19X3**
a. Actual costs incurred in year	$ 600,000	$1,000,000	$1,540,000
b. Cumulative costs to date	600,000	1,600,000	3,140,000
c. *Estimated* cost to complete	2,400,000	1,600,000	-0-
d. *Total estimated cost* (b + c)	3,000,000	3,200,000	3,140,000
e. *Total estimated profit* ($3,400,000 − d)	400,000	200,000	260,000

(continued)

	19X1	19X2	19X3
f. Amount of profit recognized in the year			
19X1: $\frac{600{,}000}{3{,}000{,}000} \times 400{,}000 =$	80,000		
19X2: $\frac{1{,}600{,}000}{3{,}200{,}000} \times 200{,}000 =$			
$100{,}000 - 80{,}000 =$		20,000	
19X3: $260{,}000 - 100{,}000 =$			160,000

In the example above items a and b are actual amounts, and items c, d, and e are estimates in years 19X1 and 19X2. The project is completed in 19X3, so those items (c, d, and e) are actual amounts in that year. The profit in 19X1 is estimated by dividing the actual costs incurred to date by the total estimated costs of the project

$$\frac{600{,}000}{3{,}000{,}000} = 20\%$$

and multiplying the resulting fraction by the total estimated profit (20% × $400,000 = $80,000). Because 20% of the work was done in 19X1, 20% of the estimated total profit of $400,000 was considered to be earned in that year.

In 19X2, total costs incurred were $1,000,000 and total cumulative costs incurred to date were $1,600,000 ($600,000 from 19X1 plus $1,000,000 from 19X2). As should be expected, total estimated cost to complete the project changed from 19X1, so that at the end of 19X2 total estimated costs were $3,200,000. Because 50% of the estimated costs have been incurred to date (1,600,000/3,200,000 = 50%), that proportion of the profit should be recognized. However because total estimated expenses have gone up, total estimated profit has gone down from $400,000 in 19X1 to $200,000 ($3,400,000 − $3,200,000) in 19X2. The amount of profit which should be recognized to date, then, is 50% × $200,000 = $100,000. Since $80,000 was recognized in 19X1, the balance of $20,000 ($100,000 − $80,000 = $20,000) must be recognized in the current year.

In year 19X3, the total costs of the project are known ($3,140,000), and the actual profit on the project is determined to be $260,000 ($3,400,000 − $3,140,000). Because profits of $100,000 were previously recognized, the remaining amount ($260,000 − $100,000 = $160,000) must be recognized in 19X3. The journal entries which would be made during the contract term would recognize annual profit in the amounts calculated (19X1: $80,000; 19X2: $20,000; 19X3: $160,000). It is important to note that this method is a departure from traditional revenue recognition procedures which require that the earning and realization processes be *completed* before revenue is recognized.

Completed-Contract Method

The accounting profession considers the percentage-of-completion method to be the preferable method when estimates of costs to complete on long-term projects are reasonably dependable. If cost estimates are not reasonably dependable then the recognition of total profit should be postponed until production is completed. This method is referred to as the *completed-contract method.* If the completed-contract method had been used in the preceding example, no profit would have been recognized in 19X1 and 19X2; and the entire profit of $260,000 would have been recognized in 19X3.

The percentage-of-completion method and the completed-contract method produces similar results when a loss is anticipated on a long-term construction project. If, at the end of any accounting period, it appears that a loss will be incurred on a long-term project, the entire loss is recognized at once. This approach is in accordance with the well-established accounting practice of making provision for foreseeable losses.

NOTES RECEIVABLE

A promissory *note* is a written promise to pay a specific sum of money on demand or at a definite future date. The person or company owning the note is the *payee.* To the payee the note is a note receivable (an asset). The person or company that signs the note and thereby promises to pay is the *maker* and refers to the note as a note payable (a liability). Notes normally carry interest, although non-interest-bearing notes do exist.

In the note illustrated next, Bruce Cannery is the payee and Jay Printing Company is the maker.

$ 10,000.00 Chicago, Illinois February 17, 19X1

Three months AFTER DATE We

TO THE ORDER OF Bruce Cannery

Ten Thousand and 00/100 ---------------------------- Dollars

PAYABLE AT First National Bank of Chicago

WITH INTEREST AT 15% per annum

Jay Printing Company
TREASURER

Commercial practice generally treats a note as maturing (becoming payable) in the number of days specified after the date the note is made. In other words, in determining the maturity date (which is the date that payment is due on the note), the first day is not counted, but the last day is. It is also convenient and common to treat each year as consisting of only 360 days.

Illustration

The A Corporation loaned B Corporation $5,000 in cash, receiving a 60-day, 12% note for that amount dated April 18, 19X1. The entries on A Corporation and B Corporation books are as follows for the note:

A CORPORATION (PAYEE)				B CORPORATION (MAKER)		
Receipt of note:				*Issuance of note:*		
Apr. 18	Notes receivable	$5,000		Cash	$5,000	
	Cash		$5,000	Notes payable		$5,000
Collection of note:				*Payment of Note:*		
June 17	Cash	5,100		Notes payable	5,000	
	Notes receivable		5,000	Interest expense	100	
	Interest income		100	Cash		5,100

The due date is determined by noting that the specified 60-day time period includes 12 days in April, 31 days in May, and 17 days in June. The interest is computed as the product of the face value of the note (principal of $5,000), the interest rate, and the time period expressed as a fraction of a year:

$$\$5{,}000 \times .12 \times 60/360 = \$100$$

In accrual accounting, it is necessary to include all interest earned and all interest expense in an accounting period that relates to the use of borrowed funds in that accounting period, whether the interest has been paid during the period or not. To illustrate the accrual problem, assume a change in the dates in the preceding illustration so that 20 days of the note's life fall in 19X1 and 40 days fall in 19X2. In other words, the note is to be dated December 11, 19X1 and the date of maturity is February 9, 19X2.

A CORPORATION (PAYEE)				B CORPORATION (MAKER)		
Receipt of note:				*Issuance of note:*		
Dec. 11	Notes receivable	$5,000		Cash	$5,000	
	Cash		$5,000	Notes payable		$5,000
Year-end adjustments:				*Year-end adjustments:*		
Dec. 31	Interest receivable	33		Interest expense	33	
	Interest income		33	Interest payable		33

Since 20 days of the 60 days of the note's life fall in 19X1, 20/60 or one-third of the $100 of interest relates to 19X2. This accrual is recorded by a debit to Interest Receivable (or Accrued Interest Receivable) on the payee's books and Interest Payable (or Accrued Interest Payable) on the maker's books.

A CORPORATION (PAYEE)				B CORPORATION (MAKER)		
Year-end closing entry 19X1:				*Year-end closing entry 19X1:*		
Dec. 31	Interest income	$ 33		Retained earnings	$ 33	
	Retained earnings		$ 33	Interest expense		$ 33
Collection 19X2:				*Payment 19X2:*		
Feb. 9	Cash	5,100		Notes payable	5,000	
	Notes receivable		5,000	Interest payable	33	
	Interest receivable		33	Interest expense	67	
	Interest income		67	Cash		5,100
Year-end closing entry 19X2:				*Year-end closing entry 19X2:*		
Dec. 31	Interest income	67		Retained earnings	67	
	Retained earnings		67	Interest expense		67

When the note is paid (collected) on February 9, 19X2, three factors must be considered on both the maker's and the payee's books: the amount carried in the note account itself, the amount previously recognized as accrued in Interest Receivable or Interest Payable, and the amount of the interest earned since the last accrual. In this case, the note was recorded as its face value of $5,000, $33 of interest was previously accrued, and $67 of interest relates to 19X2.

In both illustrations above, the lender advanced money to the borrower and received a promise to pay in the form of a note. Notes may also arise in exchange for open accounts. When a note is taken on an account the only difference is that Accounts Receivable is credited on the lender's books instead of Cash. Accounts Payable is debited on the borrower's books.

In addition to receiving notes in cash-borrowing situations, companies also issue notes for two other common occurrences: (1) to replace an open account receivable, and (2) in a sale situation. In each case the debit in the transaction is to Notes Receivable. When the note is received in exchange for an open account, the credit is to Accounts Receivable. When the note is received when a sale is made, the credit is to Sales.

Defaulting on Notes

A promissory note which is not paid at maturity is said to be *defaulted.* As soon as it is known that a note is in default, a journal entry should be made by the payee to transfer the amount due from the Notes Receivable account to an account receivable from the maker/debtor.

Assuming that a $1,000, 90-day, 18% note receivable from Zonk, Inc., is defaulted, the following entry would be made:

Accounts receivable: Zonk, Inc.	$1,045	
Notes receivable		$1,000
Interest income		45
To record default on note by Zonk, Inc.		

If the account receivable from Zonk is ultimately uncollectible, it is written off in the manner described earlier in the chapter (that is, by debiting Allowance for Uncollectible Accounts and crediting Accounts Receivable).

Discounting Notes Receivable

If the payee of a note wishes to receive money before the maturity date, it is often possible to do so by *discounting* the note receivable at a bank or other lending institution. The payee/holder of the note simply endorses it (as with endorsing a check) and turns it over to the bank for collection. The maker of the note then pays the bank (instead of the original payee) the maturity value of the note on the due date. The bank makes a profit by charging a *discount* which is computed on the maturity value of the note for the period of time the bank will hold the note. The amount of the *proceeds* paid to the endorser (payee/holder) is the excess of the maturity value over the discount.

To illustrate, assume that on September 1, 19X1, Post Company accepted a $30,000, 10%, one-year note in payment of an open account receivable from Mak, Inc. On December 1, 19X1, Post Company discounts this note at the bank at a discount rate of 14%. The journal entries and computation by Post Company for this reference of events is presented next:

19X1			
Sept. 1	Notes receivable	$30,000	
	Accounts receivable		$30,000
	To record receipt on one-year, 10% note in place of open account receivable		

The calculation of proceeds on the discounted note receivable is:

Face of note	$30,000
Add: Interest to maturity ($30,000 × .10)	3,000
Maturity value of note	33,000
Discount ($33,000 × .14 × 9/12)	(3,465)
Proceeds	$29,535

Post Company would incur a $465 ($30,000 − $29,535) Interest Expense on the transaction. The entry made by Post to record the discounting of the Mak note would be:

19X1			
Dec. 1	Cash	$29,535	
	Interest expense	465	
	Note receivable		$30,000
	To record discount of Mak note at bank (Interest expense calculation: $30,000 − $29,535 = $465)		

The $29,535 proceeds received by Post are less than the face value of the note, therefore the transaction results in interest expense to the discounter (Post Company). If the proceeds had exceeded the face value of the note, interest revenue would have resulted. This would have been the case if Post had waited until a date closer to the maturity date to discount the note, thereby resulting in the bank holding the note for a shorter period of time. The discount rate charged by the bank also has an impact on the proceeds and therefore the "profit or loss" of a discounting transaction.

Contingent Liability

When a company endorses a note and delivers it to the bank for cash, it is committed to paying the bank if the maker should default. The endorsing company does not have a direct liability to the bank; any liability that it has is contingent on the maker not meeting its obligation. This *contingent liability* becomes a real liability only if the maker defaults. If, on the other hand, the maker pays the promised amount at maturity, the contingent liability is discharged without any action on the part of the endorser. The fact that a contingent liability exists should not be included in the body of the financial statements, but should be included in any footnotes to the financial statements.

SUMMARY

The most fundamental need of a business is revenue—the increase in assets from the sales of goods and services of the business to customers. Measuring revenues and allocating them to time periods influences the determination of profit and thereby affects the opinion outsiders have of the business firm. In general, revenues should be recorded at the real current value of the inflowing assets. Current valuation of revenues involves determining the collectibility of accounts receivable. It is generally desirable to estimate the amount of such items in valuing sales and receivables. Valuation of revenues and receivables has led to the use of valuation (contra) accounts which are deducted from sales and accounts receivable. Cash, accounts receivable, and sales are closely related in the operating process because cash and accounts receivable are produced by sales and must be financed in order to make more sales.

Generally revenues must be earned and realized before they are recognized (that is, recorded in the accounting records). The earning and realization of revenues have generally occurred at the *point of sale,* so this is the point at which most revenues are recognized. There are certain exceptions to this rule, notably the mining of precious ores and long-term construction contracts.

A note receivable is an obligation which is more formal and more easily enforceable than an open account receivable. Notes generally carry interest, although they do not have to do so. A note may be sold or discounted under normal conditions. The entity selling the note must generally guarantee payment in the event that the maker is unable to pay on the maturity date.

KEY POINTS

1. **Revenue** Revenue is generally recorded in the accounting records after it is completely earned and realized. The realization of revenue most frequently occurs at the point of sale. Accounts Receivable are the result of recognizing revenues from sales on account, and include amounts due and collectible from customers in return for goods and services the customers have received from the firm.

2. **Sales discounts** A reduction in price offered by sellers to encourage customers to pay amounts owed within a specified discount period.

3. **Allowance for uncollectible accounts** A contra-asset account which establishes a provision for anticipated bad debts. It is deducted from Accounts Receivable in the balance sheet.

4. **Bad debt expense** The account which is used to record customer bad debts. It is an expense on the income statement.

5. **Aging accounts receivable** The policy of grouping Accounts Receivable into categories, by time, since date of sale. It is then customary to estimate the percent in each category that will ultimately prove uncollectible.

6. **Credit card draft** A document which is similar to a check that is drawn upon the assets of the credit card company, rather than the personal assets of the person signing it.

7. **Percentage-of-completion method** A method of recognizing revenue on long-term construction projects in the proportion of work completed in an accounting period.

8. **Note** (receivable and payable) A written promise to pay a specific sum of money on demand or at a definite future date.

9. **Payee** The person or company owning the note. To the payee the note is a note receivable.

10. **Maker** The person or company owing the money. To the maker the note is a note payable.

11. **Defaulted note** A promissory note which is not paid at maturity.

12. **Discounting notes receivable** The process of endorsing the note receivable and transferring it to a bank (which will collect it at maturity) in exchange for immediate cash.

13. **Contingent Liability** A potential liability which will either develop into a real liability or be eliminated entirely, depending on some future event.

REVIEW QUESTIONS

1. Why is revenue usually recognized at the point of sale? Under what conditions may revenue be recognized prior to, or subsequent to, sales?

2. Identify the items which flow into a business as it sells its goods and services.

3. Why does a company sell on credit if it expects that some of the accounts will not be paid? What role might a credit department play in selling on credit?

4. What is the direct write-off method of handling bad debts (as compared to the allowance method)?

5. Explain the two methods commonly used to estimate the amount of uncollectible accounts receivable to be charged as bad debt expenses of a particular period. Discuss the advantages and disadvantages of each method.

6. What procedure for estimating uncollectible accounts also gives management a view of the status of collections and the overall quality of accounts receivable?

7. What accounting rule is violated by the direct charge-off method of recognizing uncollectible accounts? Why?

8. Explain the four phases involved in applying the allowance method of accounting for uncollectible accounts receivable.

9. What is the difference between recording accounts receivable on a gross or a net basis?

10. Explain why the allowance for uncollectible accounts never has the same balance as the bad debt expense account.

11. What advantages are there to a merchant of allowing customers to pay for purchases with a credit card?

12. Explain the difference between assigning, factoring, and pledging accounts receivable.

13. There are two possible methods which might be used in accounting for long-term construction projects. What are those two methods, and when might either be used? Is either method a departure from the traditional concept of revenue recognition?

14. How is a note receivable different from an account receivable? What facts must be present for a document to be considered a note receivable?

15. Describe a situation in which a person holding a note receivable might discount it at the bank. What factors would determine if the person discounting the note would realize interest income or expense from the transaction?

16. What is a contingent liability? Give two situations in which a company would have a contingent liability. How should the readers of financial statements be informed of the existence of contingent liabilities?

17. When might a seller be willing to accept a non-interest-bearing note receivable in exchange for an open account receivable owed by a customer?

EXERCISES

E6-1 Determine which of the following items are included as accounts receivable on a firm's balance sheet using generally accepted accounting principles.

a. Rent that has been paid in advance beyond the balance sheet date.
b. Accounts receivable pledged for a loan from a bank or other financial institution.
c. A note receivable that has been dishonored (not paid when due) by a customer.
d. Cash collected from a customer whose account had previously been written off as uncollectible.

E6-2 Hart Supply sells $16,000 in merchandise to Boreland Shops on June 10, 19X1. Terms of the sale are 2/10,n/30. Assuming that the gross method is followed, record the following transactions:

a. Sale of merchandise on June 10.
b. Receipt of cash from Boreland Shops on June 20.
c. Receipt of cash from Boreland Shops on July 9 rather than June 20.

E6-3 The unadjusted trial balance for Flour Corporation at the end of the current year includes the following accounts:

	DEBIT	CREDIT
Accounts receivable	$288,000	
Allowance for doubtful accounts		$ 2,184
Sales (25 percent represent cash sales)		1,152,000

Compute the Bad Debt expense for the current year, assuming that uncollectible accounts expense is determined as follows:

a. 1 percent of total sales.
b. 1½ percent of credit sales.
c. Allowance for doubtful accounts is increased to equal 3 percent of gross accounts receivable.

E6-4 Hillbrich, Inc., reported the following amounts on its balance sheet at the end of last year:

Notes receivable from customers	$ 24,000
Accrued interest on notes receivable	480
Accounts receivable	100,800
Less: Allowance for doubtful accounts	2,400

You are to record the following events of the current year in general journal entries:

a. Accounts receivable of $2,304 are written off as uncollectible.
b. A customer's note for $660 on which interest of $36 has been accrued in the accounts is deemed uncollectible, and both balances are written off against the Allowance for Doubtful Accounts.
c. An account receivable for $312 previously written off is collected.
d. Aging of accounts receivable at the end of the current year indicates a need for a $3,600 allowance to cover possible failure to collect accounts currently outstanding.

E6-5 The general ledger controlling account for accounts receivable of Roger Wilco, Inc., shows a debit balance of $360,000 at the end of the year. An aging method analysis of the individual accounts indicates estimated uncollectible accounts to be $16,800.

Give the general journal entry to record the uncollectible accounts expense under each of the following assumptions:

a. The Allowance for Uncollectible Accounts has a credit balance of $1,200.
b. The Allowance for Uncollectible Accounts has a debit balance of $1,200.

E6-6 Assuming that the allowance method is being used, prepare journal entries to record the following transactions:

May 10, 19X1	Sold merchandise to Sean Plunkett for $1,200 on account.
Sept. 30, 19X1	Received $100 from Sean Plunkett on account.
June 15, 19X2	Wrote off as uncollectible the balance of the Sean Plunkett account when he was declared bankrupt.
July 17, 19X2	Unexpectedly received a check for $200 from Sean Plunkett.

E6-7 Pointed Tye Corporation decides to write off the $2,600 account of Phil A. Dendron against the Allowance for Uncollectible Accounts account. Shortly after the write-off, Phil paid $600 on his account. Prepare the entry to record (a) the write-off and (b) the subsequent collection.

E6-8 The state in which the Stop 'n' Swap Store does business has a sales tax of 4 percent. Sales tax need not be remitted to the state for credit sales until the account is collected. During the current year, Stop 'n' Swap Store had cash sales of $22,000 and credit sales of $64,000, of which $48,000 have been collected. These amounts do not include sales tax. Show in T-account form the effect of these transactions on the Cash, Accounts Receivable, Sales, and Sales Tax Payable, accounts. Record the sales tax remitted to the state for the year.

E6-9 The Vallente Company reviewed its accounts receivable on December 31, 19X1. Before any adjustments were made, the accounts contained the following balances:

Net sales	$1,800,000	credit
Accounts receivable	18,000	debit
Allowance for uncollectible accounts	9,000	credit

The company decides that accounts receivable with balances totaling $8,000 are uncollectible and should be written off. Based on past experience, 5 percent of the accounts receivable prove to be uncollectible. Prepare the entries to (a) write off the bad accounts, and (b) adjust the allowance account to the correct balance.

E6-10 During 19X1 Paisley Suit Shop sold merchandise amounting to $188,000 of which $60,000 was on credit. At the start of 19X1 the Allowance for Doubtful Accounts reflected a $900 credit balance.

a. On December 31, 19X1, an account receivable of $1,000 from a prior year was determined to be uncollectible; therefore, it was written off immediately. Give the journal entry for the write-off.
b. On December 31, 19X1, on the basis of past experience, it was decided to continue the accounting policy of basing estimated bad debt losses on credit sales for the year. The rate was estimated to be 1 percent of such sales. Give the adjusting journal entry required.
c. Determine the balances in the following ledger accounts on December 31, 19X1, after the entries in (a) and (b) have been posted.

Allowance for doubtful accounts	$______
Bad debt expenses	$______

E6-11 Gopher Broke Shop sells on credit terms of 2/10,n/60. A sale of $1,000 was made to Tim Holbert on February 1, 19X1. In due time, Tim paid the account in full.

REQUIRED:

Using both the gross and net methods:

1. Give the entry to record the credit sale.
2. Give the entry assuming Tim paid the account in full on February 9, 19X1.
3. Give the entry assuming, instead, that Tim paid the account in full on March 29, 19X1.

E6-12 I. M. Good Company became the payee in three notes receivable during May, 19X1. The three situations were:

May 1	Loaned U. R. Bad $10,000 cash, terms 18%, 60-days.
May 18	Received a 10%, 30-day note in payment of an open account receivable from J. S. Smith—$2,500.
May 22	Sold merchandise to Y. U. Gripe in exchange for a $15,000, 15%, 90-day note.

REQUIRED:

Prepare the journal entry for each event.

E6-13 B. U. Small, the owner of a feed and nursery store, received a document signed by W. A. Tchout which read: "I promise to pay to B. U. Small an amount equal to one-half of the proceeds of my corn crop when it is harvested in exchange for seed, fertilizer, and other goods received on August 1, 19X1."

Does B. U. Small hold a promissory note from W. A. Tchout? What is the basis for your decision?

E6-14 On February 1, 19X1, Blue Company loaned Red Company $100,000, receiving a one-year, 10% note in exchange. On May 1, 19X1, Blue Company discounted the note at the Second State Bank. The bank charged a discount rate of 15%.

REQUIRED:

Calculate the proceeds to Blue Company in the discounting transaction.

PROBLEMS

P6-1 The following transaction was taken from the February 29, 19X0, trial balance of Phonex Co.:

	DEBITS	CREDITS
Accounts receivable	$85,000	
Sales discounts	4,600	
Sales		$373,800
Allowance for uncollectible accounts	1,000	
Sales returns and allowances	8,800	

In addition, the following events occurred during 19X0.

Feb. 29 Bad debt expense was computed under one of the following methods. Show computations for both methods and journalize the one resulting in the smaller expense:

a. Five percent of the accounts receivable are estimated to be uncollectible.
b. Two percent of net sales are estimated to be uncollectible.

Mar. 25 A check for $600 was received from Rich Shaw. Rich Shaw's account receivable, in the amount of $1,000, was previously written off.

July 3 The receivable from Bill Bailey, in the amount of $1,200, was written off as uncollectible.

REQUIRED:

1. Prepare the necessary journal entries to record the 19X0 transactions.
2. Determine the balance in the Allowance for Uncollectible Accounts as of July 3, 19X0.

P6-2 The transactions, adjusting entries, and closing entries described next are all related to uncollectible accounts receivable and were completed during the fiscal year ending December 31:

Jan. 30 Received 20 percent of amount owed by Owoe Corporation, which is bankrupt, and wrote off the remainder ($400) as uncollectible.

Feb. 14 Reinstated the account of Peter Miller that had been written off as uncollectible in the previous year and received $140 in full payment of the account.

Apr. 28 Wrote off the $250 balance of the account owed by Herman Schultz as uncollectible.

July 13 Reinstated the account of Clarence Henry (balance, $320) that had been written off as uncollectible in the previous year after reassurances and $100 are received from Henry. ($220 is still owed.)

Dec. 31 On the basis of an analysis of accounts receivable, it was estimated that $1,440 will be uncollectible. Recorded the adjusting entry.

Dec. 31 Recorded the entry to close Bad Debts Expense account.

REQUIRED:

1. Set up T-accounts for the following accounts and indicated balances as of January 1 of the fiscal year:

Allowance for uncollectible accounts	$ 1,200	cr.
Accounts receivable	38,000	dr.
Bad debts expense	-0-	
Retained earnings	89,000	cr.

2. Record in general journal form the entries for the dated transactions. Post to the accounts affected and determine the balances.
3. Assume that the estimate of uncollectible accounts receivable was based on a percentage of sales rather than an analysis of the accounts, and that 1 percent of sales of $150,000 was used for the estimate on December 31. Record the estimate under this assumption and show the effect on estimated realizable accounts receivable. (Estimated realizable accounts receivable is the balance of Accounts Receivable less the Allowance for Uncollectible Accounts balance on December 31, after end-of-year period adjustments.)

P6-3 D. W. Whirl Company prepared the following partial listing of accounts at the close of business on December 31, 19X0:

	DEBITS	CREDITS
Accounts receivable	$340,800	
Allowance for uncollectible accounts	4,800	
Cash sales		$2,000,000
Credit sales		2,000,000

Prepare the journal entries to adjust the allowance for uncollectible accounts and determine the balance in the allowance account after adjustment if:

a. the D. W. Whirl Company increases the allowance account to 6 percent of ending accounts receivable, or
b. the D. W. Whirl Company estimates bad debts at ¾ percent of total sales.

P6-4 On December 31 of last year, the balance sheet of Dragon Company had accounts receivable of $628,000 and a credit balance in the Allowance for Uncollectible Accounts of $38,800. During the current year, the company's records included the following selected activities:

Sales on account	$2,430,000
Sales returns and allowances	50,000
Collections from customers	230,000
Accounts written off as worthless	32,000
Worthless accounts unexpectedly collected	4,000

In the past, the company had found that 1.5 percent of net sales would not be collected.

a. Give the summary general journal entries to record each of the five items just listed.
b. Give the general journal entry to record the Bad Debts expense for the year.
c. Open ledger accounts for the Accounts Receivable controlling account and Allowance for Uncollectible Accounts. Enter the beginning balances in these accounts, and post the appropriate parts of the transactions in (a) and (b) to these accounts.

P6-5 At the beginning of the current year, Erving Wholesale Store, a company that uses the accounts receivable aging method to estimate uncollectible accounts, had balances in its Accounts Receivable controlling account and Allowance for Uncollectible Accounts of $454,000 and $12,000, respectively. During the year, the company had sales on account of $3,944,000; sales returns and allowances of $74,000; worthless accounts written off of $49,000; and collections from customers of $3,570,000.

As part of the end-of-year (January 31) procedures, an aging analysis of accounts receivable is prepared. The analysis is partially complete. The totals carried over to the top of page 3 of the analysis appear next.

CUSTOMER ACCOUNT	TOTAL	NOT YET DUE	1–30 DAYS PAST DUE	31–60 DAYS PAST DUE	61–90 DAYS PAST DUE	OVER 90 DAYS PAST DUE
Balance forward	$664,700	$354,560	$144,600	$85,400	$46,400	$33,740

The following accounts remain to be classified in order to finish the analysis:

ACCOUNT	AMOUNT	DUE DATE
B. Alexander	$ 9,354	Jan. 15
R. Bright	1,832	Feb. 15 (next fiscal year)
T. Crown	6,414	Dec. 20
B. Douglas	294	Oct. 1
I. Exten	5,400	Jan. 4
T. Fould	7,834	Nov. 15
S. Groam	19,172	Mar. 1 (next fiscal year)
	$50,300	

From past experience, the company has found that the following rates of estimated uncollectible accounts produce an adequate balance for the Allowance for Uncollectible Accounts:

TIME PAST DUE	PERCENTAGE CONSIDERED UNCOLLECTIBLE
Not yet due	2%
1–30 days	5
31–60 days	15
61–90 days	25
Over 90 days	50

REQUIRED:

1. Complete the aging analysis of accounts receivable.
2. Compute the end-of-year balance (before adjustments) for the Accounts Receivable controlling account and the Allowance for Uncollectible Accounts.
3. Prepare an analysis computing the estimated uncollectible accounts.
4. Prepare a general journal entry to record the estimated uncollectible accounts expense for the year. (Round adjustment to the nearest dollar.)

P6-6 The balance sheet prepared by Tracy Webb at December 31 last year included $1,008,000 in accounts receivable and an allowance for doubtful accounts of $52,800. During January of the current year selected transactions are summarized as follows:

(a)	Sales on account	$736,000
(b)	Sales returns and allowances	14,720
(c)	Cash payments by customers (no cash discounts)	729,600
(d)	Accounts receivable from Bart Company written off as worthless	18,560

After a careful aging and analysis of all customers' accounts at January 31, it was decided that the allowance for doubtful accounts should be adjusted to a balance of $58,560 in order to reflect accounts receivable at net realizable value in the January 31 balance sheet.

INSTRUCTIONS:

a. Give the appropriate entry in general journal form for each of the four items just listed, and the adjusting entry at January 31 to provide for uncollectible accounts.
b. Show the amounts of accounts receivable and the allowance for doubtful accounts as they would appear in a partial balance sheet at January 31.
c. Assume that three months after the receivable from Bart Company had been written off as worthless, Bart Company won a large award in the settlement of patent litigation and immediately paid the $18,560 debt to Tracy Webb. Give the journal entry or entries (in general journal form) to reflect this recovery of a receivable previously written off.

P6-7 Fulton Company, owned by Jane Fulton, has for the past several years been engaged in selling to retail stores. Sales are made on credit and the company has regularly estimated its uncollectible accounts expense as a percentage of net sales. The percentage used has been one-half of 1 percent of net sales. However, it appears that this provision has been inadequate, because the Allowance for Doubtful Accounts has a debit balance of $5387.80 at May 31 prior to making the annual provision. Fulton therefore decided to change the method of estimating uncollectible accounts expense and to rely upon an analysis of the age and character of the accounts receivable at the end of each accounting period.

At May 31, the end of the company's fiscal year, the accounts receivable totaled $357,632. This total amount included past-due accounts in the amount of $73,964. None of these past-due accounts was considered hopeless; all accounts regarded as worthless had been written off as rapidly as they were determined to be uncollectible. These write-offs had totaled $10,226 during the year. After careful investigation of the past-due accounts at May 31, Jane Fulton decided that the probable loss contained therein was 10 percent, and that in addition she should anticipate a loss of 1 percent of the current accounts receivable.

INSTRUCTIONS:

a. Compute the probable loss contained in the accounts receivable at May 31, based on the analysis by the owner.

b. Prepare the journal entry necessary to carry out the change in company policy with respect to providing for uncollectible accounts expense.

P6-8 The Abel Corporation shows the following account balances at the end of its fiscal year on August 31, 19X1:

Accounts Receivable	$10,000	Dr.
Allowance for Uncollectibles	500	Cr.

During the fiscal year ending August 31, 19X2, the following events took place:

a. Cash sales, $55,000
b. Credit sales, $45,000
c. Accounts determined to be uncollectible and written off in the fiscal year, $450
d. Total of all collections on account for the year, $42,000
e. Recoveries on accounts written off this year and in previous years, $200

REQUIRED:

1. Set up T-accounts for Accounts Receivable and Allowance for Uncollectibles and enter the beginning balances for the fiscal year and the events that took place in 19X1 and 19X2.

2. Prepare a journal entry to reflect the bad debt adjustment for the end of the fiscal year assuming that aging analysis indicates that 5 percent of the accounts are uncollectible.
3. Prepare a journal entry to reflect the bad debt adjustment assuming instead that statistical studies indicate that 1 percent of credit sales normally prove to be uncollectible.

P6-9 Beto Company is in the construction business. They entered into a long-term contract during 19X1 which calls for a contract price of $24,000,000 and original anticipated costs of $18,500,000. At the end of each of the three years of the contract the following cumulative actual costs and estimated costs to complete were determined:

END OF:	CUMULATIVE ACTUAL COSTS	ESTIMATED COSTS TO COMPLETE
19X1	$ 3,000,000	$15,000,000
19X2	15,000,000	5,000,000
19X3	20,500,000	-0-

REQUIRED:

1. Determine the revenue to be recognized by Beto Company under both the percentage-of-completion method and the completed-contract method for each of the three years of the contract.
2. Assume that at the end of 19X1 the estimated costs to complete were $25,000,000. What should be done at the end of that year (ignoring 19X2 and 19X3) under both the percentage-of-completion method and the completed-contract method.

P6-10 The following selected transactions occurred in Moe Company during 19X1.

Jan. 30	Accepted a $10,000, 18%, 6-month note from Bles, Inc., in payment of an open account receivable.
Mar. 1	Loaned a supplier, Bleek, Inc., $5,000 for 9 months at an annual interest rate of 10%.
July 1	Discounted both notes at the Hill Country National Bank. The bank charges a discount rate of 12%.
Aug. 1	Notified by the bank that Bles, Inc., defaulted on the note. A check was written for the amount due to the bank.
Sept. 15	Received one-half of the amount due from Bles, Inc., and wrote the remainder off as uncollectible.
Dec. 1	Notified by the bank that Bleek, Inc., paid the amount due on the note on the due date.
Dec. 15	Unexpectedly received a check for $500 from Bles, Inc., in partial payment of the account written off on September 15.

REQUIRED:

Record each of these transactions in general journal form on the books of the Moe Company.

INVENTORY AND COST OF SALES

7

ORIENTATION

The primary objectives of the first part of this chapter are to describe and assess two basic methods of accounting for and controlling merchandise on hand and sold, and certain methods for estimating merchandise inventory and cost of merchandise sold. We begin the chapter with a comment on the general nature of costs and expenses, and then go on to discuss the perpetual inventory and the periodic inventory systems, the merchandise activity accounts, and some techniques of inventory estimation. The primary objective of the second part of this chapter is to examine various alternative cost-assignment methods for inventory items, and certain accounting problems relating to the accrual and deferral of merchandise costs. The chapter includes a description and illustration of three widely used cost-assignment methods for merchandise, and an analysis of the differences in inventory valuation and cost of sales resulting from them.

Where different lots of merchandise are acquired over a period of time at different costs, it is important to allocate such varying costs to cost of goods sold and to inventory in an orderly and meaningful pattern. In some cases, specific costs can be associated with specific units. If such specific identification of costs is not feasible (or desirable), some other pattern of cost assignment must be employed.

MERCHANDISE COSTS

Cost of Goods Sold

The goods which a firm holds for sale to customers in the normal course of business are referred to as merchandise. The amount of such goods on hand at any time is referred to as *merchandise inventory* or simply inventory, while the amount of such goods sold during the period is referred to as *cost of sales* or *cost of goods sold.*

This division of merchandise held for resale between the amount sold and the amount still on hand can be illustrated as follows. Assume during an accounting period COGS, Inc., had a beginning merchandise inventory of \$180,000; during 19X1 the company purchased additional merchandise totaling \$210,000, and had an ending inventory of \$150,000. The calculation of the cost of goods sold would be as follows:

Beginning inventory	\$180,000
Add: Purchases for the period	210,000
Goods available for sale	390,000
Less: Ending inventory	150,000
Cost of goods sold	**\$240,000**

It is obvious that with a beginning inventory of \$180,000 and purchases of \$210,000, COGS, Inc., had merchandise totaling \$390,000 available for sale. In other words, if they would have sold all of their beginning inventory plus the purchases during 19X1, it would have totaled \$390,000 (hence the name, Goods Available for Sale). However, COGS, Inc., did not sell it all; they still had \$150,000 on hand as of the end of the year. So by subtracting the ending inventory (\$150,000) from the goods available for sale (\$390,000) we arrive at the cost of goods sold for COGS, Inc., for the period (\$240,000). This method of determining cost of goods sold is known as the periodic method because inventory is counted periodically and the computation just illustrated is made. This periodic method and the perpetual method of keeping track of inventory amounts are both discussed and illustrated in more detail later in this chapter.

The division of the merchandise costs between the amounts that were sold and the amounts that are still on hand in inventory is extremely important. Generally, the largest single expense factor by far for firms selling products (rather than services) is the cost of goods sold.

Gross Profit

The figure for cost of goods sold is generally set off from other expenses and deducted from sales to arrive at *gross profit or gross margin.* To illustrate, assume that during 19X1, the company from our previous example, COGS,

Inc., had sales revenue of $500,000, and total expenses (except cost of goods sold) of $175,000. The income statement for COGS, Inc., for 19X1 would appear as follows:

COGS, Inc.
Income Statement
for the year ended December 31, 19X1

Sales		$500,000
Cost of goods sold:		
Beginning inventory (1/1/X1)	$180,000	
Add: Purchases	210,000	
Goods available for sale	390,000	
Less: Ending inventory (12/21/X1)	150,000	
Cost of goods sold		240,000
Gross profit		260,000
Total other expenses (*summarized*)		175,000
Net income		**$ 85,000**

The inventory of merchandise at the end of a period is an important asset crucial to the success of the firm. While the importance of the division of the merchandise cost between the expense portion and the asset portion is obvious, this division is a difficult task for most firms. Many firms deal in hundreds or even thousands of different kinds of merchandise items which are continually being purchased and sold. For such firms, the clerical cost of tracing the costs of *individual* items purchased to their ultimate sale to customers would be extremely high.

The Importance of Accurate Inventory Valuation

Inventory is generally the largest of the current assets held by a firm. Because of its relative size, a valuation error in inventory may cause a substantial misrepresentation of the financial statements.

An error in inventory will result in other mistakes in the balance sheet, such as the total current assets, total assets, owners' equity, and the total of liabilities and owners' equity. However, unlike many other accounts, an error in inventory will also affect key figures in the income statement of the firm such as cost of goods sold, gross profit, and net income. It is important to note that the ending inventory for one year is also the beginning inventory of the following year. Therefore, the income statement of the second year will also be affected to the full extent of the inventory error made in year one.

Illustration of the Effect on the Income Statement of Error in Inventory Valuation

The effect of an inventory error on the balance sheet is obvious—the inventory will be misstated by the amount of the error. The following is an illustration of the effect on the income statement of such an error.

Assume that on December 31, 19X1, the correct inventory for the Beach Company is $50,000; however because of a clerical error the amount recorded on the income statement is $40,000. The effects of the error for the two-year period (19X1 and 19X2) are presented next:

Beach Company
Income Statement
for the year ended December 31, 19X1

		CORRECT AMOUNTS		WITH INCORRECT ENDING INVENTORY
Sales		$200,000		$200,000
Cost of goods sold:				
Beginning inventory	$ 60,000		$ 60,000	
Purchases	110,000		110,000	
Goods available for sale	$170,000		$170,000	
Ending inventory	50,000		40,000	
Cost of goods sold		120,000		130,000
Gross profit		80,000		70,000
Other expenses (total)		55,000		55,000
Net income		**$ 25,000**		**$ 15,000**

Error of $10,000 equal to inventory error

Beach Company
Income Statement
for the year ended December 31, 19X2

		CORRECT AMOUNTS		WITH INCORRECT BEGINNING INVENTORY
Sales		$220,000		$220,000
Cost of goods sold:				
Beginning inventory	$ 50,000		$ 40,000	
Purchases	125,000		125,000	
Goods available for sale	175,000		165,000	
Ending inventory	70,000		70,000	
Cost of goods sold		105,000		95,000
Gross profit		115,000		125,000
Other expenses (total)		75,000		75,000
Net income		$ 40,000		$ 50,000

Error of $10,000 equal to inventory error in previous year

This illustration shows that an understatement of ending inventory in one year will result in an equal understatement of net income for that year. In the second year the resulting understatement of beginning inventory will result in an overstatement of net income in that year. This counterbalancing effect of an inventory error will result in a correct total net income for the two-year period. Obviously an overstatement of ending inventory in the first year will result in exactly the opposite effect. The effect of inventory errors on net income may be summarized as follows:

- When *ending* inventory is *understated,* net income for the period will be *understated.*
- When *ending* inventory is *overstated,* net income for the period will be *overstated.*
- When *beginning* inventory is *understated,* net income for the period will be *overstated.*
- When *beginning* inventory is *overstated,* net income for the period will be *understated.*

ITEMS OF INVENTORY COST

All goods (regardless of location) to which the company has title and are held for resale in the normal course of business should be included in inventory. Goods in inventory are always initially recorded at cost in accordance with the *cost principle.* This would include the invoice price of merchandise, as well as other applicable expenditures incurred to bring an inventory article to its existing location and condition, such as freight and insurance.

Goods in Transit

Occasionally when an inventory is being taken, goods will be in transit, or on their way to the company. If the seller makes delivery in its own vehicle, the merchandise often remains its property while in transit. However if the merchandise is shipped by public carrier, the question of ownership while in transit is dependent upon whether the carrier is acting as an agent for the buyer or the seller. If the terms of the shipment are *F.O.B.* (free on board) *shipping point,* this indicates that title to the goods passes to the buyer at the point of shipment, and the goods are the property of the buyer while in transit. If the shipment terms are *F.O.B. destination,* title to the good transfers when the merchandise reaches its destination; therefore the goods are the property of the seller while en route.

Freight-in

When goods are purchased F.O.B. shipping point, the transportation costs paid by the purchaser should be added to the cost of the merchandise acquired. This is often accomplished by debiting the cost of transportation to a separate account called *Freight-in* or *Transportation-in*. The amount in this account is then added to Purchases for a period in arriving at Goods Available for Sale in the income statement.

Purchase Discounts

The subject of cash discounts from the viewpoint of the seller (sales discounts) was discussed in the previous chapter. These same discounts from the viewpoint of the purchaser are referred to as *purchase discounts,* and provide the opportunity for a savings of 1 percent to 2 percent of the invoiced amount by making payment within a specified period (usually 10 days). If payment is not made within the discount period, then the gross purchase amount is due by some specified future time (usually 30 days from the invoice date).

To illustrate, assume that X Company purchased goods that had an invoice price of $5,000 from a supplier, terms 2/10,n/30 on March 3, 19X1. X Company generally takes the discounts, and will therefore pay $4,900 [$5,000 less (.02 × $5,000)] for the goods. Therefore the purchase should be recorded by X Company as follows:

Mar. 3, 19X1 (Date of purchase):		
Purchases (or merchandise inventory)	$4,900	
Accounts payable		$4,900
To record acquisition of merchandise		
Mar. 12, 19X1 (date of payment):		
Accounts payable	4,900	
Cash		4,900
To record payment on account		

If for some reason X Company did not pay within the 10-day discount period, the discount of $100 would be lost, and the journal entry to record the payment must reflect that fact. The journal entry then would be:

Apr. 1	Accounts payable	$4,900	
	Discounts lost (an expense)	100	
	Cash		$5,000
	To record payment on account after discount period		

Most customers try to take advantage of a 2/10,n/30 sales discount because not doing so is to borrow money at a rate of 2% for 20 days, which results in an extremely high *annual* rate of interest. To illustrate this fact, assume that Purchaser Company purchases $1,000 worth of product from Seller Company on November 1, 19X1, under 2/10,n/30 terms. The pertinent dates in the transaction are depicted here:

NOVEMBER 1	NOVEMBER 10	NOVEMBER 30
Date of sale $1,000	Date payment is due if discount is taken. Amount due $980.	Date payment due if discount is *not* taken. Amount due $1,000.

20 DAYS

Period of time that purchaser borrowed the $20 difference in amount due on November 10 and amount due on November 30.

So a failure by Purchaser Company to take the 2% discount offered by Seller Company allows them to borrow money ($20) for 20 days at a rate of 2%. To calculate the annual interest rate that Purchaser is paying, we can divide 20 days into 365 to see how many such time periods there are in a year. By multiplying the number of time periods by 2% we get the approximate annual interest rate. This is done below:

$$\frac{365 \text{ days}}{20 \text{ days}} = 18.25 \times 2\% = \underline{\underline{36.5\%}}$$

So by its failure to take a 2/10,n/30 discount, Purchaser Company will be paying an exorbitant 36.5% effective annual rate of interest on the money.[1]

Purchase Returns and Allowances

Purchased merchandise may be returned to the seller if it is damaged or unsatisfactory in some other way. This situation from the viewpoint of the seller was discussed in the previous chapter. The purchaser will receive a cash refund or reduction in the liability if the amount is unpaid. To illustrate, assume that Company Y returned to Company Z, for credit, unsatisfactory goods costing $2,400. The return would be recorded by Company Y as follows:

Accounts payable	$2,400	
Purchase returns and allowances		$2,400

[1] The exact interest rate can be calculated as follows:

$$\$980 \times \frac{20}{365} \times i = \$20$$

$$\$53.70 \times i = \$20$$

$$i = \frac{\$20.00}{53.70} = \underline{\underline{37.2\%}}$$

Purchase Returns and Allowances would be deducted from the Purchases account in the income statement.

PERPETUAL INVENTORY SYSTEM

A perpetual inventory system is being used if the accounting entity utilizes procedures to maintain a continuous record of the cost and physical quantity of merchandise on hand. It is the perpetual method that has been employed for all merchandise accounting up to this point in this text. For each sale recorded under this system, the cost of the merchandise sold is debited to Cost of Goods Sold, and Merchandise Inventory is credited along with the regular debit to Accounts Receivable or Cash and credit to Sales. This immediate recognition of outflowing merchandise costs serves to maintain the perpetual inventory record as well as to accumulate the cost of goods sold for the period. A perpetual inventory system involves the following procedures:

1. As goods are received they are checked in by the receiving department of the firm. If they are satisfactory they are retained and the cost of the goods is debited to a control account, Merchandise Inventory (or simply Inventory) and credited to Accounts Payable. It is then necessary to enter the acquisition on a detailed ledger (subsidiary ledger) showing the quantity, cost per unit, and total cost of the goods acquired.
2. As the goods are sold, there will be debits to Cash or Accounts Receivable and credits to Sales. For each sale, reference must be made to the subsidiary ledger to ascertain the cost of the merchandise sold, and provision must be made for immediate or ultimate debits to Cost of Goods Sold and credits to the control account, Merchandise Inventory, as well as credits to the subsidiary merchandise accounts affected.
3. At convenient times, it is necessary to have the employees count the merchandise on hand and compare the count of the items with the amounts reflected in the subsidiary merchandise ledger as being on hand. Where the physical count shows that the ledger is incorrect, an entry is required to reflect the difference, and, where the error is great, inquiry must be made to determine the cause of the error. Such an inquiry may turn up evidence of carelessness in handling goods or evidence of theft.

PERIODIC INVENTORY SYSTEM

If a firm does not maintain perpetual inventory records, it can determine the cost and quantity of its merchandise inventory at any given time by a physical count of the items on hand, with the items being valued in terms of their cost to the firm. The difference between the cost of merchandise available for sale during the period (the sum of the beginning inventory of merchandise and purchases of merchandise during the period) and the cost of the unsold merchandise on hand at the end of the period, as shown by the physical inventory value, is taken to be the cost of the merchandise sold. This method was illustrated briefly earlier in the chapter.

Basically the periodic inventory system postpones the determination and recording of merchandise cost of sales until the end of the accounting period, and determines this cost by assuming that the amount of merchandise purchased that is not on hand is sold. The goods not on hand are certainly gone (if they were ever received) but it is not certain that they were sold. Undetected losses of merchandise may thus be charged to cost of goods sold. This lack of inventory control must be weighed against the fact that, in most cases, the periodic system saves clerical cost. Further, some rough tests are available to arrive at a judgment as to whether the firm is handling its goods carefully and is not subject to excessive pilferage losses. It is convenient and common to introduce an analysis of merchandise activities into the periodic system that also adds an element of cost control. Very often the periodic inventory system is designed to give extra information about merchandising problems and activities by breaking the merchandise account down into its important elements such as: purchases, returns, allowances, freight, and inventory.[2]

1. As goods are received they are checked in by the receiving department. If they are satisfactory, Purchases is debited and Accounts Payable is credited. No further entries are required in subsidiary or other records. As freight on the goods purchased is incurred or paid, Freight-in is debited. If goods are returned to the vendors because they are deficient in some manner, Accounts Payable is debited and Purchase Returns is credited.
2. At the point of the sale, Cash or Accounts Payable is debited and Sales is credited. No entry is made to reflect Cost of Goods Sold at the point of the sale nor to determine the balance of goods on hand after the sale.
3. At the end of the period, whether convenient or not, the goods on hand must be counted and valued to establish the ending inventory balance. At this time the difference between the cost of the goods available for sale and the cost of ending inventory is debited to Cost of Goods Sold. This expense is recorded in a journal entry which also closes the beginning balance and the balances of the various merchandise activity accounts while recording the correct ending inventory balance as an asset account.

Table 7-1 shows how the two inventory systems handle the various types of merchandise transactions and how the bookkeeping steps vary under the two systems.

---

[2] It is possible to provide data with respect to the various merchandise activities even if a perpetual inventory system is in use. If a perpetual inventory is maintained by a computerized accounting system, there should be no great problem in having the computer produce such data as purchases, discounts, freight, returns, and so on. The data that results from the breakdown of merchandise costs may be crucial to good merchandise management. For example, when goods are acquired from a supplier who manufactures shoddy merchandise which must be returned as unsalable, such returns may involve extra handling cost and "out of stock" conditions which reduce sales, or may make it necessary for a firm to carry extra reserve at a considerable extra warehousing cost. Many merchants like to watch returns, freight costs, and allowances very carefully. Most of this data, however, has very little meaning for the outside investor.

The income statement, through Gross Profit under the perpetual and periodic inventory systems would appear as follows:

PERPETUAL

Sales		$14,800
Less: Sales returns and allowances		550
Net sales		$14,250
Cost of goods sold	$6,970	
Add: Inventory shortage	220	7,190
Gross profit		$ 7,060

PERIODIC

Sales			$14,800
Less: Sales returns and allowances			550
Net sales			$14,250
Cost of goods sold:			
Beginning inventory		$ 8,700	
Purchases	$15,000		
Add: Freight-in	200		
Subtract: Purchase returns and allowances	(500)	14,700	
Goods available for sale		$23,400	
Less: Ending inventory		16,210	
Cost of goods sold			7,190
Gross profit			$ 7,060

Of course, in each case, expenses would be subtracted from Gross Profit to arrive at Net Income.

Other costs associated with merchandise acquisition should be mentioned. Occasionally merchants incur costs in order to package items acquired in bulk form, to refurbish used items purchased or accepted as trade-ins, or to mix two or more materials together. It is clear that precise accounting should provide for treating all the costs of getting an item of merchandise into a position and condition ready for sale as the costs of that item. If the item is on hand at the end of a period, its total cost should be carried as an inventory value; if the item has been sold, the total cost of the item should be treated as the cost of goods sold. Under a perpetual inventory system, incurring costs to improve merchandise would involve debits to Merchandise Inventory. Such costs incurred in a periodic inventory system would be debited to Merchandise Repackaging or some similar account which, like Freight-in, is a component of total merchandise cost.

TRADE DISCOUNTS

When quoting prices to their customers, vendors often supply a price list or catalog which is used as a basis for a variety of prices to different types of customers. By offering discounts to dealers (referred to as trade discounts) from this basic price list, the vendors save the expense of preparing a different price list or catalog for each type of customer. Trade discounts usually are set according to the marketing category of the buyer. The retailer may be offered a 40 percent discount off the catalog price, a wholesaler may be offered an additional

TABLE 7-1
Comparison of Perpetual and Periodic Inventory System

TRANSACTION OR EVENT	PERPETUAL SYSTEM			PERIODIC SYSTEM		
Beginning inventory of $8,700	No entry necessary; the amount would be in the accounting records			No entry necessary; the amount would be in the accounting records		
Purchase of merchandise, $15,000	Merchandise inventory	15,000		Purchases	15,000	
	Accounts payable		15,000	Accounts payable		15,000
Paid invoice, billed previously, $8,000	Accounts payable	8,000		Accounts payable	8,000	
	Cash		8,000	Cash		8,000
Paid freight-in on F.O.B. shipping point purchase, $200	Merchandising inventory	200		Freight-in	200	
	Cash		200	Cash		200
Defective goods returned to vendor, $500	Accounts payable	500		Accounts payable	500	
	Merchandise inventory		500	Purchases returns and allowances		500
Goods are sold: Selling price, $14,800	Accounts receivable	14,800		Accounts receivable	14,800	
	Sales		14,800	Sales		14,800
Cost, $7,200	Cost of goods sold	7,200		No entry		
	Merchandise inventory		7,200			
Goods are returned by customers: Selling price, $550 Cost, $230	Sales returns and allowances	550		Sales returns and allowances	550	
	Accounts receivable		550	Accounts receivable		550
	Merchandise inventory	230		No entry		
	Cost of goods sold		230	Since cost of goods sold was not recognized at the point of the sale, it need not be corrected since goods are returned		
Inventory is counted; amount on hand, $16,210	Inventory shortage	220		The inventory count		
	Merchandise inventory		220	enables cost of goods sold to be determined		
	Calculation of $220 shortage:			The inventory shortage is not determinable under the simple periodic inventory system, although it may be estimated		

	Beginning inventory	$ 8,700				
	Additions to inventory:					
	Purchase	15,000				
	Freight-in	200				
	Sales returns	230				
	Total additions	15,430				
	Subtractions from inventory:					
	Purchase returns	500				
	Sale	7,200				
		(7,700)				
	Inventory balance per perpetual records	16,430				
	Inventory per actual count	16,210				
	Shortage	$ 220				
Closing entries	Retained earnings	7,190		Merchandise Inventory		
	Cost of goods sold		6,970	(Ending)	16,210	
	Inventory shortage		220	Purchase returns and allowances	500	
				Cost of goods sold	7,190	
				Purchases		15,000
				Freight-in		200
				Merchandise inventory (Beginning)		8,700
				Retained earnings	7,190	
				Cost of Goods Sold		7,190

20 percent off, and a manufacturer's agent may be offered another 2 percent off. Thus a suggested retail price in the catalog of $100 is $60 to the retailer, $48 to a wholesaler, and $47.04 to the agent. Thus trade discounts are adjustments to price quotations, and do not introduce any complications in accounting for purchases. The price quotation less the trade discount is the relevant amount from the point of view of the accountant.

COST FLOW ASSUMPTIONS

Accounting for merchandise is complicated when a firm pays different prices per unit for items of merchandise through the course of an accounting period. Where acquisition prices have varied materially during the accounting period, there are a variety of possible solutions to the problem of how to assign such costs to goods on hand and goods sold. It is not necessary to employ a pattern for cost assignment (cost flow) which corresponds to the physical flow of the goods themselves, although the latter is sometimes feasible. Following is a list of the most common cost-assignment methods.

1. *Specific Identification Method:* The cost of each item may be specifically identified. The cost of goods sold for a period, and the cost of the merchandise inventory on hand at the end of the period, is determined by *specific identification* of the goods and their cost.
2. *Weighted Average Cost Method:* The weighted average of the costs of all units available during the period is determined. This *weighted average cost* is assigned to each unit sold and on hand to determine cost of goods sold and ending merchandise inventory, respectively.
3. *FIFO Method:* Costs may be assigned to merchandise items sold according to the same sequence in which they were incurred in the acquisition of the merchandise. This involves the assumption that the first units acquired during the period were the first units to be sold. For this reason, this approach is called "first-in, first-out," or *FIFO.* The merchandise on hand at the end of the period is costed at the most recent costs incurred.
4. *LIFO Method:* Costs may be assigned to merchandise items sold in the *reverse* of the sequence in which the costs were incurred in acquiring the merchandise. This involves the assumption that the last units acquired during the period were the first units to be sold. For this reason, this approach is called "last-in, first-out," or *LIFO.* The merchandise on hand at the end of the period is assigned the oldest costs of merchandise acquired.

All of these approaches—specific identification, weighted average, FIFO, and LIFO—are employed in practice and are acceptable accounting methods. All involve *actual* (historical) costs to the firm of acquiring merchandise. Alternatives to the use of historical cost for the valuation of merchandise have been proposed, but none have yet won acceptance for general accounting purposes.[3]

[3] Within certain constraints, it is acceptable to value inventories at their current cost if that cost is *less* than historical cost.

The illustrations that follow demonstrate the different effects of each of the valuation methods described so far.

Effects of Alternative Cost-Assignment Methods

On January 1, 19X1, X Corporation had on hand 1,000 units of ruvels. During the year 19X1, two purchases were made:

Balance Jan. 1, 19X1	1,000 units at 50¢ per unit	$ 500
Purchases: Apr. 14	400 units at 55¢ per unit	220
Aug. 26	800 units at 60¢ per unit	480
Totals	2,200	$1,200

Sales for the year total 1,800 units, leaving 400 units on hand at the end of the year. The sales price per unit remained at 80 cents through the whole year.

Specific Identification Method

Let us assume that each ruvel was labeled with its own specific cost and that the costs of the ruvels that were sold were:

950 ruvels had cost 50¢ each	$475		
380 ruvels had cost 55¢ each	209	Available at cost	$1,200
470 ruvels had cost 60¢ each	282	Cost of goods sold	966
1,800 total	$966	Inventory at end	$ 234

The general ledger of the X Corporation would show the following:

Merchandise inventory		Cost of goods sold	
Total Drs. 1,200	Total Crs. 966	Total Drs. 966	
Balance 234			

It may appear that *specifically identified cost* of the items sold and the items on hand is the ideal that other methods should approximate. This conclusion is not necessarily true. Even if the approach is viewed as ideal, there are problems of implementation, since it is not always practical to keep track of the specific costs of individual units of goods carried by a merchant. For example, when a gasoline service station makes various purchases of gasoline during the year, each new purchase is simply poured in with whatever was left over from the previous purchases. One cannot know which particular gallons of gasoline are being pumped out and which remain in the tank. If specific costs cannot be determined for the merchandise items, then some method of approximating cost per item must be devised.

Weighted Average Cost Method

Average cost is the most obvious cost approximation method. The weighted average cost method is based on the assumption that the units are uniformly mixed and that customers are issued average units. Using the same original data for ruvels as before, and assuming that a periodic inventory system is in use, we may derive merchandise cost under the average cost assumption:

$$\frac{\$1{,}200 \text{ total cost}}{2{,}200 \text{ ruvels available to sell}} = \$0.5455 \text{ per unit (per ruvel) average cost (Note that this is referred to as a } \textit{weighted average}\text{).}$$

When we use the weighted average unit cost, we obtain:

Cost of goods sold	= 0.5455 × 1,800 units =	$ 982
Merchandise inventory	= 0.5455 × 400 units =	218
Totals	0.5455 × 2,200 units =	$1,200

The accounts of the X Corporation would show the following amounts:

Merchandise inventory

Dr.		Cr.	
Total Drs.	1,200	Total Crs.	982
Bal.	218		

Cost of goods sold

Dr.		Cr.
Total Drs.	982	

Notice the difference between these accounts and those shown in the illustration for the specific identification method.

The First-in, First-out Method (FIFO)

We may illustrate the FIFO inventory method using the same data for the X Corporation as before. The FIFO method assumes that goods are sold by the firm in the same order as they were acquired. This is a reasonable assumption, since merchants usually do attempt to sell the oldest goods first to avoid deterioration and obsolescence.

The 1,800 units sold during the year are assumed to:

First, use up the beginning inventory of 1,000 units at 50¢ per unit	$500
Second, use up the first purchase of 400 units at 55¢ per unit	220
Third, use up 400 units of the second purchase at 60¢ per unit	240
Total cost of goods sold (1,800 units)	$960
Remaining in inventory are the 400 units of the second purchase at 60¢	$240

The general ledger of the X Corporation would show the following:

Merchandise inventory

Dr.		Cr.	
Total Drs.	1,200	Total Crs.	960
Bal.	240		

Cost of goods sold

Dr.		Cr.
Total Drs.	960	

The Last-in, First-out Method (LIFO)

The LIFO method appears to suggest that the last goods received are sold first, which is, in terms of the physical flow of merchandise, a very poor merchandising procedure. The explanation is that the term *last-in, first-out* does not in fact refer to the actual physical movement of goods but refers to the matching of the most recent costs of merchandise with the amounts that customers are paying for merchandise. This method may be illustrated by use of the X Corporation data:

First, use up the second purchase of 800 units at 60¢ per unit	$ 480
Second, use up the first purchase of 400 units at 55¢ per unit	220
Third, use up 600 units of the beginning balance at 50¢ per unit	300
Total cost of goods sold (1,800 units)	$1,000
Remaining in inventory are 400 units from the beginning inventory at 50¢ per unit	$ 200

The general ledger of the X Corporation would show the following:

Merchandise inventory				Cost of goods sold		
Total Drs.	1,200	Total Crs.	1,000	Total Drs.	1,000	
Balance	200					

Summary of Cost-Assignment Methods

The comparison of the effects of using the different cost assignment methods indicates that the cost-assignment method employed results in different amounts of the total cost of goods available for sale ($1,200) being assigned to cost of sales and to ending inventory.

METHOD	COST OF SALES	MERCHANDISE INVENTORY
Specific identification	$ 966	$234
Average cost	982	218
First-in, first-out (FIFO)	960	240
Last-in, first-out (LIFO)	1,000	200

FIFO and LIFO Contrasted

The first-in, first-out and last-in, first-out inventory cost-assignment methods warrant further elaboration. Under the LIFO method, the most recent costs of merchandise are used to arrive at cost of goods sold as sales occur. This results in a higher cost of goods sold when prices are rising (and a lower net income) as compared to the FIFO or the weighted average methods. At the same time, since older (lower) costs are assigned to goods in the ending merchandise inventory under LIFO, the inventory valuation is less as compared to FIFO or weighted average. The use of LIFO over a number of periods of rising prices thus results in a small dollar amount of assets (merchandise assets) and a smaller dollar amount of retained earnings on the balance sheet as compared to the other methods.

A highly simplified example may be helpful in illustrating these points. Suppose a merchant has only two identical items in his inventory, Unit A and Unit B. Unit A, which was acquired first, cost $5. Unit B cost $10. The merchant then sells one of the units for $15. What is his gross margin? What is the "cost" of the remaining unit? If LIFO costing is employed:

Gross margin =	Selling price −	Cost of goods sold
$5	$15	$10

Cost assigned to remaining unit, $5.

If FIFO costing is employed:

Gross margin =	Selling price −	Cost of goods sold
$10	$15	$5

Cost assigned to remaining unit, $10.

Net income and ending merchandise inventory are thus $5 less if LIFO is employed instead of FIFO.

Even if the merchant uses LIFO, he is likely to sell his oldest units first. If Unit A (the oldest) is indeed sold, it is assigned the cost of the more expensive Unit B (the newest) and Unit B (still on hand) is assigned the cost of Unit A. What has happened is that a $5 increase in the cost value of the inventory item has been intentionally added to the cost of goods sold and deducted from the merchandise inventory valuation; this is the effect of the use of LIFO. LIFO results in the assignment of old costs to new merchandise on hand and new costs to old merchandise.

Can the reduction of gross margin (and thus net income), which is the effect of LIFO when used during a period of rising prices, be defended? We should remember that one of the primary reasons for the measurement of net earnings is for the purpose of evaluating current business success as a basis for predicting *future* business success. Two observations can be made:

1. If the overall price level has increased in approximately the same proportion as the cost of the merchandise has increased over the period that it was held, the merchant has gained no purchasing power as a result of the increased cost of the item; and
2. The merchant must *replace* the units on which the cost increases have occurred at the new higher price. In effect, this part of his gross margin on the sale must be used up in the acquisition of new merchandise if he is to continue in business.

Figure 7-1 illustrates these points.

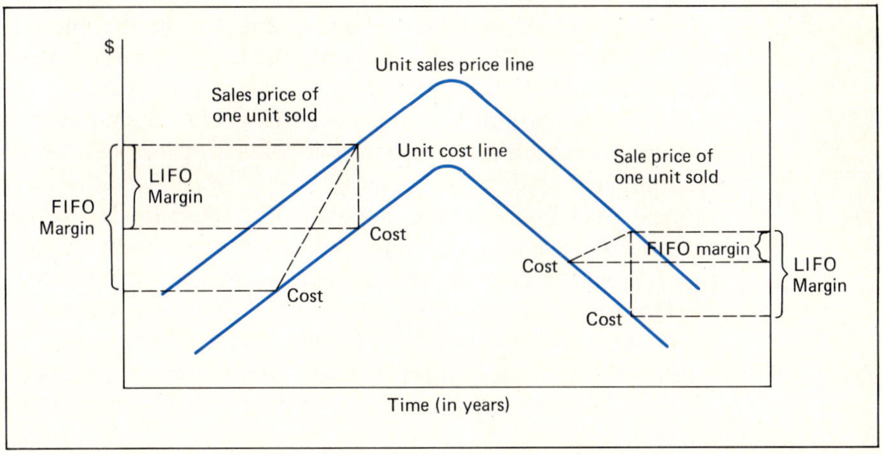

FIGURE 7-1
Cost and Revenue Matching Using FIFO and LIFO under Rising and Falling Prices. Note: *It would be rare in practice to find as precise an accord between sales prices and cost price as is assumed in the diagram. Nevertheless, the relationships illustrated are valid tendencies over periods of rising and falling prices.*

LIFO and Taxes

As we have seen, LIFO has the effect of bringing the most recent purchases to the income statement. Therefore, in an inflationary period this results in a lower reported net income. For this reason, LIFO has been popular for income tax reporting purposes. If LIFO is used for tax purposes, the Internal Revenue Service has traditionally required that it also be used for financial reporting purposes.

In January 1981, the Treasury Department issued amended regulations concerning financial reporting by companies that use LIFO. The amended regulations substantially relax the previous LIFO conformity requirements. Under the prior regulations, a company using LIFO for tax purposes was prohibited from even making reference to income or loss determined in a manner other than LIFO. The amended regulations permit companies to compute LIFO in a somewhat different manner for financial statement and income tax purposes without violating the conformity rule. In addition, companies may disclose (normally in footnotes to the financial statements) supplementary information, such as net income and cost of sales, computed using an inventory method other than LIFO.

Evaluation of Alternative Methods

The choice of the inventory costing method adopted by a particular firm will depend upon several factors:

1. For ease of calculation with reasonable accuracy one would use average cost. Average costs generally fall between FIFO and LIFO costs, since all costs related to a period are employed in the calculation of ending inventory cost.

2. The effect upon the amount of income tax payments might lead one to use LIFO because it reports a larger merchandise cost of sales deduction than any other method during periods of rising prices. Falling prices would have the opposite effect, but experience indicates that prices tend to change primarily in the *upward* direction in modern, industrialized economies.

3. Consideration of balance sheet portrayal of inventory values leads to FIFO inventory valuation as opposed to LIFO inventory valuation, since the end-of-period values under FIFO relate to the latest goods purchased and therefore approximate current values. Under LIFO inventory valuation, the ending inventory is made up of the oldest goods available (by assumption, not by fact) which would mean that the beginning inventory is assumed to remain on hand period after period. In light of this pattern, one can see that the ending inventory value of the current year may include inventory costs from the first year that the firm started using LIFO.

4. LIFO is considered by some accountants to be a superior method for income determination because it approximates a matching of *current costs* with *current revenue.* While this is generally the LIFO result, a problem is created when unit sales for a period exceed the units of merchandise purchased in that period (the number of units in inventory decreases over the period). In this case, very old costs may be matched with current revenues, resulting in an overstated net earnings figure.

LOWER OF COST OR MARKET (LCM)

The term *market* is generally defined as the *replacement cost* of an item; either the cost of reproducing it (if the entity manufactures the item), or the cost of purchasing it from the usual suppliers in the usual quantities (if the entity purchases the item for resale or for use in manufacturing a product). For many years it has been the common practice of accountants to reduce the value of ending inventory below cost to market where the latter is less than cost. This practice of reducing the inventory to the *lower of cost or market* is justified on the grounds that it results in a conservative estimate of inventory value. It is argued that balance sheet items should be valued at no more than their current cost.

Another argument for the application of the lower-of-cost-or-market rule relates to the matching principle. Proper matching requires that losses due to spoilage and obsolescence be charged against revenues of the period in which such losses occur. Less obviously, proper matching also requires the recognition of a loss where the replacement cost of the goods has simply declined. There are cases in which it appears reasonable to carry the original cost of the item into the next period to be treated as a cost of goods sold when the item is sold in that period. Such cases relate to the fact that inventory items should not be valued at an amount which exceeds that which the firm will be able to realize from its sale to customers. Nor should inventory items be valued at such a low amount that an abnormally large profit will be recognized when an item is sold. In practice, these considerations are taken into account in the use of LCM, but such technical modifications need not be treated here.

Illustration of Lower of Cost or Market

The A Corporation takes its inventory on December 31 and obtains additional information from its purchasing agents:

		PER UNIT		VALUES AT		
	Qty.	FIFO Cost	Replacement Cost	Cost	Market	Lower
On hand:						
Admixers	300	$ 5.00	$ 6.00	$ 1,500.00	$1,800.00	$1,500.00
Buchmakers	200	3.00	2.50	600.00	500.00	500.00
Cartuflin	400	4.25	3.50	1,700.00	1,400.00	1,400.00
Derklies	250	8.00	10.00	2,000.00	2,500.00	2,000.00
Etchers	600	10.00	6.00	6,000.00	3,600.00	3,600.00
				$11,800.00	$9,800.00	$9,000.00

With the inventory established on the books at cost, it becomes necessary to reduce this cost of $11,800 to $9,000 if LCM is being applied on an item basis, or to $9,800 if LCM is being applied at the lower of the two totals. The net effect of this adjustment is a reduction of inventory value by $2,800 or $2,000, and an increase of cost of goods sold by this same amount.

Where the lower of cost or market reduces the inventory value below cost, the earnings of the period are reduced because the lower inventory value produces a higher cost-of-goods-sold amount. This lower ending inventory value for the period of the write-down becomes the opening inventory of the following period, so that the cost of goods sold of this second period is lower than it would have been if cost had been maintained intact. Procedurally, there is a shift of earnings between periods as a result of the use of LCM. The effect of the lower-of-cost-or-market rule is to hasten the recognition of losses on inventory items that have undergone price decreases since their acquisition.

The lower-of-cost-or-market approach to inventory valuation recognizes losses which are not realized in sales to customers, but does not recognize gains which are not realized in sales to customers. Some accountants argue that unrealized inventory gains are as easily determined and as meaningful as losses. The theoretical justification for lower of cost or market is, at best, open to dispute. The conservative orientation of accounting that gave rise to the method is under increasing attack. It is argued, among other things, that conservatism in accounting measurement is unfair to those who are seeking to dispose of their investments in a firm and favors those who may be acquiring interests in the firm.

THE EFFECT OF INFLATION ON INVENTORIES

In 1979, the Financial Accounting Standards Board adopted Statement No. 33 "Financial Reporting and Changing Prices." This Statement requires large corporations to disclose information concerning the effect of price-level changes on certain income statement and balance sheet items. The information, which can be presented in footnotes to the traditional financial statements or in special supplementary statements, does not replace the historical cost data but rather supplements that traditional information. (FASB Statement No. 33 is covered in some detail in Chapter 15.)

One requirement of Statement No. 33 is that certain large corporations must now disclose what it would cost to replace their inventories at year-end, and what their cost of goods sold would have been had they used current replacement cost at the date of sale. To date, this disclosure requirement has revealed that the cost of goods sold computed on the basis of replacement cost often results in a much lower net income than historical cost financial statements reveal. This phenomenon, which is referred to as *inventory profits,* indicates that a large part of certain companies' net income is the result of inflation pushing up the value of inventories that they have held. Stated differently, net income tends to be overstated when companies rely solely on historical cost values during an inflationary period.

ESTIMATING ENDING INVENTORIES—THE GROSS PROFIT METHOD

When perpetual inventory records are maintained, the inventory on hand may be closely approximated at any time by reference to the perpetual inventory records. However, when these records are not maintained it may still be advantageous or necessary to be able to determine an inventory amount periodically without incurring the cost of taking a physical inventory count. If the rate of gross profit on sales is known, the ending inventory can be closely approximated by the *gross profit* method of estimating ending inventory.

The dollar amount of sales for a period can be divided into two components: (1) the gross profit and (2) the cost of merchandise sold. The cost-of-merchandise-sold component can be deducted from goods available for sale to derive an estimate of ending inventory.

To illustrate, assume that inventory on January 1, 19X1 was $60,000, net purchases during the month were $170,000, net sales for January were

$240,000, and gross profit is reasonably estimated at 40 percent of sales. The January 31 inventory can be estimated as shown here:

Sales (net)		$240,000
Cost of sales:		
Beginning inventory	$ 60,000	
Purchased (net)	170,000	
Goods available for sale	$230,000	
Ending inventory	?(3)	
Cost of goods sold		?(2)
Gross profit		?(1)

The first question mark to be filled in [? (1)] is gross profit. Although it cannot be calculated precisely, it is reasonably estimated at 40 percent of sales, so gross profit must be: $96,000 ($240,000 × 40%). This leads to the next computation —cost of goods sold, [? (2)]—which must be $144,000 or $240,000 − $96,000. (The $144,000 can be derived by multiplying $240,000 × 60% as well.) If the cost of goods sold is estimated at $144,000, then the ending inventory must be estimated at $86,000 ($230,000 − $144,000). So the ending inventory, [? (3)], has been reasonably estimated to be $86,000. These computations can be proven by the completion of the partial income statement as follows:

Sales		$240,000
Cost of sales:		
Beginning inventory	$ 60,000	
Purchases (net)	170,000	
Goods available for sale	$230,000	
Ending inventory (estimated)	86,000	
Cost of sales (estimated)		144,000
Gross profit (estimated)		$ 96,000

The gross profit method of estimating ending inventory may be used in several ways. Most frequently it is used in the preparation of monthly financial statements. By estimating the amount of ending inventory, the normally considerable cost of taking a physical inventory is avoided. The procedure may also be used after taking a physical inventory to confirm the overall reasonableness of the amount determined by the physical count and pricing process. Insurance companies also use the gross profit method to estimate the cost of inventory lost in a fire or other such disaster.

CONSIGNED MERCHANDISE

Occasionally certain types of products are marketed by using a device known as a consignment shipment. Under this arrangement, one party, *the consignor,* ships merchandise to another, *the consignee,* who is to act as an agent for the consignor in selling the goods. The consignee agrees to accept the goods without any liability, except to exercise due care and reasonable protection from loss or damage, until the goods are sold to a third party. When the goods are sold by the consignee, the sale price, less a selling commission and expenses incurred in accomplishing the sale, is remitted to the consignor.

Goods out on consignment remain the property of the consignor and must be included in the consignor's inventory at purchase price, plus the cost of handling and shipping involved in that transfer to the consignee. Occasionally, the inventory out on consignment is shown as a separate item, but unless the amount is large there is little need for this. No journal entry is made by the consignee for goods received because they are the property of the consignor. The consignee should be extremely careful not to include any of the goods consigned as a part of inventory.

SUMMARY

Comparison of merchandise cost of sales with sale price to determine the margin available for covering other operating costs and providing profit is more meaningful if the full cost of merchandise acquisitions is determined. This typically includes transportation and handling costs as well as the purchase price net of discounts. In many cases, particularly where the company handles numerous different types of items, it is too expensive to maintain the perpetual inventory system. Many companies determine cost of goods sold by counting and valuing the ending inventory, and deducting the amount of this ending inventory from the cost of goods available for sale to arrive at the cost of goods sold. This method is referred to as the periodic inventory system.

The periodic inventory system regularly supplies data about the merchandising activities which are not ordinarily supplied by the perpetual inventory system. But the simple periodic system will not indicate the amount of inventory shortages so important to merchants who experience losses from theft and careless handling of goods. The gross margin test is used under the periodic system to estimate inventory values, but provides only an approximation. The gross margin test is employed to check for material differences between the results of a physical inventory and the inventory balance as computed. It is also used to estimate the value of an inventory destroyed by fire or other disaster. Various costs should be consigned in the accounts whenever additional insight into business problems and relationships result. Thus merchandise costs should include all costs of getting the goods into position ready to sell. Accountants generally favor the tracing of specific costs of items of merchandise to inventory if the items are sold to customers. Where the tracing of specific costs to inventory or cost of goods sold is not possible or is inadvisable, some cost assumption must be made such as FIFO, LIFO, or average cost.

Merchandise purchase discounts are, logically, reductions of merchandise costs and freight costs are additions to merchandise costs. Trade discounts are given for convenience of price quotation to different classes of customers.

In practice, considerable variation in cost adjustments have resulted from using LIFO instead of FIFO. During rising prices, LIFO results in reporting lower profits and lower inventory values. The cost of goods sold under LIFO is realistically current, but the resulting inventory values are often greatly distorted. Where goods are shopworn, obsolete, or of a merchandise type on which prices have fallen, accountants have long recommended that goods be valued at the lower of cost or replacement cost (as modified by certain limits).

KEY POINTS

1. **Inventory (or merchandise inventory)** The goods which a firm holds for sale to customers in the normal course of business.

2. **Goods available for sale** Beginning inventory plus net purchases and freight-in.

3. **Cost of goods sold** Goods available for sale less ending inventory for a period.

4. **Gross profit** Net sales less Cost of Goods Sold

5. **Counterbalancing error** An error, such as an overstatement or understatement of ending inventory, which has the effect of causing net income to be misstated in one direction in the year of the error, and in the other direction in the following year.

6. **F.O.B. shipping point** Indicates that the title of the goods purchased passes to the buyer at the shipping point.

7. **F.O.B. destination** Indicates that the title to the goods purchased passes to the buyer when the merchandise reaches its destination.

8. **Perpetual inventory system** Provides a perpetual or continuous record of merchandise on hand.

9. **Weighted average cost method** A method of inventory valuation in which the weighted average unit cost is computed by dividing the total costs of goods available for sale by the total number of units available for sale.

10. **First-in, first-out (FIFO)** An inventory cost-flow method which assumes that the first units acquired during a period were the first units sold. The merchandise on hand at the end of the period is costed at the most recent cost incurred.

11. **Last-in, first-out (LIFO)** An inventory cost-flow method which assumes that the last units acquired during a period were the first units sold. The mer-

chandise on hand at the end of the period is assigned the oldest cost of merchandise acquired.

12. Lower-of-cost-or-market method A method of inventory pricing in which goods are valued at original cost or replacement cost (market), whichever is lower.

13. Gross profit method A method of estimating ending inventory in which gross profit, cost of goods sold, and ending inventory, are estimated using historical data.

QUESTIONS

1. Why does merchandise create particularly significant problems of control and cost determination?

2. What is merchandise inventory and what is the primary objective of inventory management?

3. If the merchandise inventory is mistakenly overstated at the end of 19X1, what is the effect on:

- **a.** 19X1 net income?
- **b.** 19X1 year-end balance sheet value?
- **c.** 19X2 net income?
- **d.** 19X2 year-end balance sheet value?

4. What is the difference between purchase discounts and purchase returns and allowances?

5. In measuring cost of goods sold and inventory, why is passage of title an important issue? When does title to goods usually pass? Explain.

6. Explain the application of the cost principle to the cost of an item in the ending inventory?

7. Compare and contrast the perpetual inventory system and the periodic inventory system. What are the main advantages and disadvantages of each?

8. Which type of system (perpetual or periodic) would each of the following companies find most practical?

- **a.** A retail drug store
- **b.** A grocery store
- **c.** A restaurant
- **d.** An automobile dealer
- **e.** A wholesale auto parts dealer

9. What differences occur in recording sales, purchases, and closing entries under the perpetual and periodic inventory system?

10. List the four alternative inventory valuation methods. How is each related to the actual flow of the merchandise in and out of the business firm?

11. Do FIFO and LIFO result in different quantities of ending inventory?

12. What are the significant factors involved in selection of an inventory valuation method?

13. What is meant by valuation of inventory at the lower of cost or market? When should net realizable value be used in costing an item in ending inventory? Does this approach lead to uniformly conservative results?

14. Explain the usefulness of the gross profit method of estimating inventories.

15. What is meant by consigned merchandise? Are goods on consignment the legal property of the consignee or consignor?

EXERCISES

E7-1 The condensed income statements prepared by Shorson Company for two years are shown here:

	19X2	19X1
Sales	$366,800	$336,000
Cost of goods sold	212,800	268,800
Gross profit on sales	$154,000	$ 67,200
Operating expenses	56,000	56,000
Net income	$ 98,000	$ 11,200

The inventory at the end of 19X1 was understated by $33,700 but the error was not discovered until after the accounts had been closed and financial statements prepared at the end of 19X2. The balance sheets for the two years showed owners' equity of $142,800 at the end of 19X1 and $173,600 at the end of 19X2. Compute the correct net income figures for 19X1 and 19X2 based on corrected data. What corrections, if any, should be made in owners' equity at the end of 19X1 and at the end of 19X2?

E7-2 Condensed income statements for Vandal Company for two years are as follows:

	19X2	19X1
Sales	$98,000	$84,000
Cost of goods sold	52,000	38,000
Gross profit on sales	$46,000	$46,000
Operating expenses	18,000	18,000
Net income	$28,000	$28,000

After the end of 19X2, it was discovered that an error had been made in 19X1 that resulted in an understatement of the ending inventory of 19X1 by $8,000.

Compute the corrected net income for 19X1 and 19X2. What effect will the error have on net income and owners' equity for 19X3?

E7-3 The Gallahad Corporation adjusts and closes its books each December 31. On December 31 of the current fiscal year, just prior to adjustment of the accounts, the ledger includes the following account balances (among others):

Merchandise inventory, January 1	$ 6,000
Purchases	32,000
Purchase returns	300
Freight-in	700

A physical inventory count shows $6,500 of merchandise on hand on December 31. Give the general journal entry to close the merchandise activity accounts and to record the ending inventory and Cost of Goods Sold on December 31.

E7-4 Three unrelated situations are given next. From the information provided, determine the three amounts which are missing. Note: Some of the data may not be necessary in preparing the solution.

	SITUATION 1	SITUATION 2	SITUATION 3
Beginning inventory	$ 10,000	$ 8,000	$3,000
Transportation-in	1,000	500	100
Delivery expense	none	none	150
Purchase returns	5,000	2,500	200
Purchase discounts	1,500	250	80
Purchases (gross)	?	40,000	2,000
Ending inventory	8,000	?	2,000
Sales	125,000	50,000	?
Gross margin	48,500	11,700	9,180

E7-5 The records at the end of January 19X1 for Ralph's Shop Smart for a particular kind of merchandise are shown here.

	UNITS	TOTAL COST
Inventory, Dec. 19X0	20	$200
Purchase, Jan. 9, 19X1	50	550
Sale, Jan. 11, 19X1 (at $20 per unit)	33	
Purchase, Jan. 20, 19X1	30	360
Sale, Jan. 27, 19X1 (at $21 per unit)	35	

REQUIRED:

Assuming a periodic inventory system, compute the amount of the ending inventory and the cost of goods sold at January 31, 19X1, under each of the following inventory costing methods. Show computations.

1. Specific identification (assume the sale on January 11 was "identified" with the purchase of January 9, the sale of January 27 was "identified" with the purchase of January 20, and any excess identified with the beginning inventory).
2. Weighted average cost.
3. First-in, first-out.
4. Last-in, first-out.

E7-6 Burton Company uses a perpetual inventory system. On January 1, the Inventory account had a balance of $175,000. During the first few days of January, the following transactions occurred:

Jan. 2 Purchased merchandise on credit from Bet Company for $25,000.

Jan. 3 Sold merchandise for cash, $18,000. The cost of this merchandise was $12,600.

a. Prepare entries in general journal form to record these transactions.

b. What was the balance of the Inventory account at the close of business on January 3?

E7-7 The beginning inventory balance of Item X on August 1 and the purchases of this item during August were as follows:

Aug. 1	Beginning inventory	900 units @ $1.00	$ 900
Aug. 7	Purchase	3,600 units @ $1.10	3,960
Aug. 14	Purchase	1,800 units @ $1.12	2,016
Aug. 22	Purchase	1,800 units @ $1.16	2,088
Aug. 28	Purchase	900 units @ $1.25	1,125
Totals		9,000 units	$10,089

At August 31, the ending inventory consisted of 1,350 units.

Determine the cost of the ending inventory, based on each of the following methods of inventory valuation:

a. Average cost. (Compute average cost per unit to the nearest tenth of a cent.)
b. First-in, first-out. (Round to the nearest dollar.)
c. Last-in, first-out.

E7-8 J.R.'s Gasarama had the following purchases and sales of oil during the year:

Jan. 1	Beginning inventory	100 cases @ $24 =	$ 2,400
Feb. 25	Purchased	50 cases @ $26 =	1,300
June 15	Purchased	200 cases @ $28 =	5,600
Aug. 15	Purchased	50 cases @ $26 =	1,300
Oct. 15	Purchased	150 cases @ $28 =	4,200
Dec. 15	Purchased	100 cases @ $30 =	3,000
Totals		650 cases	$17,800
Total sales		500 cases	
Dec. 31	Ending inventory	150 cases	

Assume that all of the June 15 purchase and 100 cases from each of the following were sold: the January 1 beginning inventory, the October 15 purchase, and the December 15 purchase.

Determine the costs that should be assigned to cost of goods sold and ending inventory under each of the following assumptions:

a. Costs are assigned by the specific identification method.
b. Costs are assigned on an average-cost basis.
c. Costs are assigned on a FIFO basis.
d. Costs are assigned on a LIFO basis.

What conclusions can you draw from your answers?

E7-9 The McNelly Corporation uses a periodic inventory, and purchases were as follows:

Balance on Jan. 1	600 units @ $2.40 per unit
Purchases:	
Jan. 23	100 units @ $2.50 per unit
Apr. 18	200 units @ $2.55 per unit
July 17	50 units @ $2.60 per unit
Dec. 5	50 units @ $2.60 per unit
Balance on Dec. 31	200 units @ ? per unit

Sales for the year totaled 800 units.

REQUIRED:

Calculate the ending inventory balance and the cost of sales under:

1. The FIFO inventory valuation method.
2. The LIFO inventory valuation method.
3. The weighted average inventory method.

E7-10 For the month of January, the records of the Hargrave Trading Company show the following data about Commodity A:

Balance on January 1	200 units @ $14.00
Purchases	
Jan. 6	75 units @ $15.50
Jan. 16	50 units @ $15.00
Jan. 25	100 units @ $15.50
Jan. 29	50 units @ $14.50

Sales during January totaled 375 units.

REQUIRED:

Calculate the ending inventory balance as of January 31 and the cost of goods sold for the month of January under FIFO, LIFO, and weighted average cost methods.

E7-11 Give entries in general journal form to record the following transactions of the Crachit Company. Use the "net" method of accounting for cash discounts as illustrated in this chapter. The firm uses the periodic inventory method.

a. Purchased merchandise on account for $80 on April 12, terms 1/10,n/30.
b. Purchased merchandise on account for $150 on April 16, terms 2/10,n/30.
c. Paid for the merchandise purchased on April 12 within the discount period.
d. Paid for the merchandise purchased on April 16 after the discount period.

E7-12 The Flory Company was organized and started operations on January 1, 19X1. On December 31, 19X1, the ending inventory of merchandise is determined to be:

$10,000 on the LIFO basis
$15,000 on the FIFO basis
$12,000 on the average cost basis

The accountant determined that net earnings would be $25,000 for 19X1 if he uses the FIFO basis. What would net earnings be if he used the LIFO basis? If he used the average cost basis?

E7-13 Abshire and Sons started operations on January 1, 19X1. The firm reported $10,000 net earnings per year for 19X1 and 19X2. The FIFO inventory basis is being used by the firm. The merchandise inventory at December 31, 19X1, was $20,000 and at December 31, 19X2 was $25,000, at FIFO.

What would net earnings have been if the firm had used LIFO inventory values? It is determined that LIFO inventory values were $16,000 at December 31, 19X1, and $16,000 at December 31, 19X2.

E7-14 Roost Company has compiled the following information concerning items in its inventory at December 31.

Determine the total inventory value to appear on Roost Company's balance sheet under the lower-of-cost-or-market rule, assuming (a) that the rule is applied to inventory as a whole, and (b) that the rule is applied on item-by-item basis.

ITEM	QUANTITY	UNIT PRICE COST (FIFO)	MARKET
A	120	$384	392
B	72	720	672
C	96	192	228
D	84	960	964

E7-15 The Rentz Corporation employs a periodic inventory system for merchandise. Its entire stock of merchandise was destroyed by fire on March 15, 19X1. Determine the cost of merchandise burned from the following data, using the gross profit method:

Beginning inventory of merchandise, January 1, 19X1	$ 6,000
Net merchandise purchases (January 1 through March 15)	24,000
Net sales (January 1 through March 15)	45,000
Gross profit percentage	50 percent

E7-16 Ed Craig was at home watching "The Three Stooges" on television when he received a call from the fire department. His business was a total loss from fire. The insurance company asked him to substantiate his inventory loss. Until the date of the fire, Ed's company had sales of $840,000 and purchases of $532,600. Freight-in amounted to $27,400, and the beginning inventory was $72,000. It was Ed's custom to price goods in such a way as to have a gross margin of 40 percent on sales.

Compute Ed's estimated inventory loss.

PROBLEMS

P7-1 Walker Corporation, a wholesaler, received an invoice totaling $40,000 for merchandise purchased. The terms are 2/10,n/30. The invoice is dated December 5, 19X1. The firm has an arrangement with a local bank whereby it can borrow up to $50,000 on short-term loans at a rate of 8% per annum interest. The firm often borrows money to take advantage of cash discounts. The firm will have the money to repay the loan in 30 days.

a. What is the last day on which the discount can be taken?
b. How much will Walker Corporation need to borrow?
c. What will be the amount of the interest cost if the firm substitutes borrowed funds from the bank for the funds it might use if it took full advantage of the credit terms offered by the vendor?
d. How much would the firm save by taking the discount?

P7-2 Foolish Ventures is being offered for sale as a going concern. Its income statements for the past three years are highlighted as follows:

	YEAR 3	YEAR 2	YEAR 1
Net sales	$1,040,000	$650,000	$520,000
Cost of goods sold	696,800	442,000	364,000
Gross profit on sales	$ 343,200	$208,000	$156,000
Gross profit percentage	33%	32%	30%

In discussion with prospective buyers, the owner emphasized the rising trend of the gross profit percentage as a very favorable factor.

Assume that you are retained by a prospective purchaser of the business to make an investigation of the fairness and reliability of the Foolish Ventures' accounting records and financial statements. You find everything in order except for the following: The inventory was understated by $13,000 at the end of Year 1, and it was overstated by $71,600 at the end of Year 3. The company uses the periodic inventory system and these errors had not been brought to light prior to your investigation.

INSTRUCTIONS:

a. Prepare a revised three-year schedule along the lines of the one just illustrated.
b. Comment on the trend of gross profit percentage after the revision.

P7-3 Wilkerson Corporation sells only one product, and the $20 selling price per unit has been unchanged throughout the past year. The total sales for the year amounted to $1,680,000. The beginning inventory at January 1 consisted of

15,000 units valued at cost of $222,500. Purchases during the year were as follows:

20,500 units at $15.50
33,000 units at $16.00
23,000 units at $16.60
8,500 units at $16.88

INSTRUCTIONS:

a. Compute the year-end (December 31) inventory using (1) the first-in, first-out method, (2) the last-in, first-out method and (3) the weighted-average method. (Compute average unit cost to the nearest cent.)

b. Prepare partial income statements for each of these three methods of pricing inventory. The income statements are to be carried only to the determination of gross profit on sales.

c. Which of the three methods of pricing inventory would be most advantageous from an income tax standpoint during a period of rising prices? Comment on the significance of the inventory figure under the method you recommend with respect to current replacement cost.

P7-4 Information relating to one of the items which appear in the ending inventory of the Textire Company at the end of June is shown below:

June	1	Balance	200 units @ $2.00	$ 400
	11	Purchases	200 units @ $1.90	380
	15	Purchases	300 units @ $1.90	570
	27	Purchases	300 units @ $1.80	540
				$1,890

Determine the amount to be shown as ending inventory under each of the following situations:

a. There are 500 units in ending inventory and the company prices its inventory under the first-in, first-out method.

b. There are 300 units in ending inventory and the company prices its inventory under the last-in, first-out method.

c. There are 400 units in ending inventory and the company prices its inventory under the weighted average method.

P7-5 The beginning inventory of Product STR, and data on purchase and sales for a two-month period are presented next.

June	1	Inventory	20 units @ $80
	15	Purchase	60 units @ $88
	18	Sale	40 units
	25	Sale	15 units
July	3	Purchase	30 units @ $84
	10	Sale	20 units
	16	Purchase	60 units @ $90
	19	Sale	50 units
	21	Purchase	20 units @ $94
	24	Sale	15 units
	31	Sale	20 units

Assume that the company uses a periodic inventory system. The company closes its books at the end of each month.

REQUIRED:

1. Compute the value of the ending inventory at June 30 and July 31 on a FIFO basis.
2. Compute the value of the ending inventory at June 30 and July 31 on a LIFO basis.
3. Prepare a general journal entry to record the sale on July 31 to Art Hoker, on credit, for $4,000.

P7-6 Dorsal Company merchandises a single product called DC10. The following data represent beginning inventory and purchases of product DC10 during the past year:

January 1 inventory	17,000 units @ $12.00
February purchases	20,000 units @ $13.00
March purchases	40,000 units @ $12.40
May purchases	30,000 units @ $12.60
July purchases	50,000 units @ $12.80
September purchases	40,000 units @ $12.60
November purchases	15,000 units @ $13.20

Sales of product DC10 totaled 192,000 units at $20 per unit. Selling and administration expenses totaled $1,184,000 for the year.

REQUIRED:

1. Prepare a schedule to compute cost of goods available for sale.
2. Prepare an income statement under each of the following assumptions:
   (a) Costs are assigned to inventory on an average-cost basis.
   (b) Costs are assigned to inventory on a FIFO basis.
   (c) Costs are assigned to inventory on a LIFO basis.

P7-7 Purchase and sales transactions of the MNO Corporation for January are shown next. The corporation started operations on January 1.

DATE	UNITS PURCHASED	AMOUNT	UNITS SOLD
Jan. 3	10 @ $4 each	$ 40	
11	12 @ $5 each	60	
19			20
26	6 @ $6 each	36	—
Totals	28	$136	20

Compute the cost of goods sold and the ending inventory on the FIFO basis and on the LIFO basis using periodic inventory.

P7-8 Analysis of the merchandise accounts of the Baker Corporation shows:

Inventory Jan. 1	500 units @ $3 each	$1,500
Purchases Feb. 8	700 units @ $3.20 each	2,240
Purchases July 28	800 units @ $4 each	3,200
	2000	$6,940

At the end of the year, a count of the number of units still on hand showed that 600 units were in the warehouse. Determine the ending inventory and the cost of goods sold for the year using the FIFO, LIFO, and weighted average methods. The firm operates on a periodic inventory basis (that is, if goods are not on hand at the end of the period they are assumed to be sold on the last day of the period).

P7-9 The Furniture King Company manager desires to change the method followed in valuating the company's inventory. Since he does not understand the alternatives under the lower-of-cost-or-market method, he requests your help in collecting the ending inventory for the following items:

INVENTORY		PER UNIT	
Item	Units	Cost	Market
Lamps:			
A-1	1	$15.00	$17.00
A-2	2	12.00	12.00
Ash Trays:			
B-1	4	10.00	8.00
B-2	6	12.00	13.00
Various:			
C-1	3	6.00	6.50
C-2	7	8.00	7.00
C-3	5	9.00	9.50

REQUIRED:

Determine the ending inventory under the lower-of-cost-or-market method using:

1. The item-by-item method.
2. The category method.
3. Total inventory method.

P7-10 The physical inventory for Lochnor Company appears next.

	Quantity	PER UNIT Cost	Market
Category A:			
Item A1	70	$25.00	$23.00
Item A2	40	47.00	51.00
Item A3	90	31.00	30.00
Category B:			
Item B1	250	17.00	18.40
Item B2	300	15.50	16.00
Item B3	120	12.00	11.00
Category C:			
Item C1	850	3.50	3.70
Item C2	910	4.00	3.80
Item C3	250	11.00	9.00

REQUIRED:

Determine the value of the inventory at lower of cost or market using each of the following methods:

1. The item-by-item method.
2. The major category method.
3. The total inventory method.

P7-11 Notsosafe Tire Company is a wholesale tire dealer that sells mainly to commercial trucking companies. The company maintains an office in the front of the large warehouse where it keeps its inventory. On the night of November 11, the night watchman was overpowered by armed robbers who backed a large truck up to the warehouse and stole several hundred large and expensive tires. Because the company does not maintain perpetual inventory records, the accountant for the company must estimate the amount of the loss.

By noon, the accountant was able to collect the following information:

a. Merchandise inventory on October 1, $234,000
b. Purchases, October 1 through November 11, $612,540
c. Purchase returns, October 1 through November 11, $4,440
d. Freight-in for the period, $42,920
e. Sales, October 1 through November 11, $974,416

f. Sales returns, October 1 through November 11, \$19,576
g. Merchandise inventory still on hand (not stolen), November 11, at cost, \$104,600
h. Average gross profit margin, 33⅓ percent

REQUIRED:

Prepare a schedule showing the amount of inventory that should have been in the warehouse on November 11, and estimate the amount of the loss.

P7-12 Forester Company suffered a serious fire which destroyed all but \$10,000 worth of its inventory. The fire occurred on the night of December 31, 19X1, before the inventory counts had been completed. The following information is available from the Forester Company's accounts:

	DECEMBER 31	
	19X0	19X1
Accounts receivable	\$ 25,000	\$ 30,000
Inventory, beginning	50,000	60,000
Inventory, ending	60,000	?
Accounts payable	12,500	15,000
Administrative expenses	38,000	46,000
Selling expenses	28,000	33,000
Delivery expense (outgoing merchandise)	4,000	5,000
Financial expense	8,000	10,000
Purchases	229,000	395,000
Purchase discounts	3,000	7,000
Sales	300,000	430,000
Sales commissions	10,000	16,000
Sales returns and allowances	12,000	15,000

REQUIRED:

1. Calculate the gross margin percentage based on the 19X0 information.
2. Irrespective of your answer to 1., determine the Forester Company's fire loss, assuming that the gross margin rate was 20 percent.

P7-13 Accounting records of the LarryBucko Company disclose the following information on October 6, 19X1:

Inventory, December 31, 19X0	\$ 69,230
Purchases to October 5, 19X1	269,540
Net sales to October 5, 19X1	394,800

On October 5, 19X1, the inventory of LarryBucko Company was partially destroyed by fire. The insurance company agrees that the company's gross margin percentage has averaged 20 percent in recent years.

Compute the approximate amount of inventory destroyed in the fire if some of it is salvaged for $11,000.

P7-14 Butch Blook recently opened a retail store, and has contacted you for some accounting advice. One of the things that you discover in your work is that he never takes sales (cash) discounts on purchases. When you ask him about it, he responds that on the average the discounts offered are "only 2%" and therefore he does not think that it is to his benefit to do so.

REQUIRED:

Write a short report to Mr. Blook explaining your recommendations concerning his policy of not taking cash discounts.

PLANT ASSETS: Acquisition and Depreciation

8

ORIENTATION

In this chapter, we will examine various aspects of accounting for plant assets, including the determination of acquisition cost and the allocation of that cost over the periods benefited (depreciation).

The chapter also includes a discussion of accounting problems relating to uses of different accounting methods for income tax and for financial reporting purposes and a description of the treatment in the accounts of expenditures which extend the useful life of plant assets or improve the quality of their services.

All enterprises must be located somewhere, so all enterprises are users of land; all enterprises require shelter of some sort, so all are users of buildings; and all enterprises require furniture and equipment. However, not all enterprises own land, building, and equipment; some choose to rent or lease some or even all these items. We are here concerned with those firms that own at least some of their plant assets. Since plant assets represent the framework in which the enterprise must operate and since these assets represent a substantial commitment of funds as well as a valuable investment, the well-being of the firm is significantly related to such assets and their administration in many cases. Plant assets are both a limiting factor and an enabling factor. The capacity of the plant to handle the activities in which the firm is engaged limits the firm's activities, but the plant as a modern tool often makes it possible to produce large quantities of a product efficiently. We are concerned here with the acquisition of plant assets through outright purchase or exchange, the construction of plant assets, the use of plant assets to carry on business affairs, and the repair and rehabilitation of plant assets. Further, once plant assets are acquired they must be depreciated, and that subject is of concern to us as well.

ACQUISITION OF PLANT ASSETS

The cost of any asset includes all expenditures involved in getting the asset into position and condition ready to use. Plant asset costs would thus include:

1. The amount paid to the seller of the property
2. The amount paid to obtain good title to the property and to pay off obligations applying to the property at the time of purchase
3. The amount paid to clear the property to make it ready for construction or the amount paid to put it into good operating condition immediately after acquisition
4. Construction and installation costs

To illustrate, assume the Baker Company wishes to build a new bank building. The management selects a corner lot which already has a building on it. They hire a contractor to remove the old building and construct the new building. The accountant exhibits the property costs as follows:

Land price	$ 80,000	
Legal fees for transfer	2,000	
Back taxes assumed	4,000	
Cost of removing old building	6,000	
Total land cost		$ 92,000
Total contract cost for new building	$600,000	
Architect's fee	20,000	
Total building cost		$620,000
Total property cost		$712,000

The following items are not included in the property cost, but are treated as current period losses or expenses:

Losses from changes in building design	$15,000
Losses from damages to neighboring property during construction	25,000
Total losses reported in current income statement	$40,000

Outlays such as the $15,000 and $25,000 paid for losses add no value to the fixed assets, and are not a direct cost of acquisition or installation, and should therefore be debited to either a loss or an expense account for the period.

Noncash Acquisitions

When plant assets are acquired in exchange for other noncash property (such as stock), a problem arises as to the proper amount to record as the cost of the asset. Generally, the amount to be recorded as the cost of an asset acquired in a noncash exchange is the fair market value of the asset acquired or the asset given up, *whichever is more readily determinable.*

For example, assume Carson Company decides to purchase a piece of land adjacent to their present location for possible future expansion. In lieu of paying cash for the land, Carson Company issues 1,000 shares of common stock. If the company stock is an actively traded stock, then a fair market value would be used in the determination of the amount to assign to the land acquisition. If, however, the company is closely held and the stock not actively traded, then a more readily determinable value might be an appraisal of the land acquired, in which case that value would be assigned to the property.

Lump-Sum (Basket) Purchases

Occasionally a firm acquires several assets for one "lump-sum" price in what is commonly referred to as a "basket" purchase. In this situation the total cost of the several assets is known, but the distribution of the cost to the individual assets may be uncertain. A method which is commonly employed to allocate the total acquisition cost to the individual assets involves assigning a portion of the cost to each asset according to the proportion of its current value to the total current value of all the assets acquired. Various clues as to individual asset values may be used. For example, prices of new items, reduced for wear and tear, may offer an indication of current value. Current construction costs may be useful. If the type of assets acquired is commonly bought and sold in a secondary (used) market, current prices in this market can be used.

To illustrate, assume the W Company purchased the land, buildings, and equipment of the D Company for a total price of $234,000 in cash. An investigation shows that:

A similar land site would cost	$ 40,000
The buildings, which are halfway through their useful life, would cost $300,000 to build today. Their current value is thus estimated to be	150,000
On the used-equipment market, the equipment would cost	70,000
Total value of individual assets acquired	**$260,000**

It appears that the W Company has paid $234,000 for a "basket" of assets that might have cost $260,000 if acquired separately. The actual cost of $234,000 may be allocated to the various assets on the basis of their relative values as follows:

To land site:	$40,000/$260,000 × $234,000 =	$ 36,000
To buildings:	$150,000/$260,000 × $234,000 =	135,000
To equipment:	$70,000/$260,000 × $234,000 =	63,000
Total cost assigned		**$234,000**

Note that these computations involve multiplying each individual asset value by the ratio $234,000/$260,000 (or .90):

Land site	$ 40,000 × .9 =	$ 36,000
Building	150,000 × .9 =	135,000
Equipment	70,000 × .9 =	63,000
		$234,000

The journal entry to record the acquisition would then be:

Land	36,000	
Buildings	135,000	
Equipment	63,000	
Cash		234,000
To record acquisition of various assets		

DEPRECIATION

Buildings and equipment have finite lives. The cost of a building or an item of equipment less the amount expected to be recovered at the end of the projected life of the item is the cost of the use of the item obtained by the business enterprise. The assignment of this use-cost is termed *depreciation,* but one must be careful to realize that use-cost, or depreciation, recognized by a firm does not necessarily reflect the decline in the market value of the item. The ideal allocation of depreciation would assign it over the productive life of the asset in the pattern of the productive use made of the asset. Such an allocation would result in an optimal matching of costs and benefits. Further, to the degree that depreciation is assigned on the basis of this ideal, the amount of depreciation taken on an item, when compared to the cost of the item, offers some insight into the future values expected to be utilized and the future plans of management.

Accordingly, accountants prefer to credit a contra account to the plant asset, as depreciation is recognized, in order to facilitate the determination of the total depreciation taken to date on the plant assets still in service:

Depreciation expense	XXX	
Accumulated depreciation		XXX

Book Value

The contra account, Accumulated Depreciation, which appears as a deduction from the related asset in the Balance Sheet, reports the total amount of the depreciation taken to date on the asset being used. The amount of the asset cost carried in the accounts less the accumulated depreciation is properly referred to as *net book value* (or simply *book value*)—meaning the value on the books. Other titles such as "reserve for depreciation" and "allowance for depreciation" have been used and are occasionally still encountered. Even the title "accumulated depreciation," now widely accepted, has confusing connotations, since "accumulate" means to add to, while "depreciate" means deduct from. The complete title means the sum of the subtractions, and this is what accountants mean by the term. The Depreciation Expense amount appears in the income statement and is closed (along with all other expenses) into Retained Earnings at the end of each accounting period.

DEPRECIATION METHODS

Through the course of the past centuries, various attitudes have been taken toward the deterioration of asset values. For a time it was felt that depreciation need not take place if an asset was carefully used and well maintained. This approach led to ignoring depreciation until the item reached the end of its useful life, and then expensing it all in the year in which it was disposed of. Another approach was to charge the asset cost as an expense at the time of acquisition. All sorts of variations in between these extremes have been suggested or applied in practice. At the present time, generally accepted accounting for depreciable assets requires the use of a rational and systematic depreciation plan based on asset cost, estimated useful life, and estimated scrap value. There are several depreciation methods which result in such an acceptable depreciation plan. The five methods which we discuss are as follows:

1. Straight line
2. Double declining balance
3. Sum of the years' digits
4. Production unit
5. Service hours

The following data with respect to an item of equipment acquired by the A Corporation on January 1, 19X1, are used to illustrate the five common depreciation methods:

- Cost: \$1,000
- Estimated scrap (or residual) value at the end of the life of the item: \$100
- Estimated useful life: 5 years (1,000 service hours)
- Expected number of units of output: 1,800 widgets

Actual operation distributed by years of service were:

	SERVICE HOURS	WIDGETS PRODUCED (UNITS OF OUTPUT)
19X1	200	400
19X2	400	700
19X3	180	300
19X4	120	200
19X5	150	300
Totals	**1,050**	**1,900**

Straight-Line Method

The straight-line method is based on the assumption that each accounting period receives the same benefit from using the asset as every other period. The formula allocating depreciation to time periods is:

$$\frac{\text{Cost} - \text{Scrap value}}{\text{Number of periods of expected life}} = \text{Depreciation per period}$$

This formula gives

$$\frac{\$1{,}000 - \$100}{5} = \$180 \text{ per year depreciation charge}$$

In our assumed example, the depreciation expense each year from 19X1 through 19X5 will be \$180, thus resulting in a total of \$900 depreciation expense over the five year period.

Double Declining-Balance Method

The *declining-balance method* is based on a formula which systematically allocates more depreciation to the early part of the life of an asset than to the later part. It is thus an *accelerated depreciation* method. The method calls for the use of a fixed percentage applied to the asset cost (without subtracting the scrap value), less the accumulated depreciation as of the beginning of each year (the declining book value of the asset). The precise declining-balance formula percentage rate required to spread the depreciable cost over the life of the asset is little used.[1] Instead, an arbitrary formula has been adopted for tax and accounting purposes, according to which the depreciation rate is set at twice the straight-line rate:

$$2 \times \frac{100\%}{\text{Number of periods of expected use}} = \text{the fixed percentage}$$

The depreciation method based on this formula is called the *double declining-balance method.*

The fixed percentage is applied at each period to the cost of the asset less the amount already included in accumulated depreciation (that is, the net book value) as of the beginning of the period. The cost of the asset is not reduced by the scrap value.

In terms of the example, this formula gives

$$2 \times \frac{100\%}{5} = 40\% \text{ (the fixed depreciation rate).}$$

The method of applying this formula is:

YEAR	BOOK VALUE AT THE BEGINNING OF THE YEAR	FIXED RATE	DEPRECIATION EXPENSE FOR THE YEAR	ACCUMULATED DEPRECIATION AT THE END OF THE YEAR
19X1	$1,000.00	.40	$400.00	$400.00
19X2	600.00	.40	240.00	640.00
19X3	360.00	.40	144.00	784.00
19X4	216.00	.40	86.40	870.40
19X5	129.60	.40	29.60[a]	900.00

[a] Note that the asset value must not be reduced below the scrap value.

[1] The "true" declining-balance method allocates the depreciable cost of a plant asset to expense over its estimated life, leaving the scrap value undepreciated. The depreciation rate to be applied to the declining book value of the asset is given by the formula:

$$\text{Declining-balance depreciation rate} = 1 - \sqrt[N]{\frac{\text{Scrap value}}{\text{Cost}}}$$

Where N is the number of periods of useful life of the asset.

Sum-of-the-Years'-Digits Method

The *sum-of-the-years'-digits* method applies a declining rate to the depreciable cost in order to compute depreciation. This method is another *accelerated depreciation* method which results in high depreciation charges in the early life of an asset and low depreciation charges in the later life. The declining rate is orderly but arbitrary. To understand how the rates are computed it is necessary only to recognize that a digit is a number, and a year's digit is the number representing the year of life of the asset. An asset acquired on January 1, (19X1) and expected to last four years would have 19X1 as year 1, 19X2 as year 2, 19X3 as year 3, and 19X4 as year 4. The sum of these numbers would be $1 + 2 + 3 + 4 = 10$. The declining rate is then established by taking the years' numbers in reversed order as successive numerators, with the total of the numbers as the common denominator. All of these fractions are applied to the cost of the asset less its estimated scrap value. The formula for a given year would be:

$$\frac{\text{Number selected from reversed order of years}}{\text{Sum of the years' digits}} = \text{That year's rate}$$

For the example, the calculation from the on-going illustration is as follows:

— Sum of years' digits in reversed order: $5 + 4 + 3 + 2 + 1 = 15$

Depreciation expense per year:

19X1	5/15 × $900 =	$300
19X2	4/15 × 900 =	240
19X3	3/15 × 900 =	180
19X4	2/15 × 900 =	120
19X5	1/15 × 900 =	60
	15/15	**$900**

Units-of-Production Method

The *units-of-production method* can be employed where the asset acquired is used directly in producing a specifically identifiable product, such as units of goods or miles driven. It is assumed that the purchaser of the item acquires a certain number of units of service when he or she acquires the asset. The formula to calculate the depreciation rate under this method is:

$$\frac{\text{Cost} - \text{Scrap value}}{\text{Expected number of units of output}} = \text{Depreciation expense per unit of output}$$

This formula gives

$$\frac{\$1{,}000 - \$100}{1{,}800} = 50¢ \text{ per unit in terms of the assumed data}$$

The units-of-production method then gives depreciation expense for each year as follows:

19X1	400 × 50¢ =	$200
19X2	700 × 50¢ =	350
19X3	300 × 50¢ =	150
19X4	200 × 50¢ =	100
19X5	200 × 50¢ =	100
Totals	**1,800**	**$900**

It is important to note that although *actual* usage of the asset resulted in 1,900 widgets being produced, it is only possible to depreciate the asset up to the estimate of 1,800 which was established at the beginning of the asset's life. Therefore, although the equipment actually produced 300 widgets in 19X5, it is only depreciated on the basis of 200 units of production.

Service-Hours Method

The *service-hours method* is similar to the production-unit method. The depreciable cost is allocated to the number of units of time that the item was in use. The formula to determine the rate to be used in allocating the depreciable cost on a time-use basis is:

$$\frac{\text{Cost} - \text{Scrap value}}{\text{Expected number of service hours}} = \text{Depreciation per service hour}$$

This formula gives

$$\frac{\$1{,}000 - \$100}{1{,}000 \text{ hours}} = 90¢ \text{ depreciation cost per hour of use}$$

The service-hours method gives depreciation expense for the assumed example:

19X1	200 × 90¢ =	$180
19X2	400 × 90¢ =	360
19X3	180 × 90¢ =	162
19X4	120 × 90¢ =	108
19X5	100 × 90¢ =	90
Total	**1,000**	**$900**

A similar situation prevails here as with the previous method. The depreciation calculation is limited to the number of hours established as an estimate; therefore, although the equipment was actually used for 200 hours in 19X5, it is only depreciated on the basis of 100 hours of usage.

Comparison of Depreciation Methods

The contrast between the methods can be seen in comparing the five different patterns of depreciation expenses:

YEAR	STRAIGHT-LINE METHOD	DOUBLE DECLINING-BALANCE METHOD	SUM-OF-YEARS'-DIGITS METHOD	PRODUCTION-UNIT METHOD	SERVICE-HOURS METHOD
19X1	$180	$400.00	$300	$200	$180
19X2	180	240.00	240	350	360
19X3	180	144.00	180	150	162
19X4	180	86.40	120	100	108
19X5	180	29.60	60	100	90
	$900	**$900.00**	**$900**	**$900**	**$900**

All five methods of depreciation are acceptable in contemporary accounting practice. All involve a systematic and rational allocation of the use-cost of a fixed asset over its useful life, and yet all are somewhat arbitrary.

We will reiterate the use of the five different depreciation methods by calculating the first two years of depreciation of the following asset using each of those methods:

- Cost: $2,500
- Estimated scrap value: $200
- Estimated life: 10 years
- Estimated service hours: 25,000 hours
- Estimated number of units of product to be obtained: 24,000

YEAR	SERVICE-HOURS USED	UNITS PRODUCED
19X1	2,400	800
19X2	2,600	1,400

		DEPRECIATION EXPENSE		
		19X1		*19X2*
1. Straight-line method:				
$\frac{2{,}500 - 200}{10} = 230$ yearly		$230		$230
2. Double declining-balance method:			2,500 − 500 =	2,000
$\frac{100\%}{10} \times 2 = .20$	.20 × 2,500 =	$500	.20 × 2,000 =	$400
3. Sum-of-the-years'-digits method:				
10 + 9 + 8 + 7 + 6 + 5 + 4 + 3 + 2 + 1 = 55	10/55 × 2,300 =	$418	9/55 × 2,300 =	$376
4. Production-unit method:				
$\frac{2{,}500 - 200}{24{,}000} = .096$	.096 × 800 =	$76	.096 × 1,400 =	$134
5. Service-hours method:				
$\frac{2{,}500 - 200}{25{,}000} = .092$	.092 × 2,000 =	$184	.092 × 2,600 =	$239

The depreciation methods we discussed are not the only acceptable methods. Other approaches which have been used, and which generally meet the test of being sufficiently systematic and rational, include the sinking-fund method and the annuity method. These are somewhat complex methods involving the application of compound interest calculations, and they have had a limited amount of application in the public utility industry. Various other methods have been employed to deal with unusual practical situations and have won acceptance.

Depreciation for Less than One Year

When depreciable assets are acquired during the year, it is customary to calculate depreciation to the nearest month. For example, if an asset was acquired on March 22, it would normally be depreciated beginning on April 1 of the current year. Frequently, however, businesses will record a full year's depreciation in the year of acquisition, and no depreciation in the year of retirement; or, alternatively, they take one-half of a year's depreciation in the year of acquisition, and one-half of a year's depreciation in the year of retirement.

To illustrate the calculation of depreciation for a fraction of a year, assume Cupco, Inc., purchased a machine for $50,000 on October 9, 19X1. The asset has an anticipated useful life of five years, and an anticipated salvage value of $5,000. Cupco follows the policy of depreciating assets acquired to the nearest month. The depreciation schedule for the machine under the straight-line, double declining-balance, and sum-of-the-years'-digits methods would be:

YEAR	STRAIGHT LINE	DOUBLE DECLINING BALANCE	SUM OF THE YEARS' DIGITS
19X1	$ 2,250	$ 5,000	$ 3,750
19X2	9,000	18,000	14,250
19X3	9,000	10,800	11,250
19X4	9,000	6,480	8,250
19X5	9,000	3,888	5,250
19X6	6,750	832[a]	2,250
	$45,000	$45,000	$45,000

[a] To bring balance to $45,000.

The calculation of the straight-line depreciation is as follows:

19X1:	$50,000 − $5,000 = $45,000 ÷ 5 = $9,000 × 1/4 (of a year) = $2,250
19X2–19X5:	$9,000 (a full year)
19X6:	9,000 × 3/4 (of a year) = $6,750

The depreciation calculation using the double declining-balance method is as follows:

19X1:	$50,000 × .4 = $20,000 × 1/4 (of a year) =	$5,000
19X2:	$50,000 − $5,000 = $45,000 × .4 =	$18,000
19X3:	$45,000 − $18,000 = $27,000 × .4 =	$10,800
19X4:	$27,000 − $10,800 = $16,200 × .4 =	$6,480
19X5:	$16,200 − $6,480 = $9,720 × .4 =	$3,888
19X6:	*To bring total depreciation to $45,000:*	
	$45,000 − ($5,000 + $18,000 + $10,800 + $6,480 + $3,888) =	$832

The depreciation calculation using the sum-of-the years'-digits method is as follows:

The depreciation amount is:

$45,000 ($50,000 − $5,000)

The depreciation rate per year are:

5/15
4/15
3/15
2/15
1/15
15/15

19X1:	$45,000 × 5/15 = $15,000 × 1/4 (of a year) =	$3,750
19X2:	$45,000 × 5/15 × 3/4 (of a year) $45,000 × 4/15 × 1/4 (of a year)	$14,250
19X3:	$45,000 × 4/15 × 3/4 (of a year) $45,000 × 3/15 × 1/4 (of a year)	$11,250
19X4:	$45,000 × 3/15 × 3/4 (of a year) $45,000 × 2/15 × 1/4 (of a year)	$8,250
19X5:	$45,000 × 2/15 × 3/4 (of a year) $45,000 × 1/15 × 1/4 (of a year)	$5,250
19X6:	$45,000 × 1/15 × 3/4 (of a year) =	$2,250

There would be no change in the calculation of the production-unit method or the service-hours method of depreciation for less than a year. It is obvious that under either method, depreciation is calculated based on output, not time. The output for a given period will be affected by the date on which the asset was acquired (or retired), as well as by other factors.

Two Common Misconceptions Concerning Depreciation

Many readers of financial statements operate under two misconceptions concerning depreciation. Probably the most common misconception is that depreciation is a process of valuing assets. The second common misconception is that depreciation represents money being accumulated to buy new assets.

Depreciation is a process of cost allocation, not a process of valuation. Depreciation, as the term is used in accounting, does not mean the physical deterioration of the asset. Rather, depreciation is an effort to spread (or allocate) the cost of an asset purchased over the anticipated useful life of that asset. If the accounting profession had not "invented" depreciation, then when a depreciable asset was purchased, the entire purchase price would be considered an expense in the year of acquisition. Because we have depreciation, this purchase price can be spread out of the anticipated asset life, and charged against income over that period of time. Therefore the balances in a company's Plant Asset section of a balance sheet do not represent the market values of those assets listed. Rather, those balances represent the cost less accumulated depreciation (or book value) of those assets.

In summary, it should be emphasized that depreciation is essentially a process of allocating the cost of an asset over a number of periods to the operating costs of those periods and is not intended to be a process of valuation of the assets being depreciated. At this stage in the continuing development of accounting theory and practice, it is only acceptable to accomplish this allocation by means of essentially arbitrary arithmetic calculations which are systematically and rationally applied.

Depreciation differs from most other expenses in that it does not require a cash payment at or near the time it is recorded. This anomaly leads many to believe that (in some magical way) accumulated depreciation provides funds for the acquisition of future assets. One fundamental way to correct this misconception is to emphasize that the balance in accumulated depreciation theoretically could have been credited directly to the asset being depreciated. The only real difference that would have resulted is that the depreciation to date on any particular asset (that is, accumulated depreciation) would not be a readily available figure. Instead it would be hidden in the asset figure. It appears obvious then, that accumulated depreciation represents the expired cost of the asset, and nothing more. An Accumulated Depreciation account has a credit balance. It does not represent an asset of any kind, and cannot be used to acquire new equipment.

CAPITAL AND REVENUE EXPENDITURES

When expenditures are made on plant assets after their acquisition, it is often difficult to recognize the difference between expenditures which benefit only the current period, and those which add to the permanent utility of the asset. Expenditures that add to the utility of the asset are debited to the asset and referred to as *capital expenditures*. Those costs that benefit only the current period are debited to expense accounts and are termed *revenue expenditures*. The expense account commonly debited in a revenue expenditure is Repairs and Maintenance.

Expenditures for an addition to a plant asset are clearly capital expenditures. For example, the cost of adding a new wing to an office building, or an air-conditioning unit to a company vehicle should be debited to the respective asset accounts. On the other hand, the cost of fixing a flat tire on a company truck or replacing a minor worn-out part of a company-owned machine should be debited to the appropriate expense account.

Expenditures that increase the operating capacity or efficiency of an asset should be capitalized. In that same regard, expenditures that increase the useful life of an asset beyond the original estimate are also capital expenditures. Minor expenditures that have the characteristic of capital expenditures are generally treated as repairs expense because of the savings in time and clerical costs. Some businesses actually establish a minimum amount (such as $100 or $500) required to classify an item as a capital expenditure.

REPAIRS, RENEWALS, AND IMPROVEMENTS OF PLANT ASSETS

The projected depreciable life of an asset must be set on the basis of a plan of maintenance. Even a short technological life would not be attained for an item of equipment without some regular upkeep costs. Thus the management should plan the capital expenditure for the asset and the upkeep cost to achieve the maximum effectiveness of total costs in producing revenues. Many motorists do this, in effect, when they plan to do very little maintenance and trade in their cars every two years.

Scrap Value and Maintenance Cost in Optimum Life Determination: Illustration

Equipment is purchased for $8,000 to produce 3,000 units per year:

	SCRAP VALUE AT END OF YEAR	VALUE DECLINE	MAINTENANCE
1st year	$6,000	$2,000	$ 300
2nd year	5,000	1,000	700
3rd year	4,500	500	1,500
4th year	4,000	500	2,000

Combined costs:

	TOTAL VALUE DECLINE AND MAINTENANCE COST	ANNUAL PER UNIT COST	PER UNIT COST CUMULATIVELY
1st year	$2,300	$0.77	$0.77
2nd year	1,700	0.57	0.67
3rd year	2,000	0.67	0.67
4th year	2,500	0.81	0.71

Presumably, the item should be disposed of at the end of the third year. Other factors, such as the effect on labor costs of using the old equipment, will also be very important.

Maintenance costs in this illustration are expected to be incurred according to the plan of use of the item for three years, with 3,000 units per year being produced. If it becomes desirable to change the plan, and costs are incurred which extend the life or make it possible to increase the number of units produced, then such costs are treated as additions to the asset value (capitalized). A portion of such costs may be thought of as, in effect, an erasure of part of the depreciation taken to date. To illustrate, suppose that at the end of the third year, the management finds that the item of equipment could be put back into nearly new condition by an expenditure of \$2,000 to rebuild the motor and rebush the bearings, and that the item would then last another two years with moderate maintenance costs.

Equipment		Accumulated Depreciation		Cash	
Bal. 8,000		(1) 2,000	Bal. 3,500		(1) 2,000

After recording the renewal as a reduction of the accumulated depreciation, the net book value of the equipment becomes \$6,500 (\$8,000 − \$1,500) which will be used as the basis for depreciation charges over the new two years. Assuming that scrap value at the end of this two-year period is expected to be \$3,800, then the remaining depreciable cost is \$6,500 − \$3,800, or \$2,700. On a straight-line basis, each of the next two years will be charged with \$1,350 (\$2,700 ÷ 2) depreciation.

An improvement of the asset involves an outlay to improve or expand its performance. An amount paid out to enable the machine to produce 4,000 units per year rather than the expected 3,000 units, for example, would be added to the asset value and would also require a modified depreciation calculation. Suppose that \$3,000 was expended at the end of the first year to increase the potential output of the machine. We would record the expenditure:

Equipment		Accumulated Depreciation		Cash	
Bal. 8,000			Bal. 1,167		(1) 3,000
(1) 3,000					

(Note: \$1,167 = 1/3 × \$3,500)

If the estimated scrap value at the end of the next two years now becomes \$5,800, depreciation per year would be:

$$\frac{11{,}000 - 1{,}167 - 5{,}800}{2} = 2{,}017$$

When major replacements of old parts of an asset with new parts occur, the appropriate accounting treatment depends on whether the replacement constitutes a renewal or an improvement (or both). In general, the cost of the old parts should be removed from the asset value and the accumulated depreciation and the new parts costs should be added to the asset value.

DEPRECIATION AND INCOME TAXES

Accelerated Cost Recovery System (ACRS)

The Economic Recovery Tax Act of 1981 responds to concerns that the United States economy is faltering because of reduced capital investments by business. A major part of that act, the *accelerated cost recovery system (ACRS)* permits businesses to "recover" costs for tax purposes over predetermined recovery periods which are generally shorter than actual useful lives. Thus, because of ACRS it is anticipated that there will be greater incentives for increased capital investment, which should eventually result in higher national productivity.

Under prior law, taxpayers were allowed to depreciate the cost of property used in a trade or business over the useful life of the property. Under the new law, instead of depreciation deductions, businesses are entitled to "recovery deductions" as a means of recouping capital outlays made after 1980. The concept of ACRS eliminates the need to determine each asset's useful life. To qualify for recovery deductions under ACRS, capital expenditures must be for "recovery property." Recovery property is any depreciable, tangible property used in a business or held for the production of income. Capital expenditures are generally recovered over a period of three, five, ten, or fifteen years. The recovery period depends on the type of recovery property.

Three-year Property Class

This class consists of tangible personal property such as automobiles, light-duty trucks, machinery and equipment used for research and development, and some other short-lived assets.

Five-year Property Class

This property class generally includes all other tangible personal property not included in other property classes, including most machinery and equipment.

Ten-year Property Class

This class includes certain public utility personal property, amusement park property, railroad tank cars, and certain short-lived real property.

Fifteen-year Property Class

This class covers certain public utility property, and most real property.

Generally the recovery deductions (write-offs) are accelerated through the use of "accelerated recovery tables" provided by the Internal Revenue Service. Following a phase-in period, these deduction percentages for personal property were intended to approximate the results of double declining-balance depreciation (switching to straight-line when it becomes advantageous to the taxpayer), but with a slightly lower rate for real property. However, the Tax Equity and Fiscal Responsibility Act, signed into law on September 2, 1982, moderates the amounts which are recoverable. Thus the maximum rate which will be recoverable under current law is now equal to 150% of the straight-line recovery rate. Salvage value is frequently ignored; and there is usually no distinction made between new and used property.

Under ACRS, the amount of "depreciation" taken on the income tax return will be different from the depreciation recorded in the accounting records. This will result in taxable income being different from income reported in the annual financial statements. Generally accepted accounting principles require that the income tax reported on the earnings statement supplied to the public reflect the tax on the earnings reported in that statement, whether that tax was actually paid in the current period or not. This frequent difference between income tax expense reported in published financial statements, and the income tax actually paid, gives rise to an item referred to as deferred income tax. This topic will be covered in some detail in Chapter 10.

LEASING PLANT ASSETS

A *lease* is a contractual agreement between a *lessee* and a *lessor* in which the lessee obtains the right to use a specific asset (or assets), owned by the lessor, for a period of time in return for stipulated cash payments (rents). When plant assets are rented for short periods of time, the accounting procedures described in earlier chapters are adequate to account for the rent. However, long-term leases, which may amount to disguised purchases of property under certain conditions, often require more complex treatment. If the lessee has the option to buy the leased asset at a nominal price at the termination of a long-term lease and if the lessee agrees to pay taxes, maintenance, and renewal of the property, he is in very much the same position as an owner. After all, ownership of property gives no more than the right to use and to sell property.

A lease that *in substance* is in fact a purchase, instead of a rental, is referred to as a *capital lease.* Leases that are in substance true leases in the traditional sense of the word are referred to as *operating leases.* Accounting for leases will be illustrated in Chapter 10 in conjunction with the discussion of liabilities.

SUMMARY

Many firms are committed to large amounts of plant assets. Sometimes as much, or more, capital is employed in plant assets as in current resources. Special problems develop with respect to accounting for and controlling plant assets because of the length of the lives of these items and the manner in which they are used and disposed of. Cost of plant assets at the date of acquisition should follow the general rule for inclusion of all costs necessary to place the asset into position ready for use in the business. Where several items are acquired in one "package," the cost must be allocated among the individual items for later accounting purposes. Once cost is established on the books, some rational and systematic depreciation method should be adopted for assigning the cost to expense. Several depreciation methods are available which may provide systematic and reasonable allocation of the cost of the items over their useful lives. Changes in the accounting records may be necessary as assets are modified to extend their lives or improve their services.

The Economic Recovery Tax Act of 1981 revises the depreciation provision of the tax laws. The "useful life" concept is dropped, and the "accelerated cost recovery system" (ACRS) is adopted. ACRS generally results in a faster write-off of assets, and is effective for most property placed in service after 1980. ACRS was modified somewhat by the Tax Equity and Fiscal Responsibility Act of 1982.

KEY POINTS

1. **Depreciation** The allocation of asset costs over the periods benefited.
2. **Basket purchases** The lump-sum purchase of several assets (requiring the allocation of costs to individual asset accounts).
3. **Accumulated depreciation** The total amount of depreciation taken to date.
4. **Book value** Asset cost minus accumulated depreciation.
5. **Straight-line depreciation** A method of depreciation which is based on the assumption that each accounting period receives the same benefit from using the asset as every other period.
6. **Accelerated depreciation methods** Methods based on formulas which systematically allocate more depreciation to the early part of the life of an asset than to the later part. The two most common methods are the double declining-balance method and the sum-of-the-years'-digits method.
7. **Production-unit and service-hours methods of depreciation** Depreciation methods which focus on the output (units or hours) of the asset, rather than the time it is held.
8. **Capital expenditure** An expenditure which adds utility to an asset and is debited to the asset account.
9. **Revenue expenditures** An expenditure which will benefit only the current accounting period, and is debited to an expense account.
10. **ACRS—*A*ccelerated *C*ost *R*ecovery *S*ystem** Recovery deductions which replace depreciation for tax purposes. Under the system, capital expenditures are normally recovered over a period of three, five, ten, or fifteen years.

QUESTIONS

1. Which of the following items would be classified as plant assets on the balance sheet?

   a. A truck held for sale by a truck dealer.
   b. A typewriter used by a secretary of the company.
   c. A machine used in production but which has been fully depreciated.
   d. Pollution control equipment that does not reduce the cost or improve the efficiency of the factory.
   e. A parking lot for company employees.

2. Discuss the approach taken by accountants for the valuation of plant assets at acquisition. What basic rules are involved and how can the approach be justified?

3. Of the following costs related to the purchase and installation of new production machinery, which should be charged to the cost of the asset?

   a. Sales tax on the machine.
   b. Freight charges.
   c. Wages of employees for time spent on installation and testing before machine was placed in service.
   d. Cost of damage to floor during installation.
   e. Wages of employees to maintain and perform adjustments to machine one year after it is placed in service.

4. How are plant assets that are acquired, in whole or part, by the exchange of property or the issuances of stock to be valued in the accounts?

5. Why, for accounting purposes, is land different from other plant assets?

6. What is a "basket purchase" and what valuation problems does it pose?

7. "Depreciation is a process of allocation, not valuation." Explain.

8. Depreciation expense is sometimes referred to as a "noncash expense." Discuss.

9. Should depreciation continue to be recorded on a building when sufficient information is available indicating that market value exceeds original cost? Explain.

10. Explain the similarities and differences between the following pairs of depreciation methods.

    a. Straight-line method and units-of-production method.
    b. Sum-of-years'-digits and double declining-balance method.
    c. Units-of-production and service-hours methods.

11. If a plant asset is sold during the year, why should depreciation be computed for the partial year prior to the date of sale?

12. What is the distinction between capital expenditures and revenue expenditures?

13. Distinguish between ordinary and extraordinary repairs. What is the proper accounting treatment for each?

14. What important consideration is absent in the following statement: "Since we have more than four times the necessary amount in the depreciation reserves at present, payment for the $25,000 in expected capital outlays should present no problem during the current year."

15. How do leases of assets differ from purchases of assets? Can a situation exist in which the form of a transaction is a lease, but in substance the transaction is a purchase?

16. What is meant by ACRS? Does it have any impact on depreciation which appears in published financial statements? Explain.

EXERCISES

E8-1 The Willis Corporation needed a new office building. They selected the site and purchased the land where construction will take place. Before construction could begin, an old building had to be removed from the lot. The price of the land was $85,000 and a contractor charged $75,000 for removing the old building and clearing the land. The construction fee for the new building was $650,000 and the architect's fee was $25,000. Willis Corporation was obliged to pay $4,000 to the owner of neighboring property for damages occurring during the process of clearing the land site.

What is the cost that should be charged to the Office Building account?

E8-2 The Palmetto Company issued capital stock having a current market value of $5,000 in exchange for a land site.

a. Give the entry in general journal form for the acquisition of the property.
b. What alternative for recording the acquisition of the land was available to Palmetto if a current market price for their stock was not readily obtainable?

E8-3 New office equipment was purchased by the Plunkett Company at a list price of $172,800 with credit terms of 2/10,n/30. Payment of the invoice was made within the discount period; it included 5% sales tax on the new price. Transportation charges of $5,760 on the new equipment were paid by Plunkett Company as well as labor cost of $11,520 for installing the equipment in the appropriate locations. During the unloading and installation work, some of the equipment fell from a loading platform and was damaged. Repair of the damaged parts cost $8,640. After the equipment had been in use for 3 months, it was thoroughly cleaned and lubricated at a cost of $1,920.

Prepare a list of the items which should be capitalized by debit to the Office Equipment account and state the total cost of the new equipment. (Round off figures to the nearest dollar.)

E8-4 The AAA Company purchased land, building, and equipment from BBB Company for $280,000 cash. An investigation indicates that a similar land site would cost $55,000; the building would cost $350,000 to reproduce new, but half of its useful life has expired; and the equipment would cost $90,000 if acquired in the used equipment market.

Give the entry in general journal form which will reflect the purchase of the "basket" of assets, and allocate the appropriate amount of the total cost to each asset category.

E8-5 Royce Corporation acquired machinery with a useful life of 5 years at a cost of $367,800. The estimated residual salvage value was $7,900.

You are to compute the annual depreciation on the machinery in each of the 5 years of useful life using the double declining-balance method. (Round all computations to the nearest dollar.)

E8-6 Rick Dock, general manager of Squarehead Company, attended an auction of used machinery. He was the successful bidder on a lot, consisting of three machines, for which he paid $141,000. Freight charges of $4,000 were incurred to have the three machines delivered to Squarehead Company's plant. In anticipation of this auction, the company had borrowed $150,000 in order to be able to make cash bids for the equipment being auctioned. The interest charge on the borrowing amounted to $5,000.

The estimated fair market value of the machines and the costs of installations and trial runs necessary to prepare them for regular operations were as follows:

	MACHINE 1	MACHINE 2	MACHINE 3
Fair market value	$70,000	$90,000	$40,000
Installation costs	4,000	8,000	3,000
Costs of trial runs	1,000	1,500	None

Determine the cost of each machine for accounting purposes, assuming that the auction and delivery cost is apportioned to the three machines on the basis of relative market value.

E8-7 Bourland Corporation purchased three machines during the year as follows:

Feb. 5	Machine A	$12,000
July 30	Machine B	9,600
Oct. 13	Machine C	14,400

The machines are assumed to last 6 years and have no estimated residual value. The company's fiscal year corresponds to the calendar year.

Compute the depreciation charge for each machine for the year using the straight-line method. The company follows the policy of calculating depreciation to the nearest month.

E8-8 On January 1, the Staley Company acquired a fixed asset which has the following characteristics:

Acquisition cost	$6,800
Scrap or residual value	400
Estimated service life: Years	4
Service hours	4,000
Production output (units)	8,000

Compute the annual depreciation for each year under each of the following methods:

a. Straight-line depreciation
b. Service-hours method. Service hours (and units of production) are:

YEAR	SERVICE HOURS	UNITS OF PRODUCTION
1	1,500	2,500
2	1,000	2,000
3	1,000	2,000
4	500	1,500

c. Productive-unit method

E8-9 The Worthington Corporation purchased a machine at a cost of $620. The estimated useful life was 4 years and the residual value $20. Assume that the estimated productive life of the machine is 60,000 units and each year's production was:

Year 1	20,000 units
Year 2	14,000 units
Year 3	10,000 units
Year 4	16,000 units

Determine the amount for each cell in the following table. Show your computations.

	DEPRECIATION EXPENSE			
Year	Straight Line	Productive Output	Sum of the Years' Digits	Double Declining Balance
1				
2				
3				
4				
Total				

E8-10 The Tye Company purchased a machine that cost $20,000. The estimated useful life was 5 years and the residual value $2,000. Assume the estimated useful life in productive units to be 90,000. Units actually produced were:

Year 1	10,000
Year 2	22,000

Determine the appropriate amounts for the table that follows. Show your computations.

	DEPRECIATION EXPENSE		BOOK VALUE AT END OF	
	Year 1	Year 2	Year 1	Year 2
Method of Depreciation:				
Straight line	______	______	______	______
Productive output	______	______	______	______
Sum of the years' digits	______	______	______	______
Double declining balance	______	______	______	______

E8-11 The Guido Sales Company purchased a delivery truck for $5,500 on January 1, 19X1. The truck has an estimated useful life of 5 years and scrap value of $500.

Compute depreciation for each year using:

a. Double declining-balance method
b. Sum-of-the-years'-digits method

E8-12 The Milner Manufacturing Company completed the following transactions during the current fiscal year:

a. Replaced a roof on a warehouse with a new one of sturdier, longer-lasting material (guaranteed for 25 years), $18,500.
b. Replaced worn-out tires on a company truck, $150.
c. Repainted an office building, $425.
d. Replaced a part in an item of equipment with a new, identical one, $150.
e. Increased the capacity of a machine by adding a new component, $1,500.

Indicate which expenditure would be capitalized, and which would be treated as current expense.

E8-13 Identify the following expenditures as capital expenditures or revenue expenditures:

a. Purchased new battery at a cost of $80 for 2-year-old delivery truck.
b. Installed an escalator at a cost of $25,000 in a three-story building which had previously been used for some years without elevators or escalators.
c. Purchased a pencil sharpener at a cost of $7.00
d. Immediately after acquiring a new delivery truck at a cost of $11,000, paid $250 to have the name of the store and other advertising material painted on the truck.
e. Painted delivery truck at a cost of $350 after 2 years of use.
f. Original life of the delivery truck had been estimated as 4 years and straight-line depreciation of 25 percent yearly had been recognized. After 3 years' use, however, it was decided to recondition the truck thoroughly, including a new engine and transmission, at a cost of $4,000. By making this expenditure it was believed that the useful life of the truck would be extended from the original estimation of 4 years to a total of 6 years.

PROBLEMS

P8-1 The management of the Growth Corporation hired you to examine its plant records in order to determine the proper accounting for its plant assets. You discover the following data, from which you are to prepare an analysis showing how the plant assets should be recorded in the accounts.

a. The corporation acquired a tract of land for $75,000. The land was cleared of trash, overgrowth, and some dilapidated old buildings, at a cost of $10,000. A back corner of the tract was not suited to the corporation's needs and was sold for $15,000. In the process of burning off the overgrowth, the local fire ordinance was broken and the corporation was required to pay a fine of $500.
b. A contractor was employed to construct a new building on the site. The total contract price was $1,200,000. The contractor allocated this figure at the completion of the building as follows:

Parking lot at rear building	$ 80,000
Excavation for basement of building, not likely to be usable for subsequent buildings	70,000
Building	1,050,000
Total per contract	$1,200,000
Premium charge for completing building ahead of schedule	100,000
Total billed	$1,300,000

c. Equipment was acquired and installed in the building as follows:

Invoice prices of the equipment	$500,000
Installation costs	150,000
Break-in costs	25,000
Depreciation allocation during break-in	5,000
Repair costs on the equipment during first year of operations	15,000

P8-2 Prepare journal entries on the books of the Carter Corporation to record the following selected transactions:

19X1

Mar. 11 A new lathe is acquired on account at an invoice price of $8,000, terms 2/10,n/60.

Mar. 22 A freight bill is received for transporting the lathe to the Carter Corporation factory, $120.

Dec. 31 Depreciation for 10 months is allowed for 19X1, out of a total estimated life of 5 years and a scrap value estimate of $500 at the end of 5 years. Use straight-line depreciation.

19X2

Dec. 31 Depreciation for 19X2 is recorded.

P8-3 Lafayette Manufacturing Company began operations on January 1, 19X1. The bookkeeper for this company was inexperienced and debited one account called Lands, Buildings, and Equipment for all expenditures involving long-term assets. The account had a balance at the end of the year of $1,196,540 made up of the following items:

Cost of land	$ 134,000
Broker's fees for land purchase	9,400
Attorney's fees for land purchase	2,400
Other fees connected with land purchase	1,300
Cost of draining a small pond from land	6,500
Cost of building up land to prevent further flooding	25,280
Cost of digging basement and foundation for building	14,960
Architect's fee for designing building	55,700

(Continued)

(Continued)

Cost of new building (payment made with $40,000 cash plus U.S. Treasury notes having a face value of $198,000 at time of purchase)	480,000
Cost of sidewalks	15,800
Cost of parking lots	31,200
Cost of parking lot lights	15,600
Cost of landscaping	7,600
Cost of machinery	356,800
Cost of delivering machinery	3,600
Cost of repairing parking lot after equipment delivery	1,000
Cost of installing machinery	24,800
Payment of lawsuit settlement to injured employee	10,000
Cost of repairing windows broken by vandals before building was in use	600
Account balance	$1,196,540

When the land was purchased, it contained several piles of scrap metal, which were sold for $3,700. This amount was credited to Miscellaneous Income. During construction, the company assigned the factory superintendent and two supervisors to the construction project. These people earn $36,000, $24,000, and $24,000 respectively, per year. They spent 6 months overseeing the construction of the building, 3 months supervising the installation of machinery, and 3 months in their regular factory duties. Their salaries were debited to factory payroll expense.

REQUIRED:

1. Prepare a schedule with the following headings: Land, Land Improvements, Buildings, Machinery, and Losses. List the items appropriate to these accounts and sort them out into their proper accounts. Negative amounts should be shown in parentheses. Total the columns.
2. Prepare an entry to adjust the accounts based on all the information given, assuming the company's accounts have not been closed at the end of the year.
3. Assume that the factory was in operation for 3 months during the year. Prepare an adjusting entry to record depreciation expense, assuming that the land improvements are depreciated over 15 years with no residual value, the buildings are depreciated over 25 years with no estimated residual value, and the machinery is depreciated over 10 years with the estimated residual value equal to 10 percent of cost. The company uses the straight-line method of depreciation.

P8-4 The Rolfs Company acquired its assets in two purchases:

Acquisition A:	
Land and buildings (cost)	$160,000
Acquisition B:	
Machinery and office equipment (cost)	72,000

The question of apportioning the cost of the purchases among the various assets arose, and an appraisal was obtained which revealed the following values:

Land	$ 40,000
Buildings	160,000
Machinery	40,000
Office equipment	20,000
Total	$260,000

REQUIRED:

Indicate the proper costs to be assigned to each of these assets:

1. Land
2. Buildings
3. Machinery
4. Office Equipment

P8-5 The Newton Corporation purchased a machine which cost $15,000, installed and ready to use. The machine is expected to have a scrap value of $1,000 at the end of its estimated useful life of 5 years. It is expected that the machine will be used as follows:

1st year	2,500 hours
2nd year	500 hours
3rd year	3,000 hours
4th year	2,800 hours
5th year	1,200 hours

REQUIRED:

Compute the depreciation for each of the 5 years according to the following methods:

1. Service-hours method
2. Straight-line method
3. Double declining-balance method
4. Sum-of-the-years'-digits method

P8-6 On January 1, 19X1, the Able Corporation purchased an item of equipment for $83,000 cash plus $3,000 installation costs. The equipment has an estimated life of 10 years with an estimated salvage value of $5,000 at the end of the 10 years. The equipment has an estimated capacity to produce 250,000 units. Production in 19X1 is expected to be 40,000 units and in 19X2 it is expected to be 30,000 units.

REQUIRED:

Compute depreciation for 19X1 and 19X2 using the following methods:

1. Production-units method
2. Straight-line method
3. Sum-of-the-years'-digits method
4. Double declining-balance method

P8-7 Compute depreciation for the estimated total life of 6 years for an item of equipment which cost $22,780 and is expected to have a scrap value of $2,200. Show the depreciation amounts using straight-line, sum-of-the-years'-digits, and double declining-balance methods. What will be the balance of the Accumulated Depreciation account for this item of equipment under each method at the end of each of the years?

P8-8 On March 31, 19X1, Armstrong Corporation purchased new machinery at a cost of $281,600. Depreciation has been computed by the straight-line method based on an estimated useful life of 5 years and residual scrap value of $25,600.

On January 2, 19X4, extraordinary repairs (which were almost equivalent to a rebuilding of the machine) were performed at a cost of $60,000. Because of the thoroughgoing nature of these repairs, the normal life of the machinery was extended materially. The revised estimate of useful life was 4 years from January 1, 19X4. The revised scrap value was zero.

INSTRUCTIONS:

Prepare journal entries to record:

a. The original purchase of the machinery.
b. The provision for depreciation on December 31, 19X1, 19X2, and 19X3.
c. The expenditure for the extraordinary repairs in January, 19X4.
d. The provision for depreciation on December 31, 19X4.

Assume payment in cash for the machine and the extraordinary repairs.

P8-9 The Jackson Company found it necessary to do some extensive repairs on its existing building and to add a new wing suitable for use during the next 10 years. The existing building originally cost $200,000, and, by the end of 19X1, it was one-half depreciated on the basis of a 20-year useful life and no residual value. During 19X2 the following expenditures were made that were related to the building:

a. Ordinary repairs and maintenance expenditures for the year, $17,000 cash.
b. A complete new roof was added to the building, $20,000 cash. This work was completed on January 1, 19X2.
c. The new wing was completed on June 30, 19X2 at a cash cost of $75,000.

REQUIRED:

1. Record each of these transactions during 19X2.
2. Give the adjusting entry that would be required at the end of the annual accounting period, December 31, 19X2, for the building after taking into account your entries in 1. Assume straight-line depreciation.
3. Show how the assets would be reported on the December 31, 19X2, balance sheet.

P8-10 During 19X1, Meano Company purchased two machines. Machine A was purchased on April 1, 19X1, at a cost of $10,000. It has an estimated life of 3 years, and an estimated salvage value of $1,000. Machine B was purchased on July 2, 19X1, at a cost of $30,000. It has an estimated salvage value of $5,000 and an estimated life of 4 years.

REQUIRED:

Prepare a depreciation schedule for each machine over its anticipated useful life using:

1. The straight-line method
2. The double declining-balance method
3. The sum-of-the-years'-digits method

P8-11 During 19X1, Parchment Company purchased four machines that performed very different operations. Because of their varied functions, the company accountant felt that four different depreciation methods were appropriate. Data on these machines are summarized as follows:

			ESTIMATED			
Machine	Date Purchased	Cost	Installation Cost	Residual Value	Estimated Life	Depreciation Method
1	1/1/X1	$25,600	$2,400	$3,800	10 years	Double declining balance
2	1/1/X1	32,400	800	3,520	7 years	Sum of the years' digits
3	4/4/X1	14,800	1,800	2,600	5 years	Straight line
4	8/25/X1	34,000	4,000	2,000	180,000 units	Production units

REQUIRED:

Assuming that the fiscal year ended December 31, compute the depreciation charges for 19X1, 19X2, and 19X3 by filling in a table with the following column heads:

		DEPRECIATION		
Machine	Computations	19X1	19X2	19X3

Assume that double the straight-line rate is used for the declining-balance method and that production for machine 4 was 24,000 units in 19X1, 46,500 units in 19X2, and 37,800 units in 19X3. Show your computations.

PLANT ASSETS: Trade-Ins, Natural Resources, Intangibles, and Other Assets

9

ORIENTATION

Because of the magnitude of investments in noncurrent assets, management must have information for choosing among investment opportunities. Certain transactions and classes of noncurrent assets require special consideration and handling because of highly subjective valuation characteristics. The purpose of this chapter is to examine in detail these transactions and noncurrent asset classifications including trade-ins and disposals, accounting for intangible assets, and accounting for natural resources.

DISPOSAL OF PLANT ASSETS

Plant assets may be disposed of voluntarily by retirement, sale, or trade-in; or involuntarily as the result of a casualty situation. Accounting for the disposal of a plant asset involves updating depreciation on the asset, removing the account balances that pertain to the item disposed of, and finally recognizing a gain or loss as the difference between the net book value of the item and the scrap value obtained.

Assume for example, that the equipment account includes $4,000 as the original cost of a machine having an anticipated life of four years and no salvage value, and depreciation to the end of last year on the machine totals $2,500. If the machine is to be sold on July 1 for $800, then the following entries must be made on July 1:

Depreciation expense	$ 500	
Accumulated depreciation		$ 500
To record depreciation for half a year at the straight-line rate		
Cash	800	
Accumulated depreciation	3,000	
Loss on disposal of asset	200	
Equipment		4,000
To record disposal of equipment		
Calculation of loss:		
Cost of equipment	$4,000	
Less accumulated depreciation ($2,500 + $500)	3,000	
Book value of equipment on July 1		$1,000
Selling price		800
Loss on sale of equipment		$ 200

A loss occurred in the situation just illustrated because the selling price was less than the book value on the date of sale. If the selling price had exceeded the book value on the date of sale, a gain would have been recognized.

The loss on disposal may be due to early termination of the machine because of accidental causes, unexpected obsolescence, elimination of the product that is produced by the machine from the firm's offerings, or because of errors in determining the scrap value or expected life. Often, the loss (or gain) is really attributable to improper depreciation determination in prior periods. Unfortunately it is usually not possible to go back to the earlier years and correct the depreciation reflected in those years. Where the loss (or gain) is substantial in amount and of an unusual and nonrecurring nature, a case can be made for treating it as an extraordinary item reported at the end of the income statement. Ordinary amounts of such losses are apt to occur frequently, and are properly treated as nonoperating expenses.

Asset Trade-Ins

When new assets are acquired, it is not unusual to trade in an old asset and pay a cash difference. In these situations, the old asset and related accumulated depreciation must be removed from the accounting records and the new asset must be recorded. Accounting for such an exchange of assets varies somewhat depending upon whether the two assets are *similar* or *dissimilar*. The trading in of an old computer for a new one would involve similar assets; whereas the trading in of a piece of equipment on a parcel of land would be a transaction involving dissimilar assets.

Generally, the accounting for asset exchanges should be based on the fair market value of either of the assets obtained or given up, whichever is more readily determinable.[1] If the assets are *similar,* this general approach is modified somewhat if there is a gain on the trade-in. In that case the cost of the new asset is considered to be the sum of the cash paid plus the *book value* of the old asset exchanged.

To illustrate the accounting for these different types of transactions, the discussion is divided into three sections as follows:

- Dissimilar assets—gain or loss
- Similar assets—loss situation
- Similar assets—gain situation

Dissimilar Assets

The cost of an asset acquired in exchange for a dissimilar asset is normally recorded at the fair market value of the asset given up, plus any cash paid. The fair market value of the asset received should be used only if it is more readily determinable than the fair market value of the asset exchanged.

To illustrate, assume Jetson Company exchanged a large piece of equipment for a tract of land to be used as a potential future factory site. In addition to the equipment, which had a book value of $34,000 (cost $48,000 less accumulated depreciation of $14,000), Jetson must pay $21,000 in cash for the land. It is determined by independent appraisal that the equipment traded in has a fair value of $41,000. The cost of the land is computed as follows:

Fair market value of equipment given up	$41,000
Cash paid	$21,000
Cost of land	$62,000

The journal entry to record the transaction is:

Land	$62,000	
Accumulated depreciation:		
Equipment	14,000	
Equipment		$48,000
Cash		21,000
Gain on exchange of plant assets		7,000
To record exchange of equipment for land		

[1] Opinions of the Accounting Principles Board No. 29, "Accounting for Nonmonetary Transactions," American Institute of Certified Public Accountants, New York, 1973.

The gain (or loss) is always the difference between the book value and fair market value of the assets exchanged. This is verified as follows:

Fair market value of equipment	$41,000
Book value of equipment ($48,000 − $14,000)	34,000
Gain recognized	**7,000**

It follows logically then, that if the book value of the asset exchanged is greater than their fair market value, a loss ensues. Assume, for example, that in our previous illustration all things are the same except that the fair market value of the equipment exchanged is $31,000 (instead of $41,000). In this case a loss of $3,000 ($34,000 − $31,000) would be reported, and the following journal entry would be made:

Land ($31,000 + $21,000)	$52,000	
Accumulated depreciation: equipment	14,000	
Loss on exchange of plant assets	3,000	
Equipment		$48,000
Cash		21,000
To record exchange of equipment for land		

Calculation of loss:

Fair market value of equipment	$31,000
Book value of equipment	34,000
Loss recognized	**$ 3,000**

Similar Assets—Loss Situations

Similar assets generally perform the same function, or are employed in the same line of business. When similar assets are exchanged at a loss, the loss should be immediately recognized (in much the same manner as when dissimilar assets are exchanged). For example, assume Jones Trucking Company trades in an old truck with a book value of $6,000 (cost of $16,000 less accumulated depreciation of $10,000) and a current fair market value of $4,500. The new truck has a list price of $23,000. In negotiations with the truck dealer, a trade-in allowance of $7,500 is granted on the old truck, resulting in a cash payment of $15,500 (list price of $23,000 less trade-in allowance of $7,500). The cost of the new truck is determined as follows:

List price of new truck	$23,000
Less trade-in allowance	7,500
Cash payment due	$15,500
Plus fair market value of old truck trade-in	4,500
Cost of new truck	**$20,000**

The journal entry to record the transaction is:

Truck (new)	$20,000	
Accumulated depreciation: Truck (old)	10,000	
Loss on exchange of plant assets	1,500	
Truck (old)		$16,000
Cash		15,500
To record exchange of trucks		

The loss on the exchange is verified as follows:

Fair market value of old truck	$4,500
Book value of old truck	(6,000)
Loss on exchange	**$1,500**

Similar Assets—Gain Situations

The most complex situation in accounting for asset exchanges occurs when similar assets are exchanged resulting in a gain situation. Generally accepted accounting requires that any gain resulting from such an exchange not be shown in the accounts, but rather it should be *deferred* by subtracting it from the fair market value of the assets received in the transaction. This procedure is required because the earning process of the assets involved is not complete in the sense that they perform the same function. Stated differently, it is felt that a company that exchanges one asset for another similar asset is in the same economic position after the swap occurs; therefore, no benefit (i.e., gain) should be perceived as occurring in such a situation.

To illustrate the accounting treatment for such a situation, assume that Glenn Clothing Manufacturer arranges with Zinger Sewing Machine Company to exchange a group of sewing machines with a fair market value of $86,000 and a book value of $74,000 (cost of $96,000 less accumulated depreciation of $22,000) for several new sewing machines. The fair market value of the sewing machines received is $90,000. Glenn agrees to pay the difference between the fair market values of the assets traded in and received of $4,000 ($90,000 − $86,000). The deferred gain to Glenn is computed as follows:

Fair market value of the old sewing machines exchanged	$86,000
Book value of sewing machines exchanged	74,000
Gain (*not* recorded)	**$12,000**

The gain on this transaction is deferred by subtracting it from the fair market value of the assets received, thus reducing the amount that the new sewing machines are recorded for in the accounting records. That computation is as follows:

Fair market value of *new* sewing machines	$90,000
Less deferred gain	(12,000)
Amount recorded	**$78,000**

The amount recorded (often referred to as the *basis*) for the new machines can also be computed as follows:

Book value of *old* sewing machine	$74,000
Add cash paid	4,000
Amount recorded	**$78,000**

This journal entry by Glenn to record the transaction is:

Sewing Machines (new)	$78,000	
Accumulated depreciation: Sewing machines (old)	22,000	
Sewing machines (old)		$96,000
Cash		4,000
To record exchange of sewing machines		

For tax purposes, neither a gain nor a loss is recognized on trade-ins of similar assets. Instead, the basis of the new asset is always adjusted by the unrecognized gain or loss. A gain is deducted, and a loss is added. In planning asset acquisitions, a company can benefit by selling old equipment if a loss is to be incurred, and by trading in old equipment (if possible) if a gain will result. In general, the rule in this regard is to "sell your losses and trade your gains."

NATURAL RESOURCES

Natural resources, frequently called *wasting assets,* include petroleum deposits, timber, minerals, and other natural deposits. Natural resources are characterized by the fact that the asset is consumed physically over a period of time, and the replacement of the asset is an act of nature. The process by which the recorded cost of a natural resource is allocated to expense is called *depletion.* The two primary considerations in accounting for plant assets are (1) determining the amount to record as a debit to the asset account, and (2) determining the annual amount of depletion expense.

Capitalization of a Natural Resource

When a natural resource is acquired, the cost of the asset is generally debited to an asset (commonly referred to as a *capitalizing*), and then those costs are prorated to depletion expense as benefits are extracted. As the resource is removed through the process of drilling, mining, or cutting, the asset account is systematically reduced. The carrying value of an oil well, for example, is reduced by a small amount for each barrel of oil extracted. The original cost of the well is thus gradually converted from an asset account to a part of the cost of the oil sold. The cost of a natural resource typically includes exploratory and developmental costs in addition to the purchase price.

Depletion

The term *depletion* is used to describe the pro rata allocation of the total cost of a natural resource to the units removed. Cost depletion is similar to the units-of-production method of depreciation, and is computed by dividing the asset cost by the estimated available units of natural resource (such as barrels of oil and tons of minerals). The total depletion expense for a year is equal to the number of units extracted multiplied by the depletion charge per unit.

To illustrate, assume DAS Company purchased land containing mineral deposits for $3,900,000. Tests indicate that approximately 400,000 tons of the mineral are present on the land, and it is estimated that once the materials are mined the land can be sold for $500,000. The depletion charge per ton is computed as follows:

Cost of the natural resource	$3,900,000
Less: Estimated salvage value	500,000
Amount to be depleted	$3,400,000
Estimated number of tons	÷400,000
Depletion per ton	$ 85.00

If we assume that 30,000 tons were extracted and sold during the first year of operation, the depletion charge for the year would be 30,000 × $85 or

$255,000. The journal entry to record the depletion expense for the year would be:

Depletion expense	$255,000	
Accumulated depletion: Mineral deposit		$255,000
To record depletion for the year		

The accumulated depletion account is a contra asset and is presented on the balance sheet as a deduction from the cost of the mineral deposit. The balance sheet presentation for this situation at the end of the first year of operation would be:

Mineral deposit (cost)	$3,900,000	
Less: Accumulated depletion	255,000	$3,645,000

Percentage Depletion

In certain situations, and subject to limitations, the Internal Revenue Service permits a tax deduction for depletion equal to a specified percent of gross income (sales) from extractive operations. This is commonly referred to as *percentage depletion.* Therefore, for income tax purposes it is possible for total depletion deductions to exceed the cost of the property being depleted.

To illustrate how percentage deletion differs from depletion based on cost, assume that Dixon Mining Company purchased an ore mine in January 19X1. The pertinent data relating to the purchase and operation of the mine in 19X1 follows:

Cost of the mine	$10,000,000
Estimated salvage value	$ 1,000,000
Estimated number of tons recoverable	20,000
Number of tons extracted in 19X1	3,000
Sales (gross income), 19X1	$10,000,000
All expenses other than depletion	$15,000,000
Percentage depletion allowable for tax purposes	15%

The income statement for financial reporting purposes will reflect depletion based on the cost of the mining property and the tons recoverable and extracted in 19X1. That calculation is

$$\frac{\$10{,}000{,}000 - \$1{,}000{,}000}{20{,}000 \text{ tons}} = \$450 \text{ per ton}$$

The tax return of Dixon Mining Company will reflect depletion calculated on a percentage of sales for 19X1. The two calculations of income are presented next.

Dixon Mining Company
Income Statement
(for financial reporting purposes)
For the year ended December 31, 19X1

Sales		$20,000,000
Depletion expense:		
3,000 tons × $450 =	$ 1,350,000	
All other expenses	15,000,000	
Total expenses		16,350,000
Pretax income		**$ 3,650,000**

Dixon Mining Company
Determination of Taxable Income
For the year ended December 31, 19X1

Gross income		$20,000,000
Depletion expense		
$20,000,000 × 15% =	$ 3,000,000	
All other expenses	15,000,000	18,000,000
Taxable income		**$ 2,000,000**

As shown, percentage depletion allowances can result in a reduction in taxable income. The asserted reasoning behind such favorable tax treatment is to provide additional incentives to companies who explore for the natural resources that are vital to the national economy.

INTANGIBLE ASSETS

Physical substance does not guarantee economic value; and similarly a lack of physical substances does not guarantee an absence of economic value. An intangible asset, like other assets, has value because of certain rights and privileges conferred by law upon its owner. Although, an intangible asset has no material substance, it does provide value in the form of special legal rights or claims that ownership confers. Examples of intangible assets are patents, trademarks, copyrights, franchises, and goodwill.

Amortization

An intangible asset may be acquired through purchase or by development within the company. For example, a company may either purchase the rights to a patent from an outside entity or develop it internally. In either situation, the patent must be recorded in the accounts at cost. This is true even if the value of the patent rights turns out to be more than the cost. Intangible assets are ordinarily presented in the balance sheet in a separate section following plant assets. The systematic write-off of the cost of an intangible asset over its useful life is referred to as *amortization.* Intangible assets are almost always amortized on the straight-line basis. (Tax laws require straight-line amortization.) When intangible assets are amortized the debit is to expense, and the credit is normally made directly to the asset account.

Patents

A patent is an exclusive right to produce, use, and sell a particular product. These rights, which are issued by the federal government, continue in effect for seventeen years. The period of time that the patent is amortized may be less than seventeen years or the remaining legal life of the asset.

To illustrate, assume that at the beginning of the current year a company bought the rights to a patent for $75,000 which was granted three years earlier. Although the patent has a remaining legal life of fourteen years, it is anticipated that technology will develop in such a way that the patent will lose its usefulness in about five years. The patent will therefore be amortized over its estimated remaining useful life of five years at a rate of $15,000 ($75,000 ÷ 5) per year. The journal entries relating to the acquisition and first years amortization of the patent would be:

Acquisition:	Patents	$75,000	
	Cash		$75,000
Amortization:	Amortization expense: Patents	15,000	
	Patents		15,000

A separate contra-asset account is normally *not* credited for the amortization of patents or other intangible assets.

Although a patent's useful life normally does not extend beyond its legal life of seventeen years, small changes or additions may result in a new patent. The effect may be to extend the life of the old patent, in which case it is permissible in most cases to apply the unamortized costs of the old patent to the new patent. Alternatively, if a patent becomes worthless because demand drops for the product produced, the asset should be written off immediately to operations.

Each year businesses spend huge sums of money on research and development activities directed at developing new or improved products and processes. In the past, these enterprises followed a variety of practices in accounting for and reporting these costs. Some capitalized all such costs, others expensed all such costs, while still other companies capitalized certain research expenditures and expensed the rest. The amounts involved were very substantial and there was no apparent conformity in accounting for research and development costs. Accordingly, soon after the Financial Accounting Standards Board was organized they issued FASB Statement No. 2, which mandated that all research and development costs are to be expensed as incurred. This essentially put to an end the lack of uniformity in accounting for research and development costs.

Trademarks

A permanent right to use a trademark or trade name rests exclusively with the original user of that asset. The trademark registration system provides for an indefinite number of renewals for periods of twenty years each; however it must be amortized for accounting purposes over a period not to exceed forty years. The trademark costs would include the purchase price, if acquired from an outsider, or such items as design cost, attorney fees, and registration fees, if developed internally.

Copyrights

A copyright is the exclusive right to publish and sell a literary, artistic, or musical composition. Copyrights are issued by the federal government and are granted for the life of the creator plus fifty years. The costs of a copyright include all costs of creating the work plus costs of obtaining the copyright.

Technology in the area of tapes and videorecorders has advanced so rapidly that there is widespread capability to infringe on many copyrights. Because of this uncertainty regarding the useful life of many copyrights, it is common that they be amortized over a relatively short period of time, although they may be amortized over a period not to exceed forty years.

Franchises

Franchises are frequently granted by a governmental body to a utility or other business to permit that entity to use public property in performing its services. Examples are the use of public land for telephone or electric lines, or the use of city streets for a bus line. In that same regard a company may sell franchises to local outlets, as in the case of McDonald's or Kentucky Fried Chicken. Franchises may be for a definite period of time, for an indefinite period of time, or perpetual. The company securing the franchise carries a Franchise account in its records only when there are costs such as a lump-sum payment in advance, or legal fees and other expenditures that are identifiable with the acquisition of the franchise. The cost of a franchise for a limited period should be amortized as operating expense over the life of the franchise. A franchise with an indefinite life, or a perpetual franchise, should be carried at cost and amortized over a reasonable period not to exceed forty years.

Annual payments made under a franchise agreement should be entered as operating expenses in the period in which they are incurred. They do not represent an asset to the concern since they do not relate to future rights to use property.

Organization Costs

Costs incurred in the formation of a corporation, such as fees to underwriters for handling stock or bond issues, legal fees of various sorts, and promotional expenditures involving the organization of a business are classified as organization costs.

These items are usually capitalized into an account called Organization Costs and may be carried as an asset on the balance sheet. Many companies amortize these costs over an arbitrary period of time (maximum forty years), since the time for which these expenditures will be beneficial is difficult or impossible to determine. Income tax regulations permit the amortization of organization costs over a period of five years or more. It is common practice in financial accounting to arbitrarily follow tax laws and amortize organization costs over a five-year period.

Goodwill

Goodwill is the most complex of all intangible assets. Recordable goodwill can occur, in an accounting context, *only* when one company purchases another. Goodwill is the excess of the cost of the business purchased over the fair market value of the net assets acquired.[2]

To illustrate how goodwill arises, assume that John Mac, Inc., purchased Hamilton Clothing Store on October 16, 19X1 for $500,000 cash. At the date of the purchase it was determined that the book values and fair market values of the assets acquired, less liabilities to be assumed, were as follows:

	BOOK VALUE	FAIR MARKET VALUE
Inventory	$265,000	$245,000
Plant assets (cost of $175,000 less accumulated depreciation $50,000)	125,000	160,000
Prepaid expenses	5,000	5,000
Other assets	50,000	50,000
	445,000	460,000
Less liabilities	22,000	22,000
	$423,000	**$438,000**

[2] Goodwill only occurs when the *purchase method* is used to account for the acquisition of one business by another. A second method, referred to as *pooling of interests,* is frequently used to account for business combinations and does not result in goodwill.

By definition, the goodwill to be recorded as a result of the acquisition is \$62,000 (\$500,000 − \$438,000). The journal entry to record the acquisition of Hamilton by John Mac, Inc., would be:

Inventory	\$245,000	
Plant assets	160,000	
Prepaid expenses	5,000	
Other assets	50,000	
GOODWILL	62,000	
Liabilities		\$ 22,000
Cash		500,000
To record acquisition of Hamilton Clothing Store.		

The intangible asset, goodwill, must be amortized over its estimated useful life, but not to exceed forty years. If we assume a forty-year amortization period, the amortization for 19X1 (and every forseeable subsequent year) would be:

Amortization expense (goodwill)	\$1,550	
Goodwill		\$1,550
To record amortization of goodwill for the year (\$62,000 ÷ 40 = \$1,550)		

It is important to note that goodwill in the accounting context is somewhat different from goodwill in a traditional context. As we have demonstrated, in accounting goodwill is the missing link between the current value of a business as a unit, and the sum of its parts. It is only recorded when a business is purchased. Certainly, some of the most acceptable evidence that goodwill exists is the ability of a business to earn a greater income than is common for a similar business. This greater return could be the result of a number of factors including location, expertise, name recognition of owners, and the like. However, regardless of how much goodwill is thought to exist in business, and regardless of the evidence that it does exist, it is never recorded until the business is purchased; and then it is recorded by the purchasing institution in the manner described previously.

If the fair market value of the assets acquired in an acquisition exceeds the purchase price, then negative goodwill occurs. If this excess over cost is present, it should be allocated to reduce the amount assigned to noncurrent assets in the entry to record the acquisition. This would be a very unusual situation and should not be expected to occur with any degree of regularity.

Inconsistencies Between Financial and Tax Accounting for Intangible Assets

This book is primarily concerned with financial accounting—preparing and disseminating financial information to shareholders and other outside parties. Frequently, accounting for *tax* purposes differs from financial accounting procedures prescribed by generally accepted accounting principles. In the area of intangible assets there are several such differences, especially regarding the period of time over which these intangibles may (or must) be amortized. The following table summarizes how financial and tax accounting can conflict in this regard:

	MAXIMUM AMORTIZATION PERIOD	
Intangible Asset	**Financial Accounting**	**Tax Purposes**
Patents	17 years	17 years
Trademarks	40 years	Amortization not permitted
Copyrights	40 years	40 years
Franchises:		
Indefinite life	40 years	Amortization not permitted
Determinable life	Length of contract	Length of contract
Organization costs	40 years	5 years
Goodwill	40 years	Amortization not permitted

OTHER ASSETS AND DEFERRED CHARGES

The asset items included in the Other Assets section of a balance sheet vary widely in practice. Occasionally investments in other companies are located here, although more commonly these items are set aside in a special Investments section of the balance sheet. Some of the items commonly included in Other Assets are deferred charges (long-term prepayments), noncurrent receivables, assets in special funds, and cash surrender value of life insurance policies.

Cash Surrender Value of Life Insurance

Corporations have an insurable interest in certain of their executives. Therefore, it is common for companies to insure the lives of these executives, with proceeds from the policy payable to the company. In accounting for a life insurance policy of this type, premiums paid and the related cash surrender value of the policy must be recorded and reported.

The *cash surrender value* of a policy is the sum payable upon the cancellation of the policy at the request of the insured. Each policy contains a schedule which indicates the cash surrender value and the loan value for each policy year. Since the policy can be cancelled and a portion of the premiums already paid may be returned in the form of the cash surrender value, not all of the premiums paid constitute expense. Thus the annual expense of the policy is the premium paid less any increase in the asset (cash surrender value) acquired.

To illustrate, assume that Noxid Corporation insured the life of its president for $150,000. The following data were taken from the insurance policy:

POLICY YEAR	ANNUAL PREMIUM (BEGINNING OF YEAR)	CASH SURRENDER VALUE (END OF YEAR)
1	$2,750	$ 470
2	2,750	960
3	2,750	1,470
. . . etc. as specified in the policy		

The journal entries to reflect the costs relating to the life insurance policy in policy years 1, 2, and 3 would be:

ACCOUNTS	AMOUNTS POLICY YEAR 1		2		3	
Beginning of year:						
Life insurance expense	$2,750		$2,750		$2,750	
Cash		$2,750		$2,750		$2,750
To record payment of life insurance premiums						
End of year:						
Cash surrender value of life insurance	470		490		510	
Life insurance expense		470		490 ($960 – $470)		510 ($1,470 – $960)
To record increase in cash surrender value						

The balance of the account Cash Surrender Value of Life Insurance is reported in the Other Assets (or Investments) section of the balance sheet each year; and the Life Insurance Expense account is obviously an expense to be reported in the company's income statement.

SUMMARY

Proper asset valuation and cost recognition is crucial to financial reporting both for managerial decision making and for presentation to stockholders. Because of the magnitude of investment in noncurrent assets, proper handling of asset valuation and periodic costing is all the more important as a reflection of financial and operational viability. Certain transactions and classes of noncurrent assets require special consideration and handling because of highly subjective valuation characteristics. Among these transactions and classifications are disposals, trade-ins, intangible assets, and natural resources. Intangible assets such as patents, trademarks, copyrights, and goodwill are common features on corporate financial statements as they reflect economic rights and advantages which will generate future revenues, even though they lack the physical characteristics of tangible assets. Natural resources are those wasting assets that are reduced as a result of their removal or sale, their primary distinguishing feature from depreciable assets is that they are consumed. The proper periodic costing of such assets—amortization for intangibles and depletion for natural resources—is crucial for meaningful income recognition.

KEY POINTS

1. Accounting for the disposal of a plant asset involves updating depreciation on the asset, removing the account balances that pertain to the item disposed of, and finally recognizing a gain or loss as the difference between net book value of the item and scrap value obtained.

2. In situations where old assets are traded in for new assets, the old asset and related accumulated depreciation must be removed from the accounting records and the new asset must be recorded. Accounting for such an exchange of assets varies somewhat depending upon whether the two assets are similar or dissimilar.

3. The accounting for asset exchanges should be based on the fair market values of either of the assets obtained or given up, whichever is more readily determinable.

4. Natural resources are characterized by the fact that the asset is consumed physically over a period of time and the replacement of the asset is an act of nature. The process by which the recorded cost of a natural resource is allocated to expense is called depletion.

5. Percentage depletion is depletion for tax purposes, based on a percentage of gross income of the company owning the depletable asset.

6. Intangible assets are economic rights and advantages which will generate revenues in the future but lack the physical characteristics of tangible assets. The systematic write-off of the cost of an intangible asset over its useful life is referred to as amortization.

7. A patent is an exclusive right to produce, use and sell a particular product.

8. A trademark is a permanent right to use an identifying characteristic of a product or a trade name granted exclusively to the original user of that asset.

9. A copyright is the exclusive right to publish and sell a literary, artistic, or musical composition.

10. Organization costs are cost incurred in the formation of a corporation. They are normally capitalized and amortized over a five-year period.

11. Goodwill, the most complex of all intangible assets, is the excess of the cost of a business acquired over the fair market value of the net assets acquired.

12. Deferred charges are long-term prepayments.

13. Cash-surrender value of life insurance is the sum payable upon the cancellation of the policy at the request of the insured.

QUESTIONS

1. If a plant asset is disposed of before the end of its useful life, how is a gain or loss determined?

2. When similar assets are exchanged, at what amount is the asset recorded?

3. Compu-Jockey Company traded in its old computer mainframe on a more advanced model. Because of the manufacturer's efforts to expand sales, the trade-in allowance exceeds the book value of the old model. Can Compu-Jockey recognize a gain on the exchange in determining net income for tax purposes or for financial reporting?

4. Explain the accounting treatment for trade-ins on similar assets in situations where a gain or loss occurs. If a loss occurs, what benefit arises in future years for tax purposes as a result of the trade-in loss being disallowed by the IRS?

5. Amalgamated Tapioca Mines recognizes $5 of depletion for each ton of tapioca ore mined. This year 200,000 tons were mined but only 150,000 tons were sold because of the international tapioca glut. How much depletion should be deducted from the current year's revenues?

6. Outward Inc., traded in an old production machine for a new one to fulfill the same function. Original acquisition cost of the old machine was $60,000 and the accumulated depreciation was $48,000. The trade-in allowance on the new unit was $16,000 with a list price of $80,000. What is the cash price to Outward? Calculate the resulting recorded or unrecorded loss or gain. For tax purposes, what is the cost basis to be used in depreciation for income determination?

7. Define each of the following types of intangible assets and indicate the maximum allowable amortization period for financial accounting and for tax purposes.

   a. Patents
   b. Trademarks
   c. Copyrights
   d. Franchises

e. Goodwill
f. Organization costs

8. When is it appropriate to record goodwill as an intangible asset?

9. For each of the following, indicate the appropriate type of cost allocation.

	AMORTIZATION	DEPRECIATION	DEPLETION	OTHER
a. Plant site (in use)				
b. Patent				
c. Machinery				
d. Building				
e. Research and development costs				
f. Franchise				
g. Trademark				
h. Mineral deposits				
i. Goodwill				
j. Organization costs				
k. Leasehold improvements				
l. Oil well				
m. Unimproved land				
n. Ordinary repairs to machinery				

10. A long-time friend of yours, Doc Chuckery, owns a small but successful clothing store. He plans to go to the bank soon to request a loan to expand his business, and he asks your help in preparing the store's financial statement to present to the bank. Doc feels that because his business has done well in the past, and has an excellent reputation in the community, that there is at least a small amount of goodwill present which should be included in the listing of company assets. What is your position on this matter?

11. A. R. Block Company recently purchased a ten-year fire and casualty insurance policy on their plant assets, paying the full ten-year premium in advance. How should the prepayment be presented in the financial statements?

12. What is cash surrender value of life insurance, and on what financial statement should it appear?

EXERCISES

E9-1 A company yacht with a book value of $60,000 was traded in on a new yacht with a list price of $600,000. The trade-in allowance (not necessarily the fair market value) for the old yacht was $90,000.

a. How much cash must be paid for the new yacht?
b. What is the cost basis of the new yacht for income tax purposes?
c. How much depreciation should be recorded on the new yacht for the first year of use, assuming a 4-year life, a residual of $66,000, and the use of straight-line depreciation?

E9-2 A company airplane which cost $57,600 had an estimated useful life of 5 years and an estimated salvage value of $9,600. Straight-line depreciation was used. Give the entry required by each of the following alternative assumptions:

a. The airplane was sold for cash of $36,000 after 2 years' use.
b. The airplane was traded in after 3 years on another airplane with a list price of $72,000. Trade-in allowance was $32,400.
c. The airplane was scrapped after 4 years' use. Since scrap dealers were unwilling to pay anything for the airplane, it was given to a scrap dealer for his services in removing it.

E9-3 A piece of equipment that cost $10,800, on which $6,000 of accumulated depreciation had been recorded, was disposed of on January 3, 19X1.

Give general journal entries to record the disposal under each of the following assumptions:

a. It was discarded as having no value.
b. It was sold for $2,000 cash.
c. It was sold for $6,000.
d. The equipment was traded in on similar equipment having a list price of $16,000. A $5,200 trade-in was allowed, and the balance was paid in cash.
e. The equipment was traded in on similar equipment having a list price of $16,000. A $2,400 trade-in was allowed, and the balance was paid in cash.

E9-4 A cattle truck owned by Hogan Cattle Company, and costing $14,800, with accumulated depreciation of $7,200, was traded in on a new model that had a list price of $12,200. A trade-in allowance of $2,000 was given.

a. Compute the book value of the old truck.
b. Determine the amount of cash required to purchase the new truck.
c. Compute the amount of loss on the exchange.
d. Determine the cost basis of the new truck for federal income tax purposes.
e. Compute the yearly depreciation on the new truck, assuming a useful life of 5 years, a residual value of $3,200, and straight-line depreciation.

E9-5 The Dougherty Company sold a large truck for cash and the records of the company reflected the following:

Delivery truck	$8,000
Accumulated depreciation	(6,000)

REQUIRED:

Give the entry for disposal of the truck, assuming the sales price was

1. $2,000
2. $1,200
3. $2,800

E9-6 The records of the Spartex Company reflected the following data relating to a fixed asset:

Delivery truck (at cost)	$7,200
Accumulated depreciation	(5,600)

The company decided to purchase a new truck; the dealer demonstrated a truck that was suitable to the needs. The new truck had a list price of $9,000. However, the cash price without a trade-in was $8,400. The dealer required a cash payment of $6,400 in addition to the old asset.

REQUIRED:

1. Give the entry to record the exchange assuming similar assets.
2. Give the adjusting entry for depreciation on the new truck for the first year after acquisition assuming a 6-year useful life and a 10 percent residual value.

E9-7 The Holloway Mining Company spent $50,000 to develop an ore deposit which contains an estimated 100,000 tons of recoverable ore. In the first year of operation, 25,000 tons of ore were mined and sold.

Compute the depletion cost for the first year of operations.

E9-8 Amalgamated Tapioca Mines started mining activities early in 19X1. At the end of the year its accountant prepared the following summary of its mining costs:

Labor	$4,760,000
Materials	490,000
Miscellaneous	1,078,560

These costs do not include any charges for depletion or depreciation. Data relating to assets used in mining the ore follow:

Cost of mine (estimated deposit, 10 million tons; residual value of the mine estimated at $840,000)	$4,200,000
Buildings (estimated life, 15 years; no residual value)	369,600
Equipment (useful life, 6 years regardless of number of tons mined; residual value $84,000)	672,000

During the year, 800,000 tons (8 percent) of ore were mined, of which 600,000 tons were sold. It is estimated that it will take at least 15 years to extract the ore.

Determine the cost that should be assigned to the inventory of unsold ore at the end of 19X1.

E9-9 The Hollington Manufacturing Company owns two patents, which are utilized in the manufacturing activities. The patents were acquired as follows:

— Patent No. 1 Purchased from John Hartley on January 1, 19X5 for a cash cost of $8,160. Hartley had registered the patent with the U.S. Patent Office on January 1, 19X0. Amortize over remaining legal life.

— Patent No. 2 During 19X4, two employees of the company developed this patent for the company, which was registered on January 1, 19X5. The company identified the following costs incurred in development and registration: salaries, $60,000; facilities used and overhead, $10,000; registration costs, $2,000. These costs were accumulated during 19X4 in an account entitled Deferred R & D Costs. It is estimated that this patent will have a useful economic life of 15 years; the legal life is 17 years.

REQUIRED:

1. Give entry to record each patent as an intangible fixed asset.
2. Give adjusting entry at December 31, 19X5 for amortization of each patent. Show computations.

E9-10 On January 2, 19X1, Amalgamated Inc., purchased Boo Company, paying $500,000 in cash. At that time, Boo Company had assets with book values totaling $520,000. The total fair market value of the assets acquired was $560,000. Boo Company had liabilities of $100,000 to be assumed by Amalgamated.

a. What amount of goodwill should Amalgamated recognize relating to the acquisition?
b. Assuming the goodwill recognized is to be amortized over a period of 40 years, present the entry on December 31, 19X1 to record the amortization.

E9-11 At the beginning of a given policy year, ABC Company paid a life insurance premium on the life of its president totaling $1,250. At the end of the same policy year, a reference to the insurance policy revealed that the cash surrender value of that policy had increased by $725.

Give the entries to record these facts.

PROBLEMS

P9-1 During 19X1, the Webb Company disposed of three different assets. On January 1, 19X1, prior to their disposal, the accounts reflected the following:

ASSETS	ORIGINAL COST	RESIDUAL VALUE	ESTIMATED LIFE	ACCUMULATED DEPRECIATION (STRAIGHT LINE)
X	$ 40,000	$ 4,000	10 years	$ 25,200 (7 years)
Y	70,800	6,000	9 years	43,200 (6 years)
Z	130,400	12,000	14 years	118,400 (14 years)

The assets were disposed of in the following ways:

Asset X Sold on January 1, 19X1, for $13,000 cash.

Asset Y Exchanged for a new asset of similar type on May 1, 19X1. The new asset had a list price of $96,000 and a cash equivalent price of $90,000. A trade-in allowance of $36,000 was agreed upon and the balance was paid in cash $60,000.

Asset Z On January 3, 19X1, the asset suffered irreparable damage from an accident. On January 5, 19X1, it was given to a salvage company at no cost. The salvage company agreed to remove the asset immediately at no cost to Webb.

REQUIRED:

1. List each asset and its book value on the date of disposal. Show computations. The company computes depreciation to even months.
2. Give all entries incident to the disposal of each asset. Show appropriate calculations.

P9-2 Flibinite, Inc., leased a store building from Bilman, Inc., on July 1 for a period of 10 years for a total contractual amount of $1,248,000. The fiscal year used by Flibinite begins on July 1. Terms of the lease called for an immediate cash payment of $124,800, representing rent for the final year of the 10-year lease period. Also on July 1, Flibinite (the lessee) paid $10,400 for the current month's rent and agreed to pay rent monthly in advance during the first 9 years of the lease. The lease also provided that Flibinite must pay for any repairs or improvements it wished to make.

An escalator was immediately installed by the lessee at a cost of $83,200, paid in cash. The normal life of the escalator was stated by the manufacturer to be 20 years. Some lighting fixtures were also installed at a cost of $10,400 paid in cash, for which the estimated life was 5 years.

INSTRUCTIONS:

Prepare journal entries to record

a. Payment of $135,200, representing $10,400 rent for July and $124,800 for the final year's rent under the 10-year lease contract.
b. Payment for the escalator and lighting fixtures.
c. First annual amortization of the cost of the escalator.
d. First annual amortization of the cost of the lighting fixtures.
e. Final disposition of the $124,800 advance payment of rent applicable to the tenth year of the lease.

P9-3 The Discovery Corporation purchased a mining claim for $900,000 including the residual rights to the land site after the ore is exhausted. Because the site is located close to a large city, it is considered to be worth $50,000. Geologists estimate that the ore content of the claim is approximately 4,500,000 tons. Mining is started in 19X1 and 500,000 tons of ore are mined at costs of:

For wages paid in 19X1	$120,000
Depreciation on equipment	15,000
For power costs paid	22,000
For depletion of ore claim	?

REQUIRED:

1. Record in a journal entry the acquisition of the claim.
2. Record the cost of mining the ore in 19X1.

P9-4 On November 20, 19X1, Surface Mining Company purchased a tract of land containing veins of coal near the surface for $726,000. The tract is estimated to contain 990,000 tons of coal; it is expected that the quantity mined during the first year of operations will be only half of that mined in each succeeding year.

Fixed installations are set up at an additional cost of $154,000. These transactions took place during the latter part of 19X1. Equipment was purchased for $352,000 early in January, 19X2 and operations started as soon as employees were hired and trained.

It is estimated that the fixed installations could be used for 20 years. However, they will, of necessity, be abandoned when the coal deposit is exhausted. The equipment is estimated to have a useful life of 8 years and it can be transferred to another location conveniently, although there will be no salvage value at the end of 8 years.

By the end of 19X2, 90,000 tons had been mined and sold. The company has adopted the units-of-production method of depreciation for fixed installations. The straight-line method is used for all other items.

REQUIRED:

Prepare the adjusting entries for depreciation and depletion for the year ended December 31, 19X2.

P9-5 On January 3, 19X2, Rich Raskley purchased a piece of property with gravel deposits for $6,310,000. He estimated that the gravel deposits contained 4,700,000 cubic yards of gravel. After the gravel is gone, the land, will be worth about $200,000.

The equipment required to extract the gravel cost $1,452,000. It has an estimated useful life of 6 years and an estimated residual value of $68,000. In addition, Rich had to build a small frame building to house the mine office and a small dining hall for the workers. The buildings cost $152,000 and have no residual value after the estimated useful life of 10 years.

Trucks for the project cost $308,000 (estimated life, 6 years; residual value, $20,000).

Rich estimated that in 5 years all the gravel would be mined and the mine would be shut down. During 19X2, 1,175,000 cubic yards of gravel were mined. The average selling price during the year was $2.66 per cubic yard, and at the end of the year 125,000 cubic yards remained unsold. Operating expenses were $852,000 for labor and $232,000 for other expenses.

REQUIRED:

1. Prepare general journal entries to record the purchase of the property and all the buildings and equipment associated with the mine.
2. Prepare adjusting entries to record depletion and depreciation for the first year of operation (19X2). Assume that the depreciation rate is equal to the percentage of the total gravel mined during the year unless the asset is movable. For movable assets, use the straight-line method.
3. Prepare an income statement for 19X2.
4. Prepare a general journal entry, assuming that the mine, gravel inventory, and all buildings and equipment, but not the trucks, are sold on January 1, 19X3, for $6,000,000 cash.

P9-6 The Krone Company has six different intangible assets to be accounted for and reported on the financial statements. At issue is a decision by the management in respect to the amortization of the cost of each of the six intangibles. Certain facts concerning each are:

a. Goodwill The Krone Company started business in January 19X2 by purchasing the assets of another business for a cash lump sum of $600,000. Included in the purchase price was the item "Goodwill, $160,000." Krone executives believe that "the goodwill is an important long-term asset to us." Amortize over maximum period permitted.

b. Organization costs The Krone Company is a corporation and was organized in January 19X2 to purchase the company mentioned in item a. During organization, $6,000 was expended for legal, accounting, charter, and other organizational activities. Debit a deferred charge and amortize over 5 years.

c. License The company secured a license on January 1, 19X4, from the city to operate a special service for a period of 5 years. Total cash expended in obtaining the license was $70,000.

d. Franchise The company obtained a franchise from the Flower Company to make and distribute a special item. The franchise was obtained on January 1, 19X4, at a cash cost of $4,000 and was for a 10-year period.

e. Patent The company purchased a patent for a cash cost of $47,600 on January 1, 19X4. The patent had a legal life of 17 years from date of registration with the U.S. Patent Office, which was January 1, 19X1. Amortize over the remaining legal life.

f. Copyright The company developed an item at a cost of $112,000 and it was copyrighted on January 1, 19X4. It is estimated that the copyrighted item will have little or no value by the end of 20 years. To simplify, credit Cash for the cost.

REQUIRED:

1. Give the entry for each of the acquisitions.
2. Give the adjusting entry for each intangible asset that would be necessary at the end of the annual accounting period, December 31, 19X4. Provide a brief explanation and show computations. If no entry is required for a particular item, explain the basis for your conclusion.
3. Determine the book value of each intangible on January 1, 19X5.

P9-7 A new patent was purchased by Moross Company from its inventor on January 2, 19X2. The full price of $560,000 was paid in cash. The patented device was promptly put to use in Moross's production operations. Although the legal life of the patent was 17 years, the company estimated that technological changes in its industry would limit the economic usefulness of the patent to 10 years.

On March 1, 19X2, the company paid $315,000 in legal fees for the services of attorneys who successfully defended an infringement suit against the patent.

In December of 19X4, Moross Company decided that the total useful life of the patent would be limited to 6 years rather than the original estimate of 10 years. This decision was reached before amortization was recorded for 19X4.

INSTRUCTIONS:

Prepare journal entries to record these events relating to the acquisition and amortization of the patent from January 2, 19X2, through December 31, 19X4.

P9-8 On January 4, 19X1, Investco, Inc., purchased the on-going company Pink, Inc. for $2,500,000, receiving all assets and assuming all liabilities. On that date Pink's balance sheet (abbreviated) appeared as follows:

Cash	-0-
Accounts receivable	$ 450,000
Inventory	1,250,000
Plant assets	3,200,000
Intangible assets	150,000
	5,050,000
Liabilities	2,900,000
Owners' equity	**$2,150,000**

An audit of Pink reveals that Accounts Receivable includes a debt totaling $75,000 from a customer who declared bankruptcy 2 years ago and is completely out of business. No allowance for Uncollectible Accounts has been established. All other receivables appear to be collectible. The Inventory amount includes $50,000 of merchandise which Pink is holding on consignment from Joe's Manufacturing Company. A letter from Joe revealed that he had accurately included the $50,000 in his inventory on December 31, 19X0. Other than the consigned merchandise, the fair market value of the inventory approximately equals the amount at which it is recorded. The carrying value of the Plant Assets equals its fair market value with the exception of land. The Land account (which is included in Plant Assets) shows a balance of $20,000. The current fair market value of the land is $110,000. The Intangible Assets are deemed to be worthless; the liabilities are properly valued.

REQUIRED:

1. Prepare a schedule calculating the amount of goodwill to be recognized by Investco in the acquisition of Pink.
2. Prepare the journal entry to record the acquisition.
3. Assuming Investco decides to amortize goodwill over the maximum time permissible, prepare the journal entry on December 31, 19X1 to record the amortization.

P9-9 You have been asked to look over and provide advice on the preparation of the financial statements of Fair Company as of December 31, 19X1, the company's first year of operation. Fair Company reported net income of $128,000 for the year.

All things appear to be "in order" until you begin your examination of the Other Assets section of the balance sheet. The following items are contained in that section:

Long-term prepayments	$36,000
Receivable from M. Mantle, Inc.	1,000
Cash surrender value of life insurance	2,800
Total other assets	$39,800

The Long-term Prepayment is the result of purchasing for cash a 10-year fire insurance policy on January 2, 19X1. The full amount of the check, $36,000, was debited into Long-term Prepayments, and it is presented in the Other Assets section because it represents a long-term, and not a short-term, prepayment.

The receivable from M. Mantle, Inc., is the result of a cash loan to a friend of the owner of Fair Company. The loan is not secured by a note, does not earn interest, and is due for repayment on April 15, 19X3. There is no reason to believe that the loan will not be repaid.

The Cash Surrender Value of Life Insurance is the result of a check written on January 2, 19X1 for the first annual premium on a life insurance policy taken out on the life of the president of Fair Company. The full amount of the check was debited to the account. An examination of the insurance policy reveals that as of the end of 19X1, the cash surrender value of the policy is $1,350.

REQUIRED:

1. Prepare the Other Assets section of the balance sheet as of December 31, 19X1 taking into consideration the facts just presented.
2. Prepare a schedule recomputing Fair Company's net income for 19X1.

PRESENT VALUES AND LIABILITIES 10

ORIENTATION

There are three primary sources from which a business generates or receives resources: contributions by owners, the sale of goods and services, and the extension of credit by creditors. Resources provided to the business by creditors through the extension of credit include cash loans as well as property, goods, and services. Liabilities can be defined as legal obligations that result from transactions requiring the future payment of assets or the future performance of services, with a definite and known date being prescribed for payment or performance. Because the balance sheet reflects the financial position of the business at a particular moment in time, the valuation and presentation of these future obligations must reflect the *time value of money.* The proper measurement and valuation of liabilities reflects the time value of money through utilization of present and future value techniques which are explained in this chapter.

PRESENT VALUES

Money has value because it constitutes command of purchasing power for resources (goods and services). Resources available *today,* all else equal, are worth more than resources to be received at some future time. It follows that money received today is worth more than money to be received sometime in the future. *Money has time value.*

To prove this idea, you might ask yourself, setting aside all risk considerations, what amount of money available *today* you would consider to be equivalent to the receipt of $1,000 a year from now? Since a dollar received today is more valuable than a dollar to be received in a year, the amount of money which you would view as equivalent today should be somewhat less than the $1,000. If, for example, you intended to put the money received today into a savings account earning 10% interest, then you could calculate precisely how much money you would need today in order to have $1,000 in a year. At the end of the year you would have the original amount (or principal) *plus* 10 percent of the principal (in interest), or [Principal + .10 (Principal)], which is 1.10 (Principal). In this case, *Principal* × *1.10 = $1,000.* To determine the Principal (*p*), the $1,000 is divided by 1.10, and is equal to $909 ($1,000 ÷ 1.10 = $909). In other words: $909 × 1.10 = $1,000. $909 left on deposit to earn 10 percent per year will amount to $1000 one year later. So the *present value* of $1,000 for a year at an assumed interest rate of 10 percent is $909.

Three things were necessary to be able to determine the $909 amount: (1) the future cash flow—$1,000; (2) the timing of the future cash flow—one year; and (3) the assumed interest rate—10%. In any situation in which these three factors are known (or can be approximated), a present value calculation can be made. For example, suppose that you wish to have $1000 in a savings account *two* years from the present time. The rate of interest on the account is 10 percent. The *principal* you would need to deposit is the *present value* of $1000 to be received two years hence at an interest rate of 10 percent. We can determine the principal amount (again) by recognizing that:

Principal × 1.21[1] = $1,000

Thus the principal amount would be equal to $826 ($1,000 ÷ 1.21). To prove the calculation just made, consider the following: If $826 were received now and invested at 10%, in one year it would have grown to $909 ($826 × 1.10); and in two years the amount would be $1,000 ($909 × 1.10). So the present value of $1,000 for *two* years, at an assumed interest rate of 10% is $826. The "factor" of 1.21 is simply the product of 1.10 × 1.10, or $(1.10)^2$.

[1] Ten % compounded for two years, or 1.10 × 1.10 = 1.21. The principal amount earns interest at the rate of 10 percent in each year, and the interest earned in the first year earns interest in the second year. (The term "compound interest" pertains to the earning of interest on interest previously earned.)

It is obvious that calculations such as these could become very cumbersome, particularly if several years of anticipated cash flows were involved. To simplify the process, Tables 10-1, 10-2, 10-3, and 10-4 (on pages 285 to 293) are provided. These four tables relate the time value of money to four different concepts:

1. Future value of $1
2. Present value of $1
3. Future value of an annuity of $1
4. Present value of an annuity of $1

These tables use $1 as a base and provide values for different periods of time (*n*) and at different interest rates (*i*).

Future Value of $1 (Table 10-1)

The future amount of $1 is the amount to which the $1 will increase at "*i*" interest rate for "*n*" periods. It is commonly referred to as compound interest. To illustrate, assume that on January 1, 19X1, you deposited $1,000 in a savings account at 8% annual interest, compounded each year. How much would you have on December 31, 19X4, four years hence? The answer can be determined by reference to Table 10-1, page 285, where we find a value (often called a "factor") of 1.36049 at the 8%, four-year point. By multiplying that value by our principal amount of $1,000 we get $1,360.49.[2] Obviously, the same procedure will work for any amount and for any time and interest rate which appears on the table.[3] (Interpolation can be used for rates and times which do not appear on the table.) For example, assume the amount to be deposited is $25,000, the interest rate is 14% and the time is 6 years. To determine the future value under those circumstances, we go to the six-year,

[2] We can prove this amount by the following computation:

	AMOUNT AT START OF YEAR	+ INTEREST DURING THE YEAR		=	AMOUNT AT END OF YEAR
Year 1	$1,000	$1,000 × .08 =	80.00	=	$1,080.00
Year 2	$1,080	$1,080 × .08 =	86.40	=	$1,166.40
Year 3	$1,166.40	$1,166.40 × .08 =	93.31	=	$1,259.71
Year 4	$1,259.71	$1,259.71 × .08 =	100.78	=	**$1,360.49**

[3] For the sake of simplicity of exposition, our discussion focuses on a "compounding period" of one year—interest is compounded annually. However, more frequent compounding (quarterly, monthly, daily, etc.) merely involves adjusting the *annual* rate of interest to reflect the particular "compounding period." For example, if interest is compounded monthly, a 12 percent annual rate is converted to *one* percent per month.

TABLE 10-1
Future Value of 1, $f = (1 + i)^n$

PERIODS	2%	2½%	3%	4%	5%	6%	7%	8%	9%	10%
1	1.02000	1.02500	1.03000	1.04000	1.05000	1.06000	1.07000	1.08000	1.09000	1.10000
2	1.04040	1.05063	1.06090	1.08160	1.10250	1.12360	1.14490	1.16640	1.18810	1.21000
3	1.06121	1.07689	1.09273	1.12486	1.15763	1.19102	1.22504	1.25971	1.29503	1.33100
4	1.08243	1.10381	1.12551	1.16986	1.21551	1.26248	1.31080	1.36049	1.41158	1.46410
5	1.10408	1.13141	1.15927	1.21665	1.27628	1.33823	1.40255	1.46933	1.53862	1.61051
6	1.12616	1.15969	1.19405	1.26532	1.34010	1.41852	1.50073	1.58687	1.67710	1.77156
7	1.14869	1.18869	1.22987	1.31593	1.40710	1.50363	1.60578	1.71382	1.82804	1.94872
8	1.17166	1.21840	1.26677	1.36857	1.47746	1.59385	1.71819	1.85093	1.99256	2.14359
9	1.19509	1.24886	1.30477	1.42331	1.55133	1.68948	1.83846	1.99900	2.17189	2.35795
10	1.21899	1.28008	1.34392	1.48024	1.62889	1.79085	1.96715	2.15892	2.36736	2.59374
11	1.24337	1.31209	1.38423	1.53945	1.71034	1.89830	2.10485	2.33164	2.58043	2.85312
12	1.26824	1.34489	1.42576	1.60103	1.79586	2.01220	2.25219	2.51817	2.81266	3.13843
13	1.29361	1.37851	1.46853	1.66507	1.88565	2.13293	2.40985	2.71962	3.06580	3.45227
14	1.31948	1.41297	1.51259	1.73168	1.97993	2.26090	2.57853	2.93719	3.34173	3.79750
15	1.34587	1.44830	1.55797	1.80094	2.07893	2.39656	2.75903	3.17217	3.64248	4.17725
16	1.37279	1.48451	1.60471	1.87298	2.18287	2.54035	2.95216	3.42594	3.97031	4.59497
17	1.40024	1.52162	1.65285	1.94790	2.29202	2.69277	3.15882	3.70002	4.32763	5.05447
18	1.42825	1.55966	1.70243	2.02582	2.40662	2.85434	3.37993	3.99602	4.71712	5.55992
19	1.45681	1.59865	1.75351	2.10685	2.52695	3.02560	3.61653	4.31570	5.14166	6.11591
20	1.48595	1.63862	1.80611	2.19112	2.65330	3.20714	3.86968	4.66096	5.60441	6.72750
21	1.51567	1.67958	1.86029	2.27877	2.78596	3.39956	4.14056	5.03383	6.10881	7.40025
22	1.54598	1.72157	1.91610	2.36992	2.92526	3.60354	4.43040	5.43654	6.65860	8.14027
23	1.57690	1.76461	1.97359	2.46472	3.07152	3.81975	4.74053	5.87146	7.25787	8.95430
24	1.60844	1.80873	2.03279	2.56330	3.22510	4.04893	5.07237	6.34118	7.91108	9.84973
25	1.64061	1.85394	2.09378	2.66584	3.38635	4.29187	5.42743	6.84848	8.62308	10.83471

(*continued*)

TABLE 10-1
Future Value of 1, $f = (1 + i)^n$ *(continued)*

PERIODS	11%	12%	14%	15%	16%	18%	20%	22%	24%	25%
1	1.11000	1.12000	1.14000	1.15000	1.16000	1.18000	1.20000	1.22000	1.24000	1.25000
2	1.23210	1.25440	1.29960	1.32250	1.34560	1.39240	1.44000	1.48840	1.53760	1.56250
3	1.36763	1.40493	1.48154	1.52088	1.56090	1.64303	1.72800	1.81585	1.90662	1.95313
4	1.51807	1.57352	1.68896	1.74901	1.81064	1.93878	2.07360	2.21533	2.36421	2.44141
5	1.68506	1.76234	1.92541	2.01136	2.10034	2.28776	2.48832	2.70271	2.93163	3.05176
6	1.87041	1.97382	2.19497	2.31306	2.43640	2.69955	2.98598	3.29730	3.63522	3.81470
7	2.07616	2.21068	2.50227	2.66002	2.82622	3.18547	3.58318	4.02271	4.50767	4.76837
8	2.30454	2.47596	2.85259	3.05902	3.27841	3.75886	4.29982	4.90771	5.58951	5.96046
9	2.55804	2.77308	3.25195	3.51788	3.80296	4.43545	5.15978	5.98740	6.93099	7.45058
10	2.83942	3.10585	3.70722	4.04556	4.41144	5.23384	6.19174	7.30463	8.59443	9.31323
11	3.15176	3.47855	4.22623	4.65239	5.11726	6.17593	7.43008	8.91165	10.65709	11.64153
12	3.49845	3.89598	4.81790	5.35025	5.93603	7.28759	8.91610	10.87221	13.21479	14.55192
13	3.88328	4.36349	5.49241	6.15279	6.88579	8.59936	10.69932	13.26410	16.38634	18.18989
14	4.31044	4.88711	6.26135	7.07571	7.98752	10.14724	12.83918	16.18220	20.31906	22.73737
15	4.78459	5.47357	7.13794	8.13706	9.26552	11.97375	15.40702	19.74229	25.19563	28.42171
16	5.31089	6.13039	8.13725	9.35762	10.74800	14.12902	18.48843	24.08559	31.24259	35.52714
17	5.89509	6.86604	9.27646	10.76126	12.46768	16.67225	22.18611	29.38442	38.74081	44.40892
18	6.54355	7.68997	10.57517	12.37545	14.46251	19.67325	26.62333	35.84899	48.03860	55.51115
19	7.26334	8.61276	12.05569	14.23177	16.77652	23.21444	31.94800	43.73577	59.56786	69.38894
20	8.06231	9.64629	13.74349	16.36654	19.46076	27.39303	38.33760	53.35764	73.86415	86.73617
21	8.94917	10.80385	15.66758	18.82152	22.57448	32.32378	46.00512	65.09632	91.59155	108.42022
22	9.93357	12.10031	17.86104	21.64475	26.18640	38.14206	55.20614	79.41751	113.57352	135.52527
23	11.02627	13.55235	20.36158	24.89146	30.37622	45.00763	66.24737	96.88936	140.83116	169.40659
24	12.23916	15.17863	23.21221	28.62518	35.23642	53.10901	79.49685	118.20502	174.63064	211.75824
25	13.58546	17.00006	26.46192	32.91895	40.87424	62.66863	95.39622	144.21013	216.54199	264.69780

14% point on Table 10-1, locate the factor value found there of 2.19497 and multiply it times the principal amount of $25,000 as follows:

$$\$25{,}000 \times 2.19497 = \$54{,}874.$$

So $25,000 invested at 14% compounded annually for six years will yield $54,874.

Present Value of $1 (Table 10-2)

The present value of $1 is the value today of a dollar to be received at some future time. The values in Table 10-2 represent these amounts. Each number in Table 10-2 is derived by taking the factor value from the corresponding point in Table 10-1, and dividing that amount into 1.

To illustrate, assume that we want to know the present value of $1,000 to be received in five years at a 10% interest rate. To determine the amount we refer to Table 10-2, and locate the five-year, 10% factor of .62092. By multiplying $1,000 × .62092 we get $621 (rounded); therefore the present value of $1,000 for five years at 10% is $621. So, if we invested $621 at 10% compounded annually for five years we would end up with $1,000. This can be proven as follows:

	AMOUNT AT START OF YEAR	+ INTEREST DURING THE YEAR =	AMOUNT AT END OF YEAR
Year 1	$621	$621 × .10 = $62	$ 683
Year 2	683	683 × .10 = 68	751
Year 3	751	751 × .10 = 75	826
Year 4	826	826 × .10 = 83	909
Year 5	909	909 × .10 = 91	**$1,000**

Future Value of an Annuity of $1 (Table 10-3)

The word *annuity* means an *equal amount* is contributed each period in the future for some designated number of periods. So Table 10-3 is similar to the future value of $1 table except that it is assumed that an equal amount is invested in each period at compounded interest.

To illustrate assume that you are forty years old and plan to start an IRA (Individual Retirement Account) by putting $2,000 per year into the bank at a guaranteed annual interest rate of 9% beginning next year on your forty-first birthday. It is your plan to continue with this investment until your retirement twenty-five years hence. To determine the amount of money that you will have at the end of twenty-five years, we refer to Table 10-3, the 9%, twenty-five-year point and get a value of 84.70090. By multiplying that value by $2,000 we get an

TABLE 10-2 *Present Value of 1,* $p = \frac{1}{(1+i)^n}$

PERIODS	2%	2½	3%	4%	5%	6%	7%	8%	9%	10%
1	.98039	.97561	.97087	.96154	.95238	.94340	.93458	.92593	.91743	.90909
2	.96117	.95181	.94260	.92456	.90703	.89000	.87344	.85734	.84168	.82645
3	.94232	.92860	.91514	.88900	.86384	.83962	.81630	.79383	.77218	.75131
4	.92385	.90595	.88849	.85480	.82270	.79209	.76290	.73503	.70843	.68301
5	.90573	.88385	.86261	.82193	.78353	.74726	.71299	.68058	.64993	.62092
6	.88797	.86230	.83748	.79031	.74622	.70496	.66634	.63017	.59627	.56447
7	.87056	.84127	.81309	.75992	.71068	.66506	.62275	.58349	.54703	.51316
8	.85349	.82075	.78941	.73069	.67684	.62741	.58201	.54027	.50187	.46651
9	.83676	.80073	.76642	.70259	.64461	.59190	.54393	.50025	.46043	.42410
10	.82035	.78120	.74409	.67556	.61391	.55839	.50835	.46319	.42241	.38554
11	.80426	.76214	.72242	.64958	.58468	.52679	.47509	.42888	.38753	.35049
12	.78849	.74356	.70138	.62460	.55684	.49697	.44401	.39711	.35553	.31863
13	.77303	.72542	.68095	.60057	.53032	.46884	.41496	.36770	.32618	.28966
14	.75788	.70773	.66112	.57748	.50507	.44230	.38782	.34046	.29925	.26333
15	.74301	.69047	.64186	.55526	.48102	.41727	.36245	.31524	.27454	.23939
16	.72845	.67362	.62317	.53391	.45811	.39365	.33873	.29189	.25187	.21763
17	.71416	.65720	.60502	.51337	.43630	.37136	.31657	.27027	.23107	.19784
18	.70016	.64117	.58739	.49363	.41552	.35034	.29586	.25025	.21199	.17986
19	.68643	.62553	.57029	.47464	.39573	.33051	.27651	.23171	.19449	.16351
20	.67297	.61027	.55368	.45639	.37689	.31180	.25842	.21455	.17843	.14864
21	.65978	.59539	.53755	.43883	.35894	.29416	.24151	.19866	.16370	.13513
22	.64684	.58086	.52189	.42196	.34185	.27751	.22571	.18394	.15018	.12285
23	.63416	.56670	.50669	.40573	.32557	.26180	.21095	.17032	.13778	.11168
24	.62172	.55288	.49193	.39012	.31007	.24698	.19715	.15770	.12640	.10153
25	.60953	.53939	.47761	.37512	.29530	.23300	.18425	.14602	.11597	.09230

PERIODS	11%	12%	14%	15%	16%	18%	20%	22%	24%	25%
1	.90090	.89286	.87719	.86957	.86207	.84746	.83333	.81967	.80645	.80000
2	.81162	.79719	.76947	.75614	.74316	.71818	.69444	.67186	.65036	.64000
3	.73119	.71178	.67497	.65752	.64066	.60863	.57870	.55071	.52449	.51200
4	.65873	.63552	.59208	.57175	.55229	.51579	.48225	.45140	.42297	.40960
5	.59345	.56743	.51937	.49718	.47611	.43711	.40188	.37000	.34111	.32768
6	.53464	.50663	.45559	.43233	.41044	.37043	.33490	.30328	.27509	.26214
7	.48166	.45235	.39964	.37594	.35383	.31393	.27908	.24859	.22184	.20972
8	.43393	.40388	.35056	.32690	.30503	.26604	.23257	.20376	.17891	.16777
9	.39092	.36061	.30751	.28426	.26295	.22546	.19381	.16702	.14428	.13422
10	.35218	.32197	.26974	.24718	.22668	.19106	.16151	.13690	.11635	.10737
11	.31728	.28748	.23662	.21494	.19542	.16192	.13459	.11221	.09383	.08590
12	.28584	.25668	.20756	.18691	.16846	.13722	.11216	.09198	.07567	.06872
13	.25751	.22917	.18207	.16253	.14523	.11629	.09346	.07539	.06103	.05498
14	.23199	.20462	.15971	.14133	.12520	.09855	.07789	.06180	.04921	.04398
15	.20900	.18270	.14010	.12289	.10793	.08352	.06491	.05065	.03969	.03518
16	.18829	.16312	.12289	.10686	.09304	.07078	.05409	.04152	.03201	.02815
17	.16963	.14564	.10780	.09293	.08021	.05998	.04507	.03403	.02581	.02252
18	.15282	.13004	.09456	.08081	.06914	.05083	.03756	.02789	.02082	.01801
19	.13768	.11611	.08295	.07027	.05961	.04308	.03130	.02286	.01679	.01441
20	.12403	.10367	.07276	.06110	.05139	.03651	.02608	.01874	.01354	.01153
21	.11174	.09256	.06383	.05313	.04430	.03094	.02174	.01536	.01092	.00922
22	.10067	.08264	.05599	.04620	.03819	.02622	.01811	.01259	.00880	.00738
23	.09069	.07379	.04911	.04017	.03292	.02222	.01509	.01032	.00710	.00590
24	.08170	.06588	.04308	.03493	.02838	.01883	.01258	.00846	.00573	.00472
25	.07361	.05882	.03779	.03038	.02447	.01596	.01048	.00693	.00462	.00378

TABLE 10-3
Future Value of Annuity of n Rents of 1 Each (ordinary), $F_o = \frac{(1+i)^n - 1}{i}$

PERIODIC RENTS (n)	2%	2½%	3%	4%	5%	6%	7%	8%	9%	10%
1	1.00000	1.00000	1.00000	1.00000	1.00000	1.00000	1.00000	1.00000	1.00000	1.00000
2	2.02000	2.02500	2.03000	2.04000	2.05000	2.06000	2.07000	2.08000	2.09000	2.10000
3	3.06040	3.07563	3.09090	3.12160	3.15250	3.18360	3.21490	3.24640	3.27810	3.31000
4	4.12161	4.15252	4.18363	4.24646	4.31013	4.37462	4.43994	4.50611	4.57313	4.64100
5	5.20404	5.25633	5.30914	5.41632	5.52563	5.63709	5.75074	5.86660	5.98471	6.10510
6	6.30812	6.38774	6.46841	6.63298	6.80191	6.97532	7.15329	7.33593	7.52333	7.71561
7	7.43428	7.54753	7.66246	7.89829	8.14201	8.39384	8.65402	8.92280	9.20043	9.48717
8	8.58297	8.73612	8.89234	9.21423	9.54911	9.89747	10.25980	10.63663	11.02847	11.43589
9	9.75463	9.95452	10.15911	10.58280	11.02656	11.49132	11.97799	12.48756	13.02104	13.57948
10	10.94972	11.20338	11.46388	12.00611	12.57789	13.18079	13.81645	14.48656	15.19293	15.93742
11	12.16872	12.48347	12.80780	13.48635	14.20679	14.97164	15.78360	16.64549	17.56029	18.53117
12	13.41209	13.79555	14.19203	15.02581	15.91713	16.86994	17.88845	18.97713	20.14072	21.38428
13	14.68033	15.14044	15.61779	16.62684	17.71298	18.88214	20.14064	21.49530	22.95338	24.52271
14	15.97394	16.51895	17.08632	18.29191	19.59863	21.01507	22.55049	24.21492	26.01919	27.97498
15	17.29342	17.93193	18.59891	20.02359	21.57856	23.27597	25.12902	27.15211	29.36092	31.77248
16	18.63929	19.38022	20.15688	21.82453	23.65749	25.67253	27.88805	30.32428	33.00340	35.94973
17	20.01207	20.86473	21.76159	23.69751	25.84037	28.21288	30.84022	33.75023	36.97370	40.54470
18	21.41231	22.38635	23.41444	25.64541	28.13238	30.90565	33.99903	37.45024	41.30134	45.59917
19	22.84056	23.94601	25.11687	27.67123	30.53900	33.75999	37.37896	41.44626	46.01846	51.15909
20	24.29737	25.54466	26.87037	29.77808	33.06595	36.78559	40.99549	45.76196	51.16012	57.27500
21	25.78332	27.18327	28.67649	31.96920	35.71925	39.99273	44.86518	50.42292	56.76453	64.00250
22	27.29898	28.86286	30.53678	34.24797	38.50521	43.39229	49.00574	55.45676	62.87334	71.40275
23	28.84496	30.58443	32.45288	36.61789	41.43048	46.99583	53.43614	60.89330	69.53194	79.54302
24	30.42186	32.34904	34.42647	39.08260	44.50200	50.81558	58.17667	66.76476	76.78981	88.49733
25	32.03030	34.15776	36.45926	41.64591	47.72710	54.86451	63.24904	73.10594	84.70090	98.34706

(continued)

TABLE 10-3

Future Value of Annuity of n Rents of 1 Each (ordinary), $F_o = \frac{(1+i)^n - 1}{i}$ *(continued)*

PERIODIC RENTS (n)	11%	12%	14%	15%	16%	18%	20%	22%	24%	25%
1	1.00000	1.00000	1.00000	1.00000	1.00000	1.00000	1.00000	1.00000	1.00000	1.00000
2	2.11000	2.12000	2.14000	2.15000	2.16000	2.18000	2.20000	2.22000	2.24000	2.25000
3	3.34210	3.37440	3.43960	3.47250	3.50560	3.57240	3.64000	3.70840	3.77760	3.81250
4	4.70973	4.92114	4.99338	5.06650	5.21543	5.36800	5.52425	5.68422	5.76563	
5	6.22780	6.35285	6.61010	6.74238	6.87714	7.15421	7.44160	7.73958	8.04844	8.20703
6	7.91286	8.11519	8.53552	8.75374	8.97748	9.44197	9.92992	10.44229	10.98006	11.25879
7	9.78327	10.08901	10.73049	11.06680	11.41387	12.14152	12.91590	13.73959	14.61528	15.07349
8	11.85943	12.29969	13.23276	13.72682	14.24009	15.32700	16.49908	17.76231	19.12294	19.84186
9	14.16397	14.77566	16.08535	16.78584	17.51851	19.08585	20.79890	22.67001	24.71245	25.80232
10	16.72201	17.54874	19.33730	20.30372	21.32147	23.52131	25.95868	28.65742	31.64344	33.25290
11	19.56143	20.65458	23.04452	24.34928	25.73290	28.75514	32.15042	35.96205	40.23787	42.56613
12	22.71319	24.13313	27.27075	29.00167	30.85017	34.93107	39.58050	44.87370	50.89495	54.20766
13	26.21164	28.02911	32.08865	34.35192	36.78620	42.21866	48.49660	55.74591	64.10974	68.75958
14	30.90492	32.39260	37.58107	40.50471	43.67199	50.81802	59.19592	69.01001	80.49608	86.94947
15	34.40536	37.27971	43.84241	57.58041	51.65951	60.96527	72.03511	85.19221	100.81514	109.68684
16	39.18995	42.75328	50.98035	55.71747	60.92503	72.93901	87.44213	104.93450	126.01077	138.10855
17	44.50084	48.88367	59.11760	65.07509	71.67303	87.06804	105.93056	129.02009	157.25336	173.63568
18	50.39594	55.74971	68.39407	75.83636	84.14072	103.74028	128.11667	158.40451	195.99416	218.04460
19	56.93949	63.43968	78.96923	88.21181	98.60323	123.41353	154.74000	194.25350	244.03276	273.55576
20	64.20283	72.05244	91.02493	102.44358	115.37975	146.62797	186.68800	237.98927	303.60062	342.94470
21	72.26514	81.69874	104.76842	118.81012	134.84051	174.02100	225.02560	291.34691	377.46477	429.68087
22	81.21431	92.50258	120.43600	137.63164	157.41499	206.34479	271.03072	356.44323	469.05632	538.10109
23	91.14788	104.60289	138.29704	159.27638	183.60138	244.48685	326.23686	435.86075	582.62984	673.62636
24	102.17415	118.15524	158.65862	184.16784	213.97761	289.49448	392.48424	532.75011	723.46100	843.03295
25	114.41331	133.33387	181.87083	212.79302	249.21402	342.60349	471.98108	650.95513	898.09164	1054.79118

amount of $169,402. This amount would be your retirement "nest egg" if you invested $2,000 per year for twenty-five years at 9%.

Table 10-3 can also be used to determine how much is needed to invest annually to end up with a specific amount at some future time. For example, assume you determine that your company will need $25,000 in four years to replace a particular machine. You also plan to deposit an equal amount at the end of each year at an interest rate of 11% for that purpose. To determine the amount that must be invested per year you refer to the 11%, four-year factor value in Table 10-3 (4.70973), and *divide* it into $25,000 to arrive at an annual investment amount of $5,308 ($25,000 ÷ 4.70973 = $5,308).

To prove this calculation, assume that on January 1, 19X1, the decision is made to invest the $5,308 annually for four years beginning on December 31, 19X1. This should result in the accumulation of $25,000 four years from the date that the decision was made. The schedule presented next shows the accumulation:

DATE OF INVESTMENT	AMOUNT OF INVESTMENT	COMPOUND INTEREST AT 11% FACTOR TO 12/31/X4 (FROM TABLE 10-1)	AMOUNT ACCUMULATED ON 12/31/X4
Dec. 31, 19X1	$5,308	× 1.36763	= $ 7,260
Dec. 31, 19X2	$5,308	× 1.23210	= 6,540
Dec. 31, 19X3	$5,308	× 1.11000	= 5,892
Dec. 31, 19X4	$5,308	× 1.00000	= 5,308
			$25,000

So the table for the future value of an annuity of $1 may be used (1) to determine how much an equal investment for "*n*" periods at "*i*" interest will yield (by multiplication); or (2) to determine how much must be invested for "*n*" periods at "*i*" interest to result in a predetermined amount at the end of that period (by division).

Present Value of an Annuity of $1 (Table 10-4)

The present value of an annuity of $1 is the value now of a series of equal amounts to be received (or paid) for some specified number of future periods. It is no more than the present value of $1 table (Table 10-2) in cumulative form.

To illustrate this, assume that we are to receive $3,000 in cash at the end of each of the next three years. How much would these three $3,000 amounts be worth now (i.e., the present value), assuming an interest rate of 14% per year?

TABLE 10-4

Present Value of Annuity of n Rents of 1 Each (ordinary), $P_o = \dfrac{1 - \dfrac{1}{(1+i)^n}}{i}$

PERIODIC RENTS (n)	2%	2½%	3%	4%	5%	6%	7%	8%	9%	10%
1	.98039	.97561	.97087	.96154	.95238	.94340	.93458	.92593	.91743	.90909
2	1.94156	1.92742	1.91347	1.88609	1.85941	1.83339	1.80802	1.78326	1.75911	1.73554
3	2.88388	2.85602	2.82861	2.77509	2.72325	2.67301	2.62432	2.57710	2.53129	2.48685
4	3.80773	3.76197	3.7170	3.62990	3.54595	3.46511	3.38721	3.31213	3.23972	3.16987
5	4.71346	4.64583	4.57971	4.45182	4.32948	4.21236	4.10020	3.99271	3.88965	3.79079
6	5.60143	5.50813	5.41719	5.24214	5.07569	4.91732	4.76654	4.62288	4.48592	4.35526
7	6.47199	6.34939	6.23028	6.00205	5.78637	5.58238	5.38929	5.20637	5.03295	4.86842
8	7.32548	7.17014	7.01969	6.73274	6.46321	6.20979	5.97130	5.74664	5.53482	5.33493
9	8.16224	7.97087	7.78611	7.43533	7.10782	6.80169	6.51523	6.24689	5.99525	5.75902
10	8.98259	8.75206	8.53020	8.11090	7.72173	7.36009	7.02358	6.71008	6.41766	6.14457
11	9.78685	9.51421	9.25262	8.76048	8.30641	7.88687	7.49867	7.13896	6.80519	6.49506
12	10.57534	10.25776	9.95400	9.38507	8.86325	8.38384	7.94269	7.53608	7.16073	6.81369
13	11.34837	10.98318	10.63496	9.98565	9.39357	8.85268	8.35765	7.90378	7.48690	7.10336
14	12.10625	11.69091	11.29607	10.56312	9.89864	9.29498	8.74547	8.24424	7.78615	7.36669
15	12.84926	12.38138	11.93794	11.11839	10.37966	9.71225	9.10791	8.55948	8.06069	7.60608
16	13.57771	13.05500	12.56110	11.65230	10.83777	10.10590	9.44665	8.85137	8.31256	7.82371
17	14.29187	13.71220	13.16612	12.16567	11.27407	10.47726	9.76322	9.12164	8.54363	8.02155
18	14.99203	14.35336	13.75351	12.65930	11.68959	10.82760	10.05909	9.37189	8.75563	8.20141
19	15.67846	14.97889	14.32380	13.13394	12.08532	11.15812	10.33560	9.60360	8.95011	8.36492
20	16.35143	15.58916	14.87747	13.59033	12.46221	11.46992	10.59401	9.81815	9.12855	8.51356
21	17.01121	16.18455	15.41502	14.02916	12.82115	11.76408	10.83553	10.01680	9.29224	8.64869
22	17.65805	16.76541	15.93692	14.45112	13.16300	12.04158	11.06124	10.20074	9.44243	8.77154
23	18.29220	17.33211	16.44361	14.85684	13.48857	12.30338	11.27219	10.37106	9.58021	8.88322
24	18.91393	17.88499	16.93554	15.24696	13.79864	12.55036	11.46933	10.52876	9.70661	8.98474
25	19.52346	18.42438	17.41315	15.62208	14.09394	12.78336	11.65358	10.67478	9.82258	9.07704

PERIODIC RENTS (n)	11%	12%	14%	15%	16%	18%	20%	22%	24%	25%
1	.90090	.89286	.87719	.86957	.86207	.84746	.83333	.81967	.80645	.80000
2	1.71252	1.69005	1.64666	1.62571	1.60523	1.56564	1.52778	1.49153	1.45682	1.44000
3	2.44371	2.40183	2.32163	2.28323	2.24589	2.17427	2.10648	2.04224	1.98130	1.95200
4	3.10245	3.03735	2.91371	2.85498	2.79818	2.69006	2.58873	2.49364	2.40428	2.36160
5	3.69590	3.60478	3.43308	3.35216	3.27429	3.12717	2.99061	2.86364	2.74538	2.68928
6	4.23054	4.11141	3.88867	3.78448	3.68474	3.49760	3.32551	3.16692	3.02047	2.95142
7	4.71220	4.56376	4.28830	4.16042	4.03857	3.81153	3.60459	3.41551	3.24232	3.16114
8	5.14612	4.96764	4.63886	4.48732	4.34359	4.07757	3.83716	3.61927	3.42122	3.32891
9	5.53705	5.32825	4.94637	4.77158	4.60654	4.30302	4.03097	3.78628	3.56550	3.46313
10	5.88923	5.65022	5.21612	5.01877	4.83323	4.49409	4.19247	3.92318	3.68186	3.57050
11	6.20652	5.93770	5.45273	5.23371	5.02864	4.65601	4.32706	4.03540	3.77569	3.65640
12	6.49236	6.19437	5.66029	5.42062	5.19711	4.79322	4.43922	4.12737	3.85136	3.72512
13	6.74987	6.42355	5.84236	5.58315	5.34233	4.90951	4.53268	4.20277	3.91239	3.78010
14	6.98187	6.62817	6.00207	5.72448	5.46753	5.00806	4.61057	4.26456	3.96160	3.82408
15	7.19087	6.81086	6.14217	5.84737	5.57546	5.09158	4.67547	4.31522	4.00129	3.85926
16	7.37916	6.97399	6.26506	5.95423	5.66850	5.16235	4.72956	4.35673	4.03330	3.88741
17	7.54879	7.11963	6.37286	6.04716	5.74870	5.22233	4.77463	4.39077	4.05911	3.90993
18	7.70162	7.24967	6.46742	6.12797	5.81785	5.27316	4.81219	4.41866	4.07993	3.92794
19	7.83929	7.36578	6.55037	6.19823	5.87746	5.31624	4.84350	4.44152	4.09672	3.94235
20	7.96333	7.46944	6.62313	6.25933	5.92884	5.35275	4.86958	4.46027	4.11026	3.95388
21	8.07507	7.56200	6.68696	6.31246	5.97314	5.38368	4.89132	4.47563	4.12117	3.96311
22	8.17574	7.64465	6.74294	6.35866	6.01133	5.40990	4.90943	4.48822	4.12998	3.97049
23	5.26643	7.71843	6.79206	6.39884	6.04425	5.43212	4.92453	4.49854	4.13708	3.97639
24	8.34814	7.78432	6.83514	6.43377	6.07263	5.45095	4.93710	4.50700	4.14281	3.98111
25	8.42174	7.84314	6.87293	6.46415	6.09709	5.46691	4.94759	4.51393	4.14742	3.98489

This present value relationship can be depicted as follows:

Present Value		(Multiply by) Discount Factor		Cash Flow in the Future Period 1	2	3
$2,632	←	.87719	←	$3,000		
2,308	←	.76947	←		$3,000	
2,025	←	.67497	←			$3,000
$6,965		**2.32163**				

Notice that we arrived at the present value of each of the $3,000 cash flows individually by reference to the present value of $1 table (Table 10-2). However, we could have arrived at the same total amount by adding up the three individual discount factors (totaling 2.32163) and multiplying that value by $3,000 (2.32163 × $3,000 = $6,965). The value of 2.32163 can be found in Table 10-4, so it is not necessary to determine the present values of each individual cash flow as long as they are the same amount. It is only necessary to refer to Table 10-4, and multiply the annual cash flow by the value found in that table. In other words, Table 10-4 is only Table 10-2 in cumulative form.

The concept and calculation of present and future values will be used extensively in the remainder of this chapter, and frequently in the remaining chapters of this book.

LIABILITIES

Liabilities are the debts of a company. The FASB has defined liabilities as "financial representations of obligations of a particular enterprise to transfer economic resources to other entites in the future as a result of a past transaction or event affecting the enterprise.[4]

Because liabilities involve future disbursement of assets (most often cash), one of the more important features of liabilities is the date on which they are payable. Obligations which mature in the near future generally represent a demand on the current assets of the enterprise. Liabilities which fall due farther into the future do not generally represent a claim on the current resources of the enterprise, and are therefore in a somewhat different category. This feature has given rise to the basic division of liabilities into (1) current liabilities and (2) long-term debt.

[4] "Objectives of Financial Reporting and Elements of Financial Statements for Business Enterprises," Proposed Statement of Financial Accounting Concepts (Stamford, Conn.: FASB, 1977), par. 49.

Current Liabilities

Current liabilities are defined as obligations that will be paid within the current operating cycle of the business or within one year, whichever is the longer. Therefore, there is an explicit assumption that current assets will be used to liquidate current liabilities.

Current liabilities which commonly appear on the balance sheet are: accounts payable, short-term notes payable, accrued liabilities, unearned revenues, taxes payable, and cash dividends payable.

Accounts Payable

Accounts payable were discussed in Chapter 7 as a part of the discussion on inventories and cost of sales. The term *accounts payable* (sometimes referred to as *trade* accounts payable) refers to balances owed to others for merchandise, services, or supplies purchased on open account. Typical entries for accounts payable are:

To record acquisition:	Purchases	$1,980	
	Accounts payable		$1,980
	(Purchase of merchandise on account; terms 1/10,n/30. Invoice amount $2,000 × .99 = $1,980)		
To record payment:	Accounts payable	1,980	
	Cash		1,980
	(Payments of account payable within discount period)		

Short-term notes payable would be treated in a similar manner by crediting a Notes Payable account to record the acquisition. The primary difference is in the form or evidence of the liability. A note payable has a written document (the note) as evidence of the debt, whereas the account payable has no such document to back it up. Another difference between notes and accounts payable is that notes are generally interest-bearing and open accounts payable generally are not.

Accrued Liabilities

Accrued liabilities are the result of expenses that have been incurred but not yet paid at the end of the accounting period. They appear in earlier chapters in conjunction with the discussion of adjusting journal entries. Typically, accrued liabilities are the result of such things as wages payable, taxes payable, and interest payable.

To illustrate a typical accrued liability, assume that on December 31, 19X1, it is determined that property taxes owed and payable on January 5, 19X2 amount to $14,000. The current liability and related expense must be reflected in the 19X1 financial statements, therefore the following journal entries must be made:

Dec. 31, 19X1	Property Tax Expense	14,000	
	Accrued property taxes payable		14,000
	Adjusting entry to record property taxes incurred but not paid at year end		
Jan. 5, 19X2	Accrued property taxes payable	14,000	
	Cash		14,000
	Payment of property tax liability		

Payroll Liabilities

Wages which are paid on a weekly or biweekly basis always result in an accrued liability at the end of the accounting period. This was illustrated in some detail in the discussion in Chapter 4. However, up to this point discussions and illustrations for salaries and wages have been simplified in that payroll taxes and other similar deductions and related liabilities have been ignored.

In addition to the obligation to pay the employee, payrolls create other obligations that are the direct result of the payment of salaries and wages. These liabilities fall into two basic categories: (1) those items *withheld* from the employees' pay to be paid to some governmental agency or other party; and (2) those items which are paid by the employer and are additional expenses to the enterprise. Obviously, those items which are withheld from the employees' pay reduce the amount of take-home (or net) pay from the gross amount earned. Examples of liabilities which result from payrolls are: Social Security taxes (FICA), federal income taxes withheld, group insurance, union dues, and state and federal unemployment taxes.

Social Security Taxes (FICA)

Funds for the operation of the federal social security system are obtained by taxes levied under the Federal Insurance Contributions Act, often referred to as FICA or social security taxes. Under the act employers are required to withhold a portion of each employee's earnings, and a tax at the same rate is levied against the employer. Stated differently, the employer "matches" the social security tax levied against the employee.

Social security taxes are paid on wages up to a specified amount, and any earnings over that amount are not subject to this tax. When the system began in 1937, the tax rate was 1% on the first \$3,000 earned by an individual. This amounted to a tax of \$30 (1% × \$3,000), which was matched by the employer. In 1951, the rate was 1.5% on the first \$3,600, for a tax of \$54. In 1966, the rate was 4.2% on the first \$6,600, for a tax of \$277; and in 1983 it was 6.7% on the first \$35,700 resulting in a tax of \$2,391.90, again paid by both employee and employer. In 1984 the rate became 6.7% on the first \$37,800 for employees, and

7.0% on the first $37,800 for employers. Although these increases are dramatic, they do not effect the accounting procedures involved. Regardless of the rate, both the amount withheld from employees' earnings and the employers' share of FICA are considered a current liability to the firm and must be paid to the Internal Revenue Service within a specified short period of time. Thus, although Congress periodically changes the base amount of earnings subject to tax, and the rate which is applied to the base, such changes do not affect the accounting procedures.

For illustrative purposes, in this book we will assume a tax rate of 7% on the first $40,000 to be borne by both employee and employer.

Federal Income Taxes

The Revenue Act of 1913, which included a fifteen-page section on income taxes, formed the basis of our current income tax system. Our pay-as-you-go tax system requires employers to withhold a portion of the earnings of their employees. The amount withheld depends upon the amount of earnings and the number of dependents (exemptions) claimed by the employee. An employee is always entitled to one exemption for himself, and an additional exemption for each person qualifying as a dependent of the employee. The Internal Revenue Service provides tax withholding tables for use by companies which indicate the amount of federal income tax to withhold for any amount of earnings and any number of exemptions.

Our system of graduated income taxes is reflected in the withholding system. Generally, the more an individual earns, the more that is withheld from his or her check for income taxes. The system is designed to closely approximate the rates used in computing the individual's tax liability at the end of the year.

Most states, and some cities levy income taxes as well. The accounting for withholdings of state and city income taxes would be similar to the procedure used for federal income taxes.

The amount of federal income taxes withheld must be paid to the Internal Revenue Service within a specified short period of time. The IRS provides companies with specifically designed forms to be used in submitting payments of taxes. These forms identify employees and amounts withheld for both social security and income taxes.

Other Payroll Deductions

Many companies withhold voluntary deductions from employees' checks. Typically these items would include union dues, insurance premiums, savings funds, charitable contributions, and repayment of loans. The employer agrees to make these deductions subject to authorization by the employee, as a matter of convenience to the employees. The amounts deducted are remitted in a short time to the organization in whose behalf the deduction was authorized.

Federal Unemployment Taxes

The Federal Unemployment Tax Act (FUTA) provides for a system of unemployment insurance on a national scale. Most employers are subject to taxes under this act. Recently the rate has been 3.4% on the first $6,000 of earnings paid to each employee during the calendar year. However, if a company has had few federal unemployment claims filed against it, a credit against the federal tax of up to 2.7% of taxable earnings is allowed for contributions which employers make to a state plan. Thus the effective federal tax rate in most instances is 0.7% (3.4% − 2.7%) on the first $6,000 earned by each employee. This tax is paid by the employer only.

State Unemployment Tax

Each state has its own law governing the tax of employers for unemployment compensation purposes. However, an important feature of all state unemployment tax laws is the merit rating provision under which a reduction in the tax rate levied by the state is granted to employers whose unemployment experience is better than a specified standard. Thus, employers whose employee turnover rate is low may be entitled to a lower state tax rate. The federal tax law provides that an employer who pays less than 2.7% to any state as a result of a favorable experience rating is still entitled to the full 2.7% credit against the federal tax. In most states this tax is levied on employers only.

Payroll Accounting Illustrated

To illustrate the recording of a payroll in the accounting records, assume that our company has four employees; we are paying wages for the month of October, and that our state unemployment tax rate is 2%. Employee earnings *through September* and earnings and deductions for October for the four employees are as follows:

		OCTOBER				
Employee	**Earnings through Sept.**	**Gross Pay**	**Withhold. Tax**	**FICA (7%)**	**Ins. Premiums**	**Net Pay**
J. White	$45,000	$5,000	$ 900	-0-	$150	$3,950
S. Black	38,000	3,000	600	$140	100	2,160
M. Green	5,700	1,000	75	70	25	830
V. Blue	4,500	500	50	35	25	390
		$9,500	$1,625	$245	$300	$7,330

The gross pay for each employee is known from payroll records. The withholding tax is determined by tables provided by the Internal Revenue Service. The FICA is calculated at a rate of 7% on the first $40,000 paid each employee in a calendar year. Therefore J. White has no deduction because he is over the $40,000 limit; and only $2,000 of the $3,000 earned by S. Black is subject to FICA tax ($2,000 × 7% = $140). All of the earnings of Green and Blue are subject to FICA taxes. The insurance premiums are voluntary deductions which we are withholding from employees' checks and forwarding to the insurance company.

Our company incurs expenses as a result of the payroll just illustrated. In our example those expenses may be summarized as follows:

PAYROLL TAXES

Employee	October Pay	FICA, 7% on 1st $40,000	FUTA, .7% on 1st $6,000	SUI, 2% on 1st $6,000
J. White	$5,000	-0-	-0-	-0-
S. Black	3,000	$140	-0-	-0-
M. Green	1,000	70	$2.10	$ 6
V. Blue	500	35	3.50	10
	$9,500	$245	$5.60	$16

The FICA amounts are self-explanatory in that these are the amounts to be paid by the employer in matching the employees' contributions. Because of a favorable past record, the FUTA is paid at a rate of .7% (3.4% less a credit of 2.7%) on the first $6,000 earned by each employee. Since White and Black are both over that $6,000 amount, there is no tax on their earnings. Only $300 of Green's earnings are taxable since he had earned $5,700 through September ($6,000 − $5,700 = $300). We therefore must pay Federal Unemployment Taxes of ($300 ×.7%) $2.10 on his earnings. All of Blue's earnings are subject to federal unemployment since he is still not over the $6,000 limit. The state unemployment column is calculated in an identical manner as the FUTA column except that a rate of 2% is used instead of .7%.

The journal entries to record the payroll illustrated would be:

To record the payroll for October:		
Wages Expense	$9,500.00	
Liability for income taxes withheld		$1,625.00
FICA taxes payable		245.00
Insurance premium payable		300.00
Accrued payroll (net pay)		7,330.00
To record payroll taxes related to the October payroll:		
Payroll taxes expense	266.60	
FICA taxes payable		245.00
Federal unemployment taxes payable		5.60
State unemployment taxes payable		16.00

Commonly the debit to Wages Expense is divided among expense categories which are more descriptive of the expense involved. For example, if in the preceding example, M. Green was a salesman, his October pay of $1,000 might be debited to Sales Salaries, and the balance would be debited to Wages Expense.

Payroll taxes on employees become a legal liability when wages are actually paid, rather than during the time services are rendered. The liquidation of these payroll-related liabilities is recorded by debiting the liability and crediting cash.

Long-term Debt

Long-term debt includes all financial obligations not classified as current liabilities. These long-term liabilities are normally the result of the acquisition of plant assets, or from the borrowing of large amounts of cash for major expansions of the business. Often, a long-term liability is supported by a mortgage on a specific asset of the borrower which has been pledged as security (or collateral) for the liability. The mortgage is actually a second document that is appended to the note payable. A liability supported by a mortgage is said to be secured; and an unsecured debt is one for which the creditor relies primarily on the integrity of the debtor.

Long-term debt generally falls into two categories: notes payable and bonds payable. Bonds payable is a very involved subject and will be covered separately in Chapter 11. All long-term debt is reported on the balance sheet under a separate caption below Current Liabilities. As a long-term liability approaches the maturity date, the portion that is to be paid in the next accounting period is reclassified as a current liability. To illustrate, assume that a long-term note payable of $150,000 was signed on January 1, 19X1. Repayment is to be in two installments: on December 31, 19X3, $75,000; and on December 31, 19X4, $75,000. On December 31, 19X1 and 19X2 balance sheets would report the following:

Dec. 31, 19X1	Long-term debt:	
	Notes payable	$150,000
Dec. 31, 19X2	Current liabilities:	
	Maturing portion of long-term note	$75,000
	Long-term debt:	
	Notes payable	$75,000

Notes Payable

A note may be interest-bearing or non-interest-bearing. Although some notes are referred to as non-interest-bearing, they almost invariably involve an implicit interest amount. An interest-bearing note is one that explicitly specifies (1) a stated rate of annual interest (such as 15%) on the face of the note, and (2) that the interest is to be paid at maturity, or in future installments, in addition to the principal amount of the note. For example, a $120,000, two-year, 15%, interest-bearing note would (1) provide the borrower with $120,000 cash; (2) have a principal amount of $120,000 upon which the interest would be calculated; and (3) require repayment of the $120,000 plus compounded interest for two years, for a total of ($120,000 × 1.3225) $158,700. The 1.3225 value was arrived at by reference to the compound interest table (Table 10-1), at the 15%, two-year point. The same $158,700 can be derived by the following computation: $120,000 × 1.15 = $138,000 and $138,000 × 1.15 = **$158,700**.

In contrast, a non-interest-bearing note is one that does not specify a rate of interest on the note itself. Instead the cash proceeds to the borrower are reduced by the amount of interest to be charged. For example, a $120,000, two-year, non-interest-bearing note, assuming an implicit interest rate of 15%, would yield the borrower cash of $90,737 ($120,000 × .75614). The .75614 value was arrived at by reference to the present value table (Table 10-2), at the 15%, two-year point.

Occasionally this calculation will be computed as follows: $120,000 × 15% = $18,000 × 2 years = **$36,000** interest

Principal	$120,000
Less interest	−36,000
Proceeds	**$ 84,000**

Under this type of calculation the borrower will only receive $84,000, instead of $90,737 as in the previous calculation. The primary reason for the difference between this calculation and the previous one is that in this calculation the interest is computed on the amount to be repaid, not on the proceeds to the borrower. Therefore, this second method, which results in proceeds of $84,000, is actually not a correct method of interest calculation, and is only illustrated here because it is still in occasional use. If this method is used the borrower is actually paying interest significantly in excess of the "stated rate" of 15%.

The accounting entries for interest-bearing and non-interest-bearing notes are presented for comparison, assuming the $120,000, 15%, two-year figures discussed previously.

TRANSACTION	INTEREST-BEARING		NON-INTEREST-BEARING	
Borrower $120,000				
Jan. 1, 19X1				
Cash	$120,000		$ 90,737	
Discount on notes payable	—		29,263	
Notes payable		120,000		120,000

(continued)

(continued)

TRANSACTION	INTEREST-BEARING		NON-INTEREST-BEARING	
Dec. 31, 19X1, end of accounting period:				
Interest expense	18,000[a]		13,611[b]	
Interest payable		18,000		—
Discount on notes payable				13,611
Repaid the loan:				
Notes payable	120,000		120,000	
Interest expense	20,700[c]		15,652[d]	
Interest payable				
Discount on notes payable		—		15,652
Cash		158,700		120,000

[a] $120,000 × 15% = $18,000
[b] $90,737 × 15% = $13,611
[c] $120,000 + $18,000 = $138,000 × 15% = $20,700
[d] $90,737 + $13,611 = $104,348 × 15% = $15,652

NOTE: At this time the note payable and related interest account would be reclassified as a current liability because it is scheduled to be repaid in the next year.

The proper financial statement presentation of a non-interest-bearing note payable is to show the net amount (gross less unamortized discount). So, for example, at the end of 19X1 the note payable and related interest under each assumption would be:

Interest bearing:		
Notes payable	$120,000	
Interest payable	18,000	
		$138,000
Non-interest-bearing:		
Notes payable	$120,000	
Less unamortized discount	15,652	
		$104,348

Deferred Income Taxes

It is permissible under the ACRS rules discussed in Chapter 8, to use a different depreciation technique for tax purposes than for financial reporting purposes. There are other situations in which tax laws and generally accepted accounting principles differ in such a way that taxable income will be different from accounting income. This difference raises a question about the amount of income tax to be treated as expense in the income statement; should it be the amount of tax to be paid currently as a result of operations of the current period as reported on the tax return, or should it be the amount that corresponds to the income reported to the income statement (tax rate applied to the reported earnings before tax)? It is the position of the accounting profession that the amount reported as income tax expense on the income statement should correspond with the income reported on the income statement, on the grounds that this determination of income tax results in the best matching of revenues and expenses.

Tax Deferral Illustrated

The accounting treatment of the tax postponement situation can be best understood by use of an example. The A Corporation acquired a fully equipped floatable oil-drilling rig for $5,000,000, paying $1,000,000 in cash and issuing notes payable for the $4,000,000 balance. Upon receipt of the equipment, A Corporation leased the rig to the North Sea Oil Exploration Corporation at an annual rental of $2,000,000 for a five-year period. At the end of five years, the equipment will be obsolete but will produce $500,000 in scrap value. The A Corporation will pay out $200,000 per year in operating expenses and interest. All other costs will be borne by the tenant.

A Corporation decided to use straight-line depreciation for financial reporting purposes and follows the ACRS rules (which we will assume approximates sum-of-the-years'-digits depreciation) for tax purposes. All relevant figures are shown to the nearest thousands of dollars:

TAX RETURNS:	19X1	19X2	19X3	19X4	19X5
Rent revenue	$2,000	$2,000	$2,000	$2,000	$2,000
ACRS recovery (sum-of-digits)	$1,500	$1,200	$ 900	$ 600	$ 300
Other expenses	200	200	200	200	200
Total tax deductions	$1,700	$1,400	$1,100	$ 800	$ 500
Taxable income	$ 300	$ 600	$ 900	$1,200	$1,500
Federal income tax (50%)	**$ 150**	**$ 300**	**$ 450**	**$ 600**	**$ 750**

FINANCIAL STATEMENTS:					
Rent revenue	$2,000	$2,000	$2,000	$2,000	$2,000
Depreciation expense (straight line)	$ 900	$ 900	$ 900	$ 900	$ 900
Other expenses	200	200	200	200	200
Total expenses	$1,100	$1,100	$1,100	$1,100	$1,100
Net earnings before income tax	$ 900	$ 900	$ 900	$ 900	$ 900
Income tax expense (50%)	450	450	450	450	450
Net Income	**$ 450**	**$ 450**	**$ 450**	**$ 450**	**$ 450**

The income tax expense reported to the stockholders is not the amount of income tax being paid currently, but is the amount of tax attributable to the earnings reported to the stockholders. The entries to record the tax show the relationships between actual tax and the reported tax very clearly:

	19X1		19X2		19X3		19X4		19X5	
Income tax expense	450		450		450		450		450	
Deferred income tax	-0-		-0-		-0-		150		300	
Deferred income tax		300		150		-0-		-0-		-0-
Cash (or accrued taxes payable)		150		300		450		600		750

The Deferred Income Tax account on A Corporation's books shows:

Deferred Federal Income Tax (Liability)

YEAR	DEBITS	CREDITS	BALANCE
19X1		300	300 CR
19X2		150	450 CR
19X3	—	—	450 CR
19X4	150		300 CR
19X5	300		-0-

The importance of this phase of income tax recognition is readily evident from checking almost any published balance sheet of a large corporation. It is not unusual to find a company reporting millions of dollars of deferred income tax.

It should be noted that deferred federal income tax "liability" is unlike any other liability in that future events must occur before it actually becomes a binding claim on the company recognizing it. One of the events that must take place is that the firm must experience a taxable profit in the future. If this takes place, the firm will have experienced an inflow of assets sufficient to pay the obligation. Thus deferred federal income tax "liability" is often excluded from the liability total when considering the ability of the firm to survive the claims of its creditors.

Long-term Leases

A lease is a contractual agreement between a lessee and a *lessor* in which the *lessee* obtains the right to use a specific asset, owned by the lessor, for a period of time in exchange for stipulated cash payments. In this chapter we will examine the accounting procedures to be used by the lessee.

The practice of leasing assets, rather than purchasing them, has increased dramatically since the early 1960s. A primary reason for this form of asset "acquisition" is that it does not require an immediate outflow of cash, or an incurrence of a large debt in the conventional sense. This trend of leasing assets has caused several problems in accounting, primarily in the area of liability measurement and reporting. For example, if the existence of a long-term lease of a plant asset is disregarded in the financial statements, it may be argued that the "liability" that results from the leasing arrangement is neglected. Others might argue that the company does not have legal title to the assets leased, so how could we have a liability associated with an asset not owned? Because of these problems, leasing has often been referred to as "off the balance sheet financing."

In an attempt to solve the accounting problems associated with leases, the FASB has determined that, for accounting purposes, lease agreements can be divided into two categories: (1) operating leases, and (2) capital leases.

Operating leases are defined by FASB Statement No. 13 as all leases that fail to meet at least one of the criteria mentioned in the next paragraph for capital leases. The customary accounting treatment of operating leases is to charge to expense all rental payments that have been incurred and expired during a specific period of time. The only significant information (other than the amount of rent expense, which appears on the income statements) which FASB Statement No. 13 requires to be disclosed in the lessee's financial statements is the future minimum rental payments required as of the latest balance sheet date. The latter should be clearly identified in the aggregate and for each of the five succeeding fiscal years.

Capital leases are those which meet at least one of the following four criteria:

1. The lease transfers title of the property to the lessee by the end of the lease term.
2. The lease contains a bargain purchase option, which allows the lessee to purchase, at its option, the leased property for a price which is sufficiently lower than the expected fair rental value of the property at the date the option becomes exercisable. An example of this situation would be if the property is transferred to the lessee at the end of the lease term after a payment of one dollar, or some other ridiculously low amount.
3. The lease term equals 75 percent or more of the estimated economic life of the leased property.
4. The present value of the minimum lease payments (excluding all executory costs such as insurance, maintenance, and taxes to be paid by the lessor) equals or exceeds 90 percent of the fair value of the leased property. The lessee normally

> computes this present value using the interest rate at the inception of the lease that would have been incurred to borrow over a similar term the funds needed to purchase the leased asset. This is referred to as the lessee's incremental borrowing rate.

It should be noted that these rather complex rules associated with accounting for leases are in reality an attempt to get the economic substance of the business agreement, regardless of its legal form. The legal document relating to the transaction may say "Lease" on the top of the page, but if in reality a company is acquiring property permanently, then the transaction is really a sale and should be accounted for as such. The objective of the FASB Statement No. 13 on leases is as follows:

> A lease that transfers substantially all of the benefits and risks incident to the ownership of property should be accounted for as the acquisition of an asset and the incurrence of an obligation by the lessee . . .[4]

In general, FASB Statement No. 13 requires that any capital lease agreement must be reported on the balance sheet of the lessee at the present value of all future lease payments, both as a plant asset and as a long-term liability. The asset is depreciated over its useful life as though it were purchased and owned by the lessee, and the liability is handled in a manner similar to non-interest-bearing notes illustrated earlier in this chapter. The following example will illustrate the entire procedure.

Byron Corp. (the lessee) entered into an agreement to lease equipment from the American Leasing Company (the lessor) under an agreement as follows:

- Period of lease: Three years, beginning December 31, 19X1, with title to the property being transferred to the lessee on December 31, 19X4.
- Lease payment: Three annual payments of $100,000, beginning December 31, 19X1. No executory costs are involved in these payments.
- Lessee's incremental borrowing rate: 12 percent compounded annually.
- Estimated life of equipment: Three years, with zero salvage value estimated at the end of that life.
- The fiscal year of the lessee ends each December 31.

The lease is a capital lease because the lease period of three years is equal to more than 75 percent of the estimated economic life of the property (which is also three years). Therefore the lease must be capitalized at the present value of the three annual future cash payments of $100,000. The present value of those payments is $269,005 which is based on Byron Corp.'s incremental borrowing rate of 12%, as shown here:

$$\$100{,}000 \text{ annual payment} \times 2.69005 = \$269{,}005$$

[4] "Accounting for Leases," Statement of Financial Accounting Standards, No. 13 (Stamford, Conn.: FASB, 1976), par. 62.

The factor 2.690005 is derived from Table 10-4 at the 12%, 2-period point after adding 1.00000 to the factor 1.69005. Another explanation of the computation of the 2.69005 is as follows: The first of the three payments required under the lease is to be made on December 31, 19X1, the beginning of the lease. The present value factor for $1 at December 31, 19X1 is, simply 1.00000 (since lease payments begin on that date); the present value factor for $1 that is spent one year later (Table 10-2) on December 31, 19X2, is .89286; and .79719 for $1 that is paid on December 31, 19X3. The sum of these three factors is 2.69005 (1.000 + .89286 + .79719).

The entry to record the capitalization of this lease agreement on December 31, 19X1, on the books of the lessee is shown next:

Leased equipment under capital leases	$269,005	
Obligations under capital leases		$269,005
To record the capitalization of lease agreement ($100,000 × 2.699005 = $269,005)		

The account Lease Equipment Under Capital Leases will appear in the asset section of the company's balance sheet; and the Obligations Under Capital Leases will appear in the liabilities section of the same financial statement. The lease liability should be divided into a current and long-term segment because a $100,000 payment is due for payment within one year.

The following *amortization schedule* presents the separation of each $100,000 lease payment between its interest and principal components during the period of the lease.

	(1)	(2)	(3)	(4)
Date	**Lease Payment**	**Interest Expense (12% × Principal Balance from Previous Year)**	**Reduction of Obligation (1) − (2)**	**Obligation Balance after Lease Payment**
12/31/X1				$269,005
12/31/X1	$100,000	-0-	$100,000	169,005
12/31/X2	100,000	$20,281[a]	79,719	89,286
12/31/X3	100,000	10,714[b]	89,286	-0-
	$300,000	**$30,995**	**$269,005**	

[a] $169,005 × 12% = $20,281
[b] $89,286 × 12% = $10,714

The entire sequence of entries that would be recorded during the term of the lease, following the original entry to record the lease, are shown next. The data were extracted from the amortization schedule presented previously.

19X1			
Dec. 31	Obligation under capital leases	$100,000	
	Cash		$100,000
	To record first lease payment		
19X2			
Dec. 31	Obligation under capital leases	79,719	
	Interest expense	20,281	
	Cash		100,000
	To record second lease payment		
19X3			
Dec. 31	Obligation under capital leases	89,286	
	Interest expense	10,714	
	Cash		100,000
	To record third (final) lease payment		

This lessee would charge the capitalized costs of these leased plant assets to expense over their expected useful lives by whichever depreciation method is used by the firm. It should be emphasized at this point, however, that the life of the leased assets need not coincide with the term of the lease. For example, the expected life of the assets may exceed (or in unusual cases, fall short of) the length of the lease. Byron Corp. uses straight-line depreciation; hence the annual depreciation expense during the equipment's estimated three-year life is $89,668 ($269,005 ÷ 3 years). The entry to be recorded at each fiscal year-end of 19X1, 19X2, and 19X3, is shown here:

Depreciation expense:		
Leased equipment	$89,668	
Accumulated depreciation: Leased equipment		$89,668
To record depreciation of capital lease		

The FASB requires that all assets obtained under capital leasing arrangements, the associated accumulated depreciation, and the related lease obligations shall be separately identified on the lessee's balance sheet. The depreciation expense recognized on such assets should also be separately disclosed on the income statement. In addition, the future lease payments as of the balance sheet date must be disclosed in the aggregate and for each of the five succeeding fiscal years. These requirements could be presented on the balance sheet for Byron Corp. as of December 31, 19X1:

ASSETS		LIABILITIES	
Plant assets:		Long-term liabilities:	
Leased equipment	$269,005	Obligations under capital leases	$169,005[a]
Less accumulated depreciation on leased equipment	89,668		
	$179,337		

[a] Note to balance sheet: Total lease payments required over the next two years amount to $200,000, payable in two annual $100,000 installments.

Pensions

A pension plan is an agreement between a company and its employees under which the company pays retirement benefits to eligible employees.

There are two basic ways a firm may operate a pension plan. A funded pension plan is one in which the employer-firm makes regular, periodic contributions to a separate pension fund. This separate fund is usually administered by a board of trustees or an organization such as an insurance company, bank, or trust company. Payment of the pension benefits to the retired workers then becomes the obligation of the organization that manages the fund. The employer-firm's only obligation is to make the regular contribution to the fund. An unfunded pension plan is one operated by the employer-firm itself, and the firm has the obligation to pay the retirement benefits directly to the retired employee.

Whether the plan is funded or unfunded, determining the amounts involved is a complex procedure that is beyond the scope of basic accounting. It involves, among other things, the terms of the individual plan, the use of mortality tables for life expectancy, estimates of numbers of employees covered and the length of employment covered by the plan, and the present value of the future payments. These calculations are made by professional actuaries who are statisticians trained in this work. The results of their calculations determine the amount of the contributions for a funded pension plan, or, for an unfunded plan, the amount of the employer-firm's expense and liability.

Funded Plans

The regular contributions to a funded pension plan are considered as expenses of the period in which the firm is obligated to make payments. For example, if the employer-firm made an annual payment of $450,000 to the fund, the journal entry shown here would be made.

investors were October 31 of each year, the entries on October 31, 19X1, would reflect the following accruals:

	F CORPORATION			VARIOUS INVESTORS		
Adjusting entries 19X1:						
Oct. 31	Interest expense	$4,667		Interest receivable	$4,667	
	Interest payable		4,667	Interest income		4,667
Closing entries 19X1:						
Oct. 31	Expense and revenue summary	4,667		Interest income	4,667	
	Interest expense		4,667	Expense and revenue summary		4,667
Interest payment 19X1:						
Dec. 31	Interest expense	2,333		Cash	7,000	
	Interest payable	4,667		Interest income		2,333
	Cash		7,000	Interest receivable		4,667

Since four months of the six months of interest to be paid on December 31 has been earned by October 31, it is necessary to recognize accrued interest on October 31 in the amount of two-thirds of the semiannual interest, or $4,667.

In the previous illustration, the bonds pay interest of $7,000 every six months, or 7% every six months (14% annually) on the $100,000 loaned to F Corporation. The lenders receive a 14% annual rate of return on their investment in the bonds. It may thus be said that the bonds yield 14%, which is the same rate in this case as the cash "interest" rate paid on the bonds.

Holdings of securities, particularly those payable to bearer, must be carefully controlled. They may be stolen outright or "borrowed" to be pledged as collateral for a personal loan of an officer or employee. Auditors, as a part of their annual audits, check out the client's portfolio of securities to be sure that all securities are present. The firm itself would establish careful procedures for adding new securities to the vault and disposing of old ones.

When debt is utilized extensively by a firm, its stockholders have less income (because of high interest expense) but also less investment—which thus produces a higher rate of return on the invested funds of the stockholder, but also greatly increases risk. Debt is risky because, unlike dividend payments, interest payments must be made whether or not the firm has earnings.

BOND VALUATION AND INTEREST DETERMINATION

Bonds are bought and sold in a highly competitive market. In effect, a new bond issue must compete for the funds of bond investors (lenders) with all other new bond issues and all outstanding bonds being traded on the market. Investors are able to select from all the available bonds, which differ in terms of particular features, and in terms of risk. A bond issue must offer bond investors the same interest yield (rate of return) on their investment as do bonds with similar features and risk. Since the investors' interest yield is a function of the relationship of the cash they receive as bondholders to the price they pay for the bonds, the bonds will be "priced" by the bond market to yield the same interest rate as is being earned on similar bonds at the time of the bond issue (the market rate).

Assume that the A Corporation plans to issue $100,000 of bonds on January 1, 19X1, to be due and payable five years later on December 31, 19X6 and to pay 15% cash "interest" on December 31 of each of the five years. If the market rate of interest on similar bonds at the time these bonds are issued is 15%, the bonds will be issued for the maturity value of $100,000. This price will yield an interest return of 15% to the bond investors. If bond investors are willing to accept a yield rate of less than 15% (because the prevailing yield rate on bonds of that type is less than 15%), they will pay *more* than the $100,000 maturity value of the bonds. If the bond investors are not willing to accept 15% but demand a higher rate of earnings (that is, similar bonds offer a yield rate greater than 15%), they can obtain a higher rate by giving the A Corporation less than the $100,000 maturity value of the bonds. Note that the debt contract calls for payments by A Corporation of:

One payment of $100,000 on December 31, 19X6	$100,000
Five payments of $15,000 through the years	75,000
Total cash to be paid by A Corporation	$175,000

The amount of these payments are contractually fixed in the bond indenture. The relationship between these payment amounts and the issue price of the bonds (the amount paid by investors) determine the *yield rate* of the bonds (the actual interest rate earned by the bond investors).

Bond investors will pay more than the maturity value of the bond issue if the bonds pay a cash "interest" rate which is greater than the prevailing yield rate on similar bonds. In this case, the bonds will be issued at a *premium;* the amount of the premium is the excess of the issue price over the face value of the bonds. However, bond investors will pay less than the maturity value of the bonds if the cash "interest" rate on the bonds is less than the prevailing yield rate. In this case, the bonds are issued at a *discount,* the amount of which is the excess of the face value over the issue price. The amount of discount or premium on a bond issue is that amount which, for the given cash rate of interest, will result in a yield rate of interest that reflects current bond market rates.

The bond indenture (contract) specifies exactly what cash will be paid to the investors and exactly when it will be paid. The investors will pay an amount for the bonds which will allow them to attain their required yield rate in each and every period on the money they loan, for the number of time periods that the money is invested in the bonds.

The amount received from the bond investors, called the *proceeds* of a bond issue, will be the same as the face value of the bonds only if the rate of interest stated in the bond indenture (referred to as the bond rate, or nominal rate) is the same as the market rate of interest (referred to as the effective rate or yield rate) that prevails when the bonds are issued. If the stated rate is less than the market rate, the bonds will be issued at less than face value. If the stated rate is greater than the market rate, the bonds will be issued at more than face value. *In every case, the bonds will be priced to yield the market rate of interest,* and this rate is the "real" rate paid by the bond issuer.

BONDS ISSUANCE AND DISCOUNT (OR PREMIUM) AMORTIZATION

The calculation of a bond issue price is quite simple when interest tables are employed. (Refer to Tables 10-2 and 10-4 on pages 288 and 292.) A bond consists of two promises made to the bond investor:

1. The promise to pay one lump sum in cash at a designated future date (the maturity value), and
2. The promise to pay, at specified intervals between the bond issue date and the maturity date (usually annually or semiannually), a series of cash "interest" payments of equal amount.

Discount

Following is an illustration of this procedure and the resulting discount (or premium) amortization. The SOPED Corporation is issuing $1,000,000 of 9%, five-year bonds, dated January 1, 19X1, with interest payable annually on December 31. Assume that the current market interest rate for similar securities is 10%, and the SOPED bonds are sold to yield that rate. At an assumed interest rate of 10%, the present values (values today) of the two types of cash flows which will result from the bond issues are:

Maturity value:	$1,000,000 × .62092 =	$620,920
	(Table 10-2, 10%, 5th period)	
Annual interest payments:	$90,000 × 3.79079 =	$341,171
	(Table 10-4, 10%, 5 periods)	
		$962,091[a]

[a] To prove that bonds sold to yield their stated rate of interest will be sold at par, assume that the bond issue illustrated here is sold to yield 9%, its stated rate of interest. The calculation of the proceeds of the sale would be identical to the this one except that the interest rate in Tables 10-2 and 10-4 will be 9% instead of 10%. This results in the following calculation of proceeds:

Maturity value: $1,000,000 × .649930	= $ 649,930	(Table 10-2)
Annual interest payments: $90,000 × 3.88965 =	350,070	(Table 10-4)
	$1,000,000	

Therefore, although the bonds have a par value of $1,000,000, they will be sold for $962,091, which will result in an annual yield to the investors of 10%. The difference between the par value and issuance price $37,909 ($1,000,000 − $962,091), is referred to as the *discount.* The journal entry to record the issuance of the bonds would be:

Jan. 1, 19X1	Cash	$962,091	
	Discount on bonds payable	37,909	
	Bonds payable		$1,000,000
	To record issuance of bonds		

Discount on Bonds Payable is a contra-liability account, and as such would appear as a deduction from the Bonds Payable account on the corporation balance sheet. An illustration of such a balance sheet presentation for SOPED would be:

SOPED CORPORATION PARTIAL
Balance Sheet
as of January 1, 19X1

Liabilities, long-term:		
Bonds payable	$1,000,000	
Less: Unamortized discount	37,909	$962,091

The difference between the face (or par) value of the bonds, and the unamortized discount, is often referred to as the *carrying value* of the bonds.

Discount Amortization

In the previous illustration, SOPED Corporation is receiving $962,091 for the bonds and will be required to pay back the full $1,000,000 five years hence. The difference ($37,909) is interest expense to SOPED, which should be spread out over the life of the bonds. In other words, it is an expense which cannot be attributed to any one accounting period, but rather is attributable to the entire life of the bond issue. There are two methods utilized to amortize this discount over the life of a bond issue: (1) the straight-line method, and (2) the effective interest method.

Straight-line Amortization

Straight-line amortization of the discount is accomplished by simply dividing the discount by the number of years that the bonds will be outstanding and then reducing the discount by that amount annually. Interest expense is increased by the amount of the amortization. Under the straight-line method, the annual amortization would be $7,581.80 ($37,909 ÷ 5). The *annual* journal entry to record the amortization which is normally made in conjunction with the interest payment, would be:

Dec. 31, 19X1–X5	Interest expense	$97,581.80	
	Discount on bonds payable		$ 7,581.80
	Cash		90,000.00
	To record interest expense and discount amortization		

The amortization of the Discount on Bonds Payable systematically reduces the amount in that account. As the amount in that account is reduced, the carrying value of the bonds is increased until, at maturity, it reaches the face (or par) value of the bonds.

Effective Interest Method

The carrying value of the bonds is defined as the par value plus or minus any unamortized premium or discount. In the effective interest method of amortization, the interest expense is equal to the carrying value of the bonds multiplied by the rate which the bonds were sold to yield. So in the SOPED Corporation illustration, a rate of 10% will be used to calculate the annual interest expense. It should be noted that as a discount is amortized, the carrying value of the bonds increases and moves toward the face value; and as a premium is amortized the carrying value of the bonds decreases. An *amortization table* for the SOPED bonds would appear as follows:

YEAR	(A) CARRYING VALUE (BEGINNING) OF YEAR)	(B) ANNUAL INTEREST EXPENSE (10% OF CARRYING VALUE)	(C) CASH PAYMENT ($1,000,000 × 9%)	(D) ANNUAL AMORTIZATION (B) − (C)
19X1	$ 962,091	$96,209	$90,000	$6,209
	6,209			
19X2	968,300	96,830	90,000	6,830
	6,830			
19X3	975,130	97,513	90,000	7,513
	7,513			
19X4	982,643	98,264	90,000	8,264
	8,264			
19X5	990,907	99,093[a]	90,000	9,093
	9,093			
End of 19X5	$1,000,000			

[a] Correction of rounding error included.

A summary of the journal entries for the five-year period to record the interest payments and annual amortization would be:

DEC 31:	19X1		19X2		19X3		19X4		19X5	
Interest Expense	$96,209		$96,830		$97,513		$98,264		$99,093	
Discount on bonds payable		6,209		6,830		7,513		8,264		9,093
Cash		90,000		90,000		90,000		90,000		90,000

The entry to record the final maturity of the bonds would be as follows:

Jan. 1, 19X6	Bonds payable	$1,000,000	
	Cash		$1,000,000
	To record maturity on bonds		

From the point of view of the bond investor (purchaser), the journal entries are almost a mirror image of those of the issuer. The only substantial difference is that instead of the purchaser establishing separate premium or discount account, that amount is reflected directly in the Bond Investment account. Since there is then no premium or discount to amortize, the amortization goes directly to the Bond Investment account. The journal entries, assuming effective interest amortization, to reflect the acquisition of SOPED's bonds by various investors are as follows:

Jan. 1, 19X1	Bonds investment	$962,091	
	Cash		$962,091
	To record acquisition		

DEC. 31, EACH YEAR:	19X1		19X2		19X3		19X4		19X5	
Cash	$90,000		$90,000		$90,000		$90,000		$90,000	
Bond investment	6,209		6,830		7,513		8,264		9,093	
Bond interest income		96,209		96,830		97,513		98,264		99,093

The entry to record the bond maturity would be as follows:

Jan. 1, 19X6	Cash	$1,000,000	
	Bond investment		$1,000,000
	To record bond maturity		

Premium

If the prevailing market interest rates at the time of a bond issue are less than the cash rate of interest to be paid by the new issue, investors will tend to bid the bond price up until the issue price is such that the bonds will yield the current market rate.

Consider the same situation as discussed previously in this chapter, however assume now that the market interest rate on similar issuances is 6% instead of the 10% in the previous example. This means that the market rate is less than the stated rate of the issue, and therefore the bonds will be sold at a premium. The computation of the issuance price for 6% yield would be:

Maturity value:	$1,000,000 × .74726 =	$ 747,260
	(Table 10-2, 6%, 5th period)	
Annual interest payments:	$ 90,000 × 4.21236 =	379,112
	(Table 10-4, 6%, 5 periods)	
		$1,126,372

The bonds would be issued at a price of $1,126,372 or at a premium of $126,372. The journal entry to record the issuance would be:

Jan. 1, 19X1	Cash	$1,126,372	
	Bonds payable		$1,000,000
	Premium on bonds payable		126,372
	To record issuance of bonds		

The account Premium on Bonds Payable will appear on the balance sheet as an addition to the Bonds Payable liability. An illustration of such a balance sheet presentation for the bonds issuance illustrated would be:

Liabilities long-term:		
Bonds payable	$1,000,000	
Add: Premium on bonds payable	126,372	$1,126,372

Premium Amortization

Straight-line Amortization

Straight-line amortization of the premium would simply require that the premium of $126,372 be divided by five ($126,372 ÷ 5 = $25,274.40) and that the resulting amount be *subtracted* from interest expense each time interest is paid. The journal entry to record the *annual* interest payment under straight-line amortization would be:

Dec. 31, 19X1–X5	Interest expense	$64,725.60	
	Premium on bonds payable	25,274.40	
	Cash		$90,000.00
	To record interest payment and premium amortization		

Effective Interest Amortization

When the effective interest method of premium amortization is used, the interest expense is equal to the carrying value of the bonds multiplied by the effective rate at which the bonds were sold to yield. Therefore, in this illustration, the first annual interest expense amount will be equal to $67,582 ($1,126,372 × 6%). The amount of the amortization, $22,418 ($90,000 – $67,582) will then be deducted from the carrying value of the bonds, and a new calculation will be made for 19X2. This can be summarized in an amortization table as follows:

YEAR	(A) CARRYING VALUE (BEGINNING OF YEAR)	(B) ANNUAL INTEREST EXPENSE (6% OF CARRYING VALUE)	(C) CASH PAYMENT ($1,000,000 × 9%)	(D) ANNUAL AMORTIZATION (B)–(C)
19X1	$1,126,372	$67,582	$90,000	$22,418
	(22,418)			
19X2	1,103,954	66,237	90,000	23,763
	(23,763)			
19X3	1,080,191	64,812	90,000	25,188
	(25,188)			
19X4	1,055,003	63,300	90,000	26,700
	(26,700)			
19X5	1,028,303	61,697[a]	90,000	28,303
	(28,303)			
End of 19X5	**$1,000,000**			

[a] Correction of rounding error included.

A summarization of the journal entries for the five-year period to record the annual interest payments and amortization would be:

DEC 31:	19X1		19X2		19X3		19X4		19X5	
Interest expense	$67,582		$66,237		$64,812		$63,300		$61,697	
Premium on bonds payable	22,418		23,763		25,188		26,700		28,303	
Cash		90,000		90,000		90,000		90,000		90,000

Accounting for bonds purchase (from the *investor's* viewpoint) is no different when bonds are issued at a premium instead of a discount. The bond investment is still recorded at the total cost, with no differentiation between face value and premium. When bonds are purchased at a premium, the periodic amortization amount is deducted from the investment account and from the related Bond Interest Income account. The technique is identical to the one illustrated earlier for bonds purchased at a discount; therefore an illustration on this situation is not provided.

SEMIANNUAL INTEREST PAYMENTS

Often bonds pay interest semiannually. This change in the timing of interest payments has little substantive effect on the amortization of a premium or discount. Amortization is normally recorded in conjunction with interest payments; therefore if interest is paid semiannually on twenty-year bonds there will be forty interest payments and amortization entries. Straight-line amortization would require that the original premium or discount be divided by forty. If effective interest amortization is used, the calculation of the premium or discount will have been made with the timing of the interest payments in mind. The amortization of a premium or discount must then be consistent with the calculation of that same amount.

COMPARISON OF EFFECTIVE INTEREST AND STRAIGHT-LINE AMORTIZATION

The straight-line method of amortization results in an even allocation of the interest expense over the life of the bonds. The focus is on the calculation of the amortization, and it is then added to or deducted from the cash payment to arrive at an Interest Expense amount. Under the effective interest amortization, the focus is on the determination of Interest Expense (calculated by multiplying the effective interest rate times the carrying value). The amortization is basically a "byproduct" of that calculation in that it is the difference between interest expense and cash paid. This method is considered a more accurate procedure in that it recognizes interest expense as computed at the effective rate at which the bonds were issued. APB Opinion No. 21 specifies a preference for the effective interest method but permits the straight-line method if the results obtained are not significantly different.

BONDS REDEEMED BEFORE MATURITY

Bonds may be issued that are callable by the issuer after a certain date at a stated price, so that the issuing corporation may have the opportunity to reduce its bonded indebtedness or take advantage of lower interest rates. At the time of the redemption, the unamortized premium or discount should be amortized up to the acquisition date and removed from the accounts. For example, assume that bonds with a par value of $8,000,000 due in twenty years, are issued on January 1, 19X1, at 95 (or $950 per bond). Ten years after the issue date the entire issue is redeemed at 102 (or $1,020 per bond) and cancelled. The loss on redemption is computed as follows (straight-line amortization is assumed):

Redemption price:			
8,000,000 × 1.02		$8,160,000	
Carrying value of bond redeemed:			
Par value	$8,000,000		
Less: Unamortized discount			
($400,000 × 10/20)	200,000	7,800,000	
Loss on redemption		$ 360,000	
The entry to record the redemption and cancellation of the bonds is:			
Bonds payable		$8,000,000	
Loss on redemption of bonds		360,000	
Discount on bonds payable			200,000
Cash			8,160,000
To record reacquisition and cancellation of bonds			

The Loss of Redemption of Bonds is normally considered to be an extraordinary item in the income statement of the company redeeming the bonds. Normally bonds due to be retired within one year are to be retired from existing current assets and should be categorized as current liabilities.

SERIAL BONDS

An entire bond issue may be due at one maturity date, or the bonds may mature serially, that is, in a series of installments with some bonds maturing each year over a period of years. Serially maturing bonds are frequently issued by cities, school districts, or other taxing bodies that borrow money that will be paid off in installments through a specifically levied tax.

A serial bond issue may be sold as though each series is a separate bond issue or it may be sold as a package. Whether sold separately or as a package, one account for the total premium or discount is used in the general ledger for that serial issue. The total premium or discount to be amortized, whether computed for each series separately or for the entire issue, is entered in one account. A method of amortization frequently referred to as the *bonds outstanding* method is often used to amortize the premium or discount on serial bonds. The bonds outstanding method is an application of the straight-line method to serial bonds and assumes that the premium or discount applicable to each bond of the issue is the same dollar amount per bond per year.

To illustrate, assume that a serial bond issue in the amount of $3,000,000 dated January 1, 19X1, bearing 8% interest payable at December 31 each year is sold by Judtown School District to yield 9% per annum. The bonds mature serially in the amount of $600,000 each year beginning on January 1, 19X2. Assume further that this results in an issue price of $2,925,000, and a discount of $75,000 ($3,000,000 − $2,925,000). Using the bonds outstanding method for amortization the discount would be allocated over the five year period as follows:

YEAR ENDING DECEMBER 31	BONDS OUTSTANDING DURING YEAR	BONDS OUTSTANDING FOR YEAR ÷ TOTAL OF COLUMNS		DISCOUNT TO BE AMORTIZED		AMORTIZATION FOR THE YEAR
19X1	$3,000,000	30/90	×	$75,000	=	$25,000
19X2	2,400,000	24/90	×	75,000	=	20,000
19X3	1,800,000	18/90	×	75,000	=	15,000
19X4	1,200,000	12/90	×	75,000	=	10,000
19X5	600,000	6/90	×	75,000	=	5,000
	$9,000,000	90/90				$75,000

The effect of the column "Bonds Outstanding During Year" is to convert all the bonds into terms of bonds outstanding for one year, or a total of $9,000,000. Accordingly, during 19X1 the discount to be amortized would be $25,000 ($3,000,000 ÷ $9,000,000 × $75,000). Similarly during 19X2 the discount to be amortized would be $20,000 ($2,400,000 ÷ $9,000,000 × $75,000).

The journal entries relating to the serial bond issuance by Judtown School District for the five-year period would appear as follows:

Date	Account	Debit	Credit
19X1			
Jan. 1	Cash	$2,925,000	
	Discount on bonds payable	75,000	
	Bonds payable		$3,000,000
	To record issuance of bonds		
Dec. 31	Interest expense	265,000	
	Discount on bonds payable		25,000
	Cash		240,000
	To record cash payment of interest ($3,000,000 × 8%) and discount amortization for 19X1		
19X2			
Jan. 1	Bonds payable	600,000	
	Cash		600,000
	To record redemption of several bonds maturing on January 1, 19X2		
Dec. 31	Interest expense	212,000	
	Discount on bonds payable		20,000
	Cash		192,000
	To record cash payment of interest ($2,400,000 × 8%) and discount amortization for 19X2		
19X3			
Jan. 1	Bonds payable	600,000	
	Cash		600,000
	To record redemption of serial bonds maturing on January 1, 19X3		
Dec. 31	Interest Expense	159,000	
	Discount on bonds payable		15,000
	Cash		144,000
	To record cash payment of interest ($1,800,000 × 8%) and discount amortization for 19X3		
19X4			
Jan. 1	Bonds payable	600,000	
	Cash		600,000
	To record redemption of serial bonds maturing on January 1, 19X4		
Dec. 31	Interest expense	106,000	
	Discount on bonds payable		10,000
	Cash		96,000
	To record cash payment of interest ($1,200,000 × 8%) and discount amortization for 19X4		
19X5			
Jan. 1	Bonds payable	600,000	
	Cash		600,000
	To record redemption of serial bonds maturing on January 1, 19X5		
Dec. 31	Interest expense	53,000	
	Discount on bonds payable		5,000
	Cash		48,000
	To record cash payment of interest ($600,000 × 8%) and discount amortization for 19X5		
19X6			
Jan. 1	Bonds payable	600,000	
	Cash		600,000
	To record final redemption of serial bonds maturing on January 1, 19X6		

BONDS ISSUED BETWEEN INTEREST PAYMENT DATES

The bond certificates specify the date and amount of each interest payment. Although bonds may be sold on an interest date, more frequently than not, market factors cause them to be sold *between* interest dates. Nevertheless, the exact amount of interest specified on the bond certificate for each interest date will be paid, irrespective of whether a bond is sold on or between an interest date. Therefore, when bonds are sold between two interest dates, the buyer must *pay the accrued interest* to date in addition to the market price of the bond. Because the next interest payment will be for a full interest period, the accrued interest is then effectively returned to him. In view of this standard practice, the investor will realize interest revenue only for the number of months the bonds were held by him from the date of sale. Similarly, the issuing corporation will incur interest expense for the same period. This presents two complexities in accounting for bonds: (1) The amount of accrued interest charged to the buyer must be included in the entry to record the sale of bonds, and (2) any premium or discount is amortized over the period from date of sale to date of maturity of the bonds.

To illustrate, assume that the Pizer Corporation issues $1,000,000 par value, twenty-year bonds, payable date June 1, 19X1, paying interest at 12%, for $952,400 (a discount of $47,600). Assume that the bonds pay interest semiannually on each May 31, and November 30 (6% each date, or $60,000). On August 1, the date of the bond sale, the Pizer Corporation would receive cash for the sales price of the bonds, plus two months' accrued interest. The total cash received would be computed as follows:

Market price	$952,400
Accrued interest for 2 months ($1,000,000 × 12/100 × 2/12)	20,000
Total cash received	**$972,400**

The entry to record the bond issue by Pizer would be as follows:

Aug. 1, 19X1 Cash	$972,400	
Discount on bonds payable	47,600	
Bonds payable		$1,000,000
Interest expense		20,000
To record bond issuance		

In this entry, Interest Expense is credited because the $20,000 accrued interest collected from the purchaser will be refunded to him when the first interest payment is made. That payment will be recorded as a credit to Cash and a debit to Interest Expense. This is illustrated next.

The bond discount debit of \$47,600 must be amortized over the *period outstanding* of 238 months; therefore, straight-line amortization would be: \$47,600 ÷ 238 months = \$200 per month. The entry to record the first interest payment would include amortization of discount only for the four months that the bonds have been outstanding. Therefore, the first interest payment would be recorded as follows:

Nov. 30, 19X1 Interest expense	\$60,800	
Discount on bonds payable (\$200 × 4 months)		\$ 800
Cash (\$1,000,000 × 6%)		60,000
To record interest expense and bond amortization		

On December 31 an adjusting entry must be made to record the accrued interest and the discount amortization from November 30 through December 31. This adjusting entry would be:

Dec. 31, 19X1 Interest expense	\$10,200	
Discount on bonds payable (\$200 × 1 month)		\$ 200
Accrued interest payable (1 month)		10,000
To accrue interest		

After this entry is posted, the Interest Expense account should contain (1) interest on \$1,000,000 at 12% for five months (August through December); and (2) the amortization of the discount for five months. Therefore the accounts should have a balance computed as follows:

Interest: \$1,000,000 × 12/100 × 5/12	=	\$50,000
Discount amortization: \$200 × 5	=	1,000
		\$51,000

The bond interest account would have the \$51,000 balance as illustrated here in T-account form:

Interest Expense

11/30/X1	60,800	8/1/X1	20,000
12/31/X1	10,200		
Bal.	**51,000**		

Obviously, the \$51,000 amount will appear as an expense in the income statement for 19X1.

SUMMARY

The issuance of bonds is one of the primary ways to obtain funds needed for acquiring fixed assets and to expand the business. The rationale is that the increased earnings from the new or expanded facilities over the terms of the issue can be used in retiring the debt. An important advantage is that the cost of the funds, interest expense, is deductible for income tax purposes, which serves to reduce the net interest cost to the business. Bonds may be sold at their face amount or par value, at a premium, or at a discount, depending upon the stated interest rate on the bonds compared with the effective or market rate of interest which the buyers demand. The price of a bond varies with the effective or market rate of interest. Discount and premium on bonds payable are accounted for as periodic adjustments to the interest expense incurred by the issuing company over the outstanding life of the bonds.

KEY POINTS

1. Bonds secured by mortgages on property give the lienholders prior claim on the property in the event the firm is unable to pay the interest and maturity value. Unsecured bonds are called **debenture bonds.**

2. **Income bonds** pay interest only if the firm earns the interest. **Subordinated debentures** are bonds that are not secured by any mortgage or collateral and that allow various other creditors to be paid off first in the event of financial difficulties.

3. Convertible bonds allow the investor to exchange his bonds for common stock at his option.

4. The issuance of the bond by the borrower and the purchase of the bond by the lender must be recorded at the proper valuation of the liability by the bond issuer, and of the asset to the bond investor. Periodic accrual and payment of interest must be recognized in the accounts on closing dates and payment dates, respectively.

5. Since the investor's interest yield (rate of return) is a function of the relationship of the cash he receives as a bondholder to the price he pays for the bonds, the bonds will be "priced" by the bond market to yield the same interest rate as is being earned on similar bonds at the time of the bond issue (the market rate).

6. Bonds will be issued at a **premium** when the cash interest rate of the bond issued is greater than the prevailing yield rate on similar bonds. The amount of the premium is the excess of the issue price over the face value of the bonds.

7. Bonds will be issued at a **discount** when the cash interest rate on bonds issued is less than the prevailing yield rate. The amount of the discount is the excess of the face value over the issue price.

8. The bond premium or discount is amortized over the life of the bond issue. Amortization may be accomplished by either the straight-line or the effective interest method.

9. Straight-line amortization of premium or discount is accomplished by dividing the discount or premium by the number of years the bonds will be outstanding and reducing the discount or premium by that amount annually. Interest expense is increased by the amount of the amortization of discount and decreased by the amount of amortization of premium.

10. In the effective interest method, the interest expense is equal to the carrying value of the bonds multiplied by the rate at which the bonds were sold to yield. Carrying value of the bonds is adjusted for the amount of premium or discount amortized.

11. **Serial bonds** are bonds which may mature in a series of installments with some bonds maturing each year over a period of years.

12. When bonds are sold between two interest dates, the buyer must pay the accrued interest since the last interest date in addition to the market price of the bond. The investor will recognize interest revenue only for the number of months the bonds were held from the date of sale. The issuing corporation will incur interest expense for the same period.

QUESTIONS

1. For each of the following types of bonds, identify the distinguishing characteristic.

   a. Secured bonds
   b. Debenture bonds
   c. Subordinated debenture bonds
   d. Serial bonds
   e. Callable bonds
   f. Convertible bonds
   g. Income bonds

2. What are some advantages and disadvantages of convertible bonds to the investor and the issuing corporation?

3. Why would a company exercise the callable provision of a bond?

4. Distinguish between the methods of interest payments made to holders of coupon bonds as compared to payments on registered bonds.

5. Why are bonds not always sold at face value?

6. How is the selling price of bonds determined?

7. If you were buying a bond on which the stated interest rate was more than the market interest rate, would the par value be greater or less than the amount you pay? Explain.

8. Distinguish between straight-line amortization and effective interest amortization.

9. What is the effect of a premium on the interest expense of the issuing company?

10. If bonds are issued between interest dates, why does the issuer collect an amount of cash to cover the Accrued Interest from the buyer as well as the issue price?

11. What is the purpose of a bond sinking fund?

12. What are serial bonds? Explain the method commonly used to amortize a premium or discount on serial bonds.

13. Under what circumstance is it possible to redeem bonds at a price which will result in a gain to the issuing corporation? Would you expect this to occur commonly? Explain.

14. What is meant by a bond sinking fund? What factors go into determining the amount of annual payments which will be made into the fund?

EXERCISES

E11-1 Compute the following issue prices:

a. $100,000 bond issue at 8% for 5 years, priced to yield 10%, with interest paid annually.
b. $100,000 bond issue at 6% for 10 years, priced to yield 8%, with interest paid semiannualy.

E11-2 Approval was given to Filler Company for $6,000,000 of 8%, 10-year bonds dated December 31, 19X8. Sale was at face value with interest payments on June 30 and December 31. Delays halted the sale until June 1 of 19X9, at which time the entire issue was sold at face value plus accrued interest. Give the journal entries for:

a. The issuance of the bonds
b. The first semiannual interest payment.

E11-3 On January 1, 19X3, the Kelner Corporation sold a 10-year, $100,000, 9% bond issue at face value. Interest payments were scheduled for June 30 and December 31.

a. For a December 31 closing for both parties, give the entries for both the Kelner Corporation and the bond purchaser through June 30, 19X4.
b. If the closing date was March 31 for both parties, give the entries relating to the bond issue through June 30, 19X4, for the Kelner Corporation and the bond purchasers.

E11-4 Red Arrow Company will issue $200,000 of 10-year, 8% bonds on January 1, 19X8. Interest payments will be made semiannually, on June 30 and December 31. Half of the issue will be distributed at face value on January 1, 19X8, the second half of the issue will be sold on August 1 of the same year. If the Red Arrow Company has an accounting period that ends on March 31, give the firm's journal entries for 19X8.

E11-5 The Rogers Company received permission to issue $450,000 in bonds on June 1. The face interest rate is 9%, with payment on June 1 and December 1. Prepare journal entries for both the issuer and investor, for the date of the issue. Given the following conditions:

a. The bonds are sold at face value on Sept. 1,
b. The bonds are issued June 1 at 105.

E11-6 Reliable Roofing Corporation sold $200,000, 7%, 10-year bonds issued on January 1, 19X1, at a price of $220,000. On December 31, 19X5, the following was noted on the balance sheet of Reliable:

Bonds payable	$200,000
Premium	10,000
	$210,000

Make the following journal entries:

a. The firm, on January 1, 19X6, calls the bonds at 108.
b. The firm purchases half of the outstanding bonds from the open market for $103,000 on January 1, 19X6.

E11-7 The Twilight Corporation issued $1,000,000 par value 8% bonds on July 1, 19X0. The issue price was $980. The bonds' maturity date is 10 years from issuance. Twilight's accounting periods end on December 31. The firm also uses straight-line method. For the bond discount amortization, make the following journal entries (Assume that interest is paid semi-annually):

a. The issuance of the bonds
b. The first payment of interest and amortization of the bond discount
c. The final payment of interest, amortization of the bond discount, and retirement of bonds at maturity.

E11-8 On the balance sheet of Trainer Corporation is a portion, shown next, for bonds issued December 31, 19X4, at 8% interest, payable January 1 and July 1, and due December 31, 19X9.

Bonds payable	$400,000
Unamortized bond discount	−35,000
	$365,000

It may be assumed that the effective interest rate is 11%. Prepare the journal entries for the year 19X5 relevant to the interest payments.

E11-9 Sullivan Company and Rogers Company are both issuing 5-year bonds. Sullivan Company is issuing $1,000,000 of 10%, 5-year bonds. Interest is paid semiannually on June 30 and December 31. The issue is priced at 102.

Rogers Company is issuing $1,000,000, 8% bonds, with interest again being paid June 30 and December 31. This issue is priced at 97. Using the straight-line method of amortization, prepare journal entries for the first year.

E11-10 The Saber Company issued $400,000 of 8%, 20-year bonds on March 1, 19X2, at 103. Interest payments were made semiannually on March 1 and September 1. The effective interest rate for similar marketable securities is 7%. The fiscal year for Saber ends August 31. Make journal entries for the bonds up to the date of the first semiannual payment of interest.

E11-11 The Ivy Corporation issued $100,000 of 10-year, 7% bonds. Assume that the current market interest rate for similar securities is 8%. Payment of $93,205 has been received for the bonds. Interest is payable semiannually. Ivy Corporation uses the effective interest method to amortize the bond discount.

a. Prepare a journal entry to record the bond issue.
b. Prepare a journal entry to record payment of interest and amortization of the discount, at the first semiannual interest payment.
c. Prepare a journal entry for the third interest payment and amortization of the bond discount.

E11-12 Proptech Company is issuing a 10-year, $5,000,000 bond issue on January 1, 19X1. The company wishes to establish a sinking fund which will be used to pay off the bond issue at maturity. Assuming a 12% yield on its sinking fund investments to be made at the end of each year, how much should each annual sinking fund be?

PROBLEMS

P11-1 Calculate the present value of the following bond issue:

a. $200,000 par value paying 8% interest on a semiannual basis; 5-year life; market rate is 10%.

b. $200,000 par value paying 10% interest on a semiannual basis; 10-year life; market rate is 8%.
c. $400,000 par value paying 7% interest on an annual basis; 15-year life; market rate is 6%.
d. $500,000 par value paying 5% interest on an annual basis; 20-year life; market rate is 7%.
e. $2,000,000 par value paying 12% interest on an annual basis; 25-year life; market rate is 15%.

P11-2 The Royal Yacht Company issued $50,000 of 8% 20-year debenture bonds with interest payable semiannually on June 30 and December 31 of each year. Royal Yacht's accounting period ends on December 31. Give the necessary journal entries to record the firm's transactions with respect to the bonds for 19X6 in each of the following cases:

a. The bonds were issued for $51,000 on January 1, 19X6.
b. The bonds were issued for $50,000 plus accrued interest on April 1, 19X6.
c. The bonds were issued for $52,500 on January 1, 19X6, and the firm's accounting period ends on September 30.

P11-3 Rascals Company is authorized to issue $100,000 of 10-year, 8% bonds with semiannual interest payments on June 30 and December 31. Record the journal entries necessary on January 1 and June 30, 19X2, on the books of Rascals Company in each of the following cases:

a. The bonds are issued at a price of $90,000 on January 1, 19X2. Interest is paid on June 30 and December 31.
b. The bonds are issued at a price of $106,000 on January 1, 19X2. Interest is paid on June 30 and December 31.

P11-4 The Summit Corporation issues 6,000 bonds having maturity values of $1,000 each. The bonds pay interest at a 9% annual rate payable semiannually on January 1 and July 1. The bonds are to run 10 years. The market rate of interest is 9%. What is the issue value of the bonds? Record the issuance of the bonds on January 1, 19X6; the first interest payment on July 1, 19X6; the accrual entry on December 31 (closing date) assuming that interest is not actually paid until January 1, 19X7; and the January 1, 19X7, payment.

P11-5 On January 1, 19X1, the Carson Corporation issued $1,000,000 of 8% bonds due on December 31, 19X3 with interest payable annually on December 31. The bonds are issued at a price to yield 10% to the purchasers.

a. Determine the issue price of the bonds.
b. Record the issuance of the bonds, the interest payments, and the payment of the bonds at maturity on the Carson Corporation books.
c. Assuming that the Manner Company purchased three $1,000 bonds, record the purchase, the interest collections, and the ultimate collection of the bond at maturity.

P11-6 On January 1, 19X2, the Elm Corporation issued $800,000 of 10% bonds due on December 31, 19X4 with interest payable annually on December 31. The bonds are issued at a price to yield 8% to the purchasers.

a. Determine the issue price of the bonds.
b. Record the issuance of the bonds, the interest payments, and the payment of the bonds at maturity on the Elm Corporation books.
c. Assuming that the Merlin Corporation purchased one $1,000 bond, record the purchase, the interest collections, and the ultimate collection of the bond at maturity.

P11-7 On January 1, 19X4, the stockholders of Gorski Company authorized the issuance of $16,000 of 3-year, 8% bonds paying interest semiannually on June 30 and December 31. The bonds were sold on April 1, 19X4, for $16,660 plus accrued interest. On April 1, 19X5, Gorski Company retired half of the issue at 102 (plus accrued interest). Prepare all general journal entries for 19X4 and 19X5. (Use the straight-line amortization method.)

P11-8 The Oakton Corporation maintains its accounts on a calendar-year basis. On June 30, 19X2, the company issued $12,000,000 face value of 7.6% bonds at a price of 97¼, resulting in an effective rate of interest of 8%. Semiannual interest payment dates are June 30 and December 31. The bonds mature in 10 years.

Prepare the required journal entries on:

a. June 30, 19X2, to record the sale of the bonds.
b. December 31, 19X2, to pay interest and amortize the discount using the effective interest method.
c. June 30, at the bonds' maturity, to pay interest, amortize the discount, and retire the bonds. As of the beginning of this last interest period, the carrying value of the bonds is $11,976,922. (Use a separate journal entry to show the retirement of the bonds.)

P11-9 On September 1, 19X0, Western World, Inc., issued $13 million in 8% debenture bonds. Interest is payable semiannually on March 1 and September 1, and the bonds mature on September 1 in 10 years. Company policy is to amortize bond discount or premium by the straight-line method at each interest payment date. The company's fiscal year ends at December 31.

Make the necessary adjusting entries at December 31, 19X0, and the journal entry to record the payment of bond interest on March 1, 19X1, under each of the following assumptions:

a. The bonds were issued at 97.
b. The bonds were issued at 103.

P11-10 Wagner Company obtained authorization to issue $1,000,000 of 9%, 10-year bonds, dated May 1, 19X1. Interest payment dates were May 1 and November 1. Issuance of the bonds did not take place until July 1. On this date, the entire bond issue was sold to a private pension fund at a price which included the two months' accrued interest. Wagner follows the policy of amortizing bond discount or premium by the straight-line method at each interest date as well as for year-end adjusting entries at December 31.

INSTRUCTIONS:

a. Prepare all journal entries necessary to record the issuance of the bonds and bond interest expense during 19X3, assuming that the sale price of the bonds on July 1 was $1,005,000 (including accrued interest).

b. Assume that the sales price of the bonds on July 1 had been $992,400 (including accrued interest). Prepare journal entries for Year 1 parallel to those in item a.

P11-11 Condor Company issued $1,000,000 of 20-year, 9% bonds on April 1, 19X0, with interest payable on June 30 and December 31. The bonds were callable after January 1, 19X7, at 105 percent of face value and, in fact, were called on that date. The fiscal year of the company ends on September 30. Give the necessary journal entries for the first year, and for the calling of the bonds, using the straight-line method of amortization.

P11-12 Thompson Bedding Company issued $200,000 of 8% 10-year debenture bonds at face value plus accrued interest on April 1, 19X4. Interest is payable semiannually on January 1 and July 1.

Prepare the journal entries necessary to record the issuance of the bonds and to record interest expense for the first interest date subsequent to issuance.

P11-13 The following data relating to long-term liabilities appeared on the books of Sunnyside Company on December 31, 19X5:

Bonds payable: 6%, 20-year debenture bonds, $6,000 authorized interest payable semiannually on June 30 and December 31	$200,000
Discount on bonds payable	4,000
	196,000

On January 1, 19X6, half of the bonds were purchased and retired at 102 percent of face value. Prepare the necessary journal entry to record the retirement of $100,000 of bonds on January 1, 19X6.

P11-14 Craker Company, on September 1, 19X1, issued $4,500,000 par value, 8½%, 10-year bonds payable with interest dates of March 1 and September 1. The company maintains its accounts on a calendar-year basis and follows the policy of amortizing bond discount and bond premium by the effective interest method, both for the semiannual interest payments as well as the year-end adjusting of the accounts.

INSTRUCTIONS:

a. Prepare the necessary journal entries to record the following transactions, assuming that the bonds were sold for $4,350,000, a price resulting in an effective annual interest rate of 9%.
   (1) Sale of the bonds on September 1, 19X1.
   (2) Adjustment of the accounts at December 31, 19X1, for accrued interest and amortization of discount.
   (3) Payment of bond interest and amortization of discount on March 1, 19X2.

b. Assume that the sales price of the bonds on September 1, 19X1, had been $4,650,000, resulting in an effective annual interest rate of 8%. Prepare journal entries parallel to those called for in item a at the dates of September 1, 19X1; December 31, 19X1; and March 1, 19X2.

c. State the amounts of bond interest expense for 19X1 and the net amount of the liability for the bonds payable at December 31, 19X1, under the independent assumptions set forth in both items a and b. Show your computations.

P11-15 Friar's Company issued $100,000 of 8%, 10-year debenture bonds on January 1, 19X8. Interest is payable semiannually on June 30 and December 31. The following information is given on the bonds at December 31, 19X8:

Carrying value of bonds	$103,500
Interest expense for the year	7,640

a. Were the bonds issued at a premium or discount?

b. What was the amount of premium or discount on the issuance of the bonds?

c. How much of the discount or premium was amortized during the year?

P11-16 Brown Company issued $2,000,000 of 6% 20-year debenture bonds on April 1, 19X8, and received $1,982,600. The bonds were authorized on January 1, 19X8. Interest is payable semiannually on June 30 and December 31 of each year. Brown Company's accounting period ends on December 31. Give the necessary journal entries to record the firm's transactions with respect to these bonds for 19X8 and 19X9.

P11-17 The items shown here appear in the balance sheet of Comtech Industries, December 31, 19X0.

Current liabilities:		
Bond interest payable since Oct. 1		$175,000
Long-term debt:		
Bonds payable, 7% due Apr. 1, 19X9	$10,000,000	
Less: Discount on bonds payable	132,000	9,868.000

The bonds are callable on any interest date. On October 1, 19X1, Comtech called $3 million of the bonds at 105.

a. Prepare journal entries to record the semiannual interest payment on April 1, 19X1. Discount is amortized by the straight-line method at each interest payment date and was amortized to December 31, 19X0. Base the amortization on the 99-month period from December 31, 19X0 to April 1, 19X9.

b. Prepare journal entries to record the amortization of bond discount and payment of bond interest at October 1, 19X1, and also to record the calling of $2 million of the bonds at this date.

c. Prepare a journal entry to record the accrual of interest at December 31, 19X1. Include the amortization of bond discount to the year-end.

P11-18 On January 1, 19X1, Franklin Company issued $3,000,000 of 9% serial bonds maturing in three installments of $1,000,000 each beginning on December 31, 19X1. The bonds, which pay interest semiannually each June 30 and December 31, were sold at a premium of $54,000. Franklin Company amortized the premium using the bonds outstanding method.

REQUIRED:

Present all journal entries of the Franklin Company relating to the bonds for the 3-year period.

OWNERS' EQUITY 12

ORIENTATION

Companies operate under three basic forms of business organization: sole proprietorships, partnerships, and corporations. The objective of this chapter is to compare and contrast these various forms of business organization, and to describe the accounting aspects of owners' equity under each of the variations. The chapter contains a description of the basic characteristics of ownership rights in both incorporated and unincorporated firms, and an illustration of the accounting treatment of changes in owners' equity for incorporated and unincorporated firms. Included are the accounting aspects of corporate preferred stock and cash dividends; a discussion of corporate stock dividends, stock splits, and various stock transactions; and an explanation of the accounting procedures for these items.

FORMS OF BUSINESS ORGANIZATION

There are many variations in the rights and obligations of owners under the different ownership patterns available to business entities. Three forms of ownership are the most prevalent: sole proprietorship, partnership, and the corporation.

The larger and more complex a business firm, the more elaborate its accounting system must be in order to report to investors and others who have no direct contact with the firm. While there are a great many more firms owned and operated by sole proprietors or partners, the greatest volume of business is handled by firms organized as corporations. In its basic essentials, accounting remains the same whatever form the ownership of the firm may take, except for the part of accounting that relates to the ownership interests. The accountant assumes that the business unit is separate and distinct from the personal affairs or other business affairs of those who supply capital to the firm. This assumption of separation of the business unit from its residual owners, which is referred to as the *entity principle,* is consistent with legal and economic reality for corporations while it is largely hypothetical for the sole proprietorship and partnership forms of business enterprise.

UNINCORPORATED BUSINESS FIRMS

Unincorporated business firms may be either sole proprietorships (one owner) or partnerships (multiple owners). There are certain significant differences in the accounting for these two types of business organization.

Accounting for Sole Proprietorships

The sole proprietor does not share the risks of loss nor the rewards of profits with any other party. Losses from the firm's operations may wipe out a sole proprietor's entire equity in the firm and his or her entire personal estate, and there will be no recourse against any other party. Nor does the sole proprietor share control. The proprietor may appoint agents to act for him or her but this is the proprietor's choice and they act only as long as the proprietor designates. The sole proprietor has unlimited liability for the firm's debts. Creditors rely not only on the value of the property of the proprietorship but are also concerned with the value of his or her personal property and with any claims of creditors who have supplied such personal property.

The accountant should supply the sole proprietor with financial reports on the basis of decision units. If a person has a grocery store, a farm, and an auto agency, the proprietor will need to choose whether to expand, reorganize, dispose of, or refinance each one separately and will need separate data for each decision. For each decision unit, the owner will need to know the profitability of the unit relative to investment, how much can be withdrawn for personal needs or for other business ventures, and whether agents and employees have been discharging their responsibilities efficiently and honestly. On the other hand, the sole proprietor often does not need to rely as heavily on the accountant's reports for information as do stockholders. The sole proprietor can and normally does spend much time personally with proprietorship affairs, and frequently knows the firm's resources and creditors from personal contact.

Sole Proprietorship Accounting Illustrated

When an individual begins a sole proprietorship, the owner typically invests money or other assets in the business in anticipation of earning a potential profit from the investment.

To illustrate the journal entries for such a situation, assume that Brett George invests $10,000 cash, and equipment valued at $25,000 in a home computer marketing operation. The journal entry to record the investment would be:

Cash	$10,000	
Equipment	25,000	
Brett George, Capital		$35,000

Assume further that George withdraws $12,000 from the business during the first year; and that the business earns a profit of $14,500 during the year. The journal entries to record these facts would be:

To record periodic withdrawals from the business (summarized):		
George, Drawing	$12,000	
Cash		$12,000
End-of-year entries to close total drawing and annual profit into the capital account:		
George, Capital	$12,000	
George, Drawing		$12,000
Sales	XXXXXXX	
Various expenses		XXXXXXX
George, Capital		$14,500

It is important to note that all owners' equity activity of a sole proprietorship is reflected in the owners' capital account. This is in many ways a simplification relative to owners' equity accounting for a corporation, where the value of the transaction (investment, profit distribution, etc.) determines the specific owners' equity account (or accounts) to be used.

Accounting for Partnerships

A partnership is an association of two or more individuals in a business as co-owners for profit. Like a sole proprietorship, a partnership has unlimited liability, but while a partner generally cannot insulate the business risks from personal assets, he or she does share the risks of the firm with other parties and may be able to recover some portion of losses from partners' personal assets. Control of the firm is also shared with partners. Ordinarily, each partner may act for the partnership, thus making it very important that the partners have confidence in each others' abilities. Profits are divided equally among the partners unless they specify some other arrangement. In the event of dissolution, each partner recovers his contributed capital, plus his or her share of gains and less a share of losses and the amount of withdrawals.

It is common to think of partnerships in terms of smaller businesses with two or three partners. However, large partnerships with numerous partners are traditionally associated with the practice of medicine, law, public accounting, and other professions. In somes states a "professional person" is prohibited from incorporating on the grounds that the creation of a corporate entity might weaken the personal relationship between practitioner and client. However, lawsuits against doctors for malpractice, against auditors for nonfeasance, and against other professionals are sometimes instituted with little justification, so that even the best firms must protect themselves against such possible losses. Therefore, many states have approved legislation designed to permit *professional corporations* which provide limited liability to the owners, thereby limiting their losses from lawsuits, and the like, to the assets of the corporation.

Partnership Accounting Illustrated

The techniques of partnership accounting are virtually identical to sole proprietorship accounting except that in a sole proprietorship there is only one capital account, and in a partnership there is a capital account for each partner.

To illustrate, assume that two individuals, Able and Young, decide to open a clothing store on January 1, 19X1. Able invests $43,800 cash, and Young invests other assets (building, fixtures, inventory, etc.) valued at $56,980. The journal entry to record the initial investment would be:

Cash	$43,800	
Various assets	56,980	
Able, Capital		$43,800
Young, Capital		56,980

Assume further that Able and Young agree to divide profits and losses equally, and that total profit for the year amounted to $51,306 (Sales of $1,360,000 less expenses of $1,108,694). Able withdrew $12,000 from the business and Young $20,000 during 19X1.

As in sole proprietorships, partnership profit distributions are accomplished in two steps: (1) the assignment of the net income (or earnings) to the capital accounts of the individual partners, and (2) the drawing of cash from the firm against the partners' capital balances. In the case of Able and Young, the partners had agreed to share income equally. The closing entries exhibited next show the assignment of the net income to the two capital accounts, and the recognition that the drawings made by the two partners during the year reduce their capital balances:

Sales	$1,360,000	
Cost of goods sold and other operating expenses		$1,308,694
Able, capital		25,653
Young, capital		25,653
Able, capital	12,000	
Young, capital	20,000	
Able, drawings		12,000
Young, drawings		20,000

The regular balance sheet and income statement, with only slight modification, are suited to proprietary and partnership businesses. In addition, a statement of capital for each owner is normally prepared;

Able and Young Merchants
Partial Balance Sheet
December 31, 19X1

ASSETS	EQUITIES		
(Regular format)	Current liabilities		XXX
	Long-term liabilities		XXX
	Partners' capital:		
	Able, capital	$57,453	
	Young, capital	62,633	$120,086

Able and Young Merchants
Statement of Partners' Capital
for the year ended December 31, 19X1

	ABLE, CAPITAL	YOUNG, CAPITAL	TOTAL
Capital, Jan. 1	$43,800	$56,980	$100,780
Net earnings for the year (see income statement)	25,653	25,653	51,306
Totals	$69,453	$82,633	$152,086
Withdrawals during 19X1			
Drawings (as agreed)	$12,000	$20,000	$ 32,000
Capital balances, Dec. 31, 19X1	**$57,453**	**$62,633**	**$120,086**

Note that there is no differentiation in the capital accounts between the equity of a partner that originated from his investment in the firm and the equity that came about from retention of income in the firm. The balance in a partner's capital account reflects his capital contributions and drawings as well as the partner's share of income and losses.

A significant matter in both proprietorships and partnerships concerns the salaries of owners. Economists often wish to think of the income of partners or sole proprietors as being made up of a "wage" for personal services, "interest" on invested capital, and the remainder being profit from operations. It is difficult for the accountant to apply this division of income in an objective manner in view of the fact that the owners typically set their own salaries and interest (if such amounts are designated at all). It should be pointed out, however, that the value of the personal services and the amount of capital contributed by the partners are often important factors in the negotiations between the partners when they decide how profits shall be divided.

The determination of how much of the profit for the period to assign to each partner's capital account is a *matter of adhering* to the agreement made by the partners. An agreement is likely to mention that a portion of earnings should be assigned to take into account any differences in personal services rendered by the partners and differences in amounts of capital invested in the firm. In the absence of an agreement, it will be assumed that the partners agreed to share profits equally. There are almost infinite numbers of possible combinations of factors to determine a formula for division of profits among partners. The accountant must be careful to study the particular agreement and follow it closely.

An important motive for the incorporation of partnerships relates to income tax advantages. Partnerships must file federal income tax reports but such reports are only informational in nature. The partnership does not in the ordinary course of events pay an income tax on the income of the partnership. The individual partners must pay income taxes based upon their shares of the earnings reported regardless of their withdrawals from the business.

Characteristics Common to Sole Proprietorships and Partnerships

Both sole proprietors and partners are subject to unlimited personal liability for the debt of their firms. Both forms of organization frequently require personal devotion to business affairs. Risks are great and rewards may also be great.

Since the number of owners is generally small and since most individuals have only moderate wealth to devote to business ventures, neither sole proprietorships nor partnerships can ordinarily obtain enough resources to engage in large-scale enterprises. Furthermore, as such firms grow in size through retention of profits, it becomes difficult for owners to divest themselves of ownership interests because there are few people who have both the money to buy the interests and the desire to be involved in the firm. An owner of a partnership interest who wishes to sell out must find someone who not only wishes to buy his interest but who would also be accepted to all other partners. Often it is necessary to incorporate the business firm in order to dispose of the ownership interest advantageously.

In both sole proprietorships and partnerships, each owner has his individual capital account. Both owner investment and profit distribution are recorded in these capital accounts.

CORPORATION ACCOUNTING

A corporation is a separate legal unit that can act as a "person" in most areas of business endeavor. In the Dartmouth College case in 1819, Chief Justice Marshall of the United States Supreme Court stated: "A corporation is an artificial being, invisible, intangible, and existing only in the contemplation of the law." The state law and the articles of incorporation (which become the corporation charter) spell out the activities in which the corporation shall be allowed to engage. The charter ordinarily gives the corporation powers to perform all acts necessary to its purpose of carrying on a certain type of business and performing other related activities. Furthermore, the charter often is easily amended in the event that the corporation may need to broaden its scope. Like other forms of business, the corporation is an economic entity, but it is also a legal entity to a greater degree than a partnership or sole proprietorship.

A good understanding of the real nature of a corporation can be obtained by comparing the rights of partners with the rights of stockholders. A partnership is an association of two or more individuals in a business as co-owners for profit, while a corporation is a legal entity separate from its owners. The debts of a partnership apply to partnership property and to the partners' personal property. Corporations generally enjoy *limited liability,* which means that its debts apply to the corporation property but do not relate to the personal property of the stockholders except in very unusual cases. Stockholders have a voice in the management of a corporation only through their vote to elect the board of directors or to amend the charter or certain other very limited actions specified in the charter. Partners are agents of the partnership and can take direct action to bind the partnership, and they are expected to devote their best efforts to furthering the interests of the partnership. In contrast, no one expects individuals holding a few shares of corporation stock to neglect their other activities and devote their time and energies to the corporation unless they are employed specifically to work for the corporation. Partners each have a right to refuse to accept someone desiring to join the firm, whereas stockholders usually have no voice about who shall be sold stock. On the other hand, stockholders can ordinarily sell their shares to anyone without the approval of others. A partner has full access to the firm's records and premises; a stockholder has limited access to both. Partners may draw upon the firm for their share of the profits or for their capital share, whereas stockholders share in the profits through dividends only if the board of directors deems it advisable for the corporation to pay dividends.

A corporation may be classified by the nature of ownership as follows:

1. *Public corporations,* which are governmental units or businesses owned by governmental units (such as the United States Postal Service).
2. *Private corporations,* which may be *nonstock* or *stock*-issuing corporations. A nonstock corporation is nonprofit in nature, such as private colleges, churches,

and charitable institutions. Stock-issuing corporations are companies that operate for a profit and issue stock. Such companies may be either *open* or *closed* corporations. The stock of an open corporation is generally widely held and readily available for purchase by the public; whereas a closed corporation has stock which is held by a few stockholders (often a family) and not available for public purchase. Each state in the United States has its own statutory requirements regarding the organization and operation of corporations. Variations in the statutes governing corporations do exist and there are resulting minor differences in the nature of corporate equity relationships.

Issuance of Corporate Securities

The corporation obtains funds from investors by issuing securities: stocks and bonds. Investors who acquire stock of the corporation become owners, and investors who purchase its bonds become creditors of the corporation. The nature of bonds and the related accounting problems were discussed in Chapter 11. The concern here is with capital stock.

A corporation's capital stock will always include common stock. It is referred to as the *residual equity* because it ranks after other types of securities in rights to dividends and to assets distributed upon dissolution of the corporation. There are, generally, no prescribed limitations on the amount of profits which may be distributed to common stockholders. Such limitations on dividend distributions do apply to preferred stock, which is a separate class of capital stock. *Preferred stock* differs from common stock in several respects, including a prior claim to dividends and to assets upon liquidation of the business.

Many corporations issue only *common stock*. Large corporations, however, generally issue both common and preferred stock and, in some cases, more than one class of both types of stock. The issuance of preferred as well as common stock provides a corporation with a greater degree of flexibility in its financing arrangements and also an appeal to a wider range of investors.

It should be noted that while it is possible to indicate the usual rights of classes of stockholders, in the case of an actual corporation the rights of stockholders classes will depend upon the provisions of the corporation's charter and the laws of the state.

Par and No-Par Stock

Par value of stock is a nominal value per share which is specified for the stock in the corporate charter; it does not reflect the stock's economic or market value. Originally one purpose of assigning a par value to stock was to ensure that the stockholders pay at least the par value for their stock and that this minimum value not be withdrawn by the stockholders until the creditors of the corporation were paid in full. Since par value is generally a nominal value having little or no relation to a true economic value, its effectiveness as a safeguard for creditors has always been questionable. In most states, the laws have been changed so that a par value need not be assigned to corporate stock. Such *no-par stock* is frequently issued by corporations. No-par stock is sometimes assigned a stated value which, like par value, is generally unrelated to the market value of the stock. Specific accounting entries for these three types of stock—par, no-par, and no-par with a stated value—are presented a little later in the chapter.

The journal entry for the issuance of no-par stock is simply a matter of debiting cash and crediting common stock for the net proceeds of the issuance.

Legal capital for a corporation is defined by the laws of the state of incorporation and generally designates the amount of assets which cannot be distributed to the stockholders as a dividend. Legal capital is frequently the par value of the outstanding stock or, in the case of no-par stock with a stated value, legal capital is the stated value of the stock.

The maximum number of shares that can be issued by a corporation is specified in the corporate charter and is referred to as *authorized stock. Issued stock* is the number of shares which have been issued to stockholders. On occasion, a corporation may purchase shares previously issued from its own stockholders. Such reacquired stock is called *treasury stock. Outstanding stock* is the number of shares currently held by stockholders. The term *contributed capital* is often used to describe the amount received from stockholders from the issuance of stock.

Illustration

To illustrate the journal entries that would be made in the various situations just described, assume that:

1. X Corporation issues 1,000 shares of *no-par, no-stated-value* stock at $60 per share;
2. Y Corporation issues 1,000 shares of *no-par, $10 stated value* stock for $60 a share; and
3. Z Corporation issues 1,000 shares of *$10 par* stock for $60 a share.

The X Corporation entry would be:		
Cash	60,000	
Common stock (no-par)		60,000
The Y Corporation entry would be:		
Cash	60,000	
Common stock (at stated value)		10,000
Paid-in capital in excess of stated value		50,000
The Z Corporation entry would be:		
Cash	60,000	
Common stock (at par)		10,000
Paid-in capital in excess of par		50,000

The Paid-in Capital in Excess of Par account would appear, together with the Common Stock account, in the owners' (or shareholders') equity section of the corporation balance sheet. Specific balance sheet presentation and disclosure format will be discussed later in this chapter.

The amount by which the proceeds of a stock issue exceed the par (or stated) value is sometimes referred to as *additional capital* or *premium* on stock. Published statements still frequently use these titles. Since that part of the total contributed capital generally exceeds the minimum contribution required by law in some states, it is somewhat less restricted in regard to serving as a basis for dividends than the par or stated value. Though the "excess" is still a portion of the stockholders' equity (claim) arising from paying in assets to the firm, it is possible in many states, on approval of the board of directors, to make distributions of corporate property to the extent of that "excess," providing that the stockholders are informed that the distributions cause reductions of capital rather than of retained earnings.[1]

The laws of some states permit stock to be issued for less than the amount of the par value. The difference is referred to as *discount on capital stock* or, more precisely, *excess of par value over amount contributed.* This is shown as a subtraction from the par value of issued stock in the stockholders' equity section. In some cases, if the firm fails and the creditors' claims cannot be settled out of corporation properties, creditors may proceed against the stockholders' personal assets for the amount of discount on stock.

Preferred Stock and Cumulative Preferred Stock

Every holder of a share of stock has the same rights as the holder of any other share of stock except where the charter of the corporation issuing the stock restricts the rights of, or grants special rights to, a class of stockholders. For example, preferred stockholders typically have voting rights only if they have not received dividends for a specified period of time. Also, preferred stockholders are entitled to dividends before the common stockholders may receive dividends. The dividends on the preferred stock may be either *cumulative* or *noncumulative.* If the dividends are cumulative (which is often the case), the full dividends of the current year and all previous years as yet unpaid must be paid to the preferred stockholders before the common stockholders can be paid anything. Unpaid dividends on cumulative preferred stock are called *dividends in arrears.* If the dividends are noncumulative (a rare feature), the preferred stockholders will be paid their current dividend before the common stockholders can be paid anything, but undeclared dividends of previous years need

[1] In the law and in the literature of finance and accounting, unfortunate errors in the use of terms have developed over the years. The state laws commonly refer to paying dividends out of retained earnings or paying dividends out of capital in excess of par (paid-in capital). Dividends are not "paid out of" an equity any more than creditors are "paid out of" liabilities; they are paid in cash or other assets. This carelessness is common in the language of business and is sometimes the source of confusion.

not be paid to the preferred stockholders. In addition to having special dividend rights and features, preferred stockholders generally have priority over common stockholders in rights to the proceeds of liquidation of assets in the event of bankruptcy of the firm, though this priority is subordinate to that of creditors.

Illustration

The Ace Corporation has outstanding 10,000 shares of preferred stock entitled to a $5 per share cumulative dividend, and 20,000 shares of common stock. No dividends have been paid on the preferred stock for 19X1, 19X2, nor for the current year, 19X3. The board of directors finds that Ace Corporation can pay dividends of $300,000 in 19X3 without impairing the well-being of the firm. Accordingly, dividends of that amount are declared and paid. The distribution of the dividend would be:

To preferred:	
3 years ($5 × 10,000 shares) =	$150,000
To common:	
(remainder) =	150,000
Total dividend	$300,000

If the preferred stock had not been cumulative and the same total amount of dividends had been declared, the distribution would have been:

To preferred:	
1 year ($5 × 10,000 shares) =	$ 50,000
To common:	
(remainder)	250,000
Total dividend	$300,000

Whether the preferred stock is cumulative or noncumulative, the failure in any year to pay dividends on preferred stock is indicative of financial weakness and thus often has an adverse effect upon the stock market values of both the preferred stock and the common stock. Any amount of preferred stock dividends in arrears must be noted parenthetically or in a footnote to the balance sheet of the reporting firm.

The charters of some corporations give preferred stockholders the right to participate in earnings with the common stockholders in some prescribed fashion when dividends in excess of the stipulated preferred dividend rate are declared on common stock. The manner of the sharing depends upon the particular provisions of each case. Such preferred stocks, which are now quite rare, are referred to as *participating preferred.*

Dividends in General

Dividends are payable only if declared by the board of directors and must be paid (if legal) in accordance with the declaration. Once dividends are declared and the declaration becomes public information, the dividends may not be rescinded without approval of the stockholders. Indeed, the stockholders become creditors with respect to their dividend participation (if the dividends are legal). For dividends to be legal they must be based upon the earnings (retained earnings) of the corporation or, in some states, upon the capital contributed in excess of par value, and they must not reduce the resources of the corporation to such an extent that creditors cannot be paid.

There are four dates that are important in dividend declarations:

1. The *declaration date* The date the dividend is declared by the board of directors.
2. The *record date* A date specified in the dividend declaration which indicates that all stockholders who own stock according to the stockholder records on that date will receive a dividend.
3. *Ex-dividend date* A date a few days before the record date, after which new purchases of stock will not entitle buyers to receive the dividend previously declared.
4. *The payment date* The date fixed by the board of directors at the time of declaration, on which cash will be paid to stockholders as of the date of record.

Formal journal entries are made only on the declaration and payment dates. To illustrate, assume that on November 1 the board of directors declares the regular quarterly dividend of $2 on the 50,000 shares of $100 par preferred stock outstanding (total dividend of $100,000), and a quarterly dividend of 90 cents on the 200,000 shares of $20 par common stock outstanding (total dividend $180,000). Both dividends are to stockholders of record on November 15, and checks are to be issued to stockholders on December 5. The journal entries to record the declaration and payment of the dividend would be:

Nov. 1	Retained earnings	$280,000	
	Dividends payable: Preferred		$100,000
	Dividends payable: Common		180,000
Dec. 5	Dividends payable: Preferred	100,000	
	Dividends payable: Common	180,000	
	Cash		280,000

An alternative method of accomplishing the same result would be to debit an account such as "Cash Dividends" on November 1. The balance of that account would then be transferred to Retained Earnings as a part of the closing process. If a balance sheet were prepared between the dates of declaration and payment, the Dividends Payable would be listed as a current liability.

Property and Script Dividends

There are occasionally cases in which dividends declared are payable in property other than cash. Such *property dividends* are rather unusual because most property cannot be divided into parts proportionate to the holdings of the various stockholders. There is an exception, however, in the case of shares of stock in other firms held by a corporation. Such shares may be distributed as a property dividend.

A *script dividend* is merely a very special form of note payable. It means that instead of paying the dividend now, the board of directors has elected to pay it at some future date. Such dividends may be declared when the corporation has sufficient retained earnings but is short of cash. The recipient of the script dividend may hold it until the due date, if one is specified; or occasionally may discount it to obtain immediate cash. Script dividends are extremely rare.

Stock Dividends

Dividends declared which involve the issuance of additional shares of the firm's own common stock to holders of its common stock are called *stock dividends:* dividends of stock on stock. It is generally recognized that such stock dividends do not constitute a distribution of earnings and therefore are not taxable to the recipient. A holder of 10 percent of the common stock who receives a stock dividend still has a 10 percent interest in the corporation. The investor has nothing that he or she did not have before—merely a greater number of shares to represent the same ownership rights already held.

An example may make this basic point clear. Assume that a closed corporation with 1,000 shares of common stock outstanding is owned equally by four individuals (each owning 250 shares). The corporation declares a stock dividend of 20 percent and distributes the 200 additional shares (20% of 1,000 shares), with 50 shares going to each of the four individuals. Each now holds 300 shares, but each still owns one-fourth of the business. The corporation has not changed; its assets and liabilities and its total owners' equity are exactly the same as before the dividend. From the shareholder's viewpoint, the ownership of 300 shares out of a total of 1,200 shares outstanding represents no more than did the ownership of 250 shares out of a total of 1,000 shares previously outstanding.

Large and Small Stock Dividends

The effect of a stock dividend on the capital structure of the issuing corporation is to transfer retained earnings to paid-in capital. This is sometimes referred to as "capitalizing" retained earnings. In many states this amount which must be transferred is equal to the par or stated value of the shares issued. However, because many recipients of stock dividends look upon them as distributions of corporate earnings, and usually in an amount equivalent to the fair value of the shares received, the accounting profession has mandated that under certain circumstances, the amount to be transferred from retained earnings should equal the fair market value of the shares issued. Therefore the amount transferred from retained earnings will at times be equal to the current fair value of the shares issued, and at other times be equal to the par value of the share issued. When a stock dividend is deemed to be "small," the fair market value amount is used; and when it is deemed to be "large" the par value amount is used. The cutoff point between a large and small dividend has been determined to be approximately 20 percent to 25 percent of the previously outstanding shares, because dividends in excess of that amount would be expected to materially reduce the market value per share of the stock. It should be re-emphasized, that in either case (large or small stock dividend) there is no effect on the total stockholders' equity of the corporation, or on the percentage ownership of an individual stockholder.

Stock Dividends Illustrated

To illustrate the proper accounting for small and large stock dividends, assume that on January 1, 19X1, the owners' equity section of the Price Corporation appeared as follows:

Common stock (10,000 shares, $10 par)	$100,000
Paid-in capital in excess of par	235,000
Retained earnings	440,000
Total	$775,000

Assume further that on that date, when the fair market value of the common stock was $25, a 10 percent stock dividend was declared to be distributed on February 1, 19X1. The journal entries to be made relative to this small stock dividend would be:

Jan. 1, 19X1	Retained earnings	$25,000	
	Stock dividend to be distributed		$10,000
	Paid-in capital in excess of par		15,000
Feb. 1, 19X2	Stock dividend to be distributed	10,000	
	Common stock (at par)		10,000

If a balance sheet was prepared January 30, 19X1, the Stock Dividend to Be Distributed account should be shown in the stockholders equity section of the balance sheet as an addition to common stock (whereas cash dividends are shown as current liabilities).

The stockholders' equity section of the corporation *after* the distribution of the small stock dividend would appear as follows:

Common stock (11,000 shares at $10 par)	$110,000
Paid-in capital in excess of par	250,000
Retained earnings	415,000
Total	$775,000

Notice that total stockholders' equity has remained at $775,000, but the balance that comprise the total have obviously changed.

To illustrate a large stock dividend, again assume the same stockholders' equity amounts for Price Corporation on January 1, 19X1. However, now we will assume that a 40 percent (large) stock dividend was declared to be distributed on February 1, 19X1. Now retained earnings will be capitalized for the par value of the common stock to be distributed. The journal entries to record the declaration and distribution of the stock dividend would be:

Jan. 1, 19X1	Retained earnings	$40,000	
	Stock dividend to be distributed		$40,000
	(40% × 10,000 × $10)		
Feb. 1, 19X2	Stock dividend to be distributed	$40,000	
	Common stock (at par)		$40,000

The stockholders' equity section of the corporation *after* the distribution of the large stock dividend would appear as follows:

Common stock (14,000 shares at $10 par)	$140,000
Paid-in capital in excess of par	235,000
Retained earnings	400,000
Total	$775,000

From an accounting point of view, stock dividends transfer retained earnings to other elements of owners' equity, making them unavailable as the basis for a later cash dividend. Such stock dividends in effect tell the stockholder that funds of that amount arising from earnings have been employed permanently in the business, and that the stockholder should view his invested capital as having been increased by the amount of the dividend stock.

Stock Splits

It is the belief of some observers that if the price of a stock reaches very high levels it will not be bought and sold as readily as it would at a lower price. Therefore a corporation may wish to reduce the selling price of its stock in order to facilitate purchases and sales of its shares by investors. This can be accomplished by reducing the par or stated value of the stock and issuing a proportionate number of additional shares. Such a procedure is called a *stock split* (or *stock split-up*).

For example assume that a corporation has 100,000 shares of $80 par value common stock outstanding. If the company declares a 2 for 1 stock split, each shareholder would receive two new shares with a $40 par value for each share of $80 par stock he owned prior to the split. The corporation would now have 200,000 shares of $40 par value stock outstanding, and the market price of the stock would be expected to drop to approximately one-half of its value before the split.

A stock split does not affect the balance of any account, consequently *no journal entry* is made to record the transaction. Commonly, however, a memorandum notation is made in the General Journal and in the Common Stock account to record the fact that the par value and number of shares outstanding have changed.

Treasury Stock

Corporations sometimes "reacquire" some of their issued stock, which generally means that an expenditure of cash has been employed to reduce the number of outstanding shares. Reasons for such a reacquisition include (1) the need to have enough stock on hand to pay stock bonuses to employees, (2) the intention to buy out a particular ownership interest, and (3) the desire to reduce the number of shares outstanding in order to increase earnings per share.

The result of such reacquisitions is that the corporation assets increase, and there are fewer stockholders to share in its activities and in its control. If the stock is simply held in the corporation treasury for later reissue, it is referred to as *treasury stock*. Where the stock is permanently retired, action will be taken to redeem the stock and cancel it. The following example provides an illustration of treasury stock accounting.

The Kold Corporation accounts show:

Common stock: 100,000 shares, $50 par value	$ 5,000,000
Paid-in capital in excess of par	2,000,000
Retained earnings	5,800,000
	$12,800,000

One thousand shares of stock (1 percent of outstanding shares) are acquired on the market at $110 per share. The entry would be:

Treasury stock (at cost)	$110,000	
Cash		$110,000

The stockholders' equity section of the balance sheet would appear as follows:

Stockholders' equity:	
Common stock (100,000 shares, $50 par value)	$ 5,000,000
Paid-in capital in excess of par	2,000,000
Retained earnings	5,800,000
Total	$12,800,000
Less: Treasury stock (1,000 shares, at cost)	110,000
Total stockholders' equity	$12,690,000

Notice that treasury stock is *shown as a subtraction* from total stockholders' equity. In the United States, treasury stock is not shown as an asset on the basis that a corporation cannot have as an asset an ownership interest in itself. However, in several other major industrialized countries treasury stock is shown as an asset.

When treasury stock is reissued at a price different from the acquisition price, an adjustment to the paid-in capital accounts is generally required. For example, assume that Kold Corporation reissued the 1,000 shares acquired at $110 for $120 per share. The entry would be:

Cash	$120,000	
Treasury stock		$110,000
Paid-in capital from sale of treasury stock		10,000

Authorized Stock

The charter of a corporation will state the number of shares of stock and the provisions of the stock that the corporation may issue, though authorization in the charter to issue stock does not mean that the stock will be accepted by investors. Amendment of the charter to change the provisions or number of shares authorized is usually not very difficult. Since the potential number of shares that may be issued is of interest to statement users, the accountant should give the number of shares authorized by the charter in the balance sheet or in footnotes to the balance sheet.

Convertible Securities

Bonds and shares of preferred stock issued by a corporation which may later be exchanged for common stock of the corporation are called *convertible*. Convertibility makes the bond or preferred stock issue more attractive to investors, and thus easier to issue at perhaps a lower interest rate or dividend rate. The convertibility feature gives the investor the right to exchange the security for common stock, in a prescribed ratio of a certain number of common shares to be exchanged for each bond or preferred share returned to the issuing corporation. This conversion takes place at the option of the investor, although he usually must act before some date specified by the issuing firm. The following example illustrates accounting procedures for convertible preferred stock.

Bulldog, Inc., issues 2,500 shares of $100 par value preferred stock at $110 per share. Each share is convertible into two shares of common stock (par value, $40 per share). The entry to record the issue is:

Cash	$275,000	
Preferred stock		$250,000
Paid-in capital in excess of par value of preferred stock		25,000

Assume that the Bulldog, Inc., common stock increased in value to such a point that all of the preferred stockholders choose to convert to common stock. The entry to record such a conversion would be:

Preferred stock	$250,000	
Paid-in capital in excess of par value of preferred stock	25,000	
Common stock ($5,000 shares × $40)		$200,000
Paid-in capital in excess of par value of common stock		75,000

Retained Earnings

The account title Retained Earnings suggests that some part of a firm's earnings have been retained (that is, have not been "paid out" as dividends to the stockholders in the business). However, we should not view retained earnings as being related to any asset held by the corporation. It is simply a dollar amount that represents a portion of the stockholders' equity in the assets of the firm. Nor is this dollar amount necessarily the total net earnings less total cash dividends since the inception of the firm. The retained earnings balance may have been affected by stock dividends, treasury stock transactions, or various other events. We can safely assert only that retained earnings is that portion of the stockholders' interest in a firm that came about from net earnings, and which have not yet been the basis for dividends or transferred to another equity account. It is unlikely that *liquid* assets in the amount of retained earnings are available, at any point in time, for distribution to the stockholders.

However, the amount of retained earnings for a corporation is not without significance. For example, the amount of dividends that may be paid to stockholders may be affected by the balance of retained earnings. The changes in the retained earnings account balance can be useful to analysts of financial statements in studying the growth of the firm and the dividend policy followed by the management.

Appropriations of Retained Earnings

A balance of retained earnings may be accumulated for particular purposes. The stockholders' equity is increased through paying out fewer resources in dividends than the corporation has earned for the stockholders. The reasons for not paying dividends to the full extent of earnings include: accumulation of resources to expand the activities of the firm; spreading the dividends over lean years; building up reserves to carry the firm through bad times; counterbalancing capital returned to stockholders in treasury stock transactions; and other purposes. Thus, part of the balance of retained earnings should be viewed as being not available for dividends even though, legally, dividends could be paid to the extent of the balance.

Some managements feel that they should call attention to certain plans by placing restrictions on retained earnings. For example, state laws often allow treasury stock acquisitions only to the extent of the retained earnings, thus requiring the restriction of retained earnings as long as the treasury stock is held. As a means of disclosing the restriction in its financial statements, the management may choose to transfer retained earnings to an account called Retained Earnings Appropriated for Treasury Stock. Some bond indentures provide that dividends shall not be declared on the basis of existing retained earnings as long as the bonds are outstanding. In this case dividends would be limited to the current earnings of the firm.

The existence of such legal restrictions on the amount of dividends that can be declared and paid should be disclosed in a footnote to the firm's balance sheet. An alternative form of disclosure would be a formal appropriation of retained earnings in the amount of the restriction:

Retained earnings	$279,862	
Retained earnings appropriated for dividend restriction		$279,862

When retained earnings are formally appropriated in the accounts, the balance sheet will indicate both appropriated and unappropriated retained earnings as well as the total of retained earnings. Such appropriations, however, are matters of form and disclosure rather than real substance.

Unrealized Gains and Losses Taken Directly to Owners' Equity

In recent years accounting rules have begun to require that certain unrealized gains and losses be reported directly in the equity section of the balance sheet. The first such example of this occurred with the issuance of FASB Statement

No. 12, "Accounting for Certain Marketable Securities," which was issued in 1975. This statement required that if certain marketable securities held as a long-term investment declined in value, the decline would be recorded by debiting an "unrealized loss" account, and crediting an "allowance for loss" (contra-asset) account. The contra-asset account would appear on the balance sheet as a deduction from the Investment account, and the unrealized loss account appears in the equity section as a deduction from stockholders' equity.

More recently the FASB required a similar treatment for unrealized gains and losses resulting from fluctuations in currency values relating to foreign investments. These two situations have set a precedent for bypassing the income statement, and reporting selected gains and losses directly in the equity section of the balance sheet. These two situations, which are currently considered to be "exceptions to the rule," could establish a precedent which will result in many other similar unrealized items appearing in the equity section of the corporation balance sheet in the future. It seems problematic that these two situations are sufficiently unique to justify such unique treatment.

Special Stock Equity Accounts or Conditions

Warrants which entitle the holders to subscribe at a stipulated price for common stock are often issued with bonds. Options to subscribe for stock at stipulated prices are often given as compensation to officers of the company. Any assets acquired in exchange for the warrants and options mean that stockholders' equity has grown, and therefore appropriate capital accounts such as Capital Arising from Stock Warrants must be established. The number of shares issued under such agreements are said to dilute the current stockholders' share of earnings and growth, since, if it is profitable for the holders of such claims to buy stock, they will surely do so, and the issuance of new shares has the effect of reducing the amount of dividends and earnings per share. Convertible bonds and preferred stocks may also have a dilutive effect on the sharing of profits and on growth.

Some corporations issue more than one class of common stock. In some cases, special classes of common stock are set up which carry extra voting power or exclusive voting power. Where such special classes of stock exist, balance sheet footnotes are necessary to indicate to the investors or potential investors the special conditions relating to those shares.

Balance Sheet Disclosure of Corporate Equities

An acceptable format for disclosure of the rights of the various equity claimants in a corporation is shown in the following balance sheet excerpt:

Lingstrom Stores
Partial *Balance Sheet*
December 31, 19X1

Current liabilities:			
Accounts payable		$1,215,000	
etc.		550,000	
Total current liabilities			$ 1,765,000
Long-term liabilities:			
Bonds payable, 10 percent (convertible into common stock at the option of the bondholders)			12,000,000
Total liabilities			$13,765,000
Stockholders' equity:			
Preferred stock ($5 cumulative, $100 par value, 200,000 shares authorized, 100,000 issued and outstanding)		$10,000,000	
Common stock ($5 par value, 1,000,000 shares authorized, 600,000 issued and outstanding)		3,000,000	
Paid-in capital in excess of par value:			
Preferred stock	$ 500,000		
Common stock	9,000,000	9,500,000	
Retained earnings:			
Appropriated for plant expansion	$4,000,000		
Unappropriated	8,000,000	12,000,000	
		34,500,000	
Net unrealized loss on noncurrent marketable Equity securities		(350,000)	
Total		34,150,000	
Less treasury stock (1,000 shares at cost)		(125,000)	
Total stockholder's equity			$34,025,000
Total liabilities and stockholder's equity			**$47,790,000**

SUMMARY

The financial problems of corporations are treated in more detail in other accounting courses and in other business courses. For our purposes, it is sufficient to fit the overall pattern of stockholders' equity into the accounting and reporting phases of our basic model. It is useful to compare sole proprietorships and partnerships with corporations. The corporation is, in both legal and economic terms, a separate and distinct entity. It is the decision unit for investors. It is not possible to invest in a part of a corporation, although it is useful to know how the various segments are performing.

The discussion of the accounting aspects of the different types of securities provides an insight into the nature of those securities and the rights and possible investment opportunities that they carry. It should be realized that stocks have only those rights which are granted to them by state laws and by the charters of the corporations, and it should not be assumed that any particular stock has the typical rights of such stock; each security issue has its own particular rights. Special rights, such as convertibility, warrants to subscribe for stock, and options to buy stock, offer the investor opportunities for large gains—sometimes with moderate risks, but more often with large risks. These special rights have an impact on the regular stockholders that must be kept in mind when considering the possible changes in the market price of the stock that may come about in the future.

KEY POINTS

1. While there are many variations in business ownership patterns, there are three principal types: the sole proprietorship, the partnership, and the corporation.

2. Sole proprietors and partners are directly involved in the operations of their firms and risk unlimited losses from the failure of their firms, whereas stockholders of corporations have a limited voice in the management of their firms and have limited risks in the event that their firms fail. Proprietors and partners profit directly when their firms profit, whereas stockholders are restricted to dividends based on profits and to the market value growth of their holdings when their firms prosper.

3. The Corporate form of business organization makes it possible for many stockholders to contribute fairly small amounts in order to have, in the aggregate, large capital funds to carry on large enterprises, with each contributor risking only his investment in the firm and not personal assets.

4. While corporations follow common patterns, they are formed under the different laws of each state, and therefore vary in details.

5. The accountant records stock issued at par or at stated value, treating any excess paid in as a special capital balance which is added to the par or stated value to arrive at total contributed capital. This excess is generally subject to fewer restrictions than par or stated value.

6. Preferred stockholders have special rights concerning dividends, participation in liquidation, and voting. However, in the event of liquidation, such stockholders have inferior rights relative to creditors. Some issues of preferred stock are convertible into common stock at the option of the holders. The accountant is careful to maintain the preferred stock as a separate reporting category and to observe that all the special rights of the preferred stock are noted and adhered to.

7. The procedures for declaring and paying dividends follow common patterns. The accountant must report the obligations incurred by the declarations and ensure that the various stockholders receive their proper shares of dividends declared. A stock dividend is a type of stock split and bears very little resemblance to a cash dividend. Special accounting rules apply to stock dividends.

8. When a corporation reacquires some of its own stock, it means that an ownership interest has been discharged. The amount paid out in the acquisition of the stock may be carried as treasury stock and reported in the balance sheet as a subtraction from the total of the stockholders' equity.

9. Retained earnings reflects the amount of profits that have not been transferred to reflect a dividend or some other equity adjustment.

QUESTIONS

1. Explain the distinguishing differences in the ownership rights of partners versus corporation shareholders.

2. How does the closing process for the equity accounts differ between a sole proprietorship and a partnership?

3. Abe Brown is a partner in Brown & Jennings Partnership. During 19X6 the partnership had net income of $150,000. Brown is allocated one-half of the net income, and he withdrew $24,000 from the partnership during the year. How much federal income tax must Brown pay relating to his partnership interest?

4. A friend of yours was recently fired by the AYE Corporation. He plans to sue because he claims that a corporation is not a person, therefore it cannot legally take actions such as firing an individual. What is your response?

5. List and briefly discuss several of the major rights of corporate shareholders.

6. Distinguish between the following types of corporations:

- **a.** Public vs. private
- **b.** Nonstock vs. stock
- **c.** Open vs. closed

7. What is meant by the par value of a stock? What is its relationship to the market value of the stock?

8. What is the possible justification for the name "preferred stock"?

9. Explain why an investor might prefer to purchase cumulative preferred stock instead of noncumulative preferred stock?

10. List and briefly explain the dates which are important in dividend declarations.

11. Why might a corporation prefer to issue a stock dividend instead of a cash dividend? Why might a stockholder prefer to receive a stock dividend instead of a cash dividend?

12. If financial statements are prepared after the declaration of stock dividend, but before its distribution, where in the balance sheet should the account Stock Dividend to Be Distributed appear?

13. What type of journal entry, if any, should be made for a stock split?

14. What is treasury stock?

15. Explain the basic procedure in the appropriation of Retained Earnings. What effect does such an appropriation have on the activities of the corporation?

EXERCISES

E12-1 Assume that you are a practicing certified public accountant. A client of yours, who is the owner of a successful sole proprietorship, is considering either bringing in a partner or converting his business into a corporation. One of his major considerations is his concern that if he is sued for something relating to the business, he wants some legal protection, or another person to share the liability.

REQUIRED:

Write a short report to your client detailing your thoughts and recommendations regarding his plans.

E12-2 Nelson and Sandlin form a partnership on January 1, 19X8, by investing \$20,000 and \$30,000, respectively. During the year the partnership has sales of \$100,000 and total expenses of \$82,000. The partnership agreement calls for a distribution of profits in the following ratio: Nelson, 40 percent; Sandlin, 60 percent. The partners each withdraw \$6,000 from the partnership during the year.

REQUIRED:

1. Prepare the partnership closing entries for 19X8.
2. Prepare a Statement of Partners' Capital for the year ended December 31, 19X8.

E12-3 Bruno Corporation is organized on February 15, 19X1, and at that time issues 5,000 shares of no-par common stock for \$450,000; and 1,000 shares of \$100 par preferred stock for \$110,000. The preferred stock is cumulative and pays a dividend of \$6 per share. The corporation experiences a net loss in its first 2 years of operarion. However, in its third year of operation it reports a net income of $198,000 and declares a total dividend (to both preferred and common shareholders) of $99,000.

REQUIRED:

1. Calculate the amount of the dividend that will accrue to common and to preferred shareholders.
2. If the preferred stock had been noncumulative, how would that effect your answer?

E12-4 Assume that on August 30, 19X4, the equity section of the balance sheet of Hood Company appeared as follows:

Common stock, $1 par, 100,000 shares issued and outstanding	$ 100,000
Paid-in capital in excess of par	780,000
Retained earnings	1,290,000
Total stockholders' equity	**2,170,000**

Assume further that on September 1, 19X4, the company declared a 60 percent stock dividend which was distributed on September 30. On December 15, 19X4, the company declared a 10 percent stock dividend (when the market price of the stock was $5.00), to be distributed on January 15, 19X5.

REQUIRED:

1. Prepare the journal entries necessary to record the stock dividends during 19X4.
2. Prepare the equity section of a balance sheet for Hood Company as of December 31, 19X4. Assume that the company had net income of $85,000 and paid no cash dividends during the year.

E12-5 On November 10, 19X1, the Rudolph Corporation purchased 2,000 of its $10 par common stock on the open market for $24,000. One month later the company sold the same 2,000 shares for $27,500.

REQUIRED:

Prepare the journal entries to record the acquisition and sale of the company's stock.

E12-6 On November 11, 19X2, Martha, Inc., sells a large bond issue which calls for an appropriation of Retained Earnings in the amount of $2,500.000. At that time the balance in unappropriated Retained Earnings was $4,700,000.

REQUIRED:

1. Present the journal entry to record the appropriation of retained earnings.
2. What is the maximum amount of cash dividends that Martha, Inc., could declare and pay immediately after the appropriation?

PROBLEMS

P12-1 Jake Eastman holds a patent on a new biotechnical device. Although the patent has an estimated fair market value of $62,000, he is unable to obtain sufficient financing to start his own manufacturing plant. He contacts John Care who owns a building and equipment appropriate for manufacturing the new device. The building is carried on Mr. Care's records as having an original cost of $235,000 less accumulated depreciation of $98,000; and the equipment has an original cost of $52,000 less accumulated depreciation of $27,000. Currently, the fair market value of the building is $184,000, and that of the equipment is $61,000. Mr. Eastman contributes his patent and Mr. Care his building and equipment to form a partnership. They are joined in the new partnership by Joan Smith who invests $83,000 in cash.

REQUIRED:

Prepare the journal entries to record the capital contributions of each of the partners.

P12-2 Stan Barnet, Bruce Miller, and John Bardon operate a business firm as a partnership. Net income or loss is shared equally among the partners. Prior to completing the closing entries on December 31, 19X7, the firm's accounting records contained the following accounts and balances:

	DEBIT	CREDIT
Income summary		$ 96,000
Barnet, capital		172,000
Barnet, withdrawals	$30,000	
Miller, capital		182,000
Miller, withdrawals	26,000	
Bardon, capital		206,000
Bardon, withdrawals	10,000	

REQUIRED:

1. Journalize the entries to complete the closing process.
2. Prepare a statement of changes in partners' capital.
3. Prepare the owners' equity section of the balance sheet.

P12-3 The stockholders' equity section of the Small Corporation on December 1, 19X6, appears here:

Stockholders' equity	
Preferred stock (10,000 shares, $100 par value, 6%)	$1,000,000
Common stock (200,000 shares, $10 par value)	2,000,000
Paid-in capital in excess of par	200,000
Retained earnings	500,000
Total stockholders' equity	**$3,700,000**

On December 1, 19X6, the board of directors declared the regular cash dividend on the preferred stock and a $.50 per share cash dividend on the common stock, to the stockholders of record on December 10, 19X6. This was to be paid on February 1, 19X7. As the accountant for Small, prepare whatever journal entries are needed on the following dates: December 1, 19X6; and February 1, 19X7.

P12-4 Mann Manufacturing Company is authorized to issue 100,000 shares of no-par value common stock and 30,000 shares of 5 percent, $25 par value preferred stock. The board of directors has assigned a $12 per share value to the common stock. Their accounting records on April 30, 19X7, contain the following balances:

	DEBIT	CREDIT
Common stock		$396,000
Excess over stated value		47,500
Preferred stock		200,000
Premium on preferred stock		34,000
Treasury stock (100 shares of common)	$ 1,400	
Retained earnings		178,300
Income summary	62,300	
Dividends	26,500	

REQUIRED:

Prepare the stockholders' equity section of the balance sheet on April 30, 19X7.

P12-5 The stockholders' equity section of Raybon Company appeared as follows on August 15, 19X6:

Common stock, $2 stated value; authorized 200,000 shares, issued and outstanding 140,000 shares	$280,000
Excess over stated value of common stock	540,000
Total contributed capital	820,000
Retained earnings	412,000
Total stockholders' equity	**$1,232,000**

On that date, the board of directors declared a 10 percent stock dividend to be distributed on September 25 to stockholders of record on September 1. The stock was selling for $21.00 per share on the date of declaration of the stock dividend.

On November 30, Raybon Company repurchased, and held as treasury stock, 2,000 shares of its common shares at $20.50 per share.

REQUIRED:

1. Make the journal entries to record:
   a. The declaration and distribution of the stock dividend.
   b. The purchase of the treasury stock.
2. Prepare a revised stockholders' equity section of Raybon Company as of November 30, 19X6.

P12-6 Statements prepared for the Former Corporation show the following balances on June 30, 19X6:

Common stock (100,000 shares, $10 par)	$1,000,000
Capital paid in excess of par	800,000
Retained earnings	2,000,000
Treasury stock, at cost (acquired June 1, 19X6, 2,000 shares)	80,000

Set up the stockholders' equity section of the balance sheet of the Former Corporation and illustrate how the treasury stock should be displayed.

P12-7 The same Former Corporation from P12-6 also has convertible preferred stock outstanding:

Preferred stock (1,000 shares, $100 par, convertible in the ratio of 2 shares of preferred for 5 shares of common)	$100,000

All of the holders of the preferred stock elect to convert their holding to common stock. What entry do you suggest for this conversion?

P12-8 The following account balances in alphabetical order are taken from the ledger of the Foot Corporation on December 31, 19X6. You are to prepare a balance sheet in good form and adjusting and closing entries for the year ended December 31, 19X6.

Accounts receivable	$30,000	Notes receivable (due Apr. 5, 19X7	$70,000
Accounts payable	22,000	Paid-in capital in excess of par	2,000
Administrative expenses	10,000	Preferred stock (800 shares)	40,000
Accumulated depreciation	8,000	Purchases	50,000
Allowance for uncollectibles	2,000	Retained earnings (Jan. 1, 19X6)	12,000
Bonds payable	32,000	Sales	90,000
Cash	25,600	Selling expenses (total)	15,000
Common stock (1,000 shares)	40,000	Stock dividends distributable	8,800
Dividends payable	4,400	Supplies on hand	3,000
Equipment	28,400	Treasury stock (at cost)	10,000
Interest expense	1,000		
Interest income	1,800		
Merchandise inventory	20,000		

All adjusting entries have been made except the one to reflect the ending inventory. On December 31, 19X6, the merchandise on hand was $25,000.

STATEMENT OF CHANGES IN FINANCIAL POSITION

13

ORIENTATION

The purpose of this chapter is to evaluate and interpret the statement of changes in financial position.

The chapter contains a description and evaluation of the statement of changes in financial position as prepared both on a working capital basis, and on a cash basis. The chapter also serves as a review of what we have learned from the preceding chapters, since the preparation of a financial changes statement requires the analysis of, and an understanding of, all the accounting information reported on the earnings statement, balance sheet, and statement of retained earnings.

INTRODUCTION TO THE STATEMENT

To obtain an appreciation of what the statement of changes in financial position is designed to do, it is useful to ask the following: Is it possible for a company to report net income for the year of $1,000,000, for example, and during the same year experience a reduction in cash from $20,000,000 to $100 on the firm's balance sheet?

To answer that question, it is obvious that a company could, for example, report substantial earnings but then utilize all its cash receipts, and more, on investments in buildings, stock of other companies, and debt payments, thereby liquidating its cash holdings.

On the other hand, is it possible for a company to report a substantial sustained loss, but still invest heavily in fixed assets during the period? The answer to this question is evident by reference to the automotive industry during the recent past. During a period in which the industry sustained enormous losses, the automotive firms still, through financing activities and liquidation of certain asset reserves, invested very heavily in a major retooling of their manufacturing facilities.

These types of questions are often asked by parties interested in the operations and financial management of a firm. However, it is obvious that none of the major financial statements that have been presented thus far provide ready answers to these and similar types of questions.

In a response to this perceived void in financial reporting, the Accounting Principles Board issued its Opinion No. 19 in March of 1971, requiring most firms to include a statement of changes in financial position along with their published balance sheet, earnings statement, and statement of retained earnings.

Prior to APB Opinion No. 19, many firms voluntarily provided funds-flow statements which were quite similar to the financial changes statement. These funds-flow statements essentially showed either the sources and uses of cash, or the sources and uses of working capital (current assets less current liabilities) during the reporting period. The statement of changes in financial position may be prepared on either a cash or working capital basis, but it must show all the financing and investing activities of the firm (even if cash or working capital were not directly affected) during the reporting period. Financing activities involve the acquisition of resources (inflow of funds) and investing activities involve the use of these resources (outflow of funds).

The statement of changes in financial position is essentially an explanation of the changes in assets, liabilities, and owners' equity accounts that occurred over the course of a reporting period as the result of financing activities (such as the issuance of bonds payable) and as the result of investing activities (such as the purchase of equipment). The key to the preparation of a financial changes statement is the analysis of the changes in the various balance sheet items that occurred during the period. Since the income statement and retained earnings statement provide further information relating to those changes, it is necessary to analyze them also in the preparation of the statement of changes.

The statement of changes in financial position must show all significant financial flows, whether or not they directly affected working capital or cash. However, since most financial activities of the firm do involve changes in cash or other components of working capital, sources and uses of either cash or overall working capital is ordinarily the core of the statement of changes. The preparation of the statement from a working capital approach will be considered first.

WORKING CAPITAL APPROACH TO STATEMENT OF CHANGES

Working capital is defined as the difference between current assets and current liabilities. To illustrate, assume that the following amounts were taken from a corporation's balance sheets on December 31, 19X1 and 19X2:

	19X1	19X2
Cash	$100,000	$150,000
Accounts receivable	120,000	125,000
Inventory	150,000	135,000
All other current assets	75,000	55,000
Total current assets	$445,000	$465,000
Accounts payable	$ 75,000	$ 85,000
All other current liabilities	85,000	145,000
Total current liabilities	$160,000	$230,000
Working capital	$285,000	$235,000

Therefore, working capital as of December 31, 19X1, was $285,000; and as of December 31, 19X2, it was $235,000—a decrease of $50,000 for the year. The statement of changes in financial position, prepared on a working capital basis, will provide an analysis of the financial activities that resulted in these changes in working capital.

Let us now consider certain activities which would cause a change (either increase or decrease) in the working capital of a firm.

1. *Increase in long-term liabilities.* Suppose the firm issues bonds in the amount of $100,000. Long-term liabilities (Bonds Payable) increase by $100,000 and cash (a current asset) increases by $100,000. Thus working capital increases by $100,000.
2. *Decrease in long-term liabilities.* Suppose the firm retires bonded indebtedness in the amount of $50,000. Long-term liabilities (Bonds Payable) decrease by $50,000 and cash (a current asset) decreases by $50,000. Working capital decreases by $50,000.
3. *Increase in stockholders' equity.* If capital stock is issued for $25,000, both cash and stockholders' equity increase by $25,000. Working capital increases by $25,000.
4. *Decrease in stockholders' equity.* If a dividend of $15,000 is declared but not yet paid, stockholders' equity (Retained Earnings) is decreased in the amount of $15,000 and a current liability (Dividends Payable) is increased by $15,000. Working capital decreases by $15,000. (When the dividend is paid, there is no effect on working capital because both a current asset—cash—and a current liability—dividends payable—are reduced.)
5. *Increase in noncurrent assets.* Suppose that equipment is acquired by payment of $3,000 cash and issuance of a $2,000 note payable due in six months. Working

capital decreases by $5,000: the result of a $3,000 decrease in cash and a $2,000 increase in current liabilities.

6. *Decrease in noncurrent assets.* If a long-term investment in the common stock of another company is sold, working capital will increase by the proceeds of the sale.

Financial activities which involve only current assets and liabilities will not result in a change in working capital. For example, if cash is increased by borrowing on a short-term basis, then current assets and current liabilities change by the same amount and there is no change in working capital. The same is true for such activities as collection of accounts receivable and payment of accounts payable. Such transactions involve only a change in composition of working capital, not a change in the amount.

It is obvious that some basic, general "natural laws" are applicable regarding the relationship between non-working-capital items and working capital. Basically, we can say:

NON-WORKING-CAPITAL ITEM	CHANGE IN NON-WORKING-CAPITAL ITEM AND EFFECT ON WORKING CAPITAL	
	Increase	**Decrease**
Fixed assets	Use (of working capital)	Source (of working capital)
Long-term liabilities	Source	Use
Owners' equity	Source	Use

So an increase in a fixed asset will indicate a use of working capital, an increase in long-term liabilities will indicate a source of working capital, and so on.

Another way of looking at the effect on working capital of various transactions is to classify all transactions into three categories:

1. Both the debit and credit side of the transaction occur within working capital (for example, collection of an account receivable). This type of transaction has no effect on working capital.
2. Both the debit and credit side of the transaction occur outside of working capital (for example, exchange of long-term bonds for a building). This type of transaction has no effect on working capital.
3. One-half of the entry affects working capital, and the other half does not (for example, purchase of equipment for cash). This type of transaction does affect working capital.

Determining the Activities Affecting Working Capital

For the principal part of the statement of financial changes, only changes in long-term items are included; that is, elements not reported as current assets or current liabilities. Those changes and their amounts are identified by relating the beginning and ending balances of items reported on the balance sheet. The changes (increases and decreases) in the balances of the long-term elements must then be analyzed. The nature of that analysis, and the presentation of the analytical results in the financial changes statement, is best described by the use of an illustrative example.

Statement of Changes in Financial Position Prepared on Working Capital Basis: Illustration 1

The preparation of a statement of changes in financial position for the Adams Corporation is shown in Figure 13-1. Note that the data necessary to prepare the statement is taken from: the *balance sheet* for the Adams Corporation for the beginning and end of the accounting period; the *combined statement of earnings and retained earnings* for the Adams Corporation for the accounting period; and certain *supplementary information* relating to financing and investing activities during the accounting period.

One possible step-by-step approach to the preparation of the financial changes statement is as follows:

1. Compare beginning and ending balances of items on the balance sheet to determine the amounts of changes that occurred over the course of the accounting period.
2. List the changes in current asset and current liability items in a *working capital schedule,* as shown in the illustration. This schedule will show the change in the amount of working capital and in its composition, but will not show the causes of the change.
3. Extract from the combined statement of earnings and retained earnings the amount of net earnings before extraordinary items, the extraordinary items (if any), dividends, and depreciation expense (and any other expense items which have no effect on working capital).
4. Determine the amount of working capital provided by operations by adding depreciation expense (and any other expense items which have no effect on working capital) to net earnings before extraordinary items.
5. Relate the information gathered from the combined statement of earnings and retained earnings and the changes in the balances of the noncurrent items on the balance sheet (and any supplementary information relating to financing and investing activities during the period), to identify the sources (other than operations) and uses of working capital during the period.

Each of these steps warrants elaboration with reference to the illustration for the Adams Corporation (see Figure 13-1). Note first the various items on the beginning and ending balance sheets for the firm (step 1). As indicated, changes in the working capital items (cash, merchandise inventory, and accounts payable) are shown in the working capital schedule which appears at the bottom of the statement of changes in financial position (step 2). Consider, for example, the \$20,000 increase in cash that occurred during the period. This constitutes a \$20,000 increase in working capital. Accounts payable was increased by \$12,000 and this constitutes a reduction in working capital by \$12,000. Mer-

Adams Corporation
Balance Sheet
as of dates indicated in 19X1 (last three zeros omitted)

ASSETS

	Jan. 1	Dec. 31	Changes in These Items Are:
Cash	$ 30	$ 50	reported in the working capital schedule
Merchandise inventory	40	75	reported in the working capital schedule
Equipment	150	162	reported as a use of working capital to buy equipment
Accumulated depreciation	(35)	(50)	combined with net earnings to show
Totals	$185	$237	increase in working capital

EQUITIES

Accounts payable	$ 25	$ 37	reported in the working capital schedule
Bonds payable		20	reported as a source of working capital
Common stock (par)	100	110	reported as a source of working capital
Capital contributed in excess of par	22	24	
Retained earnings (see below)	38	46	split up to report the earnings (source of working capital) and dividends (use of working capital)
Totals	$185	$237	

Adams Corporation
Combined Statement of Income and Retained Earnings
for the year ended December 31, 19X1 (last three zeros omitted)

			Effect of Profit-making Activities:
Sales		$300	new current assets flowed in to this extent
Expenses			
Cost of merchandise sold	$200		merchandise (current asset) flowed
Depreciation of equipment	15		out no effect on working capital
Other expenses (including taxes)	62	277	decreased a current asset or increased a current liability
Net income		$ 23	this is reported as a source and then adjusted
Retained earnings, Jan. 1		38	for non-working-capital elements
Total		$ 61	
Dividends for 19X1		15	current assets flowed out (use of working capital)
Retained earnings, Dec. 31		$ 46	

Additional information (amounts shown in full):

1. No equipment was disposed of during 19X1.
2. New equipment worth $12,000 was acquired by issuing new common stock with a par value of $10,000.

FIGURE 13-1
Preparation of Statement of Changes in Financial Position on a Working Capital Basis (amounts shown with last three zeros omitted).

FIGURE 13-1 *(continued)*

Solution Adams Corporation
Statement of Changes in Financial Position
for the year ended December 31, 19X1 (last three zeros omitted)

			Derived from:
Sources of working capital increases			
Net income		$23	earnings statement
Add: Expenses deducted which did not require the use of working capital during the current period: Depreciation of equipment		15	earnings statement
Working capital provided by operations		$38	(a very important figure, sometimes called "cash flow")
Issuance of bonds payable		20	balance sheet
Issuance of stock (issued in exchange for equipment)		12	balance sheet
Total sources of working capital		$70	
Uses of working capital			
Equipment acquired (see above)	$12		balance sheet
Dividends for 19X1	15		retained earnings part of the earnings statement
Total uses of working capital		27	
Net addition to working capital (see below)		$43	(must agree with the schedule below)

Working Capital Schedule (last three zeros omitted)

	JANUARY 1	DECEMBER 31	INCREASE OR (DECREASE) IN WORKING CAPITAL
Cash	$30	$50	$20
Merchandise inventory	40	75	35
Accounts payable	(25)	(37)	(12)
Totals (see above)	$45	$88	$43

chandise inventory was increased by $35,000 and thus working capital is larger by this amount. The working capital schedule shows that the net effect of the various changes in the components of working capital was an increase in working capital of $43,000.

The changes in the noncurrent items on the comparative balance sheets constitute *causes* of the change in working capital. These changes correspond to financing and investing activities which generally have the effect of increasing or decreasing working capital. The identification of those activities (step 5) is an essential segment of the financial changes statement. The key to explaining changes in working capital is the explanation of *changes in noncurrent items* which cause changes in working capital.

The determination of the amount of working capital provided by operations (steps 4 and 5) is somewhat more complex and will be explained further following this illustration, but note the nature and format of the calculation for the Adams Corporation. The Adams Corporation had net earnings of $23,000 in 19X1 (as shown on its combined statement of earnings and retained earnings). This amount of net earnings is the net results of $300,000 in sales (which provided working capital—cash and receivables—in that amount) and of $277,000 in expenses (which "used up" working capital in that amount). Thus the net earnings figure of $23,000 is the starting point for the determination of the amount of working capital provided by operations of the Adams Corporation. An adjustment of this figure by a procedure called an *add-back* is necessary, however, for the depreciation expense of $15,000. The entry on the Adams Corporation books to reflect depreciation for the period was:

Depreciation expense	$15,000	
Accumulated depreciation		$15,000

This entry reflects no change in working capital; the allocation of past costs has no effect on current assets or current liabilities. Therefore, since depreciation expense is subtracted from revenues in arriving at net earnings before extraordinary items, it is necessary to *add depreciation expense back to net earnings* to arrive at the working capital provided by net earnings. As indicated in the illustration, the Adams Corporation's operations thus provided $38,000 ($23,000 + $15,000) of working capital in 19X1.

The final step (step 5) requires an analysis of the various changes in noncurrent items on the Adams Corporation balance sheets, in order to identify the sources (other than operations) and uses of working capital during 19X1. Consider first the increase in the Bonds Payable account of $20,000. Since no premium or discount on the bonds is indicated on the balance sheet, it may be assumed that they were issued for their face value. Working capital (cash in this case) is thus provided in the amount of $20,000. This is shown in the statement of changes in financial position for the Adams Corporation directly beneath the Working Capital Provided by Operations.

The balance in the Common Stock account increased by $10,000 and the balance in the Paid in Capital in Excess of Par account increased by $2,000. We can deduce that common stock was issued in the amount of $12,000. The additional information below the combined statement of earnings and retained earnings indicates that new equipment was acquired in exchange for common stock. The stock was issued, then, not for cash, but for equipment. The transaction had no *direct* effect on working capital; however, its effects are no different than if the stock had been issued for cash and the cash employed to purchase the equipment. Since the statement of changes in financial position must show all financing and investing activities of the firm for the period, the issuance of the stock is shown as a *source* of working capital and the equipment acquired as a *use* of working capital.

The $12,000 increase in the Equipment account balance is explained by the previous transaction. The $15,000 increase in the Accumulated Depreciation account is the result of the $15,000 depreciation expense reported on the earnings statement. The $8,000 increase in the Retained Earnings account is the net effect of reported earnings of $23,000 and dividends of $15,000. The latter represents a use of working capital in the amount of $15,000, as indicated on the statement.

Essentially the statement of changes in financial position on a working capital basis shows the inflows and outflows of working capital (sometimes referred to as *funds*). This information serves to point out the major financing and investing activities of the firm during the accounting period. In the case of the Adams Corporation, the working capital provided by operations *plus* the working capital provided by the issuance of bonds and stock was used to acquire equipment, pay dividends, and add to the working capital used in the business.

Working Capital Provided by Operations

The most important recurring source of working capital for a firm is generally its own operations. Sales are generally made for cash or on account. In either case, working capital is increased by the amount of the current assets (cash or receivables) acquired at the time that sales take place.

Most operating expenses reflect decreases in working capital. As such operating expenses are incurred or paid, current liabilities increase or current assets (cash) decrease. As merchandise is sold, the Cost of Goods Sold expense item relates to a decrease in a current asset (merchandise). As prepayments expire and supplies are used up, the recognition of the related expense mirrors a decrease in current assets and a decrease in working capital.

Since revenues reflect working capital increases, and most expenses reflect working capital decreases, net earnings from operations generally reflects net working capital increases (and a net loss reflects net working capital decreases) from operations. However, not all expenses reflect decreases in working capital. Such expenses must be added to net income before extraordinary items to arrive at the amount of working capital provided by operations. Such expenses include depreciation expense, depletion expense, and amortization expense relating to such intangible items as patents and goodwill. Such items are certainly expenses which are properly matched with revenues to arrive at net income, but they merely reflect allocations of past costs and thus have no effect on working capital.

Certain other expense items are related to changes in long-term elements rather than a working capital element. One such item is the portion of income tax expense which reflects an increase in long-term deferred income taxes. Suppose that, as a result of the use of straight-line depreciation for reporting purposes and ACRS "depreciation" for income tax purposes, a firm reports income tax expense of $35,000 but has an actual income tax liability of $25,000. The journal entry would be:

Income tax expense	$35,000	
Income taxes payable		$25,000
Deferred income taxes		10,000

In arriving at net earnings from operations, the reported income tax expense of $35,000 is subtracted from revenues. There is a decrease in working capital, however, of only $25,000 (the increase in the current liability, Income Taxes Payable). The process of determining the amount of working capital provided by operations therefore must include an addition to the net income figure of $10,000 ($35,000 *less* $25,000).

The effects of the amortization of a bond premium or discount on bond interest expense (or bond interest income) must also be reflected in an adjustment of net earnings to arrive at the working capital provided from operations. If bonds are issued at a discount, the amount of interest expense recorded at interest payment dates will *exceed* the amount of cash paid (the amount of the decrease in working capital); the difference between the two amounts is the *increase* in the bond liability (a change which has no effect on working capital). If bonds are issued at a premium, the amount of interest expense recorded at interest payment dates will be *less* than the amount of cash paid (the amount of the decrease in working capital); the difference between the two amounts is the *decrease* in the bond liability (a change which has no effect on working capital). The amount of the amortization of a bond *discount* must therefore be *added* to the net income before extraordinary items. The amount of the amortization of a bond *premium* must be *subtracted* from the net income figure.

Some of these complicating factors related to the preparation of a statement of changes in financial position are involved in the second, more complex, illustration that follows.

Statement of Changes in Financial Position Prepared on Working Capital Basis: Illustration 2

The statement of changes in financial position for the Baker Corporation involves many items likely to be encountered on actual published statements. To assist in tracing the items on the statement to the data used to develop them (see Figure 13-2), each item is keyed by an identifying letter to the related source on the balance sheets, statement of earnings and retained earnings, and the supplementary information. The relationships are explained by letter sequence in the list that follows. Before considering the lettered items, however, note that the working capital items on the comparative balance sheets of the Baker Corporation are indicated by the "wc" notation. These items appear in the working capital schedule. Note again that increases in current assets are increases in

Baker Corporation
Balance Sheets
19X1 (last three zeros omitted)

ASSETS

	January 1	December 31
Cash	$ 1,000	$ 1,300 wc
Marketable securities	3,000	2,800 wc
Accounts receivable (net)	5,000	5,600 wc
Merchandise inventory	8,000	9,700 wc
Prepayments	200	360 wc
Long-term investments	6,000	7,000 (a)
Equipment	10,000	20,000 (b)
Accumulated depreciation	(3,000)	(3,100) (c)
Patents (net)	800	740 (d)
	$31,000	$44,400

wc = working capital item

EQUITIES

	January 1	December 31
Accounts payable	$ 3,000	$ 4,000 wc
Accrued wages	500	328 wc
Deferred federal income tax liability	4,000	4,300 (e)
Bonds payable (6%)	6,000	6,000
Discount on bonds payable (6%)	(500)	(448) (f)
Bonds payable (7%)	-0-	5,000 > (g)
Premium on bonds payable (7%)	-0-	200
Common stock ($100 par)	8,000	11,000 > (h)
Paid in capital in excess of par	3,000	5,000
Retained earnings (see below)	7,000	9,020
	$31,000	$44,400

wc = working capital item

FIGURE 13-2
Preparation of Statement of Changes in Financial Position on a Working Capital Basis (amounts shown with last three zeros omitted).

working capital, increases in current liabilities are decreases in working capital, and vice versa.

It is the changes in the long-term items that *cause* increases and decreases in working capital, and their effects on working capital flows are considered here:

a. *Long-term investments increased by $1,000,000.* This constitutes a use of working capital in the amount of $1,000,000, as shown on the statement of changes in financial position.

FIGURE 13-2 *(continued)*

Baker Corporation
Combined Statement of Income and Retained Earnings
for the year ended December 31, 19X1 (last three zeros omitted)

Sales		$50,000	
Operating expenses			
Merchandise cost of sales	$27,000		
Depreciation	1,800		(c)
Patent amortization	60		(d)
Other operating expenses	14,000	42,860	
Net operating earnings		$ 7,140	
Bond interest expense		412	
Net earnings before income tax		$ 6,728	
Federal income tax currently payable	$ 2,930		
Federal income tax deferred	300	3,230	(e)
Net income before extraordinary items		$ 3,498	(k)
Loss on disposal of equipment		78	(j)
Net income		$ 3,420	
Retained earnings, Jan. 1		7,000	
Total		$10,420	
Dividends		1,400	(l)
Retained earnings, Dec. 31		$ 9,020	

Supplementary Information:

1. Equipment acquired during the year was $12,000.
2. The entry for the disposal of the equipment was:

Cash	222		(i)
Loss on disposal of equipment	78		(j)
Accumulated depreciation	1,700		(c)
Equipment		2,000	(b)

Notice that accumulated depreciation was increased by $1,800 (depreciation expense) but ended up increasing only $100. Thus $1,700 (c) must have been deducted. The loss (j) is given directly in the income statement. Since $12,000 of new equipment was acquired and the equipment balance increased by only $10,000, there must have been a decrease of $2,000 (b) in this account.

3. No interest was paid or accrued on the 7 percent bonds.

b. *Equipment increased by $10,000,000.* The supplementary information indicates that $12,000,000 of equipment was acquired during the year (use of working capital) and that $2,000,000 of equipment was sold. In the case of the sale, the only effect on working capital is the amount of cash provided by the disposal of the equipment. This is shown to be $222,000, which appears on the statement of changes in financial position as a source of working capital.

c. *Accumulated depreciation increased by $100,000.* As indicated in the supplementary information, this net change is the result of $1,800,000 of current period depreciation and the charge-off of $1,700,000 of accumulated depre-

FIGURE 13-2 *(continued)*

Baker Corporation
Statement of Changes in Financial Position
for the year ended December 31, 19X1 (last three zeros omitted)

Sources of working capital increases:	
Net income before extraordinary items	$ 3,498 (k)
Add: Expenses not requiring outlay of working capital in the current period:	
Depreciation of equipment	1,800 (c)
Amortization of patents	60 (d)
Bond discount amortization	52 (f)
Increase in deferred federal income tax liability	300 (e)
Funds provided by operation for the period	$ 5,710
Issuance of bonds	5,200 (g)
Issuance of stock	5,000 (h)
Disposal of equipment	222 (i,j,c,b)
Total working capital provided	$16,132
Uses of working capital:	
Purchase of equipment	$12,000 (b)
Acquisition of long-term investments	1,000 (a)
Dividends on common stock	1,400 (l)
Total use of working capital	$14,400
Net addition to working capital (see below)	$ 1,732

	January 1	December 31	Increase (or Decrease) in Working Capital
Cash	$ 1,000	$ 1,300	$ 300
Marketable securities	3,000	2,800	(200)
Accounts receivable	5,000	5,600	600
Merchandise inventory	8,000	9,700	1,700
Prepayments	200	360	160
Accounts payable	(3,000)	(4,000)	(1,000)
Accrued wages	(500)	(328)	172
	$13,700	$15,432	$1,732

ciation on the equipment sold. The $1,800,000 depreciation expense charge is an expense item which did not reduce working capital during the period. It is therefore added back to net income before extraordinary items in the financial changes statement.

d. *Patents decreased by $60,000.* This decrease reflects current period amortization of patents which, like depreciation expense, was subtracted from revenues to arrive at net income before extraordinary items but did not reduce working capital. Thus it is also added back to net earnings before extraordinary items to arrive at working capital provided by operations.

e. *Deferred federal income tax liability increased by $300,000.* This item, too, requires the add-back treatment. Only $2,930,000 of federal income taxes were paid in 19X1, although $3,230,000 is reported as income tax expense (as indicated on the income statement).

f. *Discount on bonds payable decreased by $52,000.* This decrease reflects the current year amortization of the discount, which results in reported bond interest of $412,000 rather than the $360,000 (.06 × $6,000,000) of cash interest actually paid to the bondholders. Since the expense amount exceeds the working capital decrease by $52,000, this amount is also an add-back to net earnings before extraordinary items.

g. *A 7 percent bond issue was sold* at the end of 19X1 (since, as indicated in the supplementary information, no interest was paid or accrued on these bonds). Proceeds were $5,200,000 (the sum of the face value and the premium) and this appears on the statement of changes in financial position as a working capital source.

h. *The common stock account ($100 par value) increased by $3,000,000 and capital contributed in excess of par increased by $2,000,000.* It is apparent that new shares of common stock have been issued for $5,000,000—a source of working capital in that amount.

i. and j. These items appear in the *supplementary information* relating to the equipment disposal. Item (i) is simply the cash provided by the sale. Item (j) is the loss on the disposal of the equipment. This loss is reported as an extraordinary item on the Baker Corporation's combined statement of earnings and retained earnings. Since extraordinary items, by definition, are not operating items, they must not be included in the reported figure for working capital provided by operations. This reported figure is the *sum of the net income before extraordinary items and the various adjustments for expense items which did not affect working capital in the current period.* If the loss on the equipment sale were not treated as an extraordinary item, it might be one such adjustment (added back to net earnings before extraordinary items).

k. This is the *amount of net income before extraordinary items,* $3,498,000 which is the starting point for the determination of working capital provided by operations.

l. *Dividends of $1,400 were declared and paid in 19X1,* as indicated on the combined statement of earnings and retained earnings. The dividend payment is a use of working capital in that amount.

Although the statement of changes in financial position in this second illustration is more complex than the first, actual statements often involve considerably more complicating factors. Such situations require an orderly worksheet approach that is treated in advanced accounting courses.

CASH BASIS APPROACH TO STATEMENT OF CHANGES

In its official pronouncement concerning the reporting of changes in financial position (Opinion No. 19), the Accounting Principles Board indicated that a certain amount of flexibility in the format of the statement was permissible. While it is required that *all* important financing and investing activities of the entity be disclosed in the statement, either a *working capital* approach (as previously illustrated) or *cash* flow approach may be employed as the format basis. This cash flow approach is sometimes referred to as a cash flow statement.

The working capital approach is most prevalent in practice. Firms which, because of the nature of their activities, do not distinguish between current and noncurrent assets and liabilities are, of course, obliged to use the cash flow approach. Many accountants argue that the cash basis results in a more understandable and informative statement of changes in financial position than does the working capital approach.

It is noteworthy that a cash flow statement could be prepared by reference to a company's checkbook(s). The sources of cash would be the deposits, and the uses would be the checks written. Although this approach to the construction of a cash flow statement sounds simple, it would actually be a monumental task in most instances because of the volume of activity involved. Therefore, to simplify the preparation of the statement, a very basic assumption is made. This assumption is that cash will be increased by increases in liabilities and stockholders' equity, and by decreases in noncash assets (provided that there are no offsetting changes). The reverse will also be the case. We can readily perceive that cash can be increased by borrowing or issuing stock, decreased by paying debts and dividends, and increased and decreased by the disposal and acquisition, respectively, of assets. A more difficult aspect of determining the sources and uses of cash over an accounting period relates to the determination of cash provided by operations during that period.

Cash Provided by Operations

While net earnings from operations is often a useful predictor of future cash flows from operations, the income figure itself is not simply the result of operating cash inflows and outflows. The net earnings amount includes the effect of various noncash revenues, which are reflected in current assets other than cash, and various noncash expenses, some of which are reflected in current liabilities and some of which are simply allocations of past costs. In order to arrive at the amount of cash provided by operations, it is necessary to adjust the net earnings before extraordinary items for these noncash elements of revenues and expenses. (In effect, it is necessary to revert from an accrual basis of net income measurement to a cash basis of "net income" determination.) The nature and necessity of the various adjustments may be made clear by the following examples:

1. Sales to customers during the period must be converted to cash collected from customers during the period. This is accomplished by deducting an increase in accounts receivable that took place over the course of the operating period or by adding a decrease in accounts receivable. In formula form:

   Sales + (Accounts receivable, beginning − Accounts receivable, ending)
   = Cash collected from customers

2. The cost of goods sold expense item must be converted to cash paid to vendors during the period. The adjustment involves changes both in merchandise inventory and in accounts payable. An increase in merchandise inventory may indicate (depending on the change in accounts payable) that cash has been paid to vendors which is not yet reflected in cost of goods sold; therefore, that amount must be added to cost of goods sold as part of the process of determining cash paid to vendors. The reverse is true for inventory decreases, which represent a noncash component of cost of goods sold.

   The amount of an increase in accounts payable may indicate that this amount of goods sold has not yet had an effect on cash; therefore, the amount of that increase in accounts payable should be deducted from cost of goods sold as one necessary adjustment to arrive at cash paid to vendors. The reverse is true for a decrease in accounts payable, which might indicate that cash was paid out to pay for goods acquired and sold in a prior period. In formula form:

   Cost of goods sold + (Accounts payable, beginning − Accounts payable, ending) − (Inventory, beginning − Inventory, ending) = Cash paid to vendors

3. Expenses which involve prepayments and accruals must be adjusted to determine the amount of cash outflow related to a particular expense. To the extent that an expense for a period involves only the expiration of a prepaid element at the beginning of the period, no cash is involved. Nor is cash involved for an accrued element at the end of the period. On the other hand, cash payments are not reflected in the expense amount for prepayments which occur during the period but which do not fully expire by the end of the period. The same is true for accrued expenses at the end of the prior period which are paid in the current period.

   Again, the formula may be helpful. It is expressed here as pertaining to wages expenses, but is applicable generally:

   Wages expense − Prepaid wages, beginning + Prepaid wages, ending + Accrued wages, beginning − Accrued wages, ending = Cash paid to workers

   or:

   Wages expense − (Prepaid wages, beginning − Prepaid wages, ending) + (Accrued wages, beginning − Accrued wages, ending) = Cash paid to workers

4. As in the case of the working capital approach, expenses such as depreciation expense and amortization expense which represent allocations of past costs must be added to the net income before extraordinary items in order to arrive at the amount of cash provided by operations. The adjustments for bond discount and premium amortization are also the same as for the working capital basis, as is the adjustment for changes in long-term deferred income taxes.

   All the adjustments necessary to arrive at the cash flow effects of revenues and expenses can be made directly to the net earnings before extraordinary items to arrive at cash provided for operations. Table 13-1 indicates various account changes which should be added to or subtracted from net income before extraordinary items in order to arrive at the cash provided by operations.

Note in Table 13-1 that the adjustments to net income before extraordinary items to arrive at cash provided by operations are identical to those made to revenues to arrive at cash collected from customers, and are the reverse of those made to operating expenses to arrive at cash outflows from operations.

TABLE 13-1
Determination of Cash Provided by Operations

SALES	− OPERATING EXPENSES	= NET INCOME BEFORE EXTRAORDINARY ITEMS
Less: Increase in accounts receivable		*Less:* Increase in accounts receivable
or		or
Plus: Decrease in accounts receivable		*Plus:* Decrease in accounts receivable
	Less: Depreciation expense	*Plus:* Depreciation expense
	Less: Increase in accounts payable	*Less:* Decrease in accounts payable
	or	or
	Plus: Decrease in accounts payable	*Plus:* Increase in accounts payable
	Less: Decrease in inventory	*Less:* Increase in inventory
	or	or
	Plus: Increase in inventory	*Plus:* Decrease in inventory
	Less: Decrease in prepayments	*Less:* Increase in prepayments
	or	or
	Plus: Increase in prepayments	*Plus:* Decrease in prepayments
	Less: Increase in accrued expenses	*Less:* Decrease in accrued expenses
	or	or
	Plus: Decrease in accrued expenses	*Plus:* Increase in accrued expenses
	Less: Increase in deferred taxes	*Less:* Decrease in deferred taxes
	or	or
	Plus: Decrease in deferred taxes	*Plus:* Increase in deferred taxes
	Less: Bond discount amortization	*Less:* Bond premium amortization
	Plus: Bond premium amortization	*Plus:* Bond discount amortization
CASH COLLECTED FROM CUSTOMERS	− CASH PAID FOR OPERATING EXPENSES	= CASH PROVIDED BY OPERATIONS

This follows, of course, from the fact that expenses are deducted from revenues in arriving at net income before extraordinary items.

Statement of Changes in Financial Position Prepared on a Cash Basis: Illustration

Figure 13-3, which follows essentially the same format as the previous illustrations relating to the working capital basis for the financial changes statement, offers a simplified example of the cash basis approach. Each item appearing on the balance sheets and combined statement of earnings and retained earnings, and particularly each *change* in the balance sheet items, must be analyzed to determine its effect, if any, on the cash flows during the period.

Note also that one may arrive at the cash effect of operations either by modifying the individual items in the income statement or by modifying the net earnings figure. Modifying the *income statement data* for changes in Accounts Receivable produces cash collected from customers. Modifying the Cost of Goods Sold for the changes in Inventory and Accounts Payable produces the

Carter Corporation
Balance Sheet, 19X1 (last three zeros omitted)

ASSETS	January 1	December 31	NOTES ON EFFECTS OF CHANGES ON CASH STATEMENT
Cash	$ 30	$ 50	Cash increase $20
Accounts receivable	33	48	See income statement conversion below
Merchandise	40	77	See income statement conversion below
Equipment	150	162	Cash paid out for equipment $12
Accumulated depreciation	(35)	(50)	See income statement conversion below—depreciation
Totals	$218	$287	
EQUITIES			
Accounts payable	$ 45	$ 52	See income statement conversion below
Deferred federal income tax	13	15	See income statement conversion below
Bonds payable		40	Bonds issued for $40 cash
Common stock (par)	100	110	Stock issued for $12 cash
Paid in capital in excess of par	22	24	(Stock issued for $12 cash)
Retained earnings (see below)	38	46	Dividends paid in cash $15 and $23 of earnings
Totals	$218	$287	

FIGURE 13-3
Preparation of Statement of Changes in Financial Position on a Cash Basis (amounts shown with last three zeros omitted)

FIGURE 13-3 *(continued)*

Carter Corporation
Combined Statement of Income and Retained Earnings for the year ended December 31, 19X1 (last three zeros omitted)

Earnings Statement Conversion to the Cash Basis According to the Rules of Chapter 5

						CASH EFFECT
Sales		$300	*Less:* increase in accounts receivable $15			$285
Expenses			*Plus:* increase in inventory $37			
Merchandise cost of sales	$200		*Less:* increase in accounts payable $7	$230[a]		
Depreciation of equipment	15		Omit			
Other expenses	56		No change	56		
Total expenses		271				286
Net earnings before income tax		$ 29				$ (1)
Federal income tax: Current	$ 4		No change			4
Deferred	2	6	Omit			
Net earnings		$ 23	Net cash outflow from operations			$ (5)
Retained earnings, Jan. 1		38				
Total		$ 61	Note that if these same adjustments are made against Net income the same net effect is obtained:			
Dividends declared and paid		15				
Retained earnings, Dec. 31		$ 46	Net earnings		$23	
			Adjust for noncash changes			
			Add back: Depreciation		15	
			Increase in deferred tax		2	
			Increase in accounts payable		7	
			Total		$47	
			Deduct: Increase in inventory		(37)	
			Increase in accounts receivable		(15)	
			Net cash outflow		$(5)	

[a] The amount paid to vendors on account is calculated as follows:
Ending inventory + Cost of goods sold − Beginning inventory = *Purchases*
Accounts payable, Jan. 1 + *Purchases* − Accounts Payable, Dec. 31 = Payments

This becomes: (Ending inventory − Beginning inventory) + Cost of goods sold = Purchases
(Accounts payable, Jan. 1 − Accounts Payable, Dec. 31) + Purchases = Payments

Or: ($77 − $40) + $200 = $237 (Purchases)
($45 − $52) + $237 = $230 (Payments)

FIGURE 13-3 *(continued)*

Carter Corporation
Statement of Changes in Financial Position Cash Basis
for the year ended December 31, 19X1 (last three zeros omitted)

Sources of cash			
Net income before extraordinary items			$23
Adjust for noncash changes:			
Add back: deductions which did not require cash payments during 19X1			
Depreciation		$15	
Increase in deferred income tax		2	17
Total			$40
Deduct:			
Increase in accounts receivable to adjust sales to a cash collection basis		$15	
Extra cash needed to increase inventory			
Increase in inventory	$37		
Less: increase in accounts payable	(7)	30	45
Net decrease in cash from operations			$(5)
Cash proceeds of new bond issue			40
Cash proceeds of new stock issue			12
Total sources of cash			$47
Uses of cash			
Acquisition of equipment			$12
Dividends			15
Total uses of cash			$27
Increase in cash balance for 19X1			$20

cash paid to vendors. Eliminating the long-term item changes, depreciation and deferred federal income tax, puts the remainder of the expense items on a cash payments basis. In this manner we arrive at a net cash outflow of $5,000. Adjusting the *net income figure* for these same changes produces this same net outflow of $5,000.

The formal statement of changes for this method should not exhibit an excessive number of *minor* adjustments of net earnings. Some combining of associated items may clarify the modifications of net earnings.

In the illustration, only the disclosure of cash sources and uses is necessary to inform the statement user of the major financing and investing activities of the Carter Corporation in 19X1. If there had been any such activities which did not involve cash (for example, conversion of bonds to stock, exchange of stock for plant assets, and so forth), it would be necessary to report them in the body of the statement. This could be accomplished by a separate segment of the statement directly beneath the indicated change in the cash balance for the period entitled, perhaps, "Financing and Investing Activities Not Involving the Receipt or Use of Cash." However, a better approach would be to include noncash financing activities with sources of cash as "Total Financial Resources Generated," and noncash investing activities with uses of cash as "Total Financial Resources Used."

EVALUATION OF THE STATEMENT OF CHANGES IN FINANCIAL POSITION

Whether the statement of changes in financial position is prepared on a working capital or a cash basis, it does not report information that is unavailable in the other accounting statements. Essentially it serves to highlight changes that are reflected in the income statement and the balance sheet. The requirement that either working capital or cash changes be used as the base for the statement results from the crucial importance of liquidity to the business firm. The ability of a firm to generate "funds" to pay its debts and strengthen and expand its operating capabilities is crucial to its success. Vital information about the firm's capacity to generate funds is reported in the statement of changes in financial position.

One cautionary note should be made in regard to the statement. Under both the working capital and cash approaches, depreciation charges are added back to net income before extraordinary items as part of the process of arriving at "funds" generated by operations. This step parallels a procedure employed by many financial analysts: the adding of depreciation expense to net income to arrive at *cash flow* for the period. Such an adjustment reflects analyst skepticism in regard to the meaningfulness of depreciation charges. It also reflects the fact that firms which have substantial commitments to plant assets, and thus have large depreciation charges, may generate very large amounts of funds from operations even when reporting net losses. This fact is important, since the availability of the funds enhances the short-term viability and long-term adaptability of the firm. Nonetheless, a firm which cannot recover all its expenses—including those that reflect the expiring values of its plant assets—through the revenues it generates is very likely headed for serious financial difficulties.

It should also be noted that the cash basis variation of the statement of changes in financial position does not show the actual cash flow. The actual cash flows consist of the activity of the cash account over the operating period, and include many cash changes that are not reflected in the statement of changes in financial position. These include amounts borrowed and repaid on short-term notes, the amounts invested and realized on temporary investments in marketable securities, refunds to customers, transfers between banks, and many other changes. While many of such changes are of little or no value for financial analysis purposes, some are significant.

Cash Basis versus Working Capital Basis for the Financial Changes Statement

It was noted previously that the working capital basis is employed much more frequently in practice than the cash basis for the preparation of the statement of changes in financial position. One reason for this is that a firm's working capital position is a better measure of *liquidity* than its cash position. This can be particularly important for firms holding large amounts of inventories. On the other hand, firms such as banks, finance companies, and insurance companies should, and must, employ the cash approach, since working capital is either nonexistent or of trivial importance to those enterprises.

The working capital basis has its shortcomings. Many financial statement readers have difficulty in understanding the meaning of working capital. It has limitations as a measure of liquidity since only net changes in working capital for the year are shown, which will not reveal any seasonal liquidity squeezes that might have occurred during the year.

The most serious objection to the cash basis is, quite simply, that it does not show working capital flows. The cash approach tends to merge funds provided with funds needed to maintain the firm's current position (adequate working capital position). It does not disclose many cash flows that would be useful for statement analysis purposes in many cases.

Regardless of which approach is taken to the preparation of the financial changes statement, this accounting report serves a highly useful purpose. It serves to supplement and complement the information presented on the earnings statement and balance sheet. It offers a summary of the financing and investing activities of the reporting entity over the accounting period, as well as a measure of the extent to which the firm has generated funds from operations during that period.

SUMMARY

There are three principal statements that accountants prepare: the balance sheet, the combined statement of earnings (or income) and retained earnings, and the statement of changes in financial position. While the income statement reflects the activities engaged in to produce a profit, the statement of changes reflects all activities that have produced changes in the balance sheet data. A little "detective work" is needed to develop the data for the statement of changes, since the accounting system is not designed to produce directly the data that is needed for the statement of financial changes.

The statement of changes in financial position may be prepared on either a working capital basis or a cash basis. Regardless of which basis is employed, the statement must disclose all significant financing and investing activities of the reporting entity for the accounting period. Most of those activities affect either cash or some other component of working capital, so that either cash or working capital provides a logical vehicle for the disclosure format.

When the working capital basis is used for the preparation for the statement, working capital items (current assets and liabilities) are treated separately in a schedule at the end of the statement. Changes in long-term assets and long-term equities are reflected in the statement as producing increases and decreases in working capital. Working capital provided by operations is a particularly important figure. It is arrived at by starting with net income before extraordinary items, and adding back to this figure amounts that were deducted that did not represent the use of working capital during the period. In effect, this "funds provided by operations" is the amount of sales to customers in excess of the working capital consumed in the process of making the sales. It includes the amount needed to maintain the present level of plant assets but may be available temporarily for other purposes. It is useful in determining the adaptability of the firm to changing circumstances.

Preparation of the financial changes statement on a cash basis requires a somewhat different approach. All balance sheet and earnings statement items must be analyzed to determine their effect on cash during the period. Determination of the amount of cash generated by operations requires the adjustment of the net income before extraordinary items for noncash revenue and expense amounts. Cash generated by operations is combined with cash provided from other sources to arrive at total cash provided during the period. The various nonoperating uses of cash during the period are then deducted to arrive at the net change in the cash balance for the period.

In a sense, the statement of changes in financial position, in conjunction with the other two principal required statements, "completes the circle" of financial disclosure for a reporting entity. While it contains no information which is not otherwise available, it offers a summary of the major financing and investing activities of a firm and, within limits, a means of appraising a firm's liquidity.

KEY POINTS

1. A statement of changes in financial position must be included with the balance sheet and income statement in the annual report of corporations. This statement must disclose all the major financing (resource inflows) and investing (resource uses) activities of the firm for the reporting period.

2. Most financing and investing activities affect either cash or other components of working capital. Therefore, disclosure of the causes of changes in either cash or working capital serves to disclose most of the financing and investing activities. (However, activities not directly affecting cash or working capital, such as exchanges of common stock for plant assets, must also be disclosed.) At the same time, a measure of the firm's ability to generate funds is obtained.

3. The "funds" (cash or working capital) generated by the normal operations of a firm is a highly significant figure. This amount is useful for assessing the viability and adaptability of an enterprise, for such funds may be employed to replace plant assets, pay debts, pay dividends, acquire new assets, and for many other purposes. It is arrived at by adjusting net earnings before extraordinary items for various components of earnings which had no effect on either working capital (working capital basis) or on cash (cash basis).

4. The statement of changes in financial position, in conjunction with the balance sheet and the statement of earnings and retained earnings, completes the pattern of financial disclosure. While it presents no information which would otherwise be unavailable, it serves as a useful summary of the major business activities over the course of a reporting period.

QUESTIONS

1. In what sense does the statement of changes in financial position fill a gap between the earnings statement and the balance sheet in providing information in accounting reports?

2. Explain how non-working-capital items "cause" changes in working capital.

3. Discuss the implications of the statement of changes in financial position for statement analysis.

4. What do financial analysts mean by "cash flow"? Is this measure meaningful? Why or why not?

5. Explain the following statement: "The determination of cash generated by operations involves converting the measures developed by the *accrual* accounting model to *cash* measurements."

EXERCISES

E13-1 The balance sheets for Watkins Corporation show the following information (amounts shown with last three zeros omitted):

	DECEMBER 31	
	19X6	**19X5**
Cash	$ 235	$ 315
Short-term investments	490	475
Notes receivable	75	110
Accounts receivable (net)	3,000	3,200
Merchandise inventory	11,000	14,000
Prepaid expenses	45	60
Long-term investments	8,000	8,000
Plant and equipment (net)	20,000	22,000
Patents	500	450
	$43,345	$48,610

(continued)

	DECEMBER 31	
	19X6	19X5
Notes payable, short-term	$ 100	$ 25
Accounts payable	4,200	4,100
Accrued wages	145	160
Accrued interest payable	100	110
Deferred federal income tax liability	400	500
Bonds payable	10,000	10,000
Premium on bonds payable	900	1,000
Common stock	15,000	15,000
Capital contributed in excess of par	5,000	5,000
Retained earnings	7,500	12,715
	$43,345	$48,610

REQUIRED:

From the data shown in the Watkins balance sheets, set up a working capital schedule. You need not prepare a statement of changes in financial position.

E13-2 Prepare a statement of changes in financial position under the working capital assumption for the Jay Corporation for the year 19X6 from the following data (amounts shown with last three zeros omitted):

Balance Sheets (Summarized)

ASSETS

	January 1	December 31
Cash	$ 25	$ 15
Accounts receivable (net)	50	40
Inventory	60	50
Plant and equipment	90	100
Accumulated depreciation	(20)	(25)
Total assets	$205	$180

EQUITIES

	January 1	December 31
Accounts payable	$ 25	$ 30
Capital stock	100	100
Retained earnings	80	50
Total equities	$205	$180

Earnings Statement (Summarized)

Sales	$ 500
Operating expenses (including depreciation)	(530)
Net loss for 19X6	$ 30

No dividends were paid in 19X6. Equipment costing $10,000 was purchased for cash. There were no sales of plant or equipment in 19X6 and no extraordinary gains or losses.

E13-3 Prepare a statement of changes in financial position under the working capital assumption for the Salter Company for the year 19X6 from the following data (amounts shown with last three zeros omitted):

Balance Sheet Data

	January 1	December 31
Working capital	$ 55	$ 70
Land	75	85
Buildings	100	125
Machinery and equipment (net)	125	150
	$355	$430
Notes payable (long-term)	$ 10	$ 15
Bonds payable	100	100
Capital stock (no-par)	180	200
Retained earnings	65	115
	$355	$430

ADDITIONAL DATA (AMOUNTS SHOWN IN FULL):

- **a.** Net earnings for 19X6 were $60,000. (This includes the effect of a $6,000 loss on the sale of an old machine.) Dividends of $10,000 were declared and paid.
- **b.** Depreciation expense for 19X6 was $8,000 on the buildings and $10,000 on the machinery and equipment.
- **c.** A building was acquired by the payment of $13,000 cash and the exchange of capital stock having a current market value of $20,000.
- **d.** Machinery and equipment costing $45,000 were acquired for $40,000 cash and a long-term 6% note (due in two years) for $5,000.

E13-4 Using the data in Exercise 13-2, prepare a statement of changes in financial position for the Jay Corporation using the cash basis.

E13-5 Prepare a statement of changes in financial position using the cash basis for the Rainey Company for the year 19X2 from the following data:

Rainey Company
Balance Sheets
December 31, 19X1, and December 31, 19X2 (last three zeros omitted)

ASSETS

	December 31, 19X1	December 31, 19X2
Cash	$ 800	$ 1,100
Notes receivable	25	35
Accounts receivable (net)	2,400	2,700
Merchandise inventory	5,200	5,100
Prepaid insurance	15	10
Furniture and fixtures (net)	6,000	6,500
Plant and equipment (net)	19,400	19,000
Total assets	$33,840	$34,445

EQUITIES

	December 31, 19X1	December 31, 19X2
Notes payable, short-term	$ 15	$ -0-
Accounts payable	3,200	3,500
Accrued wages	500	650
Deferred federal income taxes	2,800	3,700
Bonds payable	5,000	-0-
Common stock	10,000	12,000
Paid in capital in excess of par	2,000	3,000
Retained earnings	10,325	11,595
	$33,840	$34,445

Rainey Company
Combined Statement of Earnings and Retained Earnings
for the year ended December 31, 19X2 (last three zeros omitted)

Sales		$45,000
Operating expenses:		
Merchandise cost of sales	$28,000	
Depreciation	2,000	
Other operating expenses	12,250	42,250
Net operating earnings		$ 2,750
Bond interest expense		150
Net earnings before income tax		$ 2,600
Federal income tax reported	$ 100	
Federal income tax deferred	900	1,000
Net earnings before extraordinary items		$ 1,600
Loss on sale of equipment		100
Net earnings		$ 1,500
Retained earnings, Dec. 31, 19X1		10,325
Total		$11,825
Dividends		230
Retained earnings, Dec. 31, 19X2		$11,595

ADDITIONAL DATA:

a. One-fourth of total depreciation taken in 19X2 is on the Furniture and Fixtures and three-fourths is on the Plant and Equipment.
b. Equipment costing $1,700 was acquired for cash during 19X2.
c. Furniture and Fixtures costing $1,000 were acquired for cash during 19X2.

E13-6 From the following data, determine the total amount of *cash* taken in from customers during the year 19X3 on sales and collection on account:

a. Accounts receivable:

January 1, 19X3	December 31, 19X3
$8,000	$8,800

b. Total sales to customers on account, $55,000.
c. Accounts Receivable written off as uncollectible during 19X3, $1,800.
d. Cash sales, $25,000.

PROBLEMS

P13-1 Answer the following questions:

a. If the bonds payable and discounts on bonds payable decreased by a net amount of $5,679,500 and if common stock and contributed capital in excess of par increased by a total of $5,679,500, what would you conclude happened?
b. If wages expense for the year was $87,000 and wages payable decreased by $3,000 from the beginning to the end of the period, what amount of *cash* was paid to employees during the period?
c. If insurance expense was $5,600 for the year, what amount was paid out in *cash* to insurance companies if prepaid insurance decreased by $1,300 from the first of the year to the end of the year?

P13-2 Prepare a statement of changes in financial position under the working capital basis for the Chester Corporation for the year 19X6 from the following data:

Balance Sheet Data

	January 1	December 31
Working capital	$ 90,000	$ 99,000
Land	30,000	30,000
Buildings and equipment	200,000	230,000
Accumulated depreciation	(80,000)	(92,000)
	$240,000	$267,000
Bonds payable	$100,000	$ 20,000
Capital stock	70,000	120,000
Capital contributed in excess of par	30,000	50,000
Retained earnings	40,000	77,000
	$240,000	$267,000

Chester Corporation Earnings Data for 19X6

Sales	$600,000
Operating expenses (including $12,000 of depreciation)	560,000
Net operating earnings after tax	$ 40,000
Gain on retirement of bonds	4,000
Net earnings	$ 44,000
Dividends declared and paid in 19X6	7,000
Addition to retained earnings for 19X6	$ 37,000

P13-3 Prepare a statement of changes in financial position for 19X6 on a working capital basis for the Drake Corporation from the data presented in the comparative balance sheet presented next:

Drake Corporation
Balance Sheet
December 31, 19X6

	January 1	December 31
Cash	$18,000	$ 16,000
Accounts receivable (net)	20,000	30,000
Merchandise inventory	29,000	45,000
Equipment (net of depreciation)	30,000	25,000
	$97,000	$116,000
Accounts payable	$17,000	$ 11,000
Notes payable (short-term)	15,000	20,000
Bonds payable	15,000	5,000
Capital stock	40,000	60,000
Retained earnings	10,000	20,000
	$97,000	$116,000

No equipment was purchased or sold during the period. Dividends for 19X6 were $6,000. Net earnings for 19X6 were $16,000.

P13-4 Answer the following questions with reference to the data shown for the Drake Corporation in P13-3.

a. If sales for the Drake Corporation for 19X6 were $190,000, what was the total amount of *cash* taken in from the customers on sales and collections?

b. If merchandise cost of sales of the Drake Corporation for 19X6 was $120,000, what was paid out in *cash* for merchandise in 19X6?

P13-5 Prepare a statement of financial changes on a working capital basis for the A Corporation for 19X6.

A Corporation
Balance Sheet
(last three zeros omitted)

	DECEMBER 31	
	19X5	**19X6**
Cash	$ 300	$ 52
Accounts receivable (net)	800	900
Inventory (FIFO)	700	1,800
Prepayments	10	15
Pension fund	50	60
Land	100	100
Buildings and equipment (none acquired in 19X6)	900	700
Accumulated depreciation	(300)	(360)
Total assets	$2,560	$3,267
Accounts payable	$ 150	$ 450
Notes payable to banks (short-term)	250	600
Accrued liabilities	50	60
Bonds payable (at present value; no new bonds were issued in 19X6)	960	967
Pension obligation	50	60
Total liabilities	$1,460	$2,137
Common stock ($100 par)	$ 500	$ -0-
Common stock ($50 par)	-0-	500
Additional contributed capital	350	350
Retained earnings	250	280
	$2,560	$3,267

A Corporation
Earnings Statement
for the Year 19X6 (last three zeros omitted)

Sales		$3,000
Operating expenses:		
Cost of goods sold	$1,400	
Salaries	850	
Advertising	200	
Delivery	50	
Depreciation	100	
Miscellaneous	150	
Total operating expenses		2,750
Net operating income		$ 250
Interest on bonds payable		67
Income before federal income taxes		$ 183
Federal income taxes		65
Net income before extraordinary items		$ 118
Gain on sale of equipment		62
Net income		$ 180
Retained earnings, Jan. 1, 19X6		250
Total		$ 430
Dividends		150
Retained earnings		$ 280

Note: While the Accounting Principles Board recommended in Opinion No. 19 that all financial changes be reported, it did recognize that stock dividends and stock splits are not real changes and should be excluded from the statement of financial changes.

P13-6 Prepare a statement of changes in financial position on a cash basis for the A Corporation in Problem 13-5.

14 FINANCIAL STATEMENT ANALYSIS

ORIENTATION

For many years it was generally assumed that the accountant's role ended with the formal preparation of the financial statements. During that era many accountants felt that the financial statements were their "manufactured product," and little regard was given to the ultimate consumer of the product, the reader of the financial statements. Now, however, contemporary accountants are aware of the fact that their responsibility frequently does not end with the preparation of financial statements, but extends to the analysis and evaluation of financial data as well.

Obviously the type of financial analysis that occurs depends on the particular interest that the analyst has in the company. For example, management, creditors, investors, labor unions, and governmental agencies might each concentrate on particular aspects of a company's financial picture. It is a function of the accountant to aid in this analysis and interpretation just as it is to prepare the financial statements that are being analyzed.

BASIC ANALYTICAL PROCEDURES

Horizontal Analysis

Horizontal analysis is a term often used to describe percentage changes in corresponding items of comparative financial statements. An amount in the most recent statement is compared with the corresponding item on one or more of the earlier statements. Normally the increase or decrease of the item is listed together with the percentage of increase or decrease for the period. The earliest year presented is usually used as a base year in the computation of percentage increase or decrease. A comparative balance sheet and comparative income statement are presented here for Straub Company to illustrate horizontal analysis.

Several comments are in order concerning the comparative data for Straub Company. The changes in current assets are negligible, with cash decreasing by $15,000 and other current assets increasing by $40,000. However, there was a substantial increase of $200,000 (25.8%) in plant assets. This change accounted for almost all of the increase of $215,000 (18.3%) in total assets.

In analyzing the credit side of the balance sheet, it is easy to spot the major source of funding for the plant asset purchases—long-term liabilities. That account increased by $150,000 (37.5%), whereas retained earnings increased by only $15,000 (12.5%). It is obvious that the plant asset acquisition was not financed by stock issued as there was no change in that account for the period. (A statement of changes in financial position would, of course, provide more detailed information concerning the changes in the composition of balance sheet items.)

Straub Company
Comparative Income Statement
for years ended December 31, 19X2 and 19X1

			INCREASE OR DECREASE*	
	19X2	**19X1**	**Amount**	**Percent**
Sales	$3,300,000	$3,000,000	$300,000	10.0%
Cost of goods sold	1,470,000	1,560,000	90,000*	5.8*
Gross profit	$1,830,000	$1,440,000	$390,000	27.1
Selling expenses	580,000	460,000	120,000	26.1
General and administrative expenses	1,200,000	960,000	240,000	25.0
Total operating expenses	$1,780,000	$1,420,000	$360,000	25.4
Operating income	$ 50,000	$ 20,000	$ 30,000	150.0
Income tax	15,000	8,000	7,000	87.5
Net income	$ 35,000	$ 12,000	$ 23,000	191.7

(continued)

Straub Company
Comparative Balance Sheet
December 31, 19X2 and 19X1

	19X2	19X1	INCREASE OR DECREASE* Amount	Percent
Assets:				
Cash	$ 35,000	$ 50,000	$ 15,000*	30.0%*
Other current assets	290,000	250,000	40,000	16.0
Plant assets (net)	975,000	775,000	200,000	25.8
Intangible assets (net)	90,000	100,000	10,000*	10.0*
Total assets	$1,390,000	$1,175,000	$215,000	18.3
Liabilities and Owners' Equity:				
Current liabilities	$ 205,000	$ 155,000	$ 50,000	32.3
Long-term liabilities	550,000	400,000	150,000	37.5
Total liabilities	$ 755,000	$ 555,000	$200,000	36.0
Common stock, no-par	$ 500,000	$ 500,000	$ -0-	0
Retained earnings	135,000	120,000	15,000	12.5
Total owners' equity	$ 635,000	$ 620,000	$ 15,000	2.4
Total liabilities and owners' equity	$1,390,000	$1,175,000	$215,000	18.3

An analysis of the Straub Company income statement reveals an increase in sales of $300,000 (10.0%). It is noteworthy that cost of goods sold actually decreased by $90,000 (5.8%) for the period, even with the increase in sales. At the same time selling expenses increased by $120,000 (26.1%); general and administrative expenses also increased dramatically by $240,000 (25.0%); and net profits increased by $23,000 (191.7%). It sounds impressive to state that Straub Company net income increased by 191.7%; however, that percentage is based on such a low base that the absolute dollar increase is insignificant.

From reviewing the two comparative financial statements, it appears that Straub Company borrowed a subtantial sum on long-term notes, and essentially used that funding to acquire plant assets. This could have caused a more efficient production operation which in turn would cause cost of goods sold to drop. However, operating expenses increased substantially during the period, which is probably due partially to interest charges on the long-term debt incurred.

Obviously the financial statements presented are in condensed form. Such a condensed form is often sufficient for most financial analyses, with the possible exception of analysis done by management. It is often possible to obtain more detailed financial statements or supplemental schedules to present details of cost of goods sold, expenses, asset and liability accounts and other items.

Vertical Analysis

Vertical analysis is often used to show the relationship of the component parts to the total in a single statement. Although the percentage relationships are confined within each individual statement, the significance of both the amounts and percentages is often enhanced by presenting comparative statements. Accordingly, comparative income statements and balance sheets for Straub Company, using vertical analysis, are presented next.

Straub Company
Comparative Income Statement
for years ended December 31, 19X2 and 19X1

	19X2		19X1	
	Amount	**Percent**	**Amount**	**Percent**
Sales	$3,300,000	100.0%	$3,000,000	100.0%
Cost of goods sold	1,470,000	44.5	1,560,000	52.0
Gross profit	$1,830,000	55.5	$1,440,000	48.0
Selling expenses	580,000	17.6	460,000	15.3
General and administrative expenses	1,200,000	36.4	960,000	32.0
Total operating expenses	$1,780,000	54.0	$1,420,000	47.3
Operating income	$ 50,000	1.5	$ 20,000	.7
Income tax	15,000	.4	8,000	.3
Net income	$ 35,000	1.1%	$ 12,000	.4%

Straub Company
Comparative Balance Sheet
December 31, 19X2 and 19X1

	19X2		19X1	
	Amount	**Percent**	**Amount**	**Percent**
Assets:				
Cash	$ 35,000	2.5%	$ 50,000	4.2%
Other current assets	290,000	20.9	250,000	21.3
Plant assets (net)	975,000	70.1	775,000	66.0
Intangible assets (net)	90,000	6.5	100,000	8.5
Total assets	$1,390,000	100.0	$1,175,000	100.0
Liabilities and Owners' Equity:				
Current liabilities	$ 205,000	14.7	$ 155,000	13.2
Long-term liabilities	550,000	39.6	$ 400,000	34.0
Total liabilities	$ 755,000	54.3	$ 555,000	47.2
Common stock, no-par	$ 500,000	36.0	$ 500,000	42.6
Retained earnings	135,000	9.7	120,000	10.2
Total owners' equity	$ 635,000	45.7	$ 620,000	52.8
Total liabilities and owners' equity	$1,390,000	100.0%	$1,175,000	100.0%

In the balance sheet each asset is expressed as a percentage of total assets, and each liability and owners' equity item is stated as a percentage of total liabilities and owners' equity. In the income statement each item is stated as a percentage of net sales.

The major relative changes in assets were, obviously, plant assets. On the equity side, it is noteworthy that total liabilities increased from 47.2% of equities to 54.3% for the period, while total owners' equity decreased from 52.8% to 45.7% for the same period. Stated differently, as of the end of 19X2 slightly more than one-half (54.3%) of the business assets are being financed through borrowing.

In the vertical analysis of the income statement it is important to point out the substantial drop in cost of goods sold and the corresponding increase in general and administrative expenses. By reference to the horizontal analysis we can see that the cost of goods sold decreased by 5.8% for the period (in absolute terms). However, the vertical analysis possibly provides an even better picture of what actually happened in that area. In 19X1 cost of goods sold was 52.0% of sales, while in 19X2 it dropped to 44.5% of sales. At the same time other expenses increased as a percentage of sales.

Common-Size Statements

Horizontal and vertical analyses are often useful in pointing out certain relationships and trends in financial statements. Vertical analysis for one company can be extended to encompass the preparation of common-size statements, that is, statements in which all items are stated in terms of percentages or ratios. Common-size statements are normally used in comparing one company with another or with industry averages. Common-size statements may also be used to compare percentages of current periods with several past periods. A comparative common-size income statement for Straub Company and its competitor, Bump Enterprises, for 19X2 is presented next.

Straub Company and Bump Enterprises
Common-Size Income Statement
for the year ended December 31, 19X2

	STRAUB CO.	BUMP ENTERPRISES
Sales	100.0%	100.0%
Cost of goods sold	44.5	45.1
Gross profit	55.5	54.9
Selling expenses	17.6	17.1
General and administrative expenses	36.4	28.1
Total operating expenses	54.0	45.2
Operating income	1.5	9.7
Income tax	.4	4.1
Net income	1.1%	5.6%

An evaluation of the statement reveals that although Straub Company had a slightly higher gross profit percentage than Bump, and selling expenses were comparable, its general and administrative expenses were substantially higher than those of its competitor. As a consequence, the operating income for Straub was only 1.5% of sales compared to 9.7% for Bump. From this abbreviated analysis, it appears that the general and administrative expense area should be of some concern to Straub Company.

Standards of Comparison

The analysis of a company's financial statements cannot be accomplished without reference to other information. We have briefly looked at a comparison of current financial statements to the past performance of the company through horizontal analysis. However, a weakness of horizontal analysis is that it does not provide the reader with any idea of what the figures should have been. The fact that sales increased by 10% may be excellent in that the average company in the industry may have suffered a 12% drop in sales. Or, on the other hand, the industry may be booming and the average company in the industry may have improved sales by 30%. In that case a 10% sales increase looks much less impressive. Therefore the inherent limitations of horizontal analysis may be overcome to some extent by comparing the financial statements of a given firm to an industry standard, or to some other predetermined yardstick of performance.

When a given company is compared with its competitors or with industry averages, it is important to realize that the comparison means little unless the companies in question are reasonably comparable. Because of the many companies currently engaging in diversified activities, the term *industry* must be interpreted with caution.

Additionally, the use of different accounting methods may make direct comparisons of two companies more difficult. For example, two otherwise "comparable" companies may use different methods of depreciation or inventory valuation, as well as different asset lives. Even though comparing a given company's financial statements with industry averages or with other companies' financial statements must be done with some caution, studying comparative performance is a generally useful method of financial analysis.

Quality of Earnings

So far throughout this book there has been some focus on the determination of the quantity of profits for a firm. Obviously, no entity can long afford a continuous drain on its invested capital. Because of this fact, financial analysts are not only concerned with the absolute amount of net income but also with the prospect for a continuation of that profit. For example, an erratic stream of earnings is generally less desirable (poses more risk for investors) than a steady level of earnings.

It is often said that a given company has a "higher quality" of earnings than a similar, otherwise comparable competitor. This idea of a high quality of earnings is often the result of accounting principles and methods selected by management which lead to a conservative representation of earnings and net assets. (For example, the use of LIFO in an inflationary period would result in a conservative earnings estimate and a lower inventory amount than if FIFO were used.)

Other items to look for in evaluating the quality of a company's earnings are: How much of the net income is the result of nonrecurring or nonoperating items? Have there been recent accounting changes that have had an impact on earnings? Are earnings largely the result of sales in a given *product line* that might be considered a fad item?

RATIO ANALYSIS

One of the more common methods of financial analysis is through the use of ratios. Ratio analysis is often the starting point in developing information for the financial analyst. Frequently there is a tendency on the part of some analysts to rely too heavily on one or two financial ratios as an accurate and complete representation of the financial picture of a company. By now in our study of accounting it should be obvious that even the best accounting records would not depict everything of importance that relates to a given company. In other words, to rely solely on accounting records as a representation of all that is important in a given company is an oversimplification. Important things happen to the company which are outside of the scope of the accounting function and are consequently not reported in the financial statements. Similarly, to attempt to reduce financial statements to a series of a few ratios to "simplify" the analysis is something that should be done with caution. Reliance on one or two ratios as a representation of the financial picture of the firm results in an oversimplification of the financial statements (which are themselves an oversimplification of the status of the company). So, although financial ratios are a useful analytical technique, they should be used and interpreted with some degree of care.

Ratios are often classified as follows:

— *Tests of profitability* Indicators of the degree of success or failure of a given company for a specified period of time.

— *Tests of liquidity and solvency* Measure of the short-run (liquidity) and long-run (solvency) ability of an enterprise to pay its maturing obligations.

— *Asset utilization, market measures, and other tests* Measures of how effectively a company is utilizing its assets; and other measures.

The use of these ratios is illustrated through the following example of a hypothetical, closely held, automotive parts wholesaler—Karparts Corporation. The following is an income statement and balance sheet for Karparts for 19X1 and 19X2.

Karparts Corporation
Condensed Income Statement for the years ended December 31, 19X2 and 19X1
(last three zeros omitted)

	19X2	19X1
Sales (net, all on credit)	$1,000	$1,050
Cost of goods sold	750	760
Gross profit	250	290
Operating expenses	150	165
Interest expense	75	60
Total expenses	225	225
Pretax income	25	65
Income taxes	10	25
Net income	$ 15	$ 40

Karparts Corporation
Comparative Balance Sheet
as of December 31, 19X2 and 19X1
(last three zeros omitted)

	19X2	19X1
Assets:		
Cash	$ 100	$ 25
Accounts receivable (net)	175	225
Inventory	700	300
Prepaid expenses	100	50
Total current assets	1,075	600
Plant assets (net)	1,800	1,725
Total assets	$2,875	$2,325
Liabilities and Owners' Equity:		
Current liabilities	$ 300	$ 452
Long-term liabilities	1,400	700
Total liabilities	$1,700	$1,152
Common stock (5,000 shares)	$ 750	$ 750
Preferred Stock (100 shares)	250	250
Retained earnings	175	173
Total owners' equity	$1,175	$1,173
Total liabilities and owners' equity	$2,875	$2,325

You are provided with the following additional information concerning Karparts:

Market price of the common stock on December 31, 19X2		$50
Dividends for the year:		
Common	$5,000	
Preferred	$8,000	

Tests of Profitability

Profitability ratios are indications of how well the enterprise operated during the year. These ratios address such issues as the rate of net income, the return to owners on a percentage basis, and the adequacy on net income from other perspectives. Generally these tests are computed on the basis of net sales or an investment base such as owners' equity.

1. Profit Margin on Sales

The profit margin on sales is computed by dividing net income by net sales for the period. Karparts' ratio is:

$$\text{Profit margin on sales} = \frac{\text{Net income}}{\text{Net sales}} = \frac{\$15}{\$1{,}000} = \underline{\underline{1.5\%}}$$

We cannot be absolutely sure of the adequacy of Karparts' profit margin without reference to some standard, such as an industry standard. However, it is unlikely that any industry could survive long with a profit margin of much less than Karparts is reporting.

2. Return on Total Assets

This ratio is computed by using total net income as the numerator and average total assets as the denominator. It is a measure of the effectiveness of the company in putting their assets to work to earn income for the company. The ratio for Karparts is:

$$\text{Return on total assets} = \frac{\text{Net income}}{\text{Average total assets}} = \frac{\$15}{(\$2{,}875 + \$2{,}325) \div 2} = \underline{\underline{.58\%}}$$

Frequently this ratio is computed by adding interest expense back to net income. This results in an approximation of earnings before payment of interest to creditors but after income taxes. Again, this ratio for Karparts appears to be unsatisfactory. A .58% return on assets is considerably below the return that could be achieved from many relatively safe investments (such as a passbook savings account or government securities).

3. Return on Owners' Investment (or Equity)

This ratio is defined as net income less preferred dividends divided by average common stockholders' equity. Karparts' ratio computed in this manner is:

$$\text{Return on common stock equity} = \frac{\text{Net income} - \text{Preferred dividends}}{\text{Average common stockholders' equity}}$$

$$= \frac{\$15 - \$8}{(\$925 + \$923) \div 2}$$

$$= \underline{\underline{.76\%}}$$

Net income *minus* preferred dividends is used in this ratio to provide an approximation of the net income that is available to the common shareholders. This ratio appears to be quite low for the common stockholders of Karparts, irrespective of industry averages. For example, if the common stockholders had put their money in a certificate of deposit at a bank, their rate of return would have been much in excess of 1.65%, and with very little risk.

4. Earnings per Share

The earnings per share (EPS) calculation is probably the most commonly referred to ratio in financial analysis. Since an investor generally thinks in terms of a certain number of shares owned, the reduction of corporate financial information to per-share terms puts it in a useful perspective to the investor.

The computation for Karparts is:

$$\text{Earnings per share} = \frac{\text{Net income} - \text{Preferred dividends}}{\text{Weighted average number of common stock shares outstanding}}$$

$$= \frac{\$15{,}000 - \$8{,}000}{5{,}000}$$

$$= \underline{\underline{\$1.40}}$$

Although it is widely used, the earnings-per-share figure must be evaluated with caution. For example, earnings per share can be increased simply by reducing the number of shares outstanding through the purchase of treasury stock.

Tests of Liquidity and Solvency

The ability of an enterprise to meet its current and future debts is an important aspect of an overall evaluation of the firm. Karparts had liabilities for

$1,700,000 at the end of 19X2. There should be some way to obtain a tentative indication of their ability to pay those obligations. Certain basic ratios can be computed which will provide a guide in these determinations.

5. Current (or Working Capital) Ratio

The current ratio (sometimes called the working capital ratio) is the ratio of total current assets to total current liabilities. The computation of the current ratio for Karparts is:

$$\text{Current ratio} = \frac{\text{Current assets}}{\text{Current liabilities}}$$
$$= \frac{\$1{,}075}{\$300}$$
$$= \underline{\underline{3.6 \text{ to } 1}} \text{ or } \underline{\underline{3.6:1}}$$

A current ratio of 3.6 : 1 (often expressed as 3.6 times) seems to indicate that Karparts has some degree of safety in meeting maturing short-term obligations. Of course, this ratio is only one measure of determining liquidity, and does not answer all questions in this regard. For example: How salable is the inventory; and how readily collectible are the receivables? To what extent do prepaid items affect the ratio? To help answer these questions, a second test of liquidity, referred to as the quick ratio or acid-test ratio, is often performed.

6. Quick (or Acid Test) Ratio

A satisfactory current ratio would not reflect the fact that a part of the current assets might not be readily convertible into cash to meet maturing obligations. With inventories, especially raw materials' inventory in a manufacturing operation, there is often a question of how long it will take to convert them into a finished product and ultimately sell the product and make collections. The elimination of inventories and prepaid expenses from the current assets might provide better information for the short-term creditor. The quick ratio computation for Karparts is:

$$\text{Quick ratio} = \frac{\text{Cash} + \text{Net receivables} + \text{Marketable securities}}{\text{Current liabilities}}$$
$$= \frac{\$100 + \$175 + 0}{\$300}$$
$$= \frac{\$275}{\$300}$$
$$= \underline{\underline{.92 \text{ to } 1}} \text{ or } \underline{\underline{.92:1}}$$

Marketable securities are generally included in the computation of the quick ratio because it is obviously management's intent to convert them into cash within a year or they would not have been classified as a current asset. The sizable drop in the quick ratio from the current ratio (3.6 : 1 to .92 : 1) may be a source of concern for the short-term creditors. However the quick ratio of .92 : 1 tells the analyst that Karparts has 92% of their current liabilities covered by assets which almost assuredly will be available for the liquidation of those debts.

Debt and Equity Ratios

Financial analysts frequently condense the relationship between the debts and equities of a firm into one of three related ratios: The *debt to equity ratio;* the *owners' equity to total assets ratio;* or *the debt to total assets ratio.* Any one of the three ratios provides the essentials of the debt-equity relationship of the firm. The choice among them is a matter of personal preference. The three ratios are computed as follows for Karparts:

7. Debt to Equity Ratio

$$\text{Debt to equity ratio} = \frac{\text{Total liabilities}}{\text{Total owners' equity}} = \frac{\$1{,}700}{\$1{,}175} = \underline{\underline{1.45 \text{ to } 1}}$$

8. Owners' Equity to Total Assets Ratio

$$\text{Owners' equity to total assets ratio} = \frac{\text{Total owners' equity}}{\text{Total assets}} = \frac{\$1{,}175}{\$2{,}875} = \underline{\underline{40.9\%}}$$

9. Debt to Total Assets Ratio

$$\text{Debt to total assets ratio} = \frac{\text{Total liabilities}}{\text{Total assets}} = \frac{\$1{,}700}{\$2{,}875} = \underline{\underline{59.1\%}}$$

All of the three ratios present the same data in different ways. Probably the most common way of presenting it is by using the debt to total asset ratio. This ratio tells the analyst that creditors have claim to 59.1% of the assets of Karparts. It is virtually meaningless to interpret the significance of this relationship without reference to industry average or company trends over time. In general, however, high debt ratios suggest greater risk of insolvency for the firm.

10. Times Interest Earned

The times interest earned ratio is computed by dividing income earned before interest expense and taxes by the interest charge.This ratio highlights the importance of a company earning a sufficient profit to pay all interest charges. The ratio uses income before income taxes because the ability to pay interest is not a function of the income taxes to be paid. (The firm will have taxable income only if all interest expense has been paid.) The ratio for Karparts is:

$$\text{Times interest earned} = \frac{\text{Income before income taxes and interest expense}}{\text{Interest expense}}$$
$$= \frac{\$15 + \$10 + \$75}{\$75}$$
$$= \frac{\$100}{\$75}$$
$$= \underline{\underline{1.33 \text{ times}}}$$

It is obvious that Karparts is barely earning enough to cover interest charges.

The term *trading on the equity* (or leverage) describes using borrowed money at fixed rates in anticipation of obtaining a higher rate of return on the money used than the interest paid. If this can be done, the capital obtained from creditors earns enough to pay the interest and then leaves a margin for common stockholders. In this case trading on the equity is profitable.

Market and Other Tests

There are certain additional tests which can be performed to indicate a company's position in the capital marketplace. One such common test is the *price earnings ratio.*

11. Price Earnings Ratio

The price earnings (P/E) ratio is a statistic which iswidely used by the investing public in analyzing investment opportunities. It is computedby dividing the market price of the stock by its earnings per share. For Karparts, the ratio is:

$$\text{Price Earnings Ratio} = \frac{\text{Market price of stock}}{\text{Earnings per share}}$$
$$= \frac{\$50}{\$1.40}$$
$$= \underline{\underline{35.7}} \text{ or } \underline{\underline{35.7:1}}$$

The average price earnings ratio for all stocks traded on the New York Stock Exchange as of the end of 1983 was 13.2. This compares with an average as of the end of 1982 of 10.1, and reflects the resurgence of the stock market during that year. Some individual companies have high P/E ratios, while some have low multiples. For example, in late 1983 Polaroid had a high ratio of 33, while Xerox had a low ratio of 10. Many factors cause this difference in P/E ratios. Commonly, analysts who believe that a company will be able to improve future earnings dramatically may value the stock higher than its present earnings may stify. Obviously, the opposite situation is also true.

12. Dividend Yield

$$\text{Dividend yield} = \frac{\text{Dividends per share}}{\text{Market price per share}} = \frac{\$1}{\$50} = \underline{\underline{2\%}}$$

The importance of dividends varies among investors. Federal income tax laws require that most dividends be taxed at rates well in excess of rates which generally apply when a gain is realized on stock sold. Consequently, some investors prefer to have earnings reinvested in the business to produce an increase in the firm's earnings, which is hopefully followed by a rise in the stock price. Others may be more interested in dividend income despite the tax disadvantage.

Another measure of the dividend-paying property of the firm is the dividend payout ratio. This ratio is computed by dividing earnings per share into dividends per share. Thus if this ratio were computed for Karparts for the year it would be:

$$\text{Dividend payout ratio} = \frac{\text{Dividends per share}}{\text{Earnings per share}} = \frac{\$1}{\$1.40} = \underline{\underline{71\%}}$$

13. Accounts Receivable Turnover

The accounts receivable turnover is computed by dividing net sales by average net accounts receivable. This provides the analyst with an indication of the average time required to convert receivables into cash. Unless seasonal factors are significant, average receivables can be computed using beginning and ending trade receivables. The average receivables figure is computed net of any allowance (contra-asset) account. Only sales on credit should be used in the computation; however, if relative amounts of credit and cash sales remain fairly constant, the use of total sales figure will provide a useful trend analysis. The accounts receivable turnover computation for Karparts is:

$$\text{Accounts receivable turnover} = \frac{\text{Net credit sales}}{\text{Average net accounts receivable}}$$
$$= \frac{\$1{,}000}{(175 + 225) \div 2}$$
$$= \underline{\underline{5 \text{ times}}}$$

14. Average Age of Receivables

The average age of the Karparts' accounts receivable can be approximated by dividing the turnover factor into 365 days. That computation for Karparts would appear as follows:

$$\text{Average age of receivables} = \frac{365 \text{ days}^{1}}{\text{Accounts receivable turnover}}$$
$$= \frac{365 \text{ days}}{5}$$
$$= \underline{\underline{73 \text{ days}}}$$

It appears that the accounts receivable turnover for Karparts is low. Generally, 30-day credit terms for the industry are common, however, even if the company granted an extremely generous 60-day credit period, the average age of receivables exceeds that period by thirteen days. It should be noted that if the sales on the last day of the month were unusually high (or low), the average of receivables as computed above can be misleading. It is also important to note that the 19X2 accounts receivable balance is down from last year, possibly indicating an improving situation regarding the collection of receivables.

15. Inventory Turnover

Inventory turnover is computed by dividing the average inventory into the cost of goods sold. The cost of goods sold figure represents the total *cost* of goods that have been sold during a period. Therefore using that figure instead of the sales figure (which includes markup) means that both the numerator and the denominator of the ratio will be at *cost.* This relationship between the cost of goods sold and average inventory indicates the number of times that inventories "turned over" during the year. The computation for Karparts is:

$$\text{Inventory turnover} = \frac{\text{Cost of goods sold}}{\text{Average inventory}}$$
$$= \frac{\$750}{(\$700 + \$300) \div 2}$$
$$= \underline{\underline{1.5 \text{ times}}}$$

[1] Commonly, the figure used in this computation is 360 days

The inventory turnover measures how quickly inventory is sold; generally, the faster the better. With inventory turnover it is normally useful to relate the number computed to an industry average. For example, an inventory turnover of 1 in the retail jewelry business is acceptable, but such a turnover in the retail grocery business would be disastrous. (Would you want to buy bread from a grocery store that only turned over their bread inventory once a year?)

16. Average Age of Inventory

As with receivables, the average age of inventory can be computed by dividing the turnover figure into 365 days. That computation for Karparts is:

$$\text{Average age of inventory} = \frac{\text{365 days}}{\text{Inventory turnover}} = \frac{\text{365 days}}{\text{1.5 days}} = \underline{\underline{\text{243 days}}}$$

This calculation tells the analyst that Karparts maintains an average inventory of 243 days of sales. This is, almost certainly, an excessive amount of inventory. Reference to industry averages could help determine a more acceptable inventory level.

It appears that the inventory situation is not improving for the company. The inventory figure increased from $300,000 to $700,000 in one year. This appears to be a major area of concern for the company.

Summary Evaluation of Karparts Corporation

The liquidity tests for the company were generally good, indicating little trouble in liquidating immediate future debts. The company's stock is also offering a moderately good dividend yield, based on the current market price of the stock. However, the good news ends there; most of the other indicator ratios are not favorable for the company.

Certainly the inventory turnover is low for such a company. Their returns on assets and owners' investments are low, as is the turnover rate for accounts receivable. Although Karparts is not in any *immediate* danger of severe financial problems, it could be heading in that direction. If you were asked to make recommendations to the management of Karparts concerning their company, you would probably begin your investigation with further analyses of the inventory and receivables positions. There is an indication from the preceding analysis that both are too high and need attention.

It is important to reiterate that ratios are simplifications of financial statements which are themselves simplified representations of the business entity's operating results and financial position. Although ratios are very useful in spotting strong and weak points of a company, they should not always be relied upon as the final word in the evaluation of a company. Often the ratios can only lead to the *questions* to ask about a company; they do not provide the *answers*.

SUMMARY

The function of the accountant has changed in recent years from strictly a *preparer* of financial statements to a more pervasive role in the use of financial statements. In that regard it is important that the accountant be knowledgable in the analysis of financial statements. There are many basic analytical procedures which are useful to a wide variety of interest groups. Almost all of these techniques rely on a frame of reference of some kind. That reference point is often industry averages, or previous year's performance.

Probably the most common type of financial analysis is ratio analysis. Ratios are often classified as: tests of profitability, tests of solvency and liquidity, asset utilization, market measures, and other tests. Different user groups will rely on different ratios more than others. One problem inherent with ratio analysis is the tendency to rely too heavily on one or two ratios as a barometer of the condition of the entire company being analyzed. Ratios are simplifications of financial statements which are themselves simplifications.

KEY POINTS

1. Horizontal analysis is a term often used to describe percentage changes in corresponding items of comparative financial statements.

2. Vertical analysis is a term often used to show the relationship of the component parts to the total in a single statement.

3. Common-size statements are financial statements in which all items are stated in terms of percentages or ratios.

4. A common yardstick of performance for a company is industry averages or standards. However, because of the many companies currently engaging in diversified activities, the term *industry* must be interpreted with caution.

5. Ratio analysis is probably the most common method of financial statement analysis. Ratios are frequently classified as follows:

RATIO	CALCULATION	USE OR MEANING
A. Tests of Profitability	Indicators of the degree of success or failure of a given company for a specified period of time.	
1. Profit margin on sales	$= \dfrac{\text{Net income}}{\text{Net sales}}$	Income produced by each dollar of sales
2. Return on total assets	$= \dfrac{\text{Net income}}{\text{Average total assets}}$	Overall measure of the profitability of all assets used in business
3. Return on owners' investment (or equity)	$= \dfrac{\text{Net income} - \text{Preferred dividends}}{\text{Average common stockholders' equity}}$	Profitability of owners' investment
4. Earnings per share	$= \dfrac{\text{Net income} - \text{Preferred dividends}}{\text{Weighted average number of common stock shares outstanding}}$	A widely used method of placing earnings on a common basis for comparison
B. Tests of Liquidity and Solvency	Tests of the short- and long-run ability of an enterprise to pay its maturing obligations.	
5. Current (or working capital) ratio	$= \dfrac{\text{Current assets}}{\text{Current liabilities}}$	Measure of short-term debt-paying ability
6. Quick (or Acid Test) ratio	$= \dfrac{\text{Cash} + \text{Marketable securities} + \text{Net receivables}}{\text{Current liabilities}}$	Measure of short-term liquidity
7. Debt to equity ratio	$= \dfrac{\text{Total liabilities}}{\text{Total owners' equity}}$	Measure of relationship of debt financing to equity financing
8. Owners' equity to total assets ratio	$= \dfrac{\text{Total owners' equity}}{\text{Total assets}}$	Measure of relationship of owner financing to assets
9. Debt to total assets ratio	$= \dfrac{\text{Total liabilities}}{\text{Total assets}}$	Measure of relationship of debt financing to assets
10. Times interest earned	$= \dfrac{\text{Income before income taxes and interest expense}}{\text{Interest expense}}$	Measure of protection of creditors from default on interest payments

(continued)

(Continued)

RATIO	CALCULATION	USE OR MEANING
C. Market and Other Tests	Measure of how effectively a company is utilizing assets, and other measures.	
11. Price earnings ratio	$= \frac{\text{Market price of stock}}{\text{Earnings per share}}$	Measure of the amount the market will pay for a dollar of earnings
12. Dividend yield	$= \frac{\text{Dividends per share}}{\text{Market price per share}}$	Measure of current dividend return to an investor
13. Accounts receivable turnover	$= \frac{\text{Net credit sales}}{\text{Average net accounts receivable}}$	Measure of effectiveness of credit policies
14. Average age of receivables	$= \frac{\text{365 days}}{\text{Accounts receivable turnover}}$	Measure of time it takes to collect an average receivable
15. Inventory turnover	$= \frac{\text{Cost of goods sold}}{\text{Average inventory}}$	Measure of inventory management policies
16. Average age of inventory	$= \frac{\text{365 days}}{\text{Inventory turnover}}$	Measure of average time that an item is held in inventory

QUESTIONS

1. Briefly describe the difference between horizontal and vertical analysis.

2. What are common-size financial statements? Describe the limitations and usefulness.

3. Under what circumstances might a company that has had lower earnings for the past several years be a better potential investment than a company with higher earnings?

4. What is the purpose and usefulness of ratio analysis?

5. What are the limitations of ratio analysis? What are some items other than current year ratios that a financial analyst should be aware of?

6. Under what circumstances might a profit margin on sales of 3.5% be good? Under what circumstances might it be bad?

7. Assume that you are a bank vice-president and are approached by the controller of Pace, Inc., concerning the possibility of obtaining a $100,000, 90-day loan to finance the acquisition of inventory. What ratio or ratios might you like to see for Pace, Inc., in your analysis of the company's credit worthiness?

8. Companies X and Y are in the same industry. Both have net incomes of $500,000 for the previous year. Is it safe to say that both companies are equally successful? Why or why not?

9. Under what circumstances might a company's dividend yield be a good indication of its investment worth?

10. Briefly explain the usefulness of the accounts receivable turnover and average age of receivable calculations. What additional information would be valuable in analyzing these ratios?

11. Briefly explain the usefulness of the inventory turnover and average age of inventory ratios. What additional information would be valuable in analyzing these ratios?

12. Under what circumstances might an inventory turnover of 4 be good? Under what circumstances might it be bad?

EXERCISES

E14-1 Compute the amount and percentage changes in the income statement and balance sheet shown here. Comment on the changes from 19X3 to 19X4.

Hillside Company
Comparative Income Statement
for years ended December 31, 19X3 and 19X4

	19X4	19X3
Sales	$875,000	$900,000
Cost of goods sold	525,000	600,000
Gross profit	$350,000	$300,000
Total expenses	328,000	227,000
Net income	**$ 22,000**	**$ 73,000**

Hillside Company
Comparative Balance Sheet
December 31, 19X3 and 19X4

	19X4	19X3
Cash	$ 5,000	$ 28,000
Other current assets	75,000	74,000
Plant assets (net)	600,000	520,000
Total assets	**$680,000**	**$622,000**
Current liabilities	$250,000	$228,000
Long-term debt	347,000	333,000
Total stockholders' equity	83,000	61,000
Total liabilities and stockholders' equity	**$680,000**	**$622,000**

E14-2 Express the income statements for Abbot and Black Companies for 19X1 as common-size statements. Comment on the comparison and limitations of this type of analysis.

Abbot and Black Company
Common-Size Income Statements
for the yer ended December 31, 19X1

	ABBOT	BLACK
Sales	$4,000,000	$12,000,000
Cost of goods sold	1,900,000	6,600,000
Gross profit	$2,100,000	$ 5,400,000
Selling expenses	450,000	1,440,000
General and administrative expenses	1,250,000	3,900,000
Total operating expenses	$1,700,000	$ 5,340,000
Operating income	$ 400,000	$ 60,000
Income tax	155,000	4,800
Net income	**$ 245,000**	**$ 55,200**

E14-3 Partial comparative balance sheet and income statement information for Lakeview Company appears next.

	19X2	19X1
Cash	$ 1,100	$ 1,300
Marketable securities	900	2,150
Accounts receivable (net)	5,600	4,950
Inventory	6,800	6,200
Total current assets	**$14,400**	**$14,600**
Current liabilities	**$ 5,000**	**$ 3,525**
Sales	$40,320	$27,590
Cost of goods sold	27,200	25,420
Gross margin on sales	**$13,120**	**$ 2,170**

In addition, accounts receivable and inventories were $4,050 $6,400 respectively, in 19X0. Figure the current ratio, quick ratio, receivable turnover, average age of receivables, and inventory turnover for each year. Comment on the change in liquidity position from 19X1 to 19X2. (Round computations to one decimal point.)

E14-4 Box Company had total assets of $64,000 in 19X0; $180,000 in 19X1; and $770,000 in 19X2; and a debt to equity ratio of .67 in all three years. In 19X1, the company made a net income of $77,112 on revenues of $1,224,000. In 19X2, the company made a net income of $98,952 on revenues of $1,596,000. Figure the profit margin, asset turnover, return on assets, and return on equity for 19X1 and 19X2. Comment on the apparent cause of the increase or decrease in profitability. (Round the percentages and other ratios to one decimal point.)

E14-5

Barnhill Company
Comparative Balance Sheet
December 31, 19X2 (in thousands of dollars)

ASSETS	19X2	19X1
Cash	$ 7,000	$ 4,000
Short-term investments	2,000	4,000
Accounts receivable (net)	13,000	9,000
Inventories	9,000	7,000
Plant assets (net)	69,000	66,000
Total assets	$100,000	$90,000
LIABILITIES AND STOCKHOLDERS' EQUITY		
Current liabilities	$ 14,000	$16,000
Bonds payable, due in 19X9	24,000	20,000
Common stock, $10 par	30,000	30,000
Retained earnings	32,000	24,000
Total liabilities and stockholders' equity	**$100,000**	**$90,000**

Sales for 19X2 were $100 million, and cost of goods sold amounted to $58 million. Other items from the income statement for 19X2 are: Interest expense, $2 million; income taxes expense, $10 million; and net income, $12 million.

Show how you would compute the following ratios (or measurements) for 19X2 by determining the appropriate dollar or other amounts to be used in computing each item.

a. Current ratio
b. Quick (acid test) ratio
c. Times interest earned (before income taxes)
d. Rate of gross profit on sales
e. Earnings per share

E14-6 Using the information given, complete the balance sheet below.

a. The quick ratio is 2 : 1.
b. Notes payable are long-term liabilities and are four times the dollar amount of the marketable securities.
c. Accounts receivable are $2,000 and are one-half of the quick assets, one-fourth of the current assets, and equal to plant and equipment.
d. Total stockholders' equity is equal to the working capital, and contributed capital is twice the dollar amount of the net accumulation of earnings.

ASSETS		LIABILITIES AND STOCKHOLDERS' EQUITY	
Cash	______	Accounts payable	______
Marketable securities	______	Notes payable	______
Accounts receivable	______		
Inventories	______	Capital stock	______
Plant and equipment	______	Retained earnings	______
	======		======

PROBLEMS

P14-1 Following is the condensed common-size income statement for Hawkins, Inc.

Hawkins, Inc.
Condensed Common-Size Income Statement
for the year ended December 31, 19X1

Net sales	100.0%
Cost of goods sold	68.0
Gross profit on sales	32.0
Operating expenses:	
Selling expense	16.0
Administrative expense	6.0
Total operating expense	22.0
Operating income	10.0
Interest expense	0.5
Income before income taxes	9.5
Income taxes	2.0
Net income	**7.5%**

Net sales for the priod were $2,000,000.

REQUIRED:

Prepare the income statement for Hawkins, Inc.

P14-2 The comparative condensed financial statements of Hillcountry, Inc., are given next:

Hillcountry, Inc.
Comparative Balance Sheet
December 31, 19X2 and 19X1

	DECEMBER 31	
	19X2	**19X2**
Current assets	$ 480,000	$ 585,000
Property, plant, and equipment	1,260,000	975,000
Total assets	**$1,740,000**	**$1,560,000**
Current liabilities	$ 312,000	$ 690,000
Long-term liabilities	756,000	360,000
Total liabilities	$1,068,000	$1,050,000
Common stock	$ 588,000	$ 450,000
Retained earnings	84,000	60,000
Total stockholders' equity	$ 672,000	$ 510,000
Total liabilities and stockholders' equity	**$1,740,000**	**$1,560,000**

Hillcountry Inc.
Comparative Income Statement
for the years ended December 31, 19X2 and 19X1

	YEARS ENDED DECEMBER 31	
	19X2	**19X1**
Sales (net)	$1,920,000	$1,719,000
Cost of goods sold	1,101,600	976,500
Gross margin on sales	$ 818,400	$ 742,500
Operating expenses:		
Selling expenses	409,200	330,000
General and administrative expenses	241,800	165,000
Total operating expenses	$ 651,000	$ 495,000
Net income	**$ 167,400**	**$ 247,500**

REQUIRED:

With amounts rounded to the nearest tenth of a percent:

1. Prepare:
   a. A comparative common-size balance sheet
   b. A comparative common-size income statement
2. Discuss the financial condition and operating results of the company, emphasizing favorable and unfavorable trends.

P14-3 The following information was taken from the financial statements of Block Company on December 31, 19X5.

Cash	$ 37,500
Accounts receivable	62,500
Inventory	50,000
Fixed assets (net)	250,000
Total assets	**$400,000**
Accounts payable	$ 50,000
Bond payable (due December 31, 19X9)	150,000
Capital stock ($10 par)	150,000
Retained earnings	50,000
Total liabilities & Owners' Equity	**$400,000**
Net income	**$ 25,000**

REQUIRED:

Compute the following:

1. Current ratio
2. Working capital

3. Acid test ratio
4. Earnings per share
5. Debt to equity ratio

P14-4 Fair Oaks Company's condensed financial statements provide the following information:

Balance Sheet

	DEC. 31, 19X1	DEC. 31, 19X0
Cash	$ 20,000	$ 30,000
Accounts receivable (net)	50,000	40,000
Marketable securities (short-term)	40,000	20,000
Inventories	220,000	180,000
Prepaid expenses	1,500	3,500
Total current assets	$331,500	$273,500
Property, plant, and equipment (net)	318,500	326,500
Total assets	**$650,000**	**$600,000**
Current liabilities	$100,000	$ 80,000
Bonds payable	200,000	200,000
Common stockholders' equity	350,000	320,000
Total liabilities and stockholders' equity	**$650,000**	**$600,000**

Income Statement
for the year ended 19X1

Sales	$ 500,000
Cost of goods sold	(350,000)
Gross profit	$ 150,000
Selling and administrative expense	(53,000)
Less: Income tax	$(12,000)
Net income	**$ 85,000**

INSTRUCTIONS:

a. Determine the following:
   (1) Current ratio at December 31, 19X1.
   (2) Acid test ratio at December 31, 19X1.
   (3) Accounts receivable turnover for 19X1.
   (4) Inventory turnover for 19X1.

(5) Rate of return on assets for 19X1.
(6) Rate of return on common stock equity for 19X1.

b. Prepare a brief evaluation of the financial condition of the Fair Oaks Company.

P14-5 As loan analyst for the Friendly National Bank, you have been presented the following information:

Assets

	DALE CO.	FRED CO.
Cash	$ 170,000	$ 500,000
Receivables	274,000	424,000
Inventories	900,000	920,000
Total current assets	$1,344,000	$1,844,000
Other assets	970,000	1,254,000
Total assets	**$2,314,000**	**$3,098,000**

Liabilities and Owners' Equity

Current liabilities	$ 500,000	$ 640,000
Long-term liabilities	800,000	1,000,000
Capital stock and retained earnings	1,014,000	1,458,000
Total liabilities and capital	**$2,314,000**	**$3,098,000**
Annual sales	2,000,000	3,000,000
Rate of gross profit on sales	30%	40%

Each of these companies has requested a loan of $100,000 for 6 months with no collateral offered. The bank has reached its quota for loans of this type, only one of these requests is to be granted.

INSTRUCTIONS:

Which of the two companies, as judged by the information given here, would you recommend as the better risk and why?

P14-6 Shown here are partially completed comparative financial statements for the Wardlaw Company.

Wardlaw Company
Comparative Balance Sheet
December 31, 19X5 and 19X4

	19X5		19X4		INCREASE (DECREASE)	
	Amount	**Percent of Total Assets**	**Amount**	**Percent of Total Assets**	**Dollars**	**Percent**
ASSETS						
Current assets:						
Cash	$ 110,000		$ 100,000			
Net accounts receivable	400,000		350,000			
Inventories	600,000		450,000			
Prepaid expenses	90,000		100,000			
Total current assets	$1,200,000		$1,000,000			
Land, buildings, and equipment (net)	2,800,000		2,500,000			
Total assets	**$4,000,000**		**$3,500,000**			
LIABILITIES						
Current Liabilities:						
Accounts payable	$ 600,000		$ 700,000			
Notes payable	400,000		200,000			
Total current liabilities	$1,000,000		$ 900,000			
Bonds payable	1,000,000		1,000,000			
Total liabilities	$2,000,000		$1,900,000			
STOCKHOLDERS' EQUITY						
Common stock ($20 par)	$1,200,000		$1,200,000			
Retained earnings	800,000		400,000			
Total liabilities and stockholders equity	**$4,000,000**		**$3,500,000**			

Wardlaw Company
Comparative Income Statement
for the years ended December 31, 19X5 and 19X4

	19X5		19X4		INCREASE (DECREASE)	
	Dollars	**Percent of Sales**	**Dollars**	**Percent of Sales**	**Dollars**	**Percent**
Net Sales	$6,000,000		$4,000,000			
Cost of goods sold	4,200,000		3,000,000			
Gross profit on sales	$1,800,000		$1,000,000			
Operating expenses						
Selling expenses:	$ 800,000		$ 400,000			
Administrative expenses	200,000		100,000			
Total operating expenses	$1,000,000		$ 500,000			
Operating income	$ 800,000		$ 500,000			
Interest expense	80,000		60,000			
Income before income taxes	$ 720,000		440,000			
Income taxes	$,180,000		90,000			
Net income	**$ 540,000**		**$ 350,000**			

Wardlaw Company
Comparative Statement of Retained Earnings
for the years ended December 31, 19X5 and 19X4

	19X5	19X4	INCREASE (DECREASE) Dollars	Percent
Retained earnings, Jan. 1	$400,000	$150,000		
Net income	540,000	350,000		
	$940,000	$500,000		
Less: Dividends	140,000	100,000		
Retained earnings, Dec. 31	**$800,000**	**$400,000**		

REQUIRED:

1. Complete the statements just presented for Wardlaw Company.
2. Calculate the following ratios for 19X5:
   a. Profit margin on sales
   b. Return on total assets
   c. Return on owners' investment
   d. Earnings per share
   e. Current ratio
   f. Quick ratio
   g. Debt to equity ratio
   h. Owners' equity to total assets
   i. Debt to total assets ratio
   j. Times interest earned
   k. Price earnings ratio (assume the stock is selling for $90 per share)
   l. Dividend yield (assume the stock is currently paying a dividend of $2.70 per share)
   m. Accounts receivable turnover
   n. Average age of receivables
   o. Inventory turnover
   p. Average age of inventory

15 THE EMERGING ISSUES: Inflation Accounting, Accounting for International Activity, and Accounting Theory

ORIENTATION

Accounting is a dynamic discipline—it is changing constantly. The changes that occur are largely the result of the accounting profession responding to changes in the ways companies do business and to changes in the environmental (external) factors which affect those businesses. In addition to simply reacting to change, the accounting profession is continually attempting to improve itself and the principles that govern accounting practice throughout the United States.

Certainly two of the more important external factors affecting business in recent years have been the inflation that has existed in varying degrees in recent times, and the increasing internationalization of the world economy. This chapter focuses on these two external factors and how the accounting profession has reacted to them. First, the effects of inflation on traditional accounting statements is explored, together with the prescribed remedies to combat the distortive effects that it is perceived to have on financial statements. Second, the area of accounting in an international business environment is explored. It is probably safe to say that, unlike twenty-five years ago, most companies of any size either buy or sell internationally. When goods are purchased and sold internationally it is normally necessary to deal in more than one currency, with the relative value of those currencies changing daily. This chapter deals with those problems.

Finally, the various concepts and principles which govern accounting are synopsized. Many of these principles have been introduced individually throughout the various preceding chapters. Taken together, these rules, standards, and principles are commonly referred to as generally accepted accounting principles (GAAP). The reasoning and thought processes which underlie the development of these principles are known as accounting theory.

FINANCIAL REPORTING AND CHANGING PRICES

It has been pointed out throughout this book that one of the primary purposes of the accounting function is to provide information for decision making. Sophisticated decision makers such as investors, creditors, and management realize that financial statements at times do not reflect certain current economic realities. One of the basic realities that many believe is omitted from current financial statements is changing price levels. As a result, it has been suggested that financial statements would be more meaningful if historical costs used in statement preparation were adjusted to reflect the changing value of the dollar. This sentiment on the part of accountants for these adjusted financial statements understandably becomes more acute when inflation increases, and such sentiment seems to moderate with the moderation of inflation.

As Table 15-1 indicates, the price of goods and services in the United States has been rising for many years. As the general price level increases, the purchasing power of the dollar decreases. The general price level is the weighted average of the prices of goods and services in the economy. It is measured by using a base year with an assigned value of 100. Thus if Year 1 = 100 and Year 2 = 108 the inflation rate from Year 1 to Year 2 is 8 percent

$$\frac{108 - 100}{100} = .08$$

If in Year 3 the index is 113.4, the inflation rate from *Year 1 to Year 3* is 13.4 percent

$$\frac{113.4 - 100.0}{100.0} = .134$$

However, the inflation rate from *Year 2 to Year 3* is 5 percent

$$\frac{113.4 - 108.0}{108.0} = .05^{1}$$

[1] Rate of inflation $= \dfrac{It - It_1}{It_1}$

TABLE 15-1

United States Inflation Rates
(Based on the Consumer Price Index) 1964 to 1983

YEAR	CONSUMER PRICE INDEX (1967 = 100)	INFLATION RATE	PURCHASING POWER OF DOLLAR (1983 = $1.00)
1964	92.9	1.3%	$3.27
1965	94.5	1.7	3.21
1966	97.2	2.9	3.12
1967	100.0	2.9	3.04
1968	104.2	4.2	2.91
1969	109.8	5.4	2.77
1970	116.3	5.9	2.61
1971	121.3	3.7	2.50
1972	125.3	3.3	2.42
1973	133.1	6.2	2.28
1974	147.4	10.7	2.06
1975	161.2	9.4	1.88
1976	170.5	5.7	1.78
1977	181.5	6.4	1.67
1978	195.4	7.7	1.55
1979	217.4	11.3	1.40
1980	246.8	13.5	1.23
1981	272.4	10.4	1.12
1982	289.1	6.1	1.05
1983	303.5	5.0	$1.00

The reciprocal of the general price-level index represents the purchasing power of the dollar. So if the price-level index is increasing, the purchasing power of the dollar is decreasing. Thus if the index in Year 1 = 100 and in Year 5 = 125, the inflation rate from Year 1 to Year 5 equals 25 percent, and the Year 5 purchasing power of the dollar amounts to only 80 percent (100 ÷ 125 = .80) of the base year dollar.

The most frequently used measurements of the general price level are the *Consumer Price Index* (CPI), the *Producer Price Index,* and the *Gross National Product Implicit Price Deflator.* The Consumer Price Index and related purchasing power and inflation rates are depicted in Table 15-1.

Historical Cost Profit—A "True" Profit?

It is arguable that in periods of extreme inflation, profits based on historical cost are somewhat misleading. For example, several U.S. industries, such as the steel industry, have many plant assets which were purchased and put into service many years ago when the general price level was much lower than at the present time. These assets are now being depreciated based on the costs of those assets when purchased. This results in a relatively low depreciation expense figure, which in turn results in a higher net income. However, if these plant assets were being depreciated at their current market values, or their cost to replace, the depreciation figure would be much larger, and the net income would be reduced. Therefore, many accountants believe that failure to adjust numbers in financial statements to reflect value changes stemming solely from changes in the price level constitutes a departure from current economic reality.

Another example of how the failure to adjust for inflation might distort economic reality in financial statements can be seen through an illustration involving inventory. Assume that DAS Company purchased and sold an inventory item with the following characteristics:

DATE	ACTIVITY	PRICE	PRICE-LEVEL INDEX	REPLACEMENT COST
Jan. 19X1	Bought inventory item	$200	100.0	$200
Dec. 19X1	Sold inventory item	$218	115.0	$216

Under traditional historical cost accounting, the profit on the transaction would be $18 ($218 − $200). In reporting that $18 profit there is an implicit assumption that management should "receive credit" for achieving that profit (instead of a loss). However, there is a question as to whether management should be credited for achieving a profit. Did they, in fact, operate efficiently, or did they simply ride the wave of inflation when buying and selling an inventory item would result in a "paper" inventory profit?

To illustrate let us assume that we adjusted the cost of the inventory item to reflect the general increase in the price level:

$200 × 1.15 =	$230
Selling price	− 218
Loss	($ 12)

Under this situation the company "gained" $30 by holding the inventory item, and then lost $12 by selling it.

Gain from holding inventory item ($230 − $200)	$30
Less: Loss on sale ($218 − $230)	12
Net gain on the transaction	$18

Many feel that if it were possible to present all transactions that affect a business in the manner just presented, it would allow the decision maker to know the extent to which profits reported were the result of inflation, or the result of expertise.

Another way to present the activity relating to our imaginary inventory item is to use current replacement costs. When we purchased the item it obviously had a replacement cost of what we purchased it for—$200. When we sold the item for $218 it had a replacement cost of $216. So, although the general rate of inflation for the period had been 15 percent

$$\frac{(115.0 - 100.0)}{100.0} = .15$$

the price of that particular inventory item has increased by 8 percent

$$\frac{(\$216 - \$200)}{\$200} = .08.$$

So adjusting our profit for changes in the specific price of the item we obtain the following profit figure:

Selling price	$218
Current replacement cost	216
Gain	$ 2

The amount of profit or loss determined under unadjusted historical cost, and the two "inflation accounting" alternatives are present below:

		"INFLATION ACCOUNTING"	
	Unadjusted Historical Cost	**Adjusted for General Inflation**	**Adjusted for Changes in Specific Prices**
Selling price	$218	$218	$218
Cost of goods sold	200	230	216
Profit (Loss)	$ 18	($ 12)	$ 2

Two Approaches to the Problem

The two approaches to the problem presented in the foregoing example are referred to as *constant-dollar accounting* and *current-value accounting*.

Constant-Dollar Accounting

In constant-dollar accounting, a dollar is valued in terms of its ability to purchase a number of items in general. This is commonly referred to as the "purchasing power" of the dollar. Therefore, all amounts are expressed in units of equal purchasing power. A general price level (such as the Consumer Price Index) is used to restate historical costs. This method shows the effects of changes in the *general* price level, not changes in price of particular items. Constant-dollar accounting is often referred to as *general-price-level* accounting.

Current-Value Accounting

The second approach, called current-value accounting, shifts from historical costs to some measure of the current values. Under this method items in financial statements are presented at their current value, or the current cost to replace those resources. The current replacement cost of a specific item may rise or fall at a different rate from the general price level. Therefore, current-value accounting reflects the effects of changes in specific prices, rather than changes in the general price level. Current-value accounting is often referred to as *current-cost accounting.*

It is interesting to note that although these methods are ways of adjusting for the effects of changing prices on financial statements, only one method, current-value accounting, is actually a departure from historical cost. Under current-value accounting, historical cost is abandoned in favor of some measure of current value. However, under constant-dollar accounting, financial statements continue to be measured in historical costs, but those historical costs are adjusted by a general index. Under constant-dollar accounting the measurement unit is changed but the *means* of measurement offered by the historical cost reporting model is retained.

FASB Statement No. 33 Requirements

Each of the methods just illustrated results in a different definition of cost and income. The question confronting the accounting profession is which of these alternative measures is most useful to decision makers. This question has been under consideration for some time by those responsible for the establishment of accounting standards. Thus far the most definitive pronouncement in this regard has been FASB Statement No. 33, "Financial Reporting and Changing Prices," which was issued by the Financial Accounting Standards Board in 1979.

Statement No. 33 is applied to publicly held companies that have either

— Inventories and property, plant, and equipment (before deducting accumulated depreciation) amounting to more than $125 million;

— Total assets amounting to more than $1 billion (after deducting accumulated depreciation.[2]

Statement No. 33 *does not require* that changes be made in the *primary* financial statements. Rather it requires that certain information be presented as supplementary schedules in the published financial statements. The primary supplementary disclosures required by Statement No. 33 include net income calculated using both of the two concepts (constant dollars and current value) we discussed previously. Also required by Statement No. 33 are calculations of gains or losses in purchasing power which result from holding monetary assets or having monetary liabilities.

Purchasing Power Gains and Losses

Monetary assets and liabilities are those items representing a claim in a fixed number of dollars. There is no possibility that the value of a monetary item will go up or down because of the changing value of the dollar. For example, cash, accounts and notes receivable, and most liabilities are monetary items. Cash is a monetary item because the amount deposited in a bank is fixed in terms of what a company can receive from that deposit. The same is true for an account receivable. For example, assume that Hour Company sells $1,000 worth of goods on account in January 19X1, and does not collect the amount due until January 19X2. If during that time the purchasing power of the dollar has been shrinking (that is, the general price level is rising), the $1,000 that is collected in 19X2 will not be as valuable as the $1,000 in 19X1. Hour Company has therefore incurred a *purchasing power loss.*

The opposite is true for monetary liabilities. Assume, for example, that Day, Inc., borrows $500,000 in 19X1 to be repaid in 19X5. If inflation is occurring during the five-year period, then the money repaid in 19X5 is not as valuable as the money received in 19X1. Day, Inc., has experienced a *purchasing power gain* as the result.

Purchasing power gains and losses are calculated by applying the inflation rate to monetary items at the beginning of an accounting period and comparing that result to the monetary items at the end of an accounting period. To illustrate, assume that Point, Inc., held $50,000 in cash through 19X1 when the price level rose from 280.0 to 308.0, or 10 percent $(308.0 - 280.0) \div 280.0 = .10$. By the end of 19X1, Point, Inc., will have experienced a purchasing power loss of $5,000 as illustrated next.

[2] FASB Statement No. 33, "Financial Reporting and Changing Prices" (Stamford, Conn.: FASB, 1979), par. 23–25.

Number of dollars held at end of 19X1	\$50,000
Number of dollars needed to maintain same purchasing power as the \$50,000 held at beginning of 19X1 (50,000 × $\frac{308}{280}$)	55,000
Purchasing power loss for the year	\$ 5,000

The reverse situation is true regarding monetary liabilities. To illustrate, assume that Point, Inc., has a \$150,000 note payable outstanding throughout 19X1. The company would experience a purchasing power gain which would be calculated as follows:

Number of dollars at the end of 19X1 needed to represent the same purchasing power as the \$150,000 owned at the beginning of 19X1 (150,000 × $\frac{308}{280}$)	\$165,000
Number of dollars owed at the end of 19X1	150,000
Purchasing power gain	\$ 15,000

As can be readily observed from the foregoing examples, holding monetary assets during a period of inflation results in a purchasing power loss. In contrast, owing money during a period of inflation results in a purchasing power gain because liabilities will be repaid using dollars with less purchasing power than those originally borrowed.[3]

Accounting for Inflation—A Final Comment

There have been no major industrialized societies entirely free from some inflationary periods in the twentieth century. Consequently, as things stand now, balance sheets are being presented which include an amalgamation of dollars that could go back to the 1920s in some cases. Obviously, these 1920 dollars, or even 1970 dollars, are not the same as dollars in the 1980s. These dollars are currently being mixed together in financial statements as if they represented the same purchasing power. Constant-dollar accounting, and current-value accounting are efforts to address this problem.

Current-value accounting appears to be gaining some acceptance in many countries (Great Britain, Australia, and the Netherlands, for example). One factor contributing to the support of current-value accounting is that it is based

[3] It should be noted, however, that *interest rates* can generally be expected to rise along with the general price level as lenders seek to protect themselves from a purchasing power *loss*. To the extent lenders are successful, purchasing power *gains* from being a borrower in periods of inflation are limited.

on the values of specific items, whereas constant-dollar financial statements are more generic in that they are based on the general price level. It is important to note that a significant disadvantage of current-value accounting is its lack of objectivity. One of the advantages of the historical cost model is such objectivity; and constant-dollar financial statements are an extension of (not a departure from) historical cost. Therefore, although current-value accounting has the advantage of being more "situation specific" than constant-dollar accounting, the latter has the advantage of being more objective. It is possible that indexes measuring price changes in specific items may be a logical compromise to the problem. The specific price indexes might be the most objective and satisfactory method of obtaining current-value data in the future.

It is important to note that *both* constant-dollar and current-value accounting convey potentially useful information. The two approaches are not mutually exclusive, and often may be complementary. As research into inflation accounting continues, the rules governing this topic will continue to evolve. It appears possible that the emergence of refined accounting processes to disclose more clearly the effects of inflation will include both constant-dollar and current-value accounting.

INTERNATIONAL ACCOUNTING

In recent decades the world economy has become increasingly complex and international economic interdependence has greatly increased. Accounting has been significantly affected by these developments. Indeed, accounting has long been shaped by the course of events in the international economic system as well as domestic economic trends. Although not distinctly measurable, this evolutionary process is generally depicted in graphic form in Table 15-2.

The events represented in the table, which relate to the development of the accounting profession, are worth noting again here:

- 4000 B.C. Record keeping thought to have begun
- 3500 B.C. Oldest known commercial documents
- 630 B.C. First coined money (Greece)
- 1494 *Summa,* first book containing a description of bookkeeping is published
- 1835 American Institute of Accountants organized
- 1896 Legal sanction of the accounting profession in the U.S.
- 1913 Enactment of the 16th Amendment, the income tax law
- 1929 Stock market crash
- 1939 Committee on Accounting Procedure (CAP) formed
- 1959 Accounting Principles Board (APB) formed
- 1973 FASB formed
- 1973 International Accounting Standards Committee (IASC) formed

TABLE 15-2

Selected Key Events in the Evolution of Accounting

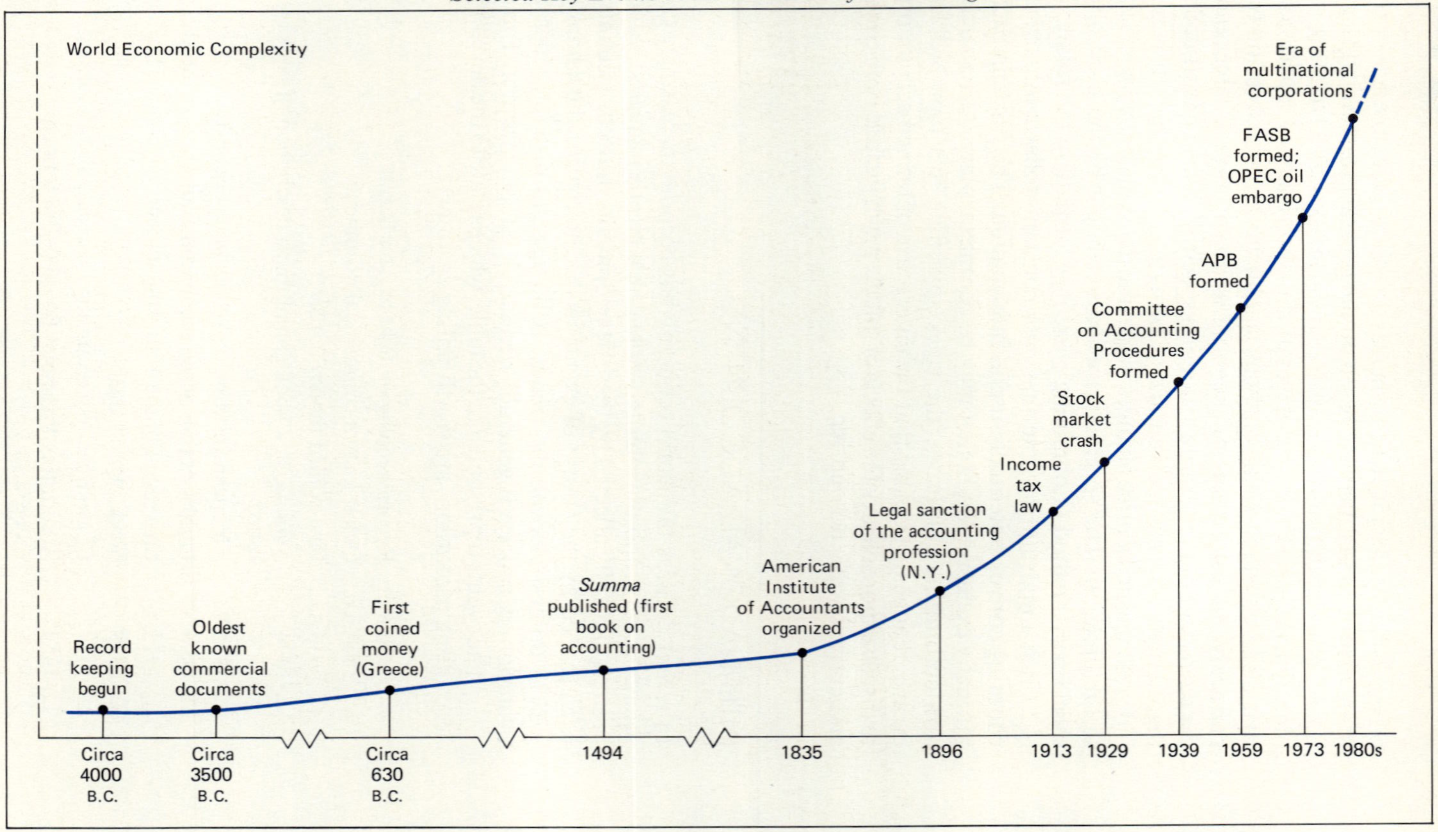

— 1973 OPEC oil embargo
— 1980 Era of multinational corporation and computer technology

To focus on economic developments in the twentieth century, we note that in the first half of this century the United States evolved from a group of regional economies to a strong national economy; and in the second half of the century this country has evolved from that position to a central role in an increasingly interdependent world economy.[4]

Although the United States is certainly an important element in the international economy, it is no longer the only economic force of major significance in the free world. Only a few years ago, when the economic well-being of the United States was still shaped primarily by events transpiring within our geographical borders, the country had a "political umbrella" over the economic system. Consequently, if economic difficulties emerged, the tools of domestic economic policy were relied upon to rectify the situation. Recent events have greatly reduced that degree of economic independence. The economic well-being of our country and other countries depends to a very large extent on international cooperation. We cannot, for example, pass a law requiring OPEC to change petroleum prices or outputs, or to reduce the attractiveness of Japanese cars or home computers to consumers in the United States. Many elements of our economic well-being now require international cooperation. We are currently in an increasingly complex and mutually reliant international economic system. Firms both within and outside the United States are becoming larger and more multinational in scope, and the world's industrial giants outside the United States are gaining strength. There is also a rise in the interchange of foreign securities — that is, there are more and more foreigners buying U.S. stocks and other U.S. securities as well as U.S. citizens investing abroad.[5]

Given these developments, it appears logical that reliable data should be available to provide information upon which to base international business decisions. Such a process of control and rational decision making requires a system of international communication. Historically, the primary formal means by which financial information of this type was transmitted was via accounting reports. However, currently each country has its own way of performing the accounting function, with some differences between countries being minor (as between Canada and the United States) and others major (as between Spain and Switzerland and the United States). It is important, therefore, if we are to operate effectively in today's business world, to recognize that

[4] A recent example of the increasingly multinational nature of contemporary businesses is the 1984 Ford Motor Company agreement to manufacture cars in Mexico, using largely Japanese parts, with the cars being sold primarily in the United States.

[5] In 1984, U.S. citizens were startled to learn that their country would apparently soon pass from the status of being a *creditor* nation to that of a *debtor* nation, as this country's debts to the rest of the world appeared well on the way to surpassing what the rest of the world owed the United States.

accounting systems differ worldwide, to understand the processes of foreign currency translation, and to understand how journal entries are to be made in international purchase and sale activities.

Basic International Monetary System

In order to completely appreciate the complexities involved in the accounting function of a company doing business internationally, one must first have a basic understanding of the organization and activities of the foreign exchange market. It is through this market that companies (and individuals) buy and sell foreign currencies with which to conduct international operations and investment.

To maximize the economic potential that is available through foreign trade, businesses should be prepared to quote sales in either U.S. dollars or the local currency of the buyer. Similarly, businesses should be prepared to bid for foreign products in local currencies.

Exchange Rate

An *exchange rate* is the price of one national currency in relation to another currency at a given time. Exchange rate quotations can be obtained from a number of sources, such as the *Wall Street Journal.* Table 15-3 provides a typical example of such quotations. The rates are listed in selling rates, and two rates are usually listed for each day: the *direct* quote, and the *indirect* quote. The first two columns contain the direct quote, which is the amount of local currency equivalent to one unit of foreign exchange. The second two columns contain the indirect quote, which is the amount of foreign currency required for one unit of the local currency. For example, in referring to Table 15-3, each French franc cost .1168 (11.68¢) on Monday, and each U.S. dollar sold for 8.561 French francs on that same day. (The "forward rates" shown in the table pertain to purchases and sales of the currency for future delivery).

The foreign currency market is similar in many respects to the stock market in that the exchange rates, like stock prices, continually fluctuate. In the stock market, good news about a listed corporation can result in increased demand for the stock and a resulting increase in its selling price, and vice versa for "bad news." The foreign exchange market is basically governed by the same principle. Such factors as balance of payments figures, rates of inflation, domestic interest rates, and national budget deficits can be important in determining the supply and demand for a given currency.

Historically this exchange rate uncertainty was thought to be a major impediment to international trade. In an attempt to surmount this problem, an agreement was signed by the major industrial nations of the world at Bretton Woods, New Hampshire, in 1944. The agreement (which also created the International Monetary Fund) established fixed exchange rates for currencies based on an official exchange rate. Using pre–World War II trade patterns as a

TABLE 15-3
Foreign Exchange

The New York foreign exchange selling rates here apply to trading among banks in amounts of $1 million and more, as quoted at 3 P.M. Eastern time by Bankers Trust Co. Retail transactions provide fewer units of foreign currency per dollar.

	U.S. $ EQUIV.		CURRENCY PER U.S. $	
Country	**Mon**	**Fri**	**Mon**	**Fri**
Argentina (Peso)	.02226	.02226	44.91	44.91
Australia (Dollar)	.8585	.8630	1.1648	1.1587
Austria (Schilling)	.05102	.05139	19.60	19.46
Belgium (Franc)				
Commercial rate	.01759	.01768	56.840	56.55
Financial rate	.01736	.01744	57.620	57.350
Brazil (Cruzeiro)	.0005977	.0005977	1673.00	1673.00
Britain (Pound)	1.3513	1.3570	.7400	.7369
30-Day Forward	1.3549	1.3606	.7381	.7350
90-Day Forward	1.3609	1.3666	.7348	.7317
180-Day Forward	1.3705	1.3759	.7297	.7268
Canada (Dollar)	.7592	.7580	1.3171	1.3193
30-Day Forward	.7591	.7579	1.3173	1.3194
90-Day Forward	.7590	.7577	1.3176	1.3198
180-Day Forward	.7586	.7573	1.3183	1.3205
Chile (Official rate)	.01101	.01101	90.84	90.84
China (Yuan)	.4461	.4461	2.2417	2.2417
Colombia (Peso)	.01015	.01015	98.57	98.57
Denmark (Krone)	.09768	.09811	10.2375	10.1925
Ecuador (Sucre)				
Official rate	.01599	.01599	62.52	62.52
Floating rate	.01125	.01125	88.85	88.85
Finland (Markka)	.1691	.1698	5.9150	5.8900
France (Franc)	.1168	.1172	8.5610	8.5300
30-Day Forward	.1168	.1172	8.5605	8.5325
90-Day Forward	.1168	.1172	8.5640	8.5355
180-Day Forward	.1165	.1168	8.5860	8.5580
Greece (Drachma)	.009074	.009091	110.20	110.00
Hong Kong (Dollar)	.1279	.1279	7.8180	7.8180
India (Rupee)	.08929	.08929	11.20	11.20
Indonesia (Rupiah)	.0009911	.0009911	1009.00	1009.00
Ireland (Punt)	1.0960	1.1005	.9124	.9087
Israel (Shekel)	.004505	.004505	222.00	222.00
Italy (Lira)	.0005813	.0005851	1720.25	1709.00
Japan (Yen)	.004193	.004213	238.50	237.35
30-Day Forward	.004215	.004234	237.24	236.18
90-Day Forward	.004257	.004234	234.90	233.88
180-Day Forward	.004328	.004344	231.05	230.22

(continued)

TABLE 15-3 (*continued*)
Foreign Exchange

	U.S. $ EQUIV.		CURRENCY PER U.S. $	
Country	**Mon**	**Fri**	**Mon**	**Fri**
Lebanon (Pound)	.1653	.1653	6.05	6.05
Malaysia (Ringgit)	.4306	.4313	2.23225	2.3185
Mexico (Peso)				
Floating rate	.004975	.004975	201.00	201.00
Netherlands (Guilder). .	.3185	.3191	3.1400	3.1335
New Zealand (Dollar). .	.6330	.6343	1.5798	2.5765
Norway (Krone)	.1247	.1252	8.0170	7.9845
Pakistan (Rupee)	.07194	.07194	13.90	13.90
Peru (Sol)	.0003163	.0003163	3161.85	3161.85
Philippines (Peso).....	.05583	.05583	17.912	17.912
Portugal (Escudo).....	.006849	.006897	146.00	145.00
Saudi Arabia (Rival)...	.2848	.2848	3.5110	3.5110
Singapore (Dollar)	.4681	.4690	2.1365	2.1320
South Africa (Rand)...	.7305	.7390	1.3689	1.3532
South Korea (Won)....	.001251	.001251	799.20	799.20
Spain (Peseta)........	.006307	.006351	158.55	157.45
Sweden (Krona)	.1220	.1222	8.1975	8.1850
Switzerland (Franc)....	.4272	.4292	2.3410	2.3300
30-Day Forward ...	.4301	.4322	2.3249	2.3140
90-Day Forward ...	.4357	.4377	2.2951	2.2845
180-Day Forward ...	.4453	.4469	2.2455	2.2375
Taiwan (Dollar).......	.02508	.02508	39.87	39.87
Thailand (Baht).......	.04351	.04351	22.985	22.985
Uruguay (New Peso)				
Financial	.01909	.01909	52.38	52.38
Venezuela (Bolivar)				
Official rate	.1333	.1333	7.50	7.50
Floating rate	.07052	.07052	14.18	14.18
W. Germany (Mark)...	.3585	.3596	2.7895	2.7810
30-Day Forward ...	.3605	.3615	2.7738	2.7661
90-Day Forward ...	.3643	.3653	2.7452	2.7375
180-Day Forward ...	.3703	.3720	2.7003	2.6885
– – –				
SDR................	1.02884	1.03121	.971971	.969734

Special Drawing Rights are based on exchange rates for the U.S., West German, British, French, and Japanese currencies. Source: International Monetary Fund.

z-Not quoted.

Source: Wall Street Journal

basis, these nations arrived at a system of exchange rate parities by defining the value of their currencies in terms of gold or certain "reserve currencies" (primarily the U.S. dollar) that were readily convertible into gold. (At that time the gold equivalent of the U.S. dollar was $35 an ounce). Once a currency's official rate was pegged, the country was required to maintain its exchange rate within a range of plus or minus 1 percent of the pegged rate.

This fixed exchange-rate system was in operation for more than twenty-five years. During that period, business was assured of relative stability in currency values, and international commerce expanded enormously. The system began to falter in the early 1970s, primarily because there was no flexible mechanism for currencies to adjust to the dynamics of the world economy. The rapid rebuilding and economic growth of Japan and Europe, and the consequent sharp shifts in trade and capital flows, were not reflected in the fixed exchange rates, which remained relatively rigid under the terms of the Bretton Woods Agreement.

In December 1971, the U.S. dollar was formally devalued and currencies were allowed to float 2¼ percent on either side of par. Continued pressure on the dollar resulted in another devaluation in 1973, and finally resulted in the abandonment of the fixed exchange-rate system. Today, foreign exchange rates are determined primarily by free market forces, or a so-called "floating" exchange-rate system. (Government intervention is termed "dirty floating.")

The International Monetary Fund

The International Monetary Fund (IMF) was established in 1944 as a permanent institution to provide the machinery for consultation and collaboration on international monetary and balance of payment adjustment problems. According to its Articles of Agreement, the purposes of the IMF were to promote international monetary cooperation, facilitate the expansion of international trade for the sake of high levels of employment and real income, promote exchange rate stability and avoid competitive depreciation, work for a multilateral system of current international payments and for elimination of exchange controls over current transactions, create confidence among member nations and give them the opportunity to correct balance-of-payments maladjustments, and make balance-of-payments disequilibriums shorter and less severe than they would be otherwise.

Essentially the IMF acts as a technical advisor to nation's experiencing currency problems. It is also a source of operating funds, created by member subscription quotas, which may be available to help overcome temporary difficulties in members' international balance of payments.

It should be noted that the IMF does not intervene directly in the foreign exchange market. It will assist the government of a member country by lending it an internationally accepted currency. The country receiving the money will then use it as a means of temporary intervention in the foreign exchange market until more fundamental economic measures return its balance of payments to equilibrium. Since the inception of the IMF, it has assisted in easing many financial crises and has generally proven to be a valuable stabilizing factor in the international monetary system.

Foreign Exchange Trading

Spot and Forward Markets

Trading in foreign exchange is an activity in which many large international banks are involved. The foreign exchange trader deals in the present *(spot)* and future *(forward)* markets.

When a sale or purchase is made spot, it means that delivery of the foreign currency must be made simultaneously at a fixed date, normally no more than two business days after the sale or purchase was contracted. A forward exchange transaction involves the purchase or sale of a foreign currency for delivery at some fixed future date. The rate at which the transaction is concluded is set at the time of the contract, but the transfer of funds does not take place until the predetermined future date. The majority of forward contracts are for a period of from 30 to 180 days, but contracts can be concluded for longer periods, particularly in the more stable currencies.

Premiums, Discounts, and Spread

If a certain foreign currency is quoted at a higher forward rate than the spot rate, its forward rate is at a *premium.* If the spot rate is higher than the forward rate, it is said to be trading at a *discount.* Different forward rates may be quoted for different periods (30, 90, 180 days). It is possible that forward rates may be at a premium for one period, and at a discount for another.

The difference between the current buying and selling rates for a currency at a particular maturity date is referred to as the *spread.* For example, if the German mark is quoted at $0.5100–$0.5102, this indicates that at that moment a bank would pay 51¢ for a mark and would sell at 51.02¢, and the spread is .02¢.

Another illustration combining the concepts of premium/discount and spread is seen in the forward contract area. On a given day a foreign exchange dealer might quote:

British Pounds—2.0400–.02
180 days—323 to 318 points discount

Therefore if a customer wanted to sell British pounds 180 days forward (the dealer buying), the dealer would bid $2.0077, or $2.0400 − .0323 (each 100 points is equal to 1¢). If the customer wanted to buy British pounds 180 days forward (the dealer selling), the dealer would offer 2.0084, or 2.0402 − .0318. The spread between the rates for which banks and other foreign exchange dealers buy and sell foreign currency is the margin upon which foreign exchange traders operate. The majority of bank transfers today are accomplished by cable communications between banks.

Instruments of Foreign Exchange

Bank Transfers

The main device for effecting foreign exchange transactions is the bank transfer. The principal method of transferring a deposit to or from a bank abroad is a cable transfer over the ocean or telegraphic transfer over land. Such transfers can also be made by mail. However, the speed of a cable or telegraphic transfer gives these methods tremendous advantage over the mail transfer.

A cable transfer is an order transmitted by cable to a foreign correspondent bank to make payment to a designated payee. It directs the foreign bank to debit the account of the seller of a particular currency and to credit the account designated by the buyer. Thus, the U.S. exporter who receives a Paris bank deposit in French francs in payment for his goods, may desire to sell the francs by means of a cable transfer to his New York bank account in dollars. The conversion rate for the transfer is determined by the current market rate between the two currencies. If the exporter has no French franc bank account, he may ask the payer to transfer the amount by cable directly to his New York bank, which purchases the exchange and credits the equivalent dollars to the exporter's account. The cost of sending the cable is charged by the bank to the sender.

Bills of Exchange

In addition to the cable, telegraphic, or mail transfers of bank balances, there are various bills of exchange used as foreign exchange instruments. Among these, checks, money orders, and sight drafts effect immediate cash payments; time drafts provide for deferred payments.

Personal checks have become increasingly important as a means of international cash payment, and those of reputable international corporations are commonly accepted in all parts of the world. Dividend and bond interest payments are often sent by check to foreign stockholders and bondholders as well as to domestic holders. Travelers checks and money orders in hard currencies are also widely accepted.

Foreign Currency Notes and Coins

Besides the use of bank transfers and bills of exchange, foreign transactions can also be settled by payment in the actual currency, that is, the currency notes and coins of the foreign country. Tourists traveling abroad use this means of international cash payment as their chief foreign exchange instrument. Also, U.S. merchants and others, particularly in the border areas, use a fairly large volume of Canadian and Mexican currency. The use of foreign currency notes as an instrument of foreign exchange is an important one, but it is practically limited to smaller transactions.

Accounting for Foreign Exchange Transactions

Often a company involved in foreign operations will engage in a cable transfer of funds to or from a foreign branch or subsidiary. This type of tansaction is generally recorded at the spot rate in existence on the date of the transfer. Other, more frequent, dealings in foreign exchange might occur as a result of buying or selling goods abroad.

The export and import business of the United States with other parts of the world originated in U.S. colonial days. The procedure for handling foreign trade shipments are rooted in early commercial practices. Modern banking, transportation, and communications has facilitated the negotiation, movement, and financing of foreign trade. The export-import balance of trade is a significant element in the international balance-of-payments position of any country.

Like domestic trade, overseas trade can be financed through open account, consignments of merchandise, or advance cash deposits. However, the greatest part of overseas trade transactions are handled through the use of letters of credit and bank drafts. Each of these financing methods, along with the specialized authority-to-purchase procedure, serves a purpose in foreign trade.

Letters of Credit

A letter of credit is an instrument issued by a bank at the request of one party authorizing that party or a designated second party to draw a check or draft against that bank, or one of its correspondents, for a designated sum payable either on demand, at a specified time, or upon presentation of specified documents which usually give title to the goods. These documents include the papers covering the shipment, such as the bill of lading, plus other documents essential to the export or import of the goods.

Drafts

A substantial volume of U.S. exports is financed by dollar drafts. For imports, drafts are used only in specific appropriate circumstances. The dollar draft as a foreign instrument may be either a time draft or a sight draft. In foreign trade transactions, such drafts are often accompanied by the shipping documents.

Advance Deposits

A very small amount of foreign trade is financed by advance deposits. This method is used when credit risks are doubtful. Certain conditions, such as foreign exchange restrictions or political and economic disturbances, may force the seller into negotiating the no-risk transaction by demanding cash in advance.

Credit on Open Account

For a few well-known, reputable international firms, foreign trade is handled on an open account basis, in the same way as domestic transactions. Besides the delayed payment risk associated with domestic transactions, there is the disadvantage in foreign trade of the added time involved in the goods shipment. Without a tangible obligation upon shipment of the goods, the exporter may be hindered in using the immediate export sale as a basis for obtaining credit from a financial institution.

Foreign Shipment Terms

In the negotiating of foreign trade transactions, the quoted price specifically excludes or includes certain related shipping costs. Besides the customary domestic freight shipment terms, FOB (free on board) shipping point and FOB destination, there are several other terms commonly used in foreign trade practice. They include FAS (free alongside), C&F (cost and freight), and CIF (cost, insurance, and freight). The standard U.S. definitions of the main foreign trade terms used are published by the International Chamber of Commerce.

Just as in domestic trade, the seller must bear all risks and, unless otherwise specified, all costs until title passes to the buyer at the stipulated point of transfer. Export costs include such items as packing, transportation to point of transfer, documentation fees, sailing registration fees, and insurance as designated by the terms. Usually the foreign duties and export taxes must be paid by the buyer.

Accounting for Foreign Trade

Foreign Sales

An exporter may bill the foreign purchaser in domestic or foreign currency. If the invoice is in domestic currency (for example, U.S. dollars for a U.S. exporter) the seller bears no risk resulting from an exchange rate fluctuation occurring between the date of invoice and the date of payment. The foreign purchaser must pay in U.S. dollars, and the transaction is recorded identically to a sale made domestically.

When export sales are billed in foreign currency, the seller assumes the risk of fluctuations in the exchange rates from the time of the sale until collection. The seller then has the option of waiting until collection is made and assuming the full risk, or entering into the forward contract market for the sale of foreign exchange in order to fix the amount of home currency to be received (at the forward rate).

Assume ACE Exporters, a U.S. company, sold goods to Black Forest Importers for 500,000 deutsche marks (DM) on March 3, 19X1 and billed the German company in deutsche marks. ACE Exporters allowed 90-day terms, and the German company pays the amount due on June 3, 19X1. The exchange rates which were in effect were as follows:

March 3, 19X1	Spot .39	
March 3, 19X1	90-day forward	.3890 (10 point discount)
June 3, 19X1	Spot .3796	

If ACE Exporters had chosen *not* to enter into the forward market, the journal entries to record the sale and collection would be:

19X1			
Mar. 3	Accounts receivable: Black Forest Importers	$195,000	
	Sales		195,000
	To record sale (DM500,000 × .39 = $195,000)		
June 3	Cash	189,800	
	Exchange gains and losses	5,200	
	Accounts receivable: Black Forest Importers		195,000
	To record remittance from Black Forest Importers (DM500,000 × .3796 = $189,800)		

In this situation, the U.S. company suffered an exchange loss of $5,200 ($195,000 − $189,800). However, it could have easily suffered a greater loss if the rate had fallen more, or it could have experienced an exchange rate gain if the deutsche mark had moved in the opposite direction.

To avoid this foreign exchange "exposure," ACE Exporters could have entered into a forward contract on March 3, 19X1. Under the terms of the contract ACE Exporters would agree to sell DM500,000, 90 days forward. If they would have done this with International Bank when the 90-day forward rate was .3890, the journal entries to record the sale, forward contract, and payment would be as follows:

19X1			
Mar. 3	Accounts receivable: Black Forest Importers	$195,000	
	Sales		$195,000
	To record sale (DM500,000 × .39 = $195,000)		
Mar. 3	Due from International Bank	194,500	
	Deferred Discount on Forward Contract	500	
	Liability for exchange sold		195,000
	To record forward contract (DM500,000 × .3890 = $194,500)		
June 3	Foreign exchange (DM)	189,800	
	Foreign exchange gains and losses	5,200	
	Accounts receivable: Black Forest		195,000

(continued)

To record remittance (DM500,000 × .3796 = $189,800)	
The loss is calculated as follows:	
Amount due in U.S. dollars:	$195,000
Amount due in U.S. dollars at current exchange rate (DM500,000 × .3796):	189,800
Loss:	$ 5,200

The loss of $5,200 would have been final had the U.S. company not entered into a forward contract. Because of the forward contract, a gain occurs which partially offsets the loss recorded above. The journal entries relating to the settling of the forward contract are as follows:

June 3:	Cash	$194,500	
	Due from International Bank		$194,500
	Liability for exchange sold	195,000	
	Foreign exchange gains and losses		5,200
	Foreign exchange		189,800
	To record Ace Company settling of forward contract		
	The gain is calculated as follows:		
	Amount due on forward contract in U.S. dollars (DM500,000 × .39)	$195,000	
	Amount paid on forward contract in U.S. dollars (DM500,000 × .3796)	189,800	
	Gain	$ 5,200	

The $5,200 gain is the result of ACE Company entering into a forward contract to "hedge" its potential losses. ACE experienced no foreign exchange gain or loss on the transaction. Nevertheless, ACE Company sustained a $500 cost because of the discount at the time of the forward contract negotiation. This discount, for hedges of monetary asset positions, is amortized over the life of the forward contract. The amount recorded as a deferred discount in the March 3 entry must be expressed as follows:

June 3:	Discount Amortization Expense	$500	
	Deferred Discount on Forward Contract		$500

Another, more simplistic way to look at the expense is to look at it as the difference between the revenue recorded from the sale on March 3, and the final cash received on June 3. This calculation is as follows:

Revenue recorded from the sale to Black Forest (March 3, 19X1)	$195,000
Cash received in settlement of the forward contract entered into hedging the sale to Black Forest (June 3, 19X1)	194,500
Loss	$ 500

If financial statements were prepared between March 3 and June 3 when the forward contract is in evidence, the account Due from International Bank would be shown as a current asset, offset by the account Liability for Exchange Sold which is considered a contra-asset account.

Foreign Purchase

If an importer is purchasing from a foreign company and is billed in U.S. dollars, the transaction is recorded the same as if it were a domestic transaction. However, if the importing company is billed in a foreign currency, it assumes the risk of the fluctuation in the currency values. One way to avoid the risk is to immediately buy the foreign currency and hold it until the payment becomes due.

To illustrate, assume the following: On May 1, 19X2, XYZ Company, a U.S. importer, purchased wooden shoes from the Netherlands and is billed in Dutch guilders (Dfls), terms net 30 days. The invoice amount is Dfls 100,000. The spot rate is .3650. To avoid an exchange rate risk, XYZ might purchase Dfls 100,000, immediately. If so, the entry to record the transaction would be as follows:

May 1, 19X2	Purchases	$36,500	
	Accounts payable: Dutch Co.		$36,500
	To record purchase (DFL100,000 × .3650)		
May 1, 19X2	Foreign exchange	36,500	
	Cash		36,500
	To record the purchase of Dfls (DFL100,000 × .3650).		
May 31, 19X2	Accounts payable: Dutch Co.	36,500	
	Foreign exchange		36,500
	To record payment		

If a balance sheet was prepared while the account payable is still outstanding, and the exchange rate had changed, both the account payable and the foreign exchange account would be revalued to the exchange rate prevailing on the balance sheet date.

Exchange Gains and Losses

In these illustrations, the exchange gains or losses were recorded as revenue or expense of the current period. Several theoretical questions may arise concerning the acceptance of this principle. They include the proper income or expense classification, and the allocation of the income or expense if the fluctuation occurs among two or more accounting periods. In connection with the allocation question, there is the problem as to when the gain or loss becomes realized and whether any unrealized gain or loss should be recorded. These are financial reporting problems.

An alternative to reporting the exchange gain or loss separately could be charging or crediting the appropriate purchases or sales account. As to import purchases, the general cost definition seems applicable. The cost means the sum of the applicable expenditures and charges directly or indirectly incurred in bringing the article to its existing condition and location.[6] Fluctuations in exchange rates occur after the article is brought to its existing location. They have no effect on the article's condition. The exchange gain or loss is not a function of procurement; it is a finance function, a decision to accept or avoid the risk involved in delayed payment. As discussed previously, the risk can be managed through hedging. As a financial expense or revenue, the exchange gain or loss should not be charged directly to the foreign sales or purchase account.[7]

Foreign Subsidiaries

When one company owns another, and the companies are operated separately, the two financial statements are essentially merged or added together at the end of each year for presentation to outsiders. This process of *consolidating* the financial statements is extremely involved, and is covered in detail in more advanced accounting books. The problems involved in consolidated financial statements are compounded when the subsidiary company is located in a foreign country and uses a foreign currency to transact business. In this case the financial statements prepared by the foreign subsidiary will be in a foreign currency, and will reflect transactions occurring at different and varying exchange rates. For example, a U.S. company might have a British subsidiary that does business primarily in Great Britain. The British company would keep its accounting records in terms of the British currency—pounds. The financial statements prepared by the British company might include a transaction such as the purchase of inventory when the British pound was selling for $1.90, the sale of a building when the pound was worth $1.75, and on and on.

---

[6] American Institute of Certified Public Accountants, *Restatement and Revision of Accounting Research Bulletins,* Accounting Research Bulletin No. 43 (New York: AICPA, 1953), p. 28.

[7] Norlin G. Rueschhoff, *International Accounting and Financial Reporting,* (New York: Praeger Publishers, 1976), p. 28.

So, the floating exchange-rate system created a problem in the translation of foreign currency financial statements into statements in U.S. dollars, in that the items contained in the foreign financial statements were commonly the result of transactions conducted at various exchange rates. To respond to this problem the Financial Accounting Standards Board issued FASB Statement No. 8 in 1975, effective for fiscal years beginning on or after January 1, 1976. This statement established standards of financial accounting and reporting for translating foreign currency financial statements into U.S. dollars for purposes of consolidation.[8]

The general provisions for the translation of foreign financial statements under FASB Statement No. 8 were:

1. The recorded amounts representing money or claims to money (e.g., cash, receivables, and payables) should be translated at each balance sheet date using the current rate.
2. Accounts carried in foreign currency financial statements on the basis of historical cost (e.g., property, land, goodwill) should be translated using historical rates.
3. Inventories should be translated at the lower of converted cost or converted market.
4. Revenues and expenses should be translated at the average rates in existence during the period.
5. With few exceptions, exchange gains and losses should be reflected in operations for the period in which the rate changes occur.[9]

This approach to the problem taken in FASB Statement No. 8, which is referred to as the "temporal" method, caused considerable criticism from certain members of the accounting profession and from the business community as well. Largely the criticism centered around the fact that companies felt that they often experienced "paper losses" from exchange rate changes which they were forced to report in their income statements.

An example of this type of situation would be when a U.S. company's German subsidiary borrowed 100,000 deutsche marks and purchased inventory when a DM cost .40. Assume that on the subsequent balance sheet date, the current rate of the deutsche mark was .50. The inventory would continue to be reported at cost ($40,000, or DM 100,000 × $.40); however, the debt would be recorded at $50,000 (DMM 100,000 × $.50). The loss of $10,000 would be reported on the income statement for the period. However, if the deutsche mark had fallen in value during the same period, no gain would have resulted because

[8] The first pronouncement by the FASB, Statement No. 1, "Disclosure of Foreign Currency Information," was issued in December 1973. As the title implies, that Statement was concerned exclusively with disclosure of foreign currency translation information and did not establish accounting standards to be followed in translating amounts stated in foreign currencies.

[9] Statement of Financial Accounting Standards No. 8, "Foreign Currency Translation" (Stamford, Conn.: FASB, 1976).

the inventory would have been restated at the lower figure (e.g., lower of translated cost or translated market).

Not surprisingly, many U.S. companies began to take action so that their foreign operations would not be subject to these losses. Many of these companies began to rematch their currently translatable assets with currently translatable liabilities; in other words, they began to pay off foreign debt.

On a macroeconomic basis there appears to be reason to believe that Statement No. 8 resulted in problems for the U.S. dollar. American companies were using dollars to buy foreign currencies to pay off strong currency debt in an effort to avoid "paper losses." The obvious impact of this action was an increase in the supply of U.S. dollars and an increase in the demand for certain foreign currencies. It could be argued that this resulted in a self-fulfilling prophecy: Statement No. 8 caused companies to act in such a way that pressure was put on the U.S. dollar and caused it to decline in world monetary markets. This, in turn, caused companies to continue to act in the same way.

In May 1979, in response to a recommendation that it undertake a formal post-enactment review process, the Board issued an Invitation for Public Comment on Statement No. 8. As a result of the responses, in January 1979, the Board added the reconsideration of Statement No. 8 to its agenda. In March 1980, the Board issued a statement of tentative views on the subject, most of which were included in the Exposure Draft issued on August 28, 1980, which ultimately lead to Statement No. 52 issued on December 7, 1981.

The primary provisions of Statement No. 52 are as follows:

1. The translation process requires that the functional currency of the entity be identified first. Ordinarily it will be the currency of the country in which the entity is located or the U.S. dollar. All financial statement elements of the foreign entity must then be measured in terms of the functional currency in conformity with U.S. generally accepted accounting principles.
2. Translation from the functional currency into the reporting currency, if they are different, is to be at the current exchange rate except that revenues and expenses are to be translated at the average exchange rates prevailing during the period. The functional currency translation approach generally considers the effect of exchange rate changes to be on the net investment in a foreign entity rather than on its individual assets and liabilities (as was the focus of SFAS 8).
3. Translation adjustments are not to be included in net income but are to be disclosed and accumulated as a separate component of stockholders' equity until such time that the net investment in the foreign entity is sold or completely or substantially liquidated. To the extent that the sale or liquidation represents realization, the relevant amounts should be removed from the separate entity component and included as a gain or loss in the determination of the net income of the period during which the sale or liquidation occurs.[10]

---

[10] Statement of Financial Accounting Standards No. 52, "Foreign Currency Translation" (Stamford, Conn.: FASB, 1981).

The impact of the current rate method promulgated in FAS No. 52 as compared to the temporal method advocated in Statement 8 is illustrated in the following example:

FOREIGN CURRENCY STATEMENTS		TRANSLATED AMOUNTS	
		Temporal Method	**Current-rate Method**
Assets		**(FAS No. 8)**	**(FAS No. 52)**
Cash & receivables	FC10,000	(.24) $ 2,400	(.24) $ 2,400
Inventory	16,000	(.22) 3,520	(.24) 3,840
Fixed assets (net)	30,000	(.18) 5,400	(.24) 7,200
	FC56,000	**$11,320**	**$13,440**
Liabilities and Stockholders' Equity			
Debt	FC20,000	(.24) $ 4,800	(.24) $ 4,800
Stockholders' equity	36,000	6,520	(.18) 6,480
Translation Adjustment			2,160[a]
	FC56,000	**$11,320**	**$13,440**

Rates: Appropriate historical: .18
Current: .24
Inventory (cost): .22

[a] Under FAS No. 8, the translation loss has been reflected in income and retained earnings over the period of decline in the exchange rate. Under SFAS No. 52 the translation gain would be credited directly to the translation adjustment account.

It is very important to note that under current accounting rules for foreign currency translation, any gain or loss resulting from the translation under the current rate method is included *directly* in the Owners' Equity section of the balance sheet, thereby bypassing the income statement. This is very similar to the treatment of gains and losses on fluctuations in the value of long-term investments which was mentioned briefly in Chapter 6. This represents a rather significant departure from accounting treatments which required that the only way a gain or loss could get into the Owners' Equity section of the balance sheet was through the closing process.

International Accounting Standards

Accounting in highly industrialized countries is, to a large degree, a pragmatic art. It is based on certain concepts and principles (entity, matching, materiality, and the like). Several of these concepts may be affected by different interpretations as to their applicability to business enterprises, but these principles are much more fundamentally affected by the culture of the country. The relative importance of an accounting standard can be discussed and debated rationally by a standard-setting body. However, because culture is a person's social heritage, the effect on the interpretation of accounting standards will be understood in relation to the basic cultures of the country.

Many countries with lower levels of industrialization have accounting systems with different degrees of sophistication; and many more advanced countries have significant differences in accounting rules. This lack of worldwide uniformity has caused some problems for companies and individuals investing abroad. Firms establishing foreign subsidiaries often have difficulty obtaining adequate, reliable, and timely reports, especially when the subsidiaries are run by nationals. Individuals wishing to invest in foreign markets find it difficult to obtain useful reports on which to base their investment decisions.

To help alleviate the "uniformity" problem, accounting institutes in ten countries (Australia, Canada, France, Germany, Japan, Mexico, the Netherlands, the United Kingdom, Ireland, and the United States) established the International Accounting Standards Committee (IASC) in 1973. Its purpose is to investigate and propose a set of accounting standards to be used in the preparation of financial statements for companies involved in international operations. Further, the OECD (Organization for Economic Co-operation and Development), representing twenty-four developed Western countries, has published a "code of conduct" setting forth guidelines for multinational enterprises for the disclosure of information for improved public understanding. Also, the United Nations Economic and Social Council is continually working on a code of conduct for transnational corporations, and the Inter-Governmental Working Group of Experts on International Standards of Accounting may provide guidelines on the listing of information disclosure items for transnational financial reporting. Regional bodies, such as the European Economic Community are establishing accounting standards as well.

BASIC ACCOUNTING THEORY

Throughout this book, we have referred to certain accounting principles or rules when they pertain directly, and help explain, particular accounting treatments being covered. This section of the book is designed to pull together these principles into one concise presentation. Another objective of this section is to further amplify on these principles in an effort to present the basic accounting theory which provides a foundation for the procedures presented earlier in this book. A complete understanding of financial accounting requires a knowledge of the *g*enerally *a*ccepted *a*ccounting *p*rinciples (GAAP) that govern the accumulation and presentation of information appearing on financial statements. A common definition of the word *principle* is: "A broad fundamental truth; a primary or basic law, or the like." Consequently, generally accepted accounting principles are broad rules adhered to by the accounting profession to guide the conduct of accounting practice.

The Development of Accounting Standards

The development of generally accepted accounting principles has been a long evolutionary process, which is continuing to this day. It was pointed out earlier in this chapter that record keeping was thought to have begun in about 4000 B.C. From that time until very recently individual accountants essentially "did their own thing." They were not bound by any formal rules which required certain financial transactions be accounted for in any certain way. Certainly tradition and general acceptance in accounting practice dictated the accounting treatment of the majority of transactions; but still it was not until very recently that these principles began to be codified.

Until the mid-1960s those accounting principles which were in writing were only considered to be recommendations of GAAP. They were not binding on the profession, and there was no strict requirement for adherence. The force of those principles depended largely on their general acceptance by the accounting profession. Acceptance was encouraged by persuasion; that is, by convincing accountants that these principles represented the best solution to a particular accounting problem. By the mid-1960s many in the profession became convinced that persuasion alone was an insufficient force to insure the comparability of financial reporting. Therefore in 1964 the governing body of the American Institute of Certified Public Accountants adopted a requirement which was incorporated into the rules of ethics for CPA's as follows:

> A member shall not express an opinion that financial statements are presented in conformity with generally accepted accounting principles if such statements contain any departure from an accounting principle promulgated by the body designated by council to establish such principles which has a material effect on the statements taken as a whole, unless the member can demonstrate that due to unusual circumstances the financial statements would otherwise have been misleading. In such cases his report must describe the departure, the approximate effects thereof, if practicable, and the reasons why compliance with the principle would result in a misleading statement.

In the 1970s there was a belief on the part of many in the accounting profession that the U.S. Congress was moving toward entering the accounting standard-setting arena. As part of a broad examination of various professions, the U.S. Senate and House of Representatives had separate subcommittees studying the accounting profession. In 1976, a Senate subcommittee released the results of a staff study entitled "The Accounting Establishment." Many accountants interpreted the staff study as a step toward government control of accounting standard setting and of the accounting profession. However, the subcommittee report which followed stated "that the subcommittee members preferred that the profession itself achieve reforms in cooperation with the SEC." Therefore, standard setting in accounting continues to reside with the FASB in the private sector, but it is influenced by the SEC, a public sector body.

The Objectives of Financial Reporting

For many years accountants have sought a basic conceptual framework or a grand design to guide current accounting practice and the establishment of accounting principles in the future. However, the profession still has a mixture of rules that have slowly evolved over many years of accounting practice and regulatory effort. In the late 1970s, in an effort to address this problem, the FASB began a major effort to develop some sort of basic conceptual framework. The Board plans to issue a series of Statements on Financial Accounting Concepts. To date the board has issued two statements.

Statement No. 1, issued in November 1978, is entitled "Objectives of Financial Reporting by Business Enterprises." In general, this statement concluded that the accounting profession should attempt to develop financial statements that a broad class of decision makers could use in evaluating business enterprises. Statement No. 1 did give accountants a general idea concerning the types of items to disclose in financial statements, however it did not describe specifically the characteristics of the information to be included.

Statement No. 2, issued in 1980, attempted to become more specific about the characteristics of the data to be used to produce the desired results.

The FASB concluded in Statement No. 2 that a "hierarchy" of accounting qualities exists. This hierarchy, depicted in Table 15-4, delineates the basic factors which should be considered in evaluating information for inclusion in published financial statements.

The hierarchy developed by the FASB acknowledges that *cost/benefit* considerations are always present. In other words, the benefit to be derived from information should be commensurate with the cost of gathering that information. A particular piece of information should be gathered and communicated to users only if the total benefits exceed the total costs.

Understandability

Sometimes we tend to forget that accounting is, in the final analysis, a system of communication. The basic key to this process of communication is the concept of *understandability.* If the readers of the financial statements are unable to understand the message being communicated, they will either disregard the data and seek other sources of information, or they will be misled by the data and a poor economic decision may result. In either of the cases, the financial statements will have failed to serve their basic purpose. So a starting point in any delineating of the qualities that should be contained in financial statements is understandability.

TABLE 15-4

A Hierarchy of Accounting Qualities

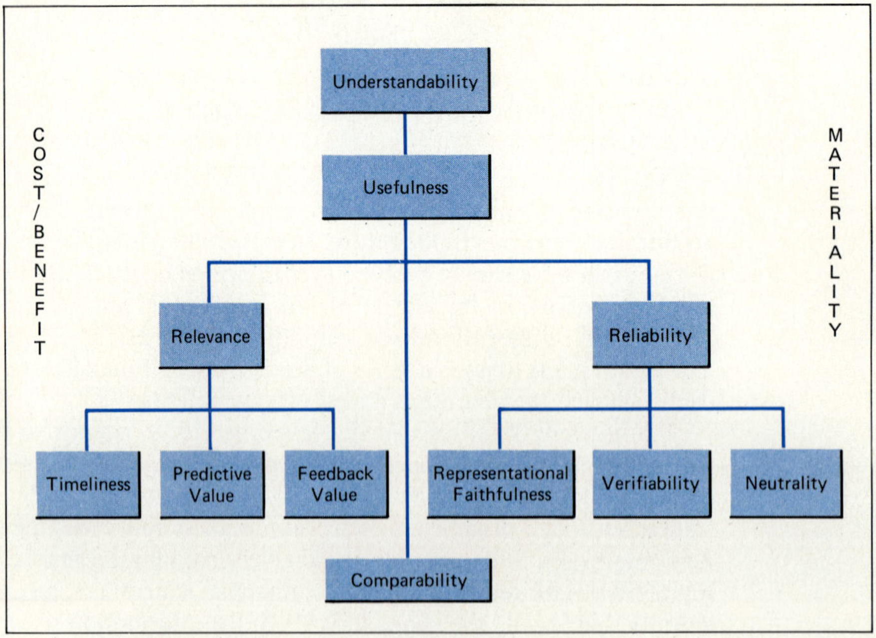

Usefulness

In addition to being understandable, the information transmitted by the accountant must be *useful.* Accountants must therefore maintain a continuing awareness of the kinds of economic decisions being made. In determining whether information is useful with respect to decisions, accountants generally consider two other qualitative characteristics of accounting information: relevance and reliability.

Relevance is defined as the capacity of the information to make a difference in a decision by helping users to form predictions about the outcomes of certain events. To be relevant the information presented must be timely and enable users to confirm or correct prior expectations.

Reliability is defined as the quality that assures that the information is reasonably free of error and bias. To be reliable the information must be neutral, verifiable, and representationally faithful (or valid).

Comparability is defined as the quality of information that enables users to identify similarities in and differences between two sets of economic phenomena. To go along with the idea of comparability, financial statements presented should be *consistent.* Consistency is defined as conformity from period to period with unchanging policies and procedures.

Materiality

Much like the cost/benefit considerations discussed earlier, *materiality* impacts on the entire hierarchy presented in Table 15-4. Even if the information presented in the financial statements is reliable, timely, and so on, that information would be useless unless it is material. Information is considered material when its inclusion or deletion would probably change the judgment of a reasonable person. For example, the omission of a note payable for $10,000 from the personal financial statement of most individuals in the United States would probably be material. However the same $10,000 note payable would certainly have no impact on the way a person might evaluate the financial statements of a major corporation. In the case of General Motors or Exxon, for example, the inclusion or omission of a $1 million amount would probably not be material. It is difficult to imagine, but the inclusion or omission of a $1 billion amount would probably not be material for the United States government. In other words, the inclusion or omission of $1 billion would probably not change the judgement of a reasonable person concerning the financial condition of the United States government.

As the foregoing examples illustrate, it is impossible to establish an arbitrary dollar amount as the level at which transactions become material. Instead, each transaction must be considered individually. It is very important to emphasize that in this area (and many others), accountants must use their professional judgment in determining the materiality of a given event.

Basic Principles

Now that we have discussed the method by which accounting principles are established, and the basic objectives of financial reporting, we shall take a look at some basic accounting principles and concepts that govern the accounting process.

The Entity Principle

One of the most basic concepts of accounting is concerned with the unit for which economic information is compiled and presented. An accounting entity is any economic unit which controls resources and is actively engaged in economic activities. For example, a corporation and its stockholders are separate and distinct entities for accounting purposes. Governmental agencies are economic entities as are not-for-profit organizations.

Under this separate entity concept, all financial reports are developed from the viewpoint of the particular entity. This provides a clear-cut distinction in analyzing transactions between the enterprise and its owners. For example, a building owned by an individual who also owns an unincorporated business is not considered an asset for the business to report, although the building and the business have a common owner.

An accounting entity may be defined as an identifiable economic unit within a larger accounting entity. For example, each separate department store of Sears, Inc., may be viewed as an accounting entity in that separate financial statements may be (and are) prepared for each store. Similarly, an economic entity may be larger than a single corporation. *Consolidated financial statements* show the financial condition of a group of affiliated corporations as though the affiliated companies were a single business organization.

The Cost Principle

Several times in this text we have alluded to the *cost principle.* Under this principle, all goods and services acquired are recorded at cost, irrespective of what the item is actually "worth." At the time an asset is originally acquired, cost normally represents the "fair market value" of the goods or services acquired. However, with the passage of time, the fair value of many assets (such as land and buildings) may change dramatically from their original cost. These changes in the fair market value of assets are generally excluded from the accounting records, and the assets are continually presented on the balance sheet at historical cost (less the portion of cost that has been allocated to depreciation expense). As we have demonstrated earlier in this chapter, it is possible to provide supplemental information relating to the changes in the value of specific assets or changes in the general price level.

It is important to note that the primary reason given in support of the cost principle is *objectivity.* In most cases the historical cost of an item is readily available and can be measured with complete objectivity (from a cancelled check or an invoice). However, evidence concerning the current fair market value of assets is usually less readily available. It is important that the users of financial statements have confidence in those statements; and many believe that this confidence might be eroded if a less-objective measure than historical cost was employed in the preparation of financial statements.

The Going-Concern Principle

The *going-concern* (or continuity) *principle* asserts that an accounting entity will continue indefinitely unless there is evidence to the contrary. We can prove that we believe in this principle by many of the things we do in accounting practice. For example, businesses typically depreciate some assets over an extended period of time because we assume that the business will continue in existence for a period of time sufficient to carry out the planned depreciation schedule. On the other hand, if we assumed that the business is likely to terminate in the future, the business would be forced to depreciate long-lived assets over the anticipated remaining life of the business, not the remaining life of the asset.

The Time-Period Principle

Although every business has a beginning and an end, in accounting we assume an indefinite existence for most business entities. Accountants are not, however, allowed the luxury of waiting until the end of a business life to prepare a "final" financial report. Users of financial information require periodic measurements for decision making. Therefore, it is commonly necessary to break up the real life of a business into several artificial time segments, and to report financial activity for those periods. These time periods are typically referred to as fiscal years. Many economic events that occur throughout the life of a business affect many different fiscal years; therefore, because accountants are forced to report by artificial time segments, numerous estimates and assumptions are required. Because of these estimates it is obvious that the period measurement of net income and financial position are only reasonable approximations. This tentative nature of periodic measurements should be understood by those who rely on periodic accounting information.

The Monetary Principle

In the United States, accounting transactions are measured in terms of dollars. In this context, the dollar is a unit of measure, like the inch, acre, or gallon. However, unlike the inch, the acre, or the gallon, the relative value of the dollar changes with changes in the general price level. To illustrate the impact of this changing value of the dollar, assume that a business reports two \$100,000 buildings on its balance sheet. One of the buildings was purchased in 1959 and the other twenty-five years later in 1984. It is obvious that although the dollars will be the same for both buildings, it is very unlikely that the two buildings will be anywhere near comparable.

So, while most units of measure are stable (remain unchanged over time), the unit of measure used in accounting is not stable in that the purchasing power of the dollar changes over time. The dollar remains, however, as the basic unit of measure in accounting. As was mentioned earlier in this chapter, FASB Statement No. 33 was adopted to address the problems associated with the unstable measuring unit.

Final Comments

It should be noted that, while the foregoing were referred to as basic accounting principles or concepts, they could have just as easily been considered to be assumptions made concerning the environment in which accounting operates. These assumptions are used fundamentally to simplify the premises about the environment. For example, with the monetary principle we assume a stable dollar. This assumption simplifies the world from what it actually is, and thereby makes the implementation of accounting more easily achievable. Accounting uses simplifying assumptions as a kind of compromise; that is, assumptions are made as a means of producing useful, but less than perfect, information about a complex system.

REVIEW QUESTIONS

1. What is the general price level?

2. Based on Table 15-1, what was the average inflation rate for the 1970s?

3. What is the reciprocal of the general price-level index? What does it mean?

4. What are three of the most frequently used measures of the general price level?

5. Companies A and B are in the same industry. Company A built its plant in the 1950s and Company B built its plant in the 1980s. What major differences would you expect to observe in the income statements of the two companies?

6. Explain the difference between constant-dollar accounting and current-value accounting. Are both methods a complete departure from historical cost accounting? Explain.

7. Does FASB Statement No. 33, "Financial Reporting and Changing Prices," apply to all publicly held companies in the United States? To which companies does it apply?

8. Briefly discuss the disclosure requirements of FASB Statement No. 33.

9. What is meant by a purchasing power gain or loss?

10. Name six events that have been important in the evolution of accounting practice.

11. What is meant by an exchange rate?

12. What is the function of the International Monetary Fund?

13. Explain the difference between "spot" and "future" markets.

14. As they relate to foreign currency, what are *discounts, premiums,* and *spreads?*

15. Briefly define or discuss the following:

- **a.** Letters of credit
- **b.** Bills of exchange
- **c.** Bank transfers

16. What problem or problems did the business community have with FASB Statement No. 8?

17. Briefly explain the provisions of FASB Statement No. 52.

18. What is the purpose of efforts to establish international accounting standards? Name several organizations that have made efforts in this regard.

19. What are generally accepted accounting principles? Are all such principles the result of the effort of the FASB? Explain.

20. Define or explain each of the components of the hierarchy of accounting qualities presented in Table 15-4.

21. Briefly explain the efforts of the FASB regarding the development of a conceptual framework of accounting.

22. Define or briefly explain the following principles:

a. Entity
b. Cost
c. Going concern
d. Time period
e. Monetary

23. Explain why the principles explained in this chapter (and in question 22) are often referred to as assumptions concerning the environment in which accounting operates.

EXERCISES

E15-1 In 19X9, Standish Mobile Home Distributor sold a model XXIG2 mobile home for $27,000. The mobile home was purchased for $19,500 in 19X8 when the consumer price index stood at 178.0. The CPI on the date of sale was 195.0, and the replacement cost of the XXIG2 on that date was $22,300.

REQUIRED:

Present the sales, cost of goods sold, and gross profit for the sale of the XXIG2 using

1. Traditional historical cost,
2. Constant-dollar accounting,
3. Current-value accounting.

E15-2 Grow, Inc., paid $800,000 cash in 19X1 to acquire land as a long-term investment. At this time, the general price level stood at 200. In 19X5, the general price index stands at 280, but the price of the land in the area in which Grow, Inc., invested has doubled in value. Rental receipts during the 5-year period were sufficient to pay all taxes and carrying charges on the land. Grow, Inc., prepares a constant-dollar income statement and discloses purchasing power gains and losses as supplementary information to its historical cost financial statements.

a. How much of a purchasing power gain or loss relating to the land will be included in the supplementary disclosures over the 5-year period? (Assume the land is still owned at the end of 19X5.)

b. Assume the land is sold in 19X5 for $1,500,000. Compute the gain or loss on the sale on a basis of (1) historical cost and (2) constant dollars.

E15-3 Briscoe Company has one monetary asset (cash: $250,000) and one monetary liability (notes payable: $300,000) which it holds during all of 19X7 when the CPI goes from 150 to 168. Calculate the purchasing power gain or loss experienced by Briscoe Company for 19X7.

E15-4 Slow Exporters of the United States sold gold to Fast French Firm for 1,000,000 French francs on January 15, 19X6, when the exchange rate was $.16 (each FFR cost $.16). The French company was billed in francs. Slow allowed 60-day terms, and the French Firm paid the amount due on March 14, 19X6, when the exchange rate was $.131.

REQUIRED:

1. Calculate the exchange gain or loss experienced by Slow Exporters on the transactions. Present the journal entries to record the transactions.
2. Assume that the French Firm paid the amount due on March 14, 19X6, and at that time the exchange rate was .192. Repeat the requirements in (1) above under that assumption.

E15-5 On August 9, 19X4, Block, Inc., a U.S. importer, purchased satillo tile from a Mexican exporting company for 3,600,000 pesos. Block is billed in pesos on August 9 when the exchange rate is .021. The invoice is paid on the due date, September 8, 19X4, when the exchange rate is .014.

REQUIRED:

1. Calculate the exchange gain or loss on the transaction. Record the necessary journal entries relating to the events.
2. Repeat the requirements in (1) assuming that the exchange rates in effect were as follows:
   Aug. 9, 19X4 .018
   Sept. 8, 19X4 .023

E15-6 For each situation described next, indicate the accounting principle or concept that is being violated.

a. The assets of the major shareholder of a closely held corporation are combined with the assets of the corporation itself.

b. A partnership is begun in an effort to explore for oil in central Alaska. The partnership acquires a lease on land for 10 years, and constructs a building on the land which it is depreciating for 25 years.

c. A Corporation purchases land in 19X1 for $15,000. In 19X5 it is appraised at $35,000 and is listed in the balance sheet at that amount.
d. A Corporation president decides that his company will not prepare annual financial statements because of the large amount of estimation that is involved. Instead he announces that the company will prepare financial statements every 4 years, in the years on which the Olympic Games are held.
e. An owner of a sole proprietorship uses the proprietorship checking account to pay for personal expenses.

PROBLEMS

P15-1 Marshall, Inc., was formed on January 4, 19X5. Selected balances from the historical-cost balance sheet on December 31, 19X5, were as follows:

Cash	$ 30,000
Short-term investments, stocks (acquired on Jan. 2 19X5)	40,000
Short-term investments, bonds, (acquired on Jan. 2 19X5, and held for speculation)	180,000
Long-term note receivable	50,000
The Consumer Price Index was 100 on Dec. 31, 19X4 (and Jan. 4, 19X5), and 110 on Dec. 31, 19X5.	

Compute the amounts at which the foregoing items would be presented in a historical-cost/constant-dollar balance sheet. Show computations.

P15-2 Daytime, Inc., paid $1,000,000 in December 19X6 for certain items of its inventory. In December 19X7, one-half of the items were sold for $1,200,000 when the current fair market value of the original items was $1,800,000.

Compute the amount to be shown as the total gain resulting from these facts in a current, fair market value income statement for 19X7. Show computations and disregard income taxes.

P15-3 On November 1, 19X4, Xebo Company, a United States importer, purchased gaskets from a Canadian exporter and is billed in Canadian dollars. The invoice amount is C$50,000, and the terms are net 30 days. The spot rate for Canadian dollars is $.8800, and the 30-day forward rate is $.8700. To avoid any exchange risk Xebo enters into a forward contract. Xebo executes the forward contract on November 1, and pays the amount due on December 1, 19X4.

REQUIRED:

Record the journal entries necessary to record the foregoing events.

P15-4 On April 3, 19X1, Cupco Exporters sold goods to a German firm for DM100,000. On that date the spot exchange rate was $.49 (each deutsche mark cost $.49), and there was a 10 point discount on the 3-month forward rate. On that date, Cupco entered into a 3-month forward contract to sell the DM100,000. On July 3, the German firm paid the amount due by depositing DM100,000 into an appropriate account in a German bank in Frankfurt. On that date the spot rate was .4896.

REQUIRED:

Present all journal entries on the books of Cupco to record these transactions.

P15-5 Each of the following independent situations relates to a decision made by the controller of a company with which you are familiar. You are asked to decide (1) if you agree with her decision, and (2) the accounting principle involved in your analysis.

a. The entire cost of a piece of equipment purchased is charged to expense in the year of acquisition.
b. A piece of land and building is purchased during the year for $116,000. The building is torn down during the year and at year-end the land is appraised at $133,000. The balance sheet at year-end shows the Land account at $116,000.
c. The company purchases 150 plastic trash cans during the year for $450. The trash cans are expected to last an average of 3 years; however it is decided that the $450 cost should be debited to maintenance expense.
d. The profit for the current year is expected to be small, therefore no depreciation is taken on plant assets for the year.
e. Because inflation was high in the current year it was decided that all items which appear on the company balance sheet will be restated in the primary financial statements to reveal the effects of inflation.
f. The company maintains a store in which employees and others can purchase merchandise manufactured locally. Total sales from the company store amount to $75,000, which is about 10 percent of all sales made annually. Because these sales are different from regular revenue, the proceeds from these sales are credited to Miscellaneous Expense. Consequently, Miscellaneous Expense has a credit balance of $63,200 for the year.

APPENDIX
Financial Statements of a Company Listed on the New York Stock Exchange

Tandy Corporation has been a leading growth company for many years. Tandy Corporations' financial statements and annual report are presented on the following pages. These financial statements have been audited by Price Waterhouse & Co., an international firm of certified public accountants. The audit report is included in the annual report.

TANDY CORPORATION ANNUAL REPORT 1983

CORPORATE PROFILE

Tandy Corporation, through its chain of Radio Shack® outlets, is one of the world's leading distributors of technology to electronics consumers.

Tandy/Radio Shack has the largest number of retail electronics outlets in the world. Through more than 5,700 company-owned retail stores and 3,000 dealer/franchise outlets, Tandy distributes a broad product line. The 1984 Radio Shack-U.S. catalog features 2,625 non-computer items plus 396 products from the full line of microcomputers, peripherals and accessories. Audio equipment, radios, magnetic audio and video tape, antennas, telephones and accessories, security devices, calculators, clocks, toys, pagers, citizens band radios, scanners, electronic parts, test equipment and the TRS-80® line of microcomputers are part of the diverse merchandise offered by Radio Shack. Fifty-four Radio Shack-U.S. service centers provide service for products sold by Radio Shack.

Tandy/Radio Shack has played a major role in the development of the microcomputer market. The Radio Shack-U.S. computer catalog for 1984 contains more than 700 items. The computer customer is offered specialized assistance in more than 1,275 Computer Centers and *Plus* Computer Centers worldwide. There are 247 special service facilities throughout the United States to service microcomputer and peripheral equipment.

Based on consumer response to the four Radio Shack Telephone Centers opened during fiscal 1983, Tandy/Radio Shack has announced plans to open additional full-line Telephone Centers and add Telephone Centers to selected Radio Shack Computer Centers. Each of these stores will offer consumer and business telephone equipment with emphasis on telephone systems with two to 16 incoming lines. Full maintenance facilities and staff technicians to install telephone systems and equipment will be provided at each Radio Shack Telephone Center.

Tandy's manufacturing capabilities allow the Company to respond quickly to changes in market conditions and technology. Tandy owns 29 factories in the United States, Asia and Canada. A manufacturing joint venture with Matra SA produces microcomputers in France for the European market. Approximately 40% of the items in the Radio Shack product line are manufactured, assembled or packaged in these plants.

Financial Highlights

YEAR ENDED JUNE 30	1983	1982	% CHANGE
Net sales ($000)	**$2,475,188**	$2,032,555	+22
Net income ($000)	**$278,521**	$224,085	+24
Net income per average common share	**$2.67**	$2.17	+23
Return on average stockholders' equity	**28.8%**	32.3%	
Average common shares outstanding (000)	**104,335**	103,395	
Working capital ($000)	**$977,199**	$715,863	
Current ratio	**4.42 to 1**	4.07 to 1	
Retail sales outlets	**8,868**	8,518	
Stockholders and nominees	**41,810**	44,347	

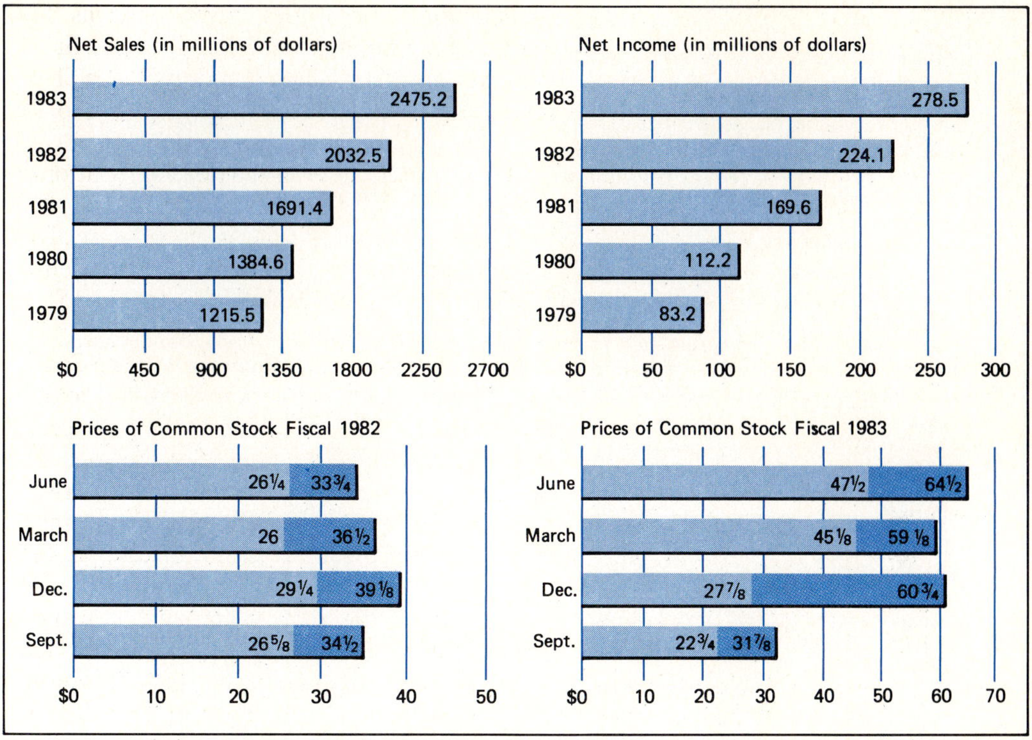

TANDY CORPORATION AND THE CONSUMER ELECTRONICS MARKETPLACE

Overview of the Market

The consumer electronics business in the United States represented an estimated \$20 billion dollars in retail volume this past year. The major ingredient attributable to this success is the high degree of innovation and continuing supply of new and affordable products for everyday living. Our business, while dominated by the computer during the recession of the past year, has shown comfortable growth or at least break-even sales in nearly all "traditional" categories.

A series of recent industry surveys claim that sales of home entertainment equipment will continually escalate during the 1980s and into the 1990s. Significant gains are expected, according to these surveys, for audio components, speakers, amplifiers, receivers and microphones. This portion of our business has been showing overall absolute dollar gains both last year and this year. The introduction of the digital audio disc has not and probably will not make any significant change in audio component sales. Once the initial, perhaps 100,000,

DEAR FELLOW STOCKHOLDERS

Our 24.3% increase in net income on a sales increase of 21.8% boosted our net income as a percent of sales to a record 11.3%. This was achieved by the strong performance of our North American operations, even though we had a significant reduction in foreign earnings.

The coming year will be one of both opportunity and challenge. The opportunities are highlighted by the continued growth of the microcomputer business, the ongoing development of the telephone business and the strengthening of the economy. The challenges are great because of the competition in the computer business, the unprecedented price reductions across most of our line and the strengthening of the dollar against foreign currencies in our international operations.

We participate in the microcomputer industry in a unique way as both a retailer and a manufacturer. It gives us not only the opportunity to monitor retail sales directly as a manufacturer, but it also gives us the opportunity to balance and promote inventories according to our needs. The good news is our unit sales continue to grow at an excellent rate. But, the selling prices have been significantly reduced due to reduced costs and competition. The trend toward improving price/performance will continue throughout 1984. We hope that our broad performance-improved, cost-reduced product line, complemented by manufacturer-supported software, training and service will keep us very competitive in the marketplace. Clearly, we do not sell just hardware. We offer an excellent support package. It is our goal to continue strong hardware and software development efforts to make our line the most complete so we can offer our customers the models that meet their needs. Our newest introduction is a portable version of our best-selling TRS-80® Model 4. This new model combines excellent price/performance, attractive styling and portability in a very compact cabinet.

The most innovative computer in our line is the "cover girl" for the annual report. The TRS-80 Model 100 combines portable usability, applications software and easy communications in a powerful combination that is possibly the most "user-friendly" machine in the market today. Our TRS-80 Color Computer for the home and education markets continues to receive high ratings for its software, performance and expandability in a section of the market where more consideration is sometimes given to price than utility. So, whether the customer is interested in a $10,000 multi-terminal, multi-user system or the latest pocket computer at $69.95, Radio Shack® has a complete line for the customer to choose from. Our goal in the microcomputer industry is the same as our goal for our whole business—profitable growth.

The telephone industry continues in transition as we continue to develop our marketing philosophy. Federal Judge Greene, who presided over the AT&T anti-trust case and then insured that the AT&T and Justice Department settlement would be in the best interest of the consumer and would create a free marketplace, has set the stage for a highly competitive telecommunications industry. The competitiveness of the industry was significantly enhanced as the ominous threat of defacto cross subsidization through advertising was lessened by placing restrictions on the use of the Bell® name. The publicity surrounding the settlement did more to build user awareness that telecommunications is now an open industry than any other single factor. We are already seeing the results of telephone equipment being provided by a large number of suppliers—lower prices to the consumer.

While our regular Radio Shack stores have our usual wide assortment of telephones, dialers, amplifiers and accessories, we are also experimenting with the telephone systems business as well. Four stores specializing in key systems for small businesses were opened during the latter part of fiscal year 1983. We will open 21 more of these stores either individually or in combination with Computer Centers during the first half of fiscal year 1984. It's our goal to develop an effective formula for the sale of small systems—a

audiophiles purchase the equipment at the $800 to $1,000 price range, the sales will probably slow down until the equipment drops in price. AM stereo has had zero impact on the audio market due to the confusion of five FCC approved transmission standards plus the fact that there is really little or no need for AM stereo. The possible market was automotive; however, most of the automotive manufacturers have chosen to ignore it.

Auto stereo has continued a pattern of steady growth both industry-wise and for us. We are experiencing significant increases in the number of con-

niche that may have limited appeal to other retailers. Our concept includes well-displayed, easy-to-demonstrate systems in a professional, but retail/showroom environment. These Telephone Centers offer equipment sales, training, installation and continuing service. Looking to the future, we anticipate phone systems may become common residential items as well.

During the last six months, as the economy has rebounded, we've seen improvements in the traditional parts of our business. This type of balanced growth builds a less volatile base than we saw in prior periods that were heavily dependent on the computer. Most of our recent computer introductions, the new video products, the telephones and pocket pagers give us the opportunity for a continuing increase in volume per location in all our stores.

The 1984 U.S. Radio Shack catalog contains more than 350 price reductions on continuing products. This is the largest number of reductions we have offered in recent years. These reductions are a function of technology, the world economy and the strong U.S. dollar. The consumer will certainly benefit and respond to these reductions, but it does require excellent increases in unit sales to maintain our momentum in dollar sales growth. Our marketing strategy hopefully will meet the challenge.

Retail operations outside North America have been significantly impacted by relatively weak foreign economies and the continuing strength of the U.S. dollar. The factors that we can control, expenses and inventories, are being controlled. These slow foreign economies and a strong U.S. dollar will continue to adversely impact sales comparisons and gross margins. Since these problems are considered to be temporary, we'll continue to add new stores but at a somewhat lower rate.

We have contracted to acquire O'Sullivan Industries, Inc., a subsidiary of Conroy, Inc., for $91,500,000 cash, effective August 31, 1983. This purchase is subject to a number of conditions and will not be closed until all conditions have been met. O'Sullivan is a leading manufacturer of consumer electronic stands, racks, desks and accessories. This transaction meets our criteria of complementary operating results, growth and synergy with our existing business. It will be operated very similar to our Memtek Products division which contributed nicely to sales and profits this year. These companies maintain their own organizations, trade names, customers and products. We will continue to look for opportunities to strengthen your Company with acquisitions in technology and distribution that we know and understand.

The ensuing pages of this annual report contain comments by key merchandising and operational executives. I think their message is very clear—we are continuing to build Tandy's business on the strong fundamentals that have yielded extraordinary operating results for a retailer in one of the most competitve segments of the retail industry. Our basic philosophies of private label merchandising, strong promotion particularly through direct mail advertising, convenient locations, vertical integration and the institutionalization of individual entrepreneurship truly make Tandy and Radio Shack unique.

Whatever the challenge or opportunity—we look forward to 1984!

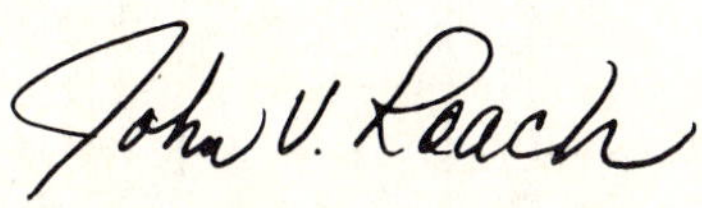

John V. Roach
Chairman of the Board,
Chief Executive Officer
and President

sumers who are purchasing their own auto stereo equipment and installing it themselves. There has also been a marked increase in the number of people who are upgrading their automotive speakers on a do-it-yourself basis.

Audio tape equipment sales are very steady and consistent. Heretofore, costly features such as logic-controlled transports, auto-reverse mechanisms and noise reduction devices that improve tape listening are now available at lower prices than ever before. Blank audio cassette sales continue to rise with an emphasis towards new improved ferric and chrome formulations as well as high-performance metal tape. Consumer taste in the tape equipment category is constantly going through a state of flux — from large portables to mini-stereos to so-called convertible home/portable products. The merchandise changes but the total volume and consumer interest continue to rise.

Microprocessor memories and electronic tuning at the touch of a finger are making our audio products friendlier and easier to use as are remote control and microprocessor programming. Obviously I am optimistic about the audio business. We are a nation in which music is an integral part of our lives and I see no reason for this to diminish in years to come.

How many times have we heard that the radio—a 62-year old consumer product—would die as a result of the introduction of TV? The Electronic Industries Association (EIA) figures indicate that a total of 40 million portable and home radios were sold this year. Some of the AM/FM radio dollars will certainly shift to personal portables or to a combination of cassettes and radio; however, the proof is there—the portable is a permanent part of the consumer industry. People want news and music wherever they go. We do foresee continued growth in the area of scanning radios, i.e., those radios used for monitoring of the public service bands. We also look forward to a proliferation of high-performance portable shortwave radios for international traveling. Innovation has certainly increased the demand for a wide range of new and specialized products.

Video has become the buzz word that connotes the transformation of the American home and lifestyle. The conventional TV set served one purpose—to receive broadcast programs. Cable TV now has added up to 100 additional channels and pay-TV is adding even more. The TV screen has become an all-purpose display device for video games, video cassette recorders and video discs. Home computers utilize the same TV display for home education, management and game programs.

We are working closely with companies in the direct satellite broadcasting area to determine if we could provide and/or sell equipment to the user—if a business develops. At some point in the not-too-distant future, stereo TV will become a reality. The requirements of new equipment and accessories represent an extraordinary growth area for us.

Programmable video games certainly made an impact on our industry and contributed to the acceptance and growth of home computers. I frankly believe that the programmable game will be a relic of the past as prices of home computers continue to fall and more and more people come to realize that the computer is more than a "game machine." The home computer is a practical household tool and can be used for word processing, electronic filing, home management and as an extraordinary educational aid. The consumer is rapidly becoming familiar with the use of additional disk drives, printers, graphics tablets and modems. A continuous flow of new game entertainment and educational and home management programs will provide continued growth of the software market. The multiple uses of microcomputers in business and education and the distribution and support services that go along with them will be covered in subsequent pages of this report. You will recognize that we are committed to maintaining strong industry position in every aspect of the microcomputer market.

The consumer electronics industry has coined the phrase "personal electronics" to cover the myriad of products that resulted from advances in integrated circuit technology. Products that range from electronic watches and clocks to calculators to security products and to electronic toys are capturing the imagination of the consuming public. The technology of the '80s is providing a greater selection of new and interesting, relatively low-cost, affordable products than ever before in the history of our industry. This flow of products will continue for years to come.

Another major consumer growth area is telecommunications. The AT&T suit was a major contributor to the public's awareness and realization of owning one's own telephones, telephone answering equipment, dialers and better telephone accessories. Cordless telephone sales have doubled and will redouble again as they remain the leading new product in the burgeoning home telephone market. Affordable electronic telephone systems for residential and commercial uses are now appearing on the market with a wide array of desirable features that in past years were only available on very expensive systems leased by the telephone companies. Other ventures into this huge growth area are covered in subsequent pages of this annual report. We have ventured, with some degree of success, into personal pocket pagers and are attempting to make this product a mass-market consumer item as well as trying to provide a low-cost system for business. We have developed a relationship with the radio common carriers that will give us the experience to deal with the possibility of getting into cellular mobile radio. Cellular offers a huge sales potential and we want to determine if there will be a market for retail distribution. With our early start in the telephone business and our experience in selling citizens band radio and other telecommunication products, we have positioned ourselves as the retail leader in this burgeoning industry.

This past year, the consumer electronics industry has had its share of uncommonly large operating losses, top management and marketing changes and price erosion. The 1984 Radio Shack catalog reflects more than 350 reduced prices from the previous catalog and a host of new products at very affordable prices. Yet, we intend to maintain our profits and improve sales. Our own product line, sold through our own distribution system via our own marketing plan to customers who appreciate our pricing, selection and service, will enable us to remain the Number One retailer of electronics to the world.

Consumer Merchandise — Ongoing Innovation

Radio Shack's 1984 catalog features 2,625 items, exclusive of computer products. There are 433 new items and 2,192 repeats from 1983. Of the 2,192 repeating items, 352 decreased in selling price while only five increased. The strong U.S. dollar, improved technology and manufacturing efficiencies continue to bring our customers more advanced products at lower retail prices.

Radio Shack's audio, or hi-fi, category continues to receive major emphasis in this year's catalog. Another year of sales gains have been recorded for this category. It includes stereo receivers, tuners, amplifiers, speakers, turntables, tape decks and accessories.

Five stereo receivers are new this year. The cost of digital-synthesized tuning continues to decline, bringing today's consumer superior product for less money. For example, the new Realistic® STA-2270, a 65-watt-per-channel AM/FM stereo receiver priced at $399.95, replaces last year's 50-watt-per-channel model that retailed for $439.95.

The newest technology in conventional turntables is linear-tracking tonearms. For 1984 Radio Shack is introducing two more linear-tracking turntables—a direct-drive, microprocessor-controlled turntable for $219.95 ($40.00 less than last year's model) and a lowcost, belt-drive unit for $159.95.

Speakers have always been a significant part of our hi-fi business. Five new speaker systems have been added for 1984. Continuing a Radio Shack tradition, four of the new models are finished in genuine walnut veneer, rather than the vinyl used by many of our competitors. The fifth speaker system is in a die-cast metal enclosure for superb sound from a small unit.

Increased competition among tape deck manufacturers and continuing improvement in manufacturing technology have reduced the cost of premium features such as auto-reverse and logic-controlled transports. Four new tape decks have been introduced this year. Our top-of-the-line SCT-42 has auto-reverse, solenoid logic control, programmable memory system and Dolby® B-C noise reduction. That's a lot of bells and whistles for only $299.95.

Audio accessories have helped us earn our reputation as the Nationwide Supermarket of Sound®. Our new 10-band audio equalizer with a control center for tape dubbing at a price of $119.95 replaces the 1983 model that was $159.95. There are four new phono cartridges and three new microphones, one of which includes a breakthrough in microphone technology. The new Realistic PZM® microphone utilizes the revolutionary pressure-zone principle that essentially allows the microphone to hear what the human ear would hear without annoying distortion.

Reflecting industry trends for personal stereo products, we've introduced seven new STEREO-MATE® personal portables for use with lightweight headphones. Four are stereo tape players. The top-of-the-line, the SCP-10 even has an AM/FM stereo tuner and Dolby® B noise-reduction circuitry built in although it is only 1⅜ inches thick and only slightly larger than a cassette.

Eleven tape recorders are new this year. Seven have built-in AM/FM radios. Highlighting the 1984 line are two portable AM/FM stereo cassette recorders that look like portables but have detachable stereo speakers. A new portable cassette recorder, the Realistic VSC® 1000 has a unique patented circuit that permits you to listen to voice recordings at twice the normal speed without pitch changes, a time-saver for professionals, students and the visually impaired.

Industry statistics show increased growth for autosound as people are discovering the pleasure of driving with a quality sound system. Seven new in-dash AM/FM stereo cassettes and one new AM/FM stereo eight-track player position Radio Shack at every major price point from $69.95 to $249.95. As with home hi-fi, Radio Shack has all the accessories to complete the system from power boosters and equalizers to speakers and antennas.

Industry sales of video equipment and accessories continue to explode. More than 11 pages of the 1984 catalog display a wide array of video products —antennas, antenna amplifiers, distribution amplifiers, cables, mounts and more. Everything necessary for a first rate antenna or video installation is offered by Radio Shack. Many new products have been added this year. Additions include the Realistic Model 10 remote-controlled VHS video cassette recorder at a competitive $499.95 and the new self-manufactured, high grade VHS T-120 video cassette recording tape.

Two new models have been added to our smallscreen TV collection—a 9″ black-and-white AC/DC portable and a compact 5″ color AC/DC television that can be used as a monitor for a computer or a portable video cassette recorder.

Radar detector sales increased dramatically for the industry and Radio Shack this past year. In response, Radio Shack has introduced three new dual-conversion, superheterodyne radar detectors Dual-conversion superheterodyne technology greatly increases reception range and decreases false "triggering."

The home security equipment business has been flat for the industry. However, Radio Shack continues to explore this potentially large market by introducing new products. Nine items were added this year, including a new-technology passive infrared motion-sensor alarm system for the home. This system detects both the body heat and movement of an intruder and is highly resistant to false alarms.

The radio line has always been an important category at Radio Shack. This year there are sixteen new models including seven novelty, five clock, three portable and a desktop weather and time receiver.

Electronic clocks, watches and timers are for everyone. There are thirty-seven varieties this year. The eighteen new clocks include a talking clock and one that projects the time on the ceiling. There are clocks you hang on the wall, carry in your pocket, wear on your wrist or you even write with. There is even a digital seven-day, programmable timer for complex timing needs.

Industry statistics show the calculator business declined in 1982. However, we increased sales and market share. The first practical consumer use of solar energy has been in powering the calculator. The low energy requirements of today's calculators are ideally suited to silicon solar cell technology. There are twelve new calculators in this year's catalog including five solar types. The line is priced from $6.95 to $79.95.

The electronics hobbyist and professional has always shopped Radio Shack for parts and test equipment. This all-important category has more than one hundred new items this year from the latest integrated circuits to the new clamp-on AC ammeter.

Last, but certainly not least, is our seasonal toy merchandise. Radio Shack continues to bring to the market unique and innovative Christmas toy values. This year sixteen new items are offered—six new radio-controlled vehicles, nine electronic games, and even a robotic arm that works just like an industrial robot.

It is obvious that the breadth of new product offerings throughout the merchandise line at more affordable prices will provide the opportunity for a successful sales year.

The Computer Marketplace

Fiscal 1983 has been an exciting year for computers at Tandy Corporation. Datamation Magazine ranks us as the 16th largest data processing company worldwide with all the higher ranking companies being in the mainframe or mini-computer market. We have the broadest line of small computers, and we support them with more software, printers, peripherals and supplies than anyone. There are 765 items in our 1984 computer catalog, 264 of which are new. Of the repeating items, 52 have price decreases while only eight have increases.

Topping our line is the powerful TRS-80® Model 16B, a dual-processor, multi-user computer. The "B" sports new low-profile styling, added expansion capability, a much-improved keyboard and double the memory—all at last year's price. Early in fiscal 1984, we will introduce a 16B with a built-in, 15-megabyte hard disk. The 16B's MC-68000 CPU is the most advanced microprocessor available, featuring 32-bit internal processing with a 16-bit data path. An upgrade to allow six (instead of three) users to share the Model 16B via lowcost TRS-80 DT-1 terminals is slated for fall delivery.

The Model 16B and its sister computer, the Model 12, offer the industry's only hardware and software upgrade path, from 8-bit single-user to 16-bit single-user to 16-bit multi-user systems. The Model 12 converts easily to a 16B, and compatible software eliminates the need to re-enter data as you grow.

Our new TRS-80 Model 12 was introduced in January as a more expandable, powerful replacement for the TRS-80 Model II. A low-profile case and keyboard, green screen, new white color, more disk capacity, cost reduction and a lower price made the Model 12 instantly popular in the marketplace. A number of ARCNET® local area networks are now in operation, tying together Model II's and Model 12's for sharing of common data. Up to 256 computers can be added to a single network, creating a very powerful distributed system at reasonable cost.

One of the biggest winners on our new TRS-80 team has been the Model 4 that replaced our popular Model III as the ideal productivity machine for executives and professionals and as the most popular TRS-80 in U.S. schools. We added the popular 80 × 24 screen format, increased memory to 64K (ex-

---

Dolby is a trademark of Dolby Laboratories Licensing Corp.
PZM is a trademark of Crown International.
VSC is a trademark of Variable Speech Control Company.

pandable to 128K), added sound, improved the keyboard and included a most powerful and feature-rich new disk operating system, TRSDOS® Version 6. Yet, we maintained 100% compatibility with all existing Model III programs by providing a "Model III mode". All this, and we reduced the price to $1,999 with two disk drives. And we provided an upgrade so Model III owners can turn their computers into Model 4's. We expected a winner . . . we got a best seller!

There isn't much that can be said about our Model 100 portable (see cover) that hasn't already been said for us by the industry. Money Magazine said in its May 1983 issue ". . . the Model 100 is so packed with goodies that it could well become the machine of the year . . ." Built-in software handles text processing, notes and schedules and also maintains address and telephone number files. Connected to a telephone through its internal modem, the Model 100 will dial a number from your phone list, automatically log you onto another computer system and let you send or receive memos, electronic mail or data such as news, weather, up-to-the minute airline schedules and fares, the latest Wall Street happenings and quotes and much more . . . all at the touch of a function key. It is perhaps the most unique data communications device ever conceived. Up to 32,000 bytes of memory (a byte is roughly one typewritten character) are battery maintained. And the "100" is a lightweight notebook-sized, battery-powered, full-featured computer with a professional-quality typewriter keyboard that's easy to carry and use anywhere. Of course it contains BASIC programming language. Model 100 is truly a new concept in computers for individuals.

Industry analysts have proclaimed our declining market share of the low-end "home computer" market, where the Color Computer has been Tandy's primary entrant. Management believes we are capturing our share of the *profitable* business in this segment, as witnessed by our continued profitability in the low-end market, compared to announcements of major losses during the year by TI and Atari. Questionable "market share" statistics notwithstanding, the number of Color Computers we sold in fiscal 1983 more than doubled from the previous year.

Our new Color Computers for 1984 have been reduced in price, both at retail and cost, with no sacrifice in margins. They now boast improved keyboards and our new white TRS-80 color. In addition, we've added the much-requested 64K memory capability to the top-of-the-line unit, and we've introduced a very low-end, entry-level model, the MC-10 Micro Color Computer.

Pocket computers are gaining momentum as prices decline. Our $69.95 PC-4 has been especially successful. We expect these BASIC-programmable alphanumeric computers to eventually replace the less-capable, numeric-only programmable calculators.

Our printer line, another major area for us, has been exciting too. We introduced the DMP-2100 printer this past year. It advances dot-matrix printing to a new standard with its ability to produce output quality comparable to an electric typewriter. It also offers a higher speed "data processing" mode and a high-density graphics mode. We've just introduced a low-cost 7-color, ink-jet printer (another "first"), and we've reduced our cost and selling prices on several models.

Amid all of the hardware development, we haven't overlooked the continuing need for software. Radio Shack has a major commitment to a well-rounded selection of quality programs. Our Education Division currently offers 83 products. Twenty-five of those items are new since last year's catalog. Additionally, we have cooperative agreements with fifty major educational publishers, who are developing software for TRS-80 microcomputers.

We have also seen a large demand for educational software for use in the home. In response, we have acquired rights to two outstanding series of programs for the Color Computer . . . one from Walt Disney Educational Media Co. and one from Children's Computer Workshop, a subsidiary of Children's Television Workshop and Sesame Street. The 1984 catalog will list fifteen packages in these two series and more will be coming during the year. We have also signed an agreement with CBS for co-development of software which will appear during the coming year.

Near the end of calendar year 1983, Radio Shack will introduce the CP/M® operating system version 3.0 for the Models 4 and 12. With it, users will gain access to more than 3,000 additional applications programs written under this very popular operating system.

Of course there is a continuing development effort for additional software for our Models 4 and 12 (and their predecessors the Models III and II). A new and improved accounting series for the Models III and 4 has been developed in-house and is now becoming available in the stores. All of our word-processing software is developed in-house. As in the past, we will be working with some outside vendors on proprietary TRS-80 software such as our popular Profile® Plus data base manager packages. This coming year, we will be working with more outside vendors than ever to convert market-proven "hits" to our computers.

In November 1982 we initiated a third party software support operation to work with software publishers who write programs for TRS-80 microcomputers, but who market them through their own efforts. This program has been well received with about 1,800 software vendors currently participating. We also initiated a software review program for third-party programs. Information on programs reviewed and accepted is available to our customers in the Computer Centers. Potential customers are then referred to the vendors of these programs by our sales personnel.

Our computer merchandising and research and development teams continue to develop new hardware, peripheral and software products to assure Radio Shack's position as an industry and technology leader.

Computers and Education

During the 1983 fiscal year, Tandy Corporation/Radio Shack has continued to experience strong growth in sales of the TRS-80® product line to schools. For the third consecutive year, total educational sales of our microcomputers, peripherals and software have more than doubled each previous year's sales, making education the fastest growing market for the TRS-80 product line.

The education market in the United States is a big business. For the past several years, total annual expenditures by elementary and secondary schools, as well as post-secondary institutions, have been 7% of the U.S. gross national product. A part of that total annual expenditure for education includes federal dollars distributed to schools under the various federal education programs. Recent changes in these programs are giving schools more latitude in how they spend these dollars. During the past twelve months, many school districts have elected to spend more of these dollars for microcomputers and instructional software to help them effectively meet the needs of their students.

Radio Shack's Education Division has been able to provide valuable and effective support to our retail store system in reaching the growing educational market by implementing and administering a national education marketing program and by developing a broad line of high-quality instructional software.

Our Education Division has become one of the largest educational publishers in this specialized area of electronic publishing. Our commitment to support schools who are using TRS-80 computers in their classrooms with a dedicated national staff of regional educational coordinators, a national customer service organization and a major effort to provide teacher training has kept us in the forefront of a growing market.

At a press conference in Washington, D.C., in March 1983 John Roach and William Gattis, Director of the Radio Shack Education Division, announced America's Educational Challenge®, which dramatically expanded the Company's offer to train teachers to include every teacher in the United States.

Immediately following the announcement in March, the Company sent a free package to 104,000 school principals in the United States. This packet contained a certificate for free classes, information on computer uses in education, computer literacy materials for elementary and secondary students and an order form offering a second free package to principals on request. The second package contained two audio-visual presentations on filmstrips for use in teacher workshops and staff development sessions to introduce computer concepts to teachers, a directory of educational software available for the TRS-80 product line from a variety of sources and additional certificates for our free classes for teachers. Tandy/Radio Shack is particularly pleased that Secretary of Education Terrell Bell was able to attend and participate in the press conference announcing America's Educational Challenge. Secretary Bell described the Tandy offer as ". . . a significant contribution" to increasing the computer literacy of America's children. The Secretary further stated that "Tandy/Radio Shack has picked the correct target and goal—helping the nation's elementary and secondary school teachers become computer literate."

The response to the America's Educational Challenge offer has been unprecedented. More than 32,000 requests for the second package have been received to date, and the response shows every sign of continuing.

We can look forward to continued growth in educational sales during the 1984 fiscal year as the Education Division continues to add to our growing list of educational software, as we continue to expand our educational marketing program and as we continue to surround our TRS-80 product line with the best service and support in the industry.

The Emerging Telephone Market

Telephone and related accessory sales are very strong again this year. According to industry data, newphone sales will reach 10 million units this year in the United States — more than double last year's business. Early entry (nearly three decades ago) into the telephone product area has given Radio Shack a strong position in the marketplace.

Radio Shack's line covers several market segments: standard telephones, decorator telephones, automatic dialers, amplifiers, cordless telephones, answering systems and accessories.

The basic replacement telephone area offers standard desk and wall telephones. Electronic telephones, however, have proven to be Radio Shack's best sellers. Decorator telephones have also shown sales gains.

Automatic dialer sales have improved this year due partially to the growth of alternate long distance and bank-by-phone services. A pocket dialer with 32-number memory for use at home or on the road has been added to our line. Telephone amplifiers for handsfree convenience have also shown steady sales gains.

Cordless phone sales are tremendous. Industry analysts estimate unit sales will double this year and will total over a billion dollars in 1985. Radio Shack's 1984 line of cordless models has even lower prices. A new item is the Chronofone® ET-380, a full-feature AM/FM clock radio with a built-in cordless telephone.

Based on U.S. industry figures, approximately one million answering machines were sold in 1982. Early entry into this marketing area coupled with continual upgrading and new-product development have allowed us to establish a strong position.

Accessories continue to grow with the overall business. New additions to the Radio Shack line include: a light-weight, hands-free telephone headset, a two-line controller with hold that replaces the need for two phones, and a multi-line controller that can replace a standard five-line phone. The availability of plugs and jacks in our stores represents another source of sales.

At last year's annual stockholders' meeting, Radio Shack announced its entry into the smallbusiness telephone systems market. According to industry data, the potential market for all key telephone systems will exceed six billion dollars by 1986. Based on national statistics, the average number of telephone lines per business is 2.8. While Radio Shack offers systems of larger capacity, the bulk of the business is in systems of ten lines or less. This portion of the market has been unappealing to the interconnect industry — most would rather sell larger systems. And, it appears to have been ignored by the telephone companies since they offer no sophisticated equipment in small systems.

To begin implementation of our plan, four pilot stores have been opened in Dallas and Fort Worth, Texas, and in Lexington and Louisville, Kentucky. The concept of a retail telephone environment offered by a well-known electronics leader is the basis of our market plan. These stores are staffed by professional sales personnel to service the business customer. They can assist the prospect through an on-site visit or through a "hands-on" demonstration in the store. This type of operation is virtually unknown in the industry. A potential residential market may exist and the concept we have adopted puts Radio Shack at the forefront of this market if it develops.

Products offered in the pilot stores fall into three groups. The first group is the existing Radio Shack telephone product line. Group two is composed of specialized and enhanced telephone products. Group three contains small to medium-sized, multi-line electronic telephone systems.

Plans were announced August 1 to enter the second phase of the telephone center development program. Twenty-one additional centers will be opening in major markets within the next few months. Ten of these will be in combination with existing Radio Shack Computer Centers.

With additional experience and fine-tuning in the stores, we plan to be the first national interconnect company.

Manufacturing and Product Development

The primary function of Tandy Electronics is to bring new and innovative products to our stores. These products need to be reliable and affordable for our customers. Our prices need to be competitive with similar product offerings from outside vendors and our factories need to make an adequate return on investment at these competitive prices.

To support our plants in this function we maintain two major design centers. Tandy Systems Design is located in Fort Worth and TC Electronics Corporation is located in Tokyo. In general, Tandy Systems Design supports our North American plants with major emphasis on computer products. TC Electronics supports our plants in Korea and Taiwan. Recently, this distinction has tended to blur. For example, the new Micro Color Computer is a joint engineering development which is being manufactured in Korea.

Tandy Systems Design now has more than 180 people engaged primarily in hardware and software development for the TRS-80® computer line. The software group is responsible for the development of both operating systems and applications software and also provides liaison and direction for our growing list of outside suppliers of software.

During the past year this group has played a major role in the almost complete update of our computer line. Virtually every model has been replaced with a new one that has higher performance and enhanced features at lower cost. Also introduced during the past year were new high-technology peripherals like the 5¼-inch Winchester hard disk drives and the ARCNET® local area network.

While the primary function of Tandy Systems Design is computer development, there is also significant involvement in product development in telephones, speakers and video accessories.

TC Electronics, Japan, was initially a manufacturing facility in Japan. Over the years it has evolved into an engineering center for our manufacturing facilities in Korea and Taiwan. It is responsible for the design of more than 100 consumer products. More recently the group is developing an expertise in computer products which will enhance our worldwide efforts in the computer area.

In some of our plants where product activities are more specialized, the plant development activity can rival that of our design centers. Our antenna plants are largely responsible for their own product development. At Tandy Magnetic Media a research and development staff is engaged in primary research on magnetic media and particle phenomenon. Several patents in these areas were issued last year and the group has an industry-wide reputation in magnetic media development.

Traditionally, the consumer electronics business has been an anomaly in the retail marketplace. Despite inflation, each year has brought better products at lower prices. Maintaining competitiveness in the consumer electronics business requires an awareness of this. As each product comes to market, engineering needs to be thinking of how to improve the existing product and how to reduce its cost.

One of the ways used to reduce cost in our computer facilities has been to increase our level of vertical integration. Our Lika plant supplies printed circuit boards to Tandy Instruments which then uses automatic equipment to insert most of these boards with components. Our computer assembly plants use the boards from Tandy Instruments and plastic cabinets from Tandy Molded Products to assemble and test the final products. This process, while steadily increasing, is intentionally not complete. Our ability to respond to rapid market fluctuations requires access to outside vendors as needed. Each facility that contributes to the final product is required to show an adequate profit while being competitive with outside vendors. The result is obviously a lower overall production cost.

During the past year several costly power supplies used in some of our computers, which previously were bought from outside vendors, have been reengineered by Tandy Systems Design and are now being produced by Tandy Apparatus. These switching-type power supplies are an improvement over the old product and are considerably cheaper to build. TC Elecronics in Taiwan now supplies a large and growing part of the video monitors used in several of our computers. Again, the result is a better monitor and a lower cost. TC Electronics, Korea, now supplies the TV modulators used in the Color Computers assembled at Tandy Home Computers. This effort to vertically integrate is an ongoing one.

Since such a large part of the cost of many of our products is influenced by semiconductor content, close contact with these suppliers is vital. An awareness of new semiconductor developments is necessary both to reduce cost and to enhance our products, as well as assuring our plants of deliveries in a timely and cost effective manner. Tandy has rapidly incorporated new standard large scale integrated (LSI) circuits into our designs.

This year saw the introduction in our products of such LSI developments as 64K RAMs, a floppy-disk controller chip, a Winchester disk controller chip set and an *ARCNET chip. All of these devices have resulted in improved performance at lower cost and with greater product reliability.

In addition to using the standard LSI components that have become available to the industry, there is a growing use of custom and semi-custom semiconductor devices. These include devices custom designed for Tandy as well as programmable logic arrays and gate arrays. The use of these devices reduces the component count of our products which in turn reduces the size. The net result is better quality and lower cost to build. Virtually every product in our computer line uses some of these devices and there are several major projects under way to incorporate more of these devices in several of our existing products.

Another area of ongoing cost reduction and product improvement involves streamlining of plant processes and facilities. Automatic insertion of components on printed circuit boards is now used at Tandy Instruments and at TC Electronics, Korea. Not only are the boards less costly but, since many of these machines also check for the quality or correctness of the part being inserted, there is considerable improvement in the quality of the finished board and fewer rejects which require expensive trouble shooting. The cost of repairing defective boards has also been reduced by the use of automatic testing equipment.

The ongoing growth of our sales and our range of products continues to require new facilities and updated equipment. Typical of this growth is the Lika printed circuit board facility in California. Approximately 16,000 square feet were added and equipped with the most modern equipment available to produce multi-layer printed circuit boards, one of the industry's fastest growing products. A 25,000 square-foot facility was constructed in Azle, Texas — Lika, Southwest.

Very substantial investments have been made in both equipment and new facilities in our California video and audio tape facility and in our joint venture tape-loading facility in Chicago. These include about 100,000 square feet of space and state-of-the-art techniques for tape production and loading, using automatic material handling, robotic assembly and computer-controlled quality assurance of process control.

TC Electronics, Taiwan, has added 138,000 square feet. This increased space and equipment will be used to support our growing line of telephone equipment and to increase our video monitor capacity.

---

* ARCNET is a trademark of Datapoint Corporation.

Tandy Electronics has an ongoing commitment to the consumer to bring high technology from the laboratory to the living room affordably. In this process we are also committed to improving the profitability of Tandy Corporation through efficient manufacturing.

Distribution — Continuing to Build

Fiscal year 1983 marked the opening of Tandy Corporation's 500th full-service Computer Center worldwide. More than 400 of these stores are located in the United States. These total-support retail service and training units have rapidly become the standard in microcomputer retailing. The reason is quite simple. Radio Shack's formula for marketing computers is successful.

A Radio Shack Computer Center begins with a choice location that is easily accessible to both the business community and the individual consumer. Typically around 3,000 square feet, a Computer Center incorporates a sales area designed for individual hands-on demonstration, a training room, in-store repair service, storage space and offices. Staffing varies depending on the actual sales volume of the store. A typical employee complement for an average volume store is a manager, one manager trainee, three full-time marketing representatives, a customer service representative, a full-time instructor and a repair service technician.

Radio Shack designed its Computer Centers with the thought in mind that our computer customer's experience only *begins* with the purchase. We have to provide a solution for our customer's problem — not just sell a piece of hardware. We know that by providing after-the-sale training, service and support our customer's confidence in Radio Shack will ring the cash drawer for subsequent purchases.

We believe no other distributor can match the level of sales support, training and service that we offer through our chain of computer stores. And, we expect these same standards will be key factors in developing the new Radio Shack Telephone Centers that are described on page 11.

In addition to the stand-alone Radio Shack Computer Center program, more than 775 expanded computer departments, or "*Plus* Computer Centers," have been placed in Tandy/Radio Shack retail stores worldwide. Six hundred of these centers are in the United States. In order to avert customer confusion, all full-service Computer Centers and expanded computer departments will henceforth be called Computer Centers with *Plus* placed before those housed within a Radio Shack retail store. The *Plus* Computer Center marketing concept places one or more trained computer marketing representatives in an approximately 200 square-foot area of a Radio Shack store. These *Plus* Computer Centers stock most of the items in our computer line. Originally the *Plus* Computer Center concept was designed to penetrate those markets deemed too small for stand-alone Computer Centers. However, these *Plus* Computer

Centers have recently been placed successfully in larger, metropolitan areas to augment penetration of specific population zones. With a very small capital investment, the *Plus* Computer Centers have proven tremendously successful.

Looking forward to fiscal 1984, Radio Shack will open 50 additional stand-alone Computer Centers in the United States and 15 Tandy Computer Centers internationally. Approximately 100 *Plus* Computer Centers will be placed in U.S. retail stores along with 20 internationally. Therefore, we anticipate having more than 1,400 Computer Centers by the end of fiscal 1984.

Providing support for our front-line Computer Centers and *Plus* Computer Centers is an ongoing effort. The backup team has been strengthened and now includes, in each of our 23 geographical regions in the United States, a regional computer marketing manager whose duties include the coordination of hiring and field training, as well as supervising a specialized marketing force. This regional marketing support group also includes one or more national account representatives whose responsibilities are initiating contact with Fortune 1000 companies and one or more regional educational coordinators providing expertise in marketing to the educational community. Individuals selected to fill these important positions have all been elevated from within the computer organization for their demonstrated abilities and they stand ready to assist the Computer Center and *Plus* Computer Center personnel whenever needed.

Probably the best news from Tandy/Radio Shack's computer marketing units has come through instituting various operational changes. Most units have become more efficient through tighter payroll scheduling, better inventory controls and greater utilization of training personnel. Radio Shack Computer Centers made significant improvement on bottom-line profitability during fiscal 1983. The outlook for next fiscal year is for continued, positive profit improvement on a per-store basis.

Radio Shack-U.S. also increased the number of full-line retail consumer electronics stores without *Plus* Compuer Centers by 93 during fiscal 1983 to a total of 4,179. Their average annual volume during the fiscal year increased over 12% with solid gains in both the computer and most of the non-computer merchandise lines. Radio Shack has always considered itself a distribution system for technology, so it comes as no surprise to see various product categories stand out with sizable volume gains. However, when gains are also accomplished in dollar volume of such "bread and butter" categories as radios, tape recorders, phonographs, and even TV antennas, we know consumers are relying more and more on Radio Shack for their complete electronic needs.

Opening new retail stores has long been a Radio Shack tradition. We will open 150 to 175 traditional Radio Shack stores this next year. Additionally, the careful scrutiny of existing store leases at expiration is playing an ever-increasing role in our store planning. Relocating from deteriorating areas, along with better positioning within viable shopping centers, is being heavily emphasized. More than 600 stores had facelifts during fiscal 1983, with at least that many planned for the current year. Attractive, well-merchandised, expertly staffed

Consolidated Statements of Income
Tandy Corporation and Subsidiaries
In thousands, except per share amounts.

	1983	1982	1981
Net sales	**$2,475,188**	$2,032,555	$1,691,373
Other income	**38,109**	28,657	15,697
	2,513,297	2,061,212	1,707,070
Costs and expenses:			
Cost of products sold	**1,008,187**	826,842	701,777
Selling, general and administrative, net of amounts allocated to spun-off operations in fiscal 1976 and prior	**930,244**	780,378	645,934
Depreciation and amortization	**38,679**	29,437	23,288
Interest expense, net of interest income and interest allocated to spun-off operations in fiscal 1976 and prior	**8,905**	1,168	15,454
	1,986,015	1,637,825	1,386,453
Income from continuing operations before income taxes	**527,282**	423,387	320,617
Provision for income taxes	**248,761**	199,302	151,015
Income from continuing operations	**278,521**	224,085	169,602
Loss from discontinued operations, net of income taxes	—	—	—
Net income before income from operations spun off	**278,521**	224,085	169,602
Income from operations spun off, net of income taxes	—	—	—
Net income	**$ 278,521**	$ 224,085	$ 169,602
Income (loss) per average common share and common share equivalent:			
Continuing operations	**$2.67**	$2.17	$1.65
Discontinued operations	—	—	—
Spun-off operations	—	—	—
Net income	**$2.67**	$2.17	$1.65
Average common shares and common share equivalents outstanding	**104,335**	103,395	102,578

The Review of Operations and Financial Information is an integral part of these statements.

stores, strategically placed in every viable consumer population zone is the common goal of each member of Radio Shack's field management team.

The final link in providing availability of Radio Shack products to every U.S. household is our associate store program. The fiscal 1983 sales and educational referral sales through our 2,010 franchisees and dealers exceeded $200,000,000. Mostly located in communities too small to support a company unit, our dealers have become an increasingly important part of our total

YEAR ENDED JUNE 30,						
1980	1979	1978	1977	1976	1975	1974
$1,384,637	$1,215,483	$1,059,324	$949,267	$741,722	$528,286	$411,241
11,360	11,403	5,629	3,763	2,649	3,963	2,153
1,395,997	1,226,886	1,064,953	953,030	744,371	532,249	413,394
594,841	535,549	491,509	434,031	331,400	249,006	198,067
546,325	484,249	403,173	350,878	270,308	204,107	158,792
19,110	17,121	13,879	11,140	8,034	7,392	5,461
25,063	28,466	30,260	15,192	7,282	14,044	8,544
1,185,339	1,065,385	938,821	811,241	617,024	474,549	370,864
210,658	161,501	126,132	141,789	127,347	57,700	42,530
98,423	78,272	59,986	69,970	63,066	29,078	20,669
112,235	83,229	66,146	71,819	64,281	28,622	21,861
—	—	—	(2,777)	—	(1,820)	(7,072)
112,235	83,229	66,146	69,042	64,281	26,802	14,789
—	—	—	—	3,243	7,794	5,657
$ 112,235	$ 83,229	$ 66,146	$ 69,042	$ 67,524	$ 34,596	$ 20,446
$1.12	$ .81	$ .69	$ .54	$ .44	$ .20	$ .13
—	—	—	(.02)	—	(.01)	(.04)
—	—	—	—	.02	.05	.03
$1.12	$ .81	$ .69	$ .52	$ .46	$ .24	$ .12
103,644	106,004	96,136	132,336	144,824	145,408	169,992

marketing picture. Tandy/Radio Shack hopes to increase the number of dealer locations by almost 200 units by the end of fiscal 1984.

The Radio Shack Store Operating System (SOS) proved an invaluable link this year between retail operating units, home office accounting and warehouse operations. Each retail store is able to transmit daily on a TRS-80 microcomputer sales and financial data and, as required, payroll, inventory and merchandise orders. Not only has the SOS streamlined store operations, the accounting functions in Fort Worth and the regional warehouse operations have benefited greatly from this system. During the second quarter of fiscal 1984, a hard disk will be added to each store's SOS to provide memory for additional functions planned for the SOS.

Providing our customers with products they want at a convenient location and then giving them the after-the-sale service they have come to expect is why Radio Shack continues to be the leader in consumer electronics.

REPORT OF INDEPENDENT ACCOUNTS

To the Board of Directors and Stockholders of Tandy Corporation

In our opinion, the consolidated balance sheets and the related consolidated statements of income, of stockholders' equity and of changes in financial position appearing on pages 16 to 47 present fairly the financial position of Tandy Corporation and its subsidiaries at June 30, 1983 and 1982, and the results of their operations and the changes in their financial position for each of the three years in the period ended June 30, 1983, in conformity with generally accepted accounting principles consistently applied. Our examinations of these statements were made in accordance with generally accepted auditing standards and accordingly included such tests of the accounting records and such other auditing procedures as we considered necessary in the circumstances. Also, in our opinion, the consolidated statements of income and of changes in financial position for the seven years ended June 30, 1980, which have been prepared from the applicable statements covered by our opinions in each of those years, present fairly the financial information included therein.

Price Waterhouse

Fort Worth, Texas
August 18, 1983

INCOME STATEMENT REVIEW

Net Sales

Tandy Corporation's consolidated sales increased 22% in fiscal 1983—an increase of $442,633,000 from the prior year's sales. For the five years ended June 30, 1983, sales have grown at a rate of 18%. Year-to-year sales gains of 20%, 22%, 14% and 15% were recorded in 1982, 1981, 1980 and 1979. Tandy Corporation has recorded sales gains in excess of 10% for each of the ten years ended June 30, 1983. These gains have ranged from a low of 12% in fiscal 1978 to a high of 40% in 1976.

The Company's sales volume has grown through expansion of the store system, increases in sales of old stores, growth of new product categories and development of the international operations.

Retail outlet openings, net of closings, totaled 350 during fiscal 1983. Although 260 company-owned stores were added during fiscal 1983, this number was less than the 372 company-owned stores opened in 1982 or the 388 stores opened in 1981. Tandy/Radio Shack's retail outlets are primarily located in the United States, Canada, Europe and Pacific/Asia. The Company's store opening plans were revised during fiscal 1983 when the economies of the countries in which the Company operates, particularly in Europe, did not

Retail Outlets

			JUNE 30,		
	1983	1982	1981	1980	1979
Radio Shack-U.S.					
Company-owned	**4,584**	4,398	4,132	3,881	3,645
Dealer/franchise	**2,010**	1,983	2,046	2,074	2,197
	6,594	6,381	6,178	5,955	5,842
International Operations					
Canada					
Company-owned	**453**	442	424	403	395
Dealer/franchise	**384**	364	386	381	386
	837	806	810	784	781
Europe					
Company-owned	**538**	491	416	319	272
Dealer/franchise	**272**	234	212	178	142
	810	725	628	497	414
Pacific/Asia					
Company-owned	**204**	188	175	156	141
Dealer/franchise	**216**	226	206	193	104
	420	414	381	349	245
Other International Outlets	**207**	192	164	130	71
	8,868	8,518	8,161	7,715	7,353

Consolidated Monthly Sales (Unaudited) In thousands.

	YEAR ENDED JUNE 30, 1983		1982		1981	1980	1979
July	**$ 165,467**	**6.7%**	$ 131,671	6.5%	$ 100,802	$ 88,240	$ 79,427
August	**178,481**	**7.2%**	147,773	7.3	117,008	101,268	88,363
September	**173,163**	**7.0**	145,577	7.2	117,055	101,461	95,193
October	**189,324**	**7.6**	159,456	7.8	128,631	104,018	93,242
November	**213,782**	**8.6**	176,227	8.7	151,811	133,918	112,245
December	**375,049**	**15.2**	302,586	14.9	253,854	209,728	189,782
January	**200,785**	**8.1**	160,458	7.9	140,567	112,275	93,952
February	**181,696**	**7.3**	146,949	7.2	125,596	104,624	82,130
March	**207,379**	**8.4**	163,200	8.0	142,182	108,133	100,035
April	**196,773**	**8.0**	154,991	7.6	137,793	105,179	88,873
May	**189,685**	**7.7**	168,464	8.3	135,802	105,919	90,884
June	**203,604**	**8.2**	175,203	8.6	140,272	109,874	101,357
	$2,475,188	**100.0%**	$2,032,555	100.0%	$1,691,373	$1,384,637	$1,215,483
Sales by quarter:							
September		**20.9%**		21.0%	19.8%	21.0%	21.7%
December		**31.4**		31.4	31.6	32.3	32.5
March		**23.8**		23.1	24.1	23.5	22.7
June		**23.9**		24.5	24.5	23.2	23.1
		100.0%		100.0%	100.0%	100.0%	100.0%

improve to desired levels. The Canadian store system increased by 11 company-owned stores and 20 dealer/franchise outlets in fiscal 1983. Sixty-three company-owned stores and 28 dealer/franchise outlets were added to the European and Pacific/Asian store systems in 1983. A network of international dealers has been established to serve countries that do not have company-owned stores. This system, supported by Radio Shack-U.S. operations, added 15 new outlets during fiscal 1983.

Increasing sales of existing stores and dealers is a high priority for management. The average monthly sales increase for Radio Shack-U.S. stores in existence more than one year was 12% in fiscal 1983 compared to 10% for fiscal 1982. Old store sales increased 11% in 1981, 6% in 1980, 10% in 1979 and 3% in 1978. Technological advancements, particularly in computers and telecommunications, have provided new and innovative products that have enabled many mature stores to continue their sales growth.

As shown in the chart above, Tandy's business is relatively stable throughout the year. The December quarter has historically been the peak selling season; but in recent years some of the additions to the product line, such as computers, have been less seasonal than the traditional lines because they are sold to businesses, schools and governmental agencies as well as to individuals.

The 1983 sales to U.S. dealers and franchisees were $193,581,000, a 14% increase from the 1982 sales of $169,431,000. In 1982 a 30% increase was recorded from the 1981 sales of $130,141,000. Average annual purchases by U.S. dealers have increased from $15,500 in 1974 to $53,800 in 1981, $72,400 in 1982 and $81,300 in 1983. The addition of computer merchandise to many dealers' inventories has increased the overall average of Radio Shack's sales to dealers.

Enhancement of the traditional merchandise line through technological advancements plus the introduction of new products such as telephones, answering devices, security equipment and the TRS-80® line of microcomputers have provided a basis for the Company's sales growth even during difficult economic times. The accompanying chart illustrates the Company's merchandising flexibility. This table is based on shipments from the warehouses to the Company's retail outlets at suggested retail prices. It does not reflect markdowns or discounts as a result of special promotions.

Every class of products, except one, showed gains from 1982 to 1983. The strongest gains in dollars and percentages were posted by computers, telephones and intercoms and the toy, antenna and security classification. The publicity surrounding the telephone deregulation issue and advancements in telephone features have provided the Company with an excellent marketing opportunity for telephones and related accessories. Video and cable accessories and electronic toys and games showed strong growth in fiscal 1983. The only classification on the chart that did not show absolute dollar gains in fiscal 1983 was citizens band radios, walkie-talkies, scanners and public address systems. This category declined 3%. Management believes that one of the Company's strengths is its ability to adapt its product line quickly to include new product offerings to meet the demands and needs of its customers. The accompanying chart illustrates how the product line and sales emphasis have been modified to accommodate the changes in the consumer electronics marketplace during the last five years.

The warehouse shipments of microcomputers, software, peripheral equipment and accessories were almost 35% of 1983's total warehouse shipments and also showed a year-to-year increase of 34%. The following chart gives a perspective on the composition of the computer and computer-related shipments in the United States.

Other Income

Income arising from the Company's normal business operations that is not appropriately classified as sales of products is included in other income. Contract and repair service income and lease income, primarily from computers, are now the largest items included in this classification. Rent income, computer training program fees, dealer fees, data processing revenues, equity earnings from joint ventures and other miscellaneous revenues are also included in other income. The year-to-year increase in other income for fiscal 1983, $9,452,000,

Worldwide Warehouse Shipments
(Unaudited) Class of Products

	YEAR ENDED JUNE 30,				
	1983	1982	1981	1980	1979
Radios, phonographs and televisions	**8.6%**	9.4%	11.6%	12.1%	13.3%
Citizens band radios, walkie-talkies, scanners and public address systems	**4.9**	6.0	6.8	9.3	13.2
Audio equipment, tape recorders and related accessories	**18.2**	21.5	25.4	29.5	33.8
Electronic parts, batteries, test equipment and related items	**13.2**	13.9	14.5	15.8	16.4
Toys, antennas, security devices, timers and calculators	**12.5**	12.0	14.1	12.6	10.3
Telephones and intercoms	**8.0**	6.5	5.8	5.6	3.5
Microcomputers, software and peripheral equipment	**34.6**	30.7	21.8	15.1	9.5
	100.0%	100.0%	100.0%	100.0%	100.0%

(Unaudited)

	YEAR ENDED JUNE 30,		
	1983	1982	1981
Model I/III/4	**28.1%**	27.2%	30.5%
Model II/12/16	**21.4**	25.7	25.3
Color computers	**9.8**	7.2	3.3
Portable/pocket computers	**3.1**	2.5	2.7
Printers	**16.5**	16.7	17.5
Software	**9.2**	8.5	7.5
Other	**11.9**	12.2	13.2
	100.0%	100.0%	100.0%

resulted from growth in computer contract and repair service income, fees from computer training courses and computer lease income. More than $10,000,000 of the $12,960,000 increase in other income from fiscal 1981 to 1982 was related to computer contract and repair service income and computer lease income. The $4,337,000 increase between 1980 and 1981 was caused by the same principal factors as the 1981-82 increase.

Gross Profit and Cost of Products Sold

Gross profit as a percent of sales remained steady at 59.3% for fiscal 1983 and 1982 after four years of increases in gross margins. The gross profit percentage has increased from 55.9% in 1979 to the current 59.3% level for several reasons.

Factors that have favorably influenced the gross profit trend are the continuing increase in the dollar volume of self-manufactured products and an increase in manufacturing profits, particularly in computer lines. Greatly expanded production combined with technological advancements in production and product design have boosted the North American manufacturing profit margin significantly in recent years. In fiscal 1983, however, there was a slight decline in the gross profit percentage of the North American manufacturing division. An increase in gross margins of the Radio Shack-U.S. retail operations offset this decline.

Several factors have prevented gross margins from reaching even higher levels. Radio Shack-Canada's gross margins improved from 1981 to 1982 but declined slightly during 1983. Gross profit percentages for the European and Pacific/Asian retail operations have declined for three years. The strength of the U.S. dollar has increased merchandise costs, particularly in Europe. Also, general market conditions, competition and legal restrictions in certain countries have prevented the Company from raising prices sufficiently to maintain gross margins.

The Company's operations are primarily retail with manufacturing, warehousing, distribution and other services to support the retail store system. Gross profit percentages for this type of operation are typically higher than for strictly wholesale companies. In late fiscal 1982 the Company acquired the domestic portion of the Consumer Products Division of Memorex Corporation (now called Memtek Products), a manufacturer and wholesaler of audio and video tape products, as a complement to its retail operations. Memtek's lower gross profit percentage had a negative impact on the comparison of the 1982 and 1983 gross profit percentages.

Price competition in the Company's product categories affects the Company's gross margin. The strength and direction of this competition varies from year to year. During fiscal 1983 the small computer and electronic game industries were very competitive.

Selling, General and Administrative Expenses

The year-to-year increase in selling, general and administrative expenses was held to 19% compared to a 22% increase in sales. During the five years ended June 30, 1983, the percentage increase in selling, general and administrative expenses has always been less than the percentage increase in sales except for fiscal 1982 when the year-to-year increases were almost the same. These expenses dropped to 37.6% of sales for fiscal 1983, the lowest percentage of sales since fiscal 1977. As a percent of sales, selling, general and administrative expenses were 38.4% in 1982 and 38.2% in 1981.

Payroll, the largest category in the selling, general and administrative expenses, was 16.0% of sales for fiscal 1983. This is the lowest percentage of payroll costs to sales since the 16.2% level in fiscal 1977 and 1978. The dollar amount of payroll increased 16.4% to $395,135,000 in fiscal 1983 from

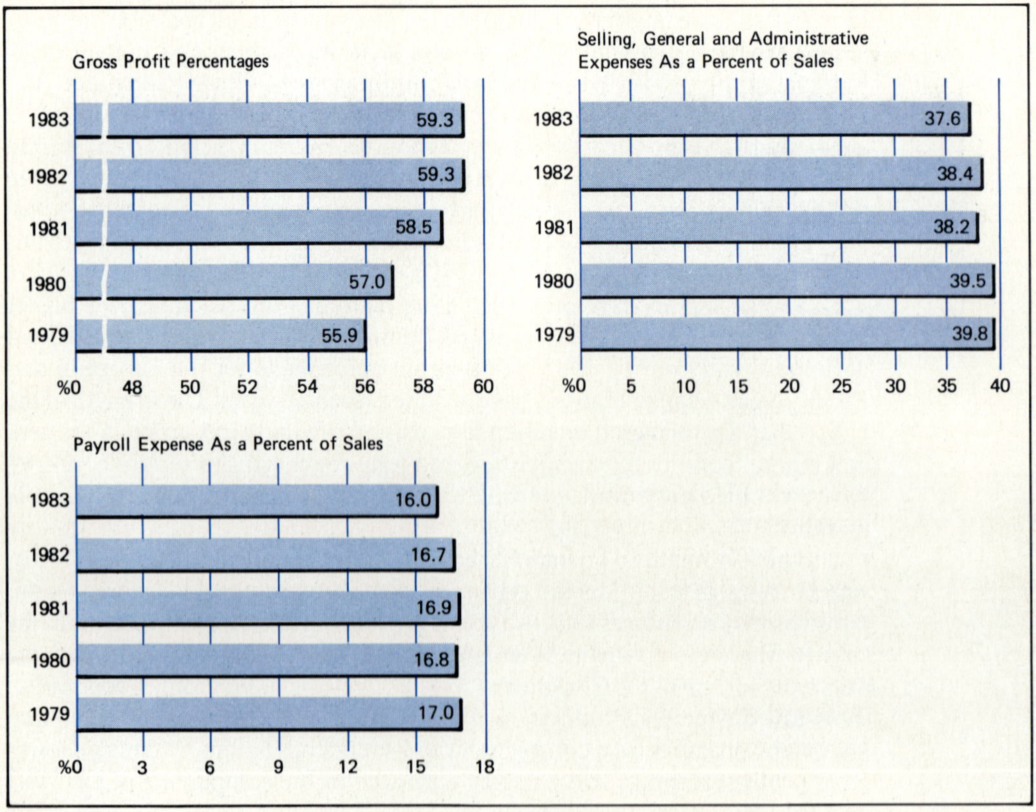

$339,559,000 in 1982. The relationship of payroll costs to sales was fairly steady for the four years ended June 30, 1982 with a high of 17.0% and a low of 16.7%. Payroll costs for 1981 were $286,494,000 compared to $232,569,000 in 1980 and $206,507,000 in 1979. Manufacturing payroll costs included in cost of products sold were $71,892,000 in 1983, $53,105,000 in 1982, $42,128,000 in 1981, $32,958,000 in 1980 and $28,344,000 in 1979. The growth of the manufacturing payroll is directly related to the increase in self-manufacturing that is discussed on pages 44 and 45. Approximately 24% of the more than 32,000 people employed by Tandy Corporation are involved in the manufacturing operations.

Advertising expense for newspaper, television, radio and other media, including catalog preparation and distribution costs, was $199,128,000 in 1983, a 23.8% increase from the expenditures of $160,905,000 in 1982. For the first time since 1979 the percentage increase in advertising expense was greater than the sales increase. Heavy competition in the computer marketplace coupled with the difficult sales environment of a recession required an increased level of advertising expenditures during fiscal 1983 to maintain sales at accept-

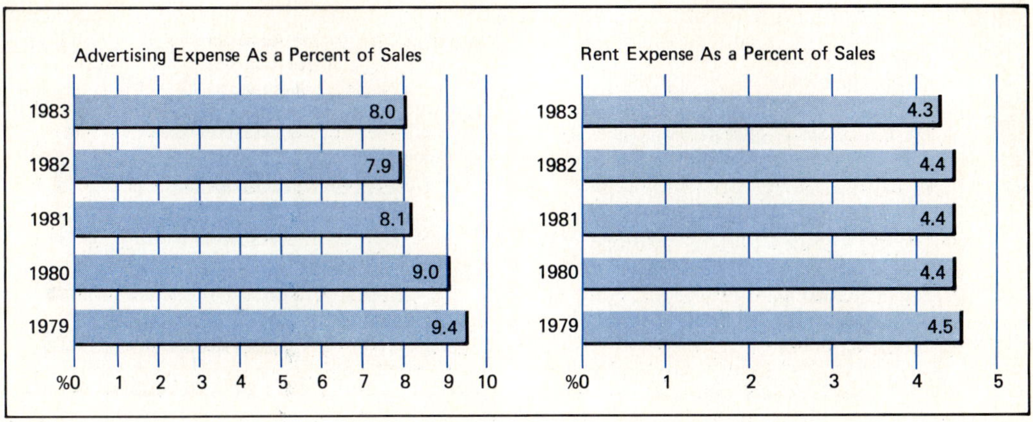

able levels. Fiscal 1982 sales gains of 20% were achieved with a 17% increase in advertising expenditures while fiscal 1981 and 1980 advertising expenditures increased only 11% and 9% but produced sales gains of 22% and 14%. Because sales grew faster than advertising expenses during this three year period, advertising expense as a percentage of sales declined from a high of 9.4% in 1979 to 7.9% in 1982. In 1983 advertising expense as a percentage of sales increased slightly to 8.0%. Advertising costs were $137,722,000 in 1981, $124,138,000 in 1980 and $114,238,000 in 1979. These amounts exclude salaries and other overhead expenses related to the Company's advertising departments.

Rent expense as a percent of sales has remained stable at 4.3% to 4.5% of sales for the five years ended June 30, 1983. The expansion of the Company's operations, particularly the retail store system, and escalations in base rents for old stores as lease agreements expire have increased the dollar amount of rent expense. The average base rent per square foot for U.S. stores opened in fiscal 1983 was $9.38, slightly lower than the $9.43 in fiscal 1982. The average square-foot base rent for stores opened in 1981 was $7.82. The overall average base rent per square foot for all U.S. stores was $6.34 in fiscal 1983, $5.77 in fiscal 1982 and $5.12 in 1981.

The retail store leases are the most significant portion of rent expense and are generally for 10 years, some having renewal options. These leases are normally based on a minimum rental plus a percentage of the store's sales in excess of a stipulated base figure. The Company also leases offices, warehouses, land and equipment.

As shown in the accompanying schedule, the Company leases rather than owns most of its facilities. Retail space is generally leased because the store locations are primarily in major shopping malls or shopping centers that are owned by other companies. The Company owns a twin-tower office complex in Fort Worth, Texas. More than half of the leasable office space in this complex is occupied by the Company. There are 12 major warehouse locations. Eight of these are in the United States. Canada, Great Britain, Belgium and Australia also have warehouses. Manufacturing operations are located in five different countries—25 in the United States and one each in Canada, Japan, Korea and Taiwan.

Rent Expense In thousands

	YEAR ENDED JUNE 30, 1983	1982	1981	1980	1979
Minimum rents	**\$101,886**	\$86,003	\$71,057	\$59,600	\$53,397
Contingent rents	**7,046**	5,470	4,452	3,674	3,498
Sublease rents	**(1,962)**	(1,741)	(1,652)	(1,783)	(2,289)
Total rent expense	**\$106,970**	\$89,732	\$73,857	\$61,491	\$54,606

The total space owned and leased by the Company at June 30, 1983 was as follows:

In thousands

	APPROXIMATE SQUARE FEET OWNED	LEASED	TOTAL
Retail	563	12,860	13,423
Warehouse and office	2,363	2,373	4,736
Manufacturing operations	1,226	1,208	2,434
Total	4,152	16,441	20,593

Capital leases, as defined by the Financial Accounting Standards Board's Statement No. 13, were not material in total at June 30, 1983. The Company's operations are basically structured in a manner that precludes the need for financing or capital leases.

Minimum rent commitments at June 30, 1983 for all long-term noncancellable leases (net of immaterial amounts of sublease rent income) were:

	IN THOUSANDS.
1984	\$ 83,649
1985	78,615
1986	70,572
1987	61,564
1988	52,556
1989 and thereafter	206,806

Taxes, other than income taxes, were \$43,431,000 in 1983 compared to \$37,135,000 in 1982, \$29,078,000 in 1981, \$22,530,000 in 1980 and \$19,412,000 in 1979. Payroll taxes are approximately two-thirds of this category and property taxes account for most of the balance of this expense category.

Stock purchase and savings plans are offered by the Company for its employees. These plans are designed to provide the Company's employees a consistent investment program to provide for their retirement and an opportunity to participate in the growth of the Company. The Company's contributions to these plans were $19,004,000 in 1983, $13,323,000 in 1982, $11,565,000 in 1981, $9,091,000 in 1980 and $7,258,000 in 1979.

Effective July 1, 1982, the Tandy Employees Investment Plan was replaced by the Tandy Employees Deferred Salary and Investment Plan. The significant change between these plans is the taxability of the employee's contribution to the plan. Under the old plan, the employee's contribution was considered taxable income to the employee. The first 5% contribution under the new plan is considered deferred compensation and is not taxed to the employee as long as it is kept in the plan. The employee investment plan is available to most employees who have been employed two years. An employee who elects to join the plan can contribute either 5% or 10% of annual compensation. The Company matches 80% of the employee's first 5% contribution. The Company's contributions are fully invested upon payment to the trustee. Administrative committees appointed by the Company's Board of Directors invest the plans' assets. A substantial majority of the plans' assets are invested in Tandy Corporation securities.

The Company also has a stock purchase program available to most employees. Each participant may contribute 1% to 10% of annual compensation. The Company matches 40%, 60% or 80% of the employee's contribution depending on the length of the employee's participation in the program. The Company periodically purchases treasury stock on the open market and then sells the number of shares required by the program each month at a price equal to the average of the daily closing prices for that month. The stock purchased by each participant is distributed annually after the close of the program's year, December 31. In the event treasury shares are not available, authorized but unissued shares can be used. However, to date the Company has always funded the program with open market purchases and it is the present intention of management to continue this procedure.

The expense categories discussed account for more than 80% of the total selling, general and administrative expenses for the five years ended June 30 1983. Other selling, general and administrative expenses were $166,576,000 for fiscal 1983, $139,724,000 for fiscal 1982, $107,218,000 for 1981, $96,506,000 for 1980 and $82,228,000 for 1979. The Company's growth and inflation have contributed to the year-to-year increases in these other costs. Postage, office supplies, reproduction expenses, utilities telephone costs, insurance and other items are included in these amounts. FAS No. 52 foreign currency transaction gains or losses for fiscal 1983 and 1982 and FAS No. 8 translation and exchange gains and losses for 1981 are discussed under International and Domestic Operations.

Depreciation and Amortization

Depreciation and amortization expense for fiscal 1983 was $38,679,000, an increase of $9,242,000 from the 1982 depreciation and amortization of $29,437,000. Depreciation was 1.6% of sales for 1983 compared to 1.4% of sales in each of the four year ended June 30, 1982. One reason for the increased depreciation as a percentage of sales for fiscal 1983 was the acquisition of Memtek Products in the latter part of fiscal 1982. The dollar amount of depreciation has more than doubled since 1979 because the retail store system, manufacturing plants and distribution facilities have been expanded or remodeled to meet the Company's growth.

Components of Interest Expense
In thousands.

	YEAR ENDED JUNE 30,				
	1983	1982	1981	1980	1979
10% debentures due 1991	**$ 9,808**	$ 9,808	$ 8,808	$ 9,807	$ 9,811
10% debentures due 1994	**3,516**	3,481	3,450	3,424	3,403
6½% convertible debentures	—	—	—	6,499	4,369
$110,000,000 revolving credit line	—	—	—	—	4,046
Foreign indebtedness	**4,714**	6,066	4,204	3,285	3,792
Other	**6,006**	2,759	5,171	4,382	4,279
	24,044	22,114	22,633	27,397	29,700
Less interest income	**15,139**	20,946	7,179	2,334	1,234
	$ 8,905	$ 1,168	$15,454	$25,063	$28,466

Net Interest Expense

Net interest expense increased in fiscal 1983 after four consecutive years of declines. The decline in interest rates during fiscal 1983 had an adverse effect on income from short-term investments. The increase in average short-term debt from $39,100,000 in fiscal 1982 to $48,700,000 in 1983 made interest expense rise even though the weighted average interest rate for this debt declined from 15.8% in 1982 to 11.8% in 1983. Average short-term debt levels during fiscal 1981, 1980 and 1979 were approximately $57,900,000, $46,600,000 and $74,500,000 respectively. The weighted average interest rates for these borrowings were 13.3% in 1981, 13.1% in 1980 and 9.9% in 1979. The most significant transaction affecting interest expense in recent years was the conversion of the 6½% convertible subordinated debentures in the first quarter of fiscal 1981. Under the terms of the indenture, no interest was paid on any debentures converted into common stock even though they were outstanding during part of the first quarter. Substantially all of the debenture holders elected to convert their debentures into stock.

The Company's cash and short-term investment position increased during fiscal 1983—averaging more than $188,000,000 for the twelve months ended June 30, 1983 compared to $155,000,000 for fiscal 1982. The Company's cash position fluctuates significantly because of seasonal cash requirements and sales. Purchases of inventory for the Christmas selling season uses much of the cash flow during the early part of the fiscal year while the heavy influx of cash from Christmas sales adds to the available cash. The decline in interest rates during fiscal 1983 reduced interest income despite an increase in average funds invested. The combination of rising interest rates combined with more funds invested caused interest income to grow during the four years ended June 30, 1982. The accompanying table shows the principal components of interest expense.

Provision for Income Taxes

The Company provides for income taxes on all items included in the consolidated statements of income regardless of the period when such items are reported for tax purposes. The Company uses the "flow-through" method for investment tax credits for all items except certain leveraged leases. Under the "flow-through" method income taxes are reduced in the year an asset is placed in service by the amount of the investment credit. Generally accepted accounting principles require that the investment tax credit on leveraged leases be recognized over the life of the lease. The domestic and foreign components of pretax income and the differences between the effective tax rate and the statutory rate are detailed in the accompanying charts. The U.S. statutory tax rate for the four years ended June 30, 1983 was 46%. The fiscal 1979 rate was 47%, a weighted average of the 48% rate in effect during the first half of fiscal 1979 and the 46% rate that became effective January 1, 1979 under the Revenue Act of 1978.

Certain provisions of the income tax laws and regulations result in some income and expense items being recorded in one period for financial accounting purposes and in another period for income tax purposes. Such items, which are included in the provision for income taxes as deferred taxes, relate primarily to differences between tax and book depreciation, income from installment sales and provisions for future losses; changes in intercompany profits in ending inventories not eliminated for tax purposes; taxes provided on net undistributed earnings of certain foreign subsidiaries not currently taxable in the United States; and unrealized gains or losses on foreign currency translation. The tax effect of each of these timing differences was less than 5% of the amount computed by multiplying pretax income for the year by the statutory tax rate. Deferred taxes and investment tax credits related to computer installment sales have increased as these sales have increased.

Net Income and Earnings Per Share

For the five years ended June 30, 1983, net income has increased at a rate of 35%, calculated by the least squares method. The five-year growth rate of net income per share was 33%. Net income increased 24% from fiscal 1982 to 1983 compared to a 32% increase from 1981 to 1982, a 51% increase from 1980 to 1981 and a 35% increase from 1979 to 1980.

Income Tax Expense
In thousands

	YEAR ENDED JUNE 30, 1983	1982	1981	1980	1979
Current					
Federal	**$200,492**	$159,007	$122,678	$ 84,992	$64,858
State	**19051**	15981	10568	6,552	5,147
Foreign	**25,007**	21,604	15,882		
		196,592	149,128	101540	75,520
Deferred					
Federal	**3,118**	3,879	2,318	(1,223)	1,649
Foreign	**1,093**	(1,169)	(431)	(1,894)	1,103
Total Income tax expense	**$248,761**	$199,302	$151015	$ 98,423	$78,272

Statutory vs. Effective Tax
In thousands.

	YEAR ENDED JUNE 30, 1983	1982	1981	1980	1979
Components of pretax income:					
United States	**$474,776**	$367,970	$285,089	$183,342	$146,827
Foreign	**52,506**	55,417	35,528	27,316	14,674
Income before income taxes	**527,282**	423,387	320,617	210,658	161,501
Statutory tax rate	**×46%**	×46%	×46%	×46%	×47%
Federal income tax at statutory rate	**$242,550**	$194,758	$147,484	$ 96,903	$ 75,905
Investment tax credit	**(5,494)**	(5,310)	(2,992)	(1,499)	(695)
State and provincial income taxes, less federal income tax benefit	**12,075**	10,177	6,970	4,418	3,430
Other, net	**(370)**	(323)	(447)	(1,399)	(368)
Total income tax expense	**$248,761**	$199,302	$151,015	$ 98,423	$ 78,272
Effective tax rate	**47.2%**	47.1%	47.1%	46.7%	48.5%

Per share amounts are based on the weighted average shares of common stock and common stock equivalents, if any, outstanding during the year. Treasury stock purchases in fiscal 1980 and 1979 had favorable effects on per share amounts in those years. The convertible debentures issued in October

1978 were considered common stock equivalents for calculating earnings per share during the time they were outstanding. Various transactions from 1974 to 1978 reduced the number of shares outstanding. The per share amounts reflect two-for-one stock splits in December and May of fiscal 1981 and two-for-one stock splits in fiscal 1978 and 1976.

Historically the Company has not paid cash dividends. The Board of Directors periodically reviews the dividend policy. No change is contemplated at this time.

International and Domestic Operations

Sales to unaffiliated customers by operations outside the United States were 15.6% of 1983's consolidated sales, or $386,337,000 in U.S. dollars. In 1982 the non-U.S. sales were $348,015,000 or 17.1% of total sales. Non-U.S. sales for 1981 totaled $307,864,000, or 18.2% of consolidated sales.

During fiscal 1982 the Financial Accounting Standards Board issued Statement No. 52, Foreign Currency Translation. The Company adopted this statement during the third quarter of fiscal 1982. Under this standard, most of the effects of translation rate changes related to net assets located outside the United States, previously included in income, are now recorded in a separate account in stockholders' equity. Foreign currency translation adjustments included in stockholders' equity were $3,980,000 net of deferred taxes of $3,390,000 in fiscal 1983 and $6,835,000 net of $1,789,000 in deferred taxes for fiscal 1982. Under FAS No. 52 only net gains or losses from foreign currency transactions are included in selling, general and administrative expenses. There were net losses of $590,000 in 1983 and $3,216,000 in 1982. Both translation and exchange gains and losses were included in selling, general and administrative expenses under FAS No. 8 rules. There were net translation and exchange gains of $5,295,000 in fiscal 1981. Certain balance sheet accounts, primarily inventories and property and equipment, previously translated from foreign currencies into U.S. dollars at historical exchange rates, are now translated at year-end rates. Income and expenses are translated at the weighted average exchange rate for the year. Under the old method, cost of goods sold and depreciation were translated using historical exchange rates, not weighted average rates. The financial statements for the first six months of fiscal 1982 were restated to conform to the provisions of FAS No. 52. This restatement increased net income for the six months ended December 31, 1981 by $5,887,000. Financial statements of the foreign operations for prior years have not been restated because operating decisions in those prior years were based upon the rules of FAS No. 8 and restatement is not required by FAS No. 52.

Canadian sales gains for fiscal 1983 were 19.1% in Canadian dollars and 16.8% in U.S. dollars. In fiscal 1982 the Canadian dollar increase in sales was 12.1% while the increase in U.S. dollars was 9.7%. Sales increases were greater in Canadian dollars than in U.S. dollars because the Canadian dollar dropped in

Operations by Geographic Area
Tandy Corporation and Subsidiaries In thousands.

	UNITED STATES	CANADA	EUROPE	PACIFIC/ ASIA	ELIMINATIONS	CONSOLIDATED
1983						
Sales to unaffiliated customers	$2,088,851	$187,129	$130,856	$ 68,352	$ —	$2,475,188
Transfers between geographic areas	75,936	5	91	398,300	(474,332)	—
Total revenue	$2,164,787	$187,134	$130,947	$466,652	$(474,332)	$2,475,188
Operating profit	$ 498,340	$ 26,349	$ (8,212)	$ 26,624	$ (1,012)	$ 542,089
General corporate expenses						(5,902)
Interest expense, net						(8,905)
Income before taxes						$ 527,282
Identifiable assets at June 30, 1983	$ 966,305	$ 79,671	$100,792	$ 96,098	$ (20,999)	$1,221,867
Corporate assets						360,041
Total assets at June 30, 1983						$1,581,908
1982						
Sales to unaffiliated customers	$1,684,540	$160,198	$117,816	$ 70,001	$ —	$2,032,555
Transfers between geographic areas	87,349	—	65	347,269	(434,683)	—
Total revenue	$1,771,889	$160,198	$117,881	$417,270	$(434,683)	$2,032,555
Operating profit	$ 398,917	$ 22,657	$ 2,313	$ 19,218	$ (11,100)	$ 432,005
General corporate expenses						(7,450)
Interest expense, net						(1,168)
Income before taxes						$ 423,387
Identifiable assets at June 30, 1982	$ 764,119	$ 66,693	$ 88,631	$ 98,982	$ (19,987)	$ 998,438
Corporate assets						229,206
Total assets at June 30, 1982						$1,227,644

Note: Operating income represents all revenues of the geographic segment less all operating expenses attributable to that segment. The operating profits of a geographic location exclude corporate expenses, net interest expense and income taxes. Transfers between geographic areas are generally recorded at market price.

Operations by Geographic Area
Tandy Corporation and Subsidiaries In thousands.

	UNITED STATES	CANADA	EUROPE	PACIFIC/ ASIA	ELIMINATIONS	CONSOLIDATED
1981						
Sales to unaffiliated customers	$1,383,509	$146,079	$112,034	$ 49,751	$ —	$1,691,373
Transfers between geographic areas ...	65,817	—	—	280,865	(346,682)	—
Total revenue ...	$1,449,326	$146,079	$112,034	$330,616	$(346,682)	$1,691,373
Operating profit ...	$ 303,951	$ 18,623	$ 13,235	$ 10,511	$ (2,161)	$ 344,159
General corporate expenses						(8,088)
Interest expense, net						(15,454)
Income before taxes						$ 320,617
Identifiable assets at June 30, 1981	$ 544,015	$ 52,657	$ 65,582	$ 61,592	$ (8,886)	$ 714,960
Corporate assets ...						221,585
Total assets at June 30, 1981						$ 936,545

value relative to the U.S. dollar during these years. Canadian operating profits were 14.1% of sales in 1983 and 1982 compared to 12.7% in 1981. The Canadian operations of Memtek Products that were acquired in January 1983 are included in the 1983 schedule of Operations by Geographic Area.

European sales and operating results have been adversely affected by the strengthening of the U.S. dollar against European currencies, general market conditions, competition and legal restrictions on price increases in certain countries. The European operations of Memtek Products, which were acquired in fiscal 1983, are included in the Operations by Geographic Area for 1983 but not in 1982 and 1981. Although sales gains were posted in all of the European retail operations, these gains were considerably smaller when translated into U.S. dollars. The European operations showed losses in both local currencies and U.S. currencies for fiscal 1983. Transaction losses for fiscal 1983 included in the European operating losses were $1,304,000. The fiscal 1982 operating profits for Europe included more than $2,000,000 in transaction losses under FAS No. 52 rules compared to almost $3,000,000 in translation and exchange gains in fiscal 1981 under FAS No. 8.

Retail operations in Australia have also been affected by a devaluation of the Australian dollar. Sales gains of 27.1% in Australian dollars were recorded in fiscal 1983. After translation into U.S. dollars these gains were reduced to 8.5%. In fiscal 1982 sales gains of 29.8% in Australian dollars translated into

24.3% gains in U.S. dollars. Australian operating profits actually increased from 1982 to 1983 in local and U.S. dollars after a moderate decline between 1981 and 1982.

The Company has manufacturing and purchasing operations in several Asian countries. Manufacturing operations are located in Japan, Korea and Taiwan. A&A International, a U.S. subsidiary of the Company, purchases approximately 40% of the products in the 1984 Radio Shack catalog as well as some parts used in the Company's manufacturing operations. A&A has affiliates in Hong Kong, Japan, Taiwan and Korea. Transfers between geographic areas shown on the table highlighting operations by geographic areas are essentially intercompany transfers of goods out of the Asian region. The domestic and foreign manufacturing operations transfer goods to A&A International in the United States or to A&A's affiliates in the Orient. Also, A&A's affiliates purchase goods from outside suppliers to transfer to A&A International. A&A then transfers these products to Radio Shack and Tandy International Electronics.

Tandy Corporation's line of business is consumer electronics retailing. The Company's consolidated financial statements include the accounts of the Company and its wholly owned subsidiaries. All significant intercompany transactions and balances have been eliminated. The Company's primary domestic operations are Radio Shack, A&A International and the domestic manufacturing operations. During fiscal 1982 and 1983 the domestic and international operations of the Consumer Products Division of Memorex Corporation were acquired. This added video tape manufacturing to the Company's manufacturing operations. Memtek Products, the sales organization of this manufacturing unit, markets a line of Memorex audio and video products under the Memorex tradename.

The Company obtains merchandise from a large number of suppliers, not one of which accounted for more than 10% of the cost of products sold in fiscal 1983. Alternatives sources of supply exist for all of the merchandise purchased by the Company.

The consumer electronics business is highly competitive. Tandy competes in the sale of its products with department stores, mail order houses, discount stores, general merchants, home appliance stores and gift stores which sell comparable products manufactured by others. Domestic competitors range in size from the local drug and hardware stores to large chains and department stores. Computer store chains and franchise groups, such as Computerland Corporation, as well as a growing number of independent computer stores compete with the Company in the microcomputer marketplace. Several major retailers have also entered the microcomputer market. Competition is also encountered from manufacturers, such as IBM, selling directly to consumers. The products which compete with those sold by the Company are manufactured by numerous domestic and foreign manufacturers and many of them carry nationally recognized brand names or private labels. Many of the Company's competitors have financial resources equal to or greater than the Company's resources.

Management believes that among the factors that are important to its competitive position are price, quality, service and the wide selection of electronic products carried at conveniently located retail outlets. The Company's utilization of trained personnel and its ability to use national and local advertising media are important to the Company's ability to compete in the consumer electronics market.

Supplementary Inflation Data (Unaudited)

Statement of Financial Accounting Standards No. 33, Financial Reporting and Changing Prices, requires disclosure of certain supplementary information concerning the impact of inflation on the Company's primary financial statements which are prepared under the concept of historical cost. FAS No. 33 requires disclosure of selected data under two sets of assumptions—current cost and constant dollars.

Current cost disclosures require adjustment of inventories, property and equipment, cost of products sold and depreciation expense. This method is based on the assumption that the Company would replace its entire inventory and facilities with identical assets at fiscal year end. The computation of current cost information was made using internally and externally generated indices using methods similar to those in the primary financial statements.

In December 1982 the Financial Accounting Standards Board issued FAS No. 70, Financial Reporting and Changing Prices: Foreign Currency Translation. This statement conforms FAS No. 33 to FAS No. 52, Foreign Currency Translation, which was adopted by the Company during fiscal 1982. In addition, FAS No. 70 exempted companies that measure a significant part of their foreign operations in one or more functional currencies other than the U.S. dollar from the constant dollar requirements of FAS No. 33. Considering the significance of the Company's foreign operations that are measured in local functional currencies, constant dollar disclosures are not presented for the current or prior periods with the exception of certain data contained in the Selected Supplemental Financial Data.

The effects of inflation on current cost data is based upon the Consumer Price Index-All Urban Users (CPI-U) for domestic and foreign operations. The current cost foreign translation effects are net of the same amount of deferred income taxes, $5,179,000, as in the primary financial statements.

As required by FAS No. 33, current cost net income is before holding gains or losses. The holding gains experienced by the Company the last four years are a result of having a net monetary liability position during an inflationary period. These gains have been affected by the slowing of the inflation rate as measured by the CPI-U. The increase in the average CPI-U for fiscal 1983 was 4.3% compared to 8.7% in 1982, 11.5% in 1981 and 13.4% in 1980.

Adjusted pre-tax earnings under the current cost method were below that reported in the primary financial statements. Since FAS No. 33 does not provide for restatement of income taxes, the effective tax rate under the current cost method was 49.7% compared to 47.2% in the primary financial statements.

Income Statement Adjusted for Changing Prices (Unaudited)
Tandy Corporation and Subsidiaries In thousands.

	YEAR ENDED JUNE 30, 1983	
	AS REPORTED IN THE PRIMARY STATEMENTS	ADJUSTED FOR CHANGES IN SPECIFIC PRICES (CURRENT COSTS)
Net sales	$2,475,188	$2,475,188
Other income	38,109	38,109
	2,513,297	2,513,297
Cost and expenses:		
Cost of products sold	1,008,187	1,016,535
Selling, general and administrative	930,244	930,244
Depreciation and amortization	38,679	56,700
Interest expense, net of interest income	8,905	8,905
	1,986,015	2,012,384
Income before income taxes	527,282	500,913
Provision for income taxes	248,761	248,761
Net income	$ 278,521	$ 252,152
Net income per average common share	$2.67	$2.42
Stockholders' equity at year end	$1,120,872	$1,209,229
Purchasing power gain from holding net monetary liabilities during the year		$ 1,160
Foreign currency translation effects, net of income taxes		$ (6,530)
Inventories and property and equipment held during the year*:		
Effect of increase in specific prices (current costs)		$ 40,232
Effect of increase in general price level		28,157
Excess of increase in specific prices over increase in general price level		$ 12,075

* At June 30, 1983, the current cost of inventory was $826,208,000 (historical amount—$844,097,000) and the current cost of property and equipment, net of accumulated depreciation, was $380,049,000 (historical amount—$257,620,000).

Selected Supplemental Financial Data (Unaudited)
Tandy Corporation and Subsidiaries

	YEAR ENDED JUNE 30,				
	1983	1982	1981	1980	1979
Net sales:					
As reported	**$2,475,188**	$2,032,555	$1,691,373	$1,384,637	$1,215,483
Adjusted for general inflation	**$2,475,188**	$2,120,519	$1,917,628	$1,750,738	$1,742,074
Net income:					
As reported	**$ 278,521**	$ 224,085	$ 169,602	$ 112,235	$ 83,229
Adjusted for specific price changes	**$ 252,152**	$ 209,287	$ 152,864	$ 104,242	
Net income per average common share and common share equivalent:					
As reported	**$2.67**	$2.17	$1.65	$1.12	$ .81
Adjusted for specific price changes	**$2.42**	$2.02	$1.49	$1.04	
Excess of increase in specific prices over increase in general price level	**$ 12,075**	$ (5,006)	$ (35,490)	$ (58,869)	
Purchasing power gain from holding net monetary liabilities during the year	**$ 1,160**	$ 8,678	$ 24,219	$ 55,210	
Foreign currency translation effects net of income taxes	**$ (6,530)**	$ (24,843)			
Net assets at year end:					
As reported	**$1,120,872**	$ 812,677	$ 571,863	$ 283,125	$ 208,353
Adjusted for specific price changes	**$1,209,229**	$ 917,286	$ 704,586	$ 428,302	
Total assets (as reported)	**$1,581,908**	$1,227,644	$ 936,545	$ 710,298	$ 609,589
Total long-term liabilities (as reported)	**$ 174,937**	$ 182,099	$ 160,902	$ 258,456	$ 263,383
Cash dividends per common share	**NONE**	NONE	NONE	NONE	NONE
Market price per common share at year end:					
Historical	**$50.75**	$27.75	$30.88	$10.38	$5.34
Adjusted for general inflation	**$50.07**	$28.09	$33.47	$12.32	$7.26
Average consumer price index	**294.1**	281.9	259.4	232.6	205.2

In thousands, except per share and index amounts. Per share amounts restated for two-for-one stock splits in May 1981, December 1980 and June 1980. Amounts adjusted for specific price changes are in average 1983 dollars.

Quarterly Data (Unaudited)
Tandy Corporation and Subsidiaries In thousands, except per share amounts.

			QUARTER ENDED					
	SEPTEMBER 30, 1982	SEPTEMBER 30, 1981	DECEMBER 31, 1982	DECEMBER 31, 1981	MARCH 31, 1983	MARCH 31, 1982	JUNE 30, 1983	JUNE 30, 1982
Net sales	$517,111	$425,021	$778,155	$638,269	$589,860	$470,607	$590,062	$498,658
Other income	8,782	5,752	7,999	6,937	8,513	6,470	12,815	9,498
	525,893	430,773	786,154	645,206	598,373	477,077	602,877	508,156
Costs and expenses:								
Cost of products sold	205,820	174,683	324,218	268,230	246,445	190,510	231,704	193,419
Selling, general and administrative	209,044	169,017	272,943	228,004	232,960	195,047	215,297	188,310
Depreciation and amortization	8,998	6,476	9,544	6,795	10,210	7,347	9,927	8,819
Interest expense, net of interest income	1,669	(141)	5,651	3,129	1,496	(1,231)	89	(589)
	425,531	350,035	612,356	506,158	491,111	391,673	457,017	389,959
Income before income taxes	100,362	80,738	173,798	139,048	107,262	85,404	145,860	118,197
Provision for income taxes	46,668	37,866	80,816	65,214	49,877	40,054	71,400	56,168
Net income	$ 53,694	$ 42,872	$ 92,982	$ 73,834	$ 57,385	$ 45,350	$ 74,460	$ 62,029
Net income per average common share	$.52	$.42	$.89	$.71	$.55	$.44	$.71	$.60
Average common shares outstanding	104,034	103,075	104,286	103,302	104,432	103,503	104,577	103,706

Tandy Home Computers' final test station for the TRS-80® Color Computer.

Consolidated Balance Sheets
Tandy Corporation and Subsidiaries In thousands.

	JUNE 30, 1983	1982
Assets		
Current assets:		
Cash and short-term investments	**$ 279,743**	$ 167,547
Accounts and notes receivable, less allowance for doubtful accounts	**107,530**	83,616
Inventories	**844,097**	670,568
Other current assets	**31,928**	27,000
Total current assets	**1,263,298**	948,731
Property and equipment, at cost:		
Consumer electronics operations, net of accumulated depreciation	**194,004**	158,678
Tandy Center, net of accumulated depreciation	**63,616**	66,317
	257,260	224,995
Other assets	**60,990**	53,918
	$1,581,908	$1,227,644
Liabilities and Stockholders' Equity		
Current liabilities:		
Notes payable	**$ 55,737**	$ 24,942
Accounts payable	**64,640**	63,641
Accrued expenses	**115,054**	92,125
Income taxes payable	**50,668**	52,160
Total current liabilities	**286,099**	232,868
Notes payable, due after one year	**15,482**	20,642
Subordinated debentures, net of unamortized bond discount	**122,938**	122,666
Store managers' deposits	**8,490**	9,306
Deferred income taxes	**17,682**	18,886
Other non-current liabilities	**10,345**	10,599
Total other liabilities	**174,937**	182,099
Stockholders' equity:		
Preferred stock, no par value, 1,000,000 shares authorized, none issued or outstanding	—	—
Common stock, $1 par value, 250,000,000 shares authorized with 105,645,000 shares issued	**105,645**	105,645
Additional paid-in capital	**68,111**	39,627
Retained earnings	**969,626**	691,105
Foreign currency translation effects	**(16,297)**	(12,317)
Common stock in treasury, at cost, 976,000 and 1,789,000 shares, respectively	**(6,213)**	(11,383)
Total stockholders' equity	**1,120,872**	812,677
Commitments and contingent liabilities		
	$1,581,908	$1,227,644

Final testing for hard disk drives on the quality control line at Tandy Apparatus.

The Review of Operations and Financial Information is an integral part of these statements.

Consolidated Statements of Stockholders' Equity
Tandy Corporation and Subsidiaries
Three Years Ended June 30, 1983 In thousands.

	SHARES		
	ISSUED	TREASURY STOCK	OUTSTANDING
Balance at July 1, 1980	25,152	(3,095)	22,057
Conversion of 6½% convertible subordinated debentures	3,443	—	3,443
Two-for-one split of common stock in December 1980	25,638	—	25,628
Two-for-one split of common stock in May 1981	51,412	—	51,412
Sale of treasury stock to employee stock purchase program	—	421	421
Other	—	(49)	(49)
Net income	—	—	—
Balance at June 30, 1981	105,645	(2,723)	102,922
Effect of restating asset and liability balances as of July 1, 1981 for adoption of FAS No. 52	—	—	—
Foreign currency translation adjustments for the period	—	—	—
Sale of treasury stock to employee stock purchase program	—	934	934
Other	—	—	—
Net income	—	—	—
Balance at June 30, 1982	105,645	(1,789)	103,856
Foreign currency translation adjustments for the period	—	—	—
Sale of treasury stock to employee stock purchase program	—	813	813
Net income	—	—	—
Balance at June 30, 1983	**105,645**	**(976)**	**104,669**

The Review of Operations and Financial Information is an integral part of these statements.

In Duval Co., Florida, Radio Shack's network controllers turn individual student workstations into cost-effective, shared learning systems.

BALANCE SHEET REVIEW

Current Assets

Cash and short-term investments increased $112,196,000 between June 30, 1982 and June 30, 1983. The short-term investments are carried at cost, which approximates market value. The decline in money market rates since the end of the 1982 fiscal year reduced the weighted average interest rate for the $259,239,000 invested at June 30, 1983 to 9% from 15% for the $137,513,000 invested at June 30, 1982.

AMOUNT					
COMMON STOCK	ADDITIONAL PAID-IN CAPITAL	RETAINED EARNINGS	FOREIGN CURRENCY TRANSLATION EFFECTS	TREASURY STOCK	TOTAL
$ 25,152	$ 33,992	$297,418	$ —	$(73,437)	$ 283,125
3,443	95,109	—	—	—	98,552
25,638	(61,051)	—	—	35,413	—
51,412	(69,369)	—	—	17,957	—
—	14,846	—	—	6,231	21,077
—	2,996	—	—	(3,489)	(493)
—	—	169,602	—	—	169,602
105,645	16,523	467,020	—	(17,325)	571,863
—	—	—	(5,482)	—	(5,482)
—	—	—	(6,835)	—	(6,835)
—	23,104	—	—	5,944	29,048
—	—	—	—	(2)	(2)
—	—	224,085	—	—	224,085
105,645	39,627	691,105	(12,317)	(11,383)	812,677
—	—	—	(3,980)	—	(3,980)
—	28,484	—	—	5,170	33,654
—	—	278,521	—	—	278,521
$105,645	$ 68,111	$969,626	$(16,297)	$ (6,213)	$1,120,872

Accounts and notes receivable have increased significantly in recent years. The retail stores generally sell their products for cash or through major bank credit cards, but the Company's growth in the microcomputer market has required that the Company provide 30-day charge accounts and leases for sales to large and small businesses, schools, governmental agencies, professional firms and other purchasers of high-dollar computer equipment. Trade accounts receivable for retail sales increased approximately $20,000,000 between June 30, 1982 and June 30, 1983. The current portion of computer lease receivables was $15,447,000 at June 30, 1983 compared to $11,550,000 at June 30, 1982. The acquisition of Memtek Products increased accounts receivable because it is primarily a wholesale business with accounts receivable for its customers.

Inventories at June 30, 1983 were 26% higher than the 1982 fiscal year-end inventory level. All inventories are valued at cost or market, whichever is lower. Inventory cost is determined primarily by the average cost method. The accompanying chart gives the components of the inventories.

The average inventory of a U.S. company-owned store, including Computer Centers, was approximately $69,900 in 1983 compared to $59,400 in 1982. Most of this increase is related to computer merchandise. Additions were made to the computer line throughout the year and availability of certain items increased so that the stores were able to add this merchandise to their store inventories rather than special ordering. This average does not include the warehouse inventories required to support the store network. The 5% increase in company-owned stores worldwide added to store and warehouse inventories. Inventories also have grown with the expansion of self-manufacturing. Inventory turnover (unaudited) was 1.28 in fiscal 1983 compared to 1.41 in 1982 and 1.39 in 1981.

Other current assets include prepaid expenses such as rent, catalog costs and property taxes. The June 30, 1983 balance also included $7,415,000 of prepaid income taxes. At June 30, 1982 these prepaid taxes were $10,441,000. The prepaid income taxes primarily result from the elimination of intercompany profits for financial purposes that are reported currently for tax purposes.

Inventories In thousands.

			JUNE 30,		
	1983	1982	1981	1980	1979
Finished merchandise	**$773,093**	$604,124	$475,377	$398,287	$354,059
Raw materials and work in progress	**71,004**	66,444	38,332	36,873	27,590
	$844,097	$670,568	$513,709	$435,160	$381,649

Property and Equipment

A review of capital expenditures by operating function and a three-year analysis of property and equipment was presented previously.

When depreciable assets are sold or retired, the related cost and accumulated depreciation are removed from the accounts. Any gains or losses are included in other income. Major additions and betterments are capitalized. Maintenance and repairs which do not materially improve or extend the lives of the respective assets are charged to operating expenses as incurred.

For financial reporting purposes, depreciation and amortization are calculated primarily using the straight-line method, which amortizes the cost of the assets over their estimated useful lives. The ranges of estimated useful lives are:

Buildings	10–40 years
Machinery and equipment	3–15 years
Leasehold improvements	the shorter of the life of the improvements or the term of the related lease

Other Assets

Other assets increased $7,072,000 from June 30, 1982 to June 30, 1983. The major item in this account at June 30, 1983 was the long-term portion of computer lease receivables which totaled $16,991,000. This account also included investments in joint ventures and unconsolidated subsidiaries, a long-term loan to a company for partial financing of construction of a hotel on property owned by one of the Company's joint ventures and goodwill.

Current Liabilities

Notes payable outstanding and due within one year were:

In thousands.

	JUNE 30, 1983	1982
Short-term indebtedness, principally relating to foreign operations	**$53,603**	$19,803
Current portion of notes payable	**2,134**	5,139
	$55,737	$24,942

The Company had available domestic seasonal bank credit lines of approximately $24,000,000 and $33,500,000 at June 30, 1983 and 1982. For $4,000,000 of the June 30, 1983 lines, the interest rate is negotiated at the time of borrowing. The rate is generally understood to be no more than the floating prime rate of the lending bank. The interest rate on the remaining lines is the floating prime rate. Interest on all the borrowings is payable at maturity. With respect to certain lines, the Company is expected to maintain compensating balances of a certain percentage of the seasonal line of credit plus a percentage of the amount actually borrowed. The compensating balance percentages for the lines were $13,500,000 at 10% + 10%, $2,000,000 at 10% + 0%, $8,000,000 at 2.5% + 2.5% and $500,000 with 5% + 0% compensating balance requirements. Compensating balances, when required, are not legally restricted. For fiscal 1983 and 1982 there were instances where part or all of the requirements for compensating balances were waived. At June 30, 1983 and 1982, the Company had no domestic seasonal borrowings outstanding.

The weighted average of domestic seasonal loans outstanding in 1983 was $3,700,000 and the weighted average interest rate, based on interest costs incurred was 11.2%. The maximum amount outstanding at any month end was approximately $31,000,000. During 1982 the weighted average of domestic seasonal loans outstanding was nominal.

The Company's short-term bank indebtedness relating to foreign operations is primarily unsecured borrowings on overdraft and other short-term lines, some of which provide for foreign acceptances. Short-term foreign lines of credit were approximately $171,000,000 at the end of 1983 and $150,000,000 at the end of 1982. No compensating balances are required. The weighted average interest rate on amounts outstanding was 11.0% at the end of 1983 and 13.1% at the end of 1982. Average monthly foreign short-term bank borrowings were approximately $38,900,000 in 1983 and $39,100,000 in 1982. The weighted average interest rates, based on interest costs incurred, were 12.2% in 1983 and 15.5% in 1982. The maximum amounts of such borrowings outstanding at any month end during fiscal 1983 and 1982 were $51,389,000 and $49,188,000, respectively.

Accounts payable are primarily amounts owed for merchandise. Amounts outstanding, if any, under letters of credit and acceptance lines of credit are included in this account. These instruments can be used as a method of short-term borrowing. During 1983 and 1982 strong cash flow from operations and strong vendor relationships in the Orient have allowed the Company to utilize letter of credit transactions to a lesser degree than in the past.

The Company's letters of credit and acceptance lines of credit were approximately $186,500,000 at June 30, 1983 and $165,000,000 at June 30, 1982. No acceptances were outstanding at June 30, 1983 or June 30, 1982. The weighted average of domestic banker's acceptances outstanding during fiscal 1983 was $6,100,000. There were no acceptances outstanding at any time during fiscal 1982. The weighted average interest rate in 1983, based on interest costs incurred, was 10.1% and the maximum amount outstanding at any month end was approximately $36,400,000. No compensating balances are required on these acceptance lines. Letters of credit open against outstanding purchase orders were approximately $64,400,000 at June 30, 1983 and $116,300,000 at June 30, 1982.

Accrued expenses include amounts owed in the normal course of operations for payroll costs, property taxes, rent, insurance and other expenses. Deferred income from computer service contracts is also included in this account. Accrued payroll and bonuses were $54,422,000 at June 30, 1983 and $46,259,000 at June 30, 1982. Property taxes accrued at the end of fiscal 1983 and 1982 were $12,491,000 and $13,274,000, respectively.

Income taxes payable were $50,668,000 at June 30, 1983 and $52,160,000 at June 30, 1982. The Company makes quarterly federal income tax deposits based on the prior fiscal year's income. A change in the tax law now requires a greater portion of the estimated taxes to be paid in by the end of the fiscal year than in prior years.

Long-term Debt

Maturities of the $17,616,000 of notes payable at June 30, 1983 are:

1984	$2,134,000
1985	2,258,000
1986	1,917,000
1987	6,531,000
1988	297,000
1989 and thereafter	4,479,000

In December 1976 the Company issued $98,082,000 of 10% subordinated debentures due 1991 for 19,607,800 shares of common stock (adjusted for the stock splits in fiscal 1981 and 1978). The 10% subordinated debentures due 1994 were issued in fiscal 1975 in exchange for 19,504,000 shares (adjusted for the stock splits in fiscal 1981, 1978 and 1976) of common stock. The shares acquired in these exchanges were retired. Debt discount of $9,894,000 relating to the debentures due 1994 was recorded based on an effective interest rate of 14.25% and is being amortized over the life of the bonds.

Long-Term Debt In thousands.

	JUNE 30 1983	1982
Notes payable with interest rates ranging from 6% to 18% at June 30, 1983 and 1982	**$ 17,616**	$ 25,781
Less portion due within one year included in current notes payable	**(2,134)**	(5,139)
	$ 15,482	$ 20,642
Subordinated debentures:		
10% due 1991	**$ 98,082**	$ 98,082
10% due 1994, less unamortized discount of $7,575,000 and $7,847,000, respectively	**24,856**	24,584
	$122,938	$122,666

Store managers' deposits are cash deposits from certain classes of store managers. Unlike regular store managers, these managers operate company-owned stores under written contracts which incorporate a different method of compensation.

Consolidated Statements of Changes in Financial Position
Tandy Corporation and Subsidiaries In thousands.

	1983	1982
Financial Resources Were Provided By:		
Income from continuing operations	**$278,521**	$224,085
Items in income and not affecting working capital:		
Depreciation and amortization	**38,679**	29,437
Other	**3,272**	7,318
Working capital provided by continuing operations	**320,472**	260,840
Conversion of debentures into common stock	—	—
Issuance of debentures	—	—
Additions to long-term borrowings	**370**	18,209
Sale of treasury stock to employee stock purchase program	**33,654**	29,048
	354,496	308,097
Financial Resources Were Used For:		
Additions to property and equipment, net of retirements	**72,675**	67,678
Foreign currency translation adjustments, net	**6,928**	10,688
Reductions of long-term debt	**5,530**	1,470
Decrease in 6½% convertible subordinated debentures	—	—
Purchase of common stock related to tender offer	—	—
Purchase of treasury stock	—	—
Retirement of common stock in exchange for debentures	—	—
Other, net	**8,027**	17,825
	93,160	97,661
Increase in Working Capital of Continuing Operations	**261,336**	210,436
Working capital provided (used) by discontinued operations	—	—
Working capital provided (used) by operations spun off	—	—
Increase in Working Capital	**$261,336**	$210,436
Increases (Decreases) in Working Capital:		
Cash and short-term investments	**$112,196**	$ 25,553
Accounts and notes receivable, net	**23,914**	41,528
Inventories	**173,529**	156,859
Other current assets	**4,928**	15,584
Short-term debt, including current portion of long-term debt	**(30,795)**	9,920
Accounts payable	**(999)**	(9,081)
Accrued expenses	**(22,929)**	(24,919)
Income taxes payable	**1,492**	(5,008)
Increase in Working Capital	**$261,336**	$210,436

The Review of Operations and Financial Information is an integral part of these statements.

YEAR ENDED JUNE 30,							
1981	1980	1979	1978	1977	1976	1975	1974
$169,602	$112,235	$ 83,229	$ 66,146	$ 71,819	$64,281	$28,622	$21,861
23,288	19,110	17,121	13,879	11,140	8,034	7,392	5,461
7,637	(536)	3,772	3,437	3,572	2,936	(159)	(121)
200,527	130,809	104,122	83,462	86,531	75,251	35,855	27,201
98,552	—	—	—	—	—	—	—
—	—	98,875	—	98,039	—	25,443	—
903	—	5,081	110,000	—	—	5,000	29,553
21,077	15,833	12,954	10,000	8,632	7,343	655	—
321,059	146,642	221,032	203,462	193,202	82,594	66,953	56,754
48,494	31,063	26,579	50,357	41,518	26,420	13,651	10,216
—	—	—	—	—	—	—	—
3,523	2,165	111,750	3,208	4,130	49,571	26,432	21,108
99,954	—	—	—	—	—	—	—
—	—	—	101,487	—	—	—	—
—	53,342	27,396	—	21,180	5,306	6,044	12,028
—	—	—	—	98,038	—	25,443	—
26,003	7,578	(7,032)	(7,663)	(5,114)	(6,441)	(4,987)	(3,410)
177,974	94,148	158,693	147,389	159,753	74,856	66,583	39,942
143,085	52,494	62,339	56,073	33,449	7,738	370	16,812
—	—	—	—	5,084	—	(560)	(10,422)
—	—	—	—	—	(4,916)	13,208	310
$143,085	$ 52,494	$ 62,339	$ 56,073	$ 38,533	$ 2,822	$13,018	$ 6,700
$ 85,629	$ 18,744	$ 1,843	$ 14,848	$(23,354)	$11,625	$(4,247)	$ 1,773
16,363	9,884	5,206	3,553	(2,360)	(1,096)	(1,758)	2,766
78,549	53,511	48,584	32,786	66,895	50,350	25,540	22,505
(2,393)	1,219	(1,562)	(2,400)	9,018	2,842	1,273	997
(8,944)	11,271	15,775	9,706	(20,001)	(15,243)	(5,714)	(5,113)
4,366	(24,536)	15,543	(1,965)	(14,725)	(11,345)	1,241	(4,752)
(8,036)	(6,827)	(9,958)	(2,449)	(4,727)	(15,914)	(1,754)	(2,764)
(22,449)	(10,772)	(13,092)	1,994	27,787	(18,397)	(1,563)	(8,712)
$143,085	$ 52,494	$ 62,339	$ 56,073	$ 38,533	$ 2,822	$13,018	$ 6,700

Litigation

There are various claims, lawsuits, investigations and pending actions involving allegations of negligence, product defects, discrimination, patent infringement, tax deficiencies and breach of contracts against the Company and its subsidiaries incident to the operation of its business. The liability, if any, associated with these matters is not determinable at June 30, 1983. While certain of the lawsuits involves substantial amounts, it is the opinion of management that the ultimate resolution of such litigation will not have a material adverse effect on the Company's financial position or the results of operations.

Proposed Acquisition

On August 18, 1983 the Company announced plans to acquire O'Sullivan Industries, Inc., a subsidiary of Conroy, Inc., for $91,500,000 in cash. O'Sullivan, located in Lamar, Missouri, is a manufacturer of consumer electronic stands, racks, desks and accessories. This transaction has been approved by both boards of directors, but it is subject to the approval of Conroy's stockholders and the fulfillment of certain other conditions. The effective date of the sale is August 31, 1983 although closing will not occur until all approvals are obtained. Closing is not expected to occur until December 1983 or January 1984. The fiscal year for O'Sullivan is August 31. For the nine months ended May 31, 1983, O'Sullivan reported sales of $55,800,000 and net income of $7,600,000.

WORKING CAPITAL, LIQUIDITY AND CAPITAL RESOURCES REVIEW

Working capital provided by operations increased 23% from $260,840,000 for 1982 to $320,472,000 for 1983. The strong growth pattern of net income has produced this expanded source of working capital. The current ratio (current assets – current liabilities) was 4.42 to 1 at June 30, 1983 compared to 4.07 to 1 at June 30, 1982. Working capital provided by operations in fiscal 1983 was approximately twelve times the 1974 level of $27,201,000.

The largest use of working capital for the last two years has been capital expenditures. As shown in the three-year analysis of fixed assets, fixed asset additions totaled $74,876,000 in fiscal 1983, $69,898,000 in 1982 and $50,757,000 in 1981. Most of the Company's retail operations are in leased facilities. Therefore, most of the Company's capital outlays are for store fixtures and leasehold improvements rather than land and buildings. The average cost of leasehold improvements, store fixtures and signs for company-owned stores, excluding Computer Centers, opened in the United States in fiscal 1983 was approximately $70,700. The comparable cost to open a store in fiscal 1982 was $59,700. The present cost to furnish and equip a new store, excluding inventory is almost four times the 1978 cost of $18,000. Escalating construction costs and expanded display systems have raised these costs significantly. Fixed asset costs for new Computer Centers are not significantly different from the expenditures for regular Radio Shack stores. New stores opened, net of closings, in fiscal 1983 were 260 compared to 372 in fiscal 1982 and 388 in 1981. The largest individual expenditures for fixed assets in fiscal 1983 were for a new warehouse/office complex in Australia, expansion of the offices and warehouse in Belgium and additions to manufacturing plants in Texas, California and Taiwan.

Self-manufacturing has been a major factor in the Company's ability to react quickly to changes in the consumer electronics marketplace. The increases in working capital provided by operations have permitted the Company to not only expand manufacturing capacity, but to expand the types of products it can manufacture without incurring substantial amounts of indebtedness. As illustrated by the accompanying chart, sales of self-manufactured products have increased significantly since 1979. Sales of computer products have been a major reason for the increase in the percentage of sales of self-manufactured products to total sales. Telephone manufacturing capabilities have been developed to allow the Company to design and produce merchandise with selected and sometimes unique features. The sharp increase in the average non-cash assets invested in manufacturing was caused by the aquisition of Memtek Products in the latter part of fiscal 1982 and expansion of existing plants.

Capital Expenditures by Operating Areas
In thousands.

	YEAR ENDED JUNE 30,				
	1983	1982	1981	1980	1979
Stores	**$37,915**	$41,288	$34,013	$20,716	$12,222
Manufacturing	**18,461**	20,370	8,460	5,294	4,248
Warehouse	**8,201**	1,414	451	470	1,402
Other	**10,097**	5,903	6,342	4,537	3,564
	74,674	68,975	49,266	31,017	21,436
Tandy Center	**202**	923	1,491	2,611	8,056
Net retirements	**(2,201)**	(2,220)	(2,263)	(2,565)	(2,913)
	$72,675	$67,678	$48,494	$31,063	$26,579

The analysis of changes in working capital on pages 42 and 43 indicates that the most significant changes in working capital in recent years have been the increases in cash and short-term investments, inventory and accounts receivable. Between the end of fiscal 1982 and 1983, cash and short-term investments increased $112,196,000. The average of month-end cash and short-term investments during fiscal 1983 was approximately $188,000,000. During 1982 the cash and short-term investments averaged about $155,000,000. The cash flow from operations that was invested in inventories allowed the Company to expand sales. The average investment in inventories for new Radio Shack-U.S. stores increased from $45,400 in 1981 to $58,400 in 1982 and to $62,600 in 1983. Initial inventories for new Radio Shack Computer Centers in the United States averaged more than $132,000 in fiscal 1983 compared to $124,000 in 1982 and $100,000 in 1981. These amounts do not include the warehouse inventories required to support the store system. Expansion of the computer product line and additions to the regular product line raised the average store inventory. As sales and the store system have increased, the warehouse and manufacturing inventories required to support this growth have also increased. As sales to large and small businesses, professional firms, schools, governmental agencies and other purchases of high-dollar computer equipment have grown, the dollar amount of 30-day charge accounts, trade receivables and lease receivables have increased.

The Company's long-term borrowing capability is enhanced by its low long-term debt-to-equity ratio. This ratio was .12 to 1 at June 30, 1983 and .18 to 1 at June 30, 1982. The debt-to-equity ratio was reduced from .81 to 1 at June

Working Capital Provided by Operations (in millions of dollars)

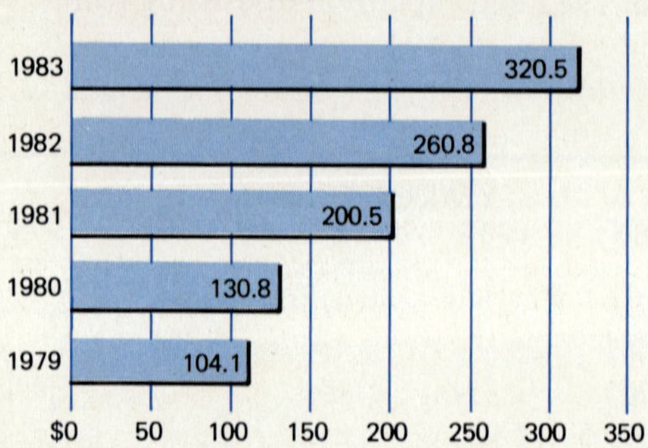

Sales of Self-Manufactured Products As a Percent of Sales (unaudited)

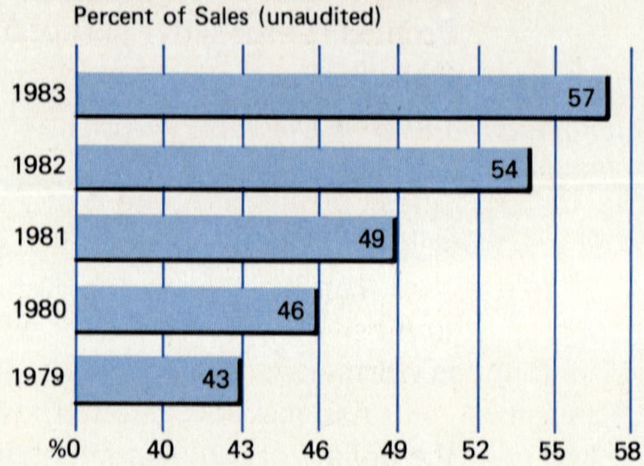

Average Non-Cash Assets Invested in Manufacturing (unaudited) (in millions of dollars)

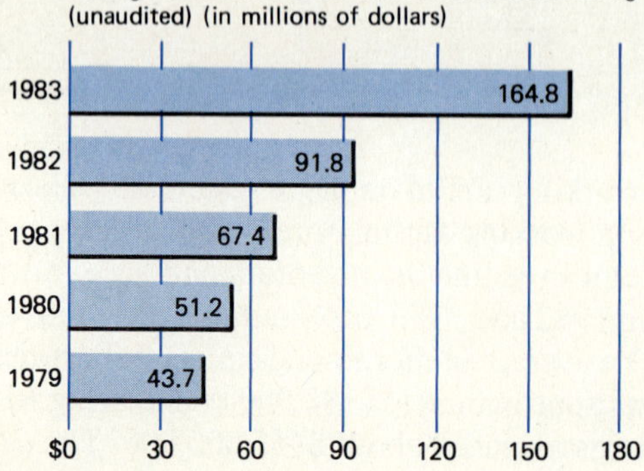

30, 1980 to .22 to 1 at June 30, 1981 because of the redemption of the 6½% convertible debentures in fiscal 1981. More than $98,000,000, or essentially all of the debentures, were converted into common stock. This transaction is shown in the Statements of Changes in Financial Position as a source and a use of funds and therefore had only a nominal effect on working capital. Essentially all of the Company's outstanding funded long-term debt is subordinated, a positive factor in negotiating interest rates and availability of funds if the Company should need senior borrowings. No significant long-term debt reductions are required until 1991. The financial strength of the Company, based on historical and current operations and balance sheets, is such that management is confident adequate funds could be raised in the long-term debt market at competitive rates if necessary. However the Company has no immediate plans for any long-term financing—debt or equity.

The Company had available domestic seasonal bank credit and acceptance lines totaling more than $210,000,000 at June 30, 1983 and $195,000,000 at June 30, 1982. No borrowings were outstanding on these lines at the end of either period. In addition, foreign lines of credit as of June 30, 1983 were $171,000,000 with less than $50,000,000 outstanding at that time. Management believes the Company's short-term credit lines can be expanded as needed. A more complete outline of the Company's year-end borrowings is detailed in the discussion of the Balance Sheet. The Corporate and Financial Objectives addresses management's philosophy on how the Company's financial framework should be structured to achieve the best results for the stockholders. Tandy has been able to continue its growth during a difficult economic period primarily because of the stream of working capital provided by strong sales and earnings gains.

Tandy Corporation has used the following investment equation for a number of years as a framework to discuss various aspects of our financial performance.

Asset turnover (sometimes called operating leverage) is the ratio of sales to the dollars of assets employed during the year. Asset turnover declined modestly in fiscal 1983 to 1.76 from 1.88 in 1982. Inventory is Tandy's largest single operating asset, accounting for more than half of total assets. The majority of our other asset investments have been made to enhance the return on our inventory investment. We are willing to accept a lower asset turnover for a higher gross margin. Our continuing investment in self-manufacturing and vertical integration is indicative of this approach. Future investments and/or acquisitions which increase technological manufacturing integration are and will continue to be high priority, even though such investment may temporarily impede asset turnover.

Return on sales (or net profit margin) is the percentage of profit earned on sales. For the fifth consecutive year, Tandy improved the net margin to a record 11.3% after taxes. Lower selling, general and administrative expenses as a percent of sales were the primary source of the improvement.

Return on assets, the percentage of net profits earned on average assets for

Property and Equipment In thousands.

	BALANCE AT BEGINNING OF PERIOD	ADDITIONS AT COST	RETIREMENTS AND SALES	OTHER	BALANCE AT END OF PERIOD
Year Ended June 30, 1983					
Consumer electronics operations:					
Land	$ 3,825	$ 1,356	$ —	$ (192)	$ 4,989
Buildings	22,497	11,662	—	(359)	33,800
Furniture, fixtures and equipment	141,312	35,706	(5,326)	(771)	170,921
Leasehold improvements	94,044	25,950	(1,164)	(1,420)	117,410
	261,678	74,674	(6,490)	(2,742)	327,120
Tandy Center:					
Land	8,611	—	—	—	8,611
Buildings and other	69,066	202	(1)	—	69,267
	77,677	202	(1)	—	77,878
	$339,355	$74,876	$(6,491)	$(2,742)	$404,998
Year Ended June 30, 1982					
Consumer electronics operations:					
Land	$ 3,079	$ 577	— —	$ 169	$ 3,825
Buildings	20,143	2,673	—	(319)	22,497
Furniture, fixtures and equipment	113,675	38,528	(7,523)	(3,368)	141,312
Leasehold improvements	70,914	27,197	(847)	(3,220)	94,044
	207,811	68,975	(8,370)	(6,738)	261,678

Tandy Center:					
Land	8,611	—	—	—	8,611
Buildings and other	68,172	923	(29)	—	69,066
	76,783	923	(29)	—	77,677
	$284,594	$69,898	$(8,399)	$(6,738)	$339,355
Year Ended June 30, 1981					
Consumer electronic operations:					
Land	$ 2,985	$ 134	$ (40)	$ —	$ 3,079
Buildings	18,006	2,192	(55)	—	20,143
Furniture, fixtures and equipment	93,543	24,958	(4,826)	—	113,675
Leasehold improvements	49,912	21,982	(980)	—	70,914
	164,446	49,266	(5,901)	—	207,811
Tandy Center:					
Land	8,256	355	—	—	8,611
Buildings and other	67,123	1,136	(87)	—	68,172
	75,379	1,491	(87)	—	76,783
	$239,825	$50,757	$(5,988)	$ —	$284,594

Accumulated Depreciation In thousands.

	BALANCE AT BEGINNING OF PERIOD	DEPRECIATION EXPENSE	RETIREMENTS AND SALES	OTHER	BALANCE AT END OF PERIOD
Year Ended June 30, 1983					
Consumer electronics operations:					
Buildings	$ 3,985	$ 927	$ —	$ 20	$ 4,932
Furniture, fixtures and equipment	65,844	22,686	(3,593)	(178)	84,759
Leasehold improvements	33,171	11,369	(697)	(418)	43,425
	103,000	34,982	(4,290)	(576)	133,116
Tandy Center:					
Buildings and other	11,360	2,902	—	—	14,262
	$114,360	$37,884	$(4,290)	$ (576)	$147,378
Year Ended June 30, 1982					
Consumer electronics operations:					
Buildings	$ 3,183	$ 736	$ —	$ 66	$ 3,985
Furniture, fixtures and equipment	56,030	16,782	(5,622)	(1,346)	65,844
Leasehold improvements	26,390	8,634	(528)	(1,325)	33,171
	85,603	26,152	(6,150)	(2,605)	103,000
Tandy Center:					
Buildings and other	8,562	2,827	(29)	—	11,360
	$ 94,165	$28,979	$(6,179)	$(2,605)	$114,360
Year Ended June 30, 1981					
Consumer electronics operations:					
Buildings	$ 2,594	$ 630	$ (41)	$ —	$ 3,183
Furniture, fixtures and equipment	45,286	13,700	(2,956)	—	56,030
Leasehold improvements	20,926	6,170	(706)	—	26,390
	68,806	20,500	(3,703)	—	85,603
Tandy Center:					
Buildings and other	5,879	2,705	(22)	—	8,562
	$ 74,685	$23,205	$(3,725)	$ —	$ 94,165

Note: With the adoption of FAS No. 52, Foreign Currency Translation, the foreign fixed assets and related accumulated depreciation are translated into U.S. dollars at the rates in effect at the date of the balance sheet. The amounts shown in the "Other" column for fiscal 1983 and 1982 reflect the changes in currency values between the balance sheet dates.

fiscal 1983 was 19.8% compared to 20.7% in fiscal 1982. Higher cash balances and lower short-term interest rates (less interest income) contributed to this decline. However, the more narrowly defined return on non-cash assets also fell to 23.6% from 24.2%. One factor adversely affecting the returns on assets and non-cash assets has been the decline in operating profits of some foreign retail operations. The strength of the dollar, general market conditions, competition and legal restrictions on pricing have negatively impacted consolidated net income.

Financial leverage is the ratio of a company's asset base to the stockholders' equity investment. Tandy again reduced its leverage in fiscal 1983 to 1.45, the lowest level since 1972. Tandy's balance sheet is strong. In fact, if present earnings trends continue, long-term debt could drop to less than 10% of equity during fiscal 1984.

Return on equity is net income expressed as a percentage of the stockholders' investment. Return on equity was 28.8% after taxes in fiscal 1983. This marks the eight consecutive year that Tandy has been able to earn an after-tax return in excess of 25%. This has been achieved despite the fact that financial leverage is lower than in earlier years (less than half of what it was five years ago).

JUNE 30	ASSET TURNOVER SALES / AVG. ASSETS	×	RETURN ON SALES NET INCOME / SALES	=	RETURN ON ASSETS NET INCOME / AVG. ASSETS	×	FINANCIAL LEVERAGE AVG. ASSETS / AVG. EQUITY	=	RETURN ON EQUITY NET INCOME / AVG. EQUITY
1974	1.47	×	3.6%	=	5.3%	×	2.41	=	12.8%
1975	1.71	×	5.1	=	8.7	×	2.53	=	22.0
1976	2.04	×	8.7	=	17.7	×	2.18	=	38.7
1977	2.16	×	7.3	=	15.7	×	2.37	=	37.2
1978	2.06	×	6.2	=	12.8	×	3.39	=	43.6
1979	2.09	×	6.9	=	14.3	×	3.35	=	47.9
1980	2.10	×	8.1	=	17.0	×	2.69	=	45.7
1981	2.06	×	10.0	=	20.6	×	1.93	=	39.7
1982	1.88	×	11.0	=	20.7	×	1.56	=	32.3
1983	**1.76**	×	**11.3**	=	**19.8**	×	**1.45**	=	**28.8**

INDEX

Accelerated cost recovery system (ACRS), 240–41, 302, 303
Accelerated depreciation, 229–31, 233–36
Accountants, 4–6
Accounting, 1–11
- accounting information, uses of, 2–3
- business organization forms (*see* Business organization forms)
- concept of, 1–2
- defined, 1
- governmental, 6
- methodology (*see* Accounting equation)
- private, 6
- profession of, 3–4
- public, 5
- role of, 2
- standards and principles, development of, 6–7, 466–67
- terms, 2

Accounting controls, 42
Accounting cycle, 42–58, 74–108
- adjusting entries (*see* Adjusting entries)
- closing entries, 53–57, 88–93, 163
- financial statement preparation, 46, 53, 87–88, 101–3
- general journal entries, 43–44, 75–76
- post-closing trial balance, 93–94
- posting to ledger, 44–46, 76–81
- steps in, 43, 74–75
- trial balance, 46, 81

Accounting equation, 9–10, 15–27
- accounts and, 24–27
- accrual concept and, 19
- balance sheet and, 17–18
- basic, 9–10
- debits and credits and, 24–26
- entity principle and, 15–17
- expenses and, 18–23
- income statement and, 23–24
- revenues and, 18–23

Accounting machines, 106
Accounting Principles Board (APB), 7 (*See also APB Opinions*)
Accounting Research Bulletins, 7
Accounting Standards:
- development of, 6–7, 466–67
- international, 464–65

Accounting system, basic elements of, 41–58
- accounting controls, 42
- accounting cycle (*see* Accounting cycle)
- source documents, 42

Accounting theory (*see* Generally accepted accounting principles)
Accounts:
- aging of, 162, 164
- classifications of, 26–27
- control, 95
- defined, 2
- illustration of, 24–25
- nominal, 54–57
- open, 157, 457
- real, 54
- T-, 45
- (*See also* General journal; General ledger)

Accounts payable, 191–93, 295
Accounts receivable:
- assigning, 166
- factoring, 166–67
- pledging, 166
- recording, 157–59
- uncollectible, 159–65

Accounts receivable subsidiary ledger, 95
Accounts receivable turnover, 423–24, 428
Accrual-basis accounting, 130, 132–35, 155
Accrual concept, 19
Accrued, defined, 47
Accrued interest, 338–39

Accrued liabilities, 47, 295–96
Accrued revenue, 47
Accumulated depletion, 262
Accumulated depreciation, 237, 239
Acid test ratio, 420–21, 427
Acquisition of plant assets, 225–27
Add-back, 386
Additional capital, 359
Adjusting entries, 46–53
  allowance for uncollectible accounts, 163, 164
  bad debts expense, 163, 164
  bank reconciliation and, 129–30
  illustration of, 47–53, 81–86
  matching principle and, 46–47
  need for, 53
  periodicity principle and, 46
  posting to ledger, 82–86
  recorded costs and, 47–49
  recorded revenue and, 47, 51–52
  transaction types requiring, 47
  unrecorded costs and, 47, 50–51
  unrecorded revenue and, 47, 52–53
Advance deposits, foreign trade financed by, 456
Aging of accounts, 162, 164
Allowance for uncollectible accounts, 161–65
American Institute of Certified Public Accountants (AICPA), 4, 7, 42, 466
  Committee on Accounting Procedure, 7
Amortization:
  bond, 329–39, 388, 394
  intangible asset, 263–68
Amortization schedule, 307
Annuities:
  future value of, 287, 289–91
  present value of, 291–94
APB Opinions:
  defined, 7
  No. 19, 380, 393
  No. 21, 335
Articles of copartnership, 8
Assets:
  account classifications for, 26
  accrual concept and, 19
  on balance sheet, 17, 18
  in basic accounting equation, 9, 15–17
  changes in (*see* Statement of changes in financial position)
  defined, 9
  (*See also* Accounts receivable; Cash; Inventory; Plant assets)
Asset utilization tests, 416, 422–25, 428
Assigning accounts receivable, 166
Attest function, 5
Auditing, 5
Authorized stock, 358, 366
Average age of inventory, 425, 428

Bad debt expense, 159–64
Balance sheet, 17–18
  cash-basis vs. accrual-basis accounting and, 132–33
  comparative, 411–14
  corporate, 366, 369–70
  partnership, 354
  preparation of, 46, 88, 103
  statement of changes in financial position and, 383, 384, 386–87, 389, 396
Bank reconciliations, 127–30
Bank service charge, 128
Bank transfers, international, 455
Basket purchases, 226–27
Bearer bonds, 324
Bills of exchange, 455
Board of directors, 8
Bond indenture, 324, 327
Bonds, 323–40
  amortization of, 329–39, 388, 394
  basic accounting for, 324–26
  convertible, 366–67
  discount, 327–32, 388, 394
  interest determination, 327–28
  issued between interest payment dates, 338–39
  issue price, 328–34
  premium, 332–34, 388, 394
  redeemed before maturity, 335
  semiannual interest payments, 334
  serial, 335–37
  terminology, 323–24
  valuation of, 326–28
Bonds outstanding amortization, 336–37
Bonds payable (*see* Bonds)
Bookkeeping machines, 106
Book value, 228
Bretton Woods agreement, 450
Budgeting cash, 135
Buildings:
  acquisition of, 225–27
  depreciation of (*see* Depreciation)
  leasing of, 241
Business organization forms, 7–9, 350–71
  corporations (*see* Corporations)
  partnerships, 8, 352–55
  sole proprietorships, 7, 351–52, 355

Cable transfer, 455
Callable bonds, 324
C&F (cost and freight), 457
Capital:
  additional, 359
  contributed, 358
  legal, 358
  paid-in, 10, 358, 362–67
  working (*see* Working capital)
Capitalization of a natural resource, 261
Capital accounts, 352–55
Capital expenditures, 237–38
Capital leases, 241, 305–8
Capital stock, 10
Carrying value, 138
Cash, 122–36
  administration of, 124
  analysis of cash position, 135
  bank reconciliations, 127–30
  budgeting, 135
  cash-basis accounting, 130–35
  control of, 124–30
  defined, 123
  electronic funds transfer, 135–36
  petty, 125–27
  point-of-sale (POS) terminals, 136
  statement of cash receipts and disbursements, 131–34
  valuation of, 123
  (*See also* Marketable securities)
Cash-basis accounting, 19*n*, 130–35
Cash-basis approach to statement of changes, 393–400
  cash provided by operations, 393–98
  illustration of, 396–98
  vs. working capital basis, 399–400
Cash over and short account, 126–27
Cash payments journal, 99
Cash payments vs. expenses, 19
Cash planning, 135
Cash receipts journal, 98–100
Cash surrender value of life insurance, 268–69
Certificate in Management Accounting (CMA), 4
Certified public accountants (CPAs), 4
CIF (cost, insurance, and freight), 457
Closing entries, 53–57, 88–93, 163
Common-size statements, 414–15
Common stock, 357–66
Comparability, 468
Comparison, standards of, 415
Compensating balance, 123
Completed-contract method, 169
Compound entry, 55
Computers, 45, 103–6
Consigned merchandise, 208
Consistency, 468
Consolidated financial statements, 470
Constant-dollar accounting, 444–47
Construction contracts, long-term, 167–69
Consumer Price Index (CPI), 441
Contingent liability, 173, 311
Contributed capital, 358
Control account, 95
Controller, 6
Convertible securities, 324, 366–67
Copyrights, 265, 268
Corporations, 8–9, 356–71
  classification of, 356–57
  defined, 356
  owner's equity (*see* Stockholder's equity)
Cost-assignment methods, 198–204
Cost/benefit considerations in accounting, 468
Cost depletion, 261–62
Cost of goods sold:
  calculation of, 187
  consigned merchandise and, 208
  defined, 187
  estimation of, 206–7
  FIFO (first-in, first-out) cost assignment method and, 198, 200–204
  gross profit and, 187–88

Cost of goods sold (*cont.*)
inflation, effect of, 206
inventory valuation errors and, 188–89
LIFO (last-in, first-out) cost assignment method and, 198, 201–4
lower-of-cost-or-market (LCM) rule and, 204–6
periodic inventory systems, and 187, 193–97
perpetual inventory systems and, 193, 196–97
specific identification cost assignment method and, 198, 199, 201
weighted-average cost-assignment method and, 198, 200, 201
Cost of sales (*see* Cost of goods sold)
Cost principle, 9, 470
Costs:
recorded, 47–49
unrecorded, 47, 50–51
CPAs (certified public accountants), 4
Credit, foreign trade, 457
Credit card draft, 166
Credit card sales, 165–66
Credit memoranda, 128
Credits, 24–26
Cumulative preferred stock, 359–60
Current assets, 26
(*See also* Accounts receivable; Cash; Inventory)
Current liabilities, 26, 27, 295–300
Current ratio, 420, 427
Current-value accounting, 444–47

Data processing, 103–6
Debit memoranda, 128
Debits, 24–26
Debt ratios, 421, 427
Debt-to-equity ratio, 421, 427
Debt-to-total-assets ratio, 421, 427
Declaration date, 361
Defaulting on notes, 171–72
Deferred, defined, 47
Deferred income taxes, 302–4
Deferred revenue, 47
Depletion, 261–63
Deposits in transit, 127
Depreciation, 227–37
adjusting entries for, 48
asset disposal and, 255–60
book value and, 228
defined, 227
double declining-balance method, 229–30, 233–35
income taxes and, 240–41, 302, 303
leases and, 308
for less than one year, 234–36
misconceptions concerning, 236–37
service-hours method, 232–34
straight-line method, 229, 233–35
sum-of-the-years'-digits method, 231, 233–36
units-of-production method, 231–34
Direct write-off method, 159–61
Discounting notes receivable, 172–73
Discounts:
bond, 327–32, 388, 394
capital stock, 359
foreign exchange, 454
purchase, 191–92
sales, 158–59
trade, 158, 195, 198
Disposal of plant assets, 255–60
Dissimilar asset exhanges, 257–58
Dividends, 25–26, 359–64
in arrears, 359
defined, 10
Dividend yield, 423, 428
Double declining-balance method, 229–30, 234–35
Double-entry bookkeeping, 6
Drafts, exports financed by, 456

Earnings:
quality of, 415–16
retained, 10, 87, 362–68
Earnings per share (EPS), 419, 427
Economic Recovery Tax Act of 1981, 240
Effective-interest amortization:
bond discount, 330–32
bond premium, 333–34
compared to straight-line amortization, 334–35
Electronic data processing (EDP), 45, 103–6
Electronic funds transfer (EFT), 135–36
Employment Retirement Income Security Act of 1974 (ERISA), 310–11
Entity principle, 15–17, 351, 469–70
Equipment:
acquisition of, 225–27
depreciation of (*see* Depreciation)
disposal of, 255–60
leasing of, 241, 305–9
maintenance costs for, 238–39
Equities:
defined, 9–10
(*See also* Liabilities; Owner's equity)
Equity ratios, 421, 427
Errors:
in accounting for bad debts, 164
bank reconciliation and, 128
in inventory valuation, 188–90
trial balance and, 106–7
Exchange rates, 450–53
Ex-dividend date, 361
Expense accounts, closing, 55–57
Expenses:
account classifications for, 26
accounting equation and, 18–23
accrual concept and, 19
defined, 18
on income statement, 24
matching principle and, 46–47, 155
(*See also* Cost of goods sold)
Expired costs, 18
Export sales, 457–60
F.O.B. (free on board) destination, 190, 457
F.O.B. (free on board) shipping point, 190, 457
Face value, bond, 324
Factoring accounts receivable, 166–67
FAS (free alongside), 457
Federal income taxes, 297
(*See also* Income taxes)
Federal Insurance Contributions Act, 296
Federal Unemployment Tax Act, 298
Federal unemployment taxes, 298, 299
Feedback value, 468
FICA taxes, 296–97
FIFO (first-in, first-out) cost assignment method, 198, 200–204
Fifteen-year property class, 240
Final entry, 44
Financial Accounting Standards Board (FASB), 7
Statement No. 2, 265
Statement No. 8, 462–63
Statement No. 12, 137–40, 369
Statement No. 13, 305, 306
Statement No. 33, 206, 444–45
Statement No. 52, 463–64
Financial reporting objectives, 467–69
Financial statement analysis, 410–28
common-size statements, 414–15
horizontal analysis, 411–12
quality of earnings, 415–16
ratio analysis, 416–28
standards of comparison, 415
vertical analysis, 413–14
Financial statements:
analysis of (*see* Financial statement analysis)
accrual-basis accounting and, 130, 132–35, 155
cash-basis accounting and, 19*n*, 130–35
common-size, 414–15
consolidated, 470
defined, 2
foreign, 461–64
interim, 103
preparation of, 46, 53, 87–88, 101–3
uses of, 2–3
(*See also* Balance sheet; Income statement; Statement of changes in financial position)
Fiscal year, 46
Five-year property class, 240
Floating exchange-rate system, 453, 461–62
Foreign currency, 124, 455–56
Foreign exchange (*see* International accounting)
Foreign purchases, 460
Foreign sales, 457–60
Foreign shipment terms, 457
Foreign subsidiaries, 461–64
Forward market, 454
Franchises, 265–66, 268
Freight-in, 190–91
"Frozen" cash, 123

Funded plans, 309-10
Future value:
  of an annuity, 287, 289-91
  of $1, 284-87

Gains:
  exchange, 458, 459, 461
  foreign currency translation, 462-64
  plant asset disposal, 256-60
  purchasing power, 445-46
  unrealized, taken directly to owner's equity, 368-69
General journal, 43-44
  accounts payable in, 295
  accrued liabilities in, 296
  adjusting entries and (*see* Adjusting entries)
  allowance for uncollectible accounts in, 161
  asset trade-ins in, 257-60
  assignment of accounts receivable in, 166
  bad debt expense in, 160, 161
  bond amortization in, 330-39
  closing entries and, 55, 57
  factoring of accounts receivable in, 166-67
  foreign purchases in, 460
  foreign sales in, 458-60
  goodwill in, 267
  income tax expense in, 388
  leases in, 307-8
  marketable securities in, 137-42
  notes payable in, 301-2
  notes receivable in, 170-73
  owner's equity (corporations) in, 358-61, 363-67
  owner's equity (partnerships) in, 353-55
  owner's equity (sole proprietorships) in, 352
  payroll expenses in, 299-300
  petty cash in, 125-27
  posting from (*see* Posting)
  purchase discounts in, 191-92
  purchase returns and allowances in, 192
  sales in, 157-59
General Accounting Office (GAO), 6
General ledger, 44-46
  (*See also* Posting)
Generally accepted accounting principles (GAAP), 465-72
  cost principle, 9, 470
  defined, 7
  development of, 466-69
  entity principle, 15-17, 351, 469-70
  financial reporting objectives, 467-69
  going-concern principle, 470
  monetary principle, 471
  time-period principle, 471
General-price-level accounting (*see* Constant-dollar accounting)
Going-concern principle, 470
Goods available for sale, 187
Goods in transit, 190
Goodwill, 266-68
Governmental accounting, 6
Gross margin (*see* Gross profit)
Gross National Product Implicit Price Deflator, 441
Gross profit, 187-88
Gross profit method, 206-7

Historical cost profit, 441-43
Horizontal analysis, 411-12

Imprest system, 125-27
Income, net (*see* Profit)
Income bonds, 324
Income statement, 23-24
  cash-basis vs. accrual-basis accounting and, 133
  common-size, 414-15
  comparative, 411-13
  preparation of, 46, 87, 101
  statement of changes in financial position and, 380, 383, 384, 390, 397
Income taxes:
  deferred, 302-4
  depreciation and, 240-41, 302, 303
  federal, 297
  intangible assets and, 268
  LIFO (last-in, first-out) cost-assignment method and, 203
  partnerships and, 355
  working capital and, 387-88
Industrial Revolution, 7
Inflation accounting, 439-47
  constant-dollar accounting, 444-47
  current-value accounting, 444-47
  historical-cost profits, 441-43
  inflation rates, 440-41
  inventories and, 206
  purchasing power gains and losses, 445-46
Institute of Management Accounting, 4
Insurance, adjusting entries for, 49
Intangible assets, 263-68
Interest, bond, 327-39
Interest payable, 50-51, 170-71
Interest receivable, 52-53, 170-71
Inter-Governmental Working Group of Experts on International Standards of Accounting, 465
Interim financial statements, 103
Internal Revenue Service (IRS), 6, 203, 240, 297
International accounting, 439-40, 447-65
  accounting for foreign exchange transactions, 456-57
  accounting for foreign trade, 457-60
  basic international monetary system, 450-53
  discounts, 454
  evolution of, 447-49
  exchange gains and losses, 458, 459, 461
  exchange rates, 450-53
  foreign exchange trading, 454
  foreign shipment terms, 457
  foreign subsidiaries, 461-64
  instruments of foreign exchange, 455-56
  international accounting standards, 464-65
  International Monetary Fund, 453-54
  premiums, 454
  spread, 454-55
International Accounting Standards Committee (IASC), 465
International Chamber of Commerce, 457
International Monetary Fund (IMF), 453-54
Inventory, 186-209
  consigned merchandise as, 208
  cost flow assumptions, 198-204
  defined, 187
  estimation of, 206-7
  FIFO (first-in, first-out) cost assignment method, 198, 200-204
  freight-in, 190-91
  goods in transit, 190
  importance of valuation of, 188-90
  inflation, effect of, 206
  LIFO (last-in, first-out) cost assignment method, 198, 201-4
  lower-of-cost-or-market (LCM) rule, 204-6
  periodic system of, 187, 193-97
  perpetual system of, 193, 196-97
  purchase discounts, 191-92
  purchase returns and allowances, 192-93
  specific identification cost-assignment method, 198, 199, 201
  trade discounts, 195, 198
  weighted-average cost-assignment method, 198, 200, 201
Inventory profits, 206
Inventory turnover, 424-25, 428
Investment decisions, 3

Journal entry, 44
Journalizing, 2, 44
Journals:
  defined, 2, 43
  general (*see* General journal)
  special, 95, 101

Land:
  acquisition of, 225-27
  disposal of, 255-60
  leasing of, 241
Leases, 241, 305-9
Ledgers:
  general (*see* General ledger)
  subsidiary, 94-95
Legal capital, 358
Lessee, 241, 305

Lessor, 241, 305
Letters of credit, foreign trade financed by, 456
Liabilities, 282–311
account classifications for, 26
accrued, 47, 295–96
on balance sheet, 17, 18
in basic accounting equation, 9–10, 15–17
changes in (*see* Statement of changes in financial position)
contingent, 311
current, 26, 27, 295–300
defined, 9–10, 294
long-term (*see* Long-term liabilities)
present value and (*see* Present value)
Life insurance, cash surrender value of, 268–69
LIFO (last-in, first-out) cost-assignment method, 198, 201–4
Limited liability, 8, 356
Liquidity, 136
tests of, 416, 419–22, 427
Long-term construction contracts, 167–69
Long-term liabilities:
bonds (*see* Bonds)
deferred income taxes, 302–4
leases, 305–9
notes payable, 300–302
Losses:
exchange, 458, 459, 461
foreign currency translation, 462–64
plant asset disposal, 256–59
purchasing power, 445–46
unrealized, taken directly to owner's equity, 368–69
Lower-of-cost-or-market (LCM) rule, 137–40, 204–6
Lump sum (basket) purchases, 226–27

Maintenance, 237–39
Management advisory services, 5
Manager, in public accounting firm, 5
Managerial decisions, 3
Marketable securities, 136–42
lower-of-cost-or-market (LCM) rule and, 137–40
sale of, 140–42
Market tests, 416, 422–25, 428
Matching principle, 46–47, 155, 204–5
Materiality, 469
Merchandise:
amount sold (*see* Cost of goods sold)
defined, 187
on hand (*see* Inventory)
Microcomputers, 45, 103–6
Monetary principle, 471

Natural resources, 260–61
Net book value, 228
Net income (*see* Profit)
Neutrality, 468
"No cash, no check" society, 136
Nominal accounts, 54–57
Noncash acquisitions, 226
Noncumulative preferred stock, 359
Non-interest-bearing note, 300–302
Notes payable, 300–302
Notes receivable, 169–73

Objectivity, 470
Open accounts, 157, 457
Operations:
cash provided by, 393–98
working capital provided by, 387–92
Operating cycle, 26–27
Operating leases, 241, 305
Organization costs, 266, 268
Organization for Economic Co-operation and Development (OECD), 465
Original entry, 44
Other assets, 268–69
Outstanding checks, 127
Owner's equity:
account classifications for, 26
on balance sheet, 17, 18
in basic accounting equation, 9–10, 15–17
changes in (*see* Statement of changes in financial position)
corporate (*see* Stockholder's equity)
defined, 9, 10
expenses and, 18–23
partnership, 352–55
revenues and, 18–23
sole proprietorship, 351–52, 355
Owner's-equity-to-total-assets ratio, 421, 427

Pacioli, Luca, 6
Paid-in capital, 10, 358, 362–67
Par stock, 357–59
Participating preferred stock, 360
Partner, in public accounting firm, 5
Partnership, 8, 352–55
Patents, 264–65, 268
Payment date, 361
Payroll liabilities, 296–300
Pensions, 309–11
Percentage depletion, 262–63
Percentage-of-completion method, 156, 167–69
Periodic inventory system, 193, 196–97
Periodicity principle, 46
Perpetual inventory system, 193, 196–97
Petty cash, 125–27
Plant assets, 224–41, 255–69
acquisition of, 225–27
capital and revenue expenditures, 237–38
comparison of methods, 233–34
depreciation of (*see* Depreciation)
disposal of, 255–60
intangible assets, 263–68
leasing of, 241, 305–9
natural resources, 260–63
optimum life determination, 238–39
other assets, 268–69
Pledging accounts receivable, 166
Point of sale, revenue recognition at, 156–57
Point of-sale (POS) terminals, 136
Pooling of interests, 266*n*
Post-closing trial balance, 93–94
Posting, 44–46, 76–86
with accounting or bookkeeping machines, 106
adjusting entries, 82–86
closing entries, 55–57, 89–93
electronic data processing and, 45, 103
from sales invoices, 98
to subsidiary ledgers, 95
Predictive value, 468
Preferred stock, 357, 359–60
Premiums:
bond, 332–34, 388, 394
foreign exchange, 454
stock, 359
Present value:
of an annuity, 291–94
concept of, 283–84
of $1, 287, 288
Price earnings (P/E) ratio, 422–23, 428
Private accounting, 6
Private corporations, 356–57
Producer Price Index, 441
Production-units depreciation, 231–34
Professional corporations, 353
Profit, 18, 23, 24
gross, 187–88
historical cost, 441–43
inventory, 206
Profitability, tests of, 416, 418–19, 427
Profit margin on sales, 418, 427
Promissory notes, 169–73
Property (*see* Plant assets)
Property dividends, 362
Public accounting, 5
Public corporations, 356
Public policy decisions, 3
Punched-card or tape equipment, 106
Purchase discounts, 191–92
Purchase returns and allowances, 192–93
Purchases:
accounts payable, 191–93, 295
foreign, 460
Purchases journal, 99
Purchasing power gains and losses, 445–46

Quality of earnings, 415–16
Quick ratio, 420–21, 427

Ratio analysis, 416–28
Real account, 54
Realized gains or losses, 140–42
Receivables (*see* Account receivable)
Record date, 361
Recorded costs, 47–49

Recorded revenue, 47, 51–52
Recordkeeping:
accounting or bookkeeping machines, 106
data processing, 103–6
locating errors, 106–7
punched card or tape equipment, 106
worksheet, 43, 101–3
(*See also* Journals; Ledgers)
Registered bonds, 324
Relevance, 468
Reliability, 468
Renewals, 238–39
Rent, adjusting entries for, 51–52
Repairs, 237–39
Replacement cost, 204
Representational faithfulness, 468
Residual equity, 357
Retained earnings, 10, 87, 362–68
combined statement of earnings and, 380, 383, 384, 390, 397
Return on owner's investment (or equity), 419, 427
Return on total assets, 418–19, 427
Revenue, 154–74
account classifications for, 26
account closing, 55–57
accounting equation and, 18–23
accrual concept and, 19
assigning accounts receivable, 166
credit card sales, 165–66
defined, 18, 155
factoring accounts receivable, 166–67
on income statement, 24
long-term construction contracts, 167–69
matching principle and, 46–47, 155
nature of, 155
notes receivable, 169–73
pledging accounts receivable, 166
recognition and measurement of, 155–57
recorded, 47, 51–52
recording of, 157–59
sales discounts, 158–59
sales taxes, 159
uncollectible accounts, 159–65
unrecorded, 47, 52–53
Revenue Act of 1913, 297
Revenue expenditures, 237
Rueschhoff, Norlin G., 461*n*

Salaries of owners, 354–55
Sales:
cost of (*see* Cost of goods sold)
credit card, 165–66
foreign, 457–60
recording of, 157–59
revenue recognition at point of, 156–57
Sales discounts, 158–59
Sales invoices, posting from, 98
Sales journals, 96–98
Sales taxes, 159
Salvage value, 48
Scrap value, 238
Script dividends, 362
Secured bonds, 324
Securities and Exchange Commission (SEC), 6
Semiannual interest payments, 334
Senior accountants, 5
Serial bonds, 335–37
Service-hours depreciation, 232–34
Shareholders, 8
Similar asset exchanges, 257–60
Slides (errors), 107
Social security taxes (FICA), 296–99
Sole proprietorships, 7, 351–52, 355
Solvency, tests of, 416, 419–22, 427
Source documents, 42
Special journals, 95–101
Specific identification cost-assignment method, 198, 199, 201
Spot market, 454
Spread, 454–55
Standards:
accounting (*see* Accounting standards)
of comparison, 415
State Boards of Accounting, 4
Statement:
defined, 2
(*See also* Financial statements)
Statement of cash receipts and disbursements, 131–34
Statement of changes in financial position, 379–401
cash basis approach to, 393–400
concept of, 379–80
evaluation of, 399
working capital approach to, 381–92
Statement on Auditing Standards No. 1, 42
State unemployment taxes, 298
Stock dividends, 362–64
Stockholders, 8, 10
Stockholder's equity, 357–70
authorized stock, 358, 366
balance sheet disclosure, 366, 369–70
convertible securities, 366–67
cumulative preferred stock, 359–60
dividends, 359–64
issuance of securities, 357
no-par stock, 358
par stock, 357–59
preferred stock, 357, 359–60
retained earnings, 10, 87, 362–68
special stock equity accounts or conditions, 369
stock splits, 364–65
treasury stock, 358, 365–66
unrealized gains and losses taken directly to, 368–69
Stock options, 369
Stocks, 357–66
Stock splits, 364–65
Stock warrants, 369
Straight-line amortization, 264
bond discount, 329–30
bond premium, 333
compared to effective-interest amortization, 334–35
Straight-line depreciation, 229, 233–35
Subordinated debentures, 324
Subsidiaries, foreign, 461–64
Subsidiary ledgers, 94–95
Summa (Pacioli), 6
Sum-of-the-years'-digits depreciation, 231, 233–36
Supervisors, in public accounting firm, 5
Supplies, adjusting entries for, 49

T-accounts, 45
Tax accounting, 5
Taxes:
federal unemployment, 298, 299
income (*see* Income taxes)
sales, 159
social security (FICA), 296–99
Temporal method, 462–63
Ten-year property class, 240
Three-year property class, 240
Timeliness, 468
Time-period principle, 471
Times-interest-earned ratio, 422, 427
Time value of money (*see* Future value; Present value)
Trade discounts, 158, 195, 198
Trade-ins, 256–60
Trademarks, 265, 268
Transit, goods in, 190
Transportation-in, 191
Transposition errors, 107
Treasury Department, 203
Treasury stock, 358, 365–66
Trial balance, 46, 81
post-closing, 93–94

Uncollectible accounts, 159–65
Understandability, 467
Unemployment taxes, 298, 299
Unfunded plans, 310–11
United Nations Economic and Social Council, 465
Units-of-production depreciation, 231–34
Unrealized gains and losses, 137–40
Unrecorded costs, 47, 50–51
Unrecorded revenue, 47, 52–53
Usefulness of accounting information, 468

Verifiability, 468
Vertical analysis, 413–14
Vouchers, petty cash, 126

Wages, adjusting entries for, 51
Wall Street Journal, 369
Wasting assets, 260–61
Weighted-average cost-assignment method, 198, 200, 201
Working capital:
activities affecting, 381–87
vs. cash basis approach to statement of changes in financial position, 399–400
defined, 381
provided by operations, 387–92
statement of changes in financial position and, 383–92
Working capital ratio, 420, 427
Worksheet, 43, 101–3

Yield rate, 327